DETENTION AND ARREST

THIRD EDITION

Other Books in the *Essentials of Canadian Law* Series

International Trade Law

Family Law

Copyright Law

The Law of Sentencing

Administrative Law

Computer Law 2/e

International Human Rights Law

Franchise Law

Legal Ethics and Professional Responsibility 2/e

Public International Law 2/e

Individual Employment Law 2/e

Civil Litigation

Canadian Telecommunications Law

Intellectual Property Law 2/e

Animals and the Law

Income Tax Law 2/e

Youth Criminal Justice Law 3/e

Bank and Customer Law in Canada 2/e

The Law of Equitable Remedies 2/e

Remedies: The Law of Damages 3/e

Freedom of Conscience and Religion

The Law of Trusts 3/e

Ethics and Criminal Law 2/e

Insurance Law 2/e

Immigration Law 2/e

Bankruptcy and Insolvency Law 2/e

Legal Research and Writing 4/e

Canadian Maritime Law 2/e

Public Lands and Resources in Canada

Conflict of Laws 2/e

Statutory Interpretation 3/e

Constitutional Law 5/e

Land-Use Planning

Refugee Law 2/e

Religious Institutions and the Law 4/e

The Law of Partnerships and Corporations 4/e

Environmental Law 5/e

Fundamental Justice 2/e

International and Transnational Criminal Law 3/e

The Law of Torts 6/e

Mergers, Acquisitions, and Other Changes of Corporate Control 3/e

Criminal Procedure 4/e

Information and Privacy Law in Canada

The Law of Evidence 8/e

The Law of Contracts 3/e

National Security Law 2/e

Canadian Competition Law and Policy

The Law of Property

Pension Law 3/e

The Charter of Rights and Freedoms 7/e

Personal Property Security Law 3/e

Criminal Law 8/e

Securities Law 3/e

Search and Seizure

ESSENTIALS OF CANADIAN LAW

DETENTION AND ARREST

THIRD EDITION

STEVE COUGHLAN
Professor, Schulich School of Law, Dalhousie University

GLEN LUTHER
Associate Professor, College of Law,
University of Saskatchewan

IRWIN LAW

Detention and Arrest, third edition

Published in 2024 by

Irwin Law Inc
14 Duncan Street
Suite 206
Toronto, ON
M5H 3G8

www.irwinlaw.com

ISBN 978-1-55221-725-2 (print) | 978-1-55221-726-9 (PDF) | 978-1-55221-727-6 (epub)

Library and Archives Canada Cataloguing in Publication

Title: Detention and arrest / Steve Coughlan (Professor, Schulich School of Law, Dalhousie University), Glen Luther (Associate Professor, College of Law, University of Saskatchewan).
Names: Coughlan, Stephen Gerard, 1957– author. | Luther, Glen, author.
Series: Essentials of Canadian law.
Description: Third edition. | Series statement: Essentials of Canadian law | Includes bibliographical references and index.
Identifiers: Canadiana (print) 20240292898 | Canadiana (ebook) 2024029291X | ISBN 9781552217252 (softcover) | ISBN 9781552217269 (PDF) | ISBN 9781552217276 (EPUB)
Subjects: LCSH: Detention of persons—Canada. | LCSH: Arrest—Canada. | LCSH: Police power—Canada.
Classification: LCC KE9265 .C68 2024 | DDC 345.71/0527—dc23

Canada

ONTARIO CREATES | ONTARIO CRÉATIF

Printed and bound by CPI Group (UK) Ltd, Croydon, CR0 4YY

1 2 3 4 5 28 27 26 25 24

SUMMARY TABLE OF CONTENTS

DETAILED TABLE OF CONTENTS

FOREWORD

In writing forewords to the first and second editions of *Detention and Arrest*, I commented on the relevance and importance of the book because of the importance of the concepts of both detention and arrest in Canadian criminal procedure. That importance remains for this, the third edition, and the new edition brings both the legislative and jurisprudential frameworks to their current level. Detention and arrest both require balancing of fair and constitutional police conduct and the autonomy and privacy interests of all members of Canadian society. Moreover, it is vital that Canadian laws on detention and arrest address such issues as the potential for excessive force, uncertainty about the reach of police powers, and, even more important, the issue of whether police conduct is disproportionately focused on minority groups such as Indigenous or African Canadians.

The structure of the book remains the same in terms of the topics that are discussed. In Chapter 2, the new content includes a discussion of *Fleming v Ontario*[1] and the controversial ancillary powers doctrine by which the courts recognize common law police powers. The chapter also has an expanded treatment of racial profiling based on *R v Le*[2] and the subsequent caselaw and expert reports, and discusses searches of the person as an incident of lawful arrest. The latter subject is discussed in light of the decision in *R v Stairs*.[3] Unfortunately, at times, some

1 2019 SCC 45.

2 2019 SCC 34 [*Le*].

3 2022 SCC 11.

confusion remains within courts of appeal about the required standard for a search as an incident of the common law power to briefly detain someone for an investigative detention and the meaning of "reasonable grounds." Professor Coughlan has been constantly vigilant in his writing in order to prevent such confusion. The new Chapter 2 reflects his contributions in this area.

Chapter 3 contains broader treatment of investigative detentions. In particular, the "brief duration" requirement is dealt with in considerable depth.

Perhaps the most comprehensive changes to the book are in the new Chapter 4. These were necessitated by the overhaul of the *Criminal Code*[4] provisions dealing with arrest powers and compelling the appearance of an accused person in court. That overhaul came in 2019 with the passage of Bill C-75, *An Act to amend the Criminal Code, the Youth Criminal Justice Act and other Acts and to make consequential amendments to other Acts.*[5]

Chapter 5 has also undergone significant changes. Its main focus is the impact of the *Canadian Charter of Rights and Freedoms*[6] on detention and arrest. *Le* and *R v Lafrance*[7] have brought modifications to the concept of psychological detention. In addition, there is now a clearer structure for assessing arbitrary detention, including the right to an additional consultation with counsel in light of changes in circumstances. Of great importance in this discussion are *R v Dussault*[8] and *Lafrance.*

This third edition of *Detention and Arrest* remains a remarkably comprehensive work despite its relative brevity. It will continue to be an important source of information for anyone working in the field or for those interested in these important topics.

Tim Quigley
Professor of Law (Emeritus)
College of Law, University of Saskatchewan

4 RSC 1985, c C-46.

5 SC 2019, c 25.

6 Part 1 of the *Constitution Act, 1982*, being Schedule B to the *Canada Act 1982* (UK), 1982, c 11.

7 2022 SCC 32 [*Lafrance*].

8 2022 SCC 16.

ACKNOWLEDGEMENTS

This book began, a bit surprisingly, because of a trip to China. In 2006, Steve Coughlan of the Schulich School of Law at Dalhousie University was invited to organize a group of Canadian criminal law scholars to attend an international seminar on the theory of criminal law at Shandong University in Jinan, China. In the wake of that conference, the chief organizer, Professor He Bingsong, expressed an interest in learning more about the law in Canada. In the course of putting together a bibliography and a collection of books, it occurred to Steve that although there were many good books covering criminal law and procedure generally, and specialist volumes in some areas such as search and seizure, bail, or sentencing, no book devoted exclusively to the topics of detention and arrest existed.

With an initial idea, Steve enlisted the help of Glen Luther of the Faculty of Law, University of Saskatchewan. Glen contributed important ideas on the structure and coverage of the book, resulting in its reframing to the form it has now. The authors each undertook half of the initial writing, but, with first drafts in hand, they consulted closely, discussing and offering suggestions on one another's work. A second edition was published in 2017, and the book now appears in its third edition, updated to take into account the significant statutory changes to powers of arrest that occurred in 2019 and the recent court decisions on various issues relating to detention and arrest. (For personal reasons, Glen was not able to be involved in updating the material for this most recent edition.)

Like any other book, however, it is not the result solely of their efforts. Steve is grateful to the Foundation for Legal Research and to the Schulich School of Law for its support over the years, in particular for the grants providing research assistance for this third edition. He would also like to thank Alex McNabb and Matt Kelly for their research assistance with the first edition, Hanna Zatzman for her zealous efforts on the second edition, and Isis Hatte and Luke McGowan for their great assistance with this latest volume. Glen would like to thank Nathan Forrester for his work on the first edition, whose insight into the many issues presented helped form the book in many ways. He also thanks Zeke Ziminock and Troy Baril for their editing assistance. In addition, both authors are indebted to many of their colleagues for their suggestions, feedback, and other assistance during the course of writing. Foremost among these is Tim Quigley, Glen's colleague at the University of Saskatchewan, who not only consulted with each of us at various times but also agreed to undertake writing the foreword to the book. Our appreciation goes as well to Don Stuart and David Tanovich. Glen would also like to thank M. Ian Savage for his timely assistance in preparing the first edition's section on the right to counsel. In addition, we would like to express our gratitude to Jeff Miller at Irwin Law, not only for agreeing to publish the book but also for his support throughout, and to Lesley Steeve and Heather Raven for their diligent work in the preparation of the book.

Finally, we wish to thank our partners, Sherry Luther and Dale Darling, not merely for their sufferance but for their moral support during the course of writing this book.

Steve Coughlan Glen Luther

CHAPTER 1

INTRODUCTION

The central goal of a proper criminal justice system must be to maintain a balance between the individual interest of private citizens to carry on their lives free from state interference and the communal interest in maintaining a safe society. One of the most visible ways in which those two goals come into conflict with each other is when agents of the state physically take control of private citizens—that is, when they exercise their powers to detain or to arrest.

Powers to detain and arrest arise at a number of points in the criminal justice system and, indeed, outside it. Travellers arriving in the country are detained at customs. Motorists can be detained for a variety of purposes, ranging from checking the mechanical fitness of the vehicle to determining the blood-alcohol level of the driver. Someone accused of an offence might be detained pending trial or to be assessed to determine fitness to stand trial or might be detained afterward, whether pursuant to a sentence, following a finding of not being criminally responsible, or for having been found to be a dangerous offender. Statutory schemes authorize detention for immigration, deportation, or security-related reasons. The police might arrest a person in order to charge them with an offence, at a later stage if a surety for the accused's bail withdraws or on a bench warrant if the accused fails to appear for trial. An absconding witness is subject to being arrested.

This book does not attempt to deal with all situations in which detentions or arrests occur. Its focus is on "street-level" encounters, detentions and arrests that occur in the course of investigating crime and laying charges. Our focus is on the initial interaction between agents of the state or others authorized to detain and arrest and the private citizens whose liberty is interfered with. At that point, the balance between societal safety and individual liberty is most keenly in play.

This book is also not focused on the issue of remedies for non-compliance with the law. Particularly in the detention context, the questions of what powers exist and whether there has been a violation of the *Canadian Charter of Rights and Freedoms*[1] are quite closely linked; many, though by no means all, powers of detention arise out of discussions of whether the police were violating an accused's rights when they stopped them. Nonetheless, our concern is with the powers of detention and arrest themselves, including, of course, those *Charter* rights that arise in these circumstances. The more well defined and understood these powers are, the less likely it is that there will be *Charter* violations, and the easier it will be to conduct the section 24 analysis. Whether an improperly arrested or detained accused might be able to obtain a remedy under section 24 of the *Charter*, or for that matter to bring a civil action, will sometimes be relevant but will not be a central focus.[2]

The law in this area comes from a variety of sources. Some investigative powers to detain have been created by statute—for example, the provisions in various provincial statutes to stop motor vehicles or the companion provisions in the *Criminal Code*[3] allowing further detentions in order to obtain breath samples. Although we do not attempt to delve into all the intricacies of the law relating to Breathalyzers, we do pursue the detention aspects of those powers. Powers of arrest are almost entirely statutory and are found primarily in sections 494 and 495 of the *Code*, which will be the focus of discussion.[4] In addition, the *Code*

---

1 Part 1 of the *Constitution Act, 1982*, being Schedule B to the *Canada Act 1982* (UK), 1982, c 11 [*Charter*].

2 The approach to analyzing s 24(2) claims for exclusion of evidence has been set out by the Court in *R v Grant*, 2009 SCC 32 [*Grant*]. On this decision, see Tim Quigley, "Was It Worth the Wait? The Supreme Court's New Approaches to Detention and Exclusion of Evidence" (2009) 66 *Criminal Reports* (6th) 88. For a discussion of the relationship between damages in tort and under s 24(1), see *Vancouver (City) v Ward*, 2010 SCC 27 and *Henry v British Columbia (Attorney General)*, 2015 SCC 24.

3 RSC 1985, c C-46 [*Code*].

4 Even beyond "later stage" arrests such as bench warrants, there are other "initial contact" arrest powers. For example, s 199(2) permits a peace officer who finds a common gaming house to take into custody the person keeping it or anyone found in it. Section 83.3(4) permits an arrest to prevent suspected terrorist activity. The discussion in this book will focus on the powers in ss 494 & 495, which are in more general use.

contains a number of statutory supporting powers, dealing with issues such as the use of force.

On the other hand, the common law is also important. Some powers to detain were created entirely at common law: the ability of police to stop vehicles randomly, for example, or the power of police to conduct investigative detentions. Indeed, to the extent that the Supreme Court has become much more willing to create common law powers, this is a phenomenon almost peculiar to the detention context. In addition, the common law remains relevant to arrest: the definition of what constitutes an arrest comes solely from the common law.

Of course, the *Charter* is significant as well. Section 9 of the *Charter* guarantees everyone the right to be free from arbitrary detention, and section 10 guarantees various rights to people who have been arrested or detained. Section 8, guaranteeing the freedom from unreasonable search and seizure, is also often relevant. Searches, like arrests, must generally be justified on reasonable grounds; the phrase does not necessarily have the same meaning in both contexts, but caselaw can be at least cautiously transferred from one context to another. Furthermore, in many cases, the purpose of a detention is to carry out some investigative technique such as a Breathalyzer test or a visual inspection of a vehicle. In that event, a *Charter* claim might plausibly be made under either section 8 or section 9, and it is not uncommon for a court to decide that the issues can be adequately dealt with simply by considering the section 8 claim.[5]

Note, too, that whether a power to arrest or detain exists can be relevant in more than one way. Most obviously, the existence or non-existence of the power settles whether a peace officer or other person can compel an individual to remain in a particular location or take part in a particular activity. However, even those are potentially different questions. In the case of a Breathalyzer, the power to detain is also a power to compel the person to provide a breath sample. An investigative detention, on the other hand, allows the police to stop an individual to ask questions but imposes no obligation on that individual to provide any answers. Even so, the questioning inherent in any detention might raise questions of whether the person has been searched or whether the privilege against self-incrimination has been called into play. A power to arrest allows the police to, if necessary, compel a person physically to attend in court. Beyond that, however, whether the police officer had a power to arrest or detain can be important in determining whether an officer is acting "in the execution of duty." This matters in assessing whether an uncooperative individual will have committed the offence

5 See, for example, *R v Shepherd*, 2009 SCC 35.

of resisting or obstructing. Whether the police officer or other person acted with legal authority will also be relevant in the private law context if an individual brings an action for false arrest, false imprisonment, or a violation of their section 9 rights.[6]

The material in this book is arranged in four chapters following this one. Chapter 2 focuses on a number of the underlying and background issues relating to arrest and detention. It begins with a discussion of the sources of powers in criminal law and then looks in detail at the supporting powers that are given to people exercising authority—for example, rules around the use of force, entry to carry out an arrest, or searches that accompany arrest or detention. It also considers the extent to which caselaw has (or has not) placed an emphasis on the purpose that is in a peace officer's mind as they perform their duty and discusses who may be considered an agent of the police for the purpose of exercising those powers. Finally, the chapter undertakes an extensive discussion of the "reasonable ground" standard that underlies the vast majority of powers to detain or arrest. This discussion gives greater emphasis to the "reasonable grounds to believe" standard but also considers the issue of "reasonable grounds to suspect."

Chapter 3 turns to a discussion of powers of detention. It looks at these powers in both the motor vehicle and other contexts and considers both statutory and common law powers. A particular focus of discussion is the tendency of the Supreme Court to create new common law powers allowing the police to detain individuals.

Chapter 4 is entitled "Arrest and Compelling Appearance," but its focus is broader than that. There are a number of ways in which the initial contact between an individual and the state can occur, including not just arrests with and without a warrant but also the use of appearance notices and summonses. A good part of the chapter, therefore, deals in some depth with those other methods, in particular with the interplay between police and justices of the peace, who are meant to act as a guardian of individual interests. These provisions underwent significant change with amendments to the *Criminal Code* in 2019, which kept the spirit of the previous approach but significantly altered many of the finer details; those changes are discussed here. In addition, the chapter examines the definition of arrest and considers the powers given to both private citizens and peace officers to make arrests.

Finally, Chapter 5 studies the *Charter* issues involved in questions of detention and arrest. In the section 9 context, *Charter* claims have ironically led to the creation of new state powers to detain. Furthermore,

---

6 See, for example, *Fleming v Ontario*, 2019 SCC 45.

section 9 jurisprudence has tended to be underdeveloped; it was only with *Grant* in 2009 that a real analytical framework for that section arose.[7] Those issues, as well as other questions around the meaning of the phrase "arbitrary detention," are pursued. In addition, we discuss section 10 of the *Charter* and the way in which the various rights listed there — to be informed of the reason for the arrest and to be informed of the right to counsel — have changed policing practice.

7 *Grant*, above note 2.

CHAPTER 2

NATURE OF THE INTERACTION BETWEEN POLICE AND INDIVIDUALS

A. SOURCES OF POLICE POWERS

1) Introduction

Police powers in Canada have long involved a lack of clarity and have engendered sharp divisions among the members of the Supreme Court of Canada. In this section, we will review the sources of police power, which involve a combination of statutory rules and common law practices. We will see that the Supreme Court of Canada has played a large role in the field as it has interpreted the various statutory police powers, all the while leaving a very large role for the common law in the delineation and exposition of such powers.

Prior to enactment of the *Canadian Charter of Rights and Freedoms* in 1982,[1] the exact nature and extent of individual police powers were not often at the forefront of the Supreme Court of Canada's reasoning. Unlawfully obtained evidence was generally admissible in criminal trials, so it was usually not necessary for a court to decide whether or not a particular police action was lawful.[2] Occasionally, an accused faced a charge of resisting arrest or obstruction of a police officer in the lawful execution of duty.[3] In such cases, the Court had to determine the lawfulness

1 Part 1 of the *Constitution Act, 1982*, being Schedule B to the *Canada Act 1982* (UK), 1982, c 11 [*Charter*].

2 *R v Wray*, [1971] SCR 272.

3 *The Queen v Biron*, [1976] 2 SCR 56 [*Biron*].

of police action, and this issue was reduced to an either/or proposition: either the police or the resisting individual acted unlawfully, and that settled all the relevant questions.

Indeed, in 1975 in *The Queen v Biron*,[4] a case to be discussed in detail elsewhere,[5] the division of the Court was precisely on this point. In dissent, Laskin CJC, supported by Dickson J (as he then was) and by Spence J, attempted to separate the question of an officer's civil liability for false arrest from that of whether the arrested individual could be said to have had the right to resist in the circumstances and thus be entitled to an acquittal on the criminal charge of resisting arrest. To Laskin, the question of civil liability was to be determined by application of section 25 of the *Criminal Code*,[6] which he held presented a shield, but not a sword, to the officer when the officer acted upon reasonable grounds. In Laskin's view, then, an officer could be said to be not acting in the lawful execution of duty (on the facts, because the officer did not "find the accused committing"[7] the summary conviction offence there in question) even though he may have been protected from civil liability by the shield of section 25 (because the officer acted on reasonable grounds). Accordingly, to Laskin, the question of lawful police action was multi-layered and multi-faceted.

The majority of five in *Biron*, on the other hand, saw the question more simply. To them, the crucial question was whether the police had the power to do what they did. Justice Martland, who wrote the majority judgment,[8] held that the focus needed to be on the time the police acted and not at some later time when the courts had had a chance to decide whether or not the officer's belief that he had found the accused committing an offence was correct.[9] In other words, to the majority, it made no sense to bifurcate the analysis. Either the officer was acting lawfully or he was not, and the majority therefore felt compelled to read in to the statute in question the word "apparently" to make clear that an officer acted lawfully if they found the eventual accused "apparently committing" an offence. The majority in *Biron*, then, rejected the shield/sword analysis of the chief justice and refused to see an officer's actions as lawful for one purpose and unlawful for another.

That approach to police powers had ramifications beyond the particular "finds committing" arrest in question. On the one hand, this

4 *Ibid.*

5 See Chapter 4, Section C(2)(b)(iii).

6 RSC 1985, c C-46 [*Code*].

7 *Biron*, above note 3 at 67–68.

8 Justice Martland wrote for four judges. Justice De Grandpré concurred with Martland J but wrote a short judgment of his own.

9 *Biron*, above note 3 at 76.

approach presented a bright-line, simple method for courts analyzing the lawfulness question. On the other hand, however, it had the effect of increasing police powers. For practical purposes, that approach amounted to concluding that if the police had not committed a crime or a tort, then they had the power to do what they did.[10]

Once the *Charter* came into effect, many wondered how Martland J's approach would apply to section 9 of the *Charter*, which says that "[e]veryone has the right not to be arbitrarily detained or imprisoned." It should be noted that the law around section 9 of the *Charter* took a long time to develop, owing in part to the fact that in a typical case, section 8 and/or section 10 of the *Charter* have also been in play, and those sections have tended to receive the most attention from the courts (see the discussion of this issue in Chapter 5, Section B). At least initially, the question became muddied as the courts struggled with the concept of "arbitrariness." The early decisions under the *Charter* allowed for the possibility of police action that was unlawful but nonetheless not arbitrary. Such unlawful but constitutional police action allowed the police to act without legal authority but without breaching the arrested person's *Charter* rights, where the police action did not depart from lawfulness by an unacceptable degree. The leading early case was the decision of the Ontario Court of Appeal in *R v Duguay*.[11] That court concluded that a police action in arresting individuals, even if unlawful, was "arbitrary" only if that action departed from the police's lawful powers in such a way that it could be considered capricious and thus arbitrary. The court said:

> It cannot be that every unlawful arrest necessarily falls within the words "arbitrarily detained." The grounds upon which an arrest was made may fall "just short" of constituting reasonable and probable

---

10 For example, see *Dedman v The Queen*, [1985] 2 SCR 2 [*Dedman*], involving a vehicle stop for breath-testing purposes. The reasoning of the Ontario Court of Appeal had explicitly been that "in signalling the appellant to stop the police officer was not committing a crime or a tort, and that since the officer had reasonable suspicion at the time the s. 234.1(1) demand was made that the appellant had alcohol in his blood and had not placed himself in a position to make the demand by the commission of a crime or a tort, the demand was valid" (at para 54). See also the discussion of this issue in Steve Coughlan, "*Charter* Protection Against Unlawful Police Action: Less Black and White Than It Seems" in Benjamin L. Berger & James Stribopoulos, *Unsettled Legacy: Thirty Years of Criminal Justice Under the Charter* (Toronto: LexisNexis Canada, 2012).

11 (1985), 50 OR (2d) 375 (CA) [*Duguay*]. The decision was upheld on the facts in *R v Duguay*, [1989] 1 SCR 93, where the majority of the Supreme Court, in three short paragraphs, dismissed the appeal, saying, *inter alia*: "The majority in the Court of Appeal for Ontario did not enunciate any principle or rule of law with which we disagree" (at para 2).

> cause. The person making the arrest may honestly, though mistakenly, believe that reasonable and probable grounds for the arrest exist and there may be some basis for that belief. In those circumstances the arrest, though subsequently found to be unlawful, could not be said to be capricious or arbitrary. On the other hand, the entire absence of reasonable and probable grounds for the arrest could support an inference that no reasonable person could have genuinely believed that such grounds existed. In such cases, the conclusion would be that the person arrested was arbitrarily detained. Between these two ends of the spectrum, shading from white to grey to black, the issue of whether an accused was arbitrarily detained will depend, basically, on two considerations: first, the particular facts of the case, and secondly, the view taken by the court with respect to the extent of the departure from the standard of reasonable and probable grounds, and the honesty of the belief and basis for the belief in the existence of reasonable and probable grounds on the part of the person making the arrest.[12]

The idea that a police action might be unlawful but not arbitrary seemed to come down strongly on the part of expansive police powers. The Supreme Court of Canada did not commit itself to this position but did initially leave the possibility open.[13] Eventually, however, the Court came to disagree with *Duguay* and clarified the limits on police powers to arrest or detain individuals under section 9 of the *Charter*. In *R v Mann*, the Court said:

> As stated earlier, the issues in this case require the Court to balance individual liberty rights and privacy interests with a societal interest in effective policing. Absent a law to the contrary, individuals are free to do as they please. By contrast, the police (and more broadly, the state) may act only to the extent that they are empowered to do so by law. The vibrancy of a democracy is apparent by how wisely it navigates

12 *Duguay*, above note 11 at para 25. It is interesting to note that a similar debate occurred early in the decisions on s 8 of the *Charter*, where early court of appeal decisions suggested that a search could be unlawful but might not as a result thereof be unreasonable. See most clearly the Alberta Court of Appeal decision in *R v Heisler* (1984), 57 AR 230. This position was rejected by the Supreme Court of Canada in its judgment in *R v Collins*, [1987] 1 SCR 265 [*Collins*], and has given rise to the clear principle that a search might be unconstitutional for one of three reasons: the search was not authorized by law, the law was unreasonable, or the manner of search was unreasonable.

13 See, for example, *R v Latimer*, [1997] 1 SCR 217 at para 26 [*Latimer*]: "Unlawful arrests may be inherently arbitrary. . . . However, it is not necessary to address that question" [citation omitted].

> through those critical junctures where state action intersects with, and threatens to impinge upon, individual liberties.[14]

The principle stated here is that the police are allowed to do what they are authorized to do by law—that is, that a lawful detention is not arbitrary. After *Mann*, the Court made clear that the converse is also true: an unlawful detention *is* arbitrary. In the subsequent decision in *R v Grant*, the majority said:

> The s. 9 guarantee against arbitrary detention is a manifestation of the general principle, enunciated in s. 7, that a person's liberty is not to be curtailed except in accordance with the principles of fundamental justice. As this Court has stated: "This guarantee expresses one of the most fundamental norms of the rule of law. The state may not detain arbitrarily, but only in accordance with the law" (*Charkaoui v. Canada (Citizenship and Immigration)*, 2007 SCC 9, [2007] 1 S.C.R. 350, at para. 88). Section 9 serves to protect individual liberty against unlawful state interference. A lawful detention is not arbitrary within the meaning of s. 9 (*Mann*, at para. 20), unless the law authorizing the detention is itself arbitrary. Conversely, a detention not authorized by law is arbitrary and violates s. 9.[15]

Nevertheless, it is clear that, following the enactment of the *Charter*, the issues have become (and will remain) much more focused and commonplace than they were before. That is because, prior to the enactment of the *Charter*, and owing to the absence of a meaningful exclusionary rule, the lawfulness of police arrests was an issue only in those cases in which the accused or the police officer was charged with an offence arising out of an altercation that gave rise to the question of whether the officer was acting in the "lawful execution of his or her duties" or in the even rarer cases where a tort action was brought against a police officer. Only in those few situations was the issue central to the litigation. Today, even without an "altercation," the lawfulness of police action can give rise

---

14 *R v Mann*, 2004 SCC 52 at para 15 [*Mann*].

15 *R v Grant*, 2009 SCC 32 at para 54 [*Grant*]. Two years before *Grant*, in *R v Clayton*, 2007 SCC 32 at para 19 [*Clayton*], the Court had said:

> If the police conduct in detaining and searching Clayton and Farmer amounted to a lawful exercise of their common law powers, there was no violation of their *Charter* rights. *If, on the other hand, the conduct fell outside the scope of these powers, it represented an infringement of the right under the* Charter *not to be arbitrarily detained or subjected to an unreasonable search or seizure.* [Emphasis added.]

However, the emphasized words were *obiter*, and the Court does not seem to have realized at the time that it was settling a point it had earlier said remained an open question. In *Grant*, the Court's intention is clear.

to arguments about the actions of the police. Post-*Charter*, and under section 9 post-*Grant*, the questions "was it unlawful?" and "was it arbitrary?" have been equated, so courts are regularly faced with deciding whether or not the police action in question might be considered lawful.

This approach to *Charter* rights makes it much easier, as well as more important, to assess whether police action is "authorized by law," which will be discussed shortly. There is one final preliminary observation to be made, however, about the importance of judicial "attitude" in deciding the scope of police powers, no matter what their source. Put simply, sometimes courts reason from the perspective of the police, while sometimes they reason from the perspective of the individual subject to police action. Even when interpreting a statute, quite different results can follow depending on which perspective is taken.

For example, *Biron* was discussed above, where the issue was whether a police officer could be said to have found the accused committing an offence when the accused was eventually acquitted of that offence. The majority, holding that the statutory "finds committing" standard was nonetheless met, focused on the problem that would face police officers if the ultimate verdict was important; if so, then "no peace officer can ever decide, when making an arrest without a warrant, that the person arrested is 'committing a criminal offence.'"[16] The dissent, in contrast, approached the issue from the perspective of the individual: what mattered to them was "the social and legal, and indeed political, principle upon which our criminal law is based, namely, the right of an individual to be left alone, to be free of private or public restraint, save as the law provides otherwise."[17]

Similarly, in *R v Tim*, the same difference in approach can be seen, in that case between the Alberta Court of Appeal and the Supreme Court of Canada. A police officer had arrested an accused, incorrectly thinking that it was unlawful to possess gabapentin. The Alberta Court of Appeal found the arrest lawful because the officer should be "assessed according to the test of the normally prudent, diligent and competent police officer in the same circumstances," and requiring "an encyclopedic knowledge of the contents of Schedules I to IV of the *CDSA* [*Controlled Drugs and Substances Act*]" would be to set an impossible standard for police officers.[18] The Supreme Court, in contrast, was not focused on fairness to police officers but fairness to individuals, who should be able to "legitimately expect that police officers who deal with him or her will comply

16 *Biron*, above note 3 at 75.

17 *Ibid* at 64.

18 *R v Tim*, 2020 ABCA 469 at paras 39 & 40, respectively [*Tim* ABCA].

with the law in force, which necessarily requires them to know the statutes, regulations and by-laws they are called upon to enforce."[19]

The impact of these differences in approach is difficult to predict, precisely because they are not so much an application of any legal doctrine as they are simply a matter of perspective: which interest will this particular court decide to give prominence to in considering this particular power? Nonetheless, this factor should be recognized as having a noticeable impact on the development of police powers. We will now therefore turn to the possible sources of those powers.

2) Statute

Clearly, the most authoritative way in which police abilities to arrest or detain are created is by statute. Statutory powers tend to be of two kinds: general powers and specific powers. The *Criminal Code* sets out general powers of arrest by police and citizens that apply to most offences, while other statutes will tend to set out particular powers for particular kinds of offences or investigations. Furthermore, both provincial governments and the federal government specify powers of arrest.[20] Later we will discuss particular statutory powers; here we wish to discuss how statutory powers are interpreted and applied by the courts. Two questions can be distinguished: how expansively individual powers should be interpreted and how courts should react to powers being used for something other than their originally intended purpose. We will discuss those questions in order.

There is not a lot of guidance on how statutory powers to arrest or detain should be interpreted, and several outstanding issues on this front remain. Initially, the issue becomes how expansively the courts should interpret particular statutory powers. As elsewhere in the criminal law, the issue is whether such powers should be read restrictively in accordance with the purported principle of "strict construction" or whether the primary issue is one of legislative purpose.

The courts have struggled with when they should read in powers to a statute that are not specifically set out. The Supreme Court has been

---

19 *R v Tim*, 2022 SCC 12 at para 30 [*Tim*], quoting Côté J in *Kosoian v Société de transport de Montréal*, 2019 SCC 59 [*Kosoian*].

20 For arrest procedures in the case of provincial offences, some provinces have adopted a general statute that incorporates the *Criminal Code* arrest provisions into provincial law. See, for example, *Provincial Offences Procedure Act*, RSA 2000, c P-34, s 3. In others, a general provincial statute sets out arrest and other powers available in the case of a provincial offence. See, for example, *Provincial Offences Act*, RSO 1990, c P.33.

faced with questions such as whether a wiretap order could authorize the entry into a home to place a listening device,[21] and even earlier—in the cases of *Eccles v Bourque*,[22] *R v Landry*,[23] and *R v Macooh*[24]—it had to decide whether a power to arrest included the right to enter a home for the purposes of arrest.

The high watermark for accused persons is likely the 1981 pre-*Charter* judgment of the Supreme Court in *Colet v The Queen*, where the Court was asked to decide whether a warrant to seize weapons included the power to enter a home to search for those weapons. Justice Ritchie for the Court declined to so hold, stating:

> I am of the opinion that any statutory provision authorizing police officers to invade the property of others without invitation or permission would be an encroachment on the common law rights of the property owner and in case of any ambiguity would be subject to a strict construction in favour of the common law rights of the owner. This is made plain from the following excerpt from *Maxwell on Interpretation of Statutes*, 12th ed., at p. 251 where it is said:
>
> > Statutes which encroach on the rights of the subject, whether as regards person or property, are subject to a strict construction in the same way as penal Acts. It is a recognised rule that they should be interpreted, if possible, so as to respect such rights, and if there is any ambiguity the construction which is in favour of the freedom of the individual should be adopted.
>
> It appears to me to follow that any provision authorizing police officers to search and enter private property must be phrased in express terms and the provisions of the *Interpretation Act* are not to be considered as clothing police officers by implication with authority to search when s. 105(1) and the warrant issued pursuant thereto are limited to seizure.[25]

Today, the Supreme Court seems to continue to view *Colet* as authoritative since it has often cited the decision, and lower courts rely on it for its particular finding.[26] However, the Court has not been consistent

---

21 See *R v Lyons*, [1984] 2 SCR 633 [*Lyons*]; *Reference re: Judicature Act (Alberta), s. 27(1)*, [1984] 2 SCR 697.

22 [1975] 2 SCR 739 [*Eccles*].

23 [1986] 1 SCR 145 [*Landry*].

24 [1993] 2 SCR 802 [*Macooh*].

25 *Colet v The Queen*, [1981] 1 SCR 2 at 10.

26 See, for example, *R v Asante-Mensah*, 2003 SCC 38 at para 41 [*Asante-Mensah*], where Binnie J says: "I accept, of course, that statutes which encroach on the liberty of the subject should be construed, where ambiguous, in favour of upholding

in its approach. In *R v Lyons*, for example, the majority contented itself with citing *Colet* for the purpose of noting that, where Parliament has regulated search and seizure, it has been express in doing so.[27] As the question before the Court in *Lyons* was whether Part VI of the *Criminal Code* allowed entry to put in place a listening device, and since such an entry was not a search, *Colet* had no application. According to the majority, then, the legislation impliedly authorized the entry to place the device. Indeed, as one reviews *Colet's* treatment by the Court, it seems clear that the intent is to limit it to circumstances involving trespass on real property and that it may now not be correct to describe the case as involving any general statutory interpretation advice involving police powers. For example, in *R v Grant* in 1993, the majority cited *Colet* only for the proposition that there was a "strong common law rule against warrantless intrusions onto private property."[28] While significant, such treatment seems to downplay the principle of strict construction there espoused. In some ways, when one thinks of the Supreme Court's treatment of statutory interpretation, one needs to ask what the Court has done as opposed to what it says it should do. Unfortunately, it is clear that the Court has often been very willing to interpret legislation expansively so as to authorize police actions.

For example, in *R v M(MR)*, a school vice-principal searched a student, finding drugs.[29] The central issue in *M(MR)* related to the search, but in that case, as in many others, the power to search also entailed a power to detain.[30] Under the analytical approach laid out by the Court for dealing with section 8, a search must have been prescribed by law.[31] In this case, the statute did not create any explicit search power for the vice-principal. However, the Court noted that the *Education Act* called for teachers and school officials to maintain proper order and discipline in the school and to attend to the health and comfort of students; this responsibility, the Court held, "by necessary implication authorizes searches of students."[32]

---

such liberty: *Colet v The Queen*, [1981] 1 S.C.R. 2, at p. 10." However, Binnie J then proceeds to find that the word "arrest" is clear and unambiguous, leaving no room for the doctrine of strict construction to operate. See also *R v Kokesch*, [1990] 3 SCR 3 [*Kokesch*]. Lower court decisions accepting that "seize" does not imply "search" include *R v Zargar*, 2014 ONSC 1415 and *R v G(J)*, 2012 ONCJ 127.

27 *Lyons*, above note 21 at 692–93.

28 *R v Grant*, [1993] 3 SCR 223 at 239.

29 *R v M(MR)*, [1998] 3 SCR 393 [*M(MR)*].

30 See, for example, *Mann*, above note 14; *R v Greaves*, 2004 BCCA 484 [*Greaves*]; *R v Ferris* (1998), 162 DLR (4th) 87 (BCCA) [*Ferris*].

31 *Collins*, above note 12.

32 *M(MR)*, above note 29 at para 51.

Similarly, in *R v Orbanski; R v Elias*,[33] the police had stopped a motorist and required him to perform various roadside sobriety tests before allowing him to contact counsel. There was no dispute that this violated the right to counsel in section 10(b), and the issue was whether that violation was justified under section 1. Within the section 1 analysis, there was only one real point of contention: whether the violation was "prescribed by law." On the surface, it was quite obvious that the relevant statute did not explicitly state that "police may delay informing a person of the right to counsel in order to perform roadside sobriety tests." Indeed, the statute did not even explicitly say that police could conduct roadside sobriety tests. However, the majority of the Court held that that power was "necessarily implicit under the general statutory vehicle stop provision."[34] They then concluded that the operational requirements of exercising that power amounted to an implied limit in the statute to the right to counsel. In that event, the section 1 requirement was met.

Obviously, finding implied powers in statutes raises some concerns. One of the benefits of statutory law is that Parliament or a legislature is in a better position to find the right balance between individual liberty and the need for police powers; therefore, that is preferable to a court finding new powers to be "necessarily implicit."[35] Another objection is that the purpose of setting out the law in a statute is to provide predictability, but finding powers to be necessarily implicit reduces the level of certainty anyone can have as to the extent of police powers. This leads to the second area of ambiguity: what happens when state agents use powers for something other than their intended purpose? This question will be discussed at much greater length below (under the heading "The Importance of Police Purpose"), but it is worth introducing the subject here.

Statutory law is replete with powers of "regulation," especially at the provincial level. It is often said that the provinces have the power to regulate dangerous activities in the interests of public safety. What should the courts do when a power that is authorized for public safety purposes is used not for the purpose of ensuring public safety but rather for the purpose of detecting and prosecuting criminal offences? All police action can be seen as fitting somewhere along a spectrum from ensuring compliance with regulatory rules to the investigation of serious crime. State action may, even in the most mundane regulatory inspection, be seen as marginally done for the purpose of protecting the public. For example, highway traffic laws require all drivers to carry with them,

---

33 [2005] 2 SCR 3 [*Orbanski*].

34 *Ibid* at para 43.

35 *R v Koma*, 2015 SKCA 92 at para 90 [*Koma*].

and to produce, a driver's licence on demand to a police officer. Clearly, driver licensing regulation is done in an overall sense to protect the public by ensuring that only qualified drivers are operating motor vehicles. However, where a properly authorized and qualified driver forgets their licence at home and is fined for not producing it, citizens will often feel that the resulting ticket is not particularly aimed at ensuring safety but at punishing the individual for forgetfulness. Nonetheless, such police actions are largely non-controversial and usually lawful. Indeed, traffic safety laws largely allow the police to stop drivers at random for the purpose of checking licences and for sobriety, and even if such actions can be seen as arbitrary or as standardless, the courts have had little difficulty upholding such actions as reasonable limits justified in a democratic society under section 1 of the *Charter*.[36]

On the other hand, where the police use traffic safety or other regulatory powers not for the predominant purpose of enforcing those laws but rather as a way to justify the stopping, detention, search, or interrogation of those they suspect of criminal offending, this practice becomes much more controversial and problematic. At one point, one could have said that the courts resisted authorizing overreaching or "misuse" of such powers created for one purpose for another purpose, particularly where the police purpose can be seen as unrelated to the purpose of the regulatory power's existence.[37] For example, while no one doubts that laws against impaired driving, even though criminal in nature, are primarily aimed at protecting highway safety, the same cannot be said of drug laws—at least when such laws are aimed at possessory and trafficking activities as opposed to driving under the influence. Similarly, where the police put up a roadblock for the purpose of catching a bank robber leaving a certain locale, it is clear that the purpose of any vehicle stops would be to catch the offender, not to ensure public safety on the roads. As we will see below, the courts have been struggling to draw a line in the sand by purposive interpretation of police statutory powers so as to attempt to keep them in check and within their "proper" spheres.[38] At one point, there was some attempt to prevent the use of regulatory or other powers when an officer's "predominant purpose" was to investigate criminal offending; however, that seems no longer to be the case. The result is that

36 See *R v Ladouceur*, [1990] 1 SCR 1257 [*Ladouceur* 1990]; *R v Hufsky*, [1988] 1 SCR 621 [*Hufsky*].

37 See *Dedman*, above note 10, particularly the Court's discussion on subterfuge or pretext. See also *R v Mellenthin*, [1992] 3 SCR 615 at para 15 [*Mellenthin*]: "Random stop programs must not be turned into a means of conducting either an unfounded general inquisition or an unreasonable search."

38 See Section B(2), below in this chapter.

statutory provisions intended for one context can frequently be used in other ways, once again expanding police power.

To combat the expansion of police powers brought about by these two trends, one might look to the *Charter* for guidance. *Charter* rights are intended to protect individuals against exercises of state power, so a broad approach to the former will result in a narrower approach to the latter. For our present purposes, it is useful to see what the Supreme Court of Canada has said about the interpretation of section 9 of the *Charter*. In 2009's *Grant*, the Court held:

> [15] As for any constitutional provision, the starting point must be the language of the section. Where questions of interpretation arise, a generous, purposive and contextual approach should be applied.
>
> [16] Constitutional guarantees such as ss. 9 and 10 should be interpreted in a "generous rather than . . . legalistic [way], aimed at fulfilling the purpose of the guarantee and securing for individuals the full benefit of the *Charter's* protection" (*R. v. Big M Drug Mart Ltd.*, [1985] 1 S.C.R. 295, at p. 344). Unduly narrow, technical approaches to *Charter* interpretation must be avoided, given their potential to "subvert the goal of ensuring that right holders enjoy the full benefit and protection of the *Charter*" (*Doucet-Boudreau v. Nova Scotia (Minister of Education)*, 2003 SCC 62, [2003] 3 S.C.R. 3, at para. 23).
>
> [17] While the twin principles of purposive and generous interpretation are related and sometimes conflated, they are not the same. The purpose of a right must always be the dominant concern in its interpretation; generosity of interpretation is subordinate to and constrained by that purpose (P.W. Hogg, *Constitutional Law of Canada* (5th ed. Supp.), vol. 2, at pp. 36-30 and 36-31). While a narrow approach risks impoverishing a *Charter* right, an overly generous approach risks expanding its protection beyond its intended purposes. In brief, we must construe the language of ss. 9 and 10 in a generous way that furthers, without overshooting, its purpose: *Big M Drug Mart*, at p. 344.[39]

It therefore behooves a court to attempt to identify the purpose of a right and then to attempt to interpret statutory language in such a way that the purpose of the *Charter* right is respected. Of course, the purpose of the *Charter* right and the purpose of the statute granting a particular power to the police may be in conflict. In such circumstances, the legislation should be struck down if it cannot be interpreted in such a way as to respect the *Charter* right in question.[40]

---

39 *Grant*, above note 15 at paras 15–17.

40 An early post-*Charter* example would be search pursuant to writs of assistance, which were struck down in *R v Noble* (1984), 48 OR (2d) 643 (CA).

A large challenge for a book such as this, then, is to identify the purpose of the right in question, and Supreme Court cases bring us closer to being able to do so. In *Grant*, the majority analyzed the purpose of section 9 in conjunction with the correlative rights under section 7 and section 10 of the *Charter*. The latter section delineates the right to be informed of the reasons for the arrest or detention and the right to retain and instruct counsel—rights that, like those in section 9, arise at the point of arrest or detention. Thus, the majority, in noting that these rights are interconnected, suggest that section 9 is intended to protect individuals from "unjustified" detentions.[41] Furthermore, the Court has held that section 8's protection against unreasonable search and seizure encompasses personal privacy[42] and amounts to the right, in the absence of express powers to invade privacy, to "be let alone."[43] This obviously has some relevance in the context of section 9 as well. Unfortunately, the reasoning remains circular in that it seems to suggest that, in order to respect the right to privacy, all the state needs to do is to specify a power while doing little in the way of protecting Canadians' freedom (other than being explicit about the limitation). We will see as well that the concept of "justified" police powers has played a large role in the *creation*, as opposed to the *limitation*, of police powers in Canada.

3) Common Law

Before the enactment of the *Charter*, the common law had started to recognize a power in the courts to create police powers. This power was based on the English decision in *R v Waterfield*, which was about whether the constable in that case was acting in the execution of his duties, and nothing more.[44] Nonetheless, the "*Waterfield* test" became, in Canada, a method of creating new police powers at common law and was frequently relied on as a basis for saying that police action was lawful when that issue became a more important one because of the *Charter*. More recently, the Court has discouraged the use of the term "the *Waterfield* test" in favour of calling it the "ancillary powers doctrine," precisely because *Waterfield* was never intended to set out a test playing the role it has taken on in Canada.[45]

---

41 *Grant*, above note 15 at para 20.

42 See *Hunter v Southam Inc*, [1984] 2 SCR 145 [*Hunter*].

43 See *R v Stillman*, [1997] 1 SCR 607 [*Stillman*]; see also Sopinka J's discussion in *Kokesch*, above note 26.

44 *R v Waterfield*, [1963] 3 All ER 659 (CA) [*Waterfield*].

45 *Fleming v Ontario*, 2019 SCC 45 at para 43 [*Fleming*].

The first citing of *Waterfield* by the Supreme Court appears to be *R v Stenning*, where in 1970 Martland J said:

> Assuming that Wilkinson did, technically, trespass on the premises, the fact remains that he was there to investigate an occurrence which had happened earlier in the evening, which involved the firing of a rifle. He had been sent out for that purpose. He was charged, under s. 47 of *The Police Act*, R.S.O. 1960, c. 298, with the duty of preserving the peace, preventing robberies and other crimes, and apprehending offenders. He was in the course of making an investigation, in the carrying out of that duty, when he was assaulted by the respondent.
>
> We were referred to a number of English authorities and some Canadian cases, all of which turned upon facts which differed from the facts found in this case. Their effect is stated in the judgment of the Court of Criminal Appeal in *R. v. Waterfield* [[1964] 1 Q.B. 164 at 170, [1963] 3 All E.R. 659, 48 Cr. App. R. 42.]:
>
>> In the judgment of this court it would be difficult, and in the present case it is unnecessary, to reduce within specific limits the general terms in which the duties of police constables have been expressed. In most cases it is probably more convenient to consider what the police constable was actually doing and in particular whether such conduct was prima facie an unlawful interference with a person's liberty or property. If so, it is then relevant to consider whether *(a)* such conduct falls within the general scope of any duty imposed by statute or recognised at common law and *(b)* whether such conduct, albeit within the general scope of such a duty, involved an unjustifiable use of powers associated with the duty.
>
> On the facts of this case, as found by the trial judge, whether Wilkinson was, technically, a trespasser, or not, he was engaged in the execution of his duties at the time when he was assaulted by the respondent, and at that time there had been no unlawful interference with either the liberty or the property of the respondent.[46]

As one can see, the English court expressly held that it is better to look at specific facts rather than to try to identify the police power being employed.[47] This point was soon forgotten as the Supreme Court of

46 *R v Stenning*, [1970] SCR 631 at 636–37 [*Stenning*].

47 *Waterfield* was also relied upon by the Supreme Court in *R v Knowlton*, [1974] SCR 443, where the Court held that the police were acting lawfully and were justified in controlling access to a public place when the Russian premier was visiting the city of Edmonton. Likewise, in *Poupart v Lafortune*, [1974] SCR 175 [*Poupart*], a case

Canada began to use the *Waterfield* formulation to declare general police powers.

Post-*Charter*, the Court started in *Dedman v The Queen* to employ *Waterfield* as "a test for whether the officer had common law authority for what he did."[48] Justice Gerald Le Dain, writing for the majority (and over the strong dissent of Dickson CJC), stated that in his opinion the test required a court to determine which police powers are "reasonably necessary" in the execution of police duties.[49] While many authors have criticized the Court for a willingness to create police powers at common law,[50] the Court has done so on many occasions. In almost all occasions where the Court has taken this step, it has rued the fact that the issue had not been dealt with by statute. Yet, in the face of a perceived failure of such parliamentary action, the Court has, for the most part, seen it as its obligation to clarify what police power exists and what police powers the courts are prepared to create and recognize. In *Dedman*, for example, the Court created the power to conduct checkstops to combat impaired driving. There, Dickson CJC complained in dissent that this was not the Court's job but rather was a job that should be left to Parliament. He

---

involving a civil suit against a police officer by an innocent bystander who was shot by the police officer, the Court noted at 183–84 that the officer was

> engaged in the hazardous performance of a grave duty imposed on him by law. In carrying out such a duty a peace officer must undoubtedly refrain from making any unjustifiable use of the powers relating to it. This principle was recognized in *Regina v. Waterfield and Another* [L.R. [1964] 1 K.B. 164.], at p. 170 et seq., and recently recalled in this Court in the as yet unpublished decision of *Knowlton v. The Queen*. However . . . the actions of Lafortune cannot, in a case like that before the Court, be evaluated as they would be if it were a case in which the precautions to be taken in accordance with the duty not to injure others were not conditioned by the requirements of a public duty. In short, the police officer incurs no liability for damage caused to another when without negligence he does precisely what the legislature requires him to do.

48 *Dedman*, above note 10 at para 67.

49 *Ibid* at para 69.

50 See Glen Luther, "Police Power and the *Charter of Rights and Freedoms*: Creation or Control?" (1986–87) 51 *Saskatchewan Law Review* 217; Patrick Healy, "Investigative Detention in Canada" [2005] *Criminal Law Review* 98; James Stribopoulos, "The Forgotten Right: Section 9 of the *Charter*, Its Purpose and Meaning" (2008) 40 *Supreme Court Law Review* (2d) 211; W. Wesley Pue & Robert Diab, "The Gap in Canadian Police Powers: Canada Needs 'Public Order Policing' Legislation" (2010) 28 *Windsor Review of Legal & Social Issues* 87; Richard Jochelson, "Ancillary Issues with Oakes: The Development of the Waterfield Test and the Problem of Fundamental Constitutional Theory" (2012–13) 43 *Ottawa Law Review* 355; Steve Coughlan, *Criminal Procedure*, 4th ed (Toronto: Irwin Law, 2020) at 17–23 [Coughlan, *Criminal Procedure*].

quoted himself in dissent in the *Wiretap Reference* as saying: "Any such principle would be nothing short of a fiat for illegality on the part of the police whenever the benefit of police action appeared to outweigh the infringement of an individual's rights."[51] As we will see, particularly when we look at police powers to detain short of arrest, this caution was prescient.[52]

The Supreme Court's actions seem a bit blinkered. Arrest powers have long been comprehensively legislated, so the failure to legislate a power of detention short of arrest could be seen as an intentional omission on the part of the legislators. Furthermore, where the Court has found gaps but has not filled them by creating a power at common law, especially in the area of search, Parliament has often responded by enacting statutory powers.[53] As well, given the broad statutory power given to courts to grant general warrants, there is expressly a power in an issuing court to authorize the police in a given situation to "do any thing" specified in the warrant.[54] To suggest, therefore, that there is no legislative action in areas of search and seizure and in arrest and detention seems somewhat unreal.

There is no question that there is a substantial body of legislation in force that authorizes arrests and detentions. Yet the Supreme Court of Canada has continued to create powers almost at will. In cases such as *R v Godoy*,[55] *Mann*,[56] *Clayton*,[57] *R v Aucoin*,[58] *R v Chehil*,[59] and *R v MacDonald*,[60] the Court created powers to enter, to detain, or to search, all as ways of avoiding having to find that the police were not authorized by law to do what they had done.[61]

---

51 *Dedman*, above note 10 at para 24. See also *Wiretap Reference*, [1984] 2 SCR 697.

52 See Chapter 3, Section C.

53 See Michal Fairburn, "Twenty-Five Years in Search of a Reasonable Approach" (2008) 40 *Supreme Court Law Review* (2d) 56. In that article, Fairburn traces how ss 184.2, 487.01, 492.2, 492.1, 487.05, and 487.092 were all enacted in response to court decisions in which police were found not to have had the power to do what they had done.

54 See Steve Coughlan, "General Warrants at the Crossroads: Limit or Licence?" (2003) 10 *Criminal Reports* (6th) 269.

55 [1999] 1 SCR 311 [*Godoy*].

56 *Mann*, above note 14.

57 *Clayton*, above note 15.

58 2012 SCC 66 [*Aucoin*].

59 2013 SCC 49 [*Chehil*].

60 2014 SCC 3 [*MacDonald*].

61 See also *R v Reeves*, 2018 SCC 56, where Moldaver J, in a concurring opinion, relied on *Waterfield* to offer a tentative view on the police power to enter a joint residence when invited by one of the occupants.

Whether this is an appropriate approach has been the subject of some debate in the Court. In *Clayton*, Binnie J described *Waterfield* as an "odd godfather for common law police powers" and relied on it only as the "least worst solution."[62] Shortly afterward in *R v Kang-Brown*, LeBel J, who spoke for four of the justices, had this to say about the creation at common law of a police power to search with a sniffer dog on less than reasonable grounds and without a warrant:

> The common law has long been viewed as a law of liberty. Should we move away from that tradition, which is still part of the ethos of our legal system and of our democracy? This case is about the freedom of individuals and the proper function of the courts as guardians of the Constitution. I doubt that it should lead us to depart from the common law tradition of freedom by changing the common law itself to restrict the freedoms protected by the Constitution under s. 8 of the *Charter*.[63]

Alas, the majority seemed prepared to create such a power. They were led—ironically—by Binnie J, who rejected the position taken by LeBel J, saying the Court had "crossed the Rubicon," by which he apparently meant that the Court should now feel its responsibility to further declare and refine police powers when it thinks it appropriate to do so.[64] Interestingly, Binnie J based his position largely on a belief that the litigants were entitled to know that a court was prepared to make law when necessary. This is quite counterintuitive as a justification. The argument seemingly rests on the notion that there ought to be more certainty in the law and that it should be knowable in advance. By their very nature, however, new common law powers are known to exist only after the fact, and the possibility of their creation renders the law uncertain.

Indeed, the lack of knowability associated with common law powers was starkly demonstrated by the Court's decision in *MacDonald*.[65] That decision saw the creation of a new common law power: a "safety search." In effect, the Court took the power to search for weapons incidental to an investigative detention that had been created in *Mann* and turned it into a free-standing power.[66] What is interesting about the decision in this context is that there was a narrow split in the Court—not over what the new power *should* be but over what *Mann* had actually *said*. Four judges thought *Mann* had created a power based on reasonable grounds, while three thought the power created there required only reasonable

62 *Clayton*, above note 15 at paras 75 & 76.

63 *R v Kang-Brown*, [2008] 1 SCR 456 at para 12 [*Kang-Brown*].

64 *Ibid* at para 22.

65 *MacDonald*, above note 60.

66 See the discussion in Section B(1)(f), below in this chapter.

suspicion. It is difficult to imagine a clearer illustration of the lack of clarity around common law powers.

Finally, there is one other aspect of the current approach to common law powers that makes them less knowable. Statutory powers are relatively specific: if particular conditions are met, then a particular power arises. For example, if (1) there are reasonable grounds to believe a person has committed an offence and (2) that offence was an indictable one, then section 495(1)(a) of the *Code* creates a power of arrest. At one point, common law powers followed that same model. For example, in *Mann*, the Court provided that if (1) there were a recent or ongoing offence, (2) a police officer has reasonable suspicion that there is a nexus between a suspect and that offence, and (3) a detention is reasonably necessary on an objective view of the totality of the circumstances, then a power of investigative detention exists. While this power is not unambiguous, it does at least set out criteria that can be separately considered in order to determine—and, importantly, to determine in advance—whether the power of investigative detention arises. As the Court has noted, "It is important for the courts to give officers the clearest possible guidance as to what common law powers are available to them within the general scope of their duties."[67]

The current approach to detention, however, is set out in *Aucoin* and simply asks whether the detention "is reasonably necessary in the totality of the circumstances."[68] That is not a power, in the sense of pre-established criteria being used to determine whether the police are authorized to take particular action. Rather, it is a conscious decision *only* to decide after the fact whether or not the police made the right decision. To adopt that approach to the law not only makes police powers unknowable even in principle, it also seems to be an abandonment of knowability as a goal of the system.

It is possible that the Court has signalled its intention to show more circumspection in the use of the ancillary powers doctrine. The most recent decision to consider the issue was *R v Fleming*, where the court below, the Ontario Court of Appeal, had concluded based on *Waterfield* that there was a common law police power to arrest an individual in order to keep the peace. The Supreme Court of Canada overturned that result, finding that no such power existed. The decision might simply be based on a conclusion that arrest powers in particular are exhaustively codified and therefore that there is no "gap" to be filled by the common law in that area. However, the decision can also be seen as showing more skepticism around the ancillary powers doctrine generally. The Court

67 *Fleming*, above note 45 at para 52.

68 *Aucoin*, above note 58 at para 36.

cites the dissenting judgment in *Dedman* for the "fundamental tenet" that police "have limited powers and are only entitled to interfere with the liberty or property of the citizen to the extent authorized by law."[69] They note that "courts should tread lightly when considering proposed common law police powers."[70] In concluding that the power sought was not reasonably necessary, they hold that "[a]n intrusion upon liberty should be a measure of last resort, not a first option. To conclude otherwise would be generally to sanction actions that infringe the freedom of individuals significantly as long as they are effective. That is a recipe for a police state, not a free and democratic society."[71] And finally, although it was not necessary to the case in front of them, the Court cast doubt on a common law power that had previously been recognized in earlier lower court decisions: a power to arrest a person who is about to commit a breach of the peace.[72]

All of this could be explained as motivated by doubts exclusive to the particular power sought to be created, one to arrest a person who had not personally breached the peace or caused harm. However, it also appears to have undertones of restraint in the use of the ancillary powers doctrine and so might suggest a shift in attitude on the part of the Court.

4) *Charter*

As noted above, since the enactment of the *Charter*, police powers have expanded greatly. This is indeed ironic in that, in its first major *Charter* decision, the Supreme Court declared the *Charter* to represent a check on state power and not a source thereof:

> I begin with the obvious. The *Canadian Charter of Rights and Freedoms* is a purposive document. Its purpose is to guarantee and to protect, within the limits of reason, the enjoyment of the rights and freedoms it enshrines. It is intended to constrain governmental action inconsistent with those rights and freedoms; it is not in itself an authorization for governmental action. In the present case this means, as Prowse J.A. pointed out, that in guaranteeing the right to be secure from unreasonable searches and *seizures*, s. 8 acts as a limitation on whatever powers of search and seizure the federal or provincial governments already and otherwise possess. It does not in itself confer any powers, even of

69 *Fleming*, above note 45 at para 38.
70 *Ibid* at para 41.
71 *Ibid* at para 98.
72 *Ibid* at para 60: "While it is not necessary to decide this in the instant case, I seriously question whether a common law power of this nature would still be necessary in Canada today."

> "reasonable" search and seizure, on these governments. This leads, in my view, to the further conclusion that an assessment of the constitutionality of a search and seizure, or of a statute authorizing a search or seizure, must focus on its "reasonable" or "unreasonable" impact or the subject of the search or the seizure, and not simply on its rationality in furthering some valid government objective.[73]

In the detention context, however, the impact of the *Charter* has tended to be the opposite of that. Section 9 guarantees a right against arbitrary detention, and it was decided at an early stage that a detention that was authorized by law was not arbitrary. This meant that the Court was often faced with a choice between two alternatives: find that the accused's *Charter* rights were violated or find that the police were authorized at common law to do what they did and therefore did not "arbitrarily" detain the accused. In cases such as *Mann*, *Clayton*, and *Aucoin*, the Supreme Court opted to create new powers rather than find an arbitrary detention, and the same approach has been taken in numerous lower court decisions.

Note as well that *Charter* analysis under either section 8 or section 9 involves asking not just whether the state action was authorized by some law but whether that law itself is *Charter* compliant.[74] However, that step can be obscured when the "law itself" is a common law power that has just been created in the very case in which the reasonableness of the law is then to be assessed. At first, the Court was careful to try to separate the steps: in the 1990 decision in *R v Ladouceur*, the Court created a roving random stop power at common law, found that it violated section 9, but then found that that violation was saved under section 1.[75] Since then, however, the Court has tended to operate on the implicit assumption that if the new rule were *not* reasonable, they would not have created it. However, this means that there is no explicit *Charter* scrutiny of the type that would be applied in other cases. As Binnie J noted in *Clayton*:

> Conflating in a *Waterfield*-type analysis the consideration of the individual's ss. 8 and 9 rights and society's s. 1 interests can only add to the problematic elasticity of common law police powers, and sidestep the

73 *Hunter*, above note 42 at 156–57 [emphasis added].

74 Section 8 analysis is governed by the approach in *Collins*, above note 12 at para 23: "A search will be reasonable if it is authorized by law, *if the law itself is reasonable* and if the manner in which the search was carried out is reasonable" [emphasis added]. Although it took some time, a parallel approach was eventually adopted for s 9. Notably in this context, in *Grant*, above note 15 at para 56, the Court held that "for a detention to be non-arbitrary, it must be authorized *by a law which is itself non-arbitrary*" [emphasis added]. See also *R v Le*, 2019 SCC 34 at para 124 [*Le*].

75 *Ladouceur* 1990, above note 36.

> real policy debate in which competing individual and societal interests are required to be clearly articulated in the established framework of *Charter* analysis.[76]

It remains a bit of a mystery as to how a court should decide whether to apply the *Waterfield* test to a given situation. Initially, the "test" was designed only to assess a particular action by a particular officer. Now that the same formulation has been employed regularly to create general police powers, it appears that we have lost sight of what the Court was attempting to do in devising the *Waterfield* test. The current attitude seems to conflate the two branches of *Waterfield* into a single question that asks, "Do the police need this power to carry out their general duties?" If so, the answer seems to be that "they shall have it." This is the point made by LeBel J in his dissent in *Orbanski*, a decision discussed above, when he said:

> The adoption of a rule limiting *Charter* rights on the basis of what amounts to a utilitarian argument in favour of meeting the needs of police investigations through the development of common law police powers would tend to give a potentially uncontrollable scope to the doctrine developed in the *Waterfield-Dedman* line of cases, which—and we sometimes forget such details—the court that created it took care not to apply on the facts before it (*R. v. Waterfield* . . .). The doctrine would now be encapsulated in the principle that what the police need, the police get, by judicial fiat if all else fails or if the legislature finds the adoption of legislation to be unnecessary or unwarranted. The courts would limit *Charter* rights to the full extent necessary to achieve the purpose of meeting the needs of the police. The creation of and justification for the limit would arise out of an initiative of the courts. In the context of cases such as those we are considering here, this kind of judicial intervention would pre-empt any serious *Charter* review of the limits, as the limits would arise out of initiatives of the courts themselves.[77]

It seems that such a formulation is not a "test" but simply a method by which police powers can forever be extended and declared, with little attention being paid to the inherent value of statutory construction and parliamentary responsibility or for the fundamental freedoms at stake. The *Charter* was surely designed to protect the latter, yet the Court's continued willingness to expand police powers has been a distinctive feature of this *Charter* era.

---

76 *Clayton*, above note 15 at para 61. See the further discussion of this issue below in Chapter 3, Section C(2).

77 *Orbanski*, above note 33 at para 81.

5) "Default" Powers

As noted earlier, the theoretical approach to police powers in Canada is that "[a]bsent a law to the contrary, individuals are free to do as they please. By contrast, the police (and more broadly, the state) may act only to the extent that they are empowered to do so by law."[78] This is true in principle, but its practical impact depends on there being a mechanism to assess whether the police were empowered to do what they did. Unless there is a way to challenge state action and hold actors accountable, it makes no practical difference whether or not that person was strictly "authorized."

Pre-*Charter*, this was a significant challenge. Unless an abuse of power was so great that it constituted an offence or a tort, there was effectively no basis upon which objection could be raised. As a result, an officer might, for example, detain a person without explicit authority to do so. But unless that became serious enough to constitute the tort of wrongful imprisonment (and the detainee had the inclination and the means to bring a civil action), there would be no consequences for the officer or the justice system. There is no right without a remedy, and the general lack of remedies effectively removed the right of people to object to some actions taken without lawful authority. As a result, although police were not strictly "empowered" to act in various ways, in effect they had the default power to do anything to which no effective complaint could be raised.

That situation is much improved because of the *Charter*, which now allows direct challenges to state action. It is further improved in the detention context by the rule that "a detention not authorized by law is arbitrary and violates s. 9."[79] That rule means that police action outside the strict limits of the given authority can be challenged even if it is not by itself so egregious as to be a tort or a crime. However, although that is a significant improvement, it has not entirely eliminated the existence of default powers.

In the context of section 8, the Court has held that if there is no reasonable expectation of privacy, then section 8 is not engaged. In *R v Tessling*,[80] the Court held that the Forward Looking Infrared Scanner (FLIR) technology as used by the police did not invade a homeowner's reasonable expectation of privacy. The result of that finding is that police are free to fly over Canadians' houses and take heat-emanation readings without repercussion; no law authorizes such an investigative step, but

78 *Mann*, above note 14 at para 15.

79 *Grant*, above note 15 at para 54.

80 2004 SCC 67.

nonetheless it is effectively permitted as there is no basis to object to it. Likewise, after *R v Patrick*,[81] the police are seemingly free to snoop through people's garbage since there is no reasonable expectation of privacy once the individual has put the garbage "out" for collection. These police actions are permitted, even though no power authorizes such activity, because there is no mechanism for objecting to them.

The same general approach applies to section 9: if what happened to the individual is not classified as a "detention," then the question of arbitrariness (that is, of whether there was legal authorization) does not arise. For example, in *R v Suberu*, the Court reached the conclusion that any person who is subject to an investigative detention has the right to counsel.[82] Suberu was not in fact told of this right to counsel during his interaction with a police officer, but, as it turned out, that did not mean that there was a breach of his rights. Rather, that interaction was simply "exploratory questioning," not a detention, so *Charter* rights did not arise.[83] As a result, although it is not strictly accurate to say that the police have a power of exploratory questioning, that might as well be true.[84]

More generally, in any circumstance where a person is found not to be detained, section 9 will not be triggered, so it will not be possible to review the state behaviour under the *Charter*. Cases have looked at whether the passenger in a vehicle that has been stopped should also be considered detained;[85] although each case ought to be considered individually, that sort of thing could easily ossify into a rule that "passengers are not detained." If that were to occur, the effect would be to state that passengers can be questioned without being told of their right to counsel.[86] Similarly, many cases take it that a person who flees is not detained; if that is so, then there is no mechanism to assess whether the police action from which the person fled was an arbitrary one.[87]

---

81 2009 SCC 17 [*Patrick*].

82 See the discussion in Chapter 5, Section B(1).

83 *R v Suberu*, 2009 SCC 33 at para 45: "[T]he definition of detention, as understood in these reasons, gives the police leeway to engage members of the public in non-coercive, exploratory questioning without necessarily triggering their Charter rights relating to detention."

84 See, for example, *R v Curry*, 2013 ONCA 420, or *R v Pearson*, 2012 ABCA 239 [*Pearson*].

85 See, for example, *R v Mooiman and Zahar*, 2016 SKCA 43.

86 In the search context, that was more or less the effect of *R v Belnavis*, [1997] 3 SCR 341 [*Belnavis*]. Although in principle every case is to be decided on the totality of the circumstances, in practice the case created the rule that "passengers do not have a reasonable expectation of privacy in a vehicle." However, there does not in fact seem to be a tendency toward concluding that passengers are not detained: see, for example, *R v Mhlongo*, 2017 ONCA 562, or *R v Loewen*, 2018 SKCA 69.

87 See the further discussion of this issue in Chapter 5, Section B(1).

Likewise, when the courts admit evidence in the face of finding a breach of rights, it often seems that the courts have de facto authorized the police to act in accord with the result of the case. It can be argued that to take away such an understanding from the cases is wrong, and indeed at times the Court has been explicit in saying to the police that particular police conduct, in the future, will result in exclusion, even though on this occasion the Court has not so decided. In *R v Silveira*, for example, Cory J explicitly said:

> Yet, the question remains, how should the police act in a situation where they have a serious and valid concern pertaining to the preservation of evidence while awaiting a search warrant. As a result of this case, police officers will be aware that to enter a dwelling-house without a warrant, even in exigent circumstances, constitutes such a serious breach of *Charter* rights that it will likely lead to a ruling that the evidence seized is inadmissible.[88]

Similarly, the Court has noted that a decision about exclusion should be dependent "not on the rights of the accused being tried, but rather on those of every individual whose rights might be violated in a similar way."[89] Put simply, a failure to exclude must not be allowed to send the message that the ends justify the means.[90] Other courts have specifically adverted to the danger of a failure to exclude seeming to amount to tacit acceptance of the police behaviour.[91]

On the other hand, where a court finds any given breach of rights not to be serious, it is easy to imagine the police seeing such a decision as in fact authorizing them to act similarly in the future. Indeed, one can sometimes read between the lines of the court decisions to see that some courts are not at all happy with the result the law has led them to in finding rights breaches. Indeed, on occasion, such disappointment by a court is even explicit.[92]

---

88 *R v Silveira*, [1995] 2 SCR 297 at para 152.

89 *Grant*, above note 15 at para 225, per the concurring reasons of Deschamps J.

90 *R v Harrison*, 2009 SCC 34 at para 40 [*Harrison*].

91 See, for example, *R v Harflett*, 2016 ONCA 248 at para 54 [*Harflett*]: the test for exclusion and specifically consideration of adjudication of the case on its merits "cannot be used to systematically require the admission of reliable evidence obtained in plain disregard of an accused's *Charter* rights."

92 Consider, for example, the position of the British Columbia Court of Appeal in *R v Martin* (1995), 97 CCC (3d) 241, where the majority said this at para 15:

> It follows from all of the above that the police constables denied the appellant's s. 8 *Charter* rights when they walked through the house. That is the unfortunate result of the inexorable operation of the Law of Unintended Consequences on the principles pronounced in *Hunter v. Southam*, *Collins*, *Kokesch*,

As well, in cases where the law is unclear, it seems that the police are often seen as acting appropriately when they push the limits of their powers. Generally, when deciding cases, the courts have intentionally not been clear in specifying what it is they expect the police to do in the future. If the police know that a given action might be illegal, are they encouraged to so act nonetheless in the absence of an express prohibition? Or, rather, is such conduct by the police to be seen as reckless in regard to the rights of the accused and therefore, in itself, to be held to represent a serious breach of rights? The Supreme Court's strong tendency has been to conclude that the lack of certainty about the existence of any particular police power makes it more likely that the evidence will be admitted. That approach, on a constantly continuing "one-off" basis, has the effect of expanding what the police were permitted to do.[93]

The existence, then, of de facto or default police power in Canada is a reality, and generally the courts have been unable or unwilling to control everyday police actions. It was only once the Supreme Court came to the realization that the police were consistently using an as of yet undeclared power to detain people for investigative purposes that it finally decided to recognize such a power in *Mann*.[94] One could equally criticize that decision for creating a power where none had existed or commend it for

---

> and other cases which apply those principles. Unfortunate because it forces police officers to become law breakers whenever they trespass while engaging in the performance of what might be called "good Samaritan" functions.

The decision was upheld by the Supreme Court in *R v Martin*, [1996] 1 SCR 463, which contented itself by saying at para 1: "We are all of the view that the appeal should be dismissed. Assuming without deciding that there was a breach of s. 8 of the *Canadian Charter of Rights and Freedoms*, we agree with the majority of the Court of Appeal that admission of the evidence would not bring the administration of justice into disrepute."

93 See the concurring judgment of Côté J in *R v Stairs*, 2022 SCC 11 at para 163 [*Stairs*]:

> As my colleague Karakatsanis J. reaffirmed in *R. v. Saeed*, 2016 SCC 24, [2016] 1 S.C.R. 518, at para. 126 (concurring in the result), "where the police act on a mistaken understanding of the law where the law is unsettled, their *Charter*-infringing conduct is considered to be less serious" (citing *R. v. Cole*, 2012 SCC 53, [2012] 3 S.C.R. 34, at paras. 86–87; *R. v. Vu*, 2013 SCC 60, [2013] 3 S.C.R. 657, at paras. 69 and 71; see also *R. v. Spencer*, 2014 SCC 43, [2014] 2 S.C.R. 212, at para. 77; *Fearon*, at para. 93. [Citation omitted.]

94 *Mann*, above note 14. Several academic articles had discussed the phenomenon of investigative detention prior to the Supreme Court's decision in *Mann*. See, for example, Alan Young, "All Along the Watchtower: Arbitrary Detention and the Police Function" (1991) 29 *Osgoode Hall Law Journal* 329; Steve Coughlan, "Search Based on Articulable Cause: Proceed with Caution or Full Stop?" (2002) 2 *Criminal Reports* (6th) 49; and James Stribopoulos, "A Failed Experiment? Investigative Detention: Ten Years Later" (2003) 41 *Alberta Law Review* 335.

reining in police behaviour by attaching limits where none had existed. As noted, courts have generally been reluctant to expressly direct police action in the future; thus, the common law has not often been effective in providing such direction to the police.

Every criminal accused that brings a *Charter* challenge to police conduct de facto represents other persons who may have been subjected to a similar police exercise of power. Therefore, it seems that the widespread use of the impugned technique by the police should become a matter of relevance, at least at the remedies stage in a *Charter* proceeding. The Supreme Court has acknowledged that the accused litigant is in fact often representative of others when arguing such points in the Court. In *Grant*, the majority expressly acknowledged this when it said:

> It should also be kept in mind that for every *Charter* breach that comes before the courts, many others may go unidentified and unredressed because they did not turn up relevant evidence leading to a criminal charge. In recognition of the need for courts to distance themselves from this behaviour, therefore, evidence that the *Charter*-infringing conduct was part of a pattern of abuse tends to support exclusion.[95]

B. PRELIMINARY ISSUES

1) Incidental and Supporting Powers and Provisions

The *Criminal Code* contains, under the heading "Protection of Persons Administering and Enforcing the Law," a number of supporting provisions relevant to the exercise of powers under the *Code*.[96] Strictly speaking, the sections are, for the most part, phrased as "justifications" rather than powers, and litigation over their meaning frequently occurs in the context of civil litigation.[97] They are therefore framed as though they are conceptually similar to, for example, the self-defence provisions in the *Code*. Nonetheless, their greater significance is the extent to which they

---

95 *Grant*, above note 15 at para 75.

96 We will here discuss ss 25 to 31, with one exception: s 25.1, which allows certain police officers to break the law in some cases, is not included in the discussion. It is quite unlike the other provisions, involving as it does the designation of particular officers and the submission of an annual report to Parliament. See the discussion of those provisions in Coughlan, *Criminal Procedure*, above note 50 at 274–79.

97 See, for example, *R v Garcia-Guiterrez* (1991), 5 CR (4th) 1 at para 37 (BCCA) [*Garcia-Guiterrez*], speaking of s 25: "[I]n the narrow sense, it provides no authority for the use of force, it merely provides a defence that may be raised when the force used is challenged as unlawful."

authorize police and others to act in ways that would not otherwise be permitted, so it is reasonable to think of them as a sort of police power.

That said, not all the provisions are limited to police. Section 25, for instance, justifying the use of force, applies as well to private persons who are required or authorized by law to do anything in the administration or enforcement of the law. And although the provisions are relevant to the powers of arrest and detention, which are the subject of this book, they are not limited to that context. The rules about warrants apply equally to search warrants, and whether the amount of force that was used in executing a search was reasonable can also be questioned.[98]

The supporting provisions will be discussed under three headings: use of force, rules regarding warrants, and breaches of the peace.

a) Use of Force

The use of force is governed by a combination of several provisions: sections 25, 26, and 27.[99]

Sections 25 and 26 have to do with the use of force in the execution of legal authority and must be read in conjunction with one another.[100] Section 25 states that anyone who is required or authorized by law to do anything in the administration or enforcement of the law (whether a private person, a peace officer, or a public officer, someone aiding one of those officers, or a person acting by virtue of some other office) "is, if he acts on reasonable grounds, justified in doing what he is required or authorized to do and in using as much force as is necessary for that purpose."[101] This must be seen in light of section 26, which states that "[e]very one who is authorized by law to use force is criminally responsible for any excess thereof according to the nature and quality of the act that constitutes the excess."[102] Note that the statutory justification attaches to anyone authorized to act, not merely to the police. This is consistent with the position at common law, which was that "the right to use reasonable force attaches at common law to the institution of an

---

98 *Ibid*; see also *R v Al-Fartossy*, 2007 ABCA 427 [*Al-Fartossy*].

99 These provisions govern the use of force in enforcing the provisions of the *Criminal Code*. A peace officer can also have the authority to use force in enforcing other statutes, such as a provincial *Highway Traffic Act*: *R v Tricker* (1995), 21 OR (3d) 575 (CA). In addition, the common law recognized a power to use force in making an arrest, an authority that attaches to the power, not to the person. Accordingly, a private citizen can also have the authority to use force in making an arrest: see, generally, *Asante-Mensah*, above note 26.

100 *R v Hebert*, [1996] 2 SCR 272 [*Hebert*].

101 *Criminal Code*, above note 6, s 25(1).

102 *Ibid*, s 26.

arrest, not to the status of the individual making the arrest."[103] Accordingly, private citizens might also be justified in using force. Similarly, correctional officers can fall under the provisions.[104]

The more significant question is what is actually authorized under section 25. The first thing to note is that the section has not been read to be nearly as broad as it might seem to be at first glance. It is *not* a broad-based grant of power for a person to do "what he is required or authorized to do"—that is, it is not a grant of ancillary powers beyond those explicitly enumerated elsewhere. As noted above, police only have the powers they are explicitly given by statute or common law; section 25 is not a source of further powers. The section does not provide a defence simply on the basis that a police officer has acted reasonably and in good faith.[105] Rather, it applies to govern the use of force when the person involved has already been authorized to act by some other power. As the Supreme Court observed in *Fleming*, "police officers cannot rely on s. 25(1) to justify the use of force if they had no legal authority — either under legislation or at common law — for their actions."[106]

Some early authority might seem to suggest that section 25 is limited to the use of force in the specific context of conducting an arrest; the Supreme Court of Canada is often taken to have concluded in *Cluett v R*[107] that the section means that "police officers are not entitled to use force unless an arrest is warranted and properly made."[108] What seems

---

103 *Asante-Mensah*, above note 26 at para 52.

104 *R v Nome*, 2015 SKCA 73.

105 *Hudson v Brantford Police Services Board* (2001), 204 DLR (4th) 645 at para 32 (Ont CA) [*Hudson*]. See also the judgment of Dickson J (as he then was) in *Eccles*, above note 22; *R v Peters* (1990), 84 Sask R 231 (CA) [*Peters*]; and *Swansburg v Canada (Royal Canadian Mounted Police)* (1996), 141 DLR (4th) 94 (BCCA) [*Swansburg*]. Note, of course, that s 25 not being a source of ancillary powers is of much less significance since courts began freely using the *Waterfield* decision as a basis for granting police ancillary powers: see the discussion above.

106 *Fleming*, above note 45 at para 117. See also *Richardson v Vancouver (City)*, 2006 BCCA 36 at para 26, quoting *Crampton v Walton*, 2005 ABCA 81 [*Crampton*], quoting *R v Asante-Mensah* (2001), 204 DLR (4th) 51 at para 51 (Ont CA), aff'd 2003 SCC 38: "Section 25 does not confer extra powers on the police, but serves as a shield from criminal or civil liability."

107 [1985] 2 SCR 216 [*Cluett*].

108 See *Swansburg*, above note 105 at para 31, describing the result in *Cluett*, above note 107. See also *Peters*, above note 105, and *R v Sheridan*, [1993] BCJ No 2784 at para 10 (SC):

> The learned Trial Judge seemed to be of the view that a peace officer, as long as he is in the execution of his or her duty, may apply force to a citizen even though that force would otherwise amount to an assault. With the greatest respect such is not the law as I read the case of *Cluett v. The Queen* (1985), 21 C.C.C. (3d) 318, a decision of the Supreme Court of Canada. In that case it

more in line with the subsequent development of the law, however, was that the Court in *Cluett* was only referring to the lack of authority (at the time) for an officer to detain short of arrest—that is, they were simply making the point noted above that section 25 is not an independent source of authority. The Court's decision in *Mann* has since created a power of investigative detention,[109] and courts generally, although not universally, take the view that section 25 is potentially applicable whether the officer's source of authority was statutory or from the common law.[110]

The Alberta Court of Appeal has held:

> Section 25(1) contains three branches. In order to access the protection of the section, a police officer must prove that he or she:
> (i) was required or authorized by law to perform an action in the administration or enforcement of the law;
> (ii) acted on reasonable grounds in performing that action; and
> (iii) did not use unnecessary force.[111]

Broadly, "the allowable degree of force to be used remains constrained by the principles of proportionality, necessity and reasonableness."[112] In considering whether the amount of force used was reasonable, courts should take into account factors such as the nature and quality of the threat, the force used in response, and the characteristics of the parties involved in terms of size, strength, gender, age and other immutable characteristics.[113]

Other guidelines have also been laid down. Actions taken under section 25 should not be assessed through hindsight but rather must be judged based on the situation as it appeared to the officer at the time. Police are not held to a standard of perfection, and their actions should be judged in light of the exigent circumstances in which they

---

was held that, notwithstanding the provisions of s. 25 of the *Criminal Code* which empower a peace officer to use reasonable force in the execution of his or her duties, such officer has no power to forcibly detain a citizen short of exercising a power of arrest.

109 See Chapter 3.

110 See, for example, *Figueiras v Toronto (City) Police Services Board*, 2015 ONCA 208 at para 147 [*Figueiras*]. This is consistent with the wording of s 25, which only requires that the person be "authorized by law." On the other hand, *JN v Horton*, 2010 ABQB 767 at para 56, specifically concludes that s 25 cannot authorize the use of force in an investigative detention, relying on the rule from *Cluett*.

111 *Crampton*, above note 106 at para 6.

112 *R v Nasogaluak*, 2010 SCC 6 at para 32 [*Nasogaluak*].

113 *R v Power*, 2016 SKCA 29 at para 35. See, for example, *Paul c R*, 2017 QCCA 245, where the type of force used was found not to be reasonable because of the lack of urgency to the situation.

work.[114] Police officers are not expected to measure the precise amount of force the situation requires and will not fall outside the protection of section 25(1) for failing to use the least amount of force actually necessary; in this regard, it is sometimes said that the officer is not required to weigh to a nicety the force required, which was the same standard used in the former section 34(1) self-defence claims.[115] Rather, allowance must be made for an officer misjudging the degree of force required given the exigencies of the moment.[116] Depending on the facts of the case, quite considerable force can be found to be justified.[117] On the other hand, the section is intended only to protect reasonable decisions; negligence precludes the application of section 25.[118] When dealing with a citizen's arrest, the assessment is also to include consideration of whether a forcible arrest was a reasonable course of action in the first place.[119] Furthermore, where excessive force is used, this can amount to a threat to the individual's security of person and therefore can result in a violation of section 7 of the *Charter*.[120]

There are further aspects to section 25, beyond the general authorization of reasonable force in section 25(1). Section 25(2) provides that a person executing process or carrying out a sentence in good faith is justified in doing so even if it later transpires that the process or sentence was defective or in excess of jurisdiction. The thrust of this section was explained by the Supreme Court in *R v Finta*:

> The purpose of s. 25(2) is to provide legal protection to a police officer, who, acting in good faith and on a reasonable belief that his or her actions are justified by law, later finds out that those actions were not authorized because the law was found to be defective.
>
> Section 25 is akin to the defence of mistake of fact. Unless, the law is manifestly illegal, the police officer must obey and implement that law. Police officers cannot be expected to undertake a comprehensive

---

114 *Nasogaluak*, above note 112 at para 35. See also *R v Chang*, 2019 ABCA 315.

115 *R v Canada (Royal Canadian Mounted Police)* (1981), 60 CCC (2d) 211 (BCCA) [*R v Canada*].

116 *Crampton*, above note 106 at para 45.

117 *R v Webster*, 2015 BCCA 286 [*Webster*], justifies the use of a police tactical team under the section. Other cases have accepted that the use of a battering ram to break down a door or the use of a chokehold in apprehending a suspect could be justified: see, for example, *R v DeWolfe*, 2007 NSCA 79; *Al-Fartossy*, above note 98 (regarding battering rams); and *Collins*, above note 12, or *Garcia-Guiterrez*, above note 97 (regarding chokeholds).

118 *Poupart*, above note 47; *Green v Lawrence* (1998), 163 DLR (4th) 115 (Man CA); *Chartier v Greaves*, [2001] 103 ACWS (3d) 1054 (Ont SCJ).

119 *Asante-Mensah*, above note 26 at para 74.

120 *Nasogaluak*, above note 112 at para 38. See also *R v Davis*, 2013 ABCA 15.

> legal analysis of every order or law that they are charged with enforcing before taking action. Therefore, if it turns out that they have followed an illegal order they may plead the peace officer defence just as the military officer may properly put forward the defence of obedience to superior orders under certain limited conditions. The qualification is that the military officer must act in good faith and must have reasonable grounds for believing that the actions taken were justified. An officer acting pursuant to a manifestly unlawful order or law would not be able to defend his or her actions on the grounds they were justified under s. 25 of the *Criminal Code*.[121]

Section 25(2) is not meant to provide a defence in the case of a mistake of law. If a peace officer is simply mistaken about what powers they have, section 25(2) is of no assistance. Thus, for example, a police officer who forces entry into a dwelling to effect an arrest in circumstances where no power to do so existed cannot rely on section 25(2).[122] The distinction between a mistake of fact and one of law can be unclear, of course, in this context as in others.[123]

Three sections deal with the use of potentially deadly force, attaching restrictions to when it is available. Section 25(3) limits the circumstances in which section 25(1) could authorize deadly force and so is available to anyone who falls within that former section. Section 25(4) is a modern version of the "fleeing felon" rule, available to peace officers

---

121 *R v Finta*, [1994] 1 SCR 701 at 842 [*Finta*].

122 See, generally, *Hudson*, above note 105 or *Figueiras*, above note 110.

123 See, for example, *Tymkin v Winnipeg (City) Police Service*, 2014 MBCA 4 [*Tymkin*], in which police officers had entered a home to arrest Tymkin, having been let in by a person who, it transpired, was an overnight guest without authority to allow such an entry. The dissenting judge would have found that *Hudson*, above note 105, governed the situation on the basis that the police made a mistake of law: they thought they had the authority to enter when they did not. The majority concluded that the police had made a mistake of fact: they thought the guest had the ability to consent to their entry when he did not.

See also *R v Devereaux* (1996), 147 Nfld & PEIR 108 (Nfld CA), in which a correctional officer placed a person back in a cell when he refused to sign a form. The Court of Appeal agreed that s 19 of the *Code* would be applicable in that the accused (the correctional officer) had made a mistake of law that would not excuse him. It then went on to conclude that his honest belief that he was acting legally entitled him to the defence in s 25, which seems inconsistent with *Finta*, above note 121. The court held that "[t]o be denied the 'peace officer defence' the conduct or act would have to be so patently illegal that a plea of acting in good faith would have absolutely no plausibility whatsoever, making no sense at all" (*Devereaux*, above in this note at para 54). It does not seem to consider whether the officer in the case could have been described as executing a process or carrying out a sentence, which is also a requirement of the section.

who are attempting to arrest a person who flees, and section 25(5) deals with the use of deadly force by peace officers in the case of a penitentiary escape.

There are some common features to the sections. All three, it should be noted, refer to force "that is intended *or is likely to cause death or grievous bodily harm*"; to refer to them as the "deadly force" provisions is a convenient shorthand, but in fact they apply whether or not death has occurred. It has been held, for example, that section 25(3) is applicable in assessing whether the use of a chokehold was acceptable.[124] Note, conversely, that whether an injury has been suffered does not settle whether the limits in these sections apply. A peace officer might use a level of force in making an arrest that in fact results in injury; if that was neither intended nor likely, then the limits in section 25(3) would not be relevant.[125] In addition, note that if the officer is justified in using deadly force under one of these provisions, then that justification applies against the world, not simply against the person the force was intended to be directed toward; that is, if an officer is justified in firing a weapon at a fleeing suspect, that justification protects them even if the person shot is an innocent bystander.[126] Of course, the force used by the officer must still meet the reasonableness requirement: "if an escaping criminal ran into a crowd of people and was obscured from the view of a pursuing police officer, it could not be suggested that it would be permissible for the latter to fire through the crowd in the hope of stopping the fleeing criminal."[127]

There are features worth discussing separately in each section. Section 25(3) is the most limited, which is partly a reflection of the fact that it potentially authorizes deadly force on the part of private citizens, not only by peace officers.[128] It sets further requirements, beyond those in

124 *Garcia-Guiterrez*, above note 97.

125 See, for example, *Mohamed v Vancouver (City) Police Department*, 2001 BCCA 290, where a police officer set his dog to chase one suspect, Mohamed, while he apprehended two others. Mohamed attempted to climb a wall to escape the dog, in the result falling and breaking his leg. The British Columbia Court of Appeal held that s 25(3) did not arise since there was no evidence that the officer intended the result or knew it was likely to ensue. See also *R v Canada*, above note 115.

126 See *Priestman v Colangelo*, [1959] SCR 615 [*Priestman*]. The facts of *Priestman* are somewhat more complex than the example suggested. The officer, Priestman, was attempting to shoot out a tire on a fleeing car. Because his own vehicle hit a bump, he fired through the back window of the vehicle, and the bullet ricocheted, knocking out the driver. That vehicle then struck and killed two pedestrians. Because the decision to try to shoot out the tire met the requirements of s 25(4) (as it stood at the time), the officer was justified and so was not liable to the estates of the deceased pedestrians. See also *Poupart*, above note 47.

127 *Priestman*, above note 126 at 624.

128 *Roberge v The Queen*, [1983] 1 SCR 312 [*Roberge*].

section 25(1), which must also be met for deadly force to be justified. In particular, it requires a belief on reasonable grounds that the force is necessary for the self-preservation of the person or the preservation of any one under that person's protection from death or grievous bodily harm. This sets a subjective-objective standard: the officer personally must hold that belief, but it must also be an objectively reasonable belief.[129] In assessing the objective portion of the test, the training and experience of the officer should be taken into account.[130]

Section 25(4) sets out a number of requirements for the use of deadly force against a fleeing felon:

(*a*) the arrest is lawful;
(*b*) the offence is one for which that person may be arrested without warrant;
(*c*) the person to be arrested takes flight to avoid arrest;
(*d*) the peace officer or other person using the force believes on reasonable grounds that the force is necessary for the purpose of protecting the peace officer, the person lawfully assisting the peace officer or any other person from imminent or future death or grievous bodily harm; and
(*e*) the flight cannot be prevented by reasonable means in a less violent manner.

Those requirements are cumulative, so all must be met to fall within the justification. As with section 25(1), the use of force must have been intentional for the justification to apply.[131]

In its original form, the section was more or less a codification of the common law "fleeing felon" rule, which allowed the use of deadly force to prevent those who had committed felonies from escaping. Until 1994, the predecessor section did not contain any equivalent to the requirement in section 25(4)(d) of a risk of death or grievous bodily harm if the felon escaped.[132] When the common law developed, this was understandable

---

129 *Nasogaluak*, above note 112 at para 34.

130 *R v Pompeo*, 2014 BCCA 317. See, more generally, the discussion of officer training and experience in Section C(2)(a), below in this chapter.

131 *R v Levert* (1994), 76 OAC 307 (CA).

132 At which point, it was amended under *An Act to Amend the Criminal Code and the Coastal Fisheries Protection Act*, SC 1994, c 12. The previous section read:

> 25(4) When protected-exception—A peace officer who is proceeding lawfully to arrest, with or without warrant, any person for an offence for which that person may be arrested without warrant, and every one lawfully assisting the peace officer, is justified, if the person to be arrested takes flight to avoid arrest, in using as much force as is necessary to prevent the escape by flight, unless the escape can be prevented by reasonable means in a less violent manner.

since anyone guilty of a felony was subject to the death penalty. However, the disproportionality of the rule in its codified form was often noted,[133] and the further limitation was eventually introduced. The rule is now much more proportionate in that deadly force is permitted only to prevent an escape when an equivalent risk would be created by the escape.

Finally, there is section 25(5), also added in 1994. Like section 25(4), it is limited to peace officers and permits the use of deadly force against an inmate attempting to escape a penitentiary. Parallel to section 25(4), the officer must believe on reasonable grounds that any of the inmates pose a threat of death or grievous bodily harm to the officer or any other person and that the escape cannot reasonably be prevented in a less violent manner.

The Supreme Court has also pronounced on the meaning of section 27, which permits the use of force to prevent the commission of an offence. The section applies only if the offence committed is one for which the person who committed it could be arrested without warrant and which would be likely to cause immediate and serious injury to the person or property of anyone. If these conditions are met (or under section 27(b), the person using force reasonably believes them to be met), then that person is permitted to use as much force as is reasonably necessary to prevent it. The Court has noted that this section potentially permits the use even of deadly force provided that that was reasonably necessary, holding:

> In determining whether the force used was reasonable the court will take into account all the circumstances of the case, including the nature and degree of force used, the seriousness of the evil to be prevented and the possibility of preventing it by other means. This provision is of general application and is not limited to arrestable or any other class of offences, but it would not be reasonable to use even slight force to prevent very trivial offences. The circumstances in which it can be considered reasonable to kill another in the prevention of crime must be of an extreme kind; they could probably arise only in the case of an attack against the person which is likely to cause death or serious bodily injury and where killing the attacker is the only practicable means of preventing the harm. It cannot be reasonable to kill another merely to prevent a crime which is directed only against property.[134]

In determining whether the force used was reasonably necessary, many factors can be relevant, but none are determinative. Whether the

133 *Roberge*, above note 128.

134 *R v Gee*, [1982] 2 SCR 286 at 302 [*Gee*], quoting Lord Hailsham of St. Marylebone, ed, *Halsbury's Laws of England*, 4th ed, vol 11 (London: Butterworths, 1974) at 630.

commission of an assault is imminent can be relevant, although it is not necessarily a requirement. Any injuries suffered by the person prevented from committing an offence could shed light on the force that was used, although a judge should not simply reason back from the existence of injuries to the conclusion that the force must have been excessive. Ultimately, the decision is one best made by the trier of fact, and considerable deference should be given by courts of appeal.[135]

The relationship between section 27 and the self-defence provisions is also worth noting. Section 27 is intended to permit a bystander who witnesses an offence being or about to be committed to use force to prevent that offence. It cannot be used by an accused who was preventing an assault against themself: as the Court has noted, that interpretation would render the self-defence provisions redundant.[136] Note as well that if a person's actions are justified under section 27, then that person will not be committing an unlawful assault; in other words, the self-defence provisions in section 34 will not be available to the person against whom force is used if they use force in return.[137]

The Court has also determined that no qualified partial defence of excessive use of force in preventing an offence, reducing murder to manslaughter, exists in Canada. Either section 27 is met and an accused was justified, or it is not met and the accused is guilty of whatever offence can be proven on the facts.[138]

Finally, on the use of force, note the more recent section 27.1 of the *Code*, which justifies every person on an aircraft in flight in using as much force as is reasonably necessary to prevent the commission of an offence that would be likely to cause immediate and serious injury to the aircraft or to any person or property on it.

b) Rules Regarding Warrants

Two supporting provisions relate to warrants: sections 28 and 29. The former provides protection to peace officers, while the latter imposes obligations on them.

Section 28(1) of the *Criminal Code* protects a person from criminal liability for arresting the wrong person under a warrant, provided that the arrest was made in good faith and on reasonable grounds. Section

---

135 *R v Guay*, 2008 NBCA 72.

136 *Hebert*, above note 100.

137 *R v Taylor* (2004), 189 OAC 388 (CA). That particular finding rested on the wording of s 34 at the time, which required an unlawful assault. The self-defence provision now in s 34 requires only a threat of force or reasonable belief that there is a threat of force.

138 *Gee*, above note 134.

28(2) extends that protection beyond peace officers making an arrest to anyone assisting in the arrest or to any keeper of a prison to which the person is taken.

The noteworthy thing about section 28 is the way in which it differs from the use-of-force provisions. It is not phrased as a justification generally; it is merely a protection from *criminal* liability. Arresting the wrong person under a warrant could amount to the tort of wrongful imprisonment depending on the facts of the case, and if that were so, then section 28 would provide no protection.[139]

Section 29 sets out rules, some of which apply to warrants generally and some to arrests specifically. Under section 29(1), everyone executing a warrant has a duty to have the warrant with them and produce it on request; this rule applies to search warrants as well as to arrest warrants.[140] A failure to comply with this requirement will render an arrest unlawful.[141]

Section 29(2) is specific to arrests, whether or not made with a warrant. It creates a duty for the arresting person to give notice of "(*a*) the process or warrant under which he makes the arrest; or (*b*) the reason for the arrest."[142] Finally, section 29(3) provides that a failure to comply with section 29(1) or 29(2) does not by itself deprive a person of protection from criminal responsibility.

The leading case on section 29(2) is *R v Gamracy*.[143] In that case, an accused was arrested by a police officer who knew that an arrest warrant existed but did not know the nature of the charge. When arresting the accused, the officer simply informed him that there was a warrant for his arrest.[144] At common law, an accused would have been entitled to know "on what charge or on suspicion of what crime he is seized,"[145] so the

139 See, for example, *Fletcher v Collins*, [1968] 2 OR 618 (HCJ). See also *Romilly v Weatherhead* (1975), 55 DLR (3d) 607 (BCSC).

140 See, for example, *R v Cornell*, 2009 ABCA 147, aff'd 2010 SCC 31. The Supreme Court held that this rule is complied with as long as at least one member of the team conducting the search has a copy of the warrant, and *R v Bohn*, 2000 BCCA 239 [*Bohn*], notes that the rule is imperative. That case concerned a search warrant, and the British Columbia Court of Appeal concluded that "[f]ailure to produce the warrant on request, without good reason, is in my view, a significant breach of s. 8" (at para 34). On the other hand, the Alberta Court of Appeal specifically rejected this conclusion in *R v Patrick*, 2007 ABCA 308 at para 49. This issue was not before the Supreme Court of Canada when it affirmed the result in *Patrick*, above note 81.

141 *Bohn*, above note 140.

142 *Criminal Code*, above note 6, s 29(2).

143 [1974] SCR 640 [*Gamracy*].

144 Section 495(1)(c) of the *Criminal Code* creates a power to arrest without a warrant based on the reasonable belief that a warrant exists.

145 *Christie v Leachinsky*, [1947] 1 All ER 567 at 567 (HL).

officer's actions would not have been sufficient. However, the Supreme Court held that the rule in Canada was that set out in section 29(2) and that sections 29(2)(a) and (b) were to be read disjunctively: an officer could comply with one or the other. In *Gamracy*, therefore, "[t]he duty was fully discharged by telling the accused that the outstanding warrant was the reason for his arrest."[146]

It is not clear that *Gamracy* still reflects the current state of the law; there is a strong argument that it does not. Specifically, it is a pre-*Charter* case, so now anyone arrested would have the right under section 10(a) to be informed of the reason for the arrest. Section 10(a) is discussed more fully below (see Chapter 5). In brief, it has been interpreted to entitle an accused to know the nature of their jeopardy so that they can decide whether to submit to the arrest and will be in a position to exercise the right to consult with counsel. Whatever section 29(2) might mean, being told "you are under arrest because there is a warrant for your arrest" seems clearly not to comply with the standard under section 10(a). Indeed, it has specifically been held that section 10(a) enshrines the common law rule in *R v Nguyen*.[147] The Court in *Gamracy* had held that section 29(2) set out a narrower rule than that common law one.

Furthermore, *Gamracy* has been held only to have settled the question of whether, for the purposes of resisting arrest, an officer will have been acting in the execution of duty. Simply saying "there is a warrant" might not be sufficient to protect an officer from civil liability in an action for personal trespass.[148]

Section 29(2) has been read narrowly in other ways. For example, it has been held that it is sufficient for an arrested person to be told in general terms the behaviour that grounds the arrest rather than the particular charge. On that basis, it has been held that a person who was told they were arrested for driving while under suspension could not complain that section 29(2) was not complied with, even though they did not know whether it was a *Criminal Code* or provincial statute they were alleged to have violated.[149] On the other hand, it has also been suggested that that approach might not comply with section 10(a).[150]

---

146 *Gamracy*, above note 143 at 644.

147 2008 ONCA 49 at para 16.

148 See *Campbell v Edmonton (City) Police Service* (1985), 66 AR 222 (CA); *Schuck v Stewart* (1978), 87 DLR (3d) 720 (BCSC).

149 *R v Fielding*, [1967] 3 CCC 258 (BCCA) [*Fielding*].

150 See *R v Smith* (1990), 53 CCC (3d) 97 at 104–7 (NSSCAD), commenting on *Fielding*, above note 149: "While that may express too narrow a view for the purposes of the *Charter* it was the practice followed under the *Code*."

c) Breaches of the Peace

Sections 30 and 31 of the *Code* create two further justifications. Section 30 justifies anyone who witnesses a breach of the peace in interfering to prevent it. In addition, that person may detain the person committing the breach of the peace for the purpose of handing them over to a peace officer. A person acting under this section is entitled to use force, but it must be no more than is reasonably necessary and must be "reasonably proportioned to the danger to be apprehended from the continuance or renewal of the breach of the peace."[151]

Accompanying this is section 31(1) of the *Code*, which justifies a peace officer who witnesses a breach of the peace arresting anyone they find committing it or whom they reasonably believe is about to join in or renew it. In addition, a peace officer is justified under section 31(2) in receiving any person delivered in accordance with section 30.

A breach of the peace "does not include any and all conduct which right thinking members of the community would regard as offensive, disturbing, or even vaguely threatening. A breach of the peace contemplates an act or actions which result in actual or threatened harm to someone."[152] The Supreme Court has said that "an act can be considered a breach of the peace only if it involves some level of violence and a risk of harm. It is only in the face of such a serious danger that the state's ability to lawfully interfere with individual liberty comes into play. Behaviour that is merely disruptive, annoying or unruly is not a breach of the peace."[153]

Although (like the use-of-force provisions) these are phrased as justifications, the sections can equally be seen as powers; this is clear from the result in *Biron*. The accused there was arrested outside a bar by one peace officer, Maissoneuve, who gave him to a second officer, Gauthier, who in turn handed him over to Dorion, a third officer. The accused ended up in a scuffle with Dorion, the third of the officers, and was charged with resisting a peace officer in the execution of his duty.[154] The dissenting judges argued that the accused was not guilty, on the basis that the officer was not in execution of his duty:

> Section 31 is not an arrest power, but a protection for the person or persons making an arrest, just as is s. 25. Moreover, it is limited to

151 *Criminal Code*, above note 6, s 30.

152 *Brown v Durham (Regional Municipality) Police Force* (1998), 43 OR (3d) 223 at para 73 (CA) [*Durham*].

153 *Fleming*, above note 45 at para 59.

154 *Biron*, above note 3 at 58–59. This case is best known for its interpretation of the "finds committing" warrantless arrest power, which is discussed in Chapter 4. A different issue is raised here.

> protection in respect of an arrest for breach of the peace, and in that respect has a connection with s. 30, which does speak expressly of detention of a person committing a breach of the peace. By no stretch of the imagination can either s. 30 or s. 31 be turned into a general power of either arrest or justification in respect of any criminal offence on the theory that all offences under the *Criminal Code* constitute breaches of the peace.[155]

The majority, however, concluded:

> Section 31(2) of the *Code* provides that Dorion was justified in receiving Biron into custody. The arrest made by Maisonneuve was because he considered Biron to be committing a disturbance, in a public place, which would be a breach of the peace. It is evident that Dorion, who was a part of the police force conducting the raid, reasonably believed that Gauthier, who turned Biron over to him, had witnessed a breach of the peace.
>
> I interpret the word "justified" in s. 31(2) as meaning that Dorion had lawful sanction to receive Biron into his custody. He received him into his custody in the course of performance of his duties as a peace officer at the scene of the raid. Biron offered resistance to him in the execution of that duty. In my opinion that is sufficient to make Biron guilty of the offence with which he was charged under s. 118(a).[156]

On this reasoning, the fact that Dorion was "justified" results in him being in the execution of his duty, which is essentially to say that he had the power to act as he did.

It is worth noting that the justifications in sections 30 and 31 are both predicated on a breach of the peace being witnessed; although the justifications extend to preventing others from joining in, there must actually be a breach of the peace. Those sections do not justify action with regard to participants in a breach of the peace that has concluded, nor do they justify preventing a breach of the peace from occurring in the first place.

There is authority holding that, independent of these *Code* sections, the police have the power at common law to arrest to prevent an *apprehended* breach of the peace.[157] This decision was controversial when made[158] but nonetheless had come to be relied on.[159] However, the

155 *Ibid* at 65–66.

156 *Ibid* at 76–77.

157 *Hayes v Canada (Royal Canadian Mounted Police)* (1985), 17 DLR (4th) 751 (BCCA).

158 Bruce P. Archibald, "*Hayes v. Thompson and Bell*: Annotation" (1985) 44 *Criminal Reports* (3d) 316.

159 *Durham*, above note 152.

Supreme Court has called into question whether that is correct. Noting the extensive statutory powers of arrest that exist and are likely to cover any situation that would amount to an apprehended breach of the peace, the Court held: "While it is not necessary to decide this in the instant case, I seriously question whether a common law power of this nature would still be necessary in Canada today."[160]

In *Fleming*, the Court also considered, in *obiter*, the possibility of a common law power short of arrest as a method of dealing with apprehended breaches of the peace. The Court noted that caselaw on the possibility held that

> such powers, if they exist, will generally not be found to be reasonably necessary unless, at a minimum, the apprehended breach of the peace is imminent, the risk of violence is sufficiently serious, the risk of it occurring is substantial, and no less intrusive measures are reasonably available . . . . Additionally, it must be demonstrated that the exercise of the power can in fact be effective in preventing the breach of the peace.[161]

They did not decide whether such a power did or did not exist, however, saying that that should be left for a case where the issue squarely arose on the facts.[162] Police forces might quite sensibly conclude that the more cautious course of action is not to attempt to use such a power, so this issue could remain unsettled for some time.

d) Entry into a Dwelling House to Effect an Arrest

As has been repeatedly observed in this book, peace officers only have the authority specifically given to them. Much of this book will deal with their power to compel a person's appearance in court, in particular through an arrest. In some cases, however, more than the power to arrest is needed. If peace officers are to enter a private dwelling, they need some authority to do so; like anyone else, peace officers can be found to be trespassers. If peace officers are trespassing, this can have several effects. First, it renders the arrest illegal.[163] Second, it can mean that the officer was not acting in the execution of duty, which can be important if that is an element of the offence with which the accused was charged.[164] Accordingly, there must be some source of authority for peace officers to

160 *Fleming*, above note 45 at para 60.

161 *Ibid* at para 107 [citations omitted].

162 *Ibid* at para 109.

163 See, generally, *Hudson*, above note 105; see also *R v Delong* (1989), 47 CCC (3d) 402 (Ont CA).

164 See *Godoy*, above note 55; *Stenning*, above note 46.

enter dwelling houses in addition to the power to arrest itself, or no one who fled into a home could be arrested.[165]

The power to enter a dwelling house to carry out an arrest is, today, largely governed by statute, in particular by sections 529 to 529.5 of the *Criminal Code*. It is not exclusively governed by those provisions since a common law exception to those rules remains. To properly understand the statutory scheme and the current state of the law, it is necessary to take something of a historical perspective on the issue: the current statutory scheme was sparked by the ways in which the former common law rules violated the *Charter*.

Pre-*Charter*, the rules for forcible entry into a dwelling house to make an arrest under a warrant were set out in *Eccles v Bourque*. That case held that

> [e]ntry can be made against the will of the householder only if (a) there are reasonable and probable grounds for the belief that the person sought is within the premises and (b) proper announcement is made prior to entry.[166]

The later decision in *Landry* extended that power to warrantless arrests as well; that is, if the requirements of section 495(1) were made out, then a reasonable belief that the person was in the premises and proper prior announcement were sufficient to authorize the police to enter a private dwelling.[167]

In *R v Feeney*,[168] the Supreme Court considered these requirements and concluded that they did not comply with the minimum standards that had subsequently come to be developed under the *Charter*. In particular, they relied upon the interplay with the law around unreasonable searches, where it had been established that a warrantless search was prima facie an unreasonable one.[169] The purpose of a warrant requirement, of course, is to obtain judicial authorization for the police action before it takes place; the major rationale for that was the desire to prevent *Charter* violations from occurring in the first place rather than simply remedying them after the fact.

Given that, the Court held, it would be anomalous if a peace officer required a warrant to be able to enter a dwelling house to conduct a

165 See *Macooh*, above note 24 at 815: "It would be unacceptable for police officers who were about to make a completely lawful arrest to be prevented from doing so merely because the offender had taken refuge in his home or that of a third party."

166 *Eccles*, above note 22 at 744.

167 *Landry*, above note 23.

168 [1997] 2 SCR 13 [*Feeney*].

169 *Hunter*, above note 42.

search but could enter to carry out an arrest based only on their own judgment of reasonable grounds and prior announcement. Indeed, given that the police might well be able to search the house incidental to the arrest, there was a direct contradiction in setting a lower standard for arrest powers compared to search powers. Accordingly, the Court concluded that, before entering a dwelling house to effect an arrest, the police would require a warrant authorizing them to do so:

> 49 In my view, then, warrantless arrests in dwelling houses are in general prohibited. Prior to such an arrest, it is incumbent on the police officer to obtain judicial authorization for the arrest by obtaining a warrant to enter the dwelling house for the purpose of arrest. Such a warrant will only be authorized if there are reasonable grounds for the arrest, and reasonable grounds to believe that the person will be found at the address named, thus providing individuals' privacy interests in an arrest situation with the protection *Hunter* required with respect to searches and seizures. Requiring a warrant prior to arrest avoids the *ex post facto* analysis of the reasonableness of an intrusion that *Hunter* held should be avoided under the *Charter*; invasive arrests without a basis of reasonable and probable grounds are prevented, rather than remedied after the fact . . . .
>
> 50 I would add that the protection of privacy does not end with a warrant; the other requirements in *Landry* for an arrest in a dwelling house must be met along with the warrant requirement. Specifically, before forcibly entering a dwelling house to make an arrest with a warrant for an indictable offence, proper announcement must be made. As Dickson C.J. stated in *Landry*, at p. 161, these additional requirements "minimize the invasiveness of arrest in a dwelling and permit the offender to maintain his dignity and privacy by walking to the doorway and surrendering himself."[170]

The Court did acknowledge that other interests competed with the privacy interest of the homeowner. In cases of hot pursuit, for example, it would be unrealistic and unnecessary to require a warrant (see the further discussion of hot pursuit, below). The Court also raised the issue of whether exigent circumstances other than hot pursuit might override the requirement for a warrant but did not decide the point. Ultimately, the Court concluded that the minimum *Charter* requirements for forcible entry into a dwelling house to carry out an arrest were as follows:

> 51 To summarize, in general, the following requirements must be met before an arrest for an indictable offence in a private dwelling

170 *Feeney*, above note 168 at paras 49–50.

> is legal: a warrant must be obtained on the basis of reasonable and probable grounds to arrest and to believe the person sought is within the premises in question; and proper announcement must be made before entering. An exception to this rule occurs where there is a case of hot pursuit. Whether or not there is an exception for exigent circumstances generally has not been fully addressed by this Court, nor does it need to be decided in the present case given my view that exigent circumstances did not exist when the arrest was made.[171]

With its decision in *Feeney*, the Court created a need for a type of warrant that did not, at the time, exist.[172] Parliament therefore enacted sections 529 to 529.5 in order to authorize entries into dwelling houses. Primarily, the statutory scheme calls for a warrant to be obtained before the police enter a dwelling house to arrest a person. Under section 529, when an arrest warrant is initially issued, the judge or justice issuing it can authorize the officer to enter a dwelling house to execute it. In this event, there are two further requirements that must be met. First, the justice must be satisfied on reasonable grounds that the person to be arrested is or will be in the dwelling house. Second, even if the warrant does authorize entry,

> the peace officer may not enter the dwelling-house unless the peace officer has, immediately before entering the dwelling-house, reasonable grounds to believe that the person to be arrested or apprehended is present in the dwelling-house.[173]

Section 529.1 deals with entry warrants obtained other than at the same time as the arrest warrant itself—namely, where (1) there is an arrest warrant, but it does not already authorize entry; (2) there are grounds to arrest the person without warrant under paragraph 495(1)(a) or (b);[174] or (3) there are grounds under some Act other than the *Criminal Code* to arrest the person without a warrant. In such cases, a judge

171 *Ibid* at para 51.

172 *Ibid* at para 48, where the Court held: "If the *Code* currently fails to provide specifically for a warrant containing such prior authorization, such a provision should be read in." This was quite a remarkable position to have taken, particularly given that the Court had quite explicitly concluded in *Hunter*, above note 42 at 156 (the case prompting the change), that the *Charter* "does not in itself confer any powers." However, the Court shortly thereafter granted a rehearing and stayed the operation of the requirement for a warrant for six months (*R v Feeney*, [1997] 3 SCR 1008), by which time the warrant provisions had been put into the *Criminal Code*.

173 *Criminal Code*, above note 6, s 529(2).

174 Excluding the warrantless arrest power in *ibid*, s 495(1)(c) means that it is only when there genuinely is an arrest warrant, not merely reasonable grounds to believe there is such a warrant, that an entry will be permitted. Section 529.1(b)

or justice may issue a warrant authorizing a peace officer to enter a dwelling house to effect the arrest. Once again, the judge or justice must be satisfied that there are reasonable grounds to believe the person is or will be present in the dwelling house, and additional conditions can be attached to the warrant "to ensure that the entry into the dwelling-house is reasonable in the circumstances."[175]

Whether the authorization to enter is obtained at the same time as the arrest warrant or later, a peace officer may apply by telewarrant if it is impracticable to appear in person.[176] In addition, the *Code* provides for the possibility of a forcible entry to be made without a warrant in certain circumstances. First, the *Code* makes clear that it is not limiting any other authorization a peace officer might have to enter; at a minimum, this preserves the hot pursuit exception to the warrant requirement, which was recognized in *Feeney*. In addition, the *Code* goes on to do what the Court had left unsettled in *Feeney*—that is, create an "exigent circumstances" exception. If all the other requirements are met, and it would be impracticable to obtain a warrant because of exigent circumstances, the officer can enter without a warrant. "Exigent circumstances" are then defined:

> [E]xigent circumstances include circumstances in which the peace officer
>
> (a) has reasonable grounds to suspect that entry into the dwelling-house is necessary to prevent imminent bodily harm or death to any person; or
>
> (b) has reasonable grounds to believe that evidence relating to the commission of an indictable offence is present in the dwelling-house and that entry into the dwelling-house is necessary to prevent the imminent loss or imminent destruction of the evidence.[177]

Note that the above is a non-exhaustive definition of the term; this is likely a reflection of the fact that hot pursuit is another exigent circumstance, and the statutory scheme does not affect the common law rules surrounding it. In addition, although reasonable grounds to *believe* are required in the case of the potential loss of evidence, entry to prevent

---

also permits entry when there is a warrantless arrest power under s 672.91, relating to the mental disorder provisions.

175 *Ibid*, s 529.2.

176 *Ibid*, s 529.5.

177 *Ibid*, s 529.3(2).

imminent bodily harm or death requires only reasonable grounds to *suspect*.[178]

In the ordinary course, the warrant provisions (and the exigent circumstances exception) do not override the common law requirement for entry that the officer is required first to make prior announcement. However, section 529.4 permits the judge or justice to authorize the officer *not* to make a prior announcement if at least one of two criteria is met, often referred to as a "no-knock entry." That is, the warrant can authorize omitting prior announcement if

> there are reasonable grounds to believe that prior announcement of the entry would
> (a) expose the peace officer or any other person to imminent bodily harm or death; or
> (b) result in the imminent loss or imminent destruction of evidence relating to the commission of an indictable offence.[179]

The judge or justice must be satisfied of one of these criteria. In addition, the officer executing the warrant must also have reasonable grounds immediately before executing the warrant.[180] However, although the "reasonable grounds to believe" standard applies to both criteria when the judge is authorizing the no-knock entry, the same is not true of the officer's required belief. The officer, at the time of the entry, must have reasonable grounds *to believe* in the case of the loss of evidence but only reasonable grounds *to suspect* in the case of bodily harm or death. These same criteria apply to the officer when they are making a no-knock entry without a warrant under the exigent circumstances exception.[181] In both cases, the standards applied to the peace officer correspond to those used in the exigent circumstances exception itself.

To summarize, the basic rule is that an officer must (1) have authority to arrest; (2) have a warrant to enter the dwelling house; and (3) make prior announcement. However, the requirement for the warrant to enter and the obligation to make prior announcement, or even both, can be dispensed with in certain cases. The statutory scheme creates exceptions in the case of exigent circumstances, and the common law creates exceptions in the case of hot pursuit.

---

178 See Heather Pringle, "Kicking in the Castle Doors: The Evolution of Exigent Circumstances" (2000) 43 *Criminal Law Quarterly* 86, for criticism of Parliament's approach to exigent circumstances in this provision.

179 *Criminal Code*, above note 6, s 529.4(1).

180 *Ibid*, s 529.4(2).

181 *Ibid*, s 529.4(3).

Various aspects of the application of these provisions have been developed by courts of appeal. It has been settled, for example, that the need for a warrant is not limited to cases where an accused is arrested in their *own* dwelling house; the issue is simply whether they are in *some* dwelling house. An accused cannot assert a *Charter* right where only a third party's right was violated—where an unreasonable search takes place in a location in which the accused has no reasonable expectation of privacy, for example.[182] However, when an accused is arrested (and in the usual course searched incidental to that arrest) in a third party's house, the accused's own rights have been violated.[183]

Some elaboration of the exigent circumstances exception has also taken place. First, note that this exception removes only the need for a warrant to enter; it does not eliminate the other requirements. In *R v Guiboche*,[184] for example, the police were investigating a murder that had occurred only hours earlier and were searching for the accused, who had been reported as the perpetrator. The murder had been committed with a bat, so the accused was likely to have bloodstains on him. The trial judge concluded that the police fell within the exigent circumstances exception on these facts when they entered the accused's father's home. However, the Court of Appeal found that to be an error. The accused's whereabouts had been unknown, and officers were looking for him in various places; some had gone to his father's house as one possible location. It was not until after they had entered and been told by the accused's father that the accused was upstairs that they knew he was there. On those facts, they did not have reasonable grounds to believe he was in the dwelling house before entering. Without that precondition for entry being met, the exigent circumstances exception to obtaining a warrant was not available.

The exigent circumstances exception talks of the risk of bodily harm to "any person."[185] This phrase includes the accused, so where the police have reason to think a person is suicidal, exigent circumstances could be made out.[186] Furthermore, it is not necessary that *all* evidence might be destroyed if the police wait to obtain a warrant. In *R v Duong*, the police entered a marijuana grow operation they had discovered by chance and arrested the accused. The accused argued that the exigent circumstances

---

182 See *R v Edwards*, [1996] 1 SCR 128. See also *Belnavis*, above note 86.

183 See *R v Adams* (2001), 203 DLR (4th) 290 (Ont CA). See also *R v Couturier*, 2004 NBCA 91 [*Couturier*], and *R v Guiboche*, 2004 MBCA 16 [*Guiboche*], in both of which the accused was arrested at another person's house.

184 *Guiboche*, *ibid*.

185 *Criminal Code*, above note 6, s 529.3(2)(a).

186 *R v Phillips*, 2006 NSCA 135.

exception did not apply since "a commercial marihuana grow operation could not be dismantled and destroyed in the hour it would have taken" to obtain a warrant.[187] The Court of Appeal rejected this argument, noting that documents and fingerprints were found in the house linking the accused to the offence and that this evidence could have been destroyed had the officers not entered immediately. The court characterized this evidence as "important," suggesting that the mere existence of *some* evidence in danger of destruction might not be sufficient.

It is also necessary to consider the hot pursuit exception, which is preserved by the statutory scheme. The Supreme Court noted in *Macooh* that the existence of a hot pursuit exception to the sanctity of the home was well settled at common law. It quoted *Halsbury's Laws of England*[188] to the effect that

> [i]f a felony has been committed and the felon is followed to a house, and there is no other means of entering, any person may, it seems, break open the door of the house, to arrest the offender. This may also be done if a felony will probably be committed unless some person interferes to prevent it.
>
> If an affray occurs in the presence of a constable, and the offenders run away and are immediately pursued by the constable and they enter a house, then the doors may be broken open by the constable to apprehend them in the course of the immediate pursuit.[189]

The Court also defined what is meant by "hot pursuit":

> Generally, the essence of fresh pursuit is that it must be continuous pursuit conducted with reasonable diligence, so that pursuit and capture along with the commission of the offence may be considered as forming part of a single transaction.[190]

The rationale for the hot pursuit exception was neatly summarized by the Ontario Court of Appeal in *R v Van Puyenbroek*:

> The court also discussed the justifications for this exception to the important principle that protects the sanctity of a private home. First, where an offender is a fugitive who has gone to his home while fleeing for the sole purpose of escaping arrest, when the police come, they

187 *R v Duong*, 2002 BCCA 43 at para 29 [*Duong*].

188 Lord Simonds, ed, *Halsbury's Laws of England*, 3d ed, vol 10 (London: Butterworths, 1954).

189 *Macooh*, above note 24 at para 13, quoting *Halsbury's Laws of England*, above note 188 at 354.

190 *Macooh*, above note 24 at para 24, quoting Roger E. Salhany, *Canadian Criminal Procedure*, 5th ed (Aurora, ON: Canada Law Book, 1989) at 44 [Salhany].

> are not unexpected or intruding on the person's "domestic tranquility." Second, from a practical point of view, offenders should not be encouraged to run or drive for home to seek refuge from the police, creating dangerous situations for members of the public . . . . Third, the police officer may have personal knowledge of the commission of an offence justifying arrest, thereby greatly reducing the risk of error. Fourth, flight usually indicates awareness of guilt. Fifth, in some circumstances it may be difficult to identify the offender without arresting him on the spot. Sixth, evidence of the offence may be lost, such as evidence of impairment. Seventh, the offender may again flee or continue the offence while the police are waiting for him to emerge.[191]

These factors are not a checklist that must be satisfied in order for the hot pursuit exception to apply. For example, if a peace officer personally witnessed the offence, it is that much more likely that "pursuit and capture along with the commission of the offence may be considered as forming part of a single transaction."[192] It is not an absolute rule that the officer must have witnessed the offence, however.[193] An officer might arrive at the scene just after the offence has taken place or might take over a pursuit begun by someone else.[194] Nonetheless, "[i]t is a necessarily narrow exception."[195] In *Van Puyenbroek*, for example, a police officer received a report of a traffic accident and drove fifty-five kilometres to the scene; after conducting an investigation, he formed a suspicion about the accused and went to his house, did a further investigation by examining the accused's truck and speaking with the accused's wife, and only then entered the house. The trial judge found that the hot pursuit exception applied on these facts, in part by discounting the officer's travel time. The Court of Appeal overturned this conclusion, holding that, if the officer had reasonable grounds to arrest the accused before entering his house, there was no reason he could not have obtained a warrant to do so. The hot pursuit exception should not be read so broadly but rather should be limited to situations "in which the officer is literally at the heels of a suspect at the moment the suspect enters a dwelling-house."[196] It remains unsettled as to whether an officer is required to give prior notice before entering in hot pursuit, in part because they seem generally to do so, so the issue does not arise.[197]

---

191 *R v Van Puyenbroek*, 2007 ONCA 824 at para 20 [*Van Puyenbroek*].

192 *Macooh*, above note 24 at 817, quoting Salhany, above note 190 at 44.

193 *R v Haglof*, 2000 BCCA 604 [*Haglof*].

194 *Macooh*, above note 24.

195 *Van Puyenbroek*, above note 191 at para 32.

196 *Ibid.*

197 *Macooh*, above note 24; *Haglof*, above note 193.

As a final point regarding police entry into premises, observe the limit on the relevance of the *Feeney* decision and the statutory scheme for entry warrants: it is not the only source of authority for police to enter a dwelling house. The Supreme Court observed in *Godoy* that "*Feeney* was concerned solely with when the police can enter a dwelling without a warrant to make an arrest."[198] In *Godoy* itself, the police received a 911 call that had been disconnected, so they went to the address to investigate. The Court relied on *Waterfield* to find that the police had the authority, at common law, to force entry into the apartment to verify that there was no emergency.[199] Similarly, in other cases, peace officers have entered a home without an entry warrant and have arrested a person therein. If they did not enter with the intention of arresting, then a precondition for the entry warrant provisions will not be made out, and those sections cannot be a source of authority for the entry.[200] It does not follow that the entry was unauthorized, however. In essence, the statutory scheme deals with forced entries, but not all entries are forced. There are at least two similar circumstances in which the statutory scheme does not apply. First, the police might have been given permission to enter by someone who had a privacy interest in the home and who was sufficiently informed about the intention of the police to consent to the entry.[201] Alternatively, police might have entered lawfully for some other investigatory purpose and then once inside formed the reasonable grounds leading to an arrest.[202] The fact that a situation subsequently develops in a way that leads to the arrest of the accused does not mean that the scheme in sections 529–529.5 governed the entry.[203] Alternatively, it might be that the statutory scheme does not apply and no other basis for entry exists, in which case the arrest will be illegal.[204]

---

198 *Godoy*, above note 55 at para 26.

199 *Godoy* is meant to create only a limited ability for police to enter a home, in response to a 911 call. As noted in *R v Davidson*, 2017 ONCA 257 at para 26:

> The police must reasonably believe that the life or safety of a person inside the home is in danger. And once inside the home, their authority is limited to ascertaining the reason for the call and providing any needed assistance. They do not have any further authority to search the home or intrude on a resident's privacy or property.

200 See *R v Custer*, [1984] 4 WWR 133 (Sask CA); *R v Thomas* (1991), 67 CCC (3d) 81 (Nfld CA).

201 *Tymkin*, above note 123 at para 78. Although this is from the dissenting judgment, the Manitoba Court of Appeal was unanimous on this portion of the decision. See also *Couturier*, above note 183, or *Guiboche*, above note 183.

202 *Tymkin*, above note 123 at paras 73–77.

203 See, for example, *R v Petri*, 2003 MBCA 1 or *R v Laliberte*, 2007 SKCA 7.

204 See *Van Puyenbroek*, above note 191.

e) Search Incident to Arrest

The power to search incidental to arrest was long recognized at common law, and in *Cloutier v Langlois*,[205] the Supreme Court affirmed its continued vitality under the *Charter*. Indeed, despite the preference for a warrant requirement for searches, the Court has noted that "[t]he practical reality is that warrantless searches of persons incident to arrest constitute the majority of searches conducted by police."[206] Having been created at common law, however, the "search incident to arrest power has been framed by nebulous parameters."[207] The basic rules have by now been relatively well established, but ambiguity still remains over exactly what will fall within the power in a given case. Some types of searches have clearly been authorized, while others have been ruled out, special restrictions have been attached to some searches, and some unanswered questions remain. We will begin with a discussion of those aspects of the power that are settled, then turn to discuss the "special cases" that have been identified, and leave the ambiguities to the end.

In *Cloutier*, the Court set out three basic rules concerning search incident to arrest:

> 1. This power does not impose a duty. The police have some discretion in conducting the search. Where they are satisfied that the law can be effectively and safely applied without a search, the police may see fit not to conduct a search. They must be in a position to assess the circumstances of each case so as to determine whether a search meets the underlying objectives.
> 2. The search must be for a valid objective in pursuit of the ends of criminal justice, such as the discovery of an object that may be a threat to the safety of the police, the accused or the public, or that may facilitate escape or act as evidence against the accused. The purpose of the search must not be unrelated to the objectives of the proper administration of justice, which would be the case for example if the purpose of the search was to intimidate, ridicule or pressure the accused in order to obtain admissions.
> 3. The search must not be conducted in an abusive fashion and in particular, the use of physical or psychological constraint should be proportionate to the objectives sought and the other circumstances of the situation. A search which does not meet these

205 [1990] 1 SCR 158 [*Cloutier*].

206 *R v Golden*, 2001 SCC 83 at para 84 [*Golden*].

207 *Ibid* at para 23.

> objectives could be characterized as unreasonable and unjustified at common law.[208]

More succinctly, the Court said in *R v Stairs* that the requirements for a search incident to arrest are that "(1) the individual searched has been lawfully arrested; (2) the search is truly incidental to the arrest in the sense that it is for a valid law enforcement purpose connected to the arrest; and (3) the search is conducted reasonably."[209]

The second requirement above is that the search must truly be "incidental," which means that the purpose of the search must be properly related to the arrest. The most commonly relied-upon statement of those legitimate purposes comes from *R v Caslake*:

> [T]he three main purposes of search incident to arrest are ensuring the safety of the police and public, the protection of evidence from destruction at the hands of the arrestee or others, and the discovery of evidence which can be used at the arrestee's trial.[210]

That entire list of three purposes has not always been used, which has led to some confusion, discussed below. However, today, that is the generally accepted list of legitimate "incidental" purposes. Whether a particular search meets one of those purposes is probably the issue most frequently in dispute in individual cases. As the Court has said, "[t]he central guiding principle is that the search must be, as the case law puts it, truly incidental to the arrest."[211]

Other rules governing this power have been settled. For example, the authority to search flows directly from the arrest itself; no separate reasonable grounds for the search are required. Indeed, this is what is meant by saying that the search is "incidental to" the arrest: its legality can stand or fall with the arrest. If the arrest is lawful, that justifies a search of some sort, but if the arrest is unlawful, then so, too, is the search. As the Court has said, "[n]o search, no matter how reasonable, may be upheld under this common law power where the arrest which gave rise to it was arbitrary or otherwise unlawful."[212]

Because the accused has been arrested, they are, of course, entitled to be informed of the right to counsel. However, the obligation to hold off from obtaining evidence until an accused has had a chance to exercise

---

208 *Cloutier*, above note 205 at 186.

209 *Stairs*, above note 93 at para 35.

210 *R v Caslake*, [1998] 1 SCR 51 at para 19 [*Caslake*].

211 *R v Fearon*, 2014 SCC 77 at para 16 [*Fearon*].

212 *Stillman*, above note 43 at para 27. See also *Caslake*, above note 210 at para 13: "[S]ince the legality of the search is derived from the legality of arrest, if the arrest is later found to be invalid, the search will be also."

that right does not mean that police are unable to search incidental to arrest. They can do so immediately in any case.[213]

Like the power to arrest itself, search incident to arrest has both a subjective and an objective requirement. Although the search does not require reasonable grounds, it must be, as the Court said in *Cloutier*, "for a valid objective in pursuit of the ends of criminal justice."[214] The subjective requirement means that the officer must personally intend that the search is aimed at one of those objectives.[215] This requirement is related to the first criterion in *Cloutier*: that each search is a discretionary one, based on an assessment of the circumstances of the case.

This is a fine line the Court is drawing, although that does not mean that drawing it is not worth the effort. The power to search flows directly from the arrest; on the other hand, the search should not be conducted automatically. In effect, a police officer might well be able to decide, each time, "I will now conduct a search"; what they *cannot* do is decide, in advance, "every time I arrest someone, I will conduct a search." A search that is simply conducted in accordance with a general policy to search will not satisfy the subjective criterion: "the police must be able to explain . . . why they searched."[216]

In *Caslake*,[217] for example, the police officer searched the vehicle but testified that he had done so in order to inventory its contents. In that event, the Court held, even though a search incident to arrest was objectively justifiable, that was not subjectively what the officer was doing, so the search was unlawful. Similarly, in *R v Rutten*, the police would have been able to conduct a search incident to the accused's arrest for having open liquor in his vehicle; however, their actual purpose in searching was to look for drugs, so the search did not qualify as a search incident to the arrest.[218]

In addition, any search incident to arrest must be objectively justified: it must be the case that a reasonable person would agree that a search involving one of the goals of search incident to arrest was justified. As the Court has stated:

> This is not a standard of reasonable and probable grounds, but simply a requirement that there be some reasonable basis for doing what the

213 *R v Debot*, [1989] 2 SCR 1140 [*Debot*]. See also *R v Lewis*, 2007 NSCA 2.

214 *Cloutier*, above note 205 at 186.

215 See *R v Lai*, 2019 ONCA 420 at para 22 [*Lai*]: "A search without subjective grounds is illegal, even where objective grounds would have existed had the officer acted on those grounds" [citation omitted].

216 *Caslake*, above note 210 at para 25.

217 *Ibid*.

218 *R v Rutten*, 2006 SKCA 17 [*Rutten*].

police did. For example, if the purpose of the search is to find evidence, there must be some reasonable prospect of finding evidence of the offence for which the accused is being arrested.[219]

This rule has two closely connected ramifications. First, it means that the objective reasonableness of the search must be related back to the given purpose for the arrest. For example, if a known drug offender is arrested for some non–drug-related offence, then the reasonableness of the search must be assessed against the actual arrest, even if in some sense it is "reasonable" to think evidence of a drug offence might also be found.[220] Second, and as a corollary of that, the actual search conducted must be aimed at that proper purpose. For example, the Court noted in *Caslake* that it is not permissible to search the trunk of a car if the arrest is for a traffic violation; nothing could be found there that would be relevant to proving the offence.[221] Exactly this situation arose in *Bulmer*, where the accused was arrested in his car because of a warrant for his arrest based on an unpaid seatbelt ticket. The officer then searched the vehicle, claiming that he did so to see whether he could find a receipt for the ticket, which the accused said he thought he had paid. The officer also suggested that he was searching for safety purposes, although the accused was at the time locked in the back of the police vehicle and other officers were on hand. This search was found to be unlawful. Because any search must be justified on one of the three purposes of search incident to arrest, it is quite explicitly not the rule that the police can always search a vehicle incidental to an arrest (although it will quite often be the case that they can search the vehicle). In *Caslake*, the Supreme Court specifically rejected the notion that there was a "vehicle inventory search" power,[222] although it should be said that police continue to try to rely upon one, and some lower courts have permitted them, although not under the search incident to arrest power.[223]

---

219 *Fearon*, above note 211 at para 22. See also *Stairs*, above note 93 at para 37.

220 See, for example, *R v Santana*, 2020 ONCA 365 [*Santana*], where the accused, suspected of involvement in drug trafficking, was arrested on a warrant relating to driving while suspended. The search in the pockets of a jacket that had been in the back of a car in which he was a passenger at the time of the arrest was not lawful. See also *R v Balendra*, 2019 ONCA 68 [*Balendra*], where the accused was arrested for having stolen a van. A search of a USB stick found in his pocket that was conducted to find evidence of a different offence for which the accused was being investigated was unlawful.

221 *Caslake*, above note 210 at para 18. See also *R v Bulmer*, 2005 SKCA 90 [*Bulmer*].

222 *Ibid* at para 30. The Court reaffirmed this point in *R v Nolet*, 2010 SCC 24 at para 30 [*Nolet*].

223 See, for example, *Harflett*, above note 91; *R v Caron*, 2011 BCCA 56; *R v Ellis*, 2016 ONCA 598 [*Ellis*]; *R v Cuff*, 2018 ONCA 276; *R v Russell*, 2018 BCCA 330;

A broad range of searches is allowed under this power. Frisk searches are permitted, and the power has been held to include the ability to perform a gunshot residue test on an accused by "dabbing" their hands with two-sided tape to get samples[224] or to take a sample of the victim's dried blood from the accused's skin.[225] In *R v Poirier*, the Ontario Court of Appeal accepted that a "bedpan vigil" waiting for an accused to excrete contraband he had secreted in his rectum could fall within the search incident to arrest power (although the search in that particular case was not conducted reasonably).[226] As well, vehicle searches can be quite extensive. Searches of vehicles in which police removed loose door panels, or in which they took interior and exterior measurements of a truck and then partly disassembled the inside to find a false compartment, have been found to fall within the scope of the power.[227]

There are no strict temporal limits on when a search incident to arrest can take place. Obviously, it must be relatively close in time to the actual arrest, although the Court held in *Caslake* that a search of a vehicle six hours later could still have been incidental to the arrest given the limited number of officers available. In *R v Balendra*, a seven-hour gap before an officer search of a USB drive was found not to be an obstacle to the search being incidental to arrest since it was conducted by the arresting officer on the same day and same shift as the arrest.[228] It has been suggested that a search incident to arrest can even precede the arrest itself provided that grounds for arrest already existed. This point has not been settled by the Supreme Court of Canada, however.[229]

R v Ahmed, 2019 SKCA 47; *R v Francis*, 2022 ONCA 729; *R v Myers*, 2022 NSCA 69; or *R v Buakasa*, 2023 ONCA 383 [*Buakasa*].

224 *R v Backhouse* (2005), 194 CCC (3d) 1 (Ont CA).

225 *R v Smyth*, [2006] OJ No 5527 (SCJ). It was found in that case that this procedure could be used to identify the source of blood (specifically, in that case, to see whether it came from the victim) but could not be used to obtain a sample of the accused's own DNA.

226 *R v Poirier*, 2016 ONCA 582 [*Poirier*]. However, the Court of Appeal also imposes an extra "reasonable grounds" requirement on such searches; see the discussion below.

227 See *R v Smellie* (1994), 95 CCC (3d) 9 (BCCA) [*Smellie*]. See also *Nolet*, above note 222.

228 *Balendra*, above note 220. Note, however, that the search was found not to be a lawful search incident to arrest for other reasons.

229 The Ontario Court of Appeal reached this conclusion in *R v Debot* (1987), 30 CCC (3d) 207 (Ont CA). The Supreme Court of Canada affirmed the decision in *Debot*, above note 213, but Wilson J (writing the majority decision on this point) found the search in question lawful based on the *Food and Drugs Act* and concluded that it was unnecessary to decide whether the search could also be justified as incidental to a valid arrest. More recently, see *R v Richards*, 2015 ONCA

There are also no strict spatial limits to a search incident to arrest, although there are some guidelines. The search might well include an accused's vehicle; where a search of the accused turns up both drugs and money and they have been stopped in an area known for drug trafficking, searching the car for more drugs is permissible.[230] However, the search of the particular vehicle must genuinely be incidental to the arrest; that police can search a vehicle the accused was driving at the time of the arrest does not mean that they can also search a car a kilometre away that the accused was driving earlier.[231] On the other hand, the search power might apply to a vehicle a block away so long as that vehicle is still spatially and temporally connected to the arrest.[232] Searches of items in a vehicle, such as looking in a box[233] or reading through documents in a briefcase,[234] might also fall within a permissible search. It seems that it is acceptable for police to arrest a person primarily in order to conduct a search incident to arrest.[235] On the other hand, a contrived arrest at a particular location as a pretext for searching that location is not allowed.[236]

Special rules govern the limits of a search incident to arrest of a home because of the enhanced privacy interest there; see the discussion below of "special cases" of search incident to arrest. An interesting question is how to treat a means of transportation that also serves as a dwelling place, such as the sleeping area in a transport truck or a vessel aboard which a person lives; should those be treated as vehicles or homes? There is

---

348 [*Richards*], or *Ellis*, above note 223, upholding a search as being incidental to arrest even though the arrest itself had not yet occurred. See also *Food and Drugs Act*, RSC 1985, c F-27.

230 *R v Polashek* (1999), 45 OR (3d) 434 (CA) [*Polashek*]. See also *Mooiman*, above note 85 at para 41.

231 *R v Frieburg*, 2013 MBCA 40 [*Frieburg*].

232 See, for example, *R v Ibrahim*, 2021 MBCA 12, where police observed the accused taking something from a vehicle that they believed he was using to stash narcotics. They decided to arrest him, but by the time they did, a few minutes later, he had driven a block away in a second vehicle and parked. The Manitoba Court of Appeal distinguished *Frieburg*, above note 231, and held that the search of the first vehicle was validly incidental to the arrest.

233 See *R v Labelle*, 2016 ONCA 110, or *R v Pino*, 2016 ONCA 389.

234 *R v Mohamad* (2004), 69 OR (3d) 481 (CA).

235 In *Stillman*, above note 43 at para 29, it is noted that "the sole purpose of the arrest was to obtain evidence from him and to question him," and that is not taken to invalidate the search since grounds for the arrest did exist.

236 See *Smellie*, above note 227, citing *R v Lim (No 2)* (1990), 1 CRR (2d) 136 (Ont Ct Gen Div) [*Lim*]. See also *R v Chubak*, 2009 ABCA 8 at para 22 [*Chubak*]: "[P]retextual searches will meet neither the subjective not [*sic*] the objective elements of the *Caslake* test."

relatively little caselaw on the subject, but the tendency seems to be to allow search incident to arrest to include those locations.[237]

What generally settles both the spatial and temporal limits is the question of whether the search is truly "incidental" to the arrest. That is, it must be both subjectively and objectively related to one of the legitimate purposes of search incident to arrest: ensuring the safety of the police and public, protecting evidence from destruction, and discovering evidence to use at trial.[238] But that is not to say that evidence of other offences would not be admissible if it were found; it would be. Both the common law "plain view" doctrine and section 489(2) of the *Code* allow police to seize evidence if they come upon it while lawfully searching for something else.[239] If an accused is validly searched incidental to arrest and evidence of some other crime is discovered—possession of a narcotic, for example—the accused can also be arrested for and charged with that offence.[240] That is quite distinct, however, from deliberately searching for evidence of some other crime.[241]

Those are the basic rules governing search incident to arrest, but they are not the end of the story in all circumstances. All search powers are meant to properly strike a balance between the state's security interest and the individual's privacy interest. The rules set out above presume that the individual has only the "normal" privacy interest of a person arrested. However, there are situations in which an accused's privacy interest is enhanced, and in such cases the ordinary rules alone are insufficient to justify a search incident to arrest. It could be found that the privacy interest is so high that the search cannot be allowed

---

237 See, for example, *R v Pedersen*, 2016 BCCA 47, where the trial judge had permitted the search of a vessel incidental to arrest. See also *Nolet*, above note 222, which is not a search incident to arrest case but which considers an accused's reasonable expectation of privacy in the sleeping compartment of a truck to be "necessarily low" (at para 31). See also *R v AB*, 2021 BCCA 20, following *Nolet*, but again not based on search incident to arrest as the particular search power.

238 *Caslake*, above note 210 at para 19.

239 See the discussion of the plain view doctrine in *Frieburg*, above note 231, or *R v Warren*, 2017 MBCA 106.

240 See, for example, *Polashek*, above note 230. See also *R v Alkins*, 2007 ONCA 264 and *Chubak*, above note 236.

241 *Rutten*, above note 218. See *R v Heatley* (2015), 327 CCC (3d) 1 (BCCA) [*Heatley*], where the officer who conducted a search of a vehicle incidental to arrest first familiarized herself with the files of several other cases in which the accused was a suspect. The British Columbia Court of Appeal noted the potential issue but, in the absence of necessary factual findings, did not settle whether this was permitted. Implicitly, however, the court seems to accept that if the officer was searching for evidence of crimes other than those for which the accused was arrested, this would mean that "the search was not entirely incidental to the arrest" (at para 67).

simply as an incident to an arrest, although, of course, some other search power—for example, through a warrant—might be available. More commonly in the face of an enhanced privacy interest, the Court will find that additional prerequisites must be met before the search can be carried out as an incident of an arrest. The Court noted in *Stairs*:

> This Court has enunciated a two-part analytical approach for determining whether the common law standard for search incident to arrest should be modified to comply with s. 8 of the *Charter* (see *Stillman*, *Golden*, *Fearon*, and *Saeed*):
>
> (1) *Stage One*: Determine whether the search satisfies the common law standard for search incident to arrest.
>
> (2) *Stage Two*: If so, determine whether the standard must be modified to comply with s. 8 of the *Charter*, given the particular privacy interests and law enforcement objectives at stake.[242]

To date, the Court has identified one type of search that is not permitted simply as an incident of arrest and four special cases where additional prerequisites must be met.

Searches for bodily samples, such as hair, blood, buccal samples (swabbing the inside of the mouth), or dental impressions, fall into the first category and therefore cannot be conducted as an incident of arrest. In *R v Stillman*, the police had performed such tests, and it was argued on appeal that this was justified as a search incident to arrest; however, the Court rejected that argument and found the search to have been unlawful. *Stillman* is a relatively early *Charter* decision, and in fact the Court's rationale for finding the search unlawful was that any search would only be incidental to an arrest if it were for safety purposes or if the evidence was in danger of going out of existence;[243] the power should not be "extended" beyond that,[244] so the search was unlawful. Equally important, the Court noted that a search that infringes upon a person's bodily integrity "may constitute the ultimate affront to human dignity."[245] It is noteworthy that in *Stillman* the Court did not recognize gathering evidence other than that which might go out of existence as an "incidental" search, although they specifically declined to express an opinion as to whether that might be acceptable in the particular case of searches of vehicles.[246]

---

242 *Stairs*, above note 93 at para 32.

243 *Stillman*, above note 43 at para 33.

244 *Ibid* at para 40.

245 *Ibid* at para 39.

246 *Ibid*.

However, their next decision was *Caslake* (a vehicle search case), and there the Court articulated what is now taken to be the three "incidental" purposes without mentioning that whether general "evidence gathering" was included had been a point deliberately left undecided before and without specifying that it was a rule aimed at vehicle searches. The result of those omissions has been that searching for evidence to use at trial has come to be seen as a generally permitted purpose, and *Stillman* is taken simply to have created an exception to the ordinary rule: specifically, the exception that bodily samples cannot be seized as a search incident to arrest.[247]

There are, so far, four types of searches where the search incident to arrest power is available but only when additional requirements are met because of the heightened privacy interest at stake. The first of these arises in the case of strip searches incident to arrest. A "strip search" was defined by the Court in *R v Golden* as "the removal or rearrangement of some or all of the clothing of a person so as to permit a visual inspection of a person's private areas, namely genitals, buttocks, breasts (in the case of a female), or undergarments."[248] Note that this definition includes the "rearrangement" of clothing, and therefore a person could be found to have been strip-searched even if they are not required to remove their clothes; however, any such rearrangement would have to result in exposing private areas of the body.[249] The Court distinguished strip searches from the less intrusive pat-down or frisk, which were permitted, and from the more intrusive body cavity search, "which involve[s] a physical inspection of the detainee's genital or anal regions."[250] The Court concluded that strip searches could, in certain circumstances, be conducted incidental to an arrest. However, it also stressed that strip searches "represent a significant invasion of privacy and are often a humiliating, degrading and traumatic experience for individuals subject to them."[251] Accordingly, it attached additional restrictions beyond those that apply to other searches incident to arrest.

---

247 See, for example, *Fearon*, above note 211 at para 44, stating that *Stillman* and *Golden* (to be discussed next) "modified the common law power in relation to particularly invasive types of searches."

248 *Golden*, above note 206 at para 47.

249 See, for example, *R v Byfield*, 2020 ONCA 515, where an officer pulled the accused's underwear away from his body and removed a package of cocaine from his groin, which was a strip search. On the other hand, in *R v Choi*, 2021 BCCA 410, the officer pulled the waistband of the accused's pants away from his body in order to inspect the waistband of his underwear, and this was found not to be a search that exposed a private area.

250 *Golden*, above note 206 at para 47.

251 *Ibid* at para 83.

First, the Court held that a strip search incident to arrest, unlike other searches incident to arrest, required reasonable grounds justifying the search itself. As they more recently put it in *R v Ali*:

> Where a strip search is conducted as an incident to a person's lawful arrest, there must be reasonable and probable grounds justifying the strip search, in addition to reasonable and probable grounds justifying the arrest (see *Golden*, at para. 99). These grounds are met for the strip search where there is some evidence suggesting the possibility of concealment of weapons or other evidence related to the reason for the arrest (see *Golden*, at paras. 94 and 111).[252]

These additional grounds must relate to the need to conduct a strip search, not merely to the grounds for arrest. In *R v Gonzales*, for example, the police had reasonable grounds to arrest the accused for trafficking in narcotics, but the discovery of an industrial-sized garbage bag containing large vacuum-sealed Ziploc bags that were "[n]ot apparently capable of secretion" did not justify a strip search.[253]

Furthermore — although the point is not entirely clear — it seems that the only purposes justifying a strip search are safety or to prevent evidence from being destroyed but *not* the more general purpose of gathering evidence to use at trial. Although *Golden* postdates *Caslake*, the three purposes articulated in *Caslake* had not yet solidified as the "ordinary case" when it was decided. Furthermore, *Golden* talks about search incident to arrest as having the purposes of safety and preventing the destruction of evidence, so it seems that strip searches are available only where there are reasonable grounds to believe that one of those two incidental purposes is in play.[254]

In addition, *Golden* set out a number of other considerations to take into account in considering whether a particular strip search was carried out reasonably. These include questions such as whether a supervisory officer authorized the search, whether officers of the same gender as the detainee conducted the search, whether a minimum number of officers and a minimum amount of force was involved, whether the search was conducted quickly and in a way that never required the detainee to be entirely unclothed, and so on.[255] A strip search might be found to be justified but nonetheless violate the accused's rights based on these

---

252 *R v Ali*, 2022 SCC 1 at para 2 [*Ali*].

253 *R v Gonzales*, 2017 ONCA 543 at para 144 [*Gonzales*].

254 *Golden*, above note 206 at paras 93–94.

255 *Ibid* at para 101.

considerations.[256] On the other hand, these considerations are only that, factors to take into account, not rigid requirements.[257]

Finally, *Golden* held that strip searches must, in most cases, be conducted at the police station, not in the field. Only if there were exigent circumstances (in addition to reasonable grounds) could a strip search take place before going to the police station. This amounts to saying that, of the legitimate purposes of safety and preventing the loss of evidence, only the former could lead to a strip search in the field:

> Strip searches conducted in the field could only be justified where there is a demonstrated necessity and urgency to search for weapons or objects that could be used to threaten the safety of the accused, the arresting officers or other individuals.[258]

It has, however, been argued that despite this clear statement, field searches for evidence might nonetheless be lawful in some circumstances.[259]

The second special case with additional requirements concerns penile swabs. This issue arose for the Court in *R v Saeed*, where the accused was arrested very shortly after a sexual assault, and police swabbed his penis for the purpose of determining whether samples of the complainant's DNA were to be found there.[260] The accused argued that this situation should be seen as analogous to *Stillman*, which observed that

---

256 See, for example, *R v Muller*, 2014 ONCA 780, where (among other things) the accused was required to stand naked in a room with the door open, next to a hallway accessible to people of both sexes, without any supervisory authority for the search having been sought.

257 See, for example, *R v Black*, 2022 ONCA 628, where a female officer was involved in the strip search of a male arrestee. However, this arose because the accused began suddenly to violently resist, causing the need for immediate assistance from other nearby officers, one of whom was female.

258 *Golden*, above note 206 at para 102. See, for example, *R v Parchment*, 2015 BCCA 417, where the accused had been arrested and two knives were confiscated from him. While still in the accused's home, the police became concerned, because of the manner in which the accused was fidgeting, that he had another weapon concealed in his pants and pulled the waistband forward to check. This strip search was found to be lawful, although in fact it turned out to be narcotics rather than another weapon that the accused was concealing.

259 See *R v Pilon*, 2018 ONCA 959 at para 27: "Notwithstanding the broad statement in para. 102 of *Golden*, that exigent circumstances are limited to safety concerns, and the absence of case law considering preservation of evidence as an exigent circumstance justifying a field strip search, it is at least arguable that the Supreme Court in *Golden* left open the possibility that the need to preserve evidence could qualify as exigent circumstances that permit a field search."

260 *R v Saeed*, 2016 SCC 24 [*Saeed*]. The actual swabbing occurred about seven hours after the incident, and the accused had been handcuffed to a wall for about an hour prior to the sample being taken so that he could not do anything to remove

searches infringing bodily integrity were "the ultimate affront to human dignity."[261] However, the Court rejected the analogy to *Stillman*—and the accompanying conclusion that this type of search was unavailable incidental to arrest—for three reasons. First, the purpose of the search was not to obtain the *accused's* DNA, so it was less intrusive than those in *Stillman*. Second, the penile swab was physically less invasive than taking dental impressions in that it was not penetrative and was accomplished quickly. Finally, while an accused's own bodily samples or impressions would not change over time and therefore did not attract any urgency, that was not true of a complainant's DNA on the accused's body, which would degrade over time and needed to be obtained relatively quickly if it were to be obtained at all.[262]

That said, the Court accepted that a heightened privacy interest was at stake and therefore that some additional requirements needed to be imposed. They concluded that the balance of individual and state interests was similar to that involved in strip searches and therefore that additional rules modelled on those in *Golden* should be imposed. Therefore, in addition to the ordinary requirements for a search incident to arrest, to perform a penile swab "the police must also have reasonable grounds to believe that a penile swab will afford evidence of the offence for which the accused was arrested."[263] Whether reasonable grounds exist will depend on such factors as whether penetrative sex was involved in the alleged offence and the length of time since it occurred.

In addition, the Court observed that the penile swab must be conducted in a reasonable manner. This is of course a requirement of all searches incidental to arrest, but the Court added some particular observations to give guidance in this context. Among these were that the penile swab should be conducted at the police station (although it was imaginable that a hospital could, in some cases, be an appropriate location); that a supervisory officer should authorize the swab; that the accused should be offered the opportunity to do the swabbing himself, failing which an officer of the same gender should do it with the minimum of force and officers present; that it should be done in a private area and as quickly as possible; and that a proper record should be kept.[264]

---

the potential sample. The accused performed the swabbing himself in the company of two male officers, although the search was not taken to be by consent.

261 *Stillman*, above note 43 at para 39.

262 *Saeed*, above note 260 at paras 48–50.

263 *Ibid* at para 75.

264 *Ibid* at para 78. See *R v Cortes Rivera*, 2020 ABCA 76, where a s 8 violation was found because a third officer was unnecessarily present, the accused was left naked during the swab, and the police had not made a complete record of the process. The accused was also not given the opportunity to swab himself, but this

Finally, the Court imposed one other limitation on penile swabs. Although they were permitted as a method of obtaining a complainant's DNA, as a practical matter the accused's DNA might also be obtained through the swab. If that were to occur and the DNA were used, the Court held, the search would have become much more intrusive and indeed would simply be a way to circumvent the requirements of *Stillman* and the DNA warrant provisions in the *Code*. As a result, if the accused's DNA were obtained through a penile swab, it could not be used for any purpose.[265]

The third special case with additional requirements is that of searching cellphones[266] found on a person at the time of arrest. As the Court noted in *R v Fearon*, such searches are not as intrusive as seizures of bodily samples or strip searches, which are always great invasions of privacy and an affront to human dignity. Also, there could be legitimate reasons to search a cellphone promptly—for example, to determine whether there were accomplices in the area, to locate weapons, or to recover stolen goods before they disappear. However, cellphone searches nonetheless have the potential to be far more intrusive than searches of other items an arrestee might be carrying or have in their car. Cellphones "may have immense storage capacity, may generate information about intimate details of the user's interests, habits and identity without the knowledge or intent of the user, may retain information even after the user thinks it has been destroyed, and may provide access to information that is in no meaningful sense 'at' the location of the search."[267]

Accordingly, special limits were placed on cellphone searches, aimed at limiting them to matters that are truly incidental to the arrest. Three particular rules were attached. First, "the nature and the extent of the search performed on the cell phone must be truly incidental to the particular arrest for the particular offence"[268]—that is, police cannot search the entire cellphone but only those parts on it likely to contain evidence that needs to be discovered in the short term, such as recent email messages, text messages, photos, or the call log. Even this is permitted only where necessary, so in the case of minor offences, cellphones

---

was reasonable given the language barrier and the lack of a male interpreter. The evidence was nonetheless admitted, largely because the events took place prior to the decision in *Saeed*.

265 *Saeed*, above note 260 at para 67.

266 The special rules were developed in the particular context of a cellphone but have been applied to similar technology. See, for example, *Balendra*, above note 220, applying the same criteria to a search incident to arrest of a USB key.

267 *Fearon*, above note 211 at para 51.

268 *Ibid* at para 76.

likely cannot be searched.[269] Second, searching for the third incidental purpose — for evidence — "must be treated restrictively."[270] Cellphone searches incident to arrest are not routinely permitted, but only where the investigation "will be stymied or significantly hampered absent the ability to promptly search the cell phone incident to arrest,"[271] and the police must be prepared to explain why it was impractical to wait for a warrant.[272] As a last requirement, officers must take detailed notes about the search, both to allow after-the-fact judicial scrutiny and to help make sure that the search stays within the limited purposes.[273]

Finally, in *Stairs*, the Court created special rules for search incident to arrest inside a home. The rule in that context had been that searches of a home as an incident of an arrest were "generally prohibited."[274]

It is well established that a person has a very high privacy interest in their home, reflected in, for example, the special rules discussed earlier attaching limits to the authority of the police to enter a home to effect an arrest.[275] The majority of the Court held that the task was to find the correct place for that interest on the "spectrum" of privacy interests that had otherwise led to special cases for search incident to arrest. They noted that although searches of the home can reveal highly personal and confidential information, they do not invariably infringe dignity and bodily integrity in the way that taking a bodily sample, conducting a strip search, or performing a penile swab would. They also held that searches in the home are more likely to raise other legitimate police objectives, such as locating potential victims needing help or aggressors posing a safety risk. Therefore, they concluded, "home searches fall lower on the spectrum than *Golden* and *Saeed*" and did not need to incorporate the additional "reasonable grounds" requirements applying to strip searches or penile swabs.[276]

---

269 *Ibid* at para 79.

270 *Ibid* at para 80.

271 *Ibid*.

272 *Ibid*.

273 *Balendra*, above note 220, found the note-taking requirement to be of less significance in the case of searching a USB key because of the narrower range of contents compared to the kinds of apps that would typically be on a cellphone.

274 *R v Golub* (1997), 117 CCC (3d) 193 at para 41 (Ont CA) [*Golub*]. The Ontario Court of Appeal had allowed for a potential exception in the case of "exceptional circumstances where the law enforcement interest is so compelling that it overrides the individual's right to privacy within the home" (*ibid*).

275 See Section B(1)(d), above.

276 *Stairs*, above note 93 at para 54. The dissenting judges argued at para 120 that this "spectrum" approach was flawed:

The Court held that it was necessary to distinguish between two areas when there was an arrest in the home: "(a) the area within the physical control of the person arrested at the time of arrest; and (b) areas outside the physical control of that person, but which are part of the surrounding area because they are sufficiently proximate to the arrest."[277] To properly understand the power created, however, it is necessary to recognize a third area implicit in those two categories—namely, the areas of the home not sufficiently proximate to the arrest. These are of course three areas with a decreasing nexus to the arrestee. What the Court decided is that in the area with the closest nexus, that in the physical control of the arrestee, no special requirements were needed, and the ordinary rules of search incident to arrest would apply. In the area with the least nexus, parts of the house not sufficiently proximate, the existing rule that search incident to arrest did not allow a search of the home would continue to apply. As a result, the additional requirements only apply to the middle category, those areas outside the arrestee's physical control but nonetheless sufficiently proximate to the arrest.[278]

The Court limited searches of those areas in two main ways. First, they imposed a "reasonable suspicion" standard: this is a stricter requirement than generally required for search incident to arrest (which requires only "some reasonable basis") but is less onerous than a "reasonable grounds" standard. Second, they limited the acceptable reasons for the search: it could only be carried out for a "valid safety purpose"[279]—that is, "the objective of police and public safety, including the safety of the accused."[280] In addition, the Court imposed as a requirement that the search should be no more intrusive than necessary to resolve the reasonable suspicion; therefore, "the nature and the extent of the search must be tailored to the purpose of the search and the heightened privacy interests in a home."[281] Finally, the Court observed that police "should keep track of the places

---

> Privacy interests come in different forms—whether personal, territorial, or informational . . . —which are not easily equated. The focus in tailoring the common law framework is to reconcile the specific privacy interests at issue with the specific law enforcement interests that counterbalance them. Whether a search of a home could be more or less invasive than body, cellphone or car searches is, in this respect, tangential; the key questions are when and how the undoubtedly strong privacy interests in a home ought to yield to varying policing objectives. [Citation omitted.]

277 *Stairs*, above note 93 at para 59.

278 The Court's reasoning on this point essentially amounts to identifying the potential "exceptional circumstances" referred to in *Golub*, above note 274.

279 *Stairs*, above note 93 at para 61.

280 *Ibid* at para 82.

281 *Ibid* at para 82.

searched, the extent of the search, the time of the search, its purpose, and its duration. In some instances, insufficient notes may lead a trial judge to make adverse findings impacting the reasonableness of the search."[282] Unlike searches of cellphones, where keeping notes was made a condition of the legality of the search, in this context the Court merely described it as a good practice.

Those are the exceptions to the ordinary search incident to arrest rules that have been created to date, although it is clear that other exceptions might also be created depending on the "proper balance between an accused's privacy interests and valid law enforcement objectives."[283]

f) Search Incident to Investigative Detention and Safety Searches

The Supreme Court of Canada created a common law power of investigative detention with its decision in *Mann*; see the discussion of this case, and this power, in Chapter 3. At the same time, it also relied on the *Waterfield* test[284] to create a common law power of "search incident to an investigative detention."[285] In this section, we will set out the rules governing that power, but it is worth saying at the start that there is fundamental confusion over a key aspect of it, so it is not possible to accurately describe the power in a way with which all courts would agree.

It is easiest to define the investigative detention search power by the ways in which it differs from search incident to arrest. The first difference relates to the acceptable purpose for the search. Search incident to arrest is permitted for safety purposes and for evidentiary purposes, but during an investigative detention, the only permissible basis for conducting a search is safety. In *Mann*, the Court relied on the *Waterfield* test, which meant that any interference had to "involve a justified use of a police power associated with a general duty to search in relation to the protection of life and property."[286] A power to search would not automatically exist, it stressed, but sometimes police would be entitled to search a detained person for reasons of safety:

> The general duty of officers to protect life may, in some circumstances, give rise to the power to conduct a pat-down search incident to an investigative detention. Such a search power does not exist as a matter of course; the officer must believe on reasonable grounds that his or her own safety, or the safety of others, is at risk.[287]

282 *Ibid* at para 81.
283 *Saeed*, above note 260 at para 5.
284 See Section B(1)(c), above in this chapter, for more on this topic.
285 *Mann*, above note 14 at paras 37 and 40.
286 *Ibid* at para 39.
287 *Ibid* at para 40.

Note that as created, the search power is initially limited to a pat-down search and no more than that. The facts of *Mann* itself make that point particularly clear. The accused was stopped near the scene of a suspected break-in, and the police patted him down. Having detected something soft in a pocket, they searched further to find what it was. It transpired that it was marijuana, so he was charged with possession. The Court found that the evidence had been unlawfully obtained. Although the initial pat-down search was legal, feeling something soft did not give rise to any concerns about safety. In that event, there was no justification for searching further, so the police acted without authority in reaching into the accused's pocket.

Similarly, in *R v Dunkley*, the accused fled from police at a gas station, following which the officers searched his vehicle. The Ontario Court of Appeal found the vehicle search to be unlawful on the basis that reasonable grounds for arrest did not exist, so the search was not incidental to an arrest, and although there was reasonable suspicion, "[t]he search of the car at that point had no nexus to a concern for officer or public safety."[288]

However, despite this power initially being quite limited, some lower courts have expanded its scope.[289] Although the Supreme Court said the power was merely one "to conduct a pat-down search,"[290] it has been held that the search might include questioning the accused for safety-related reasons[291] or looking in items carried by the accused, such as a fanny pack or purse, again if this is done for safety purposes.[292] Other decisions have expanded the search power to the area of a car in which the accused had been sitting when detained[293] or to the trunk of such

288 *R v Dunkley*, 2016 ONCA 597 at para 38. As a further example, see *R v Turpin*, 2012 SKCA 50 [*Turpin*], where police stopped a motor home in a routine traffic stop but ended up searching it quite thoroughly, which was not authorized: the search "involved police officers lifting carpet, looking under the dash and the hood of the vehicle and opening cupboards and storage compartments. It was not undertaken out of concerns for safety and was thus in no way properly incidental to an investigative detention" (at para 95).

289 See Scott Latimer, "The Expanded Scope of Search Incident to Investigative Detention" (2007) 48 *Criminal Reports* (6th) 201.

290 *Mann*, above note 14 at para 40.

291 *R v Patrick*, 2017 BCCA 57 at para 102 [*Patrick* BCCA]: "[Q]uestioning a detainee about to be frisk searched as to whether they are in possession of anything that might cause the searching officer injury is minimally intrusive .... [N]arrowly tailored questions of this kind motivated *solely* by safety concerns are permissible." [Emphasis in original.]

292 See *R v Thibodeau*, 2007 BCCA 489; *R v Sheck*, 2015 BCCA 471 [*Sheck*]; or *R v Upright*, 2020 ABCA 122.

293 See *R v Plummer*, 2011 ONCA 350, or *R v Webber*, 2019 BCCA 208 [*Webber*].

a vehicle.[294] It has also been held that *Mann* was not intended to set out a rigid "step-by-step" approach and that "searches to eliminate any imminent threat to the officer or third parties can take many forms depending on the circumstances and are not limited to pat-down searches."[295] And, of course, a search incident to investigative detention can go beyond a pat-down but only if that pat-down gives some further reason to be concerned about safety.[296]

The second way in which these types of searches differ from search incident to arrest is with regard to the standard required to justify one (and here confusion arises). As was noted above, search incident to arrest is available automatically upon arrest. It is a discretionary decision, and the officer searching must be able to point to the way in which the search is related to one of the legitimate objectives, but no separate reasonable grounds are required for the search. If an officer wants to search incidental to an arrest for safety reasons, it is not necessary for them to show reasonable grounds to believe that such a search is necessary as the reasonable grounds for the arrest justify the search.

In an investigative detention, that is not the case. Rather, as noted above, the Court said that "the officer must *believe on reasonable grounds* that his or her own safety, or the safety of others, is at risk."[297] It is tempting to say that "separate" reasonable grounds for the search must be shown, but of course part of the point here is that the detention itself did not require reasonable *grounds*, only reasonable *suspicion*.

Several observations should be made. First, one can argue that this approach is perfectly in line with the Court's approach to section 8 and unreasonable searches generally: reasonable grounds to believe should exist somewhere if the search is to be justified, so if they do not arise in the context of the detention, then they must arise independently.

Second, though, one can equally argue that this is a contradictory approach for the Court to have taken. As James Stribopoulos points out, the standard that has been set for this search is equivalent to that set for an arrest, which as a practical matter is hard to reconcile with the fact that the detention was based only on reasonable suspicion:

---

294 *R v Lee*, 2017 ONCA 654.

295 *R v McKenzie*, 2022 MBCA 3 at para 50 [*McKenzie*].

296 It was because no such reason existed that reaching into Mann's pocket was unlawful. See also *R v Del Corro*, 2019 ABCA 156, at para 48 [*Del Corro*]: "[I]n every case where a search extends beyond a pat-down, the circumstances must disclose serious safety concerns requiring something more than a pat-down." Similarly, see *Plummer*, above note 293 at para 79.

297 *Mann*, above note 14 at para 40 [emphasis added].

> The judgment in *Mann* indicates that a protective pat-down search is only permitted where a police officer has "reasonable grounds to believe" that his or her safety or that of others is at risk. This language seems to import the standard for conventional arrests, which makes little sense. If the police have such grounds, they could arrest a suspect on a charge of weapons dangerous and then conduct a far more probing search.[298]

It is important to note that the Court is not unaware of that objection. Shortly after handing down *Mann*, they were asked to reconsider their decision for precisely this reason but declined the request for a rehearing.[299]

Furthermore, one can argue that the reasonable grounds standard is an impractical one. For example, in *R v McKenzie*, the police saw a known member of a street gang running in a way giving them reasonable suspicion that he was carrying a weapon, so they stopped him for an investigative detention.[300] Reasonable suspicion was, legally, a sufficient basis for that detention. However, if the police required reasonable grounds before having the power to check for that weapon, one might wonder what the point of stopping him in the first place was. Arguably, the situation could be seen as analogous to a roadside screening; reasonable suspicion authorizes the police to investigate further, either to confirm their suspicions or dispel them, but does no more than that. However, there is a strong temptation for courts to think the stop power should include the search power.

Furthermore, the application of the reasonable grounds standard can be a bit problematic. In *Mann*, for example, the Court found that there were reasonable grounds on the basis that

> there was a logical possibility that the appellant, suspected on reasonable grounds of having recently committed a break-and-enter, was in possession of break-and-enter tools, which could be used as weapons.

298 James Stribopoulos, "The Limits of Judicially Created Police Powers: Investigative Detention After *Mann*" (2007) 52 *Criminal Law Quarterly* 299 at 311 [footnotes omitted] [Stribopoulos]. Note that that author is now Justice Stribopoulos of the Ontario Superior Court of Justice. See also the trial decision in *R v Le*, 2014 ONSC 2033 at para 99: "If a police officer possessed reasonable and probable grounds to believe a suspect was armed and dangerous, the suspect would invariably be arrested, not merely detained, and would be physically searched as incident to that arrest." On the other hand, the trial judge in *Buakasa*, above note 223, had noted that the issue of a threat existing in the abstract and the suspect's culpabiity for the threat were not identical. In that case, she found that there could be reasonable grounds to believe that there was a safety threat due to a possible firearm in a vehicle, without there being reasonable grounds to arrest the accused for possession of that firearm.

299 Stribopoulos, above note 298 at n 44 & n 45.

300 *McKenzie*, above note 295.

> The encounter also occurred just after midnight and there were no other people in the area.[301]

A "logical possibility" would not normally be seen as sufficient to meet the reasonable grounds standard. In addition, the logical possibility of the accused having break-and-enter tools itself hinges on him being the person who had committed the break and enter. By definition, the police did not have reasonable grounds to believe that.[302]

The greatest source of confusion over this power, however, arises because of the view adopted by some lower courts that *Mann* did not, as a pure matter of fact, create a reasonable grounds requirement for searches incident to investigative detention. This was the argument of the minority in *MacDonald*, which created the "safety search" power. That is not a power of detention, of course (except to the extent that the person is detained for the duration of the search), but the *MacDonald* decision is intimately bound up with the continuing confusion over search incident to investigative detention.

In *MacDonald*, police responded to a noise complaint and ended up in conversation with the accused through a partly open door. The officer formed the belief that the accused was holding a weapon in his hand, forced open the door slightly to confirm this belief, and, after a brief struggle, disarmed the accused, who was holding a loaded gun. The central issue in the case was whether the search—that is, pushing open the door to see whether the accused was armed—was a reasonable one, which would require that it be authorized by law. The Court concluded that the officer's action was authorized by a newly minted common law "safety search" power. The safety search power is, in essence, a search incident to investigative detention but without any prior investigative detention.[303]

---

301 *Mann*, above note 14 at para 48.

302 See, in contrast, *Duong*, above note 187, where a search incident to investigative detention was found to be justified because the accused was found with an apparently stolen stereo with its wires cut. The court there held that since the wires had been cut, it was reasonable to believe the accused had a knife.

303 In *R v Fountain*, 2015 ONCA 354, a panel of the Ontario Court of Appeal relied at para 25 on the finding in *MacDonald*, above note 60, that safety searches can occur "outside of an investigative detention" to conclude that the safety search power could be used even if there had been an *unlawful* investigative detention. This seems like a mistake: there is a significant difference between a search being authorized without a lawful detention and being authorized despite an *un*lawful detention. This point was noted in the later case of *R v McGuffie*, 2016 ONCA 365 at para 54, where a different panel of the Ontario Court of Appeal concluded that the power to conduct a safety search "assumes that the officer is engaged in the execution of their lawful duty" and therefore that "the police cannot, through unlawful conduct, create a circumstance said to justify a safety search of an individual." See also *R v Squires*, 2016 NLCA 54, taking the same view as *McGuffie*.

All of the judges in *MacDonald* were of the view that the standard for a safety search would be the same as the standard set in *Mann* for a search incident to investigative detention; however, they split 4:3 over the question of what standard *Mann* had actually set.

In the view of the minority, "*Mann* decided that officers may conduct safety searches when they have reasonable grounds to *suspect* an individual is armed and dangerous."[304] Their justifications for that view are complicated and included five separate reasons, but the core of the argument was that reasonable grounds to believe safety was "at risk" amounted to a probability of a possibility, which therefore should be seen simply as reasonable *suspicion*. The minority also noted that this approach had already been adopted by some lower courts:

> For example, in *R. v. Crocker*, 2009 BCCA 388, 275 B.C.A.C. 190, leave to appeal refused, [2010] 1 S.C.R. viii, the court held that "[a] lawful protective safety search . . . need only meet the legal standard of *reasonable suspicions* . . . required by *Mann*" (para. 72 (emphasis added)). Just a few months ago, the same conclusion was reached in *R. v. Atkins*, 2013 ONCA 586, 310 O.A.C. 397: "The pat-down search that followed the detention was justified on officer safety grounds" because "[t]he officers *reasonably suspected* that the appellant was in possession of a weapon" (para. 15 (emphasis added)).[305]

In addition, they noted that the Court had on later occasions described the power of search incident to investigative detention as being based on reasonable suspicion.[306]

The majority do not explicitly address the arguments of the minority. However, in creating the safety search power, they reiterate and rely on *Mann*, holding that "[g]iven the high privacy interests at stake in such searches, the search will be authorized by law only if the police officer believes on reasonable grounds that his or her safety is at stake and that, as a result, it is necessary to conduct a search (*Mann*, at para. 40; see also para. 45)."[307] There is no room for doubt that the majority in *MacDonald* sets a "reasonable grounds" rather than a "reasonable suspicion" standard, since the minority judgment exists solely to disagree with that

304 *MacDonald*, above note 60 at para 66 [emphasis in original].

305 *Ibid* at para 78.

306 Footnote 1 of *Chehil*, above note 59, says that a search accompanying an investigative detention, as set out in *Mann*, above note 14, uses the reasonable suspicion standard. It is worth noting that that footnote also says that searches by school officials, using the power found in *M(MR)*, above note 29, are available based on reasonable suspicion. Neither of those statements accurately reflects what was said in the decisions they describe.

307 *MacDonald*, above note 60 at para 41.

conclusion.[308] And it is very clear that the majority is saying that the standard for safety searches and the standard for searches incident to investigative detention are the same. The most natural conclusion would therefore be that those lower courts that had interpreted *Mann* as setting a reasonable suspicion standard were incorrect about that. That is not, however, the conclusion that lower courts have generally reached.

Rather, the decision sparked significant confusion:

> [T]he Supreme Court case law on safety searches has subsequently generated an abundance of judicial and academic commentary on the standard to be met for a safety search, and whether the applicable standard depends on whether the search is incident to investigative detention (as in *Mann*) or stand-alone (as in *MacDonald*).
>
> This court has similarly noted that the language used in *MacDonald* has given rise to confusion about what the appropriate standard is, and debate about whether there are two standards — for searches incident to detention and arrest, and free-standing safety searches.[309]

Courts of appeal that have specifically considered the issue have tended to cling to the view that *Mann* did set a reasonable suspicion standard and have asked whether *MacDonald* changed that: whether the standard has been raised "from the traditional 'reasonable suspicion'" standard.[310] That alone would be curious since *Mann* was very clear on the point in the first place. Even more curious, however, is the general reluctance of courts of appeal to conclude that the standard is, at this point, one of reasonable grounds. Many court of appeal decisions have noted this issue but found it unnecessary to decide the point on the facts of the particular case in front of them.[311] The British Columbia Court of Appeal has gone further and concluded that *MacDonald* did not "recalibrate" the standard for search incident to investigative detention, which therefore remained, in their view, based on reasonable suspicion. Even more mystifying, *R v Webber* rejects as well the suggestion that the standard for safety searches and the standard for searches incident to arrest are different from one another.[312] That could only lead to the conclusion that safety searches

308 *Ibid* at para 66: "[W]hile we agree with the majority on all three issues in this case, including Mr. MacDonald's claim under s. 8 of the *Canadian Charter of Rights and Freedoms*, we part company with our colleagues on the proper interpretation of *Mann*."

309 *Buakasa*, above note 223 at paras 38 & 39.

310 *Webber*, above note 293 at para 65.

311 See, for example, *R v Ahmed-Kadir*, 2015 BCCA 346; *R v Peterkin*, 2015 ONCA 8; *Sheck*, above note 292; *Patrick* BCCA, above note 291; *Del Corro*, above note 296; or *Buakasa*, above note 223.

312 *Webber*, above note 293 at paras 56–57.

are also based on reasonable suspicion, but the sole reason the minority judgment in *MacDonald* exists is to argue that the majority were wrong not to reach that conclusion.[313]

Accordingly, it is difficult to state with confidence the standard for search incident to investigative detention. In *Mann*, the Supreme Court was explicit that the standard was reasonable grounds, declined to reconsider that point, and repeated the conclusion in *MacDonald*. Nonetheless, some courts of appeal have expressed doubt over what the standard is, and the British Columbia Court of Appeal has concluded that it is, in fact, reasonable suspicion.

2) The Importance of Police Purpose

An issue that arises in a variety of contexts around police powers is police purpose. Police are given a variety of powers, both by statute and at common law. In either case, courts interpret those powers as having been given to police for a particular reason, and they try to interpret those powers in a way that will balance the state's needs against individual liberty. However, police do not necessarily have that same goal in mind; rather, they can be inclined simply to use the powers they have been given to achieve their goals without necessarily having regard to the underlying purpose of those powers.[314] Accordingly, courts do, at least in some cases, find themselves obliged to put particular stress on the purpose that is in an officer's mind at the time they act. As the Supreme Court noted in *R v Mellenthin*:

> Check stop programs result in the arbitrary detention of motorists. The programs are justified as a means aimed at reducing the terrible toll of death and injury so often occasioned by impaired drivers or by dangerous vehicles. The primary aim of the program is thus to check for sobriety, licences, ownership, insurance and the mechanical fitness of cars. The police use of check stops should not be extended beyond these aims.

---

313 *R v Kim*, 2016 ABPC 9 at para 52, has gone even further by concluding that the minority in *MacDonald* was wrong about what the majority decided: "I am bound by the majority in *MacDonald*, not by the interpretation of the majority's decision by the dissent."

314 See, for example, *R v Wynter*, 2005 ONCJ 516 at para 29:

> In my view, a review of Halman's evidence gives rise to a conclusion that he really had no articulable cause. And he basically concedes this. He says that he would have stopped and investigated even if Mr. Wynter had not fled. He said that his real concerns were drugs, not the *Highway Traffic Act*. The *Highway Traffic Act*, to him, seems to be some kind of a tool in his tool kit that permits him to stop people.

> Random stop programs must not be turned into a means of conducting either an unfounded general inquisition or an unreasonable search.[315]

In part, this is reflected in the simple requirement that many powers—for example, to arrest, to detain, to search—have both subjective and objective components. Typically, the objective components are in dispute (see the discussion of reasonable grounds, below), but that does not mean that the subjective component is unimportant. In *Feeney*, for example, police were found not to have made a legal arrest in part because the officer acknowledged in his testimony that he did not subjectively think he had grounds to arrest. That alone made the arrest illegal, whatever the conclusion on the objective test.[316] Similarly in *Caslake*, the Court found that a search incident to arrest of the accused's vehicle would have been objectively reasonable. The officer who had searched the car, however, testified that he was performing an inventory search, not a search incident to arrest; in that event, the search was not legal.[317]

Purpose can matter in other ways. For example, the power to search can arise in connection with both arrests and detentions. In the case of arrests, police are entitled to search either for the purpose of discovering evidence or to protect officer safety. A search incident to an investigative detention, on the other hand, can only be based on safety concerns. The result is that the officer's purpose can determine the legality or not of the search; a search conducted for the purpose of discovering evidence will violate the *Charter* in the case of an investigative detention, where the same search would be permitted if it were for the purpose of officer safety.[318] Similarly, a search incident to arrest that has the goal of seeking evidence of a crime in addition to the one for which the accused was

---

315 *Mellenthin*, above note 37 at 624.

316 *Feeney*, above note 168.

317 See, generally, *Caslake*, above note 210. But see *Latimer*, above note 13, in which the police had decided not to arrest the accused but merely to take him in for questioning; that is, they appear to have decided to do something they had no power to do. The accused claimed a violation of his s 9 right to be free from arbitrary detention. The Court rejected this claim on the basis that there had been a "*de facto* arrest." It held that "notwithstanding what the *intention* of the officers may have been, their conduct had the *effect* of putting Mr. Latimer under arrest" (at para 24 [emphasis in original]). Since that arrest was also found to be legal, it is a little hard to reconcile this result with the normal emphasis the Court places on intention. Possibly the answer lies somewhere in the fact that the police did subjectively believe they had reasonable grounds for arrest even though they did not subjectively intend to arrest; however, it is not entirely apparent that this would distinguish the case from *Caslake*. See the further discussion of this case below in Chapter 4, Section C(1)(b).

318 *Mann*, above note 14 at paras 37 and 43. An officer cannot merely assert "it was for safety," of course, and there must be reasonable grounds supporting that claim.

arrested would thereby not be incidental to the arrest.[319] As the Ontario Court of Appeal has put it, "the purpose relied on to justify the search at trial must have been the actual reason the police conducted the search. After-the-fact justifications that did not actually cause the police to conduct the search or seizure will not do."[320]

Which power the police intended to exercise can also be relevant to a *Charter* analysis in determining whether or not a detention was lawful. An arrest requires reasonable belief, while an investigative detention requires only reasonable suspicion, a more easily satisfied standard. Some courts have found a detention to be lawful where, even though the police purported to arrest an accused but there were not sufficient grounds for arrest, there nonetheless were sufficient grounds for an investigative detention.[321] That approach ignores police purpose in the analysis. The more common—and preferable—approach, especially among courts that specifically consider the issue, is that "[t]he arbitrariness of the appellant's detention must be determined having regard to the police power actually exercised and not by reference to some other police power which may have been, but was not, exercised."[322]

Purpose can play other roles relevant to arrest or detention, including helping to determine whether a detention has occurred. As the Supreme Court noted in *Grant*:

> [G]eneral inquiries by a patrolling officer present no threat to freedom of choice. On the other hand, such inquiries can escalate into situations where the focus shifts from general community-oriented concern to suspicion of a particular individual. Focussed suspicion, in and of itself, does not turn the encounter in [*sic*] a detention. What matters is how the police, based on that suspicion, interacted with the subject . . . . The police must be mindful that, depending on how they act and what they say, the point may be reached where a reasonable person, in the position of that individual, would conclude he or she is not free to choose to walk away or decline to answer questions.[323]

On the other hand, the majority in *Grant* did not let police purpose be the controlling factor settling whether an accused was detained; rather,

---

319 See, for example, *Heatley*, above note 241; *Santana*, above note 220; *Balendra*, above note 220; or *Lai*, above note 215.

320 *Santana*, above note 220 at para 28.

321 See, for example, *Richards*, above note 229.

322 See *R v Stevenson*, 2014 ONCA 842 at para 56. See also *R v Whitaker*, 2008 BCCA 174; *R v Brown*, 2012 ONCA 225 [*Brown* 2012]; *R v Dhillon*, 2012 BCCA 254 [*Dhillon*]; *Turpin*, above note 288; and *R v Moore*, 2012 BCCA 400.

323 *Grant*, above note 15 at para 41.

that question was to be settled by looking at whether "the reasonable person in the individual's circumstances would conclude that he or she had been deprived by the state of the liberty of choice."[324]

Various courts have also noted that an improper purpose can vitiate what would otherwise be legitimate police action. The Supreme Court has observed that an arrest that would otherwise be lawful might be rendered invalid if it were "made because a police officer was biased towards a person of a different race, nationality or colour, or that there was a personal enmity between a police officer directed towards the person arrested."[325] (See the further discussion of racial profiling immediately below.) Similarly, stopping a vehicle might be found to violate the *Charter*, even if the power to do so existed, if the circumstances supported the conclusion that the stop power was misused and was merely a pretext.[326] It has also been held that, even though a search incident to arrest can include the vehicle in which the accused was arrested, that power could not be used if the time and place of the arrest were contrived in order to justify the vehicle search.[327]

However, the effect of this emphasis on purpose is muted by several other rules. First, although the justification for a search might rest on having the proper purpose, that does not mean that the ultimate scope of the search is limited by that purpose. For example, a police officer can search incidental to an investigative detention only in order to try to discover a weapon. But if an officer is searching for that purpose and in fact finds narcotics, that discovery will justify laying a possession charge against the accused, and the narcotics will be admissible. More generally, so long as an officer is lawfully searching for some purpose, whatever

324 *Ibid* at para 44. Also, the Court noted that "the subjective intentions of the police are not determinative" (at para 32).

325 *R v Storrey*, [1990] 1 SCR 241 at 251 [*Storrey*]. See also *R v Byfield* (2005), 74 OR (3d) 206 at para 21 (CA) [*Byfield*], referring to a detention not being "undermined by improper purposes."

326 See *R v Calderon* (2004), 188 CCC (3d) 481 at para 67 (Ont CA) [*Calderon*].

327 See *Lim*, above note 236 at paras 49–50. But see *Stillman*, above note 43 at paras 9 and 29, where it appears that the police arrested the accused on a second occasion for the same offence primarily in order to search him incidental to that arrest. The Supreme Court does not comment one way or the other on this aspect of the police's behaviour or whether it was acceptable, but this could be because it found *Charter* violations on other grounds in relation to all the evidence gathered. Not permitting warrantless arrests for the purpose of obtaining evidence would be consistent with the way in which the ability of a justice to issue a summons has been interpreted. If the primary purpose of compelling the accused to attend court has already been satisfied in some other way, a justice cannot issue a summons for the purpose of requiring the accused to attend for the purposes of the *Identification of Criminals Act*, RSC 1985, c I-1: see *Re Michelsen* (1983), 4 CCC (3d) 371 (Man QB).

evidence is found will normally be admissible whether or not it related to that purpose.[328] Furthermore, even if the search is unconstitutional, that does not necessarily mean that the evidence will be excluded. In *Caslake*, for example, although the search violated the accused's section 8 rights because the subjective test was not met, the evidence was not excluded. One factor leading to the admission of the evidence was precisely that the objective test had been met, whatever the officer's subjective state of mind.

Finally, "police purpose" in the detention context is not as central as it might be. This can most easily be seen by contrasting the rule in this context to that in the search context.

When it comes to searches, the Supreme Court has held that different rules should govern different contexts. For example, in the criminal law context, *Canada (Combines Investigation Act Director of Investigation & Research) v Southam Inc* [*Hunter v Southam*] establishes that a search conducted without a warrant is prima facie unreasonable. However, there are many other circumstances in which individuals are required to provide information. Many of these are simple regulatory contexts, such as providing audit information with regard to income taxes. In those contexts, the panoply of procedural protections that are appropriate to criminal law are not required; there is no warrant requirement in the case of a tax audit, for example. In essence, the greater the potential consequences to the individual from the information being made available to the state, the greater the procedural protections provided.

One obvious danger of this situation, of course, is that the state could use powers created for one purpose in order to gather information to be used for another: investigators might use tax-audit powers to help produce evidence for a criminal fraud investigation, for example. In that event, the individual would not be receiving the appropriate level of protection. To guard against that possibility, in the search context the Supreme Court has created the "predominant purpose" test: where the predominant purpose of a particular inquiry is the determination of penal liability, investigators are no longer allowed to use regulatory powers.[329]

The Supreme Court seems to have concluded that the same rule does not apply in the detention context. The issue is what should happen when a stop power created for one purpose is used in pursuit of another purpose. More specifically, when police have two purposes for the stop, one proper and one improper, does the proper purpose save the search, or does the improper one render it a *Charter* violation?

---

328 See, for example, *Ferris*, above note 30; *R v Favorite* (2008), 57 CR (6th) 183 (Ont SCJ); or *R v Asp*, 2008 BCSC 794.

329 See *R v Jarvis*, 2002 SCC 73 [*Jarvis*].

Courts of appeal had disagreed over this question. A Saskatchewan Court of Appeal decision, *R v Ladouceur* (2002), had held that combining two purposes in this way would result in an unlawful detention:

> Why cannot the two aims co-exist? The notion that in conducting a check-stop a police officer can neatly compartmentalize the lawful aim separately from the unlawful one and not be influenced or affected by the latter is, in my respectful view, stretching reality to a breaking point. (This case amply illustrates this point.) Furthermore it is important not to encourage the establishment of check-stops where a nominally lawful aim is but a plausible facade for an unlawful aim.[330]

In contrast, the Ontario Court of Appeal had held in *Brown v Durham Regional Police Force* that, as long as the police had a legitimate reason for making a stop, the fact that they also had other purposes for which they would not have been permitted to make the stop did not matter:

> The trial judge rejected the submission that other purposes in addition to highway traffic concerns rendered the stops unlawful. . . .
>
> I agree with this conclusion as long as the other purposes motivating the stop are not themselves improper. For example, the police are entitled on a s. 216(1) stop to require drivers to produce their licences. That requirement is consistent with the highway safety concerns which underlie the power granted by the section. In addition to ensuring that the driver is properly licensed, the police may wish to identify the driver for other purposes. It may be, as in this case, that the police are interested in knowing the identity of all those who are connected with what they believe to be organized criminal activity. The gathering of police intelligence is well within the ongoing police duty to investigate criminal activity. As long as the additional police purpose is not improper and does not entail an infringement on the liberty or security of the detained person beyond that contemplated by the purpose animating s. 216(1) of the *HTA* [*Highway Traffic Act*], I see no reason for declaring that a legitimate police interest beyond highway safety concerns should taint the lawfulness of the stop and detention.[331]

In *Nolet*, the Supreme Court turned to consider this question, although their discussion is framed around the legality of the search conducted pursuant to a highway traffic act stop rather than the legality of the stop itself.[332]

---

330 *R v Ladouceur*, 2002 SKCA 73 at para 66 [*Ladouceur* 2002].

331 *Durham*, above note 152 at paras 30 & 31.

332 *Nolet*, above note 222. In the interests of disclosure, note that Glen Luther, one of the authors of this book, was also one of the counsel for Nolet in front of the

In that case, an RCMP officer had stopped a tractor-trailer and after some questioning of the occupants had searched it. The trial judge acknowledged that there were reasons for the officer to search connected to the improper registration offences but held that that had not in fact been his motivating factor; instead, the trial judge held, the officer's primary purpose had been to search for evidence of a criminal offence. The trial judge had therefore held that the search violated section 8 of the *Charter*. The Supreme Court disagreed, upholding the order for a new trial issued by the Saskatchewan Court of Appeal.

On the one hand, the Court recognized the legitimacy of the concern raised in *Ladouceur* (2002).[333] They agreed that highway traffic powers could not be used as a pretext, accepting that "it is important not to encourage the establishment of checkstops where a nominally lawful aim is but a plausible facade for an unlawful aim."[334] On the facts, however, they distinguished *Ladouceur*, holding that the highway traffic stop powers in *Nolet* were not merely used as a ruse as those concerns were among the ones genuinely in the officer's mind.

They went on, then, to reject the "predominant purpose" approach to the use of those powers. They held that police officers were likely to be interested in both criminal and provincial infractions most of the time, so the existence of some purpose outside the regulatory one did not invalidate the search. Rather, the issue was whether there was still some authority for the search. They held:

> [T]he question is not "determining which purpose is predominate or subordinate" (para. 85). As long as there is a continuing regulatory purpose on which to ground the exercise of the regulatory power, the issue is whether the officer's search of the duffle bag infringed the reasonable expectations of privacy of the appellants.[335]

The Court also rejected the argument that the approach in *R v Jarvis*,[336] where a question of income tax audit powers being used for a criminal investigation arose, was analogous. In *Jarvis*, the Court had spoken about "crossing the Rubicon" in moving from an audit to a criminal investigation, noting that a higher level of *Charter* protection applied in the latter situation. In this case, they held, "the context was always penal" since the initial stop concerned a provincial offence.[337]

Supreme Court.

333 *Ladouceur* 2002, above note 330.

334 *Nolet*, above note 222 at para 36, quoting *Ladouceur* 2002, above note 330 at para 66.

335 *Nolet*, above note 222 at para 41.

336 *Jarvis*, above note 329.

337 *Ibid* at para 45.

It is fair to say that the application of the law is not easy or straightforward in this area now. On the one hand, many lower courts have not taken *Nolet* simply to allow a kind of "open season" on motorists. *Nolet* permits *other* purposes to be present when a legitimate traffic stop is made, but that does not mean that merely because a traffic stop would be possible, a stop made for one of those other purposes is lawful. In essence, therefore, courts are required to decide whether they are faced with a "dual purpose" search, which is lawful, or a "pretext" search, which is not.

Some courts have held, for example, that if the real purpose police have in stopping a vehicle is suspicion (for example, because it is late at night and a secluded area), then they cannot rely upon a traffic stop power but rather must meet the test for an investigative detention. This will be so even if traffic safety concerns arise during the stop.[338] Similarly, it has been held that if an officer is only exploiting the traffic stop power as a means to pursue a different goal, this will amount to a *Charter* breach.[339] Furthermore, if the traffic stop purpose has essentially been satisfied (as opposed to the situation "developing," as in *Nolet*), further investigation will not be authorized under that power.[340]

On the other hand, other courts have held that even where it seems quite clear from the facts that police primarily have a criminal law purpose (for example, to check whether a vehicle is stolen or whether a passenger is involved in a drug offence), they can still rely on a traffic stop power if they also have a traffic-related purpose.[341] Indeed, cases with similar facts can be decided based on a credibility assessment of the police officers: if it is accepted that they genuinely were interested in a traffic matter, even if that seems peripheral to the focus of the stop,

---

338 See *R v Houben*, 2006 SKCA 129 [*Houben*], which continues to be relied upon post-*Nolet*: see, for example, *R v McCammon*, 2013 MBCA 68, or *R v Papilion*, 2014 SKCA 45. See also *Gonzales*, above note 253; *Koma*, above note 35; or *R v Bzezi*, 2022 ONCA 184.

339 See, for example, *R v Fleury*, 2014 ABQB 199 at para 26, where the trial judge found that the officer "was following the accused to 'get' a traffic violation to justify the pull over." Similarly, in *R c Koulakis*, 2012 QCCQ 4276, after the accused failed to signal a left turn, the officer examined the secondary Vehicle Identification Number (VIN) on the doorjamb with a flashlight, purportedly to investigate whether the car was stolen, and in the process peered into a slot in the door frame and discovered narcotics. Given that there was no basis to suspect that the car was stolen, the trial judge found this to be merely a pretext in order to search for drugs.

340 See the concurring judgment of Hunt J in *Pearson*, above note 84.

341 *R v Ng*, 2014 ABPC 62 [*Ng*]. See also *R v Upright*, 2020 ABCA 227 at para 10: "The fact that S/Sgt Smithman suspected Hanton to be involved in drug activities and therefore wanted the appellant's vehicle stopped for traffic violations does not make the traffic stop illegal."

then there will have been a dual purpose, and the stop will be lawful.[342] Where no such traffic purpose is found, the stop will violate section 9.[343]

Arguably, much of this confusion arises from courts failing to sufficiently take police purpose into account. On the one hand, it is accepted that that "might extend their investigations opportunistically while exercising an initial lawful authority;"[344] that is, if information comes to light during a stop that changes things, police are properly allowed to pursue that change. But it is equally accepted that a "pretext" stop is not allowed. There surely is a difference between making a stop for one purpose and extending it when new information comes to light as opposed to making a stop in the hope that it will cause new information to come to light. The caselaw in this area would probably be more consistent if that difference were always kept clearly in mind.

3) Racial Profiling

Racial profiling has been a frustratingly illusive, and elusive, phenomenon in criminal law. There is no dispute that it is an objectionable process. The Supreme Court has observed in both the arrest and the detention contexts that a racial motive will override the fact that a legitimate power might otherwise have existed if used for the proper reason. In *R v Storrey*, for example, the Court held:

> [T]here is no indication that the arrest was made because a police officer was biased towards a person of a different race, nationality or colour, or that there was a personal enmity between a police officer directed towards the person arrested. These factors, if established, might have the effect of rendering invalid an otherwise lawful arrest.[345]

Similarly, in *Chehil*, the Court declined to reject the use of profiles in the context of forming reasonable grounds but cautioned that profiles must not be stereotypical or discriminatory and must be based on an accused's actions rather than their immutable characteristics.[346]

Equally, there is no dispute that racial profiling does occur in practice. The Ontario Court of Appeal noted decades ago in *R v Brown* (2003) that

---

342 See, for example, *R v Campbell*, 2016 ONCJ 236, or *R v Peterson*, 2015 SKQB 120.

343 See, for example, *R v Mitchell*, 2019 ONSC 2613, or *R v Tully*, 2022 ONSC 1852.

344 *R v Zolmer*, 2019 ABCA 93 at para 36.

345 *Storrey*, above note 325 at 251–52. See also *Ladouceur* 1990, above note 36, noting that vehicle stops based on factors such as the race of the accused would be objectionable.

346 *Chehil*, above note 59 at paras 42–43.

> [i]n the opening part of his submission before this court, counsel for the appellant said that he did not challenge the fact that the phenomenon of racial profiling by the police existed. This was a responsible position to take because, as counsel said, this conclusion is supported by significant social science research. I quote from the *Report of The Commission on Systemic Racism in the Ontario Criminal Justice System* (Toronto: Queen's Printer for Ontario, 1995) (Co-chairs: M. Gittens and D. Cole) at 358:
>
>> The Commission's findings suggest that racialized characteristics, especially those of black people, in combination with other factors, provoke police suspicion, at least in Metro Toronto. Other factors that may attract police attention include sex (male), youth, make and condition of car (if any), location, dress, and perceived lifestyle. Black persons perceived to have many of these attributes are at high risk of being stopped on foot or in cars. This explanation is consistent with our findings that, overall, black people are more likely than others to experience the unwelcome intrusion of being stopped by the police, but black people are not equally vulnerable to such stops.[347]

If there has been clear recognition for decades that the practice occurs and that it is unambiguously objectionable, one would expect to find many successful section 9 claims based on this ground. In fact, however, successful racial profiling claims have been rare.[348]

The problem, in practice, seems to have been getting from "the phenomenon occurs sometimes" to "this is one of the times it occurred." A police officer is unlikely to admit that they acted on the basis of racial

---

347 *R v Brown* (2003), 173 CCC (3d) 23, 9 CR (6th) 240 at para 9 (Ont CA) [*Brown* 2003].

348 See David M. Tanovich, *The Colour of Justice: Policing Race in Canada* (Toronto: Irwin Law, 2006), for a discussion of racial profiling in general. Arguably, there is greater willingness, post-*Le*, above note 74, for courts to find that racial profiling has occurred: see, for example, *R v Holloway*, 2021 ONSC 6136 at para 135:

> In law, it is unnecessary to quantify the precise influence of racial profiling on the search: *Brown v. Durham Regional Police Force* (1998), 21 C.R. (5th) 1, 167 D.L.R. (4th) 672, 131 C.C.C. (3d) 1 (Ont CA) at para. 34; *Dudhi* at para. 62. Racial profiling of any degree leads to a violation of Section 8 of the *Charter*. I would go further here, however, and find that the evidence demonstrates that racial profiling played a substantial role in the conduct of the police leading to the discovery of the firearm on Holloway's person.

See also the successful claims in *R v James*, 2021 ONSC 3794, and *R v Sparks*, 2022 NSPC 51.

stereotypes, so any individual case must be decided based on inference.[349] It can be hard to persuade a court to make that inference. A variety of situations can arise.

Often, objectively, there was some basis that could authorize the detention or arrest: an accused might be speeding, for example, or a court might be persuaded that there was sufficient reasonable suspicion for an investigative detention. Indeed, something like this is the scenario imagined by the Court in *Storrey*[350]—an "otherwise lawful" arrest or detention. However, when there objectively is a basis for the stop, it can be difficult to persuade a court to infer that that objective basis was not the real reason for the stop. It has been recognized that racial profiling can occur unconsciously and need not be deliberate. Unconscious racial profiling would mean that an officer was more likely to stop a person of colour who was driving slightly over the speed limit where they would have allowed someone else to drive on. Nonetheless, it would remain the case that there was a power to stop even if it would not have been exercised against another person.

And, of course, the detention or arrest power might in fact have been used properly. Even if the particular accused has been frequently stopped by the police, even if their feeling that they are stopped more frequently than others who are not visible minorities is correct, it does not automatically follow that this particular stop was an improper one. Some people of colour, like anyone else, do commit crimes. By definition, evidence of some crime will have been found on the particular occasion in question or the case would not be in court. The accused will have the onus of proof to show that racial profiling was the motive and will often not be able to discharge that burden.

Furthermore, in many cases, it will be difficult even to pursue the question. Vehicle stops, for example, can be made randomly by any officer in any place. They do not require a reason, so it is difficult for an

---

349 See, for example, *Brown* 2003, above note 347 at para 45, in which the Ontario Court of Appeal held:

> The respondent submits that where the evidence shows that the circumstances relating to a detention correspond to the phenomenon of racial profiling and provide a basis for the court to infer that the police officer is lying about why he or she singled out the accused person for attention, the record is then capable of supporting a finding that the stop was based on racial profiling. I accept that this is a way in which racial profiling could be proven. I do not think that it sets the hurdle either too low (which could be unfair to honest police officers performing their duties in a professional and unbiased manner) or too high (which would make it virtually impossible for victims of racial profiling to receive the protection of their rights under section 9 of the *Charter*).

350 *Storrey*, above note 325.

accused to pursue the issue of whether the reason was an improper one. As the dissent in *Ladouceur* (1990) pointed out:

> [T]he roving random stop would permit any individual officer to stop any vehicle, at any time, at any place. The decision may be based on any whim. Individual officers will have different reasons. Some may tend to stop younger drivers, others older cars, and so on. Indeed, as pointed out by Tarnopolsky J.A., racial considerations may be a factor too. My colleague states that in such circumstances, a *Charter* violation may be made out. If, however, no reason need be given nor is necessary, how will we ever know? The officer need only say, "I stopped the vehicle because I have the right to stop it for no reason. I am seeking unlicensed drivers."[351]

Finally, in some cases, it might ultimately be found that there was no authority for the detention or arrest, but even then it does not necessarily follow from the illegality of the stop that it was motivated by the improper purpose of racial profiling. Especially as, since the Court's decision in *Grant*, an unlawful detention will be an arbitrary one, a further finding of racial profiling would be unnecessary, so a court might simply not decide the issue.

These obstacles have hindered the making of successful racial profiling claims or getting racial profiling incorporated into section 9 as fully as it should be. However, it is possible that the Court's decision in *Le* has shifted the grounds somewhat, making it more likely that claims will be recognized in future.

One of the foundational racial profiling cases is the 2003 Ontario Court of Appeal decision in *Brown*. That case was not a successful one, nor indeed even one assessing, on appeal, whether the racial profiling claim at trial should have succeeded. Rather, the issue on appeal was whether there was a reasonable apprehension of bias against the accused based on the trial judge's comments, which included characterizing the argument as "quite offensive" to the officer and suggesting to the accused that "you might extend an apology to the officer."[352] Similarly, the more recent Supreme Court of Canada decision in *Le* discussed racial profiling at some length and is being relied on for guidance by lower courts, but it did that in a case where the trial judge had found as a fact that there had been no racial profiling, and that conclusion was not in dispute on appeal.[353]

---

351 *Ladouceur* 1990, above note 36 at 1297.

352 *Brown* 2003, above note 347 at paras 95 and 98, respectively.

353 *Le*, above note 74 at para 80:

> Even though as early as 2006, Doherty J.A. noted that there is now "an acceptance by the courts that racial profiling occurs and is a day-to-day reality in the

Le adopted a definition of racial profiling:

> Racial profiling is any action taken by one or more people in authority with respect to a person or group of persons, for reasons of safety, security or public order, that is based on actual or presumed membership in a group defined by race, colour, ethnic or national origin or religion, without factual grounds or reasonable suspicion, that results in the person or group being exposed to differential treatment or scrutiny.
>
> Racial profiling [also] includes any action by a person in a situation of authority who applies a measure in a disproportionate way to certain segments of the population on the basis, in particular, of their racial, ethnic, national or religious background, whether actual or presumed.[354]

The Court then considered reports, dating from the 1970s until a few months before the decision, documenting the overpolicing of minority communities, eventually concluding:

> These reports represent the most current statement on the relevant issues, and they originate from highly credible and authoritative sources. They are the product of research that included the time period at issue in this case. More importantly, they document actions and attitudes that have existed for a long time. A striking feature of these reports is how the conclusions and recommendations are so similar to studies done 10, 20, or even 30 years ago. These reports do not establish any new fact, but they build upon prior studies, research and reports and present a clear and comprehensive picture of what is currently occurring. Courts generally benefit from the most up to date and accurate information and, on a go-forward basis, these reports will clearly form part of the social context when determining whether there has been an arbitrary detention contrary to the *Charter*.
>
> We do not hesitate to find that, even without these most recent reports, we have arrived at a place where the research now shows disproportionate policing of racialized and low-income communities (see

lives of those minorities affected by it" (*Peart v. Peel Regional Police Services Board* (2006), 43 C.R. (6th) 175 (Ont. C.A.), at para. 94), it is still open to a trial judge to determine that something that often occurs did not actually happen in the particular case before them. Neither of the parties have contested the trial judge's conclusion and we are not taking issue with the trial judge's determination.

354 *Ibid* at para 77, quoting *Quebec (Commission des droits de la personne et des droits de la jeunesse) v Bombardier Inc (Bombardier Aerospace Training Center)*, 2015 SCC 39 at para 33.

D. M. Tanovich, "Applying the Racial Profiling Correspondence Test" (2017), 64 *C.L.Q.* 359).[355]

It is worth adding that since the decision in *Le*, the Wortley report on street checks was published.[356] Based on data gathered by the police over a twelve-year period, and including nearly 100,000 street checks, it is the most thorough statistical analysis of data dealing with racial profiling. The study found that Black people in general were six times more likely than White people to have been subject to a street check, Black males were nine times more likely, and young Black males were twenty times more likely to have been checked.[357] Controlling for a number of factors, such as age, criminal record, location, and other factors, did not eliminate the disproportion and in some cases made it worse.

Although *Le* was not itself a racial profiling case, it has become a leading case for subsequent decisions; particular importance has been attached to the statement that racial profiling "occurs when race or racial stereotypes about offending or dangerousness are used, consciously or unconsciously, to any degree in suspect selection or subject treatment."[358]

In *R v Dudhi*, for example, police had been attempting to conduct surveillance on a blue BMW being driven by a White male. They saw a blue BMW, but it was being driven by the accused, who was not a White male. Nonetheless, they ended up stopping the vehicle and eventually arresting the accused; in the course of that, one officer was asked over the radio whether the accused was the target, and he replied, "[n]o, it's another brown guy who is a drug dealer."[359] That statement was a key part of the accused's racial profiling claim. The trial judge rejected the claim, for two main reasons. First, the trial judge found that there were reasons that would have justified the accused's arrest. Second, the trial judge took into account that the offending statement was not made until after the relevant decisions had already been made. The Ontario Court of Appeal found both ways of reasoning to be in error.

First, they noted that the articulation of racial profiling in *Le* asked whether the race of the suspect had been relevant "to any degree." They therefore held that

355 *Le*, above note 74 at paras 95 & 96.

356 Scot Wortley, "Halifax, Nova Scotia: Street Checks Report" (27 March 2019), online (pdf): *Nova Scotia Human Rights Commission*, https://humanrights.novascotia.ca/sites/default/files/editor-uploads/halifax_street_checks_report_march_2019_0.pdf.

357 *Ibid* at 115–16.

358 *Le*, above note 74 at para 76.

359 *R v Dudhi*, 2019 ONCA 665 at para 24 [*Dudhi*].

> a decision need not be motivated *solely or even mainly* on race or racial stereotypes to nevertheless be "based on" race or racial stereotypes. If illegitimate thinking about race or racial stereotypes factors into suspect selection or subject treatment, any pretence that the decision was reasonable is defeated. The decision will be contaminated by improper thinking and cannot satisfy the legal standards in place for suspect selection or subject treatment.[360]

Second, the Ontario Court of Appeal found it to be of little importance that the impugned statement was made after the fact because "attitudes or beliefs do not come and go in the moment" and that "[i]n those rare cases where conscious or unconscious racist attitudes or beliefs are exposed by evidence at trial relating to the event in question, the trial judge must closely consider whether the attitudes or beliefs—shown to be held by the officer at the time—may have contributed to the decision made."[361]

Note that *Dudhi* is clear that there is no *requirement* for such direct evidence of attitudes based on race. This was a point established much earlier, in *Brown*:

> A racial profiling claim could rarely be proven by direct evidence. This would involve an admission by a police officer that he or she was influenced by racial stereotypes in the exercise of his or her discretion to stop a motorist. Accordingly, if racial profiling is to be proven it must be done by inference drawn from circumstantial evidence.[362]

This has been referred to as the "correspondence test."

More generally, *Dudhi* summed up the proper approach to racial profiling claims:

> In sum, there are two components to racial profiling. The first is the attitudinal component, which is the acceptance by a person in authority that race or racial stereotypes are relevant in identifying the propensity to offend or to be dangerous. The second is the causation component, which requires that this race-based thinking consciously or unconsciously motivate or influence, to any degree, decisions by persons in authority in suspect selection or subject treatment.[363]

Like *Brown* and *Le*, *Dudhi* is also a case making clear the rules about racial profiling while not actually addressing whether there was racial profiling on the facts of the case. The subsequent Ontario Court of

360 *Ibid* at para 62 [emphasis in original].
361 *Ibid* at para 78.
362 *Brown* 2003, above note 347 at para 44.
363 *Dudhi*, above note 359 at para 66.

Appeal decision in *R v Sitladeen*[364] continued that pattern while adding a further gloss to assessing such claims.

In *Sitladeen*, the accused had been pulled over while driving, eventually leading to his arrest. The trial judge had rejected the racial profiling argument on the basis that the accused had not shown that the police officers were lying about their reason for pulling him over. That represented, the Court of Appeal held, a misunderstanding of the law. Racial profiling encompasses both conscious and unconscious attitudes, so the correspondence test does not require showing that the officer was deliberately misleading the court. All that is required is a basis to reject the officer's evidence to the contrary because the circumstances are indicative of racial profiling. They concluded:

> [T]he case law from *Brown* onward recognizes that in cases where an officer had objective grounds to detain a person or stop a vehicle but was also subjectively motivated by racial stereotypes, the officer is unlikely to admit his bias. The matter becomes more complicated when the officer is unaware that he was influenced by race because of unconscious bias. The officer may not be consciously lying about his motivation, but that does not mean he did not unconsciously engage in racial profiling. It is the role of the trial judge in such cases to consider all the circumstances that led to an accused's detention and/or arrest and to determine whether they correspond to the phenomenon of racial profiling, as understood in the social science literature, the reports of inquiries into race relations with police, and the case law. The trial judge can then decide whether those corresponding circumstances form a basis to infer that the record is capable of supporting a finding that the stop was based on racial profiling, contrary to the evidence of the officer. Ultimately, to reach a conclusion about racial profiling, the trial judge is not required to find that a police officer who testifies that race played no role in the decision to detain or arrest was lying.[365]

Ultimately, it seems fair to say that the Supreme Court of Canada and courts of appeal have signalled to trial courts that they ought to be more open to accepting the claim that racial profiling has occurred.

4) Agents of the Police

Not all powers of arrest and detention rest with the police; a wide variety of powers are given to a wide variety of people. Furthermore, there

364 2021 ONCA 303 [*Sitladeen*].
365 *Ibid* at para 54.

can be ambiguity in some circumstances as to exactly who has particular powers.

Many powers are given to "peace officers." It is natural to think of that category as synonymous with "police officers," and certainly they are included in the definition and as a matter of fact are the group that exercises those powers most frequently. However, the definition of "peace officer" in section 2 of the *Code* is broader than that. It includes other people with enforcement responsibilities: fisheries officers, immigration officers, customs officers, correctional workers, and military police, for instance. It also includes the captain of an airplane while it is in flight. In addition, various elected or appointed officials—mayor, warden, reeve, sheriff, deputy sheriff, sheriff's officer, and justice of the peace—fall into the definition. Furthermore, other officials might have some or all of these powers by way of the operation of other Acts.[366] See the more in-depth discussion of this issue in Chapter 4, as well as the discussion of the applicability of the *Charter* to non-state actors in Chapter 5.

Private citizens also have some powers; in particular (as will be discussed at greater length below, in Chapter 4), private citizens have the power to arrest in some circumstances. Indeed, the Supreme Court has noted that the concept of arrest predates the existence of police forces and that "it is the peace officer's powers which are in a sense derivative from that of the citizen, not the other way around."[367] The most obvious instance of citizen's arrest powers occurs in section 494, and these powers will be discussed at greater length below. The point to note here is that powers can be assigned to private citizens based on particular roles they play: some arrest powers are given to all private citizens, others to property owners.[368] Yet another arrest power is given to sureties: people who have acted as guarantors that a person released on bail will appear in court. A surety can apply to be released from that obligation, and if the application is granted, then either the surety or a peace officer can arrest the accused.[369]

In contrast, powers of detention—at least those powers of detention that are relevant to this book, aimed primarily at "street-level" encounters—are almost exclusively in the hands of the police. The reason for this is their source: for the most part, powers of detention in Canada are

366 See, for example, *R v Decorte*, 2005 SCC 9 [*Decorte*], noting that First Nations constables in Ontario have the powers of peace officers, by virtue of the *Police Services Act*, RSO 1990, c P.15, and that they can exercise these powers off-reserve so long as they are doing so in relation to the community they serve.

367 *Asante-Mensah*, above note 26 at para 40.

368 See *Criminal Code*, above note 6, s 494(1)–(2).

369 *Ibid*, s 766(2).

not statutory but rather have been created at common law through use of the ancillary powers doctrine.[370] That doctrine springs from the *Waterfield* test, which asks, first, whether the conduct falls within the general scope of any duty imposed by statute or recognized at common law and, second, whether the conduct, albeit within the general scope of such a duty, involves an unjustifiable use of powers associated with the duty.[371]

The clear result of this test is that common law powers, if created, can at least, under the existing test, rest only in the hands of police officers. This does not mean that the common law can never be relevant to private citizens; for example, the common law historically allowed private citizens to use force in effecting an arrest, and that remains the case.[372] However, to the extent that *Waterfield* has provided an "ancillary powers" doctrine allowing for the creation of new abilities to detain, search, or otherwise interfere with liberty, it is limited to creating such powers for police officers, not for others.[373]

As with anything in criminal law, however, things become murky once one delves a little below the surface. Two particular sources of ambiguity should be noted: implied statutory powers and the absence

---

370 This is a good generalization, but it is not without exceptions. For example, the power to demand a breath sample to determine whether a person has committed the offence of driving while impaired involves both a search and a detention, and the power is created by s 254 of the *Code*. Similarly, although the power to conduct random stops to check for impaired drivers exists at common law (see *Dedman*, above note 10), it can also be authorized under provincial highway traffic legislation: see, for example, *Hufsky*, above note 36; *Decorte*, above note 366.

371 *Godoy*, above note 55 at para 12.

372 See, generally, *Asante-Mensah*, above note 26.

373 This point does not always appear to have been noticed by courts. See, for example, *R v Dell*, 2005 ABCA 246 [*Dell*], in which the Alberta Court of Appeal held that the *Charter* does not apply to investigative detentions conducted by private citizens. The more important point, one would have thought, and which is not noted, is that the power of investigative detention arises at common law from the application of the *Waterfield* test in *Mann*, above note 14, and is given only to police officers; in other words, there is no such thing as a "citizen's investigative detention."

However, see also *R v Brode*, 2012 ONCA 140, dealing with border security officers (BSOs) under the *Customs Act*, RSC 1985, c 1 (2nd Supp) [*Customs Act*], who have been specially designated under s 163.5 to enforce *Criminal Code* offences relating to impaired driving. The Ontario Court of Appeal concluded at para 44 that

> BSOs do not share the general duty of police officers to prevent crime and protect life and property. Consequently, they do not have the complete set of ancillary powers of police officers that flow from that general duty. However, . . . the common law investigative powers recognized in *R. v. Waterfield*, [1963] 3 All E.R. 659 (Eng. C.A.), for police officers apply to designated BSOs exercising their authority under s. 163.5 of the *Customs Act*.

of a bright line indicating when *Charter* rights do and do not arise. It makes sense to discuss the latter of these two first.

By virtue of section 32, the *Charter* applies to Parliament and the legislatures or, put another way, applies only when there is state action. In practical terms, this can make a great difference. For example, according to section 10(b), everyone has the right to counsel on arrest or detention. However, this is true only where there is state action. It therefore definitely applies when a police officer—who is an agent of the state—uses the power in section 495 of the *Code* to arrest a person. Somewhat surprisingly, however, the question of whether the section 10(b) right arises in the case of a citizen's arrest under section 494 has yet to be authoritatively settled (see the discussion of this issue in Chapter 5, Section C(4)). Some courts of appeal have held that the common law origin of the power of arrest as a means of keeping "the King's peace" shows that even a private citizen is performing a government function when arresting.[374] Others have concluded that section 494 neither delegates the state function to private citizens nor abandons it, in which case citizens' arrests do not count as state action and so do not trigger the *Charter*.[375] The Supreme Court of Canada has so far expressly declined to settle the issue.[376]

The Supreme Court has, however, given some general guidance on how to tell when the actions of a private citizen will attract *Charter* scrutiny. In *R v Broyles*, dealing with a police informer, the Court set out a test for when a private citizen will be considered to be a state agent. It held there that

> [o]nly if the relationship between the informer and the state is such that the exchange between the informer and the accused is materially different from what it would have been had there been no such relationship should the informer be considered a state agent for the purposes of the exchange. . . . [W]ould the exchange between the accused

---

374 See, for example, *R v Lerke* (1986), 24 CCC (3d) 129 (Alta CA). Note that the Alberta Court of Appeal's later decision in *Dell*, above note 373, does not immediately seem consistent with this earlier conclusion. As noted below (Chapter 5, Section C(4)), the distinction rests on an argument that s 10 does not apply when citizens merely detain but does apply when they arrest.

375 See, for example, *R v Skeir*, 2005 NSCA 86. See also *R v S(N)*, [2004] OJ No 290 (CA), which found that the particular security guards in question in the case were not state agents and therefore were not governed by the *Charter*. That case has been taken more generally to decide that in Ontario, the *Charter* does not apply to citizen's arrests: see *R v Giamou*, 2015 ONCJ 90. See also *R v Jacobs*, 2014 ABCA 172, although it is only a decision about a particular security guard. See also *R v Nguyen*, 2016 BCCA 32.

376 *Asante-Mensah*, above note 26 at para 77. See the further discussion of this issue in Chapter 5, Section C(4).

> and the informer have taken place, in the form and manner in which it did take place, but for the intervention of the state or its agents?[377]

Broyles was decided in the particular context of an informer, but the test has been applied more broadly. It has been used, for example, to determine in *M(MR)* that a school vice-principal who searched a student for drugs was not thereby a state agent. Based on the *Broyles* test, it was found that the search would have taken place in the same way without the involvement of the police; although the vice-principal knew that criminal charges might result if he found drugs, he was searching in order to enforce a school rule, not at the behest of the officer.[378] Also, in *R v Buhay*,[379] it was found that private security guards at a bus station who searched a locker rented by the accused were not bound by the *Charter*. In *Buhay*, the Court held that "the mere fact that an entity performs what may loosely be termed a 'public function,' or the fact that a particular activity may be described as 'public' in nature, will not be sufficient to bring it within the purview of 'government' for the purposes of s. 32 of the *Charter*."[380] It also said that "[v]olunteer participation in the detection of crime by private actors, or general encouragements by the police authorities to citizens to participate in the detection of crime, will not usually be sufficient direction by the police to trigger the application of the *Charter*."[381] Yet the Court carried on to state that "[i]t may be that if the state were to abandon in whole or in part an essential public function to the private sector, even without an express delegation, the private activity could be assimilated to that of a state actor for *Charter* purposes."[382]

M(MR) is also worth considering for another aspect of *Charter* applicability. As noted, the Court concluded that the vice-principal was not, on the facts of the case, acting as an agent of the police when he

---

377 *R v Broyles*, [1991] 3 SCR 595 at 608 [*Broyles*].

378 *M(MR)*, above note 29 at para 29. See, similarly, *R v Johal*, 2015 BCCA 246, where a doctor-performed internal exam on the accused after a strip search incident to arrest turned up white powder around the accused's rectum. The court accepted that the doctor's examination was based on the medical risk to the accused if a bag of drugs had broken inside his anus, not for the purpose of assisting the police in discovering evidence. See also *R v Sidhu*, 2013 ONCA 719, where the accused's wife was found not to be a state agent.

379 2003 SCC 30 [*Buhay*].

380 *Ibid* at para 28, quoting *Eldridge v British Columbia (AG)*, [1997] 3 SCR 624 at para 43.

381 *Buhay*, above note 379 at para 30. See, for example, *Webster*, above note 117, where a property manager gave to a police officer information about one of the tenants in the building. The manager knew to whom he was giving the information, but that was not sufficient to make him a state agent.

382 *Buhay*, above note 379 at para 31.

searched one of his students, even though a police officer was present at the time. Nonetheless, the Court found that the *Charter* was applicable to the vice-principal's actions as school boards, schools, and their employees are part of government. That the *Charter* applied for this latter reason but not the former was of some significance because *Charter* rights have different meanings in different contexts.[383]

In the search context, the Court has long held that a search without a warrant will prima facie violate section 8 of the *Charter* if it is conducted for criminal law purposes. On the other hand, a more relaxed standard applies to searches in administrative contexts.[384] In *M(MR)*, therefore, a different set of rules would have applied to the search depending on why the *Charter* applied. If the vice-principal had been an agent of the police, then a stricter standard for justifying the search would have been applied.

The Court has not yet adopted any exact analog to those differing search standards in the detention context. However, a similar point arose in *M(MR)* in considering whether the accused was entitled to the right to counsel under section 10(b). Had the vice-principal been acting as an agent of the police when he took the student to the police officer on the scene, then there likely would have been a *Charter* violation since the accused was not told of his right to counsel at that point. However, the Court found that there was no section 10(b) violation because there was no "detention" within the meaning of that term in the vice-principal's actions. It was true that the accused had felt compelled to obey the vice-principal's directions, but such compulsion in the school environment, the Court held, did not constitute detention within the meaning of section 10(b).[385]

The result, then, is that it will not always be clear whether or not a given private citizen is acting as a state agent, so, to a certain extent, whether the *Charter* applies remains to be settled on a case-by-case basis. Beyond that, even if the *Charter* does apply, it will matter *why* the *Charter* applies. Different sets of rules might apply depending on whether the private citizen is generally an agent of the *state* or is more specifically an agent of the *police*.

---

383 *M(MR)*, above note 29 at paras 26–30.

384 See *Jarvis*, above note 329. See also Coughlan, *Criminal Procedure*, above note 50, ch 4.

385 *M(MR)*, above note 29 at paras 65–68.

C. GROUNDS TO ARREST AND DETAIN

1) Introduction: Belief Versus Suspicion

There are two relevant standards to be considered in discussing the basis upon which individuals can be arrested or detained: reasonable grounds to *believe* and reasonable grounds to *suspect*. The two standards share some common features, which is unsurprising since in each case "reasonableness" is in issue. The central difference between the two is the degree of certainty required, which is, of course, the difference between believing a thing and merely suspecting that thing. "Reasonable grounds to believe" is sometimes referred to simply as "reasonable belief" or "reasonable grounds," and it is very frequently referred to as "reasonable and probable grounds." The *Criminal Code* formerly used the phrase "reasonable and probable grounds" in sections setting out various search and arrest powers, and even though the words "and probable" were removed decades ago, the Court most commonly still includes them when describing the standard, no matter what the context.[386] "Reasonable grounds to suspect" is often referred to simply as "reasonable suspicion"[387] or, most recently, as "reason to suspect."[388]

These standards are used beyond the contexts of arrest and detention. A warrant to track the movements of a person can only be issued based on reasonable grounds to believe an offence has been or will be committed, while a warrant to track the movement of a thing only requires reasonable suspicion.[389] This difference is justified on the basis that the latter warrants are less intrusive on privacy and therefore can be more easily justified. Similarly, a police officer may make a demand for breath samples for an approved screening device to determine whether a person

386 See, for example, *Ali*, above note 252 at para 2: "Where a strip search is conducted as an incident to a person's lawful arrest, there must be reasonable and probable grounds justifying the strip search, in addition to reasonable and probable grounds justifying the arrest"; *Stairs*, above note 93 at para 34: search incident to arrest "is 'extraordinary' because, unlike other police powers, it requires neither a warrant nor reasonable and probable grounds"; *Tim*, above note 19 at para 24: "The arresting officer must subjectively have reasonable and probable grounds for the arrest"; *R v Lafrance*, 2022 SCC 32 at para 9 [*Lafrance*]: "It is undisputed that, at that time, Sgt. Eros did not have reasonable and probable grounds to proceed to arrest Mr. Lafrance"; *R v Beaver*, 2022 SCC 54 at para 1 [*Beaver*], where an issue on appeal was "whether the police had reasonable and probable grounds to arrest the appellants"; or *R v McColman*, 2023 SCC 8 at para 4 [*McColman*]: "the police officers did not have reasonable and probable grounds to stop him."

387 See, for example, *Kang-Brown*, above note 63; *R v AM*, 2008 SCC 19 [*AM*].

388 *Stairs*, above note 93.

389 See *Criminal Code*, above note 6, s 492.1(1) & (2).

has any alcohol in their system based on reasonable suspicion. However, a Breathalyzer demand, to determine the actual concentration of alcohol in the person's system, requires that the officer have a reasonable belief. Once again, the lower standard is justified in less intrusive circumstances; that is, failing the former test does not by itself provide evidence that the accused is guilty of an offence, whereas failing the Breathalyzer test does prove such guilt.

One would expect this same pattern to be maintained in the use of the standards in the arrest and detention context, and for the most part this is correct. Generally speaking, arrests are more intrusive than investigative detentions, and arrests depend upon reasonable grounds, while investigative detentions only require reasonable suspicion.[390] However, the division is not a perfect one. There is, for example, a specific arrest power relating to apprehended terrorist activity that depends in part only on reasonable suspicion.[391] More important (as is discussed below in Chapter 3), courts are not always careful to ensure that the investigative detention power *remains* unintrusive, despite the low standard upon which it is based. Furthermore, as will be discussed immediately below, there is some argument over exactly what "reasonable belief" requires, in a way that tries to push it closer to the reasonable suspicion standard.

Although the two standards share many common features, it is worth discussing them separately. In addition, see appendices I and II, summarizing the kinds of facts that have been taken to establish either reasonable belief or reasonable suspicion in various cases.

2) Reasonable Grounds to Believe

a) What Constitutes Reasonable Grounds to Believe?

Discussion of this subject in the caselaw can frequently end up reduced to the relatively mechanical question of whether particular facts do or do not justify reasonable belief. It is worth starting a discussion, therefore, by observing the importance of the role that this requirement plays as a protection of individual liberty interests against the state. As the Supreme Court has observed:

---

390 *Ibid*, s 495(1); *Mann*, above note 14.

391 See *Criminal Code*, above note 6, s 83.3(4), which permits an arrest without warrant where a peace officer:

> (*a*) believes on reasonable grounds that a terrorist activity will be carried out; and
>
> (*b*) suspects on reasonable grounds that the imposition of a recognizance with conditions on a person, or the arrest of a person, is necessary to prevent the carrying out of the terrorist activity.

> Without such an important protection, even the most democratic society could all too easily fall prey to the abuses and excesses of a police state. In order to safeguard the liberty of citizens, the *Criminal Code* requires the police, when attempting to obtain a warrant for an arrest, to demonstrate to a judicial officer that they have reasonable and probable grounds to believe that the person to be arrested has committed the offence.[392]

Given this acknowledged importance, it is surprising that a major confusion continues to exist over this standard. We will turn to that in a moment, but first there are some general observations that can be made about the "reasonable belief" standard.

An important point is that the belief must be a reasonable one about the *facts*, not about the *law*. In *Tim*, a police officer had observed the accused with a gabapentin pill and so arrested the accused for possession of a controlled substance; however, gabapentin is not listed in the *Controlled Drugs and Substances Act* as a controlled substance. The Alberta Court of Appeal had found that the arrest was still lawful on the basis that "reasonableness" does not require perfection, and the officer's mistake about the law was a reasonable one.[393] The Supreme Court overturned that result, finding that "[t]he concept of 'reasonable and probable grounds' for arrest relates to the facts, not the existence of an offence in law," and thus that "an arrest based on a mistake of law is unlawful, even if the arresting officer believes in good faith that the offence exists."[394]

Furthermore, note that the Court has said that "reasonable and probable grounds" can mean different things in different contexts.[395] Even in the arrest context, the standard applies both to arrests with a warrant and to those without, but it does not necessarily operate in exactly the same way in each case. The Court has said that

> [i]n the case of an arrest made without a warrant, it is even more important for the police to demonstrate that they have those same reasonable and probable grounds upon which they base the arrest.[396]

392 *Storrey*, above note 325 at 249.

393 *Tim* ABCA, above note 18.

394 *Tim*, above note 19 at paras 36 and 28, respectively, relying on *Kosoian*, above note 19, and *Frey v Fedoruk*, [1950] SCR 517.

395 *R v Jacques*, [1996] 3 SCR 312 at para 20 [*Jacques*], quoting *R v Bernshaw*, [1995] 1 SCR 254 at 304–6.

396 *Storrey*, above note 325 at 249. See also *Golub*, above note 274 at para 18, in which the Ontario Court of Appeal adopts roughly the opposite reasoning, arguing that "[t]he law does not expect the same kind of inquiry of a police officer deciding whether to make an arrest that it demands of a justice faced with an

Lastly, at least by way of introduction, note that "reasonable grounds" has both a subjective and an objective requirement; that is, "an arresting officer must subjectively have reasonable and probable grounds on which to base the arrest. Those grounds must, in addition, be justifiable from an objective point of view."[397]

The subjective standard is important: the Court has noted that "it would be inconsistent with the spirit of the *Charter* to permit a police officer to make an arrest without a warrant even though he or she does not believe reasonable grounds for the arrest exist."[398] It is unusual for the subjective aspect of the test to be at issue, but it occasionally happens. In *Feeney*, for example, the arresting officer testified that he did not subjectively feel that he had grounds to arrest, and the Court held that that alone was sufficient to render the arrest illegal.[399] In *Frieburg*, the officers testified that they arrested in order to keep the accused from the location where a search warrant was to be executed but never testified to a subjective belief that she had committed an offence. This was found to make the arrest unlawful, despite the fact that the objective test was met.[400]

Nonetheless, more commonly on the facts, a peace officer has testified that they felt they did have reasonable grounds, and the issue for a judge is whether that belief was objectively justified. The objective portion of the test will occupy the rest of this section.

A significant issue for this discussion is to understand the "reasonable grounds" and "reasonable suspicion" standards in relation to one another. They vary, of course, in the degree of certainty existing either in the officer's mind as the subjective part of the test or in the mind of a reasonable person as the objective part of the test. Surprisingly, there is confusion and disagreement among courts of appeal over exactly how much higher the reasonable grounds standard is, despite the fact that the Supreme Court's position can be understood quite clearly.

---

application for a search warrant." That is, the Supreme Court holds that a police officer acting without judicial scrutiny must be *more* careful, while the Court of Appeal is willing to let such an officer be *less* careful. The Court of Appeal's reasoning seems to place a greater emphasis on the needs of the police, while the Supreme Court in *Storrey* seems more concerned to safeguard individual liberty. See also *R v Janvier*, 2007 SKCA 147 at para 28 [*Janvier*], concluding that the "finds committing" standard for arrest without a warrant in s 495(1)(b) is stricter than the "reasonable grounds" standard for arrest in s 495(1)(a).

397 *Storrey*, above note 325 at 250–51.

398 *Feeney*, above note 168 at para 29.

399 *Ibid.* The Court also noted that the two tests are related: "Any finding that the subjective test is not met will generally imply that the objective test is not met, unless the officer is to be considered to have an unreasonably high standard" (at para 34).

400 *Frieburg*, above note 231.

In the arrest context, the standard does not require so high a standard as a prima facie case.[401] The disagreement in lower courts is over whether the "reasonable grounds" standard requires that the belief be more probable than not: despite the clear statements from the Supreme Court that that *is* a requirement, many courts of appeal hold to the view that it is *not*.

Before anything else, it is worth recalling that the standard being discussed is one of "reasonable grounds *to believe*." Discussions of this issue tend to focus on whether something can be "reasonable" without being "probable," but that is to ignore that what is required is *belief*. An intrinsic part of believing something is taking it to be more likely than not that it is true. Any other state of mind, one merely accepting that a state of affairs could be true without being committed to it on balance, could not accurately be described as a "belief" whether or not it was reasonable.[402] This gives an air of artificiality and unreality to any arguments that try to set a lower standard.

Quite apart from that, the Supreme Court has stated clearly that "reasonable belief" in the criminal context is a standard of "more likely than not." For example, at one point, the arrest and other sections in the *Code* were specifically phrased to say that an officer must have reasonable "and probable" grounds, but that wording has since been simplified to "reasonable grounds." It has been settled that this change in wording was not meant to cause a change in meaning. In *Baron v Canada*, for example, exactly the argument that "reasonable grounds" was something less than "reasonable and probable grounds" was put to the Court and rejected:

> To my mind, *Hunter, supra*, does not give rise to legitimate controversy on this point. That decision required reasonable "and probable" grounds and simultaneously established that the two words import the same standard. "Reasonableness" comprehends a requirement of probability.[403]

Also in the search context, the Court has stated that synonyms for "reasonable grounds to believe" include "reasonable probability" and "credibly-based probability."[404]

Dealing directly with the issue of the difference between the two standards, in *Chehil*, the Court distinguished reasonable suspicion from reasonable grounds to believe by saying that

---

401 See *Storrey*, above note 325.

402 See the discussion of this point in Steve Coughlan, "*R v Chapman*: Can You Believe Without Believing?" (2020) 60 *Criminal Reports* (7th) 318.

403 *Baron v Canada*, [1993] 1 SCR 416 at para 55 [*Baron*].

404 See *Debot*, above note 213 at para 47, and *Hunter*, above note 42 at 167, respectively.

> while reasonable grounds to suspect and reasonable and probable grounds to believe are similar in that they both must be grounded in objective facts, reasonable suspicion is a lower standard, as it engages the reasonable possibility, rather than *probability*, of crime.[405]

Also, as noted above, the Court routinely describes the higher standard as "reasonable and probable grounds" whether or not dealing with a statutory provision and despite the fact that none of the relevant statutory provisions include the word "probable."[406]

The most direct and unambiguous demonstration that the Court holds the reasonable grounds standard to import a requirement of "more probable than not" is their decision in *R v Loewen*. In that case, the issue was whether the accused had been lawfully arrested, which led to discussion of the reasonable grounds standard in the abstract. Justice Slatter in the Alberta Court of Appeal asked the question "Is there a difference between 'reasonable' grounds and 'probable' grounds? In other words, can grounds be reasonable if they are not also probable?"[407] He concluded that the answer was yes, they could: "'[R]easonable and probable grounds' does not necessarily mean the same thing as 'more likely than not on a balance of probabilities.'"[408] The Supreme Court of Canada upheld the *result* in *Loewen* but singled out one thing and only one thing in the court below as having been incorrect: the conclusion on that point. They specifically commented that "Slatter J.A. mistakenly held that the requirement of 'reasonable grounds' in s. 495(1)(*a*) is different from the requirement of 'reasonable and probable grounds.'"[409]

The source of the Alberta Court of Appeal's error in *Loewen* is easy to trace. In 1992, in *Sivakumar v Canada (Minister of Employment and Immigration)*,[410] the Federal Court of Appeal was called upon to interpret section F(a) of Article 1 of the *United Nations Convention Relating to the Status of Refugees*,[411] which dealt with persons "with respect to whom there are serious reasons for considering" that they had committed a war crime or a

---

405 *Chehil*, above note 59 at para 27 [emphasis added].

406 See the discussion in the Introduction to this section and the cases referred to at note 386. Cases referring to the standard as "reasonable and probable grounds" when there is no statutory provision containing the word "probable" include *Storrey*, above note 325; *Saeed*, above note 260; *Ali*, above note 252; *Stairs*, above note 93; *Tim*, above note 19; *Lafrance*, above note 386; *Beaver*, above note 386; and *McColman*, above note 386.

407 *R v Loewen*, 2010 ABCA 255 at para 14 [*Loewen* ABCA].

408 *Ibid* at para 18.

409 *R v Loewen*, 2011 SCC 21 at para 5 [*Loewen*].

410 [1994] 1 FC 433 (CA) [*Sivakumar*].

411 *United Nations Convention Relating to the Status of Refugees*, 28 July 1951, Can TS 1969 No 6 (entered into force 22 April 1954).

crime against humanity. An issue that arose was how that "serious reasons" standard should compare to section 19(1)(j) of the (at the time) *Immigration Act*,[412] which denied entry to persons "who there are reasonable grounds to believe have committed an act or omission outside Canada that constituted a war crime or a crime against humanity." Ultimately, the Federal Court of Appeal concluded that it was not important to calibrate the two standards against one another: "the international community was willing to *lower the usual standard of proof* in order to ensure that war criminals were denied safe havens," and "[b]oth of these standards require something more than suspicion or conjecture, but something less than proof on a balance of probabilities."[413] This is, notably, a decision about the reasonable grounds standard in a particular immigration context and is specifically noted to have a lower meaning than usual.

Subsequently, in *Mugesera v Canada (Minister of Citizenship and Immigration)*, the Supreme Court was also called upon to interpret that same provision of the *Immigration Act* and held that

> [t]he first issue raised by s. 19(1)(*j*) of the *Immigration Act* is the meaning of the evidentiary standard that there be "reasonable grounds to believe" that a person has committed a crime against humanity. The FCA [Federal Court of Appeal] has found, and we agree, that the "reasonable grounds to believe" standard requires something more than mere suspicion, but less than the standard applicable in civil matters of proof on the balance of probabilities.[414]

In the Alberta Court of Appeal decision in *Loewen*, all of the background about the *Immigration Act*, all of the context that the standard was explicitly said to be lower than the usual standard of proof, and all of the quotation other than saying that the standard was more than suspicion but less than proof on balance of probabilities were stripped away, and the passage from *Mugesera* was presented as a general statement by the Supreme Court about the meaning of the reasonable grounds standard in general. Of course it is not, as the Court made clear in specifically rejecting that aspect of the court of appeal's reasoning.

Nonetheless, the view that grounds can be reasonable without being probable continues to be held by many courts of appeal. Possibly more

---

412 RSC 1985 (3rd Supp), c 30, s 3, s 19(1): "No person shall be granted admission who is a member of any of the following classes: . . . (j) persons who there are reasonable grounds to believe have committed an act or omission outside Canada that constituted a war crime or a crime against humanity."

413 *Sivakumar*, above note 410 at para 18 (CA)[emphasis added].

414 *Mugesera v Canada (Minister of Citizenship and Immigration)*, 2005 SCC 40 at para 114 [*Mugesera*].

often than the standard is stated correctly one finds passages such as "it is also well-established that 'reasonable grounds' imports a test or standard that is *lower* than the standard of civil proof, or proof 'on the balance of probabilities'" or "[t]he jurisprudence is consistent that 'probability,' in this sense, does not mean 'balance of probabilities,' or even 'more likely than not.'"[415] Indeed, it is not uncommon—although it is disturbing—to see lower courts pointing specifically to the Alberta Court of Appeal judgment in *Loewen* as authority for the claim that the reasonable grounds standard is lower than reasonable and probable grounds.[416]

Indeed, the Supreme Court itself has likely contributed to ongoing confusion with its 2023 decision in *Beaver*. In a long "boilerplate" list of the rules around warrantless arrests, tucked into point number six on the list, the Court says that police need not meet the balance of probabilities standard and cites the Alberta Court of Appeal decision in *Loewen* as authority for that claim.[417] Although one issue in the case was whether the arresting officer had grounds for arrest, nothing in the decision suggests that the Court has consciously decided to adopt a lower standard than it had previously repeatedly set, and the majority conclude that the officer did have "objectively reasonable and probable grounds to arrest the appellants for murder."[418] The only plausible explanation is that this is a "slip of the pen," but it will undoubtedly muddy the water.

This is particularly the case because lower court resistance is not simply a matter of those courts being unaware of what the Court said in *Loewen*: it is often more a matter of them being unwilling to accept the conclusion that "reasonable grounds" *means* "more probable than not." For example, in *Ha*, the Alberta Court of Appeal suggested that the standard ought not to be phrased as about "probability" but rather as about "likelihood," on the basis that "'[l]ikely,' or 'not unlikely,' do [*sic*]

---

415 *R v Glendinning*, 2019 BCCA 365 at para 3 [*Glendinning*] [emphasis in original], and *R v Chapman*, 2020 SKCA 11 at para 65 [*Chapman*], respectively. For other decisions saying that the standard does not require proof on balance of probabilities, see *R v Spence*, 2011 BCCA 280 at para 33; *R v Henareh*, 2017 BCCA 7 at para 39, relied on in *R v Lotfy*, 2017 BCCA 418 at para 57, and in *R v Orr*, 2021 BCCA 42 at para 77; *R v Ha*, 2018 ABCA 233 at para 61 [*Ha*]; *R v Brayton*, 2021 ABCA 316; *R v Shinkewski*, 2012 SKCA 63 at para 13 [*Shinkewski*]; *R v Todd*, 2019 SKCA 36 [*Todd*]; *R v Santos*, 2022 SKCA 50 [*Santos*]; *R v Jacob (JA)*, 2013 MBCA 29 at para 34; *R v Omeasoo*, 2019 MBCA 43 at para 31; and *R v Kinsella*, 2022 NLCA 40 at para 23.

416 See, for example, *R c Michael*, 2019 QCCQ 5444; *R v St Clair*, 2018 ONSC 5173; *R v Cater*, 2019 NSSC 302; *R c Baptiste*, 2020 QCCQ 971; *R v Sekhon*, 2020 BCSC 2180; *R c McKenzie-Fletcher*, 2020 QCCQ 6227; *R v Coughlin*, 2012 ABPC 46; *R v Gross*, 2012 ABPC 286; *Allen v Alberta (Law Enforcement Review Board)*, 2013 ABCA 187; *R v Cook*, 2014 ABPC 70; or *R v Notay*, 2021 ABQB 706.

417 *Beaver*, above note 386 at para 72.

418 *Ibid* at para 88.

not have a technical meaning." A reasonable likelihood of something being true, they then concluded, does not require that it be more probable than not.[419] However, the obvious problem with that argument is that the Supreme Court routinely does use the phrase "credibly based probability," not "likelihood," to define the standard.[420]

Another argument made is that the word "probability" does not imply "more likely than not." *R v Glendinning*, for example, notes that "one often hears expressions such as 'There is a 30% probability of rain'"[421] and argues that statements such as "reasonable suspicion is a lower standard, as it engages the reasonable possibility, rather than probability, of crime"[422] do not imply that reasonable grounds mean "more likely than not." Again, the problem here is that the argument misrepresents what the Supreme Court usually says. Although occasionally the Court uses the term "probability," most of the time it talks about whether the belief is *probable*.[423]

Indeed, this is exactly the point the Supreme Court was making in correcting the error in the Alberta Court of Appeal decision in *Loewen*. In the Alberta Court of Appeal, Slatter JA asked, "[C]an grounds be reasonable if they are not also probable?"[424] He said that they could be, and that is precisely the thing about which the Supreme Court of Canada said he was mistaken: "Slatter J.A. mistakenly held that the requirement of 'reasonable grounds' in s. 495(1)(*a*) is different from the requirement of 'reasonable and probable grounds.'"[425]

Ultimately, the law in this area is in a very unsatisfactory state: the Supreme Court has been clear that a belief must also be probable to be reasonable, but the law as applied by many Courts of Appeal does not respect that finding.

In any event, there are other issues to discuss about establishing "reasonable grounds." One point worth noting is that the information that can enter into forming reasonable grounds need not be evidence that would be admissible in court as proof that the accused was guilty. Hearsay evidence can be used as a basis for forming reasonable grounds,

---

419 *Ha*, above note 415 at para 64.

420 See, for example, *Fearon*, above note 211; *R v Tse*, 2012 SCC 16; *Chehil*, above note 59; *R v Morelli*, 2010 SCC 8; *R v Rodgers*, 2006 SCC 15; *M(MR)*, above note 29; *Baron*, above note 403; *R v Wise*, [1992] 1 SCR 527; or *Hunter*, above note 42.

421 *Glendinning*, above note 415 at para 7.

422 *Chehil*, above note 59 at para 27.

423 See, for example, the cases listed above in notes 386 and 406.

424 *Loewen* ABCA, above note 407 at para 14.

425 *Loewen*, above note 409 at para 5.

for example.[426] Similarly, an accused's past history of involvement in violent crimes can help inform a peace officer's reasonable belief that the accused has committed an offence,[427] although for a trier of fact to rely on that same information to make the same inference at trial would be propensity reasoning, which is improper. An accused's reputation can also contribute to forming reasonable grounds, although it could not alone be enough to create them.[428] Similarly, police are entitled to rely on eyewitness identifications without cautioning themselves against the frailty of such evidence in the way that a jury would be instructed.[429]

It can also be observed that reasonable grounds are "transferable" between officers. This is more than saying that an officer can rely on hearsay; rather, the point is that more than one officer can act provided that one officer has reasonable grounds. In *R v Debot*, for example, a search was conducted by one officer after he was directed to conduct it by a prior officer. The issue, the Court held, was not whether the second officer could somehow rely on that direction as hearsay, creating reasonable grounds for him personally to search. Rather, the second officer was entitled to presume that the person who ordered the search had reasonable grounds to do so; the only legal issue was whether the first officer actually did have such grounds.[430] The same is true in the arrest context: as the Alberta Court of Appeal has put it, "[i]t is the peace officer who decides that an arrest be made who must have reasonable and probable grounds, even if that officer does not perform the actual arrest."[431] This approach is consistent with that taken to the "finds committing" arrest power (discussed in Chapter 4), where an officer who receives an accused from another officer is entitled to assume that the first officer genuinely did witness the accused commit an offence.

It is also worth noting the significance of exculpatory, or potentially exculpatory, information available at the time. As the Saskatchewan Court of Appeal has put it, "an arresting officer must consider all incriminating

---

426 See, for example, *Eccles*, above note 22; *Collins*, above note 12; *Debot*, above note 213; or *Ha*, above note 415.

427 See *Storrey*, above note 325.

428 *Debot*, above note 213.

429 *R v MAL* (2003), 173 CCC (3d) 439 (Ont CA) [*MAL*].

430 See also *Eccles*, above note 22, and *R v Quilop*, 2017 ABCA 70 [*Quilop*].

431 *Ibid* at para 22. That case also noted at para 20:

> [W]here the grounds for the arrest are based on the observations of many peace officers, the focus must be on the peace officer who made the decision to arrest. If prior to the arrest one or more of the peace officers involved in the surveillance had a properly grounded belief; and if the fact of that properly grounded belief was communicated to the peace officers who made the arrest, even if the particulars of the grounds were not communicated, the arrest was lawful.

and exonerating information which the circumstances reasonably permit, but may disregard information which the officer has reason to believe may be unreliable."[432] In *R v Kossick*, for example, the arresting officer saw a cyclist whom he had, over a week earlier, identified for a second officer as responsible for a bicycle theft. The arresting officer called that second officer to ask whether there was a warrant for the accused's arrest and was told that there was; this was incorrect since the accused had already been arrested on that warrant and released on conditions. The arresting officer then ran the accused's name through the databases available to him in his vehicle but did not read that information until after catching up to the accused and arresting him. The Saskatchewan Court of Appeal found that the arrest was unlawful. It was not automatically fatal to the reasonable grounds that the information given to the arresting officer by the second officer was erroneous. However, there was no urgency requiring the officer to carry out the arrest before reading the information he had already searched for and that would have shown that there was no outstanding warrant, so the reasonable grounds requirement was not made out.[433] On the other hand, unless there was a reasonable opportunity to make inquiries, "[a]n otherwise lawful arrest is not invalidated by the *ex post facto* discovery of deficiencies or defects in the information upon which the police have relied to effect the arrest."[434]

A related point is that whether reasonable grounds exist is to be assessed based on the information available to the officer at the time of the arrest. That officers other than the one who decided to carry out an arrest subsequently also smelled marijuana does not contribute to the objective reasonableness of the arresting officer's belief.[435] More generally, "the question of the existence of reasonable and probable grounds cannot be informed by what the police found subsequent to arrest, or on the basis of the whole of the evidence at the trial."[436]

One last issue around the objective test is worth discussing at length. In assessing whether a belief is objectively justified, the proper question is what "a reasonable person, standing in the shoes of the police officer," would believe.[437] As a result, the training and experience of an officer can

432 *Shinkewski*, above note 415 at para 13. See also *Chartier v Quebec (AG)*, [1979] 2 SCR 474 at 499: "For a peace officer to have reasonable and probable grounds for believing in someone's guilt, his belief must take into account all the information available to him. He is entitled to disregard only what he has good reason for believing not reliable."

433 *R v Kossick*, 2018 SKCA 55.

434 *Shinkewski*, above note 415 at para 19.

435 *Gonzales*, above note 253 at para 106.

436 *Ha*, above note 415 at para 23.

437 *Chehil*, above note 59 at para 45.

be helpful, but deference is not automatically owed to a police officer's view of the circumstances based on training and experience, and such claims should not be accepted uncritically.[438] This approach—recognizing the potential value of experience while not always relying on it—is a reasonable compromise position.[439]

The main rationale for incorporating training and experience is that "a fact or consideration which might have no significance to a lay person can sometimes be quite consequential in the hands of the police."[440] A person unfamiliar with street slang, for example, could overhear a conversation and be unaware that it concerned selling drugs, while a police officer's familiarity with that slang would allow them to take more information from it.[441] A person unfamiliar with clandestine chemical drug labs could see cylindrical bins being moved from one truck to another and not have their eye caught by that fact, while a police officer with such experience would be led to observe more closely.[442] At a simpler level, if an officer testified that they smelled marijuana in a vehicle, particularly if they were to identify it as raw as opposed to burnt marijuana, a judge should want to be satisfied that the officer has the experience that allows them to make that identification.[443] So there can be no question that in some contexts, officer experience is relevant to the objective test.

The difficulty is that, carried too far, incorporating the experience of the particular officer into the objective test amounts to effectively *eliminating* the objective test, leaving only the subjective test in place. If all of an officer's claimed experience is to be relevant, then the objective test becomes very close to "would a person who believes what this officer believes believe what this officer believes," which will always trivially be proven.

Claims by an officer that "in my experience, this is a reason to be suspicious" have been made in a very wide range of circumstances. Some of these claims seem quite plausible, others less so. For example,

---

438 *R v MacKenzie*, 2013 SCC 50 at para 64 [*MacKenzie*].

439 The particular standard at issue in *Chehil* and *MacKenzie* was reasonable suspicion, but the principles articulated address the objective test generally and are equally applicable to assessing whether reasonable belief is made out: *R v Wu*, 2015 ONCA 667 at para 52.

440 *MacKenzie*, above note 438 at para 62, quoting *R v Yeh*, 2009 SKCA 112.

441 See, for example, *R v Silverthorn*, 2012 ONSC 6784, where a conversation about a "Cuban" contributed to reasonable suspicion because the officer knew this to be a term referring to seven grams of cocaine.

442 *R v Canary*, 2018 ONCA 304.

443 See, for example, *R v Canlas*, 2014 ABCA 160, or *R v Valentine*, 2014 ONCA 147. See also *R v Meyers*, 2012 BCPC 50, where the trial judge did not accept the officer's claim because the officer was not shown to have enough relevant experience.

courts have allowed police officers to testify to their own experience that hydroponic drug operations use lamps that generate a great deal of heat and therefore that condensation on windows is suspicious;[444] that the smell of Bounce fabric softener sheets in luggage is an indication that the owner is transporting narcotics;[445] that a particular area is known for drug trafficking and indeed that a particular person had a history of drug use;[446] that "undesirables" are more likely to be active at night;[447] that balls of tinfoil are an indication of raw cocaine;[448] that it is "unique" in parts of Vancouver for Black and White people to be together;[449] that a particular travel agency was used by drug traffickers booking flights;[450] that particular cities are either source points or consumption points for drugs;[451] that most vehicles are stolen by young males;[452] and so on.[453] There are several possible dangers here, which is presumably why the Court has instructed judges not to accept such claims uncritically. One danger is the lack of consistency this approach can produce. A wide variety of factors have been offered by police officers as contributing to their reasonable grounds, and, indeed, contradictory factors have been offered. For example, peace officers have testified that they have been suspicious of drivers because the vehicle was exceeding the speed limit,[454] was going under the speed limit,[455]

---

444 See *R v Jacobsen* (2006), 207 CCC (3d) 270 (Ont CA).

445 *R v Rajaratnam*, 2006 ABCA 333 [*Rajaratnam*].

446 *R v Johnson* (2006), 213 OAC 395 (CA).

447 *Houben*, above note 338.

448 *R v Sinclair*, 2005 MBCA 41.

449 *Greaves*, above note 30 at paras 9 and 42.

450 *R v Bui*, 2005 BCCA 482 [*Bui*].

451 *R v Bramley*, 2009 SKCA 49 at para 11 [*Bramley*]. See also *R v Geroux*, 2008 ABPC 49 [*Geroux*].

452 *Ng*, above note 341.

453 See also *R v Sekhon*, 2009 BCCA 187; *R v Juan*, 2007 BCCA 351; *Geroux*, above note 451.

454 See, for example, *R v Bracchi*, 2005 BCCA 461 [*Bracchi*]; *R v Yaran*, 2009 ABPC 31. Note that these are not cases where an officer relied on exceeding the speed limit to justify a belief that the accused was impaired or about something related specifically to their driving. In *Bracchi*, for example, the British Columbia Court of Appeal accepted that the accused's exceeding the speed limit contributed to reasonable grounds to believe he was trying to avoid surveillance and so was acting suspiciously.

455 See *Houben*, above note 338, in which the officers offered this as a reason to be suspicious about the accused in a general way—that he might be intending to break in somewhere or otherwise be up to no good—rather than for a reason related to operation of the motor vehicle. See also *Geroux*, above note 451, where a peace officer testified that he became suspicious of a driver because he was going below the posted speed limit.

or was observing the speed limit.[456] Quite commonly, officers will testify that their experience, or their training, has taught them that whichever of these facts they are reporting is a cause for suspicion. Similarly, officers have testified that they have become suspicious—and, indeed, that their training and experience have taught them to be suspicious—of both individuals who avoid eye contact[457] and those who prolong it.[458] Indeed, individual officers have testified in the same case that they would have their suspicions aroused by a person making eye contact or by not making it.[459] Some courts have been critical of reliance on this factor in particular, describing it as "neutral" and "equivocal at best."[460] If the experience of the officer is a legitimate consideration, then it must be carefully examined to avoid these difficulties.

Another danger is that, if not kept in check, this approach can make a claim of reasonable grounds essentially irrefutable. As the Saskatchewan Court of Appeal has observed, "Police testimony should not be seen as a 'trump card' simply because officers have specialized training and relevant experience."[461] In *Brown*, for example, an officer testified that he saw the accused fully extend his right arm with a closed fist toward another person, who made no gesture in response but instead turned and walked away. The officer then arrested the accused for possession of narcotics on the basis that he had just seen a drug transaction. The officer subjectively believed that and testified that his belief was based on his experience. If that experience was taken also to satisfy the objective test, then the arrest would be lawful, but the Ontario Court of

---

456 See, for example, *R v Mouland*, 2006 SKQB 100 at para 20, in which a police officer testified that "(c) Driver's [*sic*] of vehicles containing contraband do not usually break the law, that is, they follow speed limits and drive appropriately." See also *R c White*, 2007 QCCQ 992, or *Harrison*, above note 90 at para 6, for the same suggestion.

457 See *R v Jones*, [1992] BCJ No 231 (SC): "He had been trained in the ways of detecting persons who might be carrying drugs and to be on the lookout for certain 'indicators' such as: 1) behavioural factors such as unusual speech patterns and a tendency to avoid eye contact." See also *R v Schuhknecht*, 2005 BCPC 161.

458 See *Kang-Brown*, above note 63 at para 29: "RCMP Sergeant MacPhee testified that his training in the Jetway program taught him to watch for what he referred to as an 'elongated stare,' a locked eye contact for a period of a few seconds." See also *Bui*, above note 450.

459 See *Kang-Brown*, above note 63 at para 83, referring to *R v Dinh*, 2001 ABPC 48.

460 See *Geroux*, above note 451 at paras 132–33. See also Binnie J in *Kang-Brown*, above note 63 at para 83: "If 'eye contact' or 'no eye contact' are [*sic*] both of concern to the RCMP, this seems an ambiguous basis for particularized suspicion. Everyone getting off the bus will either be making eye contact or not making eye contact."

461 *Chapman*, above note 415 at para 69.

Appeal found that it was not. While not denying the officer's claim about his own experience, the court relied upon, among other things, the fact that the officer's partner did not regard that behaviour as suspicious and found that the objective test was not satisfied.[462] On the other hand, in *R v Wilson*,[463] an officer reached the conclusion that the accused was trafficking in part because he was carrying a black pouch; he testified that, in his experience, drug traffickers carried black pouches. The British Columbia Court of Appeal in essence concluded that if that was the officer's personal experience, then that was sufficient for it to become part of the objective aspect of the test.

In both cases, either it is true or it is not that the observed fact helps support the reasonableness of the claim; extended fists or black pouches either are or are not associated with drug transactions. Limiting the question solely to that officer's experience risks missing the important point. There is, of course, the danger that some officers will simply assert, without real justification, that their experience supports their behaviour. That is one reason not to accept claims uncritically. Furthermore, some officers might quite honestly report their experience, but their experience might be atypical—that, by coincidence, one particular officer has seen several drug traffickers with the same colour bag does not necessarily show that having such a bag is typical of drug traffickers.

Furthermore, there is a quite significant reason to be careful about claims of experience, and it is one that has not received enough attention in courts to date: a person can honestly and sincerely make the claim "this is my experience" and yet be mistaken.[464] Because of confirmation bias, people tend to notice instances that support their preconceived ideas and ignore those that do not; to see equivocal evidence as confirming the hypothesis to which they already adhere; and to test a hypothesis only by seeking further confirming instances, not by looking for disconfirming instances. As a result, if a person expects to see a pattern, they might see that pattern whether or not it exists.[465]

This is not a reason to be doubtful of all claims of police experience; it is unrelated to an officer's ability to identify the smell of marijuana, for example. But where experience claims are based on having observed a

462 *Brown* 2012, above note 322.

463 2012 BCCA 517.

464 See, however, *Santos*, above note 415 at para 36, and *Chapman*, above note 415 at para 69, citing this passage from the second edition of *Detention and Arrest* in order to highlight this concern.

465 Raymond S. Nickerson, "Confirmation Bias: A Ubiquitous Phenomenon in Many Guises" (1998) 2:2 *Review of General Psychology* 175 at 181: "[P]eople sometimes see in data the patterns for which they are looking, regardless of whether the patterns are really there."

pattern—drug dealers tend to use rental cars, travel from west to east, travel from one major centre to another, and so on—there is reason to be cautious. Such claims of experience are analogous to eyewitness identification evidence, which the Court has observed "is deceptively credible, largely because it is honest and sincere."[466] This aspect of critically assessing claims of experience should be pursued in the courts.[467]

Related to but apart from the question of whether an officer's personal experience can be used in assessing the objective component, many other facts have been offered and often accepted as contributing to creating reasonable grounds. These include the fact that an airline or a bus ticket was purchased at the last minute,[468] the payment method for such tickets,[469] the use of rental cars (in particular, those rented by third parties),[470] the presence of fast-food wrappers or maps,[471] energy drinks,[472] multiple cellphones,[473] long hair,[474] the type of vehicle,[475] a strong scent of cologne or air freshener,[476] nervousness,[477] driving long distances in a short time span,[478] driving from British Columbia eastward to Regina,[479] flying from Toronto to Vancouver,[480] place of residence,[481] rubbernecking,[482] and others.

---

466 *R v Hibbert*, 2002 SCC 39 at para 50.

467 See, generally, Steve Coughlan, "Learning from Experience About Learning from Experience: Modifying the Objective Test for Arrest and Detention" (2013) 4 *Criminal Reports* (7th) 245.

468 See *Kang-Brown*, above note 63 at paras 88, 118, and 187, as well as *R v MacEachern*, 2007 NSCA 69 at para 9 [*MacEachern*]. See also *R v Ambrose*, 2008 NBPC 32 at para 3 [*Ambrose*].

469 See *Kang-Brown*, above note 63 at para 88; *MacEachern*, above note 468 at para 3. See also *Bramley*, above note 451 at paras 7 and 53; *Bui*, above note 450 at para 22.

470 See *Bramley*, above note 451 at paras 7, 11, and 47. See also *R v Burgis*, 2009 BCPC 74 at para 4 [*Burgis*]; *Ambrose*, above note 468 at para 3.

471 See, generally, *Calderon*, above note 326.

472 See *Ambrose*, above note 468 at para 3.

473 *Ibid*; see also *Burgis*, above note 470 at paras 11 and 14.

474 See *Bramley*, above note 451 at paras 6, 9, 11, 42, 47, and 53.

475 See *R v Cormier* (1995), 166 NBR (2d) 5 at para 2 (CA) [*Cormier*]; *R v Cox* (1999), 210 NBR (2d) 90 at para 2 (CA) [*Cox*].

476 *Ibid* at para 3; see also *Burgis*, above note 470 at para 11; *Ambrose*, above note 468 at para 3. See also *R v Nguyen*, 2008 SKCA 160 at para 20 [*Nguyen*], or *Todd*, above note 415.

477 See *Kang-Brown*, above note 63 at paras 31 and 187; *Bui*, above note 450 at paras 9 and 22–23; *R v Grant* (2006), 81 OR (3d) 1 at paras 19 and 29 (CA); *R v Duong*, 2006 BCCA 325 at paras 25 and 48; *Bramley*, above note 451 at para 8.

478 See *Cox*, above note 475 at para 11. See also, generally, *Nguyen*, above note 476.

479 See *Bramley*, above note 451. See also *Nguyen*, above note 476.

480 See *Bui*, above note 450 at paras 22–23.

481 See *Cormier*, above note 475 at para 3; *Bramley*, above note 451 at paras 7 and 11.

482 See *Kang-Brown*, above note 63 at paras 30, 114, and 218.

Many of these facts could be seen as quite innocuous on their own and quite neutral. That does not necessarily prevent them from contributing to reasonable grounds: it has been observed that "[f]actors which are benign in and of themselves take on some (perhaps limited) significance when ranged together with other circumstances."[483] However, this can be problematic, and indeed courts have also recognized that fact.[484] For example, in *R v Calderon*,[485] the police testified that they suspected a vehicle was being used to transport narcotics because of training they had received as to certain "indicators," which included fast food, duffel bags, a road map, cellphones, and a pager. Between the two officers concerned, they had stopped between sixty and 120 cars based on those indicators and had never before found drug couriers. The Ontario Court of Appeal concluded that, given the "neutrality and apparent unreliability of these indicators," they could not amount to reasonable grounds.[486] Similarly, in *R v Santos*, the Saskatchewan Court of Appeal found the reasonable grounds standard not to have been met in an arrest arising from a traffic stop despite the officer's testimony about the basis for his reasonable grounds:

> [A]lmost all of the factors Cst. Giannoulis cited as supporting his belief that Mr. Santos possessed cannabis for the purpose of distribution were, on their own, completely innocuous. These innocuous observations included the fact that Mr. Santos was driving a rented vehicle, the fact that he was travelling from Calgary to Winnipeg along the Trans-Canada highway, and the fact that he had an energy drink in the cup holder, fast-food wrappers on the floor, and a factory-installed luggage cover

---

483 *R v Drury*, 2000 MBCA 100 at para 90. See also *MAL*, above note 425.

484 See *Rajaratnam*, above note 445, where the Court of Appeal allowed the smell of Bounce fabric softener to contribute to reasonable grounds but acknowledged the danger of allowing ordinary household items to have this effect, stressing the other facts that were relevant in that case as well.

485 *Calderon*, above note 326.

486 *Ibid* at para 72. Note that in *Calderon* the issue was whether this evidence met the lower standard of reasonable suspicion. See also *Cox*, above note 475, where the police officer testified that his reasons for thinking a particular car was that of a drug courier was that it was an older vehicle with clothes hanging up in it, and that it was observing the speed limit. The court commented at para 11:

> Furthermore, the evidence of the smuggler's profile upon which the officer says he relied, does not meet the standard of articulable cause: (1) an older vehicle, a 1987 LTD with a large trunk area; how unusual is this in the Atlantic Provinces? (2) clothing hanging off the clothes hook in the car; the man was passing through New Brunswick and travelling hundreds of kilometres to his residence in Cape Breton in a car with Nova Scotia licence plates; and (3) he was travelling within the speed limit, a requirement of the law.

> in place. Cst. Giannoulis said these were things that, in his experience, were commonly found in conjunction with the transportation of illegal drugs. But they are also, in my view, so commonplace with travelers who are doing nothing illegal that they contribute little to the base of a reasonable belief in criminal activity.[487]

Lurking in the background here is the question of profiling—not the narrower and particularly controversial issue of racial profiling but profiling more generally. The reason why so many factors that are potentially innocuous on their own are offered as justifications is that police forces have put together "profiles" of the characteristics they feel are likely to be associated with drug couriers in particular and then consciously target those individuals. The most well-known such program is Operation Jetway, described by Binnie J in *Kang-Brown*:

> "Operation Jetway" is an RCMP program designed to curtail drug trafficking. It monitors the travelling public in transportation hubs such as airports and bus depots. It appears to be modelled on drug "courier" profiles developed since 1974 by the United States Drug Enforcement Administration. Police officers contend that certain types of behaviour, demeanour, dress and other visible personal characteristics of travellers may be indicative of criminal activity. The RCMP target these individuals as they pass through a terminal and attempt to engage them in "voluntary conversation." The aim is to have suspicious individuals consent to a search to determine whether they are carrying drugs on their person or in their luggage. In circumstances where consent is withheld or equivocal, the RCMP may decide to use a sniffer dog to try to detect any odour of narcotics around the suspect's person or belongings.[488]

---

487 *Santos*, above note 415 at para 33. To similar effect, see *Chapman*, above note 415 at para 81: "Most of the factors upon which the officers relied in this case were, individually, completely innocuous. In that regard, I am referring to Mr. Chapman's nervousness following the original stop, his route of travel, his destination, the fact that he was driving a rented vehicle, the use of a radar detector, and the presence of an empty energy drink container."

488 *Kang-Brown*, above note 63 at para 47. Operation Jetway focuses on airports as well as train and bus stations. Its counterpart, Operation Pipeline, is aimed at couriers travelling in motor vehicles and uses "pretext traffic stops": David M. Tanovich, "A Powerful Blow Against Police Use of Drug Courier Profiles" (2008) 56 *Criminal Reports* (6th) 379 [Tanovich, "A Powerful Blow"]. Tanovich argued that *Kang-Brown* severely limited the ability of the police to rely on drug-courier profiles, but that decision has been overtaken by *Chehil*, above note 59: see the discussion that immediately follows.

The types of factors that enter into a profile can concern behaviour (eye contact or rubbernecking), personal traits (sex or age), and other circumstances (luggage with no tags, country from which returning).[489]

Profiling in this sense is theoretically distinct from "racial profiling," at least given one caveat: there is no universal consistency in the use of the term "racial profiling." This has the result that denials from some agencies that they engage in racial profiling might mean a variety of things.[490] Popularly, the term has largely come to mean "singling out an individual based solely on his race," and it is not surprising that agencies would deny engaging in such behaviour. As discussed above, however, courts have moved to the view that racial profiling "occurs when race or racial stereotypes about offending or dangerousness are used, consciously or unconsciously, to any degree in suspect selection or subject treatment."[491] Looked at in that light, it seems clear that, as a practical matter, race does enter into some profiles. In *Monney*, for example, that the accused was Ghanaian was seen as a legitimate consideration; similarly, "returning from a source country for drugs" in large measure amounts to "returning from the Caribbean."[492] In this event, apparently neutral profiles will in fact target members of particular races to a greater degree.

The practice of using profiles was challenged in *Chehil*, where the police had used a sniffer dog on the accused's airline bag because he was one of the last passengers to purchase a ticket, paid for his ticket in cash, and checked only one bag, which the officers testified were, in their experience, indicators of the illegal traffic of narcotics.[493] The Court seems to have cautiously approved the practice—or, at least, refused to disapprove the practice—although they did articulate some limitations.

The Court held that it was "unhelpful" to speak of profiling as generating reasonable suspicion because the term suggested an assessment based on stereotyping and discriminatory factors.[494] The question, they held, is whether the totality of the circumstances, including the specific characteristics of the accused, reached the required threshold. The Court did caution that "profile characteristics are not a substitute for objective facts that raise a reasonable suspicion of criminal activity. Profile characteristics must be approached with caution precisely because they risk

---

489 See Tanovich, "A Powerful Blow," above note 488 at 379–80.

490 See, generally, *ibid*. See also Anna Pratt & Sara K. Thompson, "Chivalry, 'Race' and Discretion at the Canadian Border" (2008) 48 *British Journal of Criminology* 620.

491 *Le*, above note 74 at para 76.

492 Tanovich, "A Powerful Blow," above note 488 at 389. See also *R v Monney*, [1999] 1 SCR 652 at para 49 [*Monney*].

493 *Chehil*, above note 59 at para 8.

494 *Ibid* at para 39.

undermining a careful individualized assessment of the totality of the circumstances."[495] Furthermore, they attached some limits to the type of characteristics that could enter into profiles: the factors must not be stereotypical or discriminatory and must relate to the actions of the subject of an investigation, not their immutable characteristics.[496] The very fact that the Court attached these limits to the factors that can enter into a profile, however, demonstrates that they do not disapprove of the use of profiles in and of themselves. In *Chehil* itself, they accepted that the factors reported by the police as their basis for reasonable suspicion were in fact capable of supporting that conclusion.

A different point should be noted about these profiles, or "constellations" of facts, as they are sometimes referred to. A typical approach to them is found in *R v Bramley*, where the Saskatchewan Court of Appeal held:

> The point, as indicated earlier, is not that everyone who drives a third party rental vehicle, or travels from British Columbia to Saskatchewan, or hides his long hair, or has a history of drug offences, or who apparently lives in a different province than his wife, is a drug courier. The point is that, taken together, these kinds of considerations sometimes constitute a "constellation" of facts which justifies a reasonable *suspicion* an individual is involved in illegal drug activity.[497]

In fact, there is room to be skeptical as to the extent to which these types of facts really do combine to constitute reasonable grounds. The claim that travelling from British Columbia to Saskatchewan is relevant, for example, is a reflection of the belief that vehicles travelling from west to east are more likely to be transporting narcotics than those travelling from east to west. The difficulty is that the argument conflates relative likelihood with absolute likelihood, in a way that can be deceptive.

For the sake of argument, let us assume that cars travelling east are twice as likely to contain narcotics. In real numbers, this might only mean that, while one in 20,000 cars travelling west contains narcotics, one in 10,000 cars travelling east contains narcotics. "Twice as likely" makes this difference sound quite significant, but the important point is that travelling east only means that there is a 0.01 percent chance the car is carrying narcotics. That minuscule factor ought not to contribute to reasonable grounds even if it is double something much more minuscule.

Similarly, courts often rely on the fact that a vehicle is travelling from one major centre to another major centre or that it is on the Trans-Canada

495 *Ibid* at para 40.

496 *Ibid* at paras 42–43.

497 *Bramley*, above note 451 at para 47.

Highway, a route known for the transportation of narcotics. It is hard to see how these factors can really contribute to reasonable grounds as essentially everyone who crosses the country uses the Trans-Canada Highway, and virtually every car on that highway is travelling from one major centre to another.[498] As discussed above, factors that are almost inevitably true of everyone should not enter into a "constellation" satisfying the objective test.

Finally, note that, on appeal, the question of whether a police officer had reasonable grounds is a question of law. The question is based on factual findings by the trial judge, but the issue of whether the facts as found by the trial judge constitute reasonable and probable grounds is a question of law.[499]

b) The Role of "Tips" in Reasonable Grounds to Believe

A factor that frequently enters into the analysis of whether a police officer has had reasonable grounds to arrest (or, for that matter, reasonable suspicion) relates to "tips" received from informers. Some tips come from anonymous informers not previously known to the police, whereas others come from sources that have been used in the past and have proved either reliable or unreliable. The Supreme Court, in *R v Garofoli*,[500] laid down guidelines surrounding the use of such information in seeking wiretaps, although it relied on caselaw surrounding search warrants to do so. Those guidelines have since been frequently applied to assess whether reasonable grounds exist in the arrest context too.[501] The Court held:

- (i) Hearsay statements of an informant can provide reasonable and probable grounds to justify a search. However, evidence of a tip from an informer, by itself, is insufficient to establish reasonable and probable grounds.
- (ii) The reliability of the tip is to be assessed by recourse to "the totality of the circumstances." There is no formulaic test as to what

---

498 See, for example, *R v Savage*, 2009 SKPC 145 at para 60: "Mr. Savage was travelling from Alberta to Thunder Bay, a large population base, and naturally it must be a large area of consumption of drugs .... But the same can [be] and is said of any city. There was no independent evidence suggesting that Thunder Bay in particular is a destination point for illegal drugs."

499 *R v Shepherd*, 2009 SCC 35 at para 20.

500 [1990] 2 SCR 1421 [*Garofoli*].

501 See, for example, *Goodine v R*, 2006 NBCA 109 at para 23 [*Goodine*]: "There is every reason to apply those guidelines in determining whether a peace officer had the requisite reasonable and probable grounds when he or she relied upon the hearsay statements of an informer to effect a warrantless arrest." See also *R v Campbell*, 2003 MBCA 76 [*Campbell* 2003].

this entails. Rather, the court must look to a variety of factors including:

(a) the degree of detail of the "tip";
(b) the informer's source of knowledge;
(c) indicia of the informer's reliability such as past performance or confirmation from other investigative sources.

(iii) The results of the search cannot, *ex post facto*, provide evidence of reliability of the information.[502]

More simply, the criteria from *Debot* have come to be known as the "three 'C's."[503] As set out in *R v Ahmad*, any tip "should be examined to see whether its detail is compelling, the informant is credible, and its information is corroborated in any way."[504] These three criteria—compelling, credible, and corroborated—are to be considered in the "totality of circumstances." That is, all three enter into the analysis, so a weakness in one area can be compensated for by strengths in the other two.[505] For example, an anonymous tip has very little credibility since there is nothing giving it any, but there is no rule that a tip from a previously untested source cannot be relied upon. If the anonymous tip were quite detailed (compelling) and the police were able to confirm much of it (corroborated), then it might well create reasonable grounds.[506]

It is important that the test does speak of the three factors compensating for one another. That is, one can find in the caselaw tips with little to make them compelling being accepted and tips that are accepted despite the absence of very much corroboration. One must not see those cases as setting a "minimum bar" in each category; rather, the point is that an inadequacy in one area can be made up for by a strength in another area that exceeds the norm.[507]

i) Is the Tip Compelling?

To ask whether a tip is compelling is to ask about the quality of the information. Is the information so particular, precise, unique, or detailed

502 *Garofoli*, above note 500 at para 68.

503 *R v Woodworth*, 2006 NSSC 22 at para 53 [*Woodworth*].

504 *R v Ahmad*, 2020 SCC 11 at para 53 [*Ahmad*].

505 *Debot*, above note 213.

506 *Goodine*, above note 501.

507 See, for example, *R v Whyte*, 2011 ONCA 24, aff'd 2011 SCC 49, where the Court of Appeal found that the trial judge had erred in not finding reasonable grounds because he had assessed each piece of evidence independently and had not looked to whether the information the police gathered had been sufficient to confirm the tip they had received.

as to compel belief?[508] Conclusory statements from a tipster will not be sufficient, nor will a tip that lacks detail; it must be clear that the tipster is reporting more than mere rumour or gossip, and the possibility of coincidence must be excluded.[509] The standard is whether the tip has sufficient detail as to exclude the possibility that it was based upon rumour, gossip, or coincidence.

Generally speaking, the more detail a tip includes, the more compelling it will be, and this is particularly so if the tip includes information not publicly known. In *R v Wiley*, for example, an informer gave a detailed description of the residence of the accused and reported having personally seen sixty marijuana plants growing in a lab in a concrete bunker below a hot tub attached to the house.[510] This reflects that the more intimate and personal the details in the tip, the more likely it is that the information has come from a person well placed to have reliable knowledge. So, for example, reporting that a house is heated by a wood stove is not compelling evidence when a large woodpile is visible; reporting that the wood stove is on the main floor, and that the furnace was removed from the basement in order to have more room to grow marijuana plants, is compelling. It is specific, unique, and detailed, and it is not information that a member of the public would be likely to know.[511]

That the information is detailed and compelling is not, of course, sufficient alone to make a tip constitute reasonable grounds if the other two areas are weak. In *R v Lewis*,[512] for example, the police received a detailed tip identifying the accused by name, describing him and his companion accurately, stating when he would be at the airport, which airline he would be flying on, and his destination and indicating that he would be carrying cocaine. The Ontario Court of Appeal noted that the level of detail excluded the possibility that the tipster was relying on rumour or gossip and characterized the tip as compelling. Nonetheless, they found that it could not constitute reasonable grounds. The tip had been an anonymous one, so there was no basis for assessing credibility. The only corroboration had been of entirely innocent details, such as that the accused had arrived at the airport when predicted. Although the court specifically held that a tip's information about illegal conduct did

---

508 *Woodworth*, above note 503 at para 55.

509 *Ibid*; see also *Campbell* 2003, above note 501 at para 19.

510 *R v Wiley*, [1993] 3 SCR 263 [*Wiley*].

511 *Woodworth*, above note 503 at paras 58–59. See also *R v Green*, 2015 ONCA 579, where the informant had described the type of gun owned by the accused.

512 (1998), 38 OR (3d) 540 (CA) [*Lewis*].

not always require corroboration,[513] it held that in this case there were no reasonable grounds:

> Although the details provided in the tip and the confirmation of many of those details go some way to providing the requisite reasonable grounds, the danger in holding that they go the entire way is clear. Literally thousands of people go to the Pearson International Airport every day to fly to various destinations. No doubt, there are thousands more who are sufficiently familiar with a traveller's plan to know the traveller's flight, destination and who, if anyone, will accompany that traveller. Any one of those thousands could supply the police with exactly the same kind of information about any one of the thousands of travellers that this tipster provided about the respondent. It takes little imagination to conceive of situations in which a person familiar enough with another person to know his or her travel plans would also have a motive to falsely accuse that person of a serious crime.[514]

ii) *Is the Tip Credible?*

Whether a tip is credible is really a question about the informer personally and whether they are trustworthy and the disclosure reliable. It requires consideration of the informer, the informer's history of giving information, and the informer's motive for giving information.[515] If the informer is known to the police, for example, and has given information in the past that has proven reliable, then the source will likely be seen as credible.[516] If that information has resulted in criminal convictions, that fact enhances the tipster's credibility, but it is not a requirement.[517] A prior relationship between the officer receiving the information and the informer will be relevant.[518] Similarly, if there is no testimony at trial from the officer who dealt directly with the informer, that will undermine the credibility of the tip.[519] Other factors, such as whether the informer was being paid[520] or whether an officer has seen the informer with the person they report to be receiving information from, can matter.[521]

---

513 See Section C(2)(b)(iii), below in this chapter.

514 *Lewis*, above note 512 at para 18.

515 *R v Zammit* (1993), 13 OR (3d) 76 at 83–84 (CA) [*Zammit*].

516 *Wiley*, above note 510.

517 *R v Protz*, 2020 SKCA 115 at para 82 [*Protz*].

518 *R v Deol*, 2006 MBCA 39 at para 16.

519 *R v Pavlik*, 2019 SKCA 107.

520 See, for example, *Protz*, above note 517 at para 82, where the tipsters "had a financial motivation to provide accurate and therefore reliable information because the amount they were paid depended on how helpful the information was."

521 *Debot*, above note 213.

The fact that the informer is already known to the police, however, is not sufficient to make the tip constitute reasonable grounds if the actual information received remains too general to distinguish it from mere rumour and where there is no indication of the informer's means of knowledge.[522]

At the other end of the spectrum would be an anonymous informer providing a tip on a single occasion. In such a case, the tip could constitute reasonable grounds only where the information provided by the informer is detailed enough and there is enough corroborative evidence to adequately compensate for the inability to assess credibility and reliability. Furthermore, if that is the case, the police ought to seek corroborative evidence that confirms the credibility of the informer as well as of the tip itself.[523]

On this reasoning, the questions of credibility and corroboration become intermingled to some extent. To corroborate the reliability of the informer, the information confirmed should be something that suggests the informer was privy to special knowledge about the situation. For example, in *R v Zammit*, the informer had described the accused and his vehicle and had given his home address and the name and address of his workplace. The Ontario Court of Appeal held that these facts did not confirm the reliability of the informer because "[t]hey would be known to anyone familiar with the appellant and would not in any way substantiate the allegation that the appellant was involved in drugs."[524]

iii) Is the Tip Corroborated?

Whether the tip has been corroborated is the most complex question because it is hard to lay down any very precise rules. The police need not confirm every detail in an informer's tip, but there must be enough corroborative evidence "to remove the possibility of innocent coincidence."[525] A greater amount of corroborative evidence is required where the tip does not provide enough details to preclude the possibility of innocent coincidence or where the informer's credibility cannot be assessed.[526]

The most difficult situation is when there is no corroboration of criminal aspects of the tip. There is no general rule that a tip must, to form reasonable grounds, be confirmed in portions of it relating to illegal behaviour. For example, in *R v Warford*, the police received a quite

522 See *Zammit*, above note 515 at 83–84.

523 See *Debot*, above note 213; *Campbell* 2003, above note 501 at paras 22 & 23.

524 *Zammit*, above note 515 at para 84.

525 See *Debot*, above note 213 at 1144.

526 *Ibid*; see also *Campbell* 2003, above note 501 at para 20.

specific tip concerning trafficking in cocaine by the accused, giving the date the drugs had been received, prices, method of delivery, locations of sale, and a description of the accused's vehicle including the information that he always had some cocaine in it. The informer, a proven and reliable source, also indicated that the accused would be selling cocaine at a particular nightclub, giving the date and time. The police intercepted the accused in the vehicle described at the date and time in question on a route consistent with travelling to the named nightclub. The Newfoundland Court of Appeal held that this provided confirmation of the informer's tip and indeed was "as much confirmation as the police could be expected to obtain from their surveillance."[527]

That case was made easier because the informer there had provided reliable information on six previous occasions. The situation is trickier when the information comes from an anonymous source. It has been held that, where an anonymous informer is used, there should be corroboration of some criminal aspect of the tip.[528] In *Lewis*, for example, the Ontario Court of Appeal considered an anonymous tip that the accused would be carrying drugs, and the only confirmation of the tip was that the accused met the description given, including travelling with a two-year-old child, and was in fact booked on the flight the informer had indicated. The Court of Appeal held that this was not sufficient given the anonymous nature of the tip:

> The Crown's position comes down to this. If a person shows up at the airport and acts exactly as one would expect a normal traveller to act, that person is subject to arrest if an anonymous, unproven tipster has predicted that the person would attend at the airport in possession of cocaine and act like a normal traveller. I cannot accept that contention. Absent confirmation of details other than details which describe innocent and commonplace conduct, information supplied by an untested, anonymous informant cannot, standing alone, provide reasonable grounds for an arrest or search.[529]

---

527 *R v Warford*, 2001 NFCA 64 at para 27 [*Warford*].

528 See *Campbell* 2003, above note 501. The case is somewhat ambiguous. In para 26, the court says that there is no strict requirement for confirmation: "This does not mean that there must be confirmation of the accused's criminality in every case involving an anonymous informant. But where, as in this case, it is not clear whether the information provided is 'firsthand' the lack of corroborative evidence connecting the accused to the crime will be most relevant when considering the totality of the circumstances." However, in para 27, the very next paragraph, the court says: "Where an anonymous informer is used, it is my opinion that information which corroborates the 'criminal' aspect of the informer's tip in some material respect should be present."

529 *Lewis*, above note 512 at para 19.

On the other hand, it has also been held that the "totality of circumstances" test precludes a rule that an anonymous tip must be corroborated in some criminal aspects. In *Goodine*, the New Brunswick Court of Appeal held:

> [L]ack of corroboration of the "criminal" aspect of a tip by an untested anonymous source does not preclude a finding that an arrest based on that tip was lawful, at least where the following circumstances are in play: (1) there is no evidence that an improper motive underlies the tipster's report; (2) the corroborated "neutral" data would lead a reasonable and dispassionate observer to infer that the tipster is both closely acquainted with the target and privy to the criminal activity being reported; and (3) that observer would be at a loss to point to any fact-based, as opposed to speculative, justification for the conclusion that the allegation of criminal conduct is unreliable.[530]

More generally, there is also room for dispute over whether or not the confirmation of particular facts actually amounts to corroboration. In *R v Plant*,[531] for example, the informer had described the accused's house without giving its address, and the Supreme Court held that this was corroboration because the description had allowed the police to find the house in question. Lower courts have questioned whether that reasoning is sound. *Zammit* holds that confirmation of "only what would probably have been known by anyone familiar with the appellant" is not corroboration.[532]

3) Reasonable Grounds to Suspect

a) The Relationship Between Reasonable Suspicion and Reasonable Belief

Before turning to the substantive content of this standard, it is worth noting the ambiguity over the terminology used to refer to it. In the detention context, the standard first became relevant with regard to investigative detentions, and the impetus for that was the Ontario Court of Appeal decision in *R v Simpson*.[533] That decision had said that the appropriate

530 *Goodine*, above note 501 at para 20.

531 [1993] 3 SCR 281 [*Plant*].

532 *Zammit*, above note 515 at para 27. See also *Woodworth*, above note 503 at para 56, noting on facts similar to *Plant*, above note 531, that "this Court is concerned that any member of the public who knew the Woodworths or their Residence, could acquire and pass on this kind of information. While it is good information as to the location of the alleged illegal activity, it is not compelling evidence of an alleged crime."

533 (1993), 12 OR (3d) 182 (CA) [*Simpson*].

standard was "articulable cause." When the Supreme Court of Canada approved the concept of investigative detention in *Mann*, they instead used the terminology of "reasonable grounds to detain." It was noted at the time,[534] and has been subsequently observed,[535] that this terminology was likely to be confusing since "reasonable grounds" could easily sound like the standard for arrest. The decision in *Mann* also used the phrase "reasonable grounds to suspect," however, and that term, or the equivalent, "reasonable suspicion," has come to be commonly used.[536] Most recently, the Court has used the phrase "reason to suspect" as a description of the same standard.[537]

The reasonable suspicion standard applies to a number of powers. At common law, it is used in the test for entrapment, as well as to assess investigative detentions and sniffer-dog searches. It has also been employed in statutes—for example, for some searches under the *Customs Act*,[538] in issuing a warrant to track the location of a thing,[539] to justify a demand for the use of an approved screening device,[540] and in other contexts. It has been said that the standard applies to searches of students by school officials, but this is an unfortunate error now repeated.[541]

The intention is that the reasonable suspicion standard should only be used when there is a legitimate state interest to be served and the individual interest compromised by the state interference is relatively minor. Put simply, less justification for interfering with liberty is required when

---

534 See the dissenting judgment in *Mann*, above note 14 at para 64.

535 See the judgment of Deschamps and Rothstein JJ in *Kang-Brown*, above note 63 at para 164, or *MacKenzie*, above note 438 at para 38.

536 See, for example, the dissent of Deschamps and Rothstein JJ in *Kang-Brown*, above note 63 at para 164: "In my view, 'reasonable grounds to suspect' is substantively equivalent to 'reasonable suspicion.'"

537 *Stairs*, above note 93.

538 *Customs Act*, above note 373.

539 *Criminal Code*, above note 6, s 492.1(1).

540 *Ibid*, s 254(2)(b).

541 Justice Binnie in *AM*, above note 387 at para 77, listed a number of contexts in which the reasonable suspicion standard is used and included on that list *M(MR)*, above note 29. This is an error and is unfortunately one that was repeated in *Chehil*, above note 59, in footnote 1 of the decision. The Court in *M(MR)* discussed the fact that school searches in the United States have been based on reasonable suspicion and that the standard for school searches in Canada should be lower than normal. However, the test actually articulated in *M(MR)* is that "[t]he school authority must have *reasonable grounds to believe* that there has been a breach of school regulations or discipline and that a search of a student would reveal evidence of that breach" (at para 50 [emphasis added]). The Court did relax the *Hunter v Southam*, above note 42, standards by dispensing with the need for judicial pre-authorization and eliminating the need to believe an offence had been committed, but it did not change from the "reasonable belief" to the "reasonable suspicion" standard.

the stakes are lower. As the Alberta Court of Appeal has put it (in the context of an entrapment case):

> When a court determines the suitable degree of certainty that must precede state action, it is helpful to think of the consequences that attach to the determination. For example, a court cannot convict an accused of a criminal offence unless the Crown has proved the physical and mental elements of the crime beyond a reasonable doubt. This very high degree of certainty is necessary because of the severity of the consequences of a criminal conviction. An accused convicted of a crime may be incarcerated and his or her reputation will be damaged. A lesser degree of certainty is needed to validate an arrest—which, while it temporarily deprives a person of his or her liberty, it results in no verdict of criminal wrongdoing. The stigma associated with an arrest is much less than that which follows a conviction. And a still lesser degree of certainty is needed to justify a police officer interacting with a target and presenting him or her with an opportunity to commit a crime—or not. The adverse effect on any interest of a target that merits consideration is marginal.[542]

They added that the reasonable suspicion standard is "the lowest degree of certainty the criminal law utilizes."[543]

The reasonable suspicion standard shares many characteristics with reasonable belief. Indeed, it has been referred to as "a lesser but included standard in the threshold of reasonable and probable grounds to believe."[544] It, too, requires that the police have more than a hunch, but its threshold is "somewhat lower than the reasonable and probable grounds required for lawful arrest."[545] Much of what has been said about reasonable grounds—for example, the subjective and objective components,[546] the use of police training and experience in assessing the objective component, or the extent to which tips from informers constitute sufficient grounds—applies equally here. In essence, the same type of evidence is still needed, but reasonable suspicion can be justified based on less of it. Similarly, like reasonable grounds, the standard is meant to protect rights and so must be based on "objectively discernible facts" in order to "[allow] for exacting curial scrutiny of police conduct."[547] In

---

542 *R v Bank*, 2021 ABCA 223 at para 104 [footnotes omitted].

543 *Ibid* at para 106 [footnote omitted].

544 *Monney*, above note 492 at para 49.

545 *Mann*, above note 14 at para 27. See also Binnie J's judgment in *Kang-Brown*, above note 63 at para 75.

546 *Mann*, above note 14 at para 27.

547 *Ahmad*, above note 504 at para 24.

particular, "[c]ourts must be able to assess the extent to which the police, in seeking to form reasonable suspicion over a person or a place, rely upon overtly discriminatory or stereotypical thinking, or upon 'intuition' or 'hunches' that easily disguise unconscious racism and stereotyping."[548]

In dealing with reasonable grounds, the Court, as noted, has been clear that the standard varies in different contexts. With reasonable suspicion, on the other hand, there have been suggestions that the standard means the same thing in all different contexts, whether investigative detention, a customs search, or other situation. In *Mann*, for example, the Court noted that the standard of reasonable suspicion for customs searches, in *R v Jacques*,[549] was the same as the standard for investigative detention.[550] Similarly, in *Kang-Brown*, when discussing searches involving the use of sniffer dogs, Deschamps and Rothstein JJ noted: "the "reasonable suspicion" standard is readily applicable in practice, is meaningful to the police and trial judges, and is likely to be used in cases other than those involving detention."[551] They carry on to discuss the use of that same standard with regard to approved screening devices and in customs searches, with no suggestion that the standard has different meanings in different contexts. Similarly, Binnie J in *Kang-Brown* notes that "[t]he 'reasonable suspicion' standard is not a new juridical standard called into existence for the purposes of this case" and discusses its use in entrapment cases.[552]

This leads to the observation that one has to separate the questions "are there reasonable grounds to suspect" and "to suspect what?" In the former question, the standard will be the same, but suspicion with regard to what differs from context to context. In the case of approved screening devices, it is that the suspect has alcohol in their system; in the case of a customs search, it is that the person is concealing contraband; and so on. The point is that a reasonable suspicion "in the air" is never sufficient and indeed would quickly become indistinguishable from acting on a mere hunch.

---

548 *Ibid* at para 25.

549 *Jacques*, above note 395.

550 *Mann*, above note 14 at para 30.

551 *Kang-Brown*, above note 63 at para 164. Justices Deschamps and Rothstein were dissenting in the result, but it is quite difficult to say exactly what the majority rule from *Kang-Brown* is, and nothing in this passage is central to their disagreement with the majority.

552 *Ibid* at para 75. Justice Binnie was not dissenting in the result, although only McLachlin CJC actually concurred with his reasons. Four justices believed that sniffer-dog searches should not be allowed based only on reasonable suspicion. Justice Binnie felt that that was an acceptable standard but that reasonable suspicion was not made out on the facts of the case.

b) What Constitutes Reasonable Grounds to Suspect?

To begin, it is worth noting that, like reasonable grounds to believe, reasonable suspicion has both a subjective and an objective component. If a peace officer does not personally have suspicion, then the mere fact that objectively such suspicion would be reasonable is not sufficient to satisfy the standard.[553] As with reasonable belief, however, the more complicated issue is whether objectively the reasonable suspicion standard is met.

In *Chehil*, the Court for the first time engaged in a general discussion of what is necessary to meet the reasonable suspicion standard. It must be based on objectively discernible facts that can be subjected to independent judicial scrutiny. It must be more than a mere suspicion or hunch, although it is less than a belief based upon reasonable and probable grounds.[554] It therefore does not require the *probability* of crime but merely a reasonable *possibility*. As a result, in some cases, the police will reasonably suspect a person who turns out to be innocent.[555]

Reasonable suspicion is based on the totality of the circumstances, and it cannot be so broad that it descends to the level of generalized suspicion.[556] Some factors can give rise to reasonable suspicion all on their own, such as travelling under a false name. Other factors will be capable of innocent explanation and cannot give rise to reasonable suspicion alone but could contribute to reasonable suspicion if coupled with other factors. The Court observed:

> Generally, characteristics that apply broadly to innocent people are insufficient, as they are markers only of generalized suspicion. The same is true of factors that may "go both ways," such as an individual's making or failing to make eye contact. On their own, such factors cannot support reasonable suspicion; however, this does not preclude reasonable suspicion arising when the same factor is simply one part of a constellation of factors.[557]

Because all that is required is a reasonable *possibility*, reasonable suspicion need not be the only inference that can be drawn from a particular

---

553 See, for example, *Dhillon*, above note 322, where there was no evidence that the officer who conducted an investigative detention subjectively had a suspicion; therefore, the standard was not met.

554 *Chehil*, above note 59 at paras 26–27. The Supreme Court noted in *Harrison*, above note 90 at para 20, that "[w]hile an officer's 'hunch' is a valuable investigative tool . . . it is no substitute for proper *Charter* standards when interfering with a suspect's liberty."

555 *Chehil*, above note 59 at para 28.

556 This standard had been rejected by all but one judge as the basis for a sniffer-dog search in *Kang-Brown*, above note 63.

557 *Chehil*, above note 59 at para 31.

set of facts. The police are required to consider all the information that is available to them, including possible innocent explanations, but they do not have a duty to seek out exculpatory factors or to rule out possible innocent explanations. By the same token, factors learned later cannot be taken into account.[558]

The type of evidence needed to justify reasonable suspicion, as noted, does not differ in kind from that needed for reasonable grounds; all that differs is the amount. It is nonetheless worth noting some things that have been taken either to show or to fail to show that reasonable suspicion justifying an investigative detention existed.[559] In *Mann*, for example, the officers were taken to be justified in stopping the accused because he closely matched the description they had been given of a person who had just committed an offence, and he was found very shortly afterward only a few blocks from the scene of that crime. The Court stressed that what mattered about the accused's location was that he was in the vicinity of the actual reported offence. It stressed that

> [t]he presence of an individual in a so-called high crime area is relevant only so far as it reflects his or her proximity to a particular crime. The high crime nature of a neighbourhood is not by itself a basis for detaining individuals.[560]

Lying to the police or presenting false identification has also been taken to be grounds for suspicion,[561] as has changing one's story or offering an inherently implausible story. For example, in *Monney*, the accused initially denied having visited Ghana while out of the country but then later changed his story and said that he had.[562] In *R v MacKenzie*, the accused gave two different starting dates for his trip and seemed confused as to when he had left.[563] Nervousness is often seen as a contributing factor,[564] although it has also been held that it ought not to be.[565]

There is some authority suggesting that fleeing from the police can enter into creating reasonable suspicion, but this is a tricky issue.[566] In

---

558 *Ibid* at paras 32–34.

559 See also Appendix II.

560 *Mann*, above note 14 at para 47.

561 *Kang-Brown*, above note 63 at para 87.

562 *Monney*, above note 544.

563 *MacKenzie*, above note 438 at para 12.

564 *Ibid*. See, for example, *Todd*, above note 415.

565 See *Kang-Brown*, above note 63 at para 95. See also *Geroux*, above note 451.

566 See *Kang-Brown*, above note 63 at para 87, in which Binnie J notes that there is US authority for this position. In *Byfield*, above note 325, the Ontario Court of Appeal appears to accept the trial judge's reliance on this consideration. See also *R v Nesbeth*, 2008 ONCA 579 [*Nesbeth*], where the fact that the accused bolted

Chehil, the Court points to flight from the police as a factor that could create reasonable suspicion all on its own.[567] On the other hand, *Chehil* also says that the exercise of *Charter* rights, "such as the right to remain silent or to walk away from questioning made outside the context of a detention," cannot enter into forming reasonable suspicion, or those rights would become meaningless.[568] Distinguishing "fleeing" (sufficient grounds on its own) from "walking away" (irrelevant) will not always be straightforward, and cases have gone both ways on this point.[569] This is a matter that would benefit from more sustained attention from the Court.[570]

Other factors are contextual and depend on the circumstances. That a person has bought a plane ticket at the last moment and with cash might be suspicious, for example, while no similar inference should be drawn about a bus ticket.[571]

---

upon seeing the police was a factor entering into reasonable suspicion. In *R v Jackson*, [2002] OJ No 4005 (SCJ), it is held that fleeing from the police does give rise to reasonable suspicion and is unlike simply refusing to answer questions. Furthermore, *R v McKay* (2006), 200 Man R (2d) 259 (Prov Ct), suggests that an accused's *failure* to flee was relevant to deciding that reasonable grounds did not exist. See *McKenzie*, above note 295, and see also *R v Noor*, 2022 ONCA 338 at para 12: "When PC Perelli began to approach, Mr. Noor projected a startled look and he quickly attempted to walk away. Although Mr. Noor was legally entitled at this point to walk away, his reaction could only have reasonably reinforced PC Perelli's suspicion prior to the detention."

567 *Chehil*, above note 59 at para 31.

568 *Ibid* at para 44.

569 In *Reddy*, 2010 BCCA 11, the accused's flight was not permitted to enter into reasonable grounds for arrest, but this was in the particular context of fleeing an unlawful detention. On the other hand, in *Nesbeth*, above note 566, the accused bolted upon seeing the police, which was allowed to be a factor entering into reasonable suspicion.

570 See the further discussion of this issue, relating to whether a person who flees can be said to be psychologically detained, in Chapter 5, Section B(1).

571 See *Kang-Brown*, above note 63 at para 88:

> Sergeant MacPhee considered significant the appellant's acknowledgement that he had bought his bus ticket at the "last minute . . . for cash" (R.R., at p. 53). This is a factor developed in the original Jetway program at airports where ordinary travellers usually book air transportation in advance and do not pay for an expensive ticket in cash (see, e.g., *Monney*). I think we can take judicial notice of the fact that people travelling by bus frequently buy their tickets not long before boarding. There is no evidence that cash payments are unusual.

CHAPTER 3

POWERS OF DETENTION

A. INTRODUCTION

As has been noted above, powers of arrest and detention in Canada are created by statute and by the common law. In this chapter, we address powers of detention. Initially, it is worth noting that detention can be seen as a broad concept that might include arrest and subsequent detentions, surrounding issues of pretrial detention and incarceration, as well as indefinite detentions under dangerous offender legislation. Here, though, we will focus on "on-the-street" encounters where police powers short of arrest remain controversial.[1] This area of the law developed largely through caselaw owing, it seems, to the need in our law for greater specificity in police powers since the enactment of the *Canadian Charter of Rights and Freedoms*.[2]

Generally in Canada, powers of arrest arise where the police or the citizen finds the person committing an offence or, in the case of the police, have reasonable grounds to believe the person has committed certain criminal offences. These powers to arrest are discussed in Chapter 4; for now we wish to address those other powers that enable police to detain an individual on less than a reasonable belief of criminal offending. Since the

1 In *R v Thomsen*, [1988] 1 SCR 640 [*Thomsen*], and in *R v Therens*, [1985] 1 SCR 613 [*Therens*], Le Dain J speaks of detention as a "restraint of liberty other than arrest" (*Thomsen*, above in this note at para 8).

2 Part 1 of the *Constitution Act, 1982*, being Schedule B to the *Canada Act 1982* (UK), 1982, c 11 [*Charter*].

enactment of the *Charter*, the Supreme Court has been active in addressing this area of the law, particularly in its recognition of powers of detention in *Dedman v The Queen*,[3] *R v Hufsky*,[4] *R v Mellenthin*,[5] *R v Ladouceur*,[6] *R v Mann*,[7] *R v Clayton*,[8] and *R v Aucoin*.[9] The scope and requirements of such powers are of central concern to this discussion. Initially, however, we will discuss statutory powers of detention before moving to discuss the common law. As we do so, we emphasize that our discussion is intended to focus on the detention aspect of the issues and not on related issues that arise, particularly in the context of search and seizure.

One final point must be made by way of preface to this discussion. It is worth noting that the question of whether there has been a "detention" is distinct from the question of whether there is a detention *power*. As we will note, the definition of the word "detention," which appears in sections 9 and 10 of the *Charter* and plays an important role in the right to silence under section 7 of the *Charter*, has received considerable attention from the Court.[10] In *R v Grant*[11] and *R v Suberu*,[12] for example, the Court provided a great deal of guidance about the definition of those terms, but those cases were not about detention powers; rather, they addressed questions as to what rights a person has once they are, in fact, detained. A detention power, on the other hand, needs to focus upon whether the state or an individual had the authority, at law, to assume "control over the movement of a person by a demand or direction," not just whether the police did in fact detain a person in a given circumstance.[13] The failure to keep in mind the distinction can result in a misunderstanding of the principles at stake in any given situation.

B. STATUTORY POWERS OF DETENTION

The most obvious statutory power to detain arises in the impaired-driving context, where, not atypically as a feature of powers of detention, it is based on something less than reasonable belief.

3 [1985] 2 SCR 2 [*Dedman*].
4 [1988] 1 SCR 621 [*Hufsky*].
5 [1992] 3 SCR 615 [*Mellenthin*].
6 [1990] 1 SCR 1257 [*Ladouceur*].
7 2004 SCC 52 [*Mann*].
8 2007 SCC 32 [*Clayton*].
9 2012 SCC 66 [*Aucoin*].
10 See the discussion in Chapter 5, Section B(1).
11 2009 SCC 32 [*Grant*].
12 2009 SCC 33 [*Suberu*].
13 *Thomsen*, above note 1 at 649.

As we have noted above, this area is plagued by inconsistency and by varying opinions on many issues; statutory context, both federal and provincial, has been important, and the Supreme Court has allowed the common law a large role in expanding powers given by statute. Because provincial statutes are significant and because provinces have not acted in unison, each statute will need, at times, to be consulted to determine the particular powers available to enforcement officers in a given jurisdiction.

A detention may be for varying amounts of time, but generally we are here speaking of brief detentions that give rise to rights concerns. Different detention powers will sometimes be used in succession in that the exercise of one detention power might lead to the use of another or others. For example, the power to demand a roadside screening sample from a driver of a motor vehicle, which was formerly in section 254 of the *Criminal Code*,[14] gave rise to a detention, which then gave rise to rights under sections 9 and 10 of the *Charter*.[15] But that statutory power to demand a breath sample did not give rise to the power to stop a motor vehicle. Accordingly, the actual stopping of the vehicle by the police officer must have been justified under some other power. That might be a checkstop power from the common law as set out in the decision in *Dedman*[16] or, alternatively, might be set out in some provincial statute allowing police to stop vehicles.[17] Of course, that second detention might then lead to a further detention for a Breathalyzer test or an arrest under applicable police arrest powers based upon a reasonable belief in impaired driving. Likewise, where the police do not employ a checkstop but rather conduct a random stop, they will need to look elsewhere for their power to stop the vehicle even though both kinds of stops might, in the right circumstance, lead to a roadside detention and demand. The power to conduct a random stop, as we will see, is arguably less clear, although the Court has certainly discovered such a power in most of the provinces.[18] The more general point to understand is that it can be an oversimplification to speak of "a detention": for the purposes

---

14 RSC 1985, c C-46 [*Code*]. All of the provisions around breath testing, and indeed around driving offences generally, were amended in 2018: see *An Act to amend the Criminal Code (offences relating to conveyances) and to make consequential amendments to other Acts*, SC 2018, c 21. Although the specific powers have now changed, that does not affect the general point in this paragraph.

15 *Thomsen*, above note 1 at 12; *Charter*, above note 2.

16 *Dedman*, above note 3.

17 See, for example, the Ontario *Highway Traffic Act*, RSO 1990, c H.8, s 216. Some provincial legislation specifically envisions checking for impairment as one of the allowed purposes of such a stop: see, for example, the Newfoundland and Labrador *Highway Traffic Act*, RSNL 1990, c H-3, s 201.1.

18 *Ladouceur*, above note 6.

of assessing whether the power to detain existed, a single encounter between an individual and the police will often need to be understood as a series of detentions.[19]

Initially, it appears useful to separate this heading into stop powers and subsequent detention powers. In the *Criminal Code*, outside the impaired-driving context, there are few statutory detention powers short of arrests themselves. There is, for example, a specific arrest power relating to apprehended terrorist activity, which depends in part only on reasonable suspicion.[20] Significantly, there are detention powers in other federal statutes relating specifically to border crossings and customs.[21] Furthermore, there are important detention powers in provincial legislation, which in almost all cases will be centred on those who engage in various licensed or regulated activities or industries.

1) Statutory Motor Vehicle Detention Powers

Our focus here will be on motor vehicle legislation stop powers since they have received the most attention from the Court. In the section immediately following this, we will look at *Criminal Code* stops for impaired driving, while the discussion here will be about the more general power to stop to check for licensing, mechanical fitness, and other motor vehicle–related issues and therefore generally relates to provincial laws. In practical terms, this is a somewhat artificial distinction since police stopping a vehicle will frequently be checking for both sets of purposes. Nonetheless, there is some value in looking at the two types of stops separately.

Let us look, then, at what the caselaw has said about motor vehicle stops. In *Dedman*, the Supreme Court faced an argument that section 14

---

19 *R v Tim*, 2022 SCC 12, is a nice illustration [*Tim*]. A police officer approached the accused at the scene of a single-accident collision, believed he saw the accused to be in possession of illegal narcotics, and in the course of pursuing that issue found bullets and a handgun on the accused. The Court separately considered the issues of a power to detain for the initial investigation, an arrest for a drug offence, and a further arrest for a firearms offence.

20 See the *Criminal Code*, above note 14, s 83.3(4), which permits an arrest without warrant where a peace officer:

> (*a*) believes on reasonable grounds that a terrorist activity will be carried out; and
>
> (*b*) suspects on reasonable grounds that the imposition of a recognizance with conditions on a person, or the arrest of a person, is necessary to prevent the carrying out of the terrorist activity.

21 See the *Customs Act*, RSC 1985 (2d Supp), c 1, discussed in Section B(2)(b), below in this chapter.

of the then *Highway Traffic Act* of Ontario justified the checkstop in which Dedman was caught.[22] The section imposed a duty upon the driver of a motor vehicle to surrender their licence for inspection upon demand. It did not expressly provide a police power to stop the vehicle to ask to see the licence. The Crown argued that a police officer's power to stop a motor vehicle for the purpose of inspecting a licence arose by implication from the driver's duty. The majority disagreed with the Crown, ruling that the section might imply a power to demand surrender of the licence for inspection, but whether such a power should extend, by further implication, to a power to stop a motor vehicle for such purpose was "doubtful."[23] Writing for the majority, Le Dain J also said:

> It would appear to involve an unusual extension of the rule of implied powers, as a matter of statutory construction. Such a power might exist as a matter of implication from the general nature of police duties, but that is a different basis. That is what I understand by common law authority for the exercise of police power. It may seem to come down to much the same thing in the end but the rule of statutory construction must not be distorted because of its application in a great variety of other statutory contexts. In any event, even assuming for the purposes of analysis that a power to stop a motor vehicle in order to demand surrender of a licence for inspection arises by implication from the terms of s. 14 of *The Highway Traffic Act*, and need not be grounded as a matter of common law on the general duties of police officers, it is a power that must be exercised for the purpose indicated in s. 14. It cannot be validly exercised for another purpose, using the purpose indicated in s. 14 as a subterfuge or pretext. In this case, it is clear from the findings of fact as set out in the stated case that while the police officer asked the appellant for his licence, the true purpose of the signal to stop was not to demand surrender of the licence for inspection but rather to determine whether there were grounds for a reasonable suspicion that the appellant had alcohol in his blood. That

---

22 According to RSO 1970, c 202, s 14, as amended by SO 1979, c 57, s 2:

> 1) Every operator of a motor vehicle shall carry his licence with him at all times while he is in charge of a motor vehicle and shall surrender the licence for reasonable inspection upon the demand of a constable or officer appointed for carrying out the provisions of this Act.
>
> 2) Every person who is unable or refuses to surrender his licence in accordance with subsection 1 shall, when requested by a constable, give reasonable identification of himself and, for the purposes of this subsection, the correct name and address of such person shall be deemed to be reasonable identification.

23 *Dedman*, above note 3 at para 62.

> is clear from the following findings of fact: "Although police officers ask for valid driver's licences, they only do so to initiate conversation or contact to detect the drinking driver that they may not otherwise be able to detect" and "The only reason he was stopped was as part of the R.I.D.E. programme." I am, therefore, of the opinion that s. 14 of *The Highway Traffic Act* did not provide statutory authority for the signal to stop in the present case.[24]

Several significant findings appear in the above passage, at least some of which are now of doubtful validity. First, Le Dain J, for the majority, suggests that it is not appropriate to find by implication a power not expressly provided for in the statutory language. As we will see, the Court later does exactly that in *R v Orbanski; R v Elias*.[25] Next, it is suggested that a power must be used for the purpose there stated, in this circumstance, to ask for the driver's licence, and not for another purpose, such as discovering evidence of impaired driving. As will be discussed below, the Supreme Court has held that it is a valid purpose to investigate the sobriety of the driver by way of provincial motor vehicle legislation.[26] As will also be discussed below, while the Court in *Dedman* did go on to employ the common law to create a power to conduct impaired-driving checkstops, it would also in a subsequent decision return to the theme that that power must be used only for that purpose and not to investigate criminal offending generally.[27] We will discuss this common law power further, in Section C below in this chapter.

The Ontario legislature did not sit idly and accept the *Dedman* interpretation of section 14 and soon amended its Act. The issue then returned to the Court in *Hufsky* in 1988.[28] By this time, the legislature had added section 189(a) to the Ontario *Highway Traffic Act*,[29] which provided:

> (1) A police officer, in the lawful execution of his duties and responsibilities, may require the driver of a motor vehicle to stop and the driver of a motor vehicle, when signalled or requested to stop by a police officer who is readily identifiable as such, shall immediately come to a safe stop.
>
> (2) Every person who contravenes subsection (1) is guilty of an offence and on conviction is liable to a fine of not less than $100 and

---

24 *Ibid.*

25 2005 SCC 37 [*Orbanski*].

26 *Hufsky*, above note 4 at para 13, and *Ladouceur*, above note 6 at 1287.

27 *Mellenthin*, above note 5.

28 *Hufsky*, above note 4.

29 RSO 1980, c 198, as amended by the *Highway Traffic Amendment Act, 1981 (No 3)*, SO 1981, c 72, s 2.

> not more than $2,000 or to imprisonment for a term of not more than six months, or to both.

In *Hufsky*, Le Dain J had little difficulty finding the stop, based as it was on this section, to be lawful:

> It [section 189(a)] does not specify that there must be some grounds or cause for stopping a particular driver but on its face leaves the choice of the drivers to be stopped to the discretion of the officer. In carrying out the purposes of the spot check procedure, including the observation of the condition or "sobriety" of the driver, the officer was clearly in the lawful execution of his duties and responsibilities.[30]

We will return to this decision below for its important discussion on arbitrary detention, but for now note that the Court found that a stop conducted for the purposes of checking a driver's sobriety was authorized by the provincial statute, even though no express reference to sobriety or impaired driving appeared in the section. In doing so, it observed that the Crown relied upon the provincial statute and not upon the common law power available since *Dedman*.

This gloss on the statutory language was accepted in the subsequent decision in *Ladouceur*.[31] At issue in *Ladouceur* was a "roving random" stop that did not involve an organized checkstop, such as those the Court had faced in the earlier decisions.[32] Describing the stop at issue as having a broad range of purposes, "to check for sobriety, for licences, insurance and the mechanical fitness of cars," Cory J, for the majority, nonetheless upheld the stop pursuant to section 189(a) as the Court had done in *Hufsky*.[33] The majority rejected the "reading down" of this language that had occurred in the Court of Appeal, holding that there was no need to "qualify it in any way."[34] The Court refused, therefore, to see the section as requiring any kind of "cause" to exercise the stop.

While the Court, in *Mellenthin*,[35] recognized limits on the scope of the police actions that could be taken after the vehicle was stopped, it was later to read such a power expansively when deciding the case of *Orbanski*. There the Court was faced with the issue of the use of "field sobriety checks" in two cases arising from Manitoba. The Manitoba section being relied upon was a general stop provision that made no

---

30 *Hufsky*, above note 4 at para 13.

31 *Ladouceur*, above note 6.

32 *Ibid*.

33 *Ibid* at para 30.

34 *Ibid* at para 63.

35 *Mellenthin*, above note 5.

mention of sobriety checks.[36] The Court saw itself as interpreting the section of the Manitoba *Highway Traffic Act* as well as the overall legislative scheme in place to combat impaired driving, which, of course, included the federal *Criminal Code* provisions relating to breath testing and roadside breath testing. The Court stressed the "operability" of that scheme, which it seemed to assume was similar across the country. That might not have been a safe assumption. Describing the regulation of motor vehicles as affecting a "'liberty' interest in a general sense," the Court said that it "cannot be equated to the ordinary freedom of movement of the individual that constitutes one of the fundamental values of our democratic society. Rather, it is a licensed activity that is subject to regulation and control for the protection of life and property."[37]

The interpretation of the regulatory scheme seems to have moved the Court to read in to the general stop power a statutory power to conduct roadside sobriety tests:

> [I]t is important to recognize that the need for regulation and control is achieved through an interlocking scheme of federal and provincial legislation. The provincial legislative scheme includes driver licensing, vehicle safety and highway traffic rules. At the federal level, the primary interest lies in deterring and punishing the commission of criminal offences involving motor vehicles. Control of drinking and driving is not confined exclusively to the laying of criminal charges after a criminal offence has been committed. Roadside screening techniques contemplated by provincial legislation provide a mechanism for combatting the continuing danger presented by the drinking driver, even if the driver may not ultimately be found to have reached a criminal level of impairment. Examples of such provisions in the Manitoba *Highway Traffic Act* applicable at the roadside include s. 263.1(1), which permits a peace officer to suspend a driver's licence if the officer has reason to believe that the driver's blood alcohol level exceeds 80 milligrams of alcohol in 100 millilitres of blood or if the driver refuses to comply with a demand for a breath or blood sample made under s. 254 of the *Criminal Code*. Hence, although the issues on these appeals arise in the context of criminal trials, their resolution must nonetheless take into account both federal and provincial legislative schemes. The Court must carefully balance the *Charter* rights of motorists against the policy concerns of both Parliament and the provincial legislatures.[38]

36 Manitoba *Highway Traffic Act*, CCSM c H60.
37 *Orbanski*, above note 25 at para 24.
38 *Ibid* at para 27.

So, while stressing that a particular legislative scheme was under consideration, the decision in *Orbanski* was a clear signal from the Court that, at least in the context of impaired driving, the policy of the law can be more important than what the statute actually says.

The ultimate issue the Court was analyzing in *Orbanski* was whether the stop power provided a limit on the right to counsel, thereby satisfying the "prescribed by law" requirement in section 1. Such a limit would have to be found by implication from the legislative scheme in existence at the time of the offence. Relying on its earlier decision in *R v Therens*,[39] the Court said that "a prescribed limit arose in these cases by necessary implication from the operating requirements of the governing provincial and federal legislative provisions."[40] Interestingly, the Manitoba legislature had in fact moved to expressly limit the right to counsel through an amendment to its *Highway Traffic Act*,[41] but that new section did not apply to the cases before the court that had occurred before the amendment came into force. The Court in effect interpreted the general stop power in accord with the new law, which expressly went much further.

---

39 *Therens*, above note 1.

40 *Orbanski*, above note 25 at para 35. It is worth mentioning here that in *Orbanski*, the Court also suggested that the justified limit on the right to counsel was only proportional (as required by s 1 analysis) because the evidence obtained "can only be used as an investigative tool to confirm or reject the officer's suspicion that the driver might be impaired" [para 58] and not as direct evidence to incriminate the driver. Since that time, most courts have held that this limitation on the use of the evidence applies to all evidence obtained during the initial interaction between the police and the driver, including the result of the approved screening device (ASD) test. In Ontario, see *R v Huff*, [1999] OJ No 5153 (SCJ), aff'd [2000] OJ No 3487 (CA), leave to appeal to the SCC refused [2001] 1 SCR xvii, [2000] SCCA No 562; *R v Cresswell*, [2002] OJ No 2492 (CA); and *R v Boothby*, [2001] OJ No 5078 (CA). Some courts in other provinces have adopted *Huff*: *R v Penner*, 2004 ABQB 98; *R v Lieskovsky*, 2004 ABPC 153; *R v Abercrombie*, 2007 ABPC 226; and *R v Ross*, 2009 BCSC 356. On the other hand, the Saskatchewan Court of Appeal has continued to insist that *Orbanski* does not prohibit use of the ASD result or even of statements of the accused when used by the Crown for the limited purpose of testing the credibility of the accused. See *R v Fox*, 2003 SKCA 79; *R v Beston*, 2006 SKCA 131; *R v Doell*, 2007 SKCA 61; and *R v Gunn*, 2010 SKCA 44.

41 Manitoba *Highway Traffic Act*, above note 36, s 76.1(6): "A peace officer is not required to inform a driver or passenger of his or her right to counsel, or to give the driver or passenger the opportunity to consult counsel, before doing anything subsection (4) or (5) authorizes." (Section 76.1(4) permits a peace officer to demand that a driver provide information and driving documents to the officer. It also permits the officer to conduct field sobriety tests or question the driver about their drinking. Section 76.1(5) permits the officer to request relevant information from the passenger of the vehicle.)

Although *Orbanski* is based on the legislation of one province, it seems safe to say that its reasoning is applicable, in one way or another, across the country. In Nova Scotia, for example, the Court of Appeal found a random stop power in *R v MacLennan*.[42] There the court noted that while there was no express stop power, the legislation did provide that the motorist must follow all "directions" given by a police officer.[43] The court had little difficulty in finding that such a general provision provided police in that province with a general power to stop vehicles arbitrarily:

> When this is read in the context of the common law authority of police to control traffic on the highways, other provisions of the *Motor Vehicle Act* and provisions of the *Criminal Code*, and note is taken of long standing customary practices, I am left in no doubt that s. 83(1) authorizes peace officers to require vehicles on the highway to come to a stop in response to an appropriate order, signal or direction.[44]

For some period of time, Newfoundland and Labrador was a holdout on this point, requiring the police to have "articulable cause" to stop a motor vehicle under the provincial stop power.[45] This was a pre-*Orbanski* finding but was still followed after that case.[46] Since that time, however, the provincial Act has been amended, and the law in Newfoundland and Labrador now allows stops without such grounds provided that they are for the purposes set out in the statute.[47]

That raises the important point, however, that although a broad stop power for motor vehicle regulatory purposes exists, that motor vehicle regulatory purpose must be the actual purpose of the police at the time. For example, in *R v Schaeffer*, there was a factual finding at trial that the accused "was not stopped for purposes relating to vehicle or highway traffic safety," so the Saskatchewan Court of Appeal held that the highway traffic provision could not be relied upon to authorize the stopping

42 (1995), 138 NSR (2d) 369 (CA) [*MacLennan*]. See also *R v Cooper*, 2005 NSCA 47, affirming that decision.

43 The *Motor Vehicle Act*, RSNS 1989, c 293, s 83, provided: "It shall be an offence for any person to refuse or fail to comply with any order, signal or direction of any peace officer."

44 *MacLennan*, above note 42 at para 28.

45 *R v Griffin* (1996), 111 CCC (3d) 490 (Nfld CA), leave to appeal to SCC refused [1997] SCCA No 32.

46 *R v Tucker* (2008), 280 Nfld & PEIR 169 at para 17 (Prov Ct).

47 See the Newfoundland and Labrador *Highway Traffic Act*, above note 17, and *Canada v Gibbs* (2014), 354 Nfld & PEIR 146 (NL Prov Ct).

of the vehicle.[48] Similarly, in *R v Mayor*, the Ontario Court of Appeal noted that although random motor vehicle stop powers exist, "the existence of these powers does not automatically make motor vehicle stops lawful" on the grounds that "the police are not free to use these powers for some other purpose."[49] So, for example, an officer who is patrolling a neighbourhood because of concerns about break-ins cannot rely on the "random" motor vehicle stop power to stop a car. Although no standard of reasonable suspicion needs to be met for a checkstop, the purpose of the stop must be of the right sort.[50]

A decision often relied on in this context is the Ontario Court of Appeal decision in *Brown v Durham (Regional Municipality) Police Force*, where it had said:

> The detention authorized by s. 216(1) of the HTA [*Highway Traffic Act*] is circumscribed by its purpose. The detention is limited to the roadside and must be brief, unless other grounds are established for a further detention. The police may require production of the documents which drivers are required to have with them and may detain the vehicle and its occupants while those documents are checked against information available through the computer terminal in the police vehicle. The police may also assess the mechanical fitness of the vehicle, examine equipment for compliance with safety standards and from outside of the vehicle, make a visual examination of the interior to ensure their own safety in the course of the detention: *R. v. Ladouceur*, supra, at 1286-87; *R. v. Mellenthin*, [1992] 3 S.C.R. 615 at 623-24; *R. v. E. (G.A.)* (1992), 77 C.C.C. (3d) 60 (Ont. C.A.). More intrusive examinations or

---

48 *R v Schaeffer*, 2005 SKCA 33 at para 23 [*Schaeffer*]. The (then) Saskatchewan *Highway Traffic Act*, s 40(8), provided:

> A peace officer who:
> (a) is readily identifiable as a peace officer; and
> (b) is in the lawful execution of his or her duties and responsibilities;
> may require the person in charge of or operating a motor vehicle to stop that vehicle.

See also *R v Houben*, 2006 SKCA 129 [*Houben*], as well as *R v Suteau*, 2019 SKCA 115, holding at para 20 that the concern in *Houben* was "that the police not broaden the statutory power to a *general* power of detention for investigatory purposes other than those identified by statute and the case law" [emphasis in original].

49 *R v Mayor*, 2019 ONCA 578 at para 7.

50 See, for example, *R v Gonzales*, 2017 ONCA 543. To similar effect, see *R v Schell*, 2006 SKCA 128; *R v Koma*, 2015 SKCA 92; or *R v Bzezi*, 2022 ONCA 184.

> inquiries directed at matters not relevant to highway safety concerns are not authorized by s. 216(1) of the HTA: *R. v. Mellenthin*, supra.[51]

Significantly, the Ontario court was careful to say that "more intrusive" examinations or inquiries are not authorized by the highway traffic legislation. These further examinations might, of course, be authorized by other powers, such as those operative where the police obtain, during the statutorily authorized stop, reasonable cause to further detain under the authority of *Mann*.

There might be disagreement among members of the various courts of appeal as to the nature of the inquiries that can be undertaken pursuant to the highway traffic stop powers. As we have seen, the Supreme Court added "sobriety" to licensing and registration in *Hufsky* and *Ladouceur*, and, as the Ontario Court of Appeal notes in *Brown*, mechanical fitness would seem to be a valid concern under the provincial stop powers.[52] In *Brown*, the court labels these grounds to be "proper" and differentiates them from "improper" ones. But the basis of the distinction is not clear. It appears that the Saskatchewan Court is of the view that the above-listed purposes are the only proper grounds, while the *Brown* court may view the criteria as more open-ended. It is to be noted that in *Schaeffer* and *Houben*, the courts were dealing with stops that were found *not* to be for highway traffic purposes, while in *Brown*, the court found that the stops were for those purposes as well as other ones.

This raises the question of when and if a non-highway traffic purpose can override or invalidate the proper purposes. According to the Ontario Court of Appeal, this is only where the highway traffic stop is used as a "ruse" for other purposes.[53] That court in *Brown* said:

> I agree with this conclusion as long as the other purposes motivating the stop are not themselves improper. For example, the police are entitled on a s. 216(1) stop to require drivers to produce their licences. That requirement is consistent with the highway safety concerns which underlie the power granted by the section. In addition to ensuring that the driver is properly licensed, the police may wish to identify the driver for other purposes. It may be, as in this case, that the police are interested in knowing the identity of all those who are connected with what they believe to be organized criminal activity. The gathering of police intelligence is well within the ongoing police duty to investigate criminal activity. As long as the additional police purpose is not

51 *Brown v Durham (Regional Municipality) Police Force* (1998), 116 OAC 126 at para 24 [*Brown*].

52 *Ibid*.

53 *Ibid* at para 25.

> improper and does not entail an infringement on the liberty or security of the detained person beyond that contemplated by the purpose animating s. 216(1) of the HTA, I see no reason for declaring that a legitimate police interest beyond highway safety concerns should taint the lawfulness of the stop and detention. As the trial judge pointed out, known criminals should not be more immune from s. 216(1) stops than law abiding citizens who are not known to the police.[54]

There is some difficulty with this approach, which finds a stop not to be invalidated as long as the additional purpose is not "improper." In principle, the police "may act only to the extent that they are empowered to do so by law,"[55] which should mean that a purpose is improper if it is not one of those for which the power was intended. This was the attitude taken by the Court in *Mellenthin*, where the officer inquired of a driver stopped in a checkstop as to what was in a gym bag in the front seat of the vehicle, an inquiry that led to the discovery of cannabis resin. The Court said:

> [T]he subsequent questions pertaining to the gym bag were improper. At the moment the questions were asked, the officer had not even the slightest suspicion that drugs or alcohol were in the vehicle or in the possession of the appellant. The appellant's words, actions and manner of driving did not demonstrate any symptoms of impairment. Check stop programs result in the arbitrary detention of motorists. The programs are justified as a means aimed at reducing the terrible toll of death and injury so often occasioned by impaired drivers or by dangerous vehicles. The primary aim of the program is thus to check for sobriety, licences, ownership, insurance and the mechanical fitness of cars. The police use of check stops should not be extended beyond these aims. Random stop programs must not be turned into a means of conducting either an unfounded general inquisition or an unreasonable search.[56]

The approach in *Brown*, however, does not ask whether there was some authority saying the police could do what they did but rather assumes that the police *can* use a power so long as there is nothing saying they *cannot*. That interpretation of "improper" undermines the notion of limited police power.

In *R v Nolet*, the Supreme Court considered this question and reaffirmed that "it is important not to encourage the establishment of checkstops where a nominally lawful aim is but a plausible facade for

---

54 *Ibid* at para 31. See also *R v Shipley*, 2015 ONCA 914, affirming this conclusion.

55 *Mann*, above note 7 at para 15.

56 *Mellenthin*, above note 5 at para 15.

an unlawful aim."[57] As a practical matter, however, *Nolet* made it more difficult to achieve that goal. The trial judge had found a search of a duffle bag in the cab of a truck to be predominantly for the purpose of pursuing a criminal investigation, and therefore had found it violated the *Charter* for the police to use a regulatory power aimed at driving offences to conduct that search. The Supreme Court rejected the "predominant purpose" approach in this context. They held that police officers were likely to be interested in both criminal and provincial infractions most of the time and that the existence of some purpose outside the regulatory one did not invalidate the search. However, if the only requirement is that driving concerns are among the issues in a police officer's mind at the time of a search or detention, not necessarily the predominant one, then only in very rare circumstances will a random vehicle stop be perceived as a ruse. In fact, the use of such stops will have been extended beyond the original aims.

We have discussed this same point above, in Chapter 2, Section B(2). As noted there, the Saskatchewan Court of Appeal has said that an improper purpose will invalidate a proper purpose where the lawful purpose is but a "plausible façade for an unlawful aim."[58] For now, it is useful to see that the statutory powers must include a lawful purpose that is part of the highway traffic scheme, which would appear to include licensing, registration, mechanical fitness, and the sobriety of the driver.

2) Other Statutory Powers of Detention

a) Screening Demands for Impaired Driving[59]

The *Criminal Code* provisions dealing with testing for alcohol and drugs, and indeed driving offences generally, were amended quite significantly in 2018.[60] The provisions were controversial, with many arguing that the expanded testing powers—specifically, removal of the requirement for reasonable suspicion—would violate the *Charter*. Most important

57 *R v Nolet*, 2010 SCC 24 at para 36 [*Nolet*], quoting *Ladouceur* 2002, below note 58 at para 66. See a further discussion of this decision above in Chapter 2, Section C(1). In the interests of disclosure, note that Glen Luther, one of the authors of this book, was also one of the counsel for Nolet in front of the Supreme Court.

58 *R v Ladouceur*, 2002 SKCA 73 at para 66 [*Ladouceur* 2002]; see also *R v Dhuna*, 2009 ABCA 103.

59 Impaired driving is a particularly complex subject, and more information can be found in a specialist volume such as Joseph K. Kenkel, *Impaired Driving in Canada*, 4th ed (Toronto: LexisNexis Canada, 2015).

60 *An Act to amend the Criminal Code (offences relating to conveyances) and to make consequential amendments to other Acts*, SC 2018, c 21, amending the *Criminal Code*, above note 14.

for our current purposes is that the changes effected relate fundamentally to the search powers in the *Code*, not to the associated powers of detention. There have been section 8 and section 9 challenges to the new provisions in lower courts, which have been unsuccessful. In the case of the search issue, courts have generally concluded that despite the changes, the provisions still do not violate section 8. With regard to section 9 and issues of detention, however, the key point is that courts have generally concluded that nothing has changed. Although the legislation was amended significantly, those changes did nothing relevant to the powers of detention associated with the breath testing. So although the following discussion is based on caselaw which, in large part, rests on provisions that have now been repealed, it can nonetheless still be seen as accurate on the underlying detention issues.

The relevant breath testing provision for many years was section 254(2), which underwent amendment to broaden it before being repealed and replaced by even broader provisions. The earlier and narrower versions of this section were interpreted by the Court in *Therens* and in *Thomsen*. The Court had little difficulty in these cases in holding that a detention occurs when a screening-device demand is made.[61] Notably, this was contrary to its pre-*Charter* decision in *R v Chromiak*.[62] The nature of the demand pursuant to section 254(2), which was upheld under section 9 and deemed to represent a constitutional exercise of police power as a section 1 limit on the right to counsel, was found by the Court to be a detention of brief duration.

At the time of *Thomsen*, the section referred to a "road-side" screening device, and the Court, in finding a section 1 limit on the right to counsel, said that "a limit prescribed by law within the meaning of section 1 may result by implication from the terms of a legislative provision or its operating requirements. It need not be an explicit limitation of a particular right or freedom."[63] The Court proceeded then to find that there was a limit on the right to counsel that arose by implication since the "roadside screening device test is to be administered at roadside, at such time and place as the motorist is stopped, and as quickly as possible, having regard to the outside operating limit of two hours for the breathalyzer test which it may be found to be necessary to administer pursuant to section 235(1) of the *Code*."[64]

After *Thomsen*, the section was amended as Parliament authorized the screening device to be administered to airplane pilots and to operators of

61 *Therens*, above note 1; *Thomsen*, above note 1.

62 [1980] 1 SCR 471 [*Chromiak*].

63 *Thomsen*, above note 1 at para 15.

64 *Ibid* at para 19. Note that s 235 has also now been replaced.

watercraft, and thus the word "road-side" was removed. Nonetheless, in *R v Grant* (1991),[65] the Court found that the implicit limit on the right to counsel remained, finding no intention on the part of Parliament to move away from short detentions for screening purposes. The failure of the police to have the screening device available such that the test might be administered "forthwith" resulted, on the facts, in a failure to administer the test in accord with the section; thus, the right to counsel did indeed arise where the sample was provided some thirty minutes after the demand. Presumably, also, the detention became unlawful.

Later, in *R v Bernshaw*,[66] a divided Court was faced with the suggestion that since the police officer failed to delay the screening test for fifteen minutes to allow for the dissipation of mouth alcohol (which might have provided a false high reading), the result of the test could not form part of the reasonable grounds to demand the later Breathalyzer test. Justice Cory, who formed part of the majority, held,

> [t]his Court has in fact recognized that the ALERT [the screening device in use at the time] test must be administered immediately and that the detention under s. 254(2) is constitutionally justifiable under s. 1 of the *Charter* for the very reason that the detention is of such very brief duration.[67]

To Cory J, a fifteen-minute delay was unnecessary. On the other hand, Sopinka J, whose judgment made up the balance of the majority, held that the word "forthwith" in the section did not mean "immediately" but rather its interpretation required that the particular facts be taken into account and that, where there was an indication of recent drinking, the officer would be acting in accord with the section to delay the test for fifteen minutes to allow the mouth alcohol to dissipate. Therefore, to Sopinka J, the section did in some circumstances authorize a somewhat longer detention. He further held that the right to counsel would be held in abeyance in such circumstances.

Where the detention is not "brief," the Crown and police run into problems on several fronts. Particularly as discussed above in *Grant* (1991), the Court has recognized that where the detention is more than brief, the right to counsel arises.[68] Furthermore, even if the police provide the right to counsel where the demand is delayed, the Court has found the demand or the test to be *not* conducted "forthwith" and therefore presumably the detention to be unlawful. This might be seen most clearly from

---

65 [1991] 3 SCR 139 [*Grant* 1991].

66 [1995] 1 SCR 254.

67 *Ibid* at para 23.

68 *Grant* 1991, above note 65.

the 2005 decision of the Supreme Court in *R v Woods*, where a demand at the police station more than an hour after the stop was held to be coercive (and thus not voluntary nor obtained by consent) and also unlawful.[69] Once the demand and resulting detention become unlawful, the decision in 2009 in *Grant*—which holds that detentions that are unlawful are thus arbitrary—has significant application.[70] The crucial factual finding in such circumstances may be as to when the detention began rather than the question as to whether the sample was provided "forthwith."

As noted at the start, the provisions upon which the above analysis was based have been significantly altered, but the prevailing view among lower courts is that this has made no difference to the detention issues. The most controversial change, for example, was that in some cases police can make a demand for a breath sample even without reasonable suspicion.[71] This has been held to make no difference to the detention issue on the grounds that

> the reasonable suspicion threshold has not been a consideration in the analysis concerning the reasonableness of limiting an individual's rights under s 9 of the *Charter* at the roadside. The relevant considerations have always been the limited use of the roadside screening result, the duration and minimal inconvenience of a roadside stop, the non-intrusive nature of roadside sobriety testing, and the substantial risk posed by impaired drivers: see the discussions regarding detention in *R v Thomsen*, 1988 CanLII 73 (SCC), [1988] 1 SCR 640 [*Thomsen*] at p 652–53 and *R v Orbanski; R v Elias*, 2005 SCC 37 [*Orbanski*] at para 58. The fact that reasonable suspicion has been removed from the MAS [mandatory alcohol screening] regime does not change these factors, which apply with equal measure regardless of whether the police engage in mandatory or suspicion-based alcohol screening.[72]

---

69 *R v Woods*, 2005 SCC 42.

70 *Grant*, above note 11.

71 *Criminal Code*, above note 14, s 320.27(2).

72 *R v Dylan Alexander Pratt*, 2022 ABQB 407 at para 67. The decision also observes at para 69:

> The issue of whether the MAS regime infringes on a person's s 9 *Charter* interests has been considered by other provincial courts in other provinces. In all cases, the Courts have found that the MAS regime did not change the stopping power of the police, which was already upheld in the cases of *Hufsky* and *Ladouceur*. In *R v Blysniuk*, 2020 ONCJ 603 [*Blysniuk*] at paras 14 and 18 and *R v Day*, 2022 MBPC 2 [*Day*] at paras 79–86, the Courts found that, while the MAS regime breached an accused's s 9 *Charter* rights, it was not necessary to re-engage in a s 1 *Charter* analysis because there was no change to the stopping power that already exists for investigating a driver's sobriety. Other courts have found no s 9 *Charter* breach using the same principles: see *R v Morrison*,

b) Customs Detentions

The main area of litigation around stops on less than reasonable grounds and outside the highway traffic context has been that of customs. In an early series of customs cases, the Supreme Court dealt with the "reasonable suspicion" standard in the *Customs Act*. Generally, it is clear that when one is crossing international boundaries, something less than reasonable grounds can justify a stop and a limited detention. In *R v Simmons*,[73] *R v Monney*,[74] and *R v Jacoy*,[75] the Court dealt with *Customs Act* searches. Currently, section 98 of that Act reads:

> **98** (1) An officer may search
> (a) any person who has arrived in Canada, within a reasonable time after his arrival in Canada,
> (b) any person who is about to leave Canada, at any time prior to his departure, or
> (c) any person who has had access to an area designated for use by persons about to leave Canada and who leaves the area but does not leave Canada, within a reasonable time after he leaves the area,
>
> if the officer suspects on reasonable grounds that the person has secreted on or about his person anything in respect of which this Act has been or might be contravened, anything that would afford evidence with respect to a contravention of this Act or any goods the importation or exportation of which is prohibited, controlled or regulated under this or any other Act of Parliament.
>
> (2) An officer who is about to search a person under this section shall, on the request of that person, forthwith take him before the senior officer at the place where the search is to take place.
>
> (3) A senior officer before whom a person is taken pursuant to subsection (2) shall, if he sees no reasonable grounds for the search, discharge the person or, if he believes otherwise, direct that the person be searched.[76]

As a review of the section shows, the legislation contemplates a search where the "officer suspects on reasonable grounds" that the person has secreted on their person "anything that would afford evidence with respect to a contravention of [the *Customs Act*] or any goods the

---

2020 SKPC 28 [*Morrison*] at paras 136–137; *R* v *Kortmeyer*, 2021 SKPC 10 [*Kortmeyer*] at paras 32–35; *R* v *Switenky*, 2020 SKPC 46 [*Switenky*] at paras 77–79; *R* v *Brown*, 2021 NSPC 32 [*Brown*] at para 24.

73 [1988] 2 SCR 495 [*Simmons*].

74 [1999] 1 SCR 652 [*Monney*].

75 [1988] 2 SCR 548.

76 *Customs Act*, above note 21.

importation or exportation of which is prohibited, controlled or regulated under this or any other Act of Parliament." The detention aspect of this provision is presumably the length of time the detention takes the person away from their normal travel process and includes the time it takes to search the person. The statutory limit requires only "suspicion on reasonable grounds" before the person can be detained and subsequently searched. In fact, the Court authorizes a random albeit brief "detention" (and search) of all travellers, although the source of such power is unclear. The Court seems to be of the view that such "detentions," being very brief, do not raise *Charter* concerns. Also, the statute requires that any search must be conducted within a "reasonable time," which again seems to limit the detention. In *Monney*, the Court read this latter requirement in context when it held that a "passive bedpan vigil" of two hours was reasonable.[77]

The Court found in *Monney* that "border crossings represent a unique factual circumstance for the purposes of a s. 8 analysis,"[78] reasoning that presumably also applies to section 9. In the border-crossing context, "[n]ational self-protection becomes a compelling component in the calculus,"[79] according to the Court. The majority judgment in *Simmons*, written by Dickson CJC, held that there are three kinds of interactions with travellers in the customs context:

> It is, I think, of importance that the cases and the literature seem to recognize three distinct types of border search. First is the routine of questioning which every traveller undergoes at a port of entry, accompanied

---

77 *Monney*, above note 74 at para 53, where the Court said:

> On the question of whether the customs officers conducted the search within a reasonable time after the respondent's arrival in Canada, I agree with Weiler J.A.'s conclusion that the assessment of "reasonableness" must take into account not only any delay in the search process, but also the inherent time requirements of the particular search technique. Based on the evidence at trial, a delay of 30 minutes from the time a person is detained until the search begins is reasonable. In this case, however, the customs enforcement officers did not arrive until nearly two hours after the respondent was detained. As Weiler J.A. noted, however, while a delay at any point in the search process is an important consideration, it cannot be examined in isolation. Given the fact that a passive "bedpan vigil" is an inherently time-consuming process, I am of the opinion that the delayed response by the customs enforcement officers of one-and-a-half hours is not sufficient to establish that the search of the respondent was not conducted "within a reasonable time after his arrival in Canada" as required by s. 98(1) of the *Customs Act*.

78 *Ibid* at para 42.

79 *Simmons*, above note 73 at para 48, Dickson J, cited with approval in *R v Jacques*, [1996] 3 SCR 312 at para 18, Gonthier J, and in *Monney*, above note 74 at para 42.

> in some cases by a search of baggage and perhaps a pat or frisk of outer clothing. No stigma is attached to being one of the thousands of travellers who are daily routinely checked in that manner upon entry to Canada and no constitutional issues are raised. It would be absurd to suggest that a person in such circumstances is detained in a constitutional sense and therefore entitled to be advised of his or her right to counsel. The second type of border search is the strip or skin search of the nature of that to which the present appellant was subjected, conducted in a private room, after a secondary examination and with the permission of a customs officer in authority. The third and most highly intrusive type of search is that sometimes referred to as the body cavity search, in which customs officers have recourse to medical doctors, to X-rays, to emetics, and to other highly invasive means.
>
> I wish to make it clear that each of the different types of search raises different issues. We are here concerned with searches of the second type and what I have to say relates only to that type of search. Searches of the third or bodily cavity type may raise entirely different constitutional issues for it is obvious that the greater the intrusion, the greater must be the justification and the greater the degree of constitutional protection.[80]

One can see, therefore, that the majority was of the view that the first category of search allows individuals to be questioned and even searched without, according to the majority, raising a constitutional issue.

This conclusion ought to be reconsidered. In the specific context of section 8 and searches of electronic personal devices, it has been, but that reconsideration should be undertaken more generally.[81] The decision in *Simmons* is primarily about searches and the right to counsel but discusses detention in that context. The decision predates the Supreme Court jurisprudence on sections 8 and 9, which developed the framework for analyzing those rights; specifically, it was decided before it had become clear that each of those rights involves a two-step process. In the case of searches, those two steps are, first, was there a search (that is, did the accused have a reasonable expectation of privacy) and then, second, was the search reasonable. The parallel approach to section 9 asks first whether there was a detention and then whether that detention was arbitrary.

Simmons does not clearly distinguish between those two steps in the case of either right because those distinctions had not yet been clearly drawn. As a result, however, some courts treat *Simmons* as though it

80 *Simmons*, above note 73 at paras 27–28.

81 See *R v Canfield*, 2020 ABCA 383.

found that the threshold steps were not satisfied: that a person who is patted down, or is examined by a sniffer dog, is neither searched nor detained, for example.[82] It is not that nothing in the language of *Simmons* can be found to support such a reading, but to read it that way is to ignore the historical development of the rights. Subsequent caselaw on sections 8 and 9 makes it clear that the more appropriate reading of *Simmons* is that the search and detention that occurred were not unreasonable or arbitrary. To treat the cases as being about the first step when they are better understood as being about the second risks skipping the important analysis.

After the Supreme Court judgments on section 9 in *Clayton*[83] and *Grant*,[84] the lawfulness of state action is essential to the constitutionality of that action. As we have seen, section 98 of the *Customs Act* requires the officer to have at least reasonable grounds to suspect that a relevant offence is being committed.[85] If there are no such grounds, the resulting illegal search might support an argument based on sections 8 and 9 of the *Charter*. Furthermore, the proper *Charter* analysis now calls for assessment of whether the underlying law itself is unreasonable or arbitrary. The better approach, therefore, would be to not simply rely on *Simmons* but to graft onto it the full section 8 and 9 analytical frameworks.[86]

We will return to these cases in Chapter 5 in an analysis of arbitrary detention and the right to counsel, but here it is also worth mentioning that the majority in *Simmons* did find that individuals whose detentions fall within the second or third category are detained and therefore entitled to their right to counsel, even though they did admit the evidence in the given circumstance.

c) Wildlife Enforcement Detentions

Another area of statutory random stops that has been litigated in some provinces has been that of Wildlife Acts. In particular, Saskatchewan has been active in amending its *Wildlife Act* to authorize the random stopping of vehicles for the purpose of enforcing hunting and fishing regulations. The original legislation in that province read as follows:

> **49.2** (1) Where due to the circumstances, the time or the location there could reasonably be expected to be a high incidence of offences against this Act or the regulations in any area, a wildlife officer may request or

---

82 See, for example, *R v Jackman*, 2016 ONCA 121.

83 *Clayton*, above note 8.

84 *Grant*, above note 11.

85 *Customs Act*, above note 21.

86 See, for example, *R v Nagle*, 2012 BCCA 373.

> signal to the person in charge of or operating a vehicle or boat in the area to stop the vehicle or boat and may search it for evidence of an offence against this Act or the regulations and seize anything that may be evidence of such an offence.
>
> (2) The person in charge of or operating a vehicle or boat shall, upon being requested to do so by a wildlife officer pursuant to subsection (1), immediately bring the vehicle or boat to a safe stop, and the operator of the vehicle or boat shall, upon request, permit the wildlife officer to search the vehicle or boat.[87]

In *R v Denys*, the Saskatchewan Court of Appeal threw the constitutional validity of this section into some doubt when it said:

> Since, in empowering wildlife officers to take action of this nature, the subsection does not expressly require the existence of reasonable and probable grounds to believe an offence has been or is being committed, it is constitutionally suspect, as are the actions of wildlife officers taken in exercise of the powers conferred by the subsection.[88]

The court noted that the section of the Act might be saved by section 1 of the *Charter*, although the justices did not find it necessary to make that decision on the case there presented. In a subsequent judgment, a provincial court judge did rule that a very similarly worded provision in the Saskatchewan *Fisheries Act*[89] was unconstitutional.[90] In analyzing whether such random stops could be "saved" under section 1, the trial judge noted the

> fact that the initial stop and the checks made were of the travelling public at random, that is, they were not made regarding persons engaged, or apparently engaged, in the regulated activity being monitored. This is a substantial and crucial difference between this case and those involving traffic stops for the purpose of monitoring driver's licences, vehicle registrations, the condition of drivers, etc.[91]

The judge also noted that the evidence before him showed that

> [o]verall, from 1993 to the present, 3971 vehicles were stopped on the highway. Ninety charges were laid for what could be called the primary purpose of the process, the conservation of the fishery by prevention of overfishing. That is a ratio of about 2.26 per cent of substantive charges

87 *The Wildlife Act*, RSS 1978, c W-13.1.

88 *R v Denys* (1995), 131 Sask R 251 at para 28.

89 *The Fisheries Act (Saskatchewan), 1994*, SS 1994, c F-16.1, s 24.

90 *R v Stengler*, [2004] 3 WWR 739 (Sask Prov Ct) [*Stengler*].

91 *Ibid* at para 31.

to vehicles stopped and checked. Putting it another way, about 98 vehicles with no violations were stopped to discover 2 vehicles with a violation. The number of people involved is, of course, substantially higher.[92]

The Crown did not appeal the decision in *Stengler*, and the provincial government amended its *Wildlife Act* to remove the requirement in the stop power that required the stops to be in locations where there "could reasonably be expected to be a high incidence of offences against this Act or the regulations."[93] The current section, enacted in 2007, therefore allows random stopping of any vehicles for the purpose of enforcing the Act and does not seem to require any grounds for doing so.[94] The section would seem to be constitutionally invalid as allowing an arbitrary detention based on the above authorities.[95] Only section 1 could save its constitutional validity, as occurred in *Ladouceur*[96] and *Hufsky*[97] with motor vehicle stops.

The British Columbia Court of Appeal in *R v Rice*[98] dealt with a similarly worded statute in that province. The court did not analyze the stop power but did hold that statutory-compelled statements under the same legislation were admissible given that the offences being investigated were not criminal in nature and that hunters voluntarily enter into the activity and thereby agree to the statutory compulsion that the statute requires. While it appears that in *Rice* the accused did not challenge the stop power and thus it was not at issue, there is, as was found in *Stengler*, a significant difference between a hunter who agrees to the regime set out

---

92 *Ibid* at para 32.

93 *The Wildlife Act*, above note 87.

94 *The Wildlife Act, 1998*, SS 1998, c W-13.12, as amended. See, for example, *R v Schmidt*, 2014 SKPC 106, concluding that the accompanying search power in s 59 of the Act does not require any reasonable grounds. Similarly, see *R v Jones*, 2016 ABPC 168, concluding that s 22(1) of the *Fisheries (Alberta) Act*, RSA 2000, c F-16, permits stops without any requirement for reasonable grounds or any criteria and therefore (at para 45) that "any stop predicated upon its authority as is the case in this instance is arbitrary unless the section is saved by s 1 of the *Charter*." The decision does not carry on to consider s 1 but does conclude that the stop in the case violated s 9. The decision has not prompted any legislative change.

95 This issue has seemingly not arisen relating to arbitrary detention in other provinces, although similar issues have arisen in the context of the right to silence and the right to counsel in the context of wildlife investigations. See, for example, *R v Douglas*, 2002 BCPC 666; *R v Taylor*, 2001 BCPC 67; *R v Meise*, [1994] BCJ No 876 (SC); *R v Calder*, [1988] NSJ No 230 (Co Ct); *R v Lowe*, [2007] NJ No 456 (Prov Ct); *R v Sosnich*, 2003 ABPC 96; and for Saskatchewan, see *R v Rutley*, 2004 SKPC 44.

96 *Ladouceur*, above note 6.

97 *Hufsky*, above note 4.

98 2009 BCCA 569.

for hunting regulation and a driver, not being a hunter, who does not. In other words, the stop power seemingly applies to all drivers, while the statutory compulsion seems to apply only to hunters who have undertaken the regulated activity in question. If the Court of Appeal is correct in *Rice* about the admissibility of the compelled statements, which is not at issue here, the stop in question remains constitutionally suspect.[99]

C. COMMON LAW POWERS OF DETENTION

1) Introduction

For a long time, there was a phrase in law enforcement parlance that the law ignored. In various contexts, police were often heard to say that a given individual was a "person of interest" in their investigation. Until about 2000, the law had steadfastly been of the view that a citizen on the street had "the right to be let alone" and that, unless the police had reasonable and probable grounds to arrest an individual, they had no power to stop, question, or search that person unless and until the individual voluntarily agreed to stop and be questioned.

On the other hand, although the police, as a matter of law, had no authority to conduct such detentions, this did not mean that the police did not, as a matter of fact, conduct such detentions. In an influential 1991 article, Professor Alan Young argued:

> It is naive to believe that the state will restrict itself only to such non-invasive investigative procedures until such time as it acquires the requisite grounds to effect a proper arrest. Of necessity, the state will employ liberty-restraining practices of low visibility that manage to escape public and judicial scrutiny. In particular, the practice of brief investigative detention is carried out on a daily basis with little or no accountability. The police power to restrain liberty when the requisite grounds to effect an arrest are lacking is not a power that is recognized or accepted in the common law world; however, investigative detention is part and parcel of the routine activities of all police forces.[100]

---

99 On this point, see *R v Sidhu and Sweeney*, 2018 BCPC 124, which found that there would be a reduced expectation of privacy and an expectation of more intrusive enforcement in a regulated activity and therefore (at para 13) that "the stop and detention of travelers along these roads for the purpose of motor vehicle compliance or firearms inspection is less likely to be arbitrary pursuant to s. 9 of the *Charter*."

100 Alan Young, "All Along the Watchtower: Arbitrary Detention and the Police Function" (1991) 29 *Osgoode Hall Law Journal* 329.

The realization that such steps were a routine practice for police in Canada prompted Canadian courts to focus their attention on the issue. It was the Ontario Court of Appeal that first acknowledged a power to conduct a "brief investigatory detention." In *R v Simpson*,[101] that court saw a need for the common law to recognize such a power, short of arrest, a power the US Supreme Court had recognized in its 1963 decision in *Terry v Ohio*[102] (which became known south of the border as the "stop and frisk" power).

Ten years after *Simpson*, the Supreme Court of Canada decided in *Mann* that it was time to begin to regulate an activity that the law had for too long ignored. One possibility open to them, in the face of police acting in the absence of any power, was to find the practice in violation of the *Charter* and put a stop to it. In fact, the Court took the opposite approach and created a power authorizing what the police were doing. This was an area of law that developed rapidly. The accepted view at one point had been that "a police officer has no right to detain a person for questioning or for further investigation."[103] In *Mann*, the Court created a limited power of investigation in the particular context of that case but stressed that it was not creating a general power of detention for investigative purposes.[104] Only three years later, in *Clayton*, the Court then created exactly that general power of detention.[105] The Court in *Clayton* did not describe itself as creating a general power, but in *Aucoin*, that is how the Court characterized its own previous decision:

> The existence of a general common law power to detain where it is reasonably necessary in the totality of the circumstances was settled in *R. v. Clayton*, 2007 SCC 32, [2007] 2 S.C.R. 725. That case moved our jurisprudence from debating the existence of such a power to considering whether its exercise was reasonably necessary in the circumstances of a particular case.[106]

This relatively rapid evolution in the common law came about through the Court's application of the *Waterfield* test.[107] This major step in the creation of police powers was seemingly taken on the basis that

101 (1993), 12 OR (3d) 182 [*Simpson*].

102 392 US 1 (1968).

103 *R v Dedman* (1981), 23 CR (3d) 228 at para 22 (Ont CA), Martin JA. *Dedman* was appealed to the Supreme Court of Canada (*Dedman*, above note 3), which is when the Court's use of the *Waterfield* test to create new common law powers began: see Chapter 2, Section A(3).

104 *Mann*, above note 7 at para 17.

105 *Clayton*, above note 8.

106 *Aucoin*, above note 9 at para 36.

107 See the discussion in Chapter 2, Section A(3).

police were widely exercising powers that Parliament had not given them and therefore, with a sort of reverse logic, that the Court needed to authorize these actions that were occurring with or without parliamentary approval. The clearest way to understand this development is to consider those three cases individually and then turn to discuss the outstanding ambiguities.

2) Common Law Power of Investigative Detention: *R v Mann*

In *Mann*, two police officers received a radio dispatch about a break and enter in progress. They were given a description of the suspect, including his approximate height, weight, and age; his name; and a description of his clothing; he was also identified as Aboriginal. As the officers approached the scene of the reported crime, they observed the accused walking casually away. They stopped him and asked him to identify himself, in response to which he gave his name and date of birth. The officers then performed a pat-down search of his person. The accused was not connected with the break and enter, but in the course of the pat-down search, one officer felt a soft object in his pocket and reached inside. The accused was found to be in possession of narcotics and was arrested for that offence. He argued that there had been a violation of his *Charter* rights—specifically, that the police had violated his section 9 right to be free from arbitrary detention by stopping him without any power to do so and his section 8 right to be protected against arbitrary search and seizure.

Justice Frank Iacobucci, for the majority, suggested that the Court should not "recognize a general power of detention for investigative purposes"; instead, its "duty is to lay down the common law governing police powers of investigative detention in the particular context of this case."[108] Nonetheless, the majority did indeed go on to recognize that these officers had the power to detain Mann in the circumstances.[109] As noted above, the majority seemed to be of the view that the common law had an obligation to regulate this area; they noted that "the unregulated use of investigative detentions in policing, their uncertain legal status, and the potential for abuse inherent in such low-visibility exercises of discretionary power are all pressing reasons why the Court must exercise its custodial role."[110] The majority effectively presupposes the existence of a power to detain in appropriate circumstances; the major part of the

108 *Mann*, above note 7 at para 17.

109 *Ibid*.

110 *Ibid* at para 18.

judgment is focused on the extent and limits of the power in question. Justice Iacobucci says:

> Police powers and police duties are not necessarily correlative. While the police have a common law duty to investigate crime, they are not empowered to undertake any and all action in the exercise of that duty. Individual liberty interests are fundamental to the Canadian constitutional order. Consequently, any intrusion upon them must not be taken lightly and, as a result, police officers do not have *carte blanche* to detain. The power to detain cannot be exercised on the basis of a hunch, nor can it become a *de facto* arrest.[111]

The Court acknowledged the American approach and the Ontario Court of Appeal's decision in *Simpson* that adopted "articulable cause" as a standard less than the reasonable grounds needed for an arrest. On the other hand, the majority in *Mann* was not satisfied either with the phrase "articulable cause" or with its common synonym, "reasonable suspicion," but rather was of the view that a better formulation would be "reasonable grounds to detain":

> The caselaw raises several guiding principles governing the use of a police power to detain for investigative purposes. The evolution of the *Waterfield* test, along with the *Simpson* articulable cause requirement, calls for investigative detentions to be premised upon reasonable grounds. The detention must be viewed as reasonably necessary on an objective view of the totality of the circumstances, informing the officer's suspicion that there is a clear nexus between the individual to be detained and a recent or on-going criminal offence. Reasonable grounds figures at the front-end of such an assessment, underlying the officer's reasonable suspicion that the particular individual is implicated in the criminal activity under investigation. The overall reasonableness of the decision to detain, however, must further be assessed against all of the circumstances, most notably the extent to which the interference with individual liberty is necessary to perform the officer's duty, the liberty interfered with, and the nature and extent of that interference, in order to meet the second prong of the *Waterfield* test.[112]

It is necessary to "unpack" the above quotation to determine what the Court was trying to say. By using the phrase "reasonable grounds to detain," the majority seemed to want to stress the stringency of the standard that they intend to employ. On the other hand, they acknowledge that the standard in question is less than reasonable grounds to believe

111 *Ibid* at para 35.
112 *Ibid* at para 34.

and indeed can be seen as a standard of suspicion. We will discuss this requirement in Section C(2)(a) below. Furthermore, the majority says that the suspicion must be of a recent or ongoing criminal offence. This requirement ought to operate to help keep the power confined within some limits, a point that is discussed in Section C(2)(b) below. Lastly, the majority states that the detention must, in all circumstances, be "reasonably necessary" to the performance of the officer's duty. This latter requirement seems to require an objective assessment that the detention in the circumstances was justifiable as a limit on the suspect's right to be let alone. This will be discussed in Section C(2)(c), below. The Court in *Mann* also observed that investigative detentions "must be of brief duration," and that point will be pursued in Section C(2)d).[113]

a) *Mann*: The Reasonable Suspicion Standard

As noted above, the Court in *Mann* adopted the phrase "reasonable grounds to detain" as the appropriate standard for an investigative detention, although the term was not meant to set a different standard from "articulable cause."[114] It appears that this language was chosen to stress that a multi-factorial approach is necessary to make the decision. In *Mann* itself, Deschamps J in dissent expressed reservations about this terminology, arguing that it was likely to create confusion with the higher standard of "reasonable grounds to believe" for arrest.[115] A decade later in *R v MacKenzie*, Moldaver J suggested that this phrasing "has led to some confusion for the bench and bar alike."[116] As discussed in Chapter 2, Section C(3), in practice, the phrases "reasonable grounds to suspect" and "reasonable suspicion" are commonly used and capture the same standard. More recently, in *R v Stairs*, the Court has used the term "reason to suspect" as a shorthand for reasonable suspicion.[117]

As noted in Chapter 2, reasonable suspicion shares many characteristics with reasonable grounds to believe. It requires both a subjective and an objective test;[118] it must be based on the totality of the circumstances; and it must be more than a hunch—and, indeed, more than generalized

113 *Ibid* at para 22.

114 *Ibid* at para 33.

115 *Ibid* at paras 62–64.

116 *R v MacKenzie*, 2013 SCC 50 at para 38 [*MacKenzie*].

117 *R v Stairs*, 2022 SCC 11 [*Stairs*].

118 *R v Reddy*, 2010 BCCA 11 at para 67 [*Reddy*]:

> As is the case with the power of arrest, an officer invoking the power of investigative detention must subjectively believe that the requisite standard has been met, and the officer's belief must be objectively reasonable.

See also *Mann*, above note 7 at para 27.

suspicion—although unlike reasonable grounds to believe, the level of certainty required is only that of reasonable *possibility*, not *probability*.[119] As Binnie J held in *R v Kang-Brown*:

> The "reasonable suspicion" standard is not a new juridical standard called into existence for the purposes of this case. "Suspicion" is an expectation that the targeted individual is possibly engaged in some criminal activity. A "reasonable" suspicion means something more than a mere suspicion and something less than a belief based upon reasonable and probable grounds.[120]

Whether the reasonable suspicion standard is met in any given case depends on the constellation of factors present. See Chapter 2, Section C(3)(b), for further discussion of the standard and Appendix II, which sets out important decisions on the issue.

However, reasonable suspicion alone is not sufficient to allow a valid *Mann* detention. The majority held that the suspicion must be that the accused has a "nexus" to a recent or ongoing criminal offence and that the detention must be "reasonably necessary" in the circumstances. As a result, one needs to be cautious about relying on investigative detention cases that predate *Mann*. Furthermore, cases on reasonable suspicion from other contexts, such as the sniffer-dog cases[121] and those cases involving assessment of the grounds under former section 254 of the *Criminal Code* relating to roadside breath testing, are not directly applicable. Although the same *standard* of reasonable suspicion will be applied in each, it will be applied to different considerations.[122] As the Court notes in *R v Chehil*, there must be a nexus between the criminal conduct suspected and the investigative technique employed, whether that is a detention (as in *Mann*) or the use of a sniffer dog.[123]

---

119 *R v Chehil*, 2013 SCC 49 at para 27 [*Chehil*].

120 *R v Kang-Brown*, 2008 SCC 18 at para 75 [*Kang-Brown*].

121 *Ibid* and *R v AM*, 2008 SCC 19.

122 See *MacKenzie*, above note 116 at para 36:

> It is important that the detention and search issues in this case be kept analytically distinct because they stem from different police powers and must respect different *Charter* rights (*R. v. Yeh*, 2009 SKCA 112, 337 Sask. R. 1, at paras. 48–49; *R. v. Schrenk*, 2010 MBCA 38, 255 Man. R. (2d) 12, at para. 105). We have never suggested that a sniffer-dog search is authorized as a search incidental to a detention. On the contrary, the detention and the sniff must be independently justified, even if both are based on the same underlying facts that led police to reasonably suspect that the appellant was involved in a drug-related offence.

123 *Chehil*, above note 119 at para 36.

b) *Mann*: The Nexus Issue

The significance of the nexus issue should not be understated as it is a key way in which *Mann* changed the approach to investigative detention that had developed under *Simpson*. Specifically, the power in *Simpson* did not require that the police detain someone to investigate a particular offence; as a result, the power was frequently used simply to investigate general suspicions of criminality.[124] In effect, pre-*Mann*, police sometimes stopped a person on the relatively vague basis that it looked as if they were "up to something"; post-*Mann*, the requirement became that a specific crime was under investigation, and the police reasonably suspected that there was a nexus between this person and that crime. In the immediate aftermath of *Mann*, not all courts were careful to observe this requirement, perhaps because it was not immediately apparent to all that *Mann* had not simply just affirmed the approach in *Simpson*.[125] The Court has remained consistent on this point—for example, in *R v Le*, where no investigative detention power allowed police to enter a backyard because "there was no nexus between the address and any recent or ongoing complaint about trespassing."[126] Similarly, the Court has consistently been unwilling to authorize police action on a "generalized suspicion" standard.[127] Courts now are normally careful to identify the particular offence to which there is a nexus[128] or to find that a detention does not fall within the *Mann* power when that cannot be done.[129]

---

124 See the discussion in Eric V. Gottardi, "*R. v. Mann*: Regulating State Intrusions in the Context of Investigative Detentions" (2004) 21 *Criminal Reports* (6th) 27.

125 See, for example, *R v Byfield* (2005), 74 OR (3d) 206 (CA), or *R v Chaisson*, 2005 NLCA 55, rev'd on other grounds 2006 SCC 11. See also Christina Skibinsky, "Regulating *Mann* in Canada" (2006) 69 *Saskatchewan Law Review* 197.

126 *R v Le*, 2019 SCC 34 at 131 [*Le*].

127 See *Kang-Brown*, above note 120, where one of the few things that is clear from the four-way split is that eight of nine judges reject generalized suspicion as a standard authorizing sniffer-dog searches. See also *Chehil*, above note 119 at para 30, and *MacKenzie*, above note 116, rejecting that standard. See as well *Stairs*, above note 117, where the majority and dissent disagree over whether the reasonable suspicion standard as opposed to mere generalized suspicion was met but agree that generalized suspicion would be insufficient.

128 See, for example, *R v Chaif-Gust*, 2011 BCCA 528 [*Chaif-Gust*] (reasonable suspicion that the accused was connected to a marijuana grow operation); *R v Richards*, 2015 ONCA 348 (reasonable suspicion that the accused was trafficking in cocaine); *R v McGuffie*, 2016 ONCA 365 [*McGuffie*] (reasonable suspicion that the accused was in possession of a handgun); or *R v Manning*, 2019 NLCA 46 [*Manning*] (reasonable suspicion that the accused had committed assault).

129 See, for example, *R v Hebrada-Walters*, 2013 SKCA 24 [*Hebrada-Walters*].

Nonetheless, the error of failing to identify a particular offence does sometimes still arise.[130]

It is clear that the distinction between being suspicious in general terms of a person and being suspicious that the person is involved in "particular" criminal activity, as set out in *Mann* and restated in *MacKenzie*,[131] is meant to be important. It must be noted, therefore, that there are two separate ways in which some courts of appeal, at least, have somewhat weakened that standard.

Recall the facts of *Mann*: the police received a report of a break and enter in progress and found Mann, a person matching the description of the suspect, in the vicinity. These facts gave *reasonable suspicion* that Mann was connected to the crime, but the police had *reasonable grounds to believe* an offence had occurred. One could see that as the standard set by *Mann*: that there must be reasonable belief that there was an offence, but the police need only have a reasonable suspicion that the detainee was involved. That was explicitly the view of some courts immediately post-*Mann*. For example, the Saskatchewan Court of Appeal held in *R v Bramley* that "because the detentions of the respondents were conducted in relation to a *suspected* rather than a *known* offence, I shall take those detentions as having violated the respondents' rights as guaranteed by s. 9 of the *Charter*."[132]

To say instead that there need only be reasonable *suspicion* that an offence has occurred would therefore be to water down the *Mann* standard, but some courts have explicitly done exactly that. The Saskatchewan Court of Appeal, for example, reconsidered its decision from *R v Bramley*, reaching the opposite conclusion in *R v Yeh*.[133] The majority there concluded that *Mann* allows detentions where an offence is reasonably suspected as opposed to being known, which is a significant difference. As that same court has noted elsewhere:

> [T]here is a significant distinction between the test of objectively reasonable and probable grounds to believe that a crime has been

130 See *R v Wilkinson*, 2023 BCCA 3, where the trial judge had analyzed a detention by looking at whether there was a particular crime under investigation, but the British Columbia Court of Appeal found that that was unnecessary. They did so by relying exclusively on *Chehil*, above note 119, apparently not recognizing that what they were relying on simply explains what the reasonable suspicion standard is in all the various contexts in which it occurs, as opposed to setting out the criteria for some particular detention power, as *Mann* does. See the discussion in Steve Coughlan, "*Wilkinson*: Reasonable Suspicion, But About What?" (2023) 86 *Criminal Reports* 7th 348.

131 *MacKenzie*, above note 116 at para 35.

132 *R v Bramley*, 2009 SKCA 49 at para 32.

133 2009 SKCA 112 [*Yeh*].

> committed and the test of objectively reasonable suspicion that a crime is being or has been committed. The former requires that the factors relied upon have enough probative value to establish the probability that the suspect is implicated in criminal activity. . . . [T]he lower standard does not require that the officers be able to point to factors sufficient to establish the probability of the crime. Reasonable suspicion is a lower standard and can be established by less evidence, with less probative value, than reasonable and probable cause.[134]

The minority judgment in *Yeh* was decidedly of the view that the majority had expanded the reach of *Mann* beyond what was required or desirable. Interestingly, both the majority and the dissent use hypothetical situations to try to make their points. The majority speak of an individual in the early-morning hours putting a television in a car trunk when a police officer arrives on the scene. The majority use the example to suggest that the police must be able to inquire about the ownership of the television even though they do not "know" whether an offence has been committed by the television-toting individual.

In the view of the minority, the issue is not whether a crime is "known" or "suspected." To require that crimes be "known" would set too high a standard, but allowing a power based on reasonable suspicion would give police too much discretion. The power of investigative detention was meant to fill a gap when police were investigating crime (as in the majority's example) but fell short of having an arrest power. An arrest power in that scenario would rest on the "finds committing" power in section 495(1)(b) of the *Criminal Code*. The investigative detention power should therefore be based on reported crime (as in *Mann*) or on the observations of the officers themselves:

> For example, if an officer sees a woman lying on the ground crying and, seconds later, sees a man fleeing with a woman's handbag, it is probable that a trial judge would conclude that investigative detention was necessary to determine whether the detained person is linked to the recent, specific crime of theft. The arrest power under s. 495(1)(b) of the *Criminal Code* would not be available because the individual is not found committing or apparently committing an offence. An investigative detention power may be necessary, in such circumstances, to permit the police to determine whether the individual is linked to the recent crime of theft in the same way as with a reported crime. In such a case, the police need not wait for a crime to be reported if they observe, smell or hear something that causes them to believe that a particular

134 *R v Savage*, 2011 SKCA 65 at para 18.

crime has recently been committed or is being committed—assuming, of course, that the balance of the *Mann* criteria are satisfied.[135]

The *Yeh* approach has been explicitly adopted in some cases.[136] More generally, it appears to have been implicitly adopted by most courts. Generally, judges seem not to specifically turn their minds to the distinction between whether the offence occurred and whether there is a nexus to the detainee. Rather, most cases simply pose the question as to whether there was "reasonable suspicion of criminal activity" or "reasonable suspicion supporting an investigative detention," which collapses the two issues into one.[137]

Furthermore, in a great number of investigative detention cases, the police are not responding to a report of an offence by someone else but are acting based on their own observations. For example, a very common situation is for the police to make a routine traffic stop (which requires no grounds) and for the question to become whether the observations of the officers during that stop were sufficient to justify a further investigative detention, typically related to narcotics.[138] In such cases, where there is nothing but the observations of the officer to take into account, exactly the same evidence must be used to establish both the existence of an offence and the accused's nexus to it, so—whether or not they explicitly say that they have adopted the *Yeh* approach—courts must be applying the reasonable suspicion standard to both questions.[139]

The second way in which the "particular criminal activity" requirement has arguably been relaxed relates to how specific a requirement the word "particular" imposes. In *R v Nesbeth*, the police were in an apartment building and saw the accused entering a stairwell. When the police officer asked Nesbeth what he was doing, he ran away. The officer yelled "stop, police," but Nesbeth continued to run and actively attempted to impede the police in their attempt to catch him. The court held that the

135 *Yeh*, above note 133 at para 123.

136 See *R v Schrenk*, 2010 MBCA 38 [*Schrenk*].

137 See, for example, *MacKenzie*, above note 116 at para 38: "In the context of detention, "reasonable grounds" means reasonable grounds *to suspect* that an individual is involved in a particular criminal activity, which is synonymous with reasonable suspicion." [Emphasis in original.]

138 See, for example, *MacKenzie*, *ibid*. For other instances, see *R v Mooiman and Zahar*, 2016 SKCA 43; *R v Herritt*, 2015 NBCA 33; *R v MacCannell*, 2014 BCCA 254; or *R v Nartey*, 2013 ONCA 215.

139 See, for example, *R v By*, 2015 SKQB 86, where the judge noted at para 46 about the particular case: "[T]he issue is not whether there were discernible facts which demonstrated a sufficient nexus between Mr. By and that suspected crime. Rather, it is whether there were discernible facts which gave Cst. Hooker reasonable grounds to suspect that the crime of impaired driving had been committed at all."

accused was not in fact detained until he was eventually caught by the police, by which time they had formed the necessary reasonable suspicion to detain him based on his actions during the chase. One potential issue here is that although the accused's actions might have made it seem as if he was up to *something*, generalized suspicion is not enough: there must be a nexus to a particular crime.

However, the Ontario Court of Appeal held:

> While the court in *Mann* speaks of reasonable grounds to suspect that the individual is connected to "a particular crime," in my view, it is not necessary that the officers be able to pinpoint the crime with absolute precision. Given the respondent's behaviour in relation to the knapsack and the desperation with which he fled the police, the police could reasonably suspect that he was in possession of contraband: either drugs or weapons or both.[140]

By the time the police detained Nesbeth, the facts known to them, according to the Court of Appeal, were that he had immediately fled, that he had thrown a shopping cart in their path, that he had thrown away a backpack, and that "[i]t was late at night, and the respondent was in the stairwell of a building known to be a high-crime area."[141] These facts justified the investigative detention. However, it should be noted that in *Mann*, the Supreme Court was clear that being in a high-crime area does not mean that someone can be detained: "The presence of an individual in a so-called high crime area is relevant only so far as it reflects his or her proximity to a particular crime. The high crime nature of a neighbourhood is not by itself a basis for detaining individuals."[142]

There is some tension here. *Nesbeth* does not relax the standard to generalized suspicion or the feeling that the accused was committing some offence. One could say that he was suspected of a possession offence but with some ambiguity over what he possessed. That said, the decision does show some slippage compared to the *Mann* standards. Other courts of appeal have insisted more strongly on keeping to a high standard on this point.[143]

---

140 *R v Nesbeth*, 2008 ONCA 579 at para 18 [*Nesbeth*].

141 *Ibid* at para 17.

142 *Mann*, above note 7 at para 47.

143 For example, the Manitoba Court of Appeal in *Schrenk*, above note 136 at para 85, in agreeing with *Yeh* that reasonable suspicion, as opposed to reasonable belief, was sufficient, stressed:

> However, I would add that it cannot be a reasonable suspicion of any bad behaviour. It is a reasonable suspicion of specific criminal activity that gives rise to the grounds to detain. I agree with the majority of the Saskatchewan Court of Appeal when it says in *Yeh* (at paras. 84, 91):

As a matter of fact, most cases do tend to require some specificity to the crime, which is usually met by the observations of the police: if they smell marijuana, they suspect marijuana, and so on. Where the detention really does just seem to be an unfocused investigation into whether an accused was engaged in wrongdoing of some sort, the investigative detention power is usually not found to be made out.[144]

One particular context in which the line between reasonable suspicion of particular criminal activity and generalized suspicion has frequently come into play is with regard to RCMP investigations into the smuggling of drugs and weapons. Adopting practices from the United States Drug Enforcement Administration, the RCMP created various training programs for its officers to assist them in detecting contraband during various interactions with members of the public. Operations Convoy and Pipeline are aimed at the detection and seizure of contraband moving across Canada in cars and transport trucks; Operation Jetway is aimed at couriers who transport contraband via body pack, checked luggage, or carry-on luggage and travel by air, bus, or train. These operations make use of "profiles" that are thought to be indicative of smuggling activities.[145]

> . . . The reference in this passage to a "particular crime," read in context, reflects the idea that the police may not detain an individual out of a general sense he or she might be doing something unlawful. As discussed above, police suspicions must relate to specific criminal wrongdoing. . . .
>
> . . . . As noted, a generalized feeling on the part of the police that an individual is doing something wrong can not serve as the basis for a lawful detention. Thus, in this way, the prerequisites for investigative detentions help to ensure they will not be based on the sorts of hunches and intuitions which can serve as a cover for arbitrary conduct and either deliberate or unconscious profiling based on factors such as race, ethnic origin or socioeconomic status.

144 See, for example, *Hebrada-Walters*, above note 129; *R v Badger*, 2021 BCSC 2623; or *R v Vasile*, 2021 SKPC 54.

145 Justice Binnie in *Kang-Brown*, above note 120 at para 47, observed:

> "Operation Jetway" is an RCMP program designed to curtail drug trafficking. It monitors the travelling public in transportation hubs such as airports and bus depots. It appears to be modelled on drug "courier" profiles developed since 1974 by the United States Drug Enforcement Administration. Police officers contend that certain types of behaviour, demeanour, dress and other visible personal characteristics of travellers may be indicative of criminal activity.

See also Deschamps J, in dissent, at para 109. On this point, see *R v Sandhu*, 2020 ABQB 459, where the accused was unsuccessful in an attempt to get either disclosure or production of training materials relating to operations Pipeline and Convoy.

The practice of using profiles has been discussed by the Supreme Court of Canada.[146] Although some judges individually have expressed concerns, the practice as a whole has not been condemned. In *Chehil*, the Court said that the real issue was not whether reasonable suspicion could come from a profile but whether the particular characteristics, in the circumstances of the case, in fact reach the reasonable suspicion threshold:

> [P]rofile characteristics are not a substitute for objective facts that raise a reasonable suspicion of criminal activity. Profile characteristics must be approached with caution precisely because they risk undermining a careful individualized assessment of the totality of the circumstances.[147]

An important consideration here is that each accused should be seen as representing other members of the public who were also subjected to such activities by the police but who do not end up before the courts because the detention and search of them failed to yield any evidence, precisely because they are not guilty of any offence.[148] In *R v Calderon*, for example, police became suspicious of the accused because of a profile that included the presence of (among other things) maps, fast-food wrappers, and cellphones in the car. In cross-examination, it became apparent that the officers had acted on these indicators between sixty and 120 times but had on no other occasion found drugs. Given this "false positive" rate, the Ontario Court of Appeal concluded that the indicators could not be seen as generating reasonable suspicion.

On the other hand, the Supreme Court has noted that reasonable suspicion deals with possibilities, not probabilities, and therefore that the standard "necessarily means that in some cases the police will reasonably suspect that innocent people are involved in crime."[149] On that basis, it seems that even a profile that is wrong more often than it is right cannot automatically be discounted.

c) *Mann*: The Necessity Issue

In *Mann*, as we have seen, Iacobucci J said:

> The overall reasonableness of the decision to detain . . . must further be assessed against all of the circumstances, most notably the extent to which the interference with individual liberty is necessary to perform the officer's duty, the liberty interfered with, and the nature and

146 See the more complete discussion of profiles, and of racial profiling, in Chapter 2.

147 *Chehil*, above note 119 at para 40.

148 *Grant*, above note 11 at para 75.

149 *Chehil*, above note 119 at para 28. See also *R v Calderon* (2004), 188 CCC (3d) 481, 23 CR (6th) 1 (Ont CA).

> extent of that interference, in order to meet the second prong of the *Waterfield* test.[150]

The second branch of the *Waterfield* test is described by him elsewhere in the judgment in these terms: "[W]hether such conduct, albeit within the general scope of such a duty, involved an unjustifiable use of powers associated with the duty."[151] It would appear, therefore, that the *Mann* majority felt that the detention had to be necessary in the sense that it was a justifiable use of power on the facts.

This latter requirement has been criticized elsewhere herein. Above, in Chapter 2, Section A(4), it was suggested that at times it appears that the courts have simply asked under *Waterfield* whether the police need this power, and if so, they will have it. The majority decision in *Yeh* and that of the Ontario Court of Appeal in *Nesbeth* seem to fall into the same trap by stressing the "importance of the community interest served by allowing the police to pursue such practices."[152] On the other hand, and in fairness to the *Yeh* court, the majority there found that there was no reasonable suspicion on the facts before them. In the final analysis, the robustness of this standard might be the ultimate test of whether investigative detentions go too far in entrenching upon the so-called right to be left alone.

In days past, some Supreme Court judges criticized even the arrest standard of reasonable grounds (or reasonable and probable grounds) as not up to the task of adequately protecting the privacy of Canadians under section 8 of the *Charter*. For example, in *R v Landry*, Gérard La Forest J, in dissent, said, *inter alia*, about the then common law power to enter a home to arrest on reasonable grounds:

> Let me first say something about the vagueness of the proposed test of "reasonable and probable cause" and the consequential danger of giving the police power to enter into a private dwelling on that basis. The expression, no doubt, comprises something more than mere surmise, but determining with any useful measure of precision what it means beyond that poses rather intractable problems both for the police and the courts. If the principle in *Eccles v. Bourque* is to be extended to permit forcible entry into private homes, for the purpose of making arrests simply on the basis that a police officer has reasonable and probable cause, then as the Law Reform Commission put it in its working paper on *Arrest*, *supra*, at p. 115, it would allow him a "wide latitude based on vague, sometimes contradictory statements which provide police with few guidelines, individuals with few definable rights, and courts with

150 *Mann*, above note 7 at para 34.

151 *Ibid* at para 24.

152 *Yeh*, above note 133 at para 94.

little means of control"; see also John Manley's comment on *Eccles v. Bourque* in (1975), 7 *Ottawa L. Rev.* 649, at p. 656. I have found nothing in the cases or in learned commentaries that gives much assistance in giving more precision to the concept, the situations being so various. Because of the vagueness of the discretion it gives a police officer, that discretion is virtually uncontrollable. Small wonder, then, that the Law Reform Commission recommended the statutory reaffirmation of the traditional position.[153]

Of course, since that was said by the learned justice, we now have two standards that purport to be different in intensity, so the concern must be even greater. Nonetheless, the two standards seem to be here to stay. The challenge, then, is to ensure that both standards have real teeth and real value, thereby justifying the Supreme Court's faith that they can provide meaningful protection of constitutional rights.

d) *Mann*: The "Brief Duration" Issue

The Court said in *Mann* that an investigative detention "must be of brief duration."[154] They added as well that such a detention cannot turn into "a *de facto* arrest,"[155] by which they meant that it cannot impose the same types of restrictions on liberty as an arrest would. Given the facts of *Mann*, the Court seemed to have in mind a power to conduct stops on the street where a person is prevented from going on their way for a few moments as they are asked about their identity or destination as opposed to more intrusive state actions. However, some lower courts were willing to countenance detentions the lengths of which were difficult to view as "brief."[156]

In *R v McGuffie*, for example, police received a tip about a handgun in a bar, and an officer caught up to the accused shortly after he had left the scene. The officer told the accused that he was detaining him because he thought the accused might have a handgun, which the accused denied. The officer then handcuffed and searched the accused, finding nothing. Following that, he put the accused in the back of a police cruiser, leaving him there for a half-hour before returning. Subsequent events resulted in

153 *R v Landry*, [1986] 1 SCR 145 at para 72 [*Landry*]. It is to be noted that *Landry* itself was later found to have countenanced an unconstitutional entry power in *R v Feeney*, [1997] 2 SCR 13.

154 *Mann*, above note 7 at para 22.

155 *Ibid* at para 35.

156 See, for example, *Chaif-Gust*, above note 128, where the British Columbia Court of Appeal expressed qualms about a forty-two-minute detention, although they ultimately deferred to the trial judge's decision. See also the trial decision in *R v Barclay*, 2016 ONSC 2811, where the accused was detained for nearly two hours purportedly under *Mann*; this result was overturned on appeal (see below).

the accused being taken back to the police station, strip-searched, and charged with narcotics-related offences. The Ontario Court of Appeal found that the accused's section 9 *Charter* right had been violated because the officer had not acted within the limits of the investigative detention power. Specifically, although the officer had been justified in briefly detaining the accused to question him about his knowledge of the handgun, once that had been accomplished, the officer had exhausted his legal authority. The Court of Appeal held:

> The duration and nature of a detention justified as an investigative detention must be tailored to the investigative purpose of the detention and the circumstances in which the detention occurs. A brief detention on the street to question an individual implicated in a criminal investigation involving ongoing events may be justifiable under the *Mann* criteria, but under those same criteria imprisonment in a police cruiser while handcuffed for some indefinite period while an officer carries out other aspects of a criminal investigation could not be justified. The police cannot use investigative detention as an excuse for holding suspects while the police search for evidence that might justify the arrest of the suspect. Nor does investigative detention mean that the police can detain suspects indefinitely while they carry out their investigation.[157]

The Ontario Court of Appeal returned to the issue of the appropriate length of a detention in *R v Barclay*.[158] In that case, police had received a tip identifying a person reported to be transporting marijuana in his luggage as he travelled by train. The police detained the accused but could not themselves smell marijuana, so they arranged to have a sniffer dog brought to the scene. Because of the location, this meant that the accused was detained for a period of nearly two hours. The trial judge had found this detention to be authorized under *Mann*, but the Court of Appeal overturned that aspect of the decision.[159]

The length of an investigative detention, they held, was not driven by the investigative needs of the police; rather, the limiting factor was that by definition the police would only have reasonable suspicion about the accused's involvement in crime. This relates back to the Supreme Court's point that an investigative detention should not become a de facto arrest. The Ontario Court of Appeal noted that

157 *McGuffie*, above note 128 at para 38.

158 2018 ONCA 114 [*Barclay*].

159 The trial judge had found no s 9 violation. The Court of Appeal held that there was a violation but that the evidence should not be excluded and so upheld the conviction: see paras 37–40.

> all investigative detentions must be "brief" because the state interference with the individual's liberty rests on a reasonable suspicion of criminal activity, a much lower standard than the reasonable and probable grounds needed for an arrest. The relatively low "reasonable suspicion" standard cannot constitutionally sustain a detention that is not "brief."[160]

The Court of Appeal acknowledged that no precise time limit could be attached to the term "brief" but nonetheless held that even if police were reasonably and expeditiously carrying out an investigation, that might not be possible in the time permitted.[161] They offered guidelines to be used in assessing the issue:

> [31] The permitted duration of an investigative detention is case-specific. Some of the relevant factors include:
>
> - *the intrusiveness of the detention.* For example, handcuffing the suspect behind his or her back and placing the suspect in a police cruiser, or diverting the suspect from his intended path by taking him to the police detachment to continue the investigation, will generally be more intrusive of the suspect's liberty interest than asking him questions at the point of initial detention. The more intrusive the detention is to the suspect's liberty interest, the more closely its duration will be scrutinized.
> - *the nature of the suspected criminal offence.* If the suspected offense is not serious, the permitted duration will probably be at the shorter end of "brief."
> - *the complexity of the investigation.* If the investigation is not complex, one would expect that police questioning of the suspect would not reasonably need to be lengthy, and the permitted duration will probably be at the shorter end of "brief." However, if the investigation of the suspected criminal offence is complex, its complexity will only justify a longer permitted duration within the range of "brief" to the extent it is causally linked to the duration of the detention.
> - *any immediate public or individual safety concerns.* Immediate public or individual safety concerns may justify a permitted duration at the longer end of "brief."
> - *the ability of the police to effectively carry out the investigation without continuing the detention of the suspect.* If there are other reasonable means of continuing the investigation without detaining the suspect, the continued detention of the suspect would likely render continued detention unconstitutional.

---

160 *Barclay*, above note 158 at para 28.

161 *Ibid* at para 30.

- *the lack of police diligence*. For example, if a sniffer dog were immediately available, and yet the police detained the suspect for 20 minutes before employing the dog to confirm or refute their suspicion, then, depending on all of the other relevant factors, the interference with the suspect's liberty interest as a result of the lack of police diligence might render the delay unconstitutional.
- *the lack of immediate availability of the required investigative tools*. On the other hand, depending on all of the other relevant factors, if a sniffer dog were made available as soon as practicable and employed as soon as available, the same 20-minute detention might fall within the range of time that can be characterized as a "brief" detention.

> [32] The relative importance of these and other relevant factors, and thus the permissible length of an investigative detention, will vary from case to case. But it is crucial to remember that such factors merely situate the permitted duration of the detention within the range of what is "brief," and that all investigative detentions must be "brief."[162]

The factors identified in *Barclay* have been relied on in later caselaw.[163]

3) Common Law Roadblocks (and More): *R v Clayton*

After *Mann*, further issues reached the Supreme Court. As we have seen, in *Mann*, the Court appeared to see itself as largely confirming what had already occurred in practice and been approved of in the lower courts, led by the Ontario Court of Appeal in *Simpson*. In *Mann*, the Court seemingly approved of *R v Murray*,[164] a prior Quebec Court of Appeal decision that had approved the use of a roadblock to block a main exit point following an armed robbery. Justice Iacobucci said this about the Quebec case:

> The Court of Appeal of Quebec did not find it necessary to apply the articulable cause doctrine in *R. v. Murray* (1999), 136 C.C.C. (3d) 197. Relying upon the *Waterfield* test, Fish J.A. (as he then was) recognized a narrow police power at common law to set up immediate road blocks along an obvious avenue of escape from the scene of a serious crime. Fish J.A.'s comments on the exercise of this power focus specifically on its reasonable necessity in the totality of the circumstances (p. 205). The road block in *Murray* was set up immediately after the commission

162 *Ibid* at paras 31 & 32.

163 See, for example, *R v McPake*, 2019 BCSC 751; *R v Enchin-Dixon*, 2022 BCSC 1342; *R v Baglee*, 2022 YKTC 13; *R v Hayatibahar*, 2022 ONSC 1281; *R v Chopra*, 2022 ONCJ 322; and *Balde c R*, 2023 QCCQ 919.

164 (1999), 136 CCC (3d) 197.

> of a crime and was limited to an obvious escape route for the sole purpose of apprehending the fleeing perpetrators.[165]

A roadblock differs from a *Mann* stop since in a roadblock there is no individualized suspicion of a given car or its occupants but rather a "generalized" suspicion that the suspect is going to be in one of the cars passing by and to be stopped in the roadblock. After *Mann*, it was not long before the Court itself allowed a form of roadblock after a report of gun crime. At a minimum, *Clayton* found that the roadblock that took place in that case was authorized at common law. However, the case was ambiguous in its reasoning and as a result did more than simply authorize that particular roadblock, or roadblocks in certain circumstances; rather, it had the effect of creating a general common law power to detain.

In *Clayton*, the police received an emergency call reporting that about ten "black guys" were around a group of cars in a strip-club parking lot and that four of them had guns "like glocks."[166] The caller described their vehicles. The police arrived at the scene minutes later and blocked both exits. The police officers at the rear exit stopped the next car to try to leave, although it did not match the description of any of the vehicles they had been given. After stopping the car, the officers observed that the two occupants were black. Some conversation between the police and the occupants ensued, which resulted in one of the occupants running away and then being apprehended; he was searched and was discovered to be carrying a gun. The other occupant was then also arrested and searched and was also found to be armed. The two accused claimed that the detention and the searches violated their *Charter* rights. The Ontario Court of Appeal accepted this argument; however, the Supreme Court of Canada overturned that decision and found that there were no *Charter* violations. The Court was unanimous that the police roadblock in the case was a lawful exercise of police power but was divided over why this was so.

Two points about *Clayton* are worth discussing separately: the creation of a common law power and the *Charter* question of whether that power complies with section 9. We will discuss the latter question first.

For the majority of six, Abella J effectively did not explicitly discuss the *Charter* issue, confining herself to the issue of the power at common law:

> The statement that a detention which is lawful is not arbitrary should not be understood as exempting the authorizing law, whether it is common law or statutory, from *Charter* scrutiny. Previous decisions of this Court are clear that where a detention by police is authorized by law, the law authorizing detention is also subject to *Charter* scrutiny: *R. v.*

165 *Mann*, above note 7 at para 29.

166 *Clayton*, above note 8 at para 2.

> *Hufsky*, [1988] 1 S.C.R. 621; *R. v. Ladouceur*, [1990] 1 S.C.R. 1257. The courts can and should develop the common law in a manner consistent with the *Charter*: *Dagenais v. Canadian Broadcasting Corp.*, [1994] 3 S.C.R. 835, at pp. 875–78. The common law regarding police powers of detention, developed building on *R. v. Waterfield*, [1963] 3 All E.R. 659 (C.A.), and *Dedman v. The Queen*, [1985] 2 S.C.R. 2, is consistent with *Charter* values because it requires the state to justify the interference with liberty based on criteria which focus on whether the interference with liberty is necessary given the extent of the risk and the liberty at stake, and no more intrusive to liberty than reasonably necessary to address the risk. The standard of justification must be commensurate with the fundamental rights at stake.[167]

It seems that the majority are of the view that, once they have applied the *Waterfield* test to the facts, the matter is over. However, on this approach, the *Charter* gets lost in the analysis; once the common law analysis is completed, section 9 is apparently satisfied without explicit consideration, and no thought is given to section 1.

Justice Binnie, writing the minority concurring judgment, criticized this aspect of the majority's reasoning:

> It seems to me problematic in a case like this, however, to say the authorizing law is subject to *Charter* scrutiny without in fact subjecting the authorizing law to any recognizable *Charter* scrutiny.[168]

Justice Binnie followed the approach that had been adopted in the checkpoint cases of *Hufsky* and *Ladouceur*: he articulated a common law power, found that that common law power authorized a detention that was arbitrary (in that the stop was based on no criteria), but then concluded that this arbitrary detention was saved under section 1.[169]

It might be that the majority was saying that the *Waterfield* test acts as a proxy for the section 1 analysis, although one would think it is preferable to say that section 9 is breached by the stop but that the power represents a reasonable limit under section 1 based on the *Waterfield* analysis. If a stop is justified by section 1, one can agree that the stop is constitutional and thus lawful. On the prior approach and because of its generalized nature, a justified roadblock was a constitutionally valid and lawful arbitrary stop.[170] On the *Clayton* reasoning, since the stop was lawful, the stop was therefore not arbitrary. Lost in the analysis is what

---

167 *Ibid* at para 21.

168 *Ibid* at para 61.

169 See the discussion of this aspect of *Hufsky* and *Ladouceur* in Chapter 5, Section B(2).

170 It is to be noted that in *Nolet*, above note 57 at para 22, Binnie J, for a unanimous Supreme Court, seemed to rely on the random equals arbitrary view when he said:

the word "arbitrary" means. Of course, Abella J might simply have been of the view that arbitrary means unlawful, full stop.[171]

It matters which approach is taken. We are discussing separately the common law power and *Charter* issues, but of course they do combine. If being authorized by the common law is sufficient to mean that there is no *Charter* violation, as the majority approach assumes, then the relatively well-defined *Oakes* test for balancing individual and state interests will never be considered. Instead, any balancing of interests will only occur in creating the common law power and therefore in the application of the *Waterfield* test. That makes it even more important that the limits of any common law power should be set out precisely. Unfortunately, the approach to common law powers of detention by the majority in *Clayton* was exactly the opposite, creating an amorphous and unstructured test.

Justice Abella adopted the *Waterfield* analysis as set out in the court below, which she described as containing "great clarity" and requiring "no further refinement":

> The powers of police constables at common law, often described as the ancillary police power, as set out in *Waterfield* have been accepted by the Supreme Court of Canada as part of the Canadian common law in several decisions rendered both before and after the proclamation of the *Charter*: see e.g. *Knowlton v. The Queen* (1973), 10 C.C.C. (2d) 377 (S.C.C.) at 379–80; *Dedman v. The Queen* (1985), 20 C.C.C. (3d) 97 (S.C.C.); *R. v. Godoy* (1999), 131 C.C.C. (3d) 129 (S.C.C.) at 135–36; *R. v. Mann* [(2004), 185 C.C.C. (3d) 308 (S.C.C.)], at 320–1. The power of the police to detain for investigative purposes in some circumstances and the power to search as an incident of arrest are two of the better

---

A random vehicle stop on the highway is, by definition, an arbitrary detention: *Dedman v. The Queen*, [1985] 2 S.C.R. 2; *R. v. Hufsky*, [1988] 1 S.C.R. 621; *R. v. Ladouceur*, [1990] 1 S.C.R. 1257 (hereinafter "*Ladouceur (Ont.)*"); *Mellenthin*, and *R. v. Harris*, 2007 ONCA 574, 87 O.R. (3d) 214. The detention will only be justified under s. 1 of the *Charter* (*Hufsky*, at p. 637), if the police act within the limited highway related purposes for which the powers were conferred (*Ladouceur (Ont.)*, *per* Cory J., at p. 1287).

171 At the time *Clayton*, above note 8, was decided, the Court had decided that a lawful detention was not arbitrary but had deliberately left open the corresponding question of whether an unlawful detention was arbitrary. Justice Abella, however, makes a comment at para 19 of *Clayton* that amounts to saying "lawful = non-arbitrary" (the established point) and also "unlawful = arbitrary" (the point until then left open), thereby equating the two concepts. That point did not directly matter in *Clayton*, and the Court consciously committed itself to this view two years later in *Grant*, above note 11. See the discussion of this point in Chapter 5, Section B(2).

> known examples of the exercise of the common law ancillary police power: *R. v. Mann, supra*; *R. v. Caslake* (1998), 121 C.C.C. (3d) 97 (S.C.C.) at 107–108.
>
> Where the prosecution relies on the ancillary power doctrine to justify police conduct that interferes with individual liberties, a two-pronged case-specific inquiry must be made. First, the prosecution must demonstrate that the police were acting in the exercise of a lawful duty when they engaged in the conduct in issue. Second, and in addition to showing that the police were acting in the course of their duty, the prosecution must demonstrate that the impugned conduct amounted to a justifiable use of police powers associated with that duty: *Brown v. Durham Regional Police Force* (1998), 131 C.C.C. (3d) 1 (Ont. C.A.) at 23–24.[172]

However, having adopted the appeal court's statement of the correct approach, Abella J disagreed with its conclusion on the facts. While in agreement with the finding that the common law allowed such a stop of a motor vehicle, a power that "reaches beyond" the statutes, she disagreed with the Court of Appeal concerning whether this particular stop was justifiable. The Court of Appeal had held that the police could not pick and choose which aspects of the tip to believe: they had been told that a gun was in one of four vehicles and so were justified in stopping those vehicles but not all vehicles. However, Abella J concluded (quoting the trial judge) that the police were "justified in stopping 'all vehicles' emerging from the parking lot and 'would have been derelict in their duties had they sat by and watched vehicles leave.'"[173] She stressed that

> [t]he determination will focus on the nature of the situation, including the seriousness of the offence, as well as on the information known to the police about the suspect or the crime, and the extent to which the detention was reasonably responsive or tailored to these circumstances, including its geographic and temporal scope.[174]

Clayton dealt with a roadblock of a single parking lot, which was the result of a very recent 911 report alleging that several weapons were being brandished. Justice Abella held that, in all the circumstances, the roadblock was justified: there were reasonable grounds to believe there were several handguns in a public place, which was a serious offence carrying a genuine risk of serious bodily harm to the public, and the

---

172 *Clayton*, above note 8 at para 22, quoting Doherty JA in *R v Clayton* (2005), 194 CCC (3d) 289 at paras 35–37 (Ont CA) [emphasis removed].

173 *Clayton*, above note 8 at para 24.

174 *Ibid* at para 31.

police had arrived promptly enough after the tip that stopping cars emerging from the parking lot was likely to apprehend the perpetrators.[175] To the extent that the majority articulated an actual "test" governing the situation, it was by holding that

> [i]n the totality of the circumstances, therefore, the initial detention in this case was reasonably necessary to respond to the seriousness of the offence and the threat to the police's and public's safety inherent in the presence of prohibited weapons in a public place, and was temporally, geographically and logistically responsive to the circumstances known by the police when it was set up. The initial stop was consequently a justifiable use of police powers associated with the police duty to investigate the offences described by the 911 caller and did not represent an arbitrary detention contrary to s. 9 of the *Charter*.[176]

To the extent that this is a test, it is not limited to creating roadblocks.

The uncertain nature of this test can be seen by contrasting the majority judgment to that of the minority. The minority is quite clear as to what new common law power they wish to create:

> common law authority for the police (1) to form a blockade (2) on receipt of information the police consider reliable (3) about serious firearms offences underway or recently committed (4) limited to the premises where the offence allegedly occurred (5) sufficiently soon after the alleged incident to give police reasonable grounds for belief that the perpetrators may be caught.[177]

Justice Binnie acknowledges that such a specific power leaves other situations unsettled and does discuss other situations in which the common law could authorize the use of a roadblock. He suggests, for example, that a prison break or a child kidnapping would likely give rise to a power to conduct a roadblock.[178]

The majority judgment, on the other hand, is quite open-ended. It is not possible to identify any specific new power they created. Rather, for them, the question was settled by the fact that what the police officers did was "reasonably necessary" given all the facts.[179] That is not a power; it is simply an after-the-fact assessment that what the police did was desirable and justifiable. That approach seems fundamentally at odds with the Court's stated position that "the police (and more broadly, the

---

175 *Ibid* at para 33.
176 *Ibid* at para 41.
177 *Ibid* at para 89.
178 *Ibid* at para 99.
179 *Ibid* at para 41.

state) may act only to the extent that they are empowered to do so by law."[180] Indeed, more generally, "it impairs the right of citizens to know what the law is in advance and govern their conduct accordingly — a fundamental tenet of the rule of law."[181] Nonetheless, it is clear from the next case to be discussed, *Aucoin*, that that is now the test.

4) "General Common Law Power to Detain": *R v Aucoin*

In *Aucoin*, a police officer stopped a vehicle for reasons relating to its licence plate; the accused was the sole occupant of the vehicle. Having done so, the officer noticed the smell of alcohol on the accused's breath and administered a roadside screening test. As the accused had more alcohol in his system than he was permitted as a newly licensed driver, the officer decided to impound his vehicle and issue him a ticket under the Nova Scotia *Motor Vehicle Act*. Because it was dark, the officer decided to sit in the front seat of his cruiser to write the ticket, and in order to prevent the accused from wandering off, he decided to have the accused sit in the back seat of the cruiser. Because he was putting the accused in the back seat of the cruiser, he first patted him down, and on feeling something soft in the accused's pocket, he asked what it was. The accused replied that it was ecstasy, which resulted in his immediate arrest. The contents of his pockets were seized as part of a search incident to arrest and in fact transpired to be cocaine. The issue, by the time the case reached the Supreme Court, was whether the officer had the power to perform the pat-down search or whether that had violated the accused's *Charter* rights. Although the Court upheld the conviction on the basis that the evidence should not be excluded, they did find that the search was unlawful, specifically on the basis that it occurred in the context of an arbitrary detention. In reaching this conclusion, the Court commented on the detention power in *Clayton* along with discussing the detention power in other ways. However, *Aucoin* itself leaves questions in its wake.

In a sense, the decision itself can be seen as a reflection of the lack of clarity left by *Clayton*. The trial judge had concluded that in the very unusual circumstances of the case (that the officer was alone; it was late at night, with little light; allowing the accused to get back in his own vehicle arguably breached the *Motor Vehicle Act*; and there were many people present at a festival, which meant that the accused could have easily wandered off), it was reasonable for the officer to place the accused in the police vehicle and reasonable to pat him down first. The majority in the Nova Scotia Court of Appeal upheld the finding that

180 *Mann*, above note 7 at para 15.

181 *R v Ferguson*, 2008 SCC 6 at para 72.

the officer's decision was reasonable in the circumstances. The Supreme Court of Canada, however, concluded that this was the wrong test. The police officer was not entitled to detain a person merely on the basis that it was *reasonable* to do so; rather, the test was the more stringent standard of whether it was reasonably *necessary*. They held:

> The existence of a general common law power to detain where it is reasonably necessary in the totality of the circumstances was settled in *R. v. Clayton*, 2007 SCC 32, [2007] 2 S.C.R. 725. That case moved our jurisprudence from debating the existence of such a power to considering whether its exercise was reasonably necessary in the circumstances of a particular case. As Abella J., for the majority, observed:
>
> > The determination will focus on the nature of the situation, including the seriousness of the offence, as well as on the information known to the police about the suspect or the crime, and the extent to which the detention was reasonably responsive or tailored to these circumstances, including its geographic and temporal scope. This means balancing the seriousness of the risk to public or individual safety with the liberty interests of members of the public to determine whether, given the extent of the risk, the nature of the stop is no more intrusive of liberty interests than is *reasonably necessary* to address the risk. [Emphasis added; para. 31.][182]

Aucoin therefore confirms that "reasonably necessary in the totality of the circumstances" is the proper test—or at least a proper test—for determining whether the police have the authority to detain a person. Applying that test on the facts of the case, the Court determined that Aucoin had been unlawfully detained. They held:

> [T]he question to be asked is whether there were other reasonable means by which Constable Burke could have addressed his concern about the appellant disappearing into the crowd, short of doing what he did. If there were other reasonable means to ensure the appellant would not flee the scene, then detaining him in the police cruiser could not be said to be reasonably necessary and would thus have constituted an unlawful detention within the meaning of s. 9 of the *Charter*.[183]

Some observations should be made about the potentially beneficial impacts of *Aucoin*. First, to the extent that the *Clayton* power could be made more specific, *Aucoin* has done so. It was in fact unclear from

182 *Aucoin*, above note 9 at para 36.

183 *Ibid* at para 39.

Clayton itself whether it should be seen as reaching a decision on its facts or articulating a more broadly based power and, if the latter, how that power should be understood. *Aucoin* has at least clarified that there is a common law test of "whether the detention was *reasonably necessary* in the totality of the circumstances."

Furthermore, *Aucoin* makes clear that among the "circumstances" that should enter into the totality are the *Charter* rights of the accused, which is of some significance. The Court notes that

> in order to justify securing the appellant in the back seat—*knowing that this would also entail a pat-down search*—detaining the appellant in that manner had to be reasonably necessary.[184]

In effect, the lower courts' approach had been to ask first whether the detention was authorized and then to take the power to search to flow directly from that. The Court reverses that order and requires the fact that the accused will be searched to be taken into account in assessing whether to detain, or at least to detain in that particular manner. There is a significant difference between asking "given that I will put this person in my vehicle, should I search them" and asking "given that it would require me to search them, should I put this person in my vehicle." The latter approach has the potential to limit the open-ended nature of this general power of detention and make it more respectful of rights.

Aucoin makes clear that there is a general common law power of detention, created in *Clayton*, despite the avowal only three years earlier in *Mann* that it was not appropriate for the Court to create such a power. On the other hand, as we will discuss in the next section, *Aucoin* itself leaves questions.

5) Conclusion

As noted in the Introduction, common law powers of detention were a fast-developing area of the law, going quickly from "no power" to "an investigative detention power but no general common law power to detain" to "a general common law power to detain." The very speed of that change left room for some confusion over the exact nature of each power and the relationship between the cases. We will look here at two questions: (1) the relationship between the *Mann* power and the *Clayton* power and (2) the role of *Aucoin* in *Charter* analysis.

---

184 *Ibid* [emphasis added].

a) The Relationship Between *Mann* and *Clayton*

Because the powers in *Mann* and *Clayton* arose at separate times, and because the first denied that a general power to detain should be created, while the second created such a power, an issue arises. Simply put, the issue is this. *Mann* created a power to detain briefly, but only when a number of criteria were met: (1) the detention had to be reasonably necessary in the totality of the circumstances; (2) there had to be a recent or ongoing offence; and (3) there had to be a nexus between the detainee and that offence. On the other hand, the power created in *Clayton*, as explained by *Aucoin*, requires only that the detention be reasonably necessary in the totality of the circumstances. The question arises as to why police would ever try to comply with all three requirements in *Mann* to authorize their behaviour when—apparently—complying with only the first would be sufficient to authorize their behaviour under *Clayton*.[185]

Certainly, there are situations in which the *Mann* power does not apply. In *Clayton*, for example, there was no reasonable suspicion of the particular vehicles stopped,[186] and in *Aucoin*, the purpose of the stop was not investigatory.[187] It is therefore clear why a power that can apply to circumstances other than investigative detention could be required. But when the test for that more general power can be satisfied more easily than the investigative detention test—where both the *Mann* and *Clayton* tests potentially apply—it is harder to see how the more demanding power continues to exist. Why doesn't the "general power to detain" simply swallow the particular power?

Of course, this relationship would make perfect sense if one conceptualized investigative detentions as a particularly intrusive form of detention, as one of those common law detentions at the upper end of the scale; in that event, additional restrictions ought to be required to be satisfied before the power can properly be used. The situation would be similar to that with searches: additional requirements are imposed before a wiretap authorization can be issued, for example, because an unusually high privacy interest is at stake in that case. However, it is not clear that this argument is viable in the detention context. First, the *Mann* power was meant to be limited and to allow for only a brief detention in which the person detained was not required to answer any questions, so it is not

185 See, for example, *R v McClelland*, 2012 ONSC 7207 [*McClelland*], holding in an investigative detention case at para 23 that "*Clayton* moves farther away from the more exacting articulable cause requirement or 'clear nexus between the individual to be detained and a recent or on-going criminal offence' as described in *Mann*."

186 See the discussion under the heading "The Relevant Police Power Is Not Found in *Mann* (or *Simpson*)" in the minority judgment of *Clayton*, above note 8 at paras 81–83.

187 *Aucoin*, above note 9 at paras 31–33.

particularly at the high end of potential detentions. It is hard to see, for example, that a person who is stopped by police, questioned, and denied the ability to attend a public event has less at stake than a person who is briefly detained for investigative purposes, but the former would not be an investigative detention, so *Clayton* would be the analytical tool used.[188]

Alternatively, if one were to envision the *Clayton* power as limited to circumstances where particularly acute state interests were at play—for example, guns recently reported in a very contained location and likely to be recovered if quick action is taken—then it is easy to see why the proper balance in face of some immediate danger would impose fewer limitations before the detention can occur. There is some tendency among lower courts to regard the *Clayton* power as limited in that way,[189] but it is by no means consistent. And, of course, *Aucoin* reframed the *Clayton* test so that it is not limited to those factual situations but is intended as a general test. The facts of *Aucoin*—a person whose car had already been seized might wander off before he could be given a ticket—are at about as low an end of the scale as one can imagine.

All of this said, the *Mann/Clayton* distinction nonetheless tends to be respected: if the facts of the case are such that an investigative detention is at issue, then courts generally ask whether the power in *Mann* is satisfied, and only in situations to which that case does not apply do courts tend to use *Clayton*.[190] *Clayton* is often cited for various principles, but it is less common for it to be applied directly.[191] This might not, doctrinally, be perfectly consistent, but it is the workable practice at which courts have arrived.

---

188 See *Figueiras v Toronto (City) Police Services Board*, 2015 ONCA 208.

189 See, for example, *R v Yoon*, 2012 BCSC 580; *R v DAJ*, 2011 ONSC 4158; *R v JK*, 2010 ONCJ 232; or *R v Woods*, 2009 ONCJ 182.

190 See, for example, *R v Peterkin*, 2015 ONCA 8 at para 54, or *R v Sheck*, 2015 BCCA 471 at para 53. This is the tendency, but not a uniform practice: see, for example, *McClelland*, above note 185. *McClelland* identifies what occurred in the case as an investigative detention (the police approached a vehicle in a parking lot outside a bar to investigate impaired driving). The reasoning in the case also refers to the more relaxed standard in *Clayton* but arguably simply applies the *Waterfield* test from scratch to conclude that the officers were authorized. To very similar effect, see *R v McKenzie*, 2022 MBCA 3, as well as the discussion in Steve Coughlan, "*R v McKenzie*: Continuing Confusion on Common Law Powers" (2022) 77 *Criminal Reports* (7th) 330.

191 See, for example, *Tim*, above note 19, or *Fleming v Ontario*, 2019 SCC 45, both of which cite principles from *Clayton* but do not apply its test. To the same effect, see *R v Reid*, 2016 ONCA 944 at paras 28–30, or *Manning*, above note 128. See also *R v Okemow*, 2019 MBCA 37, where the trial judge relied on *Clayton* because the facts of the case were seen as analogous.

b) The Role of *Aucoin*

It was noted above, in discussing *Clayton*, that the *Charter* analysis by the majority there amounted to, at most, a finding that the detention was lawful, which was presumed to entirely settle the section 9 analysis. Subsequent to *Clayton*, the approach to *Charter* analysis in the section 9 context was developed first in *Grant* and then in *Le*. It is now clear that a full section 9 analysis must look at three issues: "the detention must be authorized by law; the authorizing law itself must not be arbitrary; and, the manner in which the detention is carried out must be reasonable."[192] However, that full articulation of the structure of the test was not made until after decades of individual section 9 cases had already been handed down, with the result that exactly how some cases fit into the analysis is not necessarily clear.[193] *Aucoin* is an example of this problem.

The majority in *Aucoin* stated that the detention itself was perfectly lawful (based on *Motor Vehicle Act* concerns) and held:

> I do not see this case as turning on whether Constable Burke had the *authority* to detain the appellant in the rear of his police cruiser, having lawfully stopped him for a regulatory infraction. Rather, the question is whether he was justified in *exercising it* as he did in the circumstances of this case.[194]

That certainly sounds like saying that the question is not whether the detention was authorized by law but whether the manner in which it was carried out complied with the *Charter*. On the other hand, the Court also stated that "the increased restriction on the appellant's liberty interests by placing him in the rear of the police cruiser required a standard of reasonable necessity," which seems like it is addressing the first step in the analysis.[195] Similarly, the very basis for the Court's decision—"detaining him in the police cruiser could not be said to be reasonably necessary"—seems as though it is addressed to the first step.[196]

In this particular case, the problem is exacerbated by the "open-ended" nature of the common law power created in *Clayton*. Because that case collapsed the common law and *Charter* analyses, applying the common law test and asking of the detention "was it reasonably necessary" would seem to settle both the first and third steps of the arbitrariness analysis.

---

192 *Le*, above note 126 at para 124.

193 See the more extensive discussion of this subject in Chapter 5, Section B(2).

194 *Aucoin*, above note 9 at para 35 [emphasis in original].

195 *Ibid*, n 2.

196 *Ibid* at para 39.

CHAPTER 4

ARREST AND COMPELLING APPEARANCE

A. METHODS OF COMPELLING APPEARANCE

The topic of arrest — the first term in this chapter's title — will occupy a great part of the discussion below. It is necessary to recognize, however, that powers of arrest are part of a larger scheme for causing an individual who is alleged to have committed a crime to appear in court to face charges. For that reason, Part XVI of the *Criminal Code*, which contains the arrest powers, is entitled "Compelling Appearance of Accused Before a Justice and Interim Release."[1]

The "compelling appearance" part of the chapter's title refers to powers of arrest but also to summonses, appearance notices, and other things. The "interim release" part refers to the various ways in which a person can, after arrest, nonetheless be released pending trial rather than held in custody. The most obvious of those ways is through the judicial interim release portion of Part XVI, popularly referred to as "bail." That is not the only form of interim release, however, since non-judicial actors are

---

1 *Criminal Code*, RSC 1985, c C-46 [*Criminal Code* or *Code*]. Part XVI is not limited to indictable offences, and indeed some of the arrest powers are specifically designed to cover any criminal offence. Nonetheless, note that s 795 of the *Criminal Code* provides, with regard to summary conviction offences, that

> [t]he provisions of Parts XVI and XVIII with respect to compelling the appearance of an accused before a justice, and the provisions of Parts XX and XX.1, in so far as they are not inconsistent with this Part, apply, with such modifications as the circumstances require, to proceedings under this Part.

also given a similar discretion. Indeed, it is worth noting at the start that significant amendments were made to Part XVI in 2019, by Bill C-75.[2] The central goal of those amendments was to make it more likely that an arrested person would be released at as early a stage as possible (or not arrested in the first place), to limit the restrictions on the liberty of persons who were released, and to streamline the procedures for such releases. This chapter will discuss the forms of interim release available prior to the bail-hearing stage, but the more complex topic of judicial interim release will be left for specialist volumes on that subject.[3]

As noted, arrest is the most well-known method of causing a person to appear in court to face charges, and the mental image most people have is probably that of a warrantless arrest. It is worth observing, therefore, that having warrantless arrest in mind as a model for that process is somewhat misleading. The most obvious actors in a warrantless arrest will be the police officers who take an accused into custody. That mental image therefore obscures the fact that the decision to make a person account for their actions to a court is generally not one made exclusively by a police officer. Rather, the decision that that is necessary must normally have been reached separately by both a police officer and a justice of the peace. Sometimes this decision by a justice of the peace will precede the police officer's interaction with the individual, and sometimes it will follow it, but except in one instance—arrest without a warrant—it does occur at some point. Even in that one exception, the accused person is then taken in front of a justice, although in a slightly different context.

Furthermore, although the image of an arrest involves taking physical control of the accused person, that too is not the only model. Summonses and appearance notices consist of a written demand to the person to appear in court; in essence, because of the nature of the charges or the situation, it is reasonable to expect that the person will comply with the request that they appear. "Request" is not an entirely accurate word since there are significant legal consequences for non-compliance, but at least initially the person is given the opportunity to comply voluntarily.[4]

These two considerations—whether the approval of the justice of the peace is sought before or after the fact and whether the individual is given an opportunity to comply or is physically compelled to appear—can be seen as creating a matrix of four possibilities, as set out

---

2 Bill C-75, *An Act to amend the Criminal Code, the Youth Criminal Justice Act and other Acts and to make consequential amendments to other Acts*, SC 2019, c 25 [Bill C-75].

3 See, for example, Gary Trotter, *The Law of Bail in Canada*, 3d ed (Toronto: Carswell, 2010) [*Trotter*].

4 *Criminal Code*, above note 1, s 145.

in Figure 4.1, below. In fact, the four methods of compelling appearance—appearance notice, summons, arrest with a warrant, and arrest without a warrant—fit neatly into that matrix.[5]

Figure 4.1: Compelling Appearance Matrix

	Justice of the Peace confirmation first	**Justice of the Peace confirmation second**
Give written notice	Summons • defined—s 2, Form 6 • lay information before JP—s 504 • issuance by JP—s 507 • issuance in private prosecution—s 507.1 • contents—s 509(1), (4) & (5) • service—s 509(2), ss 703.1-703.2 • failure to comply—s 145(4) • expiry—s 523, s 730(2)	Appearance notice • defined—s 2, Form 9 • availability—s 497 • contents—s 500(1) • judicial referral hearing—s 496 • arrest for failure to comply—s 502 • failure to comply—s 145(5) • lay information before JP—s 505 • confirmation (or not) by JP—s 508 • expiry—s 523, s 730(2)
Take physical control	Arrest with a warrant • availability—s 504, s 507(4), s 512 • contents—s 511, s 513 • execution—s 512, s 511(3) & (4) • release after arrest—s 499, s 503(1.1) • take before JP—s 503	Arrest without a warrant • power—ss 494–495 • release after arrest—s 498(1), s 503(1.1) • take before JP—s 503 • territorial validity—s 703(1) & (2)

It will be helpful at this point simply to "trace through" these various routes to compelling a person's appearance before a court. To some extent, this is an artificial division since the routes overlap at many points or follow parallel paths; still, it is useful for the purposes of clarity to examine the features of each route separately, to the extent possible. Following that, we will look in greater detail at specific issues within the compelling-appearance scheme.

5 There are other mechanisms that are relevant to compelling appearance. For example, after an accused has been arrested, a peace officer has the obligation in some circumstances to release the accused on either an appearance notice or an undertaking: see s 498(1.1) or s 503(1.1). These options, however, are more akin to the judicial interim-release provisions rather than the powers available to a peace officer in initiating contact with a person. They are discussed in more detail below, under "Restraint in Compelling Appearance."

The primary goal of this overview and subsequent consideration of specific issues is to examine the non-arrest methods of compelling an accused's appearance in court. Arrest will be the focus of the next section in this chapter.

A point to note, which will be discussed in greater detail below, is that the *Code* provisions can be looked at as varying in the degree of intrusiveness with respect to individual liberty that they entail.[6] Most obviously, liberty is infringed less when an accused person is simply handed a piece of paper requiring them to appear in court on a particular date than when the police physically take control of that person. More subtly, there is less of an infringement on liberty when both the police officer and the justice of the peace have considered beforehand whether the accused should be made to come to court rather than the justice of the peace reviewing this decision after the accused has already been dealt with. On that basis, the matrix in Figure 4.1 above is least intrusive in the upper left (summons) and most intrusive in the lower right (arrest without a warrant). We will deal with the sections in degrees of increasing intrusiveness.[7]

1) Summons

The issuing of a summons depends on two *Code* provisions: sections 504 and 507. Section 504 permits anyone to "lay an information" in front of a justice—that is, allege that a person has committed an offence.[8] Section 507 then permits the justice to decide what, if anything, to do about the allegation.

Under section 504, the information can be laid by a person having reasonable grounds and must be in writing and under oath. The information must allege one of four things: (1) that the person committed an offence anywhere that can be tried in the province where the information is laid and that the person is in the territorial jurisdiction of the justice; (2) that the person committed an offence in the territorial jurisdiction of the justice, even if the person might no longer be in that jurisdiction; (3) that property was stolen in the territorial jurisdiction of the justice

---

6 See Section B(3), below in this chapter.

7 Relevant to all of these approaches, see s 20 of the *Criminal Code*, which provides that "[a] warrant, summons, appearance notice, undertaking, release order or recognizance that is authorized by this Act may be executed, issued, given or entered into, as the case may be, on a holiday."

8 Section 504 deals with alleging that a person has committed an indictable offence. However, as noted in note 1, s 795 of the *Criminal Code* makes Part XVI, "Compelling Appearance," applicable in the case of summary conviction offences, so this section, and indeed all of the rules to be discussed, are equally applicable in the case of all crimes.

and the person has received it, anywhere; or finally (4) that the person is in the territorial jurisdiction of the justice and is in possession of stolen property, from wherever that property came.

A justice has no discretion under section 504: they "shall receive the information." However, the fact that an information has been laid before a justice is, on its own, of no consequence. It is merely a step leading to the provisions that permit a justice to decide what, if anything, to do about the information.[9]

By far the most common next step is found in section 507, which is used when the information has been laid by a police officer (as is typically the case) or Crown prosecutor. Under that section, the justice hears the allegations of the informant and of any witnesses (on oath), where they consider it desirable, and then decides what to do; this hearing is referred to as a "pre-enquete." Section 507(1)(b) permits a justice to issue a summons or warrant, but only "where he considers that a case for doing so is made out." In other words, the justice first decides whether the allegations justify requiring the person to attend court; if they do, only then does the justice choose between a summons and an arrest warrant. Section 507(4) directs the justice to issue a summons unless there are reasonable grounds to believe that it is "necessary in the public interest" to issue an arrest warrant. A summons or warrant can be issued even if the person could be arrested without a warrant; indeed, a justice is specifically barred from refusing to issue process on that basis.[10]

The alternative next step is found in section 507.1, which applies only in the case of a private prosecution—that is, an information laid by a member of the public. For the most part, the same rules apply,[11] but with some additional requirements. The primary difference is that while informations laid by a police officer can go in front of any justice, an information laid by a private citizen must be considered at the later stages either by a provincial court judge or by a justice who has been designated by the chief judge of the provincial court to receive such informations.[12] That judge or justice has the same three choices—do nothing, issue a summons, issue a warrant—but there are a few other additional requirements. The judge or justice must also be satisfied that the attorney general has received a copy of the information and notice of the hearing. Despite the fact that the prosecution is commenced privately—or, perhaps, because of that—the attorney general has a special

9 See Section B(1), below in this chapter.

10 See Section B(3), below in this chapter.

11 Indeed, s 507.1(8) incorporates s 507(2)–(8).

12 In Quebec, the relevant court is the Court of Quebec rather than the provincial court.

supervisory role, which includes the ability to cross-examine, call witnesses, or present evidence without being deemed to intervene. In addition, the attorney general can enter a stay of proceedings or withdraw the information if process is issued.[13] Furthermore, if a judge or justice decides not to issue a summons or warrant, they endorse the information to this effect. This step will not only notify other judges or justices that the information has once been considered and rejected (since it is possible to bring a new application concerning the same offence[14]), it also starts a clock ticking. Six months from the date of that endorsement, the information is deemed never to have been laid unless the informant commences proceedings to compel the judge or justice to issue process.

There is one further noteworthy distinction between sections 507 and 507.1. The former refers to a justice hearing witnesses "where he considers it desirable or necessary to do so." The private-prosecution provision, on the other hand, states that "[t]he judge or designated justice may issue a summons or warrant only if he or she . . . has heard and considered the allegations of the informant and the evidence of witnesses."[15] This makes the evidence of witnesses essential when the information is laid in a private prosecution, which "serves as an important control over invocation of the criminal process to further the fevered imaginings of a private informant."[16] Any evidence that would be relevant, material, and admissible under traditional rules of evidence at a preliminary inquiry can be led at the pre-enquete; it is uncertain whether the more relaxed rules of evidence for preliminary inquiries set out in sections 540(7) to 540(9) also apply to the pre-enquete.[17]

In addition, it has been suggested that a private informant should be sworn even when simply making allegations and that where a private

---

13 *R v Vasarhelyi*, 2011 ONCA 397 at para 49 [*Vasarhelyi*].

14 *Criminal Code*, above note 1, s 507.1(7).

15 *Ibid*, s 507.1(3)(a). *R v McHale*, 2010 ONCA 361 at para 47, observes that "[t]he *obligation* to hear witnesses under s. 507.1(3)(a) may be contrasted with the language in s. 507(1)(a)(ii), applicable when the informant is a law enforcement officer or official, where the evidence of witnesses is only taken where the justice "considers it desirable or necessary to do so" [emphasis in original]. *R v Edge*, 2004 ABPC 55 at para 100 [*Edge*], suggests that the informant personally could be that witness.

16 *Vasarhelyi*, above note 13 at para 39.

17 *Ibid* at paras 57–58. This result flows from the fact that s 507.1(8) incorporates s 507(2)–(8), and s 507(3) says that evidence shall be taken in accordance with s 540, which governs preliminary inquiries. See also *Canadian Broadcasting Corporation v Morrison*, 2017 MBCA 36, equally finding it unnecessary to settle the issue (at para 93).

informant's allegations depend on information obtained from others, the informant should be expected to call those other witnesses.[18]

---

18 *Edge*, above note 15 at para 99. *Edge* contains, at para 100, a useful summary of the approach to be taken in the case of private prosecutions:

- The receiving of an information is a ministerial act; the issuance of process is a judicial act. Where the informant is a private informant, the latter responsibility can only be exercised by a judge as defined in s. 507.1 or a justice who is designated pursuant to s. 507.1(10). Hereafter in these bullets, the judicial officer issuing process will be referred to as "judge" or "the judge."
- The judge who determines whether process must be issued must weigh two competing interests and perspectives: (a) the right of private informant to seek justice; (b) the right of the potential accused and that a person not be called before the court to respond to the charge without just cause. The public has an interest in both of those rights and that the process is balanced.
- These two competing interests are balanced by the judge applying the standard set out in s. 507.1(2), i.e. a case has been made out requiring an accused to be compelled to appear to answer to the charge. If so, a judicial officer shall issue a summons. A warrant can be issued where there are reasonable grounds to believe a warrant is necessary in the public interest: ss. 507.1(8) and 507(4).
- The informant bears the onus to establish that a summons or warrant should be issued. The onus is satisfied where there is a *prima facie* case that satisfies the elements of the offence charged.
- There are conditions that must be satisfied before the judge can issue process. The judge must be satisfied that the Attorney General has a copy of the information, notice of the hearing and had an opportunity to attend, cross-examine, and call relevant witnesses: ss. 507.1(3)(b)(c)(d).
- The judge may issue process only if he or she has heard and considered the allegations of the informant and the evidence of witnesses. This means that a witness or witnesses must testify before process is issued. Where the informant has personal knowledge to prove the required elements, the informant's recorded testimony can satisfy that onus. However, where the proof relies upon the evidence of other witnesses, those witnesses should testify. Adjournments can be granted, in appropriate circumstances, to allow witnesses who can prove the required elements to attend. Where there is insufficient evidence to establish a *prima facie* case the justice will not issue process and the information will be endorsed to that effect.
- The judge does not weigh the evidence or consider any defences to the charge in coming to a determination whether a *prima facie* case exists. If a *prima facie* case has been established, the judge must issue process. The judge has some limited discretion not to issue process where he or she decides the charge is frivolous, vexatious, or abusive. There is also such discretion when the evidence is based upon the evidence of someone who is mentally disordered.
- The informant has six-months after process has been refused to appear before the same judge or another judge to request process be issued on the information. The new process request must be based upon new evidence. If process does not issue within six months the information is deemed never to have been laid: s. 507.1(5) & (6).

The contents of a summons are described in section 509.[19] It must be directed to the accused, describe the offence charged, and indicate a time and place for the accused to appear in court. It is to be served personally by a peace officer or left at the accused's usual place of abode with a person more than sixteen years of age. The summons can also require the accused to appear at some other date for fingerprinting. In addition, the summons must indicate the consequences of failing to appear either for court or for identification purposes. In the former case, the accused will have committed an offence, and in the latter, an arrest warrant can be issued. Recent amendments to the *Code* creating "judicial referral hearings," discussed below, create the option of not treating a failure to appear for these purposes as an offence.

A summons can be served anywhere in Canada and if served is effective no matter what territorial jurisdiction it was issued in.[20] However, a summons cannot be served outside the country without specific statutory authority, so any such service will not give a court jurisdiction over the person.[21] Unless otherwise vacated, a summons, once served on an accused, remains in force until the trial is complete and the accused is acquitted, sentenced, or ordered held in custody pending sentencing.[22]

2) Arrest with a Warrant

Many of the rules that apply to summonses also apply to arrests with a warrant since they are issued by the same route of laying an information under section 504 and process potentially being issued under section 507 or 507.1. As noted above, justices are directed to prefer the use of a summons. However, even if a summons has previously been issued, or for that matter the accused has been released at some earlier stage (these possibilities are discussed below), an arrest warrant can be issued where there are reasonable grounds to believe it is necessary in the public interest.[23] Similarly, an arrest warrant may be issued where the accused fails to appear for court after another process has been used.[24]

Like a summons, an arrest warrant names the accused and briefly describes the offence.[25] An arrest warrant is directed to the peace officers

19 See also Form 6.

20 *Criminal Code*, above note 1, s 703.1.

21 *R v RJ Reynolds Tobacco Co (Delaware)*, 2007 ONCA 749; *R v Shulman* (1975), 23 CCC (2d) 242 (BCCA).

22 *Criminal Code*, above note 1, s 523. Note that the summons continues to apply even if a new information is laid or a direct indictment is preferred: s 523(1.1)–(1.2).

23 *Ibid*, s 512.

24 *Ibid*.

25 *Ibid*, s 511.

within the territorial jurisdiction in which it is issued. It may be executed by one of those officers anywhere in the territorial jurisdiction of the issuing judge or justice or anywhere in Canada in the case of fresh pursuit.[26] The warrant directs that the accused is to be arrested and brought before the issuing judge or justice or some other judge or justice having jurisdiction. The warrant remains in effect until it is executed.[27] It is possible for a judge or justice to delay execution of a warrant to allow an accused to turn themself in voluntarily; if the accused does so, the warrant is deemed to be executed.[28]

Once the accused has been arrested, there are two possibilities: either the accused will be released on some basis by the police or the accused will be taken to a bail hearing. The former possibility arises in two ways. First, a justice can, at the time of issuing the warrant, endorse it to allow a peace officer to release the accused.[29] If that is the case, the accused might be released simply with an appearance notice (see immediately below) or based on an undertaking that might contain conditions (see the discussion below under "Restraint in Compelling Appearance").[30] Alternatively, section 503(1.1) applies to all arrests, whether with or without a warrant. It provides that "a peace officer who is satisfied that the continued detention of the person in custody for an offence that is not listed in section 469 is no longer necessary shall release the person." In that case as well, the accused will be released either on an appearance notice or an undertaking. If the accused is not released on either of those bases, however, then the accused must be taken to a justice of the peace in accordance with section 503. That section requires that the accused be taken to a justice "without unreasonable delay" and in any case within twenty-four hours. It is important to recognize that the primary obligation created by this section is to avoid unreasonable delay. That is, a delay might well be unreasonable even though twenty-four hours has not passed; that time is better seen as creating the outer limit of possible reasonableness.[31] The twenty-four-hour limit does not apply where no justice is available within that time, but the unavailability must be based on some real obstacle, such as the accused being arrested in a remote area;

---

26 *Ibid*, ss 513 & 514. Note as well s 703 of the *Criminal Code*, which provides that warrants issued by a court other than a provincial court may be executed anywhere in Canada. Section 703(2) provides that an arrest warrant issued by a provincial court judge or a justice may be executed anywhere in the province in which it is issued.

27 *Ibid*, s 511(2).

28 *Ibid*, s 511(3) & (4).

29 *Ibid*, s 507(6).

30 *Ibid*, s 499.

31 *R v Storrey*, [1990] 1 SCR 241 [*Storrey*].

an administrative decision not to have justices available on weekends, for example, could not justify non-compliance with the section.[32] This requirement of section 503 will be discussed at greater length below.[33]

Once an arrested accused is taken before a justice of the peace, the issue becomes one of judicial interim release, otherwise known as "bail," a subject that will not be pursued at any length in this book.[34]

3) Appearance Notice

An appearance notice is issued by a peace officer to an accused, requiring them to appear in court on a particular date. It is used as an alternative to the more intrusive route of arresting the accused and taking them into custody. Like a summons, it contains the accused's name, describes the offence, and sets out a date for the accused to appear in court.[35] Also like a summons, an appearance notice can require an accused to appear for fingerprinting and must set out the consequences either of failing to comply with that requirement (a warrant could be issued) or of failing to appear in court on the specified date (the offence of failure to appear under section 145(5)).[36] Note, however, that these consequences flow only if the appearance notice is in fact confirmed later by a justice, an issue to be discussed shortly.

There are several circumstances in which an appearance notice might be used, all of which are aimed at minimizing the intrusiveness of police power. Section 495(2) of the *Code* directs a peace officer in certain circumstances not to use the power of arrest, even if it exists.[37] Specifically, the *Code* discourages officers from arresting for summary conviction offences, for hybrid offences, or for indictable offences for which the method of trial is in the absolute jurisdiction of a magistrate. Put more simply, one might say that police are encouraged not to arrest in the case of less serious offences.[38] In those cases, rather than arresting, the peace officer is authorized to issue an appearance notice instead.[39] Furthermore, even if the peace officer does arrest a person for one of those less serious offences, they can, after the fact, decide to issue an

32 *R v Simpson* (1994), 117 Nfld & PEIR 110 (Nfld CA), rev'd on the issue of remedy [1995] 1 SCR 449 [*Simpson*].

33 See Section B(4), below in this chapter.

34 For information on bail, see Trotter, above note 3.

35 *Criminal Code*, above note 1, s 501.

36 *Ibid*, s 502.

37 See also Section B(4), below in this chapter.

38 See Section B(3), below in this chapter.

39 *Criminal Code*, above note 1, s 497.

appearance notice rather than continue to hold the person in custody.[40] This might be appropriate, for example, where an immediate arrest was necessary in order to get control of a situation, which is then defused and calms down.

It might be noted at this point that there is a situation that can be seen as even less serious than these less serious offences. Specifically, note that peace officers do not always have the power to arrest at all: if the offence is a summary conviction one and the officer did not find the accused committing it, then there is no power to arrest. This might be seen as the very least serious of situations, at least in the criminal context, in that not only is the offence itself minor, but there is less justification to intervene immediately because the offence itself is not ongoing. In these circumstances, even the relatively unintrusive method of issuing an appearance notice is not available. Rather, the only option available to an officer is to go to a justice in order to lay an information and seek a summons or warrant.[41]

When a police officer has issued an appearance notice, a route parallel to the "section 504/507" route for issuing a summons or warrant is then followed. Under section 505, the police officer is required to lay an information relating to that offence (or another one) before a justice. This information is, according to the section, to be laid as soon as practicable and in any event before the time stated in the appearance notice for the accused to appear in court. As will be discussed further below, however, this requirement has not been interpreted strictly by courts. Once the information is laid, the justice of the peace considers it, under section 508. As with a summons or warrant, the justice of the peace is to hear the informant and can hear witnesses. The choices available to the justice at that stage are to cancel the appearance notice entirely, to confirm it, or to issue a summons or warrant in its place.[42]

Note that an officer issuing an appearance notice is to request that the accused sign a duplicate of it, although the failure to sign does not invalidate the process.[43] Whether or not they sign it, the accused is to be given a copy of the appearance notice. Furthermore, in seeking confirmation of the appearance notice in front of a justice, the police must

---

40 *Ibid*, s 497.

41 Using an appearance notice is also a non-intrusive method of compelling appearance. However, the only Part XVI provisions explicitly making that option available relate to requiring the accused to attend a judicial referral hearing (s 496) or arise when there already was an arrest (ss 498, 499, and 503(1.1)) or where there was a power to arrest that the officer chose not to exercise (s 497).

42 *Ibid*, s 508.

43 *Ibid*, s 501(4).

prove at that point that a copy was given to the accused; that is, it is not sufficient only to prove service of the appearance notice in court if the accused fails to comply with it.[44]

If confirmed, like a summons, an appearance notice remains in force until the trial is complete and the accused is acquitted, sentenced, or ordered held in custody pending sentencing.[45]

4) Arrest Without a Warrant

Various powers of warrantless arrest are created in sections 494 and 495 of the *Code*; they will be discussed in greater detail below. It is sufficient to note here that they are given to both private citizens and to peace officers and that their availability depends primarily on the type of offence and whether the person arresting has witnessed the offence or only believes on reasonable grounds that it has occurred. For the purposes of tracing through the "route" for various methods of compelling appearance, there is for the most part no significant difference between an arrest without a warrant and with one. Although different *Code* sections govern the two situations, they describe essentially parallel routes.

As already noted, if an accused has been arrested with a warrant, they might nonetheless be released by the police rather than retained in custody, if the issuing justice has authorized this. Similarly, peace officers have powers to release a person who has been arrested rather than detain the person to be brought before a justice.[46]

If the accused is released in any of these fashions in a situation where there was or could have been a warrantless arrest, then the police officer is directed to lay an information in front of a justice.[47] In that event, the ordinary rules about laying an information, discussed above, will apply. If the arrested person is not released, on the other hand, then, just as when an accused is arrested under a warrant, they must be taken under section 503 of the *Code* in front of a justice of the peace without unreasonable delay and in any case within twenty-four hours.

Arrest without a warrant can differ from the other methods of compelling appearance in one fashion, noted at the start: a justice does not oversee the officer's decision that the person should be made to come to court at all. This is quite surprising, at a conceptual level. The purpose of this review in other contexts is to "place a judicial officer between the

---

44 *R v DeMelo* (1994), 92 CCC (3d) 52 (Ont CA).

45 *Criminal Code*, above note 1, s 523. Note that the summons continues to apply even if a new information is laid or a direct indictment is preferred: s 523(1.1)–(1.2).

46 *Ibid*, ss 498(1) and 503(1.1).

47 *Ibid*, s 505.

informant and the defendant to ensure that the liberty of the subject was secure from unwarranted intrusion."[48] There is no obvious reason that those subject to arrest without a warrant — the most intrusive method of compelling appearance — should have the least protection in this regard, yet "[t]he current statutory scheme actually provides greater procedural protection for those charged with an offence whom the police choose not to arrest or release."[49]

That is, in the case of a summons or warrant, section 507 permits a justice to decide that no case for issuing any process has been made out. In the case of an appearance notice, section 508(1)(c) gives the justice the power to cancel the appearance notice on the grounds that it ought not to have been issued. But when an accused is arrested without a warrant and is not released on an appearance notice, no precise analogue to this supervisory function can be found. The officer must still lay an information under section 504 charging the accused with an offence, of course. However, although section 504 normally leads to a review under section 507, that latter section notes that it does not apply "if an accused has already been arrested." An accused is not entirely without options, but a review by a justice of the peace as to whether the charge was justified is not among them:

> It should be pointed out that the issue of whether the person arresting the accused had sufficient grounds to do so cannot be inquired into with a view to quashing the information charging the accused. That is not to say that the arrested accused could not sue the arresting party for false imprisonment and malicious prosecution where the arrest is without factual foundation. Additionally, an accused could attempt to establish that the arrest was arbitrary, thereby contravening s. 9 of the *Canadian Charter of Rights and Freedoms*.[50]

Nonetheless, the fact remains that, in the case of arrest without a warrant, no judicial screening mechanism is provided. Although the accused is brought to a justice, that justice will consider only whether

---

48 *R v Jeffrey* (1976), 34 CRNS 283 at para 9 (Ont Prov Ct (Crim Div)) [*Jeffrey*].

49 James Stribopoulos, "Unchecked Power: The Constitutional Regulation of Arrest Reconsidered" (2003) 48 *McGill Law Journal* 225 at 252–53 [Stribopoulos].

50 *R v Whitmore* (1987), 41 CCC (3d) 555 at 561 (Ont HCJ) [*Whitmore*], aff'd (1989), 51 CCC (3d) 294 (Ont CA) [*Whitmore* appeal]. The Court of Appeal accepted the trial judge's conclusions and added some observations of their own. See also *R v Ladouceur*, 2013 ONCA 328 at para 26 [*Ladouceur*], relying on *Whitmore* for the conclusion that "[i]f an accused is arrested and held for a bail hearing, no jurisdiction exists for the justice presiding at the bail hearing to inquire into the sufficiency of the allegations and quash the information or dismiss the charge."

the accused should be released pending trial, not whether the accused should have to face trial at all.

B. ISSUES WITHIN COMPELLING APPEARANCE

1) The Role of the Justice

A common feature to all of the methods of compelling appearance is the requirement for some person, at some point, to lay an information before a justice.[51] Several issues are worth noting in this regard.

The most important thing to stress about the process for laying informations and issuing process is its two-step nature. Many cases have noted the important distinction to be drawn between laying an information under section 504 and asking a justice to act on that information under section 507.

In the former task, the justice of the peace is acting "ministerially" or "administratively." That is, in receiving the information, the justice is making sure that it is valid on its face: that it is in writing, that it sufficiently describes the accused person so as to make them identifiable, that it alleges an offence known to law, that the jurisdictional requirements are met, and so on. Provided that these technical requirements are satisfied, the justice has no choice but to accept the information.[52]

---

51 Form 2 in the *Criminal Code*, above note 1, sets out the format for an information: see s 506.

52 See, for example *Re Watt*, 1999 YTTC 16 at para 5:

> Mr. Watt (the informant) will recall that he placed this Information before Justice of the Peace Studds and the Information was sworn. That step in the process is referred to as receiving an Information or swearing an Information, and it is an administrative or ministerial act. It is not a judicial act. If, on the face of it, the wording of the Information appears to make out an offence known or recognized in law, the justice of the peace has no choice but to swear the Information. But that does not result in anything being done. The Information is merely sworn. In order for something to happen on the Information a judicial officer has to make a decision that process should issue, process meaning summons that should issue and the parties should be brought to court to answer to the charge.

In the *Whitmore* appeal, above note 50, the Ontario Court of Appeal (although not making specific reference to the *Criminal Code* sections) observed at 296 that "the duty of the justice of the peace is, first, to determine if the information is valid on its face and secondly, to determine whether it discloses or there is disclosed by the evidence a prima facie case of the offences alleged." At the trial level in *Whitmore*, above note 50, Ewaschuk J had suggested that a justice's role

However, that merely means that the first step has been taken: an information has been laid. Generally speaking, unless the justice carries on to issue a summons or warrant or confirm the appearance notice, there are no consequences for the accused from the simple fact that an information has been laid. At the second step, deciding whether process should be issued based on the information, an accused begins to face potential consequences, and at this stage a justice is required to act judicially.[53] Note that although the wording of the section implies that the same justice undertakes both roles, this is not necessarily the case, and a second justice can decide whether to issue process based on an information laid before the first.[54]

This is one of the reasons that justices of the peace "occupy a critical role as the point of entry into the criminal justice system."[55] The role of the justice is to act as a check on state power, in this particular context by preventing the police from bringing to court anyone they choose. However, institutional structures have not always made it easy for justices of the peace to genuinely play this role. The Supreme Court of Canada has noted that

> the whole concept, that the office should stand as a safeguard of the civil rights of the individual against the exercise of arbitrary police power, is in many cases, and probably in most cases, little more than a sham. In saying this we do not want to be taken as condemning individuals. We are condemning a system under which many conscientious and dedicated individuals are required to work.[56]

---

in deciding the facial validity of an information did not extend to such questions as whether it was duplicitous. However, his reasoning seems to depend in part on the fact that at the time many if not most justices would not have had legal training. With the changes in qualifications for justices of the peace since then (see below), it is not clear that the same rationale would still apply.

53 See *Jeffrey*, above note 48; *Whitmore*, above note 50. See also *R v Jean Talon Fashion Centre Inc* (1975), 22 CCC (2d) 223 (Que QB). In *Whitmore*, it is noted at 564 that the justice who "hears and considers ex parte the allegations of the informant," along with any witnesses, is required to act judicially: *R v Allen* (1974), 20 CCC (2d) 447 (Ont CA).

54 *R v Southwick* (1968), 1 CCC 356 (Ont CA); *Edge*, above note 15; *Re Willisko* (1980), 13 Alta LR (2d) 298 (QB).

55 *Ell v Alberta*, 2003 SCC 35 at para 5.

56 *Ibid* at para 6, quoting from the *Royal Commission Inquiry into Civil Rights: Report No 1*, vol 2 (Toronto: Queen's Printer, 1968) ch 38. Note as well this observation from the trial level in *R v Morton* (1992), 70 CCC (3d) 244 at para 10 (Ont Ct Gen Div), aff'd (1993), 83 CCC (3d) 95 (Ont CA), dealing with the procedure for swearing informations in a jurisdiction where (as is often the case) a particular officer is designated as the court officer, responsible for swearing informations in front of a justice:

As a result, provinces have taken steps to improve the qualifications and other aspects of the role of the justice of the peace, in order to allow them to act more independently.[57] The Court has held that the concept of judicial independence does apply to justices of the peace because of the role they play. Legislative change has been intended to help protect that. Legislation varies from province to province, of course, but typically there are now two categories of justices of the peace: sitting and non-sitting or presiding and non-presiding. We will not pursue here the details of each province's scheme, but the essential distinction that has been drawn has been to separate those justices who are required to act judicially by issuing process such as summons, arrest warrants, or search warrants and to create different qualifications for them—often the requirement that they have a law degree, among other things.

We will now consider in turn the ministerial and judicial aspects of the justice's role. First, note that section 504, dealing with the ministerial act of receiving the information, requires that it be laid by someone who, "on reasonable grounds, believes that a person has committed an indictable offence." The question of what constitutes reasonable grounds has been discussed above, in Chapter 2, Section C(2). The point to note here is that the requirement that the informant personally *believes* is also crucial.

> Sergeant Neeson testified that he had sworn the information before the justice of the peace in this case. He indicated that in the course of his duties as a court officer, he would swear several informations on any given day. When this occurred, there would be a number of officers lined up to see the justice of the peace and they would get 10 or 15 seconds per information.

57 *Justice of the Peace Act*, RSA 2000, c J-4; *Provincial Court Act*, RSBC 1996, c 379; *The Provincial Court Act*, CCSM c C275 [enacted as RSM 1987, c C275]; *Provincial Court Act*, RSNB 1973, c P-21; *Justices Act*, RSNL 1990, c J-6; *Justices and Other Public Authorities Protection Act*, RSNL 1990, c J-7; *Justices of the Peace Act*, RSNWT 1988, c J-3, as amended by RSNWT 1988, c 39 (Supp) in force 2 November 1992: SI-014-92; SNWT 1997, c 3; SNWT 1998, c 15; SNWT 2003, c 9 in force 1 April 2003; SNWT 2003, c 12; SNWT 2003, c 31 in force 1 April 2004: SI-003-2004; SNWT 2007, c 16; *Justices of the Peace Act*, RSNS 1989, c 244, as amended by 1992, c 16, ss 71–76; 2000, c 28, ss 56–64; 2002, c 10, ss 7–9; 2007, c 18, s 1; *Justices of the Peace Act*, SNWT (Nu) 1998, c 34, s 2; *Justices of the Peace Act*, RSO 1990, c J.4 as amended by SO 1994, c 12, ss 50–57; SO 1999, c 12, Schedule B, s 12; SO 2002, c 18, Schedule A, s 11; SO 2002, c 17, Schedule F; SO 2006, c 21, Schedule B, ss 1–19; 2007, c 7, Schedule 20; SO 2006, c 35, Schedule C, s 56(1) and (3); SO 2011, c 1, Schedule 1, s 4; *Provincial Court Act*, RSPEI 1988, c P-25; *Code of Penal Procedure*, CQLR c C-25.1, *Courts of Justice Act*, CQLR c T-16; *The Justices of the Peace Act, 1988*, SS 1988–89, c J-5.1 (effective 1 May 1989), as amended by SS 1997, c 10; *Territorial Court Act*, RSY 2002, c 217.

The laying of an information is an important point in the criminal justice process. It is the point at which, at least conceptually, the state ceases to investigate an offence and begins to try to prove that a particular person is guilty of it.[58] The rules therefore demand that the process of laying an information should not, to the extent possible, merely be seen as a matter of paperwork to be got out of the way.

In *R v Pilcher*, for example, the accused, two police officers, were charged with theft of firearms.[59] At trial, they called as their witness the police officer who had sworn the information. He testified that he had been instructed by a superior officer and a senior Crown attorney to go before a justice of the peace and lay the information but that he was not given any details about it. His normal practice before swearing an information was to read the police reports and summaries of the investigation prepared by other officers in order to have reasonable grounds to believe the offence had been committed. In this case, he testified that he knew nothing beyond what was stated in the information itself. The trial judge held that, on these facts, the information was invalid and had to be quashed. The informant was entitled to rely on information provided by others in order to form reasonable grounds, but he was required to form them personally; simply being told by someone else that the grounds existed was not sufficient. As the Ontario High Court of Justice put it in *R v Peavoy*:

> Recognizing that the pressure of duties and administration upon police forces may quite naturally cause them, when under pressure, to manage the laying of informations as a form of routine 'paperwork,' I feel obliged to add the following comments. A person swearing an information, particularly a law enforcement officer, is not at liberty to swear the information in a perfunctory or irresponsible manner with a reckless disregard as to the truth of his assertion. To do so is clearly an affront to the Courts and is at variance with the right of the citizen to be left alone by the authorities unless there is reasonable and probable grounds for invading his liberty by compelling his attendance before the Courts. The police officer who does not satisfy himself that he can personally swear to the truth of the information according to its terms (i.e., personal knowledge or reasonable and probable grounds), yet does

58 See *Lindsay v British Columbia (AG)*, 2005 BCSC 1494 at para 11, where the court observes: "The process set out in the *Code* (see, for example, s 504 to s 597.1 of the *Code*) establishes a finely tuned set of checks and balances which, coupled with a modicum of judicial discretion, work together to provide part of the process that leads to a just determination of a criminal proceeding" and concludes therefore that there are no alternative ways of commencing criminal proceedings.

59 *R v Pilcher* (1981), 58 CCC (2d) 435 (Man Prov Ct).

> so, jeopardizes his personal position and also does a disservice to the upholding of law in the community. His oath must be beyond reproach. He need not, of course, have personal knowledge of all the facts or even most of the facts that support the allegation; indeed much of what would be available to him will, so far as he is concerned, be hearsay. He must, however, be satisfied, even if it be on the basis of reliable reports made by other persons in the course of an investigation, that there is some evidence to support the charge, that that evidence in fact constitutes reasonable and probable grounds for believing that the accused committed the offence and that he believes that the accused did so.[60]

Where the officer does swear to have knowledge but in fact does not, the information will be a nullity.[61]

Similarly, for the information to be valid on its face, it must adequately identify the accused. *Re Buchbinder and Venner* presented a rather odd situation in which the informant (the matter was a private prosecution) alleged that four RCMP members were in possession of documents that had been stolen from him, but he did not know the identity of the particular officers who had taken them. The information was laid against "an unknown person that can be pointed out"; the informant's intention was then to rely on the power of a justice in section 507 to hear the evidence of witnesses in order to compel testimony from a former RCMP superintendent who would be able to identify the particular officers.[62] The Court of Appeal held, however, that the information was fatally flawed and so could not satisfy the earlier section 504 stage; in that event, there was no jurisdiction to issue subpoenas or otherwise call witnesses for a section 507 proceeding. It rejected the suggestion that there might be some sort of "halfway house" whereby an information that was not sufficient to allow process to be issued might be sufficient to allow a hearing to be held.

On the other hand, the court in *Buchbinder* did note that something less than the accused's name might be sufficient and that an information could be valid as long as it sufficiently described the accused. Without deciding the point, the court seemed to suggest that a narrower description than "unknown person that can be pointed out"—something that identified where the officers worked, when they worked there, and other

60 *R v Peavoy* (1974), 15 CCC (2d) 97 at para 39 (Ont HCJ). This statement of the law has frequently been relied upon in the various cases where it transpires that police officers have sworn informations despite not being familiar with the underlying facts. See, for example, *R v Awad*, 2015 NSCA 10.

61 *Ibid*.

62 *Re Buchbinder and Venner* (1985), 47 CR (3d) 135 (Ont CA) [*Buchbinder*].

details—might be sufficient. In concluding that a name was not always necessary, the court held:

> If a description was given in an information that the accused was short, swarthy, had a prominent scar on his left cheek, and was referred to as "Marty," surely the Justice of the Peace could "receive" such an information and permit witnesses to be brought forth by the complainant who could further identify him for the purpose of greater specificity in the information and subsequent warrant or summons. An example closer to home would be the case of an unidentified police officer who commits an assault. The victim knows the force he belongs to, his rank and badge number, and states that he can identify him. Is the entire process of the law then to be frustrated because the Chief of Police refuses to tell the complainant the name of the police officer to whom that badge number was assigned?[63]

A further issue related to the justice's judicial function has to do with exercising the powers in the *Code* for a proper purpose. In particular, it was noted above that when a summons is issued requiring an accused to appear in court on a particular date, that summons can require the accused to appear for fingerprinting or other identification purposes. In *Re Michelsen*, the accused had been arrested, fingerprinted, and then released by a justice on a recognizance; subsequently, the police decided that they also wanted to obtain a palm print from him. They therefore obtained a summons from a justice that only required the accused to appear for the purposes of providing that palm print. The accused was successful in having that summons quashed. It was held that the only justification for a summons was as a method of compelling the accused to appear in court, a purpose that was already accomplished in this case by the recognizance he had signed. Without that primary justification for a summons, the ancillary ability to compel the accused to appear for fingerprinting did not exist as the summons procedure was not intended to be an investigative technique.[64]

Sections 507 and 508 set out the justice's judicial function of deciding whether process should issue based on the information.[65] In 1986, the Law Reform Commission suggested that there was little authority on the issue of what standard a justice is to apply in deciding whether "a case for doing so is made out," as the *Code* requires. The commission concluded that it must be at least the reasonable grounds standard

63 *Ibid* at 146–47.

64 *Re Michelsen* (1983), 4 CCC (3d) 371 (Man QB).

65 Note the quite fundamental point about acting judicially included in s 507(5)—namely, that a justice shall not sign a summons or warrant in blank.

that would apply to a warrantless arrest but that probably nothing more stringent is required.[66] Since that time, various courts have stated that a justice's task is to decide whether the information or the evidence presented discloses a prima facie case, which is a stricter standard than reasonable grounds.[67] It has been suggested that the standard is lower than that of a judge deciding whether to commit an accused at a preliminary inquiry.[68] Others suggest, however, that the standard is analogous to that for committing at a preliminary inquiry, although the rules of evidence are more relaxed.[69]

The justice must consider the evidence not only of the informant but also of any witnesses who are called in deciding whether to issue process.[70] This requirement parallels, more or less, the obligation of a police officer to consider all the evidence known to them in deciding whether they subjectively have reasonable grounds.[71] However, the application for a summons or warrant is conducted on an *ex parte* basis, so as a

---

66 Law Reform Commission of Canada, *Arrest*, Working Paper 41 (Ottawa: Law Reform Commission of Canada, 1986) at 42 [LRC, *Arrest*].

67 *R v Morton* (1993), 83 CCC (3d) 95 (Ont CA), aff'g (1992), 70 CCC (3d) 244 (Ont Ct Gen Div) [*Morton*]. The Court of Appeal does not discuss the justification for adopting the prima facie case standard, but that justification is considered at some length in the decision below, which it upholds. *Storrey*, above note 31, makes clear that the reasonable grounds standard is a lower one than that of a prima facie case: see Chapter 2. See also *R v Fry* (1998), 38 RFL (4th) 328 (BCCA), which upholds the lower court's decision based on the conclusion that process should issue only where a prima facie case is made out.

68 See the useful review of caselaw in *Re Sorenson*, [2001] BCJ No 2114 (Prov Ct) [*Sorenson*]. See also *Re Lindsay*, 2005 BCPC 176 at para 12, summarizing the conclusions in *Sorenson*:

1. under s 507 the justice of the peace "effectively fills the role of a grand jury," as regards the finding of grounds to issue a process;
2. the threshold test is that there must be tangible evidence from which one might conclude that the offence has been committed by the person named in the information;
3. the threshold test is lower than that required to commit on a preliminary inquiry;
4. the test is "whether the information or the allegations of the informant and any evidence of witnesses . . . disclose a prima facie case."

69 *Edge*, above note 15 at para 63, quoting Quigley: "[He] seemed to agree with that approach but added the following at p. 231 of his text: 'The rules of evidence are relaxed for pre-inquiries, however, so that the justice is permitted to rely on hearsay or other evidence that might not be admissible at a trial or preliminary inquiry.'"

70 *Whitmore*, above note 50 at 568: "[A] justice acting under s. 455.3 must consider not only the allegations of the informant but also the evidence of other witnesses where they are called: *Re Tait* (1950), 11 C.R. 42 at 53 (BCCA)."

71 See Chapter 2.

practical matter, the only witnesses likely to be called are those who can be expected to provide evidence that favours issuing some sort of process. Witnesses can be called even if they were discovered only after the laying of the information; the important question is what evidence is available at the time the justice decides whether to issue process. The *Code* makes the hearing of witnesses optional, not mandatory.[72]

The *Code* does not specify that this hearing must take place in camera, but caselaw has imposed that requirement for hearings held under both section 507 and section 507.1.[73] This has been justified in part on the basis that the statutory requirement for proceedings against an accused to take place in open court did not apply since until a justice had decided whether to issue process, there *was* no "accused." In addition, there was a much greater privacy interest to be protected at a stage where allegations that might turn out to be unfounded and not to justify the laying of charges were made.[74]

The holding that the standard for issuing process on an information is analogous to the test at a preliminary inquiry has an important element that should be noted. The standard for committal at a preliminary inquiry has, somewhat unusually, been largely developed in the context of extradition hearings. In *United States v Shephard*, the Supreme Court held that a justice is to commit for trial at a preliminary inquiry if "there is admissible evidence which could, if it were believed, result in a conviction."[75] That standard was taken to imply that a judge could not weigh the evidence presented and decide to reject any of it as unreliable. Subsequently, however, the Court has held that that cannot be the case. In *United States v Ferras*, again an extradition case, the Court held that it was "axiomatic that a person could not be committed for trial for an offence in Canada if the evidence is so manifestly unreliable that it would

---

72 Section 507(1)(a)(ii). There is authority suggesting that although s 795 of the *Code* makes s 507 applicable to summary conviction offences, there is no authority for a justice to hear witnesses in considering such charges. See *Whitmore* (trial level), above note 50 at 564:

> It is also interesting to note that, a justice determining whether or not to issue process in respect of a summary conviction offence has never had the jurisdiction to hear witnesses in addition to the informant: see s. 723 of the *Criminal Code* and *R. v. Sweeney* (1912), 19 C.C.C. 222 (N.S.S.C. in banco). See also *Canada v Galbraith*, 2001 BCSC 675; *R v Gibbs*, [2006] 3 CTC 223 (BCSC).

Note as well that in the case of private prosecutions, the hearing of witnesses is mandatory: see the discussion above under "Summons."

73 See *Southam Inc v Coulter* (1990), 60 CCC (3d) 267 (Ont CA).

74 *Ibid.*

75 *United States v Shephard*, [1977] 2 SCR 1067.

be unsafe to rest a verdict upon it."[76] Lower courts, even prior to *Ferras*, had concluded that essentially this same standard had to be applicable in the case of a decision by a justice whether to issue process based on an information. That is, although the question is whether a prima facie case has been made out, which in large measure requires the justice simply to accept the evidence presented, the justice is not simply a rubber stamp. Consequently, there is a discretion to refuse to act "where the basis is abusive, frivolous, vexatious, or the informant is not credible because of mental disorder."[77] However, a justice is not entitled to consider issues such as whether the accused might have a defence to the charge.[78]

The judicial role in section 507 can be thought of in two quite different ways. First, without this step, the criminal process has not really been invoked: the laying of an information by itself does not mean that an accused has been "charged" in the sense in which that term is generally understood. For example, although the attorney general has the power to stay charges, this power cannot be exercised when the only step that has been taken is to lay an information under section 505; it is only after a summons or warrant has been issued that the power to stay exists.[79] Second, once the justice has acted judicially, the criminal justice process has begun; accordingly, there are a number of requirements for that step.

Sections 507 and 508 require that the justice "hear" the allegations of the informant. There is authority suggesting that this requirement is to be taken quite literally and therefore that, beyond simply being sworn, the informant must testify in front of the justice.[80] Others take the view

---

76 *United States v Ferras*, 2006 SCC 33 at para 40 [*Ferras*]. The Court held as well, in the same paragraph: "Similarly, I take it as axiomatic that a person could not be committed to trial for an offence in Canada if the evidence put against the person is not available for trial."

77 See *Edge*, above note 15 at para 73. See also *Marcotte v Pelletier*, [1998] RJQ 3186 (Que SC).

78 *Edge*, above note 15 at para 85.

79 *R v Dowson*, [1983] 2 SCR 144. On the other hand, see also *Casey v Automobiles Renault Canada Ltd*, [1965] SCR 607, where the Court held that an accused could sue for malicious prosecution in a case where the informant had laid the information, but no process had yet been issued. The Court found there that the informant had done everything in his power to commence proceedings and was therefore liable in tort. Note, however, that the Court also seems to suggest on the facts that the justice had heard the informant and in some way acted judicially even though he had not yet issued any process.

80 *Jeffrey*, above note 48 at para 5: "I cannot interpret 'hear' to mean 'see' or 'read.'" See also *R v Brown* (1975), 28 CCC (2d) 398 (Ont Prov Ct). Note the observation in *Edge*, above note 15 at para 43, however, that "[s]ome older jurisprudence support the view that the justice is only obliged to read the information and to

that it is sufficient for the justice to read the material filed and simply ask the informant whether it is true.[81] In any case, it is agreed that no very great level of formality is expected, evidence is not recorded, and so on because the accused's interests will eventually be adequately protected by the trial process.[82] Nonetheless, it has been suggested that

> [i]n the vast majority of cases, the justice should question the informant, the more so where the informant has only hearsay knowledge of the charge, to decide whether process should issue. Often an inquiry of a few minutes will suffice. In other cases, the inquiry must be more detailed. If the justice is not satisfied that the informant has a sufficient factual basis justifying the issuance of process, the justice must hear the evidence of other witnesses. In such case, it is "necessary to do so" in accordance with s. 455.3(1)(a)(ii): *R. v. Ingwer* (1955), 113 C.C.C. 361 at pp. 365-6, [1956] O.R. 60, 22 C.R. 399 (Ont. H.C.J.), and *R. v. Jean Talon Fashion Center Inc.* (1975), 22 C.C.C. (2d) 223 at p. 228, 56 D.L.R. (3d) 296 (Que. Q.B.). Even though an informant might have sufficient grounds to justify process, the justice may still consider it "desirable" to hear the evidence of other witnesses, especially where the witnesses are alleged accomplices, of disreputable backgrounds, or closely associated to the accused.[83]

It might seem to be difficult to reconcile these requirements with the reality that in many cases a single officer is responsible for swearing informations in front of a justice and that only a very short time might be available for each. In large part, the explanation can be found in the presumption of regularity, which imposes on an accused the onus of proving that the proper procedures were not followed. In *R v Morton*, for example, a court officer testified that when he laid informations in front of a justice, he would swear several informations on any given day, that a number of officers would be lined up to see the justice of the peace, and that they would get ten or fifteen seconds per information. He also testified that he was always asked whether the information was true to the best of his knowledge but was only sometimes asked other questions. He further stated that he did not have any specific recollection of laying the

---

ask the informant if the allegations are true: *Ex parte Archambault* (1910), 16 C.C.C. 433 (Que. K.B.) at p. 438; *R. v. Mitchell* (1911), 19 C.C.C. 113 (Ont. H.C.) at pp. 121–2; *Ex parte Dolan; Kay* (1911), 26 C.C.C. 171 (N.B.S.C.)."

81 See *R v Brar*, 2007 ONCJ 359, citing Roger E. Salhany, *Canadian Criminal Procedure*, 6th ed (Aurora, ON: Canada Law Book, 1996) at 3–26.

82 *Morton*, above note 67; *R v Ingwer*, [1956] OR 60 (HCJ); *Edge*, above note 15.

83 *Morton*, above note 67 at 565, citing Ewaschuk J in *Whitmore*, above note 50 at 564–65.

information in that case.[84] On those facts, an objection to the validity of the information was rejected. It was held that the presumption of regularity required a judge to begin by presuming that the information had been properly issued. The court officer's testimony that he did not recall what had happened and that he was only sometimes asked questions did not rebut that presumption, in which case it remained intact; on that basis, the objection to validity was rejected. The court suggested that it did not intend to condone perfunctory or rudimentary hearings, but it must be said that this decision certainly does little to discourage them.

There are other factors that serve to limit the extent to which the justice's supervisory role is a real one. Most significantly, it is worth noting the consequences of a failure by the justice to perform that role; in a great many cases, there will be none. In *R v Pottle*, for example, the justice who issued the summons testified that she had not conducted the hearing that was required. The Court of Appeal held that this failure resulted in a loss of jurisdiction over the person but not over the offence. The loss of jurisdiction over the person was of no consequence since it was regained when the accused did appear for trial. In that event, it made no difference that the justice had not performed the second, and one might think more important, of the two functions.[85]

The basis upon which this conclusion is reached depends, in fact, on the separation between the ministerial and judicial functions. On the one hand, the ministerial function only involves confirming the facial validity of the information; on the other hand, it *does* confirm that validity. In other words, once the ministerial stage has been properly complied with, the information is valid and remains so, despite any later failures at the judicial stage.[86] The general position of courts is that any errors are of no consequence if the accused does in fact appear in court since it is not possible for an accused to make a "conditional appearance" simply to object to some defect in process:

> The argument is also made that if an accused is not obliged to appear by reason of a defect in process, why should he not be entitled to appear solely to make this point and to obtain the Court's declaration on it in his favour. I appreciate the apparent logic of this submission but it

---

84 *Morton*, above note 67.

85 *R v Pottle* (1978), 49 CCC (2d) 113 (Nfld CA). See also *R v Hrankowski* (1980), 54 CCC (2d) 174 (Alta CA) [*Hrankowski*].

86 To the same effect, see *R v Bachman*, [1979] 6 WWR 468 at para 14 (BCCA), where the issuing justice had not held the necessary hearing: "There may have been various reasons for this. I need not examine them or discuss them. Suffice it to say that he did not, apparently, hold the hearing contemplated by the section. The information did not thereby become a nullity. It remained valid."

> appears to me that it overlooks one of the basic functions of process and that is to bring the accused before the Court. If this purpose is accomplished, and the objection is not based on jurisdictional grounds, the balance of policy considerations is in favour of holding that the Court does have jurisdiction, regardless of protest.[87]

That passage from *R v Gougeon* has been generally relied on by other courts.[88] *Gougeon* itself suggested in *obiter* that an error in the ministerial stage—that is, while acting under section 507 or 508—would give rise to legitimate grounds for objection by an accused. However, the Ontario Court of Appeal has explicitly overruled that reading of *Gougeon* in *R v Ladouceur*.[89] *Ladouceur* concluded that whether the error relates to administrative steps in section 505 (for example, non-compliance with time limits)[90] or a failure on the part of a justice to do one of the things required under section 507 or 508, there is only a loss of jurisdiction over the person, which can be ignored if the person otherwise appears in court.[91] However, none of these errors lead to a loss of jurisdiction over the offence.

This argument has been taken to apply not merely when there is some non-jurisdictional defect in the information itself but also where

87 *R v Gougeon* (1980), 55 CCC (2d) 218 (Ont CA) [*Gougeon*]. Also quoted in *R c Manseau* (1992), 73 CCC (3d) 476 (Que CA). See also *R v Harnish* (1979), 49 CCC (2d) 190 (NSSCAD) [*Harnish*].

88 See, for example, *R v Sinopec Shanghai Engineering Company Ltd*, 2011 ABCA 331, holding that an accused cannot make a conditional appearance to contest whether there was proper service; a challenge to the jurisdiction of a court to try a matter can be made conditionally, but nothing else.

89 *Ladouceur*, above note 50.

90 See the further discussion of this issue below at Section B(4).

91 The New Brunswick Court of Appeal, in *Black v R*, 2010 NBCA 36 at para 16 [*Black*], held, in similar circumstances, that there was no loss of jurisdiction of any kind, saying that "the Provincial Court did not lose jurisdiction over the offence *or the offender* by reason of the delay in laying the information" [emphasis added]. It is noteworthy, however, that the decision in *Black* says this immediately after saying that "*R. v. Markovic* (2005)... set[s] out the current state of the law." In *R v Markovic* (2005), 200 CCC (3d) 449 (Ont CA) [*Markovic*], the Ontario Court of Appeal had held at para 24 that "the validity of the information will remain unaffected and there will be no loss of jurisdiction over the offence nor will there be a loss of jurisdiction over the person *if the accused appears for his trial*" [emphasis added]. The accused appearing is, of course, a way for a court to *regain* jurisdiction over the person, so there is good reason to doubt the broader statement in *Black* that there is no loss of jurisdiction over the person. *R v Esliger*, 2022 NBKB 245, notes at para 13 that the accused in *Black* was unrepresented and that "[w]ith respect, maybe an in-depth debate would bring a different result."

there have been other errors at the preliminary stages.[92] Accordingly, where there is some problem with an appearance notice rendering it invalid but an information has been filed, it is possible for a summons later to be issued based on that information.[93] It would be the case, however, that an accused who did not respond to an invalid summons would not be guilty of the offence of failing to appear.[94]

Note as well that if a justice acts judicially and decides not to issue process, mandamus does not lie to require the justice to do so. Mandamus lies only to require someone to perform their legal duty; if the justice has performed their judicial duty, mandamus cannot be used as a method of review of the decision reached.[95] It could be that a justice who acts based on extraneous considerations has not really performed their duty, in which case a remedy might be available. But even then that remedy would amount only to ordering the justice to hear the matter again as mandamus cannot require a particular result.[96]

The justice's role is a supervisory one, although the exact nature of that supervision varies with the context. Where an appearance notice has been laid and taken to a justice, for example, the justice is authorized under section 508(1)(c) to cancel the appearance notice and cause the accused to be informed of that cancellation; in effect, in that instance, the justice's decision does stop the process, subject, of course, to a new process being sought. Put another way, the justice says "yes" or "no" to the possibility of further proceedings in that context. On the other hand,

---

92 In a similar vein, see s 546 of the *Criminal Code*, above note 1, which provides that an irregularity in the substance or form of a summons or warrant does not affect the validity of a preliminary inquiry. See also *R v Curlew* (1981), 64 CCC (2d) 211 (Nfld CA).

93 See, for example, *R v McAskill* (1981), 58 CCC (2d) 361 (NSSCAD), or *R v Thomson* (1984), 11 CCC (3d) 435 (Alta CA). See also *R v Allen* (1974), 20 CCC (2d) 447 (Ont CA) [*Allen*], holding that a decision by a justice not to issue a summons does not render the information invalid and does not prevent the complainant from seeking a summons from another justice. That is, the justice did not have a power to *cancel* the information.

94 See, for example, *R v Gray*, [1979] OJ No 1598 (HCJ). The problem with the information in that case was that it had not been sworn as soon as practicable after the appearance notice was issued, a question that will be pursued at greater length below. That fact did not mean that he could not still be tried for the offence of impaired driving with which he had been charged. However, when he did not appear for trial, the judge had no authority to issue a warrant for his arrest based on non-attendance. See also *R v Legge* (1990), 112 NBR (2d) 11 (QB), where the accused was not guilty of failing to appear, on the basis that the appearance notice had not been confirmed in a timely manner.

95 *R v Coughlan, Ex parte Evans*, [1970] 3 CCC 61 (Alta SC); *R v Jones, Ex parte Cohen* (1969), 2 CCC 374 (BCSC).

96 *Ibid*; see also *Re Blythe* (1973), 113 CCC (2d) 192 (BCSC).

when a peace officer lays an information and seeks a summons or warrant, the justice's role is somewhat more limited. The justice can refuse to issue a summons or warrant but cannot do anything further, such as cancelling the information. In effect, the justice can say "yes" to further proceedings, or can fail to say "yes," but cannot say "no." Rather, it is always open to the officer to take the same information before a different justice to seek a summons or warrant. As the Ontario Court of Appeal has held:

> In our view the determination which is made by the Justice under section 455.3(1) [now section 507(1)] is a determination, to be made judicially, whether on the evidence which is placed before him upon that hearing a case for the issue of a summons has been made out. It has no further effect. If he refuses to issue a summons, the information still stands, and the complainant is entitled to attend before the same or another Justice of the Peace on a subsequent occasion with additional evidence, and to request the issue of a summons on the basis of the evidence which is presented on that subsequent day.[97]

However, note as well in this context section 507.1, dealing with informations laid by private citizens. In those cases, if a justice decides not to say "yes," then they endorse the information to that effect. Such an information is deemed not to have been laid six months from the date of the endorsement unless the informant commences proceedings to require a summons or warrant to be issued.[98] Furthermore, the *Code* specifically requires that any further application on the same information requires the informant to bring forward new evidence.[99]

2) Charge Screening

In principle, there is a further way in which a peace officer's decision whether to lay charges can be assessed by another person. Crown prosecutors also engage in the process of "charge screening," although the way in which it is conducted varies from province to province.

---

97 *Allen*, above note 93 at para 6.

98 *Criminal Code*, above note 1, s 507(5).

99 *Ibid*, s 507(7). There is a certain ambiguity in the fact that new evidence is explicitly required for a reapplication in the case of a private prosecution. *Allen*, above note 93, had also referred in passing to a need for new evidence in the case of reapplications by a peace officer, although no *Criminal Code* section sets out any such requirement. Other cases have spoken about a peace officer reapplying before a different justice without specifically calling for new evidence: see, for example, *Whitmore*, above note 50.

There is no dispute that, at some stage, a Crown prosecutor should consider the charges that are proposed or have been laid and decide whether to proceed with the matter. This question is a broader one than that before the justice of the peace, whether a prima facie case can be made out. Crown prosecutors certainly are looking at whether there is a reasonable prospect of conviction; however, they are typically looking as well at whether it is in the public interest to proceed with the charges. That is, in a variety of circumstances, it might be possible to obtain a conviction but preferable to not to attempt to do so. Typically, the criteria to be applied in making this assessment are set out in a policy manual for Crown prosecutors in each province. Having this second look at the charges, by an independent Crown prosecutor, can help provide greater accountability. It should be noted, of course, that having the decision whether to lay charges initially made by independent peace officers also helps guarantee accountability.[100]

The real question, therefore, is not whether Crown prosecutors should review the decision of police officers but when. In most provinces, police lay the charges, and only afterward do Crown prosecutors review them and potentially withdraw them. In three provinces, however—New Brunswick, Quebec, and British Columbia—the screening happens before the charges are laid.[101]

Briefly put, the advantage of pre-charge screening is the possibility of avoiding both technical errors and the stigma of charges that will later be withdrawn. The major potential disadvantage is that it is less open and accountable since the decision not to proceed with a charge will have been made privately. The advantages and disadvantages of post-charge screening are essentially complementary to those: it is more open and accountable but potentially less efficient.

The Supreme Court has held that either procedure is acceptable. It is important, the justices found, that the decision of the Crown prosecutor is truly independent of the police decision and is made objectively. However, pre-charge screening does not necessarily lead to a loss of objectivity, and its absence does not guarantee objectivity.[102]

In any case, it has been argued that practical considerations mean that charge screening, whether it happens pre- or post-charge, is of limited value in restricting the number of charges that go to court. Crown

---

100 See Law Reform Commission of Canada, *Controlling Criminal Prosecutions: The Attorney General and the Crown Prosecutor*, Working Paper 62 (Ottawa: Law Reform Commission of Canada, 1990) [LRC, *Controlling Criminal Prosecutions*].

101 *R v Regan*, 2002 SCC 12 [*Regan*]. See also LRC, *Controlling Criminal Prosecutions*, above note 100.

102 *Regan*, above note 101 at para 70.

prosecutors have access to limited information and often are not in a good position to seriously assess the strength of their case until much later in the process.[103]

3) Restraint in Compelling Appearance

The general purpose of the compelling-appearance section of the *Criminal Code* is, of course, to see to it that an accused who is charged with an offence will appear in court to face the charges laid. However, woven throughout the provisions has long been the assumption that this result should be assured by the least intrusive means possible; indeed, the arrest provisions fall under the subheading "arrest without warrant *and release from custody*." If necessary, a person will be arrested and held in custody until the time of trial; preferably, however, the accused will be released after arrest or, if possible, not arrested in the first place. As will be discussed in detail below, the compelling-appearance provisions create an approach meant to promote the use of the least restrictive options: "the powers of arrest and judicial interim release are a means of last resort."[104] The scheme also contains provision requiring regular reconsideration of whether intrusive measures that have already been taken can subsequently be relaxed. Most obviously, the philosophy of restraint is reflected in the "ladder" approach of the bail provisions, which start from a presumption of a release order without conditions and require the Crown to justify each greater restriction in turn.[105] Earlier in the process, however, other provisions encourage the use of methods of compelling appearance other than arrest or encourage the release of an arrested accused without the need for a bail hearing. The Court has observed that "release—at the earliest opportunity and in the least onerous manner—is the default presumption in Canadian criminal law."[106]

That implicit goal of the provisions became explicit in 2019, when section 493.1 was added to Part XVI of the *Code*. That section, entitled "Principle of Restraint," states:

> In making a decision under this Part, a peace officer, justice or judge shall give primary consideration to the release of the accused at the earliest reasonable opportunity and on the least onerous conditions that are appropriate in the circumstances, including conditions that

---

103 Stribopoulos, above note 49 at paras 64–66.

104 *R v Penunsi*, 2019 SCC 39 at para 52 [*Penunsi*]

105 *Criminal Code*, above note 1, s 515. This book will not discuss the standards or procedures at a bail hearing, but the same philosophy can be observed at the earlier stages of the process of compelling an accused's appearance.

106 *R v Myers*, 2019 SCC 18 at para 1.

> are reasonably practicable for the accused to comply with, while taking into account the grounds referred to in subsection 498(1.1) or 515(10), as the case may be.[107]

The new provisions also add that in making those decisions, the actors are to give particular attention to the circumstances of Aboriginal accused and accused who belong to a vulnerable population that is over-represented in the criminal justice system and that is disadvantaged in obtaining release, a point we will return to below.[108]

The Court has commented:

> Restraint has a constitutional dimension, a legislative footing, and is not only recognized in case law, but was also recently expressly reinforced by the amendments that came into force on December 18, 2019. Section 493.1 now explicitly sets out a "principle of restraint" for any interim release decisions.[109]

Lower courts have found that non-compliance with this principle can amount to an arbitrary detention even if the detention was not unlawful. The provision has been described as "an exhortation to peace officers," which establishes "a duty on the police officer in charge of a person in custody to consider releasing the person at the earliest reasonable opportunity. Compliance with this duty is important to stave off arbitrary detentions."[110] Failing to think about and act on the obligation to release can therefore lead to a section 9 violation of the *Canadian Charter of Rights and Freedoms*.[111]

The explicit overarching statement of principle is new, but the specific compelling-appearance provisions are also structured to give effect to that principle. In particular, there are a series of points where release, or an approach that prefers the less intrusive of two options, is specifically preferred by the statutory scheme. In the order they will be discussed here, these are:

- Section 507(4) and related provisions, preferring the use of a summons to an arrest warrant;
- Sections 507(6) and 499, permitting the release on conditions by police of a person who has been arrested under a warrant;

107 This section was added by Bill C-75, above note 2.

108 Section 493.2.

109 *R v Zora*, 2020 SCC 14 at para 26 [*Zora*].

110 *R v Dugas*, 2022 BCSC 1947 at paras 67 & 68, respectively.

111 Part 1 of the *Constitution Act, 1982*, being Schedule B to the *Canada Act 1982* (UK), 1982, c 11 [*Charter*]. See also *R v Polusmiak*, 2022 PECA 8 [*Polusmiak*]; *R v Babulal*, 2021 ONSC 3531; and *R v Al-Adhami*, 2020 ONSC 6421.

- Sections 495(2) and 497, directing a peace officer to use an appearance notice rather than to arrest without a warrant in certain cases;
- Section 498, directing peace officers to release an accused in certain cases even if an initial arrest was necessary; and
- Section 503(1.1), directing peace officers to release an arrestee in certain cases without waiting to take that person to a justice for a bail hearing.

Following discussion of those sections, we will discuss an innovation introduced in Bill C-75, the judicial referral hearing, which is meant to reduce the use of additional criminal charges as a means of compelling appearance. We will also discuss section 493.2, directing actors in the system to pay particular attention to the circumstances of accused who are Aboriginal or belong to a vulnerable and overrepresented group.

To begin with the most minimally intrusive approach to compelling appearance, let us look at the situation when a peace officer approaches a justice of the peace first to lay a charge. In that event, the justice decides under section 507 not only whether to compel the accused's appearance but also the means for doing so. That section provides that if grounds for compelling the accused's appearance have been made out, the justice is to issue a summons; that is, "[t]he default process for compelling attendance is the issuance of a summons."[112] The only exception to this rule is if the evidence led when laying the summons shows "reasonable grounds to believe that it is necessary in the public interest to issue a warrant for the arrest of the accused."[113]

The phrase "necessary in the public interest" is worth pausing to take note of since it will appear repeatedly. That phrase had appeared in section 515 of the *Criminal Code*, the bail provisions, as a tertiary ground justifying detaining an accused in custody pending trial. The primary and secondary grounds were that the accused would not otherwise appear for trial and that the accused's detention was necessary for public safety. In *R v Morales*, the Supreme Court struck down that public-interest criterion, holding that it was unconstitutionally vague.[114] The question therefore arises as to whether the same conclusion ought to follow in the context of section 507(4) or for that matter in other related sections that refer to the same consideration.

The matter has not been explicitly decided by the Supreme Court, but the caselaw seems to lead to the conclusion that the provision is constitutional as long as it is interpreted properly. It has been held that the

---

112 *Penunsi*, above note 104 at para 65.

113 *Ibid*, s 507(4).

114 *R v Morales*, [1992] 3 SCR 711 [*Morales*].

result in *Morales* does not lead to the conclusion that the phrase "public interest" will always be unconstitutionally vague; rather, its meaning and validity will depend on the context in which it occurs.[115] The specific meaning and constitutionality of the phrase in section 507(4) have been considered, but the analysis is made slightly murky because the major cases are not considering that section in its "ordinary" use. Rather, the caselaw considering section 507(4) has done so in the context of the interrelationship between that section and the various peace bond provisions in the *Code*, which can require a person to enter into a recognizance where there is a reasonable fear that they will commit one of various types of offences: sections 810 (personal injury or intimate image offence), 810.01 (criminal organization offence), 810.011 (terrorism offence), 810.02 (forced marriage offence), 810.1 (sexual offence), and 810.2 (serious personal injury offence).

The starting point is *R v Budreo*, where a section 810.1 application was brought against the accused, and he argued that section 507(4) violated the *Charter* on the grounds set out in *Morales*—namely, that it was vague. The trial judge rejected the challenge, although in doing so, he read "public interest" in a narrow fashion. The judge distinguished the use of the criterion in the two sections. Specifically, in section 515(10), the public-interest criterion had been used as a third, and separate, ground for detention beyond guaranteeing the accused's appearance and preventing the commission of more offences. In that context—what concerns other than those could justify the accused's detention—the phrase had been found to offer insufficient guidance.

In section 507(4), on the other hand, the "public interest" was not an additional and residual criterion; it was the *sole* criterion. The judge held that it ought to be interpreted in a narrow fashion, related to the justifiable reasons for detaining an accused. That is, the trial judge held that the only grounds that would mean that it was in the public interest to issue a warrant rather than a summons were that the accused otherwise would not appear or might commit another offence if a summons were used. The "public interest" was to be interpreted as shorthand for the primary and secondary grounds that had been upheld in *Morales*.[116]

The Ontario Court of Appeal upheld the trial judge's decision, but the vagueness challenge to section 507(4) was not among the grounds of appeal. What was in issue, however, was whether section 507(4), which dealt with compelling appearance for the purpose of answering to criminal charges, even applied in the case of a peace bond, which is not a criminal charge. The Court of Appeal found that the provisions could

115 *R v Farinacci* (1993), 86 CCC (3d) 32 (Ont CA).

116 *R v Budreo* (1996), 104 CCC (3d) 245 at para 177 (Ont Ct Gen Div).

be used in that different context and in essence adopted the trial judge's interpretation of "public interest."[117] Eventually, that same issue of the applicability of section 507(4) in the context of peace bond applications reached the Supreme Court, where they came to the same conclusion. They held:

> Where an Information is laid before a justice and he or she finds that there are "reasonable grounds to believe that it is necessary in the public interest," he or she may issue a warrant for the defendant's arrest. This phrase must be interpreted in light of the context (where the subject is not suspected of having committed a criminal offence) and the purpose (to bring the subject forward to a hearing) of the provision operating within the peace bond scheme. I agree with the Courts of Appeal in *Budreo C.A.* and *Nowazek* that instances when it will be
>
> > "necessary in the public interest" to issue an arrest warrant will be limited to cases in which proceeding in this fashion is necessary to preserve the integrity of the [peace bond] proceedings. *This will only be so when a case has been made out by the informant that the defendant will not otherwise attend court or that the defendant poses an imminent risk* . . . .
>
> (*Nowazek*, at para. 82 (emphasis added), citing *Budreo C.A.*, at para. 66. See also *Cachine*, at para. 26.)[118]

Strictly, all of these interpretations focus on the meaning of "public interest" when section 507(4) is used in combination with various peace bond provisions and, other than the trial decision in *Budreo*, do not expressly address the potential vagueness challenge. Still, the reasonable conclusion is that the provision is constitutional and that "necessary in the public interest" should be understood in all contexts as meaning necessary to ensure the accused's attendance or to prevent an imminent risk.

It is also not entirely clear who bears the burden of showing compliance with section 507(4) or what type of evidence is necessary. In *R v Brown*, for example, the accused had agreed to surrender himself to the police, but his lawyer had subsequently written a letter offering to make arrangements for the accused to come to court without being arrested. The police officer did not reply to the accused's counsel's letter and instead prepared a report to the Crown suggesting that the accused be arrested based on his non-appearance. A justice did issue a warrant, and the accused was arrested, but he objected that section 507(4) had

117 *R v Budreo* (2000), 142 CCC (3d) 225 at para 67 (Ont CA).

118 *Penunsi*, above note 104 at para 69.

not been complied with. The trial judge concluded that because there was no evidence of the allegations placed before the justice, the warrant had to be presumed to have been properly issued "unless there is evidence before the court that the justice improperly issued the warrant."[119]

On the other hand, in *R v Gagnon*, the police recommended an arrest to the Crown, and the Crown agreed but recommended a subsequent release on an undertaking to appear. The trial judge found this warrant to have been improperly issued because the accused had given notice of his intention to challenge the claim that a warrant was required, "[y]et there is no explanation of the basis for the existence of the reasonable and probable grounds required by s. 507(4)."[120] Nothing in the facts showed why a warrant would be necessary, and the recommendation of release on an undertaking implied the opposite. In that event, the warrant was found to have been improperly issued.

In the normal course of events, a warrant will name or describe the accused, name the charge for which they are sought, and order that they be arrested and brought before "the judge or justice who issued the warrant or some other judge or justice having jurisdiction in the same territorial division."[121] This wording does not, it has been held, allow an issuing judge to insist on an accused being brought before them personally: the "or" means that the police must take the accused before *some* justice with jurisdiction within the time period allowed.[122] Note in addition the possibility provided for in section 511(3), which is to allow the justice to delay the execution of a warrant in order to give an accused the opportunity to voluntarily surrender; this is sometimes referred to as a "bench warrant with discretion."[123] If an accused does so, the warrant is deemed to be executed.

Arguably running against the general trend of avoiding arrest, section 512 allows a justice to issue a warrant (or summons) even though the accused has previously been dealt with in some other fashion, such as by an appearance notice. Section 512 requires the justice to have "reasonable and probable grounds to believe that it is necessary in the public interest" before doing so; in this context, that phrase has been interpreted to give a justice "residual powers to be exercised in the public interest."[124] For example, where an accused who is already in custody is

---

119 *R v Brown*, 2004 BCPC 290 at para 17.

120 *R v Gagnon*, [1994] BCJ No 818 at para 22 (Prov Ct).

121 *Criminal Code*, above note 1, s 511.

122 *R v Davidson*, 2004 ABCA 337. See Section B(4), below in this chapter.

123 See *R v Sheppard*, 2020 CanLII 43917 (NL PC) at para 17 [*Sheppard*].

124 *Ex parte Chung* (1975), 26 CCC (2d) 497 (BCSC), aff'd (1976), 26 CCC (2d) 497 (BCCA); *R v Horton*, [2002] OJ No 1219 (SCJ).

not brought to court at a scheduled time, the public-interest criterion has been held to justify the issuance of an arrest warrant, despite the fact that the accused is in custody, as a means of retaining jurisdiction over the person.[125] It has also been suggested that the public interest in this context should be assessed in light of public safety, the seriousness of the offence and the nature of the charges, the effective enforcement of the criminal law, and any need to prevent the continuation or repetition of the offence.[126] Furthermore, since section 512 permits either a summons or a warrant, the principle of restraint requires that a summons be used unless that approach is contrary to the public interest.[127]

That aspect of section 512 has been used in support of adopting a restraint-based approach in other sections. Sections 512.1, 512.2, and 512.3 create related powers allowing for the issuance of an arrest warrant where an accused has failed to comply with some previous process, such as the obligation to appear for fingerprinting. Although those sections refer only to the possibility of issuing an arrest warrant, it has been held that in light of the principle of restraint in section 493.1 and the ability in section 512 to issue a summons rather than a warrant, the provisions should be interpreted to permit a justice simply to issue a summons to appear for fingerprinting.[128]

A further example of the potential restraint in the use of arrest powers is found in section 507(6), which also applies once a warrant has been issued. That section allows the justice (except in the case of section 469 offences) to endorse the warrant, authorizing the accused to be released after arrest, in accordance with section 499. Until 2019, the decision to release was directed toward "the officer in charge" of the place where the accused was kept in custody, but with the streamlining of the arrest provisions in 2019 by Bill C-75, the power is now available simply to "a peace officer." The peace officer can release the person either with an appearance notice or on an undertaking. The contents of each are set out in sections 500 and 501, respectively. An appearance notice, in essence,

---

125 See also *Criminal Code*, above note 1, s 485(2), which provides:

> (2) Where jurisdiction over an accused or a defendant is lost and has not been regained, a court, judge, provincial court judge or justice may, within three months after the loss of jurisdiction, issue a summons, or if it or he considers it necessary in the public interest, a warrant for the arrest of the accused or defendant.

126 *Sheppard*, above note 123 at para 39.

127 *Ibid* at para 41.

128 See *R v Chevalier*, 2020 ONCJ 514 [*Chevalier*]. The particular issue in the case was that, due to the COVID-19 pandemic, hundreds of people had been unable to appear for fingerprinting as ordered, and the Crown was seeking not to have to obtain arrest warrants in every case.

simply requires the accused to appear in court at the appropriate place and time and perhaps to appear for fingerprinting. An undertaking, in contrast, can be more involved. Section 501(3) provides that

> [t]he undertaking may contain one or more of the following conditions, if the condition is reasonable in the circumstances of the offence and necessary, to ensure the accused's attendance in court or the safety and security of any victim of or witness to the offence, or to prevent the continuation or repetition of the offence or the commission of another offence:
>
> (a) report at specified times to the peace officer or other specified person;
>
> (b) remain within a specified territorial jurisdiction;
>
> (c) notify the peace officer or other specified person of any change in their address, employment or occupation;
>
> (d) abstain from communicating, directly or indirectly, with any victim, witness or other person identified in the undertaking, except in accordance with any specified conditions;
>
> (e) abstain from going to any specified place or entering any geographic area related to any person referred to in paragraph (d), except in accordance with any specified conditions;
>
> (f) deposit all their passports with the peace officer or other specified person;
>
> (g) reside at a specified address, be at that address at specified hours and present themselves at the entrance of that residence to a peace officer or other specified person, at the officer's or specified person's request during those hours;
>
> (h) abstain from possessing a firearm, cross-bow, prohibited weapon, restricted weapon, prohibited device, ammunition, prohibited ammunition or explosive substance, and surrender those that are in their possession to the peace officer or other specified person and also any authorization, licence or registration certificate or other document enabling them to acquire or possess them;
>
> (i) promise to pay an amount specified in the undertaking, which shall not be more than $500, if they fail to comply with any condition of the undertaking;
>
> (j) deposit, with the peace officer specified in the undertaking, money or other valuable security whose value does not exceed $500 if, at the time of giving the undertaking, the accused is not ordinarily resident in the province or does not ordinarily reside within 200 kilometres of the place in which they are in custody; and
>
> (k) comply with any other specified condition for ensuring the safety and security of any victim of or witness to the offence.

In addition to these rules governing the context of pre-arrest and arrest with a warrant, there are a number of provisions that attempt to impose restraint on the use of arrest without warrant powers. Largely parallel provisions affect a peace officer's abilities at the time of arrest and post-arrest.

The easiest starting point is in section 495, the arrest powers section itself. Section 495(1) creates a number of warrantless arrest powers (see the discussion in Section C(2)(b)(iii), below). Between them, section 495(2) and (3) have an impact on how peace officers should exercise their powers that is not easy to encapsulate in a few words. On the one hand, the sections do not take away the power to arrest. On the other hand, they do make clear that an officer is wrong to arrest in some situations. That is, section 495(2) says that an officer "shall not arrest" if particular conditions (which will be discussed below) are met. However, section 495(3) carries on to say that the officer is "deemed to be acting lawfully and in the execution of duty" even if they do arrest despite section 495(2). Accordingly, section 495(2) is not a limit on the ability to arrest; it is in some ways merely guidance intended to increase restraint in the exercise of those powers.[129]

---

129 Some mention should be made here of the Supreme Court's decision in *Moore v The Queen*, [1979] 1 SCR 195 [*Moore*], since it runs against the general spirit of s 495(2). The accused had ridden his bicycle through a red light and was witnessed doing so by a police officer. The accused refused to stop when asked to do so by the police officer and was ultimately charged with an offence. However, he was not charged with going through the red light; rather, he was charged with obstructing an officer in the execution of duty, on the basis that he refused to give his name to the officer when the officer requested it. The issue in the case was whether the officer had the authority to demand Moore's name; in essence, the Court held that s 495(2) gave the officer that power. The Court held that the officer's only potential arrest power was under s 495(1). However, since riding through a red light was a summary conviction offence, s 495(2) would apply. In that case, the officer "had no power to arrest the accused for such offence unless and until he had attempted to identify the accused" (*Moore*, above in this note at 204). That in turn meant that the officer was acting in the execution of duty in demanding the accused's name and therefore that the accused was guilty of obstructing the officer. *Moore* runs against the general trend of obstruction cases as more commonly, courts conclude that, in the absence of a clear and express power to compel a person to provide information to the police, a person does not obstruct in refusing to do so. See, for example, *R v Greaves*, 2004 BCCA 484 at para 49: "Generally, a person cannot then be convicted of obstructing a police officer in the execution of duty for simply refusing to say or establish who he or she is when asked to do so" [citations omitted]. See also *R v Guthrie* (1982), 69 CCC (2d) 216 (Alta CA) [*Guthrie*], or *R v Fraser*, 2002 NSPC 6 [*Fraser*]. There has been a tendency to try to limit *Moore*'s application. *R v Sandy*, 2007 ABPC 173 at para 73, for example, cites *Guthrie* for the proposition that "the ruling in *R v*

That said, it is worth pausing to note that the exact impact of section 495(2) and (3) is not entirely clear. It can be seen as merely guidance in some contexts.[130] The primary impact of section 495(3)(a) in the criminal law context is to prevent an accused from invoking non-compliance with section 495(2) as a justification for resisting an arrest. One clear effect—perhaps the only clear effect—of section 495(3) is that an accused who resists an officer who is ignoring section 495(2) will nonetheless be guilty of resisting.[131] However, saying that an officer is deemed to be acting in the execution of duty does not necessarily amount to saying that the arrest was lawful for all purposes:

> The purpose of Subsection (3) is to make it impossible for a person to invoke the illegality of an arrest by reason of Subsection (2) as a defence in criminal proceedings, not to render such an arrest lawful; otherwise there would be no purpose to Subsection (2).[132]

In some cases, police officers have arrested an accused because they were acting on the basis of a particular policy: to arrest all impaired drivers, or all those charged with spousal assaults, or all street prostitutes, for example. Such policies have come under criticism from courts since they conflict with the discretion whether or not to arrest given by the word "may" in section 495(1) and can conflict with the criteria set out in section 495(2). Accordingly, some courts have found that such arrests were not lawful and that they amounted to a violation of the right to be free from arbitrary detention.[133]

Furthermore, section 495(3) distinguishes two situations. In the case of proceedings under the *Code* or other Acts of Parliament, the rule above prevails automatically. However, the section provides that for other proceedings, the rule prevails "unless in any such proceedings it is alleged and established by the person making the allegation that the

---

Moore . . . is limited to situations in which the requesting peace officer has, as a result of seeing the individual commit some act, reasonable and probable grounds to believe that that individual has committed an offence, the *actus reus* of which is the act the peace officer saw the individual commit." To similar effect, see *R v Vasile*, 2021 SKPC 54, or *R v Alderson*, 2022 BCPC 180.

130 It has been described as "a mere paper restriction": *R v Prince* (1981), 61 CCC (2d) 73 at 79 (Man Prov J Ct Crim Div).

131 *R v Schwartz* (1998), 51 CRR (2d) 277 at para 47 (BC Prov Ct) [*Schwartz*]; *R v McKibbon* (1973), 12 CCC (2d) 66 (BCCA). See also *R v Munson*, 2003 SKCA 28, and the cases listed at para 58, or *R v Adams* (1972), 21 CRNS 257 (Sask CA).

132 *Schwartz*, above note 131 at para 47.

133 See, for example, *R v Labine*, [1987] BCJ No 567 (Co Ct); *Schwartz*, above note 131; *R v Pithart* (1987), 34 CCC (3d) 150 (BC Co Ct).

peace officer did not comply with the requirements of subsection (2)."[134] In other words, in a civil action, the arrest might be illegal, although the burden of showing that the officer was not authorized to arrest will fall on the claimant. In essence, then, section 495(3) means that if there has been non-compliance with section 495(2), an accused could on the same set of facts be guilty of the offence of resisting arrest but bring a successful "false arrest" tort claim.[135]

In any event, section 495(2) applies in the case of arrests for relatively less serious offences: summary conviction offences, hybrid offences, or indictable offences that are in the absolute jurisdiction of a magistrate. In the case of those offences, presumptively a peace officer should not arrest. However, the section carries on to set out two bases that could displace that presumption: that an arrest is necessary in the public interest or that an arrest is necessary to make the person attend court.[136] An assessment of whether section 495(2) should act to limit section 495(1) in a particular case rests on an examination of "all of the circumstances existing at the moment of arrest which were apparent to the police officer."[137]

Once again we have, in this section, a potentially problematic reference to the "public interest" criterion, which was found unconstitutionally

---

134 *Criminal Code*, above note 1, s 495(3)(b). In *Schwartz*, above note 131 at para 47, the trial judge noted that the *Charter* is not an Act of Parliament but rather an imperial Act and relied on this as a justification for finding that non-compliance with s 495(2) was of consequence. This rationale does not seem to have been more generally adopted.

135 On the other hand, see also *R v Hall*, [1996] BCJ No 348 (Prov Ct (Crim Div)) [*Hall*], where the trial judge was persuaded that, on the facts of the case, ss 495(3) and 498(3) meant that the accused would be precluded from obtaining a civil remedy because the police had acted outside of s 495(2) but nonetheless in good faith. The judge relied on the likely denial of a civil remedy as one justification for granting a stay of proceedings in the criminal matter.

136 Section 495(2) is phrased as a double, and sometimes triple, negative, which makes it difficult to follow. In fact, the relevant restrictions are phrased in this fashion:

> (2) A peace officer shall not arrest a person without warrant . . . where
> (*d*) he believes on reasonable grounds that the public interest, having regard to all the circumstances including the need to
> (i) establish the identity of the person,
> (ii) secure or preserve evidence of or relating to the offence, or
> (iii) prevent the continuation or repetition of the offence or the commission of another offence,
> may be satisfied without so arresting the person, and
> (*e*) he has no reasonable grounds to believe that, if he does not so arrest the person, the person will fail to attend court in order to be dealt with according to law.

137 *R v Sieben* (1989), 51 CCC (3d) 343 (Alta CA) [*Sieben*].

vague in *Morales*. However, in this context, the *Code* carries on to give some guidance. Section 495(2) says that the public interest in this context includes

> the need to
> (i) establish the identity of the person,
> (ii) secure or preserve evidence of or relating to the offence, or
> (iii) prevent the continuation or repetition of the offence or the commission of another offence.

It has been held that an open-ended reference to the public interest in section 495(2) would violate the *Charter*; however, if the section is read as being limited to the specific considerations listed, then it is constitutional.[138] In essence, the section complies with the *Charter* if "includes" is read as "means." This approach is similar to that noted above as a way of ensuring *Charter* compliance in the case of section 507(4).

Finally with regard to section 495(2), note that there is some authority suggesting that it does not apply to every arrest made under section 495(1). Section 495(1) (discussed at greater length below) allows a peace officer to arrest if they (a) have reasonable grounds to believe that an indictable offence has occurred; (b) find a criminal offence being committed; or (c) reasonably believe there is a warrant for the accused's arrest. Some lower courts have held that the requirement to release in section 495(2) applies only to arrests made on the first two grounds. In the third case, where an arrest is made because a warrant exists, it has been suggested that the justice's ability under section 507(6) to endorse the warrant takes priority—more specifically, that if the justice did not endorse the warrant allowing the accused to be released, then the officer is not entitled to release based on the factors in section 495(2).[139]

It is not clear that this authority ought to be followed. First, of course, a literal reading of the section suggests otherwise, and the literal reading ought to prevail. Second, *Gamracy v R* makes clear that an arrest under section 495(1)(c) is not an arrest based on the warrant but rather is a warrantless arrest; in that event, there is no reason in principle that any conditions in the warrant should bind an officer since the officer is

---

138 *R v Fosseneuve* (1995), 43 CR (4th) 260 (Man QB) [*Fosseneuve*]. The Alberta Court of Appeal in *Sieben*, above note 137, had held that the public interest was not limited to the specific criteria listed, but that decision predates *Morales*, above note 114, and so is unlikely to be followed on this point. See also the discussion of *R v Saxby*, 2006 ABPC 201 [*Saxby*], below, concerning the similar provision in the former s 498, which does not differ from the current s 498 on this aspect.

139 See *Wall v British Columbia*, [1995] BCJ No 1697 (SC), or *Ilnicki v MacLeod*, 2003 ABQB 465.

not acting upon it.[140] Finally, as a practical matter, an officer who arrests based on section 495(1)(c) might know only of the existence of a warrant and will not necessarily know anything about its contents—such as, for example, whether or not it has been endorsed. Particularly as the principle of restraint has now been explicitly articulated in Part XVI, provisions favouring release over continued detention should be favoured.

Section 495(2) deals with a decision by a peace officer not to arrest (in which case, section 497 authorizes the use of an appearance notice). However, the *Code* also provides for the possibility of a person being arrested initially but then subsequently being released by the police. For many years, this was accomplished by a set of provisions that distinguished the powers of an arresting officer from those of an officer in charge and provided more specific guidelines at each stage. As noted above, Bill C-75 streamlined the compelling appearance provisions as well as giving more substance to the principle of restraint. Release after an arrest is now dealt with in two provisions, sections 498 and 503(1.1). Both provisions apply to any peace officer and allow release for more offences than did the prior scheme.

Section 498(1) directs that a peace officer shall release an arrested person as soon as practicable if the officer intends to seek a summons, the officer issues an appearance notice, or the person gives an undertaking (see the discussion above of each mechanism).[141] This release condition applies not just to the relatively minor offences covered by section 495(2) but rather to any offence not listed in section 469. This was an expansion of the power brought in by Bill C-75.

As in section 495(2), section 498(1.1) lists circumstances in which an officer shall not release. If an officer believes on reasonable grounds that it is necessary in the public interest that the person be detained in custody or that their possible release be dealt with under a different provision, the officer shall not release; however, as with section 495(2), this decision is to be based on consideration of certain circumstances. Exactly as in section 495(2), these include the need to establish the person's identity, to secure or preserve evidence relating to the offence, to prevent the continuation or repetition of an offence, or to ensure the person's attendance in court. In addition, section 498(1.1)(iv) refers to

140 *Gamracy v R*, [1974] SCR 640 [*Gamracy*].

141 The phrasing of the section, asking "if" the officer intends to do one of these things, might be taken to imply that the decision whether to release is quite discretionary. However, it has been held that "[t]hese sections and in particular s. 498(1.1) require the police to release an individual charged with an offence": see *Polusmiak*, above note 111 at para 60.

the need to "ensure the safety and security of any victim or witness to the offence."

These circumstances to be taken into account in considering the public interest in relation to non-release are unchanged from the previous version. On that prior version, it had been held that the public interest takes into account a wide variety of considerations, including not just safety concerns but also the ability of the accused to understand the process to which they are subject, an issue that arises particularly with regard to impaired-driving charges. Police cannot adopt a policy of detaining all impaired drivers until they are sober, but they are permitted to consider the individual's functional sobriety or whether there is a responsible person to whom they can be released. That an accused is belligerent does not on its own justify detention, but it can be in the public interest to detain a combative and abusive detainee until they have an opportunity to sober up and calm down.[142]

That police cannot apply a blanket policy in this context is a key aspect of the section: each detainee is entitled to an individualized assessment of the factors in section 498(1.1), and the failure to do so can amount to an arbitrary detention violating the accused's section 9 rights.[143]

There was authority, under the prior version of section 498, that gave a release power to an officer in charge, suggesting that the criteria listed in section 498(1.1) should not be seen as exhaustive of the possible justifications for the officer in charge to decline to release. It had been argued that other legal powers, such as that in provincial legislation allowing intoxicated persons to be taken into custody, might justify detention independently of the public-interest criteria specifically mentioned in section 498(1.1).[144] Two points can be made about this argument. First, it is not necessarily inconsistent with the suggestion

---

142 See the discussion in *R v Hardy*, 2015 MBCA 51 at paras 49–51. In that case, the "emotional and agitated" accused was bellicose and uncooperative with police and acting against his own best interests, so not releasing him under s 497 was lawful.

143 See, for example, *Polusmiak*, above note 111 at para 72:

> The officer is required to analyze any and all of the factors present before making an informed decision of whether it is in the public interest to detain the person for a reason listed or arising from s. 498(1.1) of the *Code*.

And at para 79:

> The *Charter* breach occurred when the officer-in-charge turned Polusmiak over to the back-up officers for transfer to be detained overnight at the Provincial Correctional Centre without giving any consideration to the factors in s. 498(1.1) and other relevant factors.

It has also been held that police will be acting unreasonably if they rely on considerations other than those set out in the section: see *R v Korecki*, 2007 ABPC 321.

144 *Saxby*, above note 138.

in the previous paragraph that detainees cannot be kept in custody on the basis of a general policy to retain all intoxicated persons. Rather, it could simply mean that the detainee's drunkenness would be a legitimate consideration — part of "all the circumstances" — in making a discretionary decision.[145] However, it is inconsistent with the suggested interpretation of section 495(2), which limited the public interest to only the listed factors, as a way of avoiding the section being vague and therefore unconstitutional.[146]

It might be that this argument should not be seen as surviving the changes brought about by Bill C-75. The text of the new provisions on this particular point is not significantly different. However, the principle of restraint has now been explicitly stated as governing the part, by section 493.1, and judges do point to that as affecting the proper interpretation of the new sections.[147]

Equally, however, perhaps this dilemma can be reconciled without the need to read "public interest" as something broader than the specific criteria listed in section 498(1.1) and yet still allow police to hold intoxicated detainees until it is safe to release them. The general obligation in section 498, under both the old and new versions, is to release the person "as soon as practicable." Some courts have held that where police decide not to immediately release an intoxicated person, they have not actually decided to detain the person. In such cases, the police might not, for example, intend to take the person in front of a justice of the peace eventually; rather, is the person simply being held until they are sober enough to be released. In that event, the person is in fact being released as soon as practicable, so no justification for detention in section 498(1.1) needs to be found.[148]

In addition to this release power, a further provision mandating the release of an accused is found in section 503(1.1). The main point of

---

145 See, for example, *R v Coulter*, [2000] OJ No 3452 (Ct J) [*Coulter*]. See also *R v Suyat-Pavalaraj*, 2017 ONCJ 657, finding a s 9 violation where no individualized assessment was done as to whether the accused could be released, who was instead detained solely based on her blood-alcohol level.

146 See *Fosseneuve*, above note 138.

147 See, for example, *Sheppard*, above note 123; *Chevalier*, above note 128; or *Polusmiak*, above note 111.

148 See, for example, *Coulter*, above note 145; *R v Smith*, 2005 ABPC 202; or *R v Campbell*, [1995] OJ No 2975 (Gen Div). In the latter case, this argument was offered as one reason making it unnecessary to decide whether the former s 498(1.1) should be found vague based on *Morales*, above note 114. Nonetheless, the judge went on to hold that he would not have found the section vague since the words "public interest" did not appear alone, as in *Morales*, but in the context of the enumerated criteria.

section 503 is to require that anyone arrested be brought before a justice for a bail hearing without unreasonable delay (see the discussion below). However, in some cases, it is apparent that the accused's continued detention will not be sought at that bail hearing, so the issue is only the conditions upon which the accused should be released. Section 503(1.1) therefore states:

> At any time before the expiry of the time referred to in paragraph (1)(a) or (b), a peace officer who is satisfied that the continued detention of the person in custody for an offence that is not listed in section 469 is no longer necessary shall release the person, if
> (a) the peace officer issues an appearance notice to the person; or
> (b) the person gives an undertaking to the peace officer.

(The contents of an appearance notice and undertaking are discussed above. The most important distinction is the range of conditions that can be attached to an undertaking.) This section differs most notably from its predecessor legislation (former section 503(2)) in that the officer "shall" release rather than "may" release.

The policy rationale for what is now section 503(1.1) was explained by the Ontario Court of Appeal in *R v Oliveira*, discussing the prior legislation:

> Although the promise to appear and other similar mechanisms for release by the police introduced into the *Criminal Code* by the *Bail Reform Act*, S.C. 1970-72, c. 37, gave the police broad powers of release, those powers were deficient in that they did not permit the police to impose conditions as a term of the release. Unless the police were satisfied that the arrested person should be released without any conditions, they had to detain that person pending appearance before a justice of the peace. The justice of the peace could then release that individual on the appropriate bail conditions. This shortcoming was eventually cured by amendments that gave a peace officer who released the person on a promise to appear, the power to require that person to enter into an undertaking before being released: *Criminal Code*, s. 503(2). That undertaking could contain one or more of the conditions set out in s. 503(2.1) of the *Criminal Code* and is aptly described as "police bail."[149]

Interestingly, section 503 contains no provision parallel to sections 495(2) and 498(1.1), setting out "public interest" criteria that would

149 *R v Oliveira*, 2009 ONCA 219 at para 6. A "promise to appear" was a method for compelling the appearance of an accused similar to an appearance notice or an undertaking, although that particular mechanism was removed with the Bill C-75 amendments.

justify non-release. Equally, it contains no equivalent to sections 495(3) and 498(3), stating that an officer who does not act in accordance with section 503(1.1) is nonetheless acting in the execution of duty. There is such a provision in section 503(5), but it applies only to non-release in accordance with section 503(4) (release of a person arrested on the basis that they were about to commit an indictable offence). This might be taken to indicate a broader obligation to release under section 503(1.1) than under section 498(1), but the point is not clear. Other than these points, however, there seems to be little difference between the obligations to release in sections 498(1) and 503(1.1). Their predecessor versions were more distinct from one another, but the streamlining from Bill C-75 has eliminated many of those differences.

To conclude this section, we should discuss two other measures introduced by Bill C-75, both of which are aimed at promoting restraint: section 523.1, creating judicial referral hearings, and section 493.2, calling for particular attention to the circumstances of Aboriginal or vulnerable accused.

Judicial referral hearings are, in large part, a response to the use of additional criminal charges as a means of compelling appearance. The *Code* contains a number of sections that piggyback on the various compelling appearance provisions; for example, section 145(4) makes it an offence for a person released on an undertaking to fail to comply with conditions in that undertaking. These types of offences—referred to as "administration of justice offences"—are primarily meant as a means of enforcing compliance with the release order, but they make the consequences of non-compliance quite severe. Their impact has been to create a kind of "revolving door" of criminal liability. The initial charge might not have been especially serious, but non-compliance with conditions or a failure to appear for the court date could mean that the accused ends up charged with two or three offences rather than just one. This can ultimately result in the person being sentenced more harshly and having a longer criminal record. Indeed, in some cases, the accused ends up being acquitted on the original charge but still convicted of the administration of justice offences. This phenomenon has been noted as having a particular impact on Aboriginal accused.[150]

---

150 See, for example, Abby Deshman & Nicole Myers, *Set Up to Fail: Bail and the Revolving Door of Pre-trial Detention* (Canadian Civil Liberties Association and Education Trust, July 2014) at 75, online (pdf): https://ccla.org/wp-content/uploads/2021/07/Set-up-to-fail-FINAL.pdf: "The over-imposition of conditions of release and subsequent breaches are identified as major contributors to the over-arrest and incarceration of Aboriginal people."

Judicial referral hearings were therefore introduced "to address concerns regarding the over-criminalization of bail breaches."[151] Section 496 of the *Code* now provides that

> [i]f a peace officer has reasonable grounds to believe that a person has failed to comply with a summons, appearance notice, undertaking or release order or to attend court as required and that the failure did not cause a victim physical or emotional harm, property damage or economic loss, the peace officer may, without laying a charge, issue an appearance notice to the person to appear at a judicial referral hearing under section 523.1.

At the judicial referral hearing, if the judge is satisfied there was non-compliance of the sort referred to in section 496, the judge can, under section 523.1(3),

> (a) take no action;
> (b) cancel any other summons, appearance notice, undertaking or release order in respect of the accused and, as the case may be,
> (i) make a release order under section 515, or
> (ii) if the prosecutor shows cause why the detention of the accused in custody is justified under subsection 515(10), make an order that the accused be detained in custody until the accused is dealt with according to law and if so detained, the judge or justice shall include in the record a statement of the judge's or justice's reasons for making the order; or
> (c) remand the accused to custody for the purposes of the *Identification of Criminals Act*.

---

151 *Zora*, above note 109 at para 27. The innovation was also meant to provide benefits to the criminal justice system as a whole. Administration of justice offences make up something in the range of one-quarter of the total caseload in criminal courts. See Laura Barnett et al, *Legislative Summary: Bill C75: An Act to amend the Criminal Code, the Youth Criminal Justice Act and other Acts and to make consequential amendments to other Acts* (Ottawa: Library of Parliament, 2019) at 15, online (pdf): https://lop.parl.ca/staticfiles/PublicWebsite/Home/ResearchPublications/LegislativeSummaries/PDF/42-1/c75-e.pdf [Legislative Summary of Bill C-75], which notes:

> According to Statistics Canada, just over a million charges were completed in criminal provincial courts in 2015–2016, of which slightly more than 350,000 were for administration of justice offences—the largest number of these being failure to comply with an order (175,170). In 2014–2015, administration of justice offences represented 23% of cases completed in adult court. [Citations omitted.]

Diverting a significant portion of these cases away from prosecution was also intended to make the system as a whole more efficient.

More simply, if there has been non-compliance with the conditions of release, the judge can vary those conditions of release in some appropriate way, but no new charges will result. Section 523.1(4) and (5) provide that when such an order is made, any charges already laid will be dismissed, and no other charges can be laid. Put more generally, the provision is aimed at making further prosecutions "a last resort measure."[152]

Unfortunately, the early indications are not as hopeful as they might be that these benefits are being realized. As of 2021, at least three provinces—Newfoundland, New Brunswick, and Manitoba—had not yet created mechanisms for holding such hearings.[153] Defence lawyers in Montreal, Toronto, and Vancouver reported not having been involved in any such hearings or hearing of any taking place, despite having made requests.[154] A judge in Nova Scotia has observed that "it is unfortunate that these provisions, which would help to reduce the numbers of minor cases getting added to already burgeoning dockets, are being under-used. Or not used at all."[155] It is possible that the COVID-19 pandemic, which had a significant impact on many things starting from the spring of 2020, could have delayed implementation, but to date judicial referral hearings seem not to have had widespread uptake.

Although distinct from judicial referral hearings in section 523.1, a similar process can be found in section 524. If an accused has been arrested for contravening, or being about to contravene, whatever mechanism was being used to compel an accused's appearance, that accused can be brought before a justice for a hearing.[156] The point of a section 524 hearing is to decide whether the terms of the accused's release will be changed as a result. The section provides that the accused will be ordered detained in custody unless they show cause why their detention is not justified under the usual judicial interim-release provisions.[157]

---

152 *Zora*, above note 109 at para 70.

153 Justin Ling, "Reform but No Follow-through" *CBA National Magazine* (11 March 2021), online: https://nationalmagazine.ca/en-ca/articles/law/in-depth/2021/reform-but-no-follow-through.

154 *Ibid.*

155 *R v Morrison*, 2021 NSPC 39, at para 25.

156 The same process applies if the accused has been arrested for having committed an indictable offence while subject to some compelling appearance mechanism: *Criminal Code*, above note 1, s 524(2)(b). See s 512.3, creating the possibility of an arrest warrant where a person has contravened or is about to contravene a summons, appearance notice, undertaking, or release order or has committed an indictable offence while so subject; such an arrest is specifically for the purpose of holding a s 524 hearing. An arrest without a warrant for the same purpose can be made under s 495.1.

157 Section 524(3) calls for the cancellation of the previous order, and s 524(4) imposes the burden on the accused to justify release in accordance with s 515(10).

One issue that has arisen is whether the accused must still be detained for section 524 to be applied. That is, the trigger for a hearing is that "the accused has been arrested": if the police have arrested the accused but subsequently released them, does the section still apply? Caselaw has gone both ways on the point, but the most recent view is that the principle of restraint in section 423.1 means that such a hearing is still available. If releasing the accused meant that the police had lost the ability to seek such a review later, they would be encouraged not to release.[158]

The last Bill C-75 innovation to be considered here is section 493.2 of the *Code*, which says:

> **493.2** In making a decision under this Part, a peace officer, justice or judge shall give particular attention to the circumstances of
> (a) Aboriginal accused; and
> (b) accused who belong to a vulnerable population that is overrepresented in the criminal justice system and that is disadvantaged in obtaining release under this Part.

This provision applies to all of Part XVI, although its likeliest impact—and the motivation for it—is in decisions about bail. As the Supreme Court noted in *R v Zora*,

> A third reality of bail is that onerous conditions disproportionately impact vulnerable and marginalized populations. . . . Those living in poverty or with addictions or mental illnesses often struggle to meet conditions by which they cannot reasonably abide. . . . Indigenous people, overrepresented in the criminal justice system, are also disproportionately affected by unnecessary and unreasonable bail conditions and resulting breach charges.[159]

The language of "particular attention to the circumstances of Aboriginal accused" is very similar to that set out in section 718.2(e), which calls for particular attention in the context of sentencing. That section had been considered by the Court in *R v Gladue*,[160] and later decisions had already held that the *Gladue* principles should apply in other contexts, including bail.[161] Nonetheless, section 493.2 is valuable for a number of reasons. First, codification by Parliament of the broader application of those principles is likely to lead to greater uptake since lawyers will more frequently point to them and judges will more frequently apply them. Second, section 493.2 applies not just to bail decisions but to all

158 See the discussion in *R v McGinnis*, 2021 YKTC 16.
159 *Zora*, above note 109 at para 79 [citations omitted].
160 [1999] 1 SCR 688 [*Gladue*].
161 See, for example, *R v Robinson*, 2009 ONCA 205, and *R v Hope*, 2016 ONCA 648.

of Part XVI and therefore is applicable to all the potential "release points" discussed above.[162] Third, the section calls for particular attention not only to Aboriginal accused but also to those belonging to any overrepresented and disadvantaged vulnerable group.

Gladue principles require some modification for use in the bail, or any release, context. In a sentencing decision, a court will typically have a "*Gladue* report" providing information about the accused's background. In a bail decision, such extensive and case-specific information is not likely to be available. Courts nonetheless "may take judicial notice of the broad systemic and background factors affecting Aboriginal people generally"[163] and "should be prepared to rely on credible and trustworthy information that may come through counsel's submissions and may be in the form of hearsay."[164] It has also been noted that the presumption of innocence is still in play in a bail hearing, so *Gladue* principles—which are, after all, about how to deal with "offenders"—must be applied in a way that takes that difference into account. Nonetheless, these principles can be, and it appears are being, applied in the release context.[165]

4) Non-compliance with Time Limits

As noted above, the statutory scheme for compelling appearance envisions the likelihood that most accused persons will not be held in custody until the time of their trial. The officer first dealing with the person might not arrest in the first place and instead issue an appearance notice under section 497. Even if the person is arrested, peace officers have a duty in some cases to release the person on an appearance notice or undertaking, under sections 498(1) and 503(1.1). But if the person is not released, they must be taken before a justice, at which point a bail hearing considering whether the person will be released, and if so on what terms,

---

162 Note that the duty imposed by the section applies to "a peace officer, justice or judge."

163 *R v Ipeelee*, 2012 SCC 13 at para 59.

164 *R v EB*, 2020 ONSC 4383 at para 32.

165 See, in particular, *Raheem-Cummings v R*, 2020 SKQB 342, noting that the section says that a judge "shall" give particular attention and therefore finding an error of law in a decision below which made no reference to the section. That decision also noted that the obligation applied equally across the country and to all decisions. In particular, it applied in the case of the Black accused there, even though there was no significant Black community in Saskatchewan and no direct evidence led of racism against that group in that province. There was also no need to show that racial profiling had played a role in the arrest.

will be held. This is a further way in which justices of the peace play an important supervisory role with the compelling-appearance scheme.[166]

Out of this scheme, three important time limits relating to the interaction between a justice of the peace and the officers who are seeking to compel the accused's appearance in court arise. First, when an appearance notice has been issued under section 497 or the accused has been released under section 498 or 507, an information must be laid in front of a justice "as soon as practicable after the issuance or release."[167] Second, such an information is, as an outer limit, required to be laid "in any event before the time stated in the appearance notice or undertaking for their attendance in court."[168] Finally, when an accused has been arrested with or without a warrant, the accused is to be brought before a justice "without unreasonable delay."[169] Caselaw has discussed all three of these requirements.

Note first that the "as soon as practicable" and "before the time stated . . . for their attendance in court" requirements are independent of one another, although both are contained in section 505.[170] Accordingly, the former requirement can fail to be met even if there is an information in court when the accused appears.[171] This is consistent with the purpose of having an information laid in front of a justice, which is in part to allow that justice to decide whether or not the accused should in fact be compelled to appear.

It has been held that the "as soon as practicable" requirement with regard to appearance notices is mandatory for some purposes but merely directory for others. If no information is laid after an appearance notice has been issued, then the accused cannot be found guilty of the offence of failing to comply with an appearance notice.[172] Nor could a warrant be issued for the accused's arrest in the event of non-compliance with the appearance notice or a failure to appear.[173] These are not trivial points.

---

166 *R v Vassell*, 2015 ABCA 409, rev'd on other grounds 2016 SCC 26 [*Vassell*], from the dissenting judgment at para 70: "The requirement of personal attendance before an independent member of the judiciary distinguishes the Canadian legal system from that of a totalitarian state where people detained by the police often simply disappear."

167 *Criminal Code*, above note 1, s 505.

168 *Ibid*.

169 *Ibid*, s 503(1)(a), although it will become apparent in the discussion below that the time limit is more complex than just that.

170 *R v Naylor* (1978), 42 CCC (2d) 12 (Ont CA) [*Naylor*].

171 See, for example, *R v Taylor*, 2005 BCSC 1257 [*Taylor*], where the accused was, on 12 June, released on a promise to appear in court on 16 September. The information was not laid before a justice until 14 September, and this was found to violate the "as soon as practicable" requirement.

172 See *Criminal Code*, above note 1, s 145.

173 *Ibid*, ss 512 and 803(3).

It means, for example, that an accused might be not guilty of failing to appear for fingerprinting even if the appearance notice has been confirmed if this review was not undertaken soon enough.[174]

However, although the requirement is mandatory in those contexts, it is merely directory about the validity of the information itself. In this regard, the approach to failure to comply with time limits is consistent with the failure to comply with other requirements concerning the laying of an information and issuance of process, which is to say that there is no impact on a court's jurisdiction to try the offence.[175] Even if it is not laid as soon as possible, the information will still be valid. This result flows from the purpose of the section in the statutory scheme. It is not meant to prevent prosecutions from taking place if the time limit is not met. Rather, its purpose is to guarantee that there will be a prompt opportunity for judicial review of the appearance notice, to see whether it should be cancelled. Non-compliance with the "as soon as practicable" time limit therefore does not lead to the information's invalidity.[176] In this event, a court will have lost jurisdiction only over the *person*, and this can be regained if the person does in fact appear in court on the required date.[177] That means that the accused is still obliged to face the charge in the information; however, since jurisdiction over the person was attained only through the accused's actual appearance, they are not bound by the conditions in any undertaking that had been issued.[178]

This leads to the question of what "as soon as practicable" means. It does not, it has been held, mean "as soon as convenient" because that would be too lax. Such a requirement might allow unduly restrictive terms of release to be imposed, which would then not be reviewed sufficiently soon.[179] On the other hand, it is less strict than "as soon as possible." There is no hard and fast numerical formula determining the meaning of the phrase, so the analysis will turn largely on the facts of each case.[180] That said, the practicable time for laying the information does not vary according to the degree of restriction placed on the accused's release or on whether they are released by way of an appearance notice or an undertaking.

---

174 See, for example, *Taylor*, above note 171.

175 See the discussion in Section B(1), above in this chapter.

176 *Gougeon*, above note 87 at paras 35–36.

177 See the discussion above and the authorities cited in notes 85–93.

178 *R v Oliveira*, [2007] OJ No 2394 (SCJ).

179 *R v Marshall*, [2003] OJ No 5501 (Ct J).

180 *Taylor*, above note 171 at para 24. Periods of eight, nine, and ten days have been seen as falling within the "as soon as practicable" limit: see *Naylor*, above note 170; *R v Wetmore* (1976), 18 NSR (2d) 292 (SCAD); and *Harnish*, above note 87. However, sixteen days has been seen as too long: see *Hrankowski*, above note 85.

The same conclusion, that the information remains valid despite the deadline not being met, has been reached with regard to the obligation to swear an information before the time stated for the accused's appearance. One might have argued that there was a difference between the two situations since in the previous case there would have been an information in court, but in the latter the accused would appear, and no charge would have been laid. However, it has been held that the same reasoning applies and that an information can still be laid under section 504 even though the accused has already appeared in court. Concluding otherwise, it has been held, would amount to allowing the section to create a statutory limitation period for the trial of a criminal offence, which was not the intention of the section.[181]

More complex is the time limit for taking an arrested accused before a justice of the peace, found in section 503(1). First, note that different interests are at stake. In the previous case, it was simply a matter of an information being laid with respect to an accused who has been released. In this context, the accused has not been released, so the deadline concerns a review of their liberty. It has been noted that

> [s]ection 503 may be one of the most important procedural provisions of the *Criminal Code*. The liberty of the subject is dominant. A person not convicted of an offence should never be held in custody except in accordance with constitutionally valid provisions of the *Criminal Code* or other legislation .... The paramountcy of the liberty of the subject has been recognized in English law from the earliest times. Freedom is a fundamental right. It is not to be taken away except in strict accordance with the law.[182]

The *Code* creates two separate deadlines in this regard. The first applies when a justice is available within a period of twenty-four hours. In that case, section 503 provides that the person "shall be taken before a justice without unreasonable delay." The section carries on to say "and in any event within that period," but caselaw has made very clear that the intention is *not* to say that the police may hold the accused for twenty-four hours before taking them to a justice. Rather, "the police must take the person before a justice without unreasonable delay and ... the twenty-four hours is simply the outer limit of the time span."[183] In other words, once twenty-four hours have passed, the delay is (in the normal case) necessarily unreasonable, but it will frequently have become

181 *Markovic*, above note 91. See also *Black*, above note 91.

182 *Simpson*, above note 32 at paras 36–37.

183 *Storrey*, above note 31 at para 31, relying on *R v Koszulap* (1974), 27 CRNS 226 (Ont CA).

unreasonable well before then. There is a possible exception to that requirement, however, which is found in section 503(b). That section simply requires that a person be taken before a justice of the peace "as soon as possible" in any case where "a justice is not available within a period of twenty-four hours."[184]

Four issues need to be discussed: (1) What does "without unreasonable delay" mean in this context? (2) What does it mean to say that a justice is "not available"? (3) What is the impact of taking the accused before a justice? and (4) What are the *Charter* implications of a failure to comply with the requirements of this section?

In general, it has been held that "without unreasonable delay" is intended to convey a relatively short period, similar to "as short as reasonably practicable" or to "forthwith."[185] However, it is clear that police are not required to take an accused to a justice of the peace immediately upon completing the arrest; inherent in the concept of "without unreasonable delay" is the notion that *some* delay will be reasonable. Specifically, it is understood that the police are likely, at a minimum, to interrogate the accused and might engage in other investigative techniques before taking the accused to a justice, and this will not infringe the "without unreasonable delay" standard. Courts sometimes speak of this as the "right" of police officers to interrogate a suspect,[186] but that overstates the situation. Rather, it is better understood as not infringing the accused's rights when the police engage in questioning or other investigations so long as the statutory conditions are still complied with.[187]

---

184 *Criminal Code*, above note 1, s 503(1)(b). There is virtually no caselaw interpreting the meaning of "as soon as possible" in s 503(1)(b) in comparison to "without unreasonable delay" in s 503(1)(a). This is in part due to the fact that very little consideration has been given to s 503(1)(b), although see the cases discussed below. There is some suggestion that "as soon as possible" implies a greater sense of urgency than does "without unreasonable delay," but it would of necessity be a greater urgency only after a longer time has already passed since seemingly it will be a period of more than twenty-four hours. See *R v Warren*, [1994] NWTJ No 82 at para 150 (SC).

185 *R v CK*, 2005 ONCJ 462 [*CK*].

186 See, for example, *R v Soh*, 2014 NBQB 14 at para 42: "Police officers have the right to interrogate a person who has expressed his intention not to make a statement."

187 As the Court said in *R v Singh*, 2007 SCC 48 at para 28 [*Singh*], in the context of the right to silence:

> What the common law recognizes is the individual's right to *remain* silent. This does not mean, however, that a person has the right *not to be spoken to* by state authorities. The importance of police questioning in the fulfilment of their investigative role cannot be doubted. One can readily appreciate that the police could hardly investigate crime without putting questions to persons from whom it is thought that useful information may be obtained. The person

For example, in *R v Storrey*, the accused had been arrested in Windsor, Ontario, at 7:25 p.m., and the police wanted to conduct an identification parade or lineup.[188] The complainants in the case lived in Michigan and so had to be brought to the jurisdiction to view the lineup; that did not occur until the following day. Immediately following the lineup, the accused was taken in front of a justice, a total of some eighteen hours after his arrest. The Court found that in the circumstances of the case, this was not an unreasonable delay. It concluded first that it was open to the police, having arrested a person, to continue their investigation. To be sure, the police must already have had reasonable grounds for arrest before arresting, but that does not mean that a continued investigation to gather more evidence, or potentially to exonerate the accused, is not permitted. In some cases, therefore, that continued investigation can justify a delay in taking the accused to a justice. In *Storrey* itself, the delay was based on the investigative needs of the particular case: the Court stressed the lack of alternatives to a lineup in the specific case and the fact that the complainants lived out of the jurisdiction.

Storrey has not been taken to mean that, as a general proposition, the investigative needs of the police trump the rights of the accused under section 503. The issue is finding the appropriate balance between the two given the unique features of each case. In *R v Viszlai*, for example, the accused was arrested but was not interviewed until fifteen hours later; the accused argued that this violated the "without unreasonable delay" requirement.[189] The British Columbia Court of Appeal noted that the delay was primarily caused by the need for the investigating officer to reach the scene. As she was the lead investigator, was a member of a specialized investigation unit, and had travelled expeditiously, holding the accused until she arrived rather than have someone else conduct the interview was reasonable. However, it has been held that the police must be able to offer some reasonable explanation for why the accused needs to be in custody while an investigation is ongoing.[190] Even where that is necessary—that the accused is being questioned, for example—the

---

suspected of having committed the crime being investigated is no exception. Indeed, if the suspect in fact committed the crime, he or she is likely the person who has the most information to offer about the incident. Therefore, the common law also recognizes the importance of police interrogation in the investigation of crime. [Emphasis in original.]

188 *Storrey*, above note 31.

189 *R v Viszlai*, 2012 BCCA 442 [*Viszlai*].

190 *R v Clarke* (2003), 184 CCC (3d) 39 at para 185 (Ont SCJ) [*Clarke*].

police do not have carte blanche.[191] In *R v CK*, the accused, two sisters, were arrested at 7:00 a.m. one morning but not taken to a justice until after 9:00 a.m. the next day. The reason for this delay was that the police were interrogating the girls until 6:00 p.m. and were unable to persuade the "after hours" justice to hear the matter. That justice did not regard the matter as an emergency; tellingly, the police had begun trying to arrange for an after-hours justice at about 1:00 p.m. on the first day, at a point when taking the accused to a justice during normal hours was still feasible.[192] The trial judge noted that throughout this time the accused were being held ten minutes away from a courthouse where any number of judges and justices were available; the fact that the police wanted to continue their investigation did not justify delaying matters past 5:00 p.m., when justices ceased to be available.[193]

Similarly, in *R v Clarke*, three accused were arrested at different points on the same day but were not taken before a justice until the following morning. As a result of being held overnight, all three accused were strip-searched. The judge noted in that case that the nature of the investigation being conducted by the police did not justify the overnight detention. Documents were found on one of the three accused, which justified some delay in order to question him concerning them. However, to the extent that those documents raised the possibility that some further charge might be laid, that point could be pursued at a later time. Although some delay was justified to question the one accused about the documents, the existence of the documents did not justify an overnight detention for all three accused, particularly since the other two were never asked about them. Related to that point, although the police wanted to bring all three accused before a justice together, there was no need to do so. Accordingly, that desire did not justify delaying the bail hearing.

In *R v Poirier*, police had, in advance of an arrest for trafficking in narcotics, obtained a general warrant permitting them to conduct a "bedpan vigil" in order to obtain drugs that they had been advised

---

191 See, for example, *R v Keats*, 2014 NSPC 108 at para 70, where an accused's interrogation was postponed until the morning after his arrest, which was found not to be reasonable:

> The justification given for postponing the interview until the morning of the 31st was that the officers wanted to be rested when they conducted this interview. In this case, complying with section 503 and ensuring that a detained person is taken before a justice "without unreasonable delay" ought to have taken precedence over the officers being rested.

192 *CK*, above note 185. Note as well that even if the police are properly investigating, this will not justify a detention beyond the twenty-four-hour outside limit: *ibid*, and *R v Dann*, 2002 NSSC 37.

193 To similar effect, see *R v Mangat* (2006), 209 CCC (3d) 225 (Ont CA) [*Mangat*].

the accused would have concealed in his rectum.[194] The Ontario Court of Appeal concluded that such a general warrant could be granted and that the wait until an accused had excreted the drugs could be more than twenty-four hours but nonetheless found a *Charter* violation in that case because of section 503. A general warrant could not supersede the statutory provision, so the police were still required to comply with its terms. That meant not only that the drugs obtained after twenty-four hours had passed were obtained unlawfully but also those obtained prior to that point because of the "without unreasonable delay" requirement.

CK suggested as a general rule that "anyone arrested in the early morning should be brought to court during its sittings on the same day, absent a very good explanation."[195] In addition, that case offered some suggestions for deciding what would be a reasonable delay in each case. Courts should consider how necessary the investigative procedure was to the investigation: the stronger the case already, the less justification for delaying taking the accused before a justice.[196] In *Storrey,* the lineup might provide evidence of guilt but also might have exonerated the accused. Also, a lineup takes a discrete amount of time; once it is done, it is done. In *CK*, on the other hand, the reason for the delay was the desire of the police to continue interrogating the accused. The judge suggested that in such cases the right to silence should be taken into account: "[O]nce the right to silence was asserted and the police were given a reasonable opportunity to persist and persuade a change of heart (as the law now permits), delay beyond that point for further interrogation was unreasonable."[197] The length of a "reasonable opportunity," of course, might be quite extensive given the subsequent decision of the Supreme Court of Canada in *R v Singh*, but that case did not raise the issue of the interplay between questioning and the requirements of section 503.[198]

Other factors besides the nature of the investigation can also be relevant to how long it takes to bring an accused before a justice and what will be seen as reasonable. In *Clarke*, for example, the three accused were held overnight but were still taken to a justice within the

---

194 *R v Poirier*, 2016 ONCA 582 [*Poirier*].

195 *CK*, above note 185 at para 41.

196 *Ibid* at para 42, where the judge suggests that courts ask, "Was it, like *Storrey*, a step to determine whether they had the right man—whether a charge would proceed at all—or was it a procedure to simply gather more evidence in respect of a charge that would be proceeding in any event?" This advice should be understood in light of the prior finding in *Storrey* that if the police had not already had reasonable grounds to arrest when they did arrest, there would have been an arbitrary detention on that basis.

197 *Ibid* at para 43.

198 *Singh*, above note 187.

twenty-four-hour time frame.[199] Nonetheless, the delay was found to be unreasonable. In part, the overnight detention resulted from the fact that bail court had closed at 3:00 p.m. that day. The trial judge concluded that the police could have finished any investigations justifying delay by roughly 4:00 p.m.; even though the bail court might have been closed by that point, the judge noted that "[i]t is hard to accept that, in a city of 2.5 million people, a justice of the peace was not available."[200] Also in that case, it was significant that there was no need for a contested bail hearing since the accused had agreed to the terms the police wanted as conditions of their release. Most of those terms could have been imposed by a peace officer, but the police were requesting a surety in an amount great enough that only a justice could make such an order. Nonetheless, the trial judge suggested that given the consent nature of the order, it would have been feasible to release the accused on the terms sought by the Crown and on an undertaking to appear in front of a justice the following morning to add the surety. If that had been done, the overnight detention (and consequent strip search) would have been unnecessary.

Other rights can also be relevant to deciding the amount of delay that will be seen as unreasonable. Strip searches, for example, are sometimes justifiable, but they have been recognized as particularly invasive. One context in which they are allowed is when an accused will be intermingling with other prisoners, such as, for example, when being held overnight before being taken before a justice. Some courts have held that this possibility of a strip search creates an added obligation on police to be expeditious in taking accused persons before a justice, to avoid the necessity of holding them overnight.[201]

Where the police do fail to bring an accused before a justice in the specified time period, it is irrelevant whether this has happened deliberately or negligently.[202] Indeed, having a general warrant permitting a

---

199 *Clarke*, above note 190. Two of the three were within the twenty-four-hour period, and one was outside it.

200 *Ibid* at para 189. See also the discussion below of the interplay between s 503 and a purported lack of resources.

201 *Ibid*; see also *R v SF*, [2003] OJ No 92 (Ct J).

202 *R v EW*, 2002 NFCA 49 [*EW*]; *Clarke*, above note 190. See also *R v Dumont*, 2005 BCPC 204 at para 50:

> I do not believe that Constable Gill nor any of the other police officers deliberately planned to defeat the rights of the accused under s. 503 of the *Criminal Code*. I do think, though, that the police utterly failed to give the rights of the detainees anything like the priority which is required by the legislative provisions. The attitude disclosed by the evidence is altogether too casual, subordinating the s. 503 requirements to other considerations related to the police investigation.

procedure that will take longer than twenty-four hours does not allow police to fail to comply with section 503.[203] In addition, it is not relevant that the accused was unlikely to be released if taken in front of a justice.[204] As has been said, "[w]hat s. 503(1) guarantees to the accused is the opportunity to seek release from custody without unreasonable delay."[205]

As noted above, the general obligation is to bring an accused before a justice without unreasonable delay, with twenty-four hours set as an outer limit on reasonableness unless a justice is "not available" in that period of time. If a justice is not available, something more than twenty-four hours might consequently be reasonable.

It is necessary to consider the second question posed above and the meaning of "not available" in this context. It could be argued that this section has been rendered redundant for practical purposes because the *Code* has for some time allowed for various types of hearings to be conducted by video link. Bill C-75 modernized and rationalized these rules and in particular added section 502.1, specifically envisioning that proceedings under Part XVI might take place by audioconference or videoconference. A large part of the motivation for these changes was to improve access to justice for remote and isolated communities.[206] Given the availability of justices in many provinces in conjunction with this option, it arguably should never be the case that a justice is not available within twenty-four hours.[207]

---

203 *Poirier*, above note 194.

204 *R v MacPherson* (1995), 100 CCC (3d) 216 (NBCA) [*MacPherson*].

205 *EW*, above note 202 at para 18. See also *R v Rodgerson*, 2016 ONSC 6094 [*Rodgerson*].

206 Legislative Background: *An Act to amend the Criminal Code, the Youth Criminal Justice Act and other Acts and to make consequential amendments to other Acts, as enacted (Bill C-75 in the 42nd Parliament)*, online: www.justice.gc.ca/eng/rp-pr/csj-sjc/jsp-sjp/c75/p3.html:

> In its Final Report, the Senate Committee recommended that the "Minister of Justice ensure that resources are invested in technological solutions to the problems presented by small, scattered populations in remote and isolated communities." The Report specifically called for increased use of videoconferencing technology "so that court appearances such as bail hearings and interlocutory applications can be conducted remotely and without the need for an accused person to be removed from his or her community."

The amendments in the Act directly respond to this recommendation by expanding the use of technology to facilitate remote appearances by all persons involved throughout the criminal justice process, including in remote and isolated communities.

207 See the dissent in *Vassell*, above note 166 at para 71:

> In this case, a justice was available by video link from Edmonton 24-hours a day with the result that it was possible for the police to bring the appellant before a justice within the 24-hour limit in section 503(1)(a). In my view, this

In any event, it has been determined that mere administrative issues will not be sufficient to meet this criterion: "[A] lack of resources or a failure to apply resources effectively, cannot be used as a justification."[208] That is, the fact that particular courts might not be sitting and so it is not possible to proceed in a routine fashion is not, by itself, sufficient to say that a justice is "not available." In *R v Simpson*, for example, the accused was arrested in St. John's on a Sunday, but as the following Monday was a holiday and the provincial court was closed, she was not taken before a justice until Tuesday, forty-eight hours after her arrest. The Newfoundland Court of Appeal concluded, with no difficulty, that the "not available" exception did not apply. There were Provincial Court judges in St. John's, as well as fifty-five justices of the peace; the fact that the courts were not open did not mean that no one was available.[209] Similarly, in *R v MacPherson*, the Province of New Brunswick had not, at the time, created a system by which judges were available on weekends. The Court of Appeal there concluded that this was a systemic defect that had routinely resulted in violations of section 9 and did not fall within the meaning of a justice not being available; it commented that "justice does not stop on weekends."[210]

Simpson and *MacPherson* both dealt with "system-wide" failures, but the same principle applies in individual cases. In *CK*, the police chose to keep questioning the two accused past the time when bail court would close and were unable to persuade the after-hours justice (before the court had closed) that hearing the matter was an emergency. As noted above, the officers' desire to continue questioning the accused did not make the delay reasonable, nor did it mean that a justice was not available.[211]

The third question to be considered is the impact of taking an accused before a justice. Specifically, of course, the effect is that there

---

> precludes reliance on subsection 503(1)(b) because that subsection, seen in context, is designed to cover the situation where it is not possible to comply with subsection 503(1)(a) because a justice is not available *at all* within the 24-hour period. The subsection was not designed to allow institutional backlog to interfere with a detainee's right to be brought before a justice within a reasonable time of his arrest. [Emphasis in original.]

208 *Clarke*, above note 190 at para 192.

209 *Simpson*, above note 32.

210 *MacPherson*, above note 204 at para 13.

211 *CK*, above note 185 at para 35: "At its highest, the Crown/police position is that a justice was not available when they were ready to take the accused before a justice. The defendants were being held 10 minutes or less from the courthouse in which any number of judges and justices were sitting from 9 a.m. onwards. A justice was most definitely available within twenty-four hours."

will be a bail hearing and the accused will either be detained or will be released on some basis. It is also possible that the accused will be ordered remanded for up to three days before the bail hearing takes place if the Crown is seeking to show cause why they should be detained.[212] The broader question, however, is whether having been taken in front of a justice necessarily ends, if even for the moment, the ability of the police to question the accused. If the accused is released by the justice, then, of course, as a practical matter, questioning is at an end, barring further cooperation from the accused. However, there are two schools of thought as to how to respond if the accused is not released.

One view is that once the accused is taken before a justice, they have "come into the judicial sphere and out of the hands of the investigating authorities."[213] The purpose of section 503 is not merely to review the accused's detention but is also "to transfer control of the accused from police to the courts and the prosecution.[214] In that event, if the accused is remanded into custody, then they should be transferred to a prison; that is the authority given to a justice by the *Code*.[215] That is, upon being remanded, an accused should not be returned to police custody to allow the continuation of whatever investigation had been going on. The primary source for this approach is the Ontario Court of Appeal decision in *R v Precourt*:

> When the accused has been taken before a judicial officer and remanded on an information the investigative process incidental to arrest, previously referred to, has terminated, a decision to invoke the machinery of the criminal law to try the accused has been made, and he is thereafter under the jurisdiction of the Court.[216]

The court added that, in appropriate circumstances, police could still interview the accused or conduct an identification parade but that, nonetheless, the accused was to be held in a separate location following remand. Some delay—for example, to allow other accused also to be dealt with in court—might be justified, but the requirement to take the accused to prison "forthwith" meant that it must be done as soon as possible in the circumstances.

Under this view, if the accused cannot immediately be transported to a prison, they must nonetheless be treated differently following the appearance before a justice. It has been held, for example, that

---

212 *Criminal Code*, above note 1, ss 515 & 516.

213 *R v Ansari*, 2008 BCSC 1492 at para 48 [*Ansari*].

214 *R v Mendez*, 2014 ONSC 498 at para 109 [*Mendez*].

215 *Criminal Code*, above note 1, s 515(5).

216 *R v Precourt* (1976), 18 OR (2d) 714 at 725 (CA) [*Precourt*].

> [t]he general police investigative power to interrogate the accused person has terminated. The right to question the accused in the absence of counsel without his consent and the use of police persuasion to convince the accused to waive his or her right to silence do not exist at this stage, because the accused is under the jurisdiction of the court.[217]

Furthermore, if an accused is not taken immediately to prison, they must be given an opportunity to consult with counsel in order to be informed of the change in their status, and the police no longer have the right to interrogate the accused as though they are in investigative custody.[218] Once taken in front of a justice, the nature of the accused's detention changes, from one authorized by whatever legal power the police exercised to "a court monitored detention that ensured the ongoing protection of the appellant's *Charter* rights."[219]

In *R v Ansari*, for example, the accused was not taken before a justice until more than twenty-four hours had passed, and even then the hearing was conducted only by telephone. The trial judge noted that the effect was that "the police simply took the accused back to cells as if nothing of any importance had happened, and had another go at him."[220] The accused, who had been actively seeking an opportunity to speak with his lawyer again, obtained none of the protections that ought to have flowed from being taken in front of a justice. The justice had recommended to the police that they should let the accused contact his lawyer but had behaved as though the accused were still under the authority of the police rather than having passed into judicial hands. The trial judge found this to be a serious breach of section 9.

The other school of thought holds that a remand order holds no particular significance with regard to the ability of the police to continue questioning. In *R v Ashmore*, for example, the accused was arrested on a Friday and, having spent the night in a police cell, had a teleconference hearing with a justice the next morning, in which he was ordered remanded until the following Monday.[221] He was kept in the police cells until that Monday and over the course of the weekend was interviewed in several locations in the station, as well as being taken to several locations outside in order to take part in a re-enactment of the murder with which he was charged. The accused argued that, based on *Precourt* and *Ansari*, the police were required to treat an accused differently following

217 *R v Daunt*, [2005] YJ No 23 at para 143 (SC) [*Daunt*]. See also *Bacon v Surrey Pretrial Services Centre (Warden)*, 2010 BCSC 805, relying on *Daunt*.

218 *Daunt*, above note 217.

219 *Poirier*, above note 194 at para 58.

220 *Ansari*, above note 213 at para 54.

221 *R v Ashmore*, 2011 BCCA 18 [*Ashmore*].

a remand order. In particular, he argued that as he was under the jurisdiction of the court, the police were required to readvise him of his right to counsel before they were permitted to interrogate him again.

The British Columbia Court of Appeal rejected this position, at least for the most part. First, the court distinguished *Precourt*: in their view, that decision was about the voluntariness of a statement given by the accused in that case, and any statements made should be understood in that context. They held that it only addressed the *place* at which an accused could lawfully be held following a remand order; the location might have a practical impact on whether the police could continue to question an accused, but no more than that. They held that "a remand order does not have the effect of shielding an accused from otherwise lawful investigative action."[222] Nor did the remand grant the accused additional constitutional rights, so the police were not required to rewarn him of his right to counsel.[223] On the particular facts, however, the police had behaved unlawfully in one way. The remand order said that he should be taken to a "prison" but included a police lock-up among the possibilities meeting that definition. The accused argued that this meant that he had to be kept in the cells, but in fact he had been taken to several other rooms in the building for questioning. It would be drawing too fine a distinction, the Court of Appeal held, to find a problem with the police questioning the accused in a different room within the building where he was lawfully held. However, when the accused accompanied the police in order to take part in a re-enactment, they acted unlawfully: the remand order "did not give the police the unilateral right to remove Mr. Ashmore from one of those places and keep him in their custody elsewhere for investigative purposes."[224]

The *Ashmore* approach is firmly entrenched in British Columbia[225] and has also been applied by lower courts in other provinces. This includes lower courts in Ontario, where in principle *Precourt* ought to be seen as binding.[226] It has also been relied on by other courts of appeal for

222 *Ibid* at para 98. See also *Poirier*, above note 194, holding that although the police were required to take an accused before a justice before continuing with the bedpan vigil authorized by general warrant, the justice could have ordered the accused remanded to the police lock-up for the vigil to continue.

223 *Ashmore*, above note 221 at para 97.

224 *Ibid* at para 106.

225 See, for example, *R v Bhander*, 2012 BCCA 441 [*Bhander*], or *R v Chung*, 2011 BCCA 131 at para 29 [*Chung*]: "I do not read the case as holding that an appearance before a judicial officer cloaks the accused in some sort of protection from proper police investigative enquiry."

226 See, for example, *Rodgerson*, above note 205 at para 170; *Mendez*, above note 214 at 109–10; or *R v Al Zaharna*, 2021 ONSC 3295 at para 44. *Rodgerson* cites *Ashmore* without reference to *Precourt*. *Mendez* and *Al Zaharna* both cite *Precourt*

the specific finding that a remand is not a new circumstance entitling the accused to be readvised of the right to counsel.[227] That particular finding does not require courts to adopt the view that there is functionally no difference whatsoever between an accused's situation pre- and post-remand. At a minimum, if police do have an unchanged right to investigate post-remand, then courts should show considerably less sympathy to a failure on the part of police to comply with the deadline for taking an accused to a justice; if they continue to be allowed to interrogate after that hearing, then delaying the hearing in order to interrogate will be even less reasonable. However, especially given that the police sometimes deliberately make an arrest on a Friday in order to be able to investigate over an entire weekend,[228] which is contrary to the purpose of section 503, this is a matter that would benefit from clarification by the Supreme Court.

Finally, then, we arrive at the fourth question, the *Charter* implications of non-compliance with a deadline in section 503. Some older cases had suggested that failure to meet the deadline would not necessarily result in an arbitrary detention — that is, that there might be a valid explanation for the failure to comply with the statutory requirement, which would mean that the detention, although unlawful, was not arbitrary.[229] This argument has now been foreclosed by the Supreme Court's decision in *R v Grant*, holding that "a detention not authorized by law is arbitrary and violates s. 9."[230] There is no longer any doubt that a failure to release as soon as practicable, or within twenty-four hours at the outside, is a section 9 violation.[231]

---

but nonetheless rely on *Ashmore* for the conclusion that "a remand order does not shield an accused from further investigative action." In contrast, see *R v Baptiste*, 2020 ONSC 5677 at paras 78–90, discussing and seeming to prefer *Ashmore* but concluding that *Precourt* was binding in Ontario.

227 See, for example, *R v Briscoe*, 2015 ABCA 2. See also the discussion of readvising in Chapter 5, Section C(3)(a).

228 This was the finding of the trial judge in *Bhander*, above note 225.

229 See, for example, *R v Tam* (1995), 100 CCC (3d) 196 (BCCA).

230 *R v Grant*, 2009 SCC 32 at para 54 [*Grant*].

231 See, for example, *Vassell*, above note 166; *Chung*, above note 225; or *Ashmore*, above note 221. The issue of the proper remedy for a s 9 violation can also arise in contexts related to s 503 but not specifically based on it. In both *R v Cutforth* (1987), 40 CCC (3d) 253 (Alta CA), and *R v Weaver*, 2005 ABCA 105, the accused was arrested and eventually released without being taken in front of a justice; both accused had been intoxicated when arrested and were held overnight for that reason. Each accused was held longer than necessary for that purpose, so s 9 violations were found. In addition, there are other sections of the *Code* calling for an accused to be released at various stages of the process (see the discussion in Section B(3), above in this chapter), and arguments for a section 9 violation can also be based on failure to release in accordance with those sections: see, for example, *Viszlai*, above note 189.

The remedy for such a violation will be settled under section 24 and will depend on the particular circumstances of the case.[232] In *Simpson*, in the context of a systemic failure to provide the possibility of bail hearings within twenty-four hours, the trial judge ordered a stay of proceedings; this decision was upheld by the Supreme Court of Canada. Similarly, in *R v Reilly*, the trial judge found a systemic problem leading to many accused being detained for more than twenty-four hours and ordered a stay; this decision was upheld by the Supreme Court of Canada.[233] Stays have also been granted as a remedy in other cases that are not reflections of any systemic failure.[234] Other cases have excluded evidence that was obtained as a result of the detention.[235] Still other cases have taken the arbitrary detention into account on sentencing, imposing a significantly shortened period of imprisonment.[236] Yet other courts have given the accused no remedy despite a finding of a breach: if no evidence was discovered as a result of the arbitrary detention and the test for a stay is not met, the accused might not receive any relief.[237] Similarly, it might simply be found that the *Charter* breach was merely the result of administrative error and that no remedy of exclusion is called for.[238]

5) Lineups and Time Limits

One particular investigative technique that can have an impact on the length of a reasonable delay is an identification parade, or lineup. In practical terms, this is less of an issue than in the past because photo lineups have increasingly replaced in-person lineups, so the accused's

---

232 It is interesting to note that a series of trial decisions in Saskatchewan have entered stays as a remedy in cases where an accused has been initially detained for a breath test but then held overnight in cells, in violation of the *Code* release provisions. In these decisions, trial judges have quite explicitly pointed to the goal of changing this improper police practice as a justification for the remedy of a stay. See *R v Fox*, 2007 SKPC 61; *R v Holbrook*, 2008 SKPC 133; and *R v Poletz*, 2009 SKPC 121. Note that the Crown chose not to appeal any of these trial decisions.

233 See *R v Reilly*, 2018 ABPC 85. The Alberta Court of Appeal overturned the remedy of a stay (2019 ABCA 212), but the Supreme Court held that as the trial judge had found that the breach of s 503 "was an instance of a systemic and ongoing problem that was not being satisfactorily addressed, we are all of the view that there was no basis for the Court of Appeal to interfere with the trial judge's exercise of discretion" (2020 SCC 27 at para 1).

234 See, for example, *R v Gagea*, [1989] YJ No 90 (SC), or *Hall*, above note 135.

235 *Mangat*, above note 193; *CK*, above note 185.

236 *MacPherson*, above note 204.

237 *Clarke*, above note 190; *EW*, above note 202.

238 *Chung*, above note 225.

personal involvement is not required.[239] Where an in-person lineup is used, however, it is likely to extend the period for which the accused is detained. In *Storrey*, for example, the Court relied on the wish of the police to conduct a lineup as part of the justification for holding an accused overnight. That case made clear the point noted above, that the police can continue their investigation, although they have already arrested the accused, and specifically stated that "[t]he constable can put him up on an identification parade to see if he is picked out by the witnesses."[240] Other cases have made statements suggesting that the police have some sort of authority to place an accused in a lineup.[241]

On the other hand, the Court has also explicitly noted, in *R v Ross*, what appears to be the contrary of this view: there, it held that there is no legal obligation to participate in a lineup, either statutorily or by judicial creation.[242] An accused can be compelled to allow their picture to be taken, and that picture could later be used for a photo lineup.[243] However, there is no basis upon which an accused can be forced physically to participate in a lineup.

That is not to say that an accused would always be well advised not to participate. The underlying rationale of asking a witness to identify the accused from a group of others is to protect the accused's interests. If an accused refuses to participate in the lineup, a less favourable method of identification might be used as an alternative. In *R v Marcoux*, the accused refused to take part in a lineup, so the police instead conducted a "showup": the witness was allowed to see the accused and only one other person in a hallway and then subsequently was shown the accused alone and asked whether he could identify him.[244] The Court did not question the appropriateness of this action, and indeed in *Storrey*, it also seems to affirm this type of action as appropriate.[245]

That is not to say, of course, that an accused's refusal to participate in a lineup gives free rein to the police. In *R v Henry*, for example, the

---

239 See, for example, Ryan J. Fitzgerald, Heather L. Price & Tim Valentine, "Eyewitness Identification: Live, Photo, and Video Lineups" (2018) 24:3 *Psychology, Public Policy, and Law* 307 at 309: "photo identification has become the most widely used lineup method in Canada."

240 *Storrey*, above note 31 at para 26, quoting *Dallison v Caffery*, [1964] 3 WLR 385 at 398 (CA).

241 See, for example, *Precourt*, above note 216.

242 *R v Ross*, [1989] 1 SCR 3 [*Ross*].

243 *Identification of Criminals Act*, RSC 1985, c I-1, s 2.

244 *R v Marcoux*, [1976] 1 SCR 763 [*Marcoux*].

245 *Storrey*, above note 31 at para 32: "This is clearly not a case where the victim could, for example, be taken to the place of employment of the suspect to see if an identification could be made."

accused refused to participate in a lineup and as a result was physically forced to do so: he was pushed into the line and held in a headlock by one officer.[246] The trial judge had instructed the jury that the accused's refusal to take part could be taken as evidence of consciousness of guilt, but the British Columbia Court of Appeal found that to be an error. They pointed out that in *Marcoux*, the issue was the accused's objection to what he claimed was an unfair identification procedure; the evidence of his refusal to take part in a lineup was admitted in response to that argument. *Marcoux* did not, they held, stand for the proposition that the refusal could directly be evidence relating to guilt or innocence and indeed rejected that position.[247]

Conceptually, an accused who participates in a lineup should be seen as doing so voluntarily. Indeed, in *Ross*, the Court stressed the importance of allowing an accused the opportunity to have access to counsel before a lineup is conducted, precisely so that they will have the ability to make an informed choice. The obligation to "hold off" (see Chapter 5, Section C(3)(c)) was triggered by the accused's request to speak to counsel, and the lineup was among the evidence-gathering techniques foreclosed to the police in the interim. If the delay involved in taking an accused before a justice were analyzed from this perspective, on the assumption that an accused had consented to the delay, it might well have an impact on what period of time was seen as reasonable. Alternatively, it seems equally plausible that many accused who end up in lineups, particularly those who have not requested counsel, are simply unaware that they have no obligation to participate. In either case, this question seems not to arise in the caselaw very often.

In fact, the question of the interaction between lineups and reasonable delay has never been seriously analyzed, and this area would benefit from more judicial attention. Although the Court has held that an accused has no legal obligation to participate in a lineup, it has suggested that this is distinct from the accused having a positive right to refuse to participate, a point it takes to be unsettled.[248]

Presumably, the Court has in mind some type of analogy to the right to silence: that if an accused has a positive right to refuse to participate, then non-refusal could not be made the subject of comment even in circumstances such as those in *Marcoux*. In that case, the accused had objected to the admission of evidence about his refusal to participate in a lineup, but the Court held that the evidence was admissible since

246 *R v Henry*, 2010 BCCA 462 [*Henry*].

247 *Ibid* at para 55.

248 *Ross*, above note 242 at 13.

he had specifically criticized the police for using a showup rather than conducting a lineup.

Since *Marcoux* is a pre-*Charter* case, it is an open question as to what conclusion would be reached today; on the same facts, a court might well find a violation of *Charter* rights.[249] This conclusion could be based either on a violation of section 7 or on the more direct ground that admitting identification evidence created in an unfair way would violate the accused's right to a fair trial. In *R v Walker*, for example, the accused was subpoenaed to a co-accused's preliminary inquiry, at which point several witnesses saw him in the hallway outside the courtroom and pointed him out to police; this method of identification was held to violate his *Charter* rights, and the evidence was excluded.[250]

One might well argue that the circumstances should be seen as analogous to the Court's reasoning in *R v Turcotte*: if it would be "a snare and a delusion" to say that an accused has the right to silence but then to use that silence as evidence of the accused's guilt, then equally it would be objectionable to say that an accused has no obligation to be in a lineup but then place the accused in a worse position for refusing.[251] On the other hand, one might also analogize to *Singh*. That case seems to limit the extent to which the right to silence can be asserted as a positive protection, in the face of acquiescence to a police investigative technique.[252]

Entirely apart from the question of a *Charter* violation, there is increased skepticism over identification evidence since *Marcoux* was decided. The Sophonow Inquiry, for example, laid down a number of guidelines for identification parades and photo lineups, which have been referred to with approval by the Supreme Court in *R v Hibbert*.[253] Pre-trial identification evidence, however gathered, now tends to be evaluated against those criteria and to be treated more carefully. In *R v FA*, for example, a witness was shown a lineup of only two people and was told that suspects were in the group; the Ontario Court of Appeal found that convicting the accused based on the identification evidence in that case was unreasonable.[254] In *R v Miaponoose*, the police created a ruse whereby they drove the accused past the complainant in the case, who was waiting to see whether she could identify him. She did, but the Ontario Court of

249 However, note that *Henry*, above note 246, accepts *Marcoux* as authoritative on the "response evidence" approach.

250 *R v Walker*, [2005] OJ No 6159 (SCJ).

251 *R v Turcotte*, 2005 SCC 50 at para 44.

252 *Singh*, above note 187.

253 2002 SCC 39.

254 *R v FA* (2004), 183 CCC (3d) 518 (Ont CA).

Appeal described that evidence as "very dubious and of very little weight" and once again overturned the conviction as unreasonable. It also noted:

> [I]t is crucial that procedures which tend to minimize the inherent dangers of eyewitness identification evidence be followed as much as possible in any given case . . . . In all cases, the suspect should be presented to the complainant in circumstances that minimize any suggestion that the police believe the suspect is the offender.[255]

The procedures used in *Marcoux* seemingly would not meet today's standards, so the impact of that case as an incentive for an accused to agree to take part in a lineup is very much up in the air.

6) Remote Appearances

Appearances by telecommunications in criminal proceedings have undergone a sea change. Initially, of course, the only real choice to be made was whether or not an accused had to be present, but as technology developed, other choices became available and were incorporated into the *Code*. In 2019, Bill C-75 made a number of changes to the provisions allowing for remote appearances. Following that, in 2023, further expansions of that possibility came into effect, triggered by the COVID-19 pandemic and the need at the time to find ways to make the system continue to operate. These most recent changes are intended to "give courts increased flexibility in how they hold criminal proceedings and issue orders."[256] Those changes are subject to review after three years to assess whether they "(a) enhance, preserve or adversely affect access to justice; (b) maintain fundamental principles of the administration of justice; and (c) adequately address the rights and obligations of participants in the criminal justice system, including accused persons."[257]

For the most part, these provisions, especially the most recent changes, relate to trial issues. They create rules around pleas, preliminary inquiries, jury selection, the trial itself, and sentencing, among other matters. They create a complicated interconnected set of rules that have

---

255 *R v Miaponoose* (1996), 110 CCC (3d) 445 at paras 17 and 28 (Ont CA).

256 Michaela Keenan-Pelletier, *Legislative Summary: Bill S-4: An Act to amend the Criminal Code and the Identification of Criminals Act and to make related amendments to other Acts (COVID-19 response and other measures)* (Ottawa: Library of Parliament, 2023), online (pdf) at 1: https://lop.parl.ca/staticfiles/PublicWebsite/Home/ResearchPublications/LegislativeSummaries/PDF/44-1/44-1-S4-E.pdf.

257 *An Act to amend the Criminal Code and the Identification of Criminals Act and to make related amendments to other Acts (COVID-19 response and other measures)*, SC 2022, c 17, s 78.1.

caused courts some difficulty in interpretation.[258] The various provisions at times distinguish between the accused and witnesses, witnesses in and out of Canada, summary conviction versus indictable offences, whether or not the accused is represented, whether or not the accused is in custody, whether the remote appearance will be by videoconference or audioconference, whether or not the proceeding involves evidence, and whether the accused can be required or only allowed to proceed remotely.

Two sets of provisions in the compelling appearance part are most worth noting in this respect: sections 502.1 and 515(2.2) to (2.3), both under separate subheadings, "Appearance of the Accused." Section 502.1 refers to appearances "in a proceeding under this Part," while section 515(2.2) to (2.3) deal with appearances "for the purposes of judicial interim release." The more general provision, section 502.1, provides that

> [e]xcept as otherwise provided in this Part, an accused who is required to appear in a proceeding under this Part shall appear in person but may appear by audioconference or videoconference, if arrangements are made with the court in advance and those arrangements are satisfactory to the justice.

Some remote appearance provisions have wording that makes clear that a remote appearance cannot take place against the wishes of the accused; for example, section 715.231 provides that "[t]he court may, with the consent of the prosecutor and the accused, allow an accused to appear by videoconference at the preliminary inquiry." Other sections make clear that the accused's consent is not required: section 715.241 provides that "[d]espite sections 715.231 to 715.233, the court may allow *or require* an accused who is in custody and who has access to legal advice to appear by videoconference in any proceeding referred to in those sections, other than a part in which the evidence of a witness is taken" (emphasis added). Section 502.1, however, is not very clear on this point. It says that the accused "may appear by audioconference or videoconference," but the only preconditions are that "arrangements are made with the court in advance and those arrangements are satisfactory to the justice." Seemingly, this wording permits a justice to require a

---

258 See, for example, the thorough discussion of various issues in *R v Twoyoungmen*, 2021 ABPC 88; the disagreement over whether an accused can plead guilty by phone in *R v Candelaria*, 2020 ONCJ 194 and *R v Daley*, 2020 ONCJ 201, or the discussion of whether a person who appears remotely is or is not "present" as required by s 650(1) in *In Re: Court File No. 19/578*, 2020 ONSC 3870. These decisions all predate the 2023 changes, but those changes are likely to have created as many new issues as they have cleared up.

remote appearance whether or not the accused agrees, but the issue has not been authoritatively determined.[259]

Section 502.1 also deals with remote appearances by witnesses in and out of Canada, by the justice, and by participants. "Participants" are defined in section 715.25(1) as "any person, other than an accused, an offender, a witness, a juror, a judge or a justice, who may participate in a proceeding," a definition that seems primarily aimed at court staff. As with the accused, the provisions generally state that the person "shall" appear in person but "may" appear remotely in some cases. Usually, the requirement is that the remote appearance is "satisfactory to the justice." However, for witnesses outside Canada, the provisions in sections 714.2 to 714.8 also apply here, and the justice personally can only preside remotely "if the justice considers it necessary in the circumstances."

The provisions concerning remote appearances for a judicial interim-release hearing also appear in general not to require the accused's consent. Section 515(2.2) provides:

> If, by this Act, the appearance of an accused is required for the purposes of judicial interim release, the accused shall appear in person but the justice may allow the accused to appear by videoconference or, subject to subsection (2.3), by audioconference, if the technological means is satisfactory to the justice.

Consent is required in one specific circumstance: where "the accused cannot appear by closed-circuit television or videoconference and the evidence of a witness is to be taken at the appearance." In that particular situation, the accused can appear by audioconference, but only with the consent of both the accused and the prosecutor.[260]

C. ARREST

Several issues need to be discussed in looking at powers of arrest. First, we will consider the meaning of the word "arrest" itself, which allows a determination of whether a particular person has or has not been

---

259 *R v Wright*, 2002 BCPC 488 at para 31, for the argument that the accused's consent is not required under s 515(2.2). On the other hand, *Ansari*, above note 213 at para 37, expressed the view that there is a "strong argument" that the accused's consent is required and that at a minimum it requires "an exercise of judicial discretion ensuring that there will be no compromise of the rights of the accused by virtue of the character of the hearing." Both cases dealt with a previous version of the section, but the wording on this issue was effectively the same.

260 *Criminal Code*, above note 1, s 515(2.3).

arrested. Following that, we will consider the circumstances in which various persons are authorized to make arrests. This will entail discussion of "citizen's arrest" and arrests by peace officers. In the latter case, there are powers of arrest both with and without warrants.

It is worth noting at the start that powers of arrest are extensively codified and indeed probably *exhaustively* codified. As was noted in Chapter 2, the common law is a potential source of police power and has been used as the foundation for some powers, such as investigative detention or search incident to arrest. However, the most plausible view is that there are no common law powers of arrest.

In *Fleming v Ontario*, the Supreme Court considered and rejected the possibility of recognizing a common law power "to arrest someone who is acting lawfully in order to prevent an apprehended breach of the peace"—that is, to prevent an apprehended breach of the peace by someone other than the person arrested.[261] They also acknowledged that a common law power of arrest to prevent an apprehended breach of the peace by the person being arrested might historically have existed at common law but suggested that it should no longer do so: "While it is not necessary to decide this in the instant case, I seriously question whether a common law power of this nature would still be necessary in Canada today."[262] In general, the decision shows a certain antipathy toward the expansion of police powers other than through statute, holding, for example, that "[t]he courts of this country, as custodians of the common law, must act cautiously when asked to use it to authorize actions that interfere with individual liberty."[263] Any argument for a non-statutory power of arrest, therefore, would face a steep uphill climb.

1) Definition of "Arrest"

Powers of arrest for criminal law purposes are now set out statutorily, in section 494 for private citizens and in section 495 for peace officers. However, the concept of an arrest was initially a common law one. Partly because of this history, the meaning of the word "arrest" is drawn from the common law.

The definition of "arrest" in Canadian criminal law stems from the 1970 decision of the Supreme Court in *R v Whitfield*.[264] In that case, a police officer saw Whitfield, the accused, in a car and stopped at a stoplight. The officer knew that there was a warrant for Whitfield's arrest and

261 *Fleming v Ontario*, 2019 SCC 45 at para 57 [*Fleming*].

262 *Ibid* at para 60.

263 *Ibid* at para 5.

264 [1970] SCR 46 [*Whitfield*].

went over, telling the accused to remain. Whitfield in fact tried to drive away, although he was not immediately able to flee because of other traffic. At one point, the officer managed to reach in through the open window of the accused's car, grab Whitfield's shirt, and say to him, "You are under arrest." Shortly thereafter, the accused was able to accelerate and drive away, breaking free from the officer, who fell to the ground and suffered minor injuries. The accused was not charged with resisting arrest, although it would seem unambiguously true that he was guilty of that offence, and in the eyes of the dissenting judges in the case that would have been the proper charge. Instead, he was charged with "escaping lawful custody." He could be guilty of that offence, of course, only if he was actually "in custody" when the officer was reaching through the open car window and gripping his shirt. That is the conclusion the majority reached.

The majority concluded that there was no distinction to be drawn between being arrested and being in custody. In essence, they held, the two states were the same:

> There is no room for what seems to be a new subdivision of "arrest" into "custodial" arrest and "symbolical" or "technical" arrest. An accused is either arrested or he is not arrested. If this accused was arrested, he escaped from lawful custody.[265]

That, then, led to the question of exactly what constitutes an arrest. The Court held that an arrest could be accomplished in one of two ways:

> [A]n arrest consists either of (i) the actual seizure or touching of a person's body with a view to his detention, or (ii) the pronouncing of "words of arrest" to a person who submits to the arresting officer.[266]

Both definitions of arrest create some oddities in practice. The former fixes the point of arrest quite precisely—almost too precisely, in a sense, since it is capable of making the process of arrest appear to be a game of tag.[267] If the person arresting can touch the arrestee, the arrest

---

265 *Ibid* at 48.

266 *R v Latimer*, [1997] 1 SCR 217 at para 24 [*Latimer*], characterizing the result in *Whitfield*, above note 264.

267 In *R v Asante-Mensah*, 2003 SCC 38 at para 45 [*Asante-Mensah*], the Court quotes with approval from *Genner v Sparks* (1704), 6 Mod Rep 173, 87 ER 928 at 929 (QB): "If here he had but touched the defendant even with the end of his finger, it had been *an arrest*" [emphasis in original]. See, for example, *Gentles v Toronto (City) Non-Profit Housing Corp*, 2010 ONCA 797 at para 130 [*Gentles*]: "[T]he arrest took place when Collins touched Gentles on the shoulder and said 'you are under arrest.'" See also *R v Costain*, 2011 ONCJ 559 at para 9: "I am forced to conclude that due to the complete absence of any physical touching accompanying the ensuing declaration of arrest, in law, this accused was never actually under arrest."

is made, but if the arrestee can dodge successfully, they are not guilty of the offence of escaping lawful custody. This is essentially the fact pattern in *R v Asante-Mensah*, to be discussed in a moment.[268]

In contrast, the latter basis for arrest is not always precise enough because it might not be clear whether the words that preceded an arrestee's submission constituted "words of arrest." The term "words of arrest," in the second branch of the test, is not interpreted narrowly. As a result, it is not always easy to know whether someone has been arrested or instead has had their liberty restrained in some other way.

These two branches of the definition of arrest are worth discussing separately.

a) Touching with a View to Detention

Asante-Mensah was primarily about the use of force, in particular in the context of arrest by private citizens. However, the facts neatly illustrate the use of the definition of arrest. The accused was a "scooper"—that is, a taxi driver who picked up fares at the Toronto International Airport even though he was not licensed to do so. Security guards at the airport arrested him on a number of occasions, although he fled each time. Their power to arrest flowed from provincial legislation, but that did not matter in terms of deciding the factual question of whether or not the accused was arrested: the Court held that "arrest" is a term of art and that the definition from *Whitfield* therefore applied when the word was used in the provincial statute.[269]

The case concerned three particular charges. In the first two, the accused had been tapped on the shoulder by a security guard before fleeing; he was convicted of escaping lawful custody in connection with both incidents. The third incident went as follows:

> Later in the afternoon of July 25, 1991, another incident at the airport led to charges against the appellant of dangerous driving, use of a weapon in committing an assault, and escaping lawful custody. The charges arose in this way. A different inspector, aware of the appellant's previous arrest the same day, saw the appellant's taxi "trolling" past the arrivals level at Terminal 3. He stepped out in front of the appellant's taxi with his hand raised, holding his badge, and ordered the appellant to stop. The appellant kept on coming and, to avoid personal injury, the inspector jumped onto the hood of the appellant's car, from where he

---

268 In *Asante-Mensah*, above note 267 at para 45, the Court notes that "[t]here is no doubt the appellant understood the significance of the inspector's touch because, according to the trial judge, he made every effort to avoid being touched."

269 *Ibid* at paras 28 and 41.

> was dislodged as the appellant accelerated to get clear of the terminal. The inspector had made no physical contact to arrest the appellant. There was clearly no submission by the appellant to the inspector's authority. The trial judge held that no arrest had occurred and, having a reasonable doubt on other aspects of the evidence, dismissed all charges in connection with this incident.[270]

In the first two incidents, the accused had been under arrest from the moment he was first touched; in the third, in the absence of any touch or submission, he was not arrested.

Although an arrest begins instantaneously, as it were, the Court describes it as a continuing act, in the sense that the accused remains in the state of arrest from the moment of the touch (or submission) "until the person so restrained is either released from custody or, having been brought before a magistrate, is remanded in custody by the magistrate's judicial act."[271] This definition, it should be observed, is the counterpart to the observation in Section B(4) above that once the accused is taken before a justice, she has "come into the judicial sphere and out of the hands of the investigating authorities."[272]

In the particular context of *Asante-Mensah*, the continuing nature of an arrest helped the Court reach the conclusion that a private citizen arresting under provincial legislation was entitled to use force to effect the arrest.[273] The arrest was initiated by a touch, but the power to arrest was not exhausted once the touch was made; that is, the arrest was not over. Rather, the security guard was entitled to use necessary force to achieve the purpose of the arrest: to deliver the accused to a peace officer. To conclude otherwise, the Court held, would be to resurrect the "custodial arrest" and "technical arrest" distinction that had been rejected in *Whitfield*.

b) Words of Arrest Plus Submission and "De Facto Arrest"

Two separate issues will be discussed here, one relatively straightforward: "words of arrest plus submission" as a method of effecting an arrest and the other a complication arising from it, "de facto arrest."

The term "words of arrest plus submission" is, in many cases, a perfectly sensible definition of arrest leading to no ambiguity and justified on a policy basis. In many cases, the police might say words to the effect of "you are under arrest; get in the car," following which the arrestee

---

270 *Ibid* at para 15.

271 *Ibid* at para 33, quoting *Holgate-Mohammed v Duke*, [1984] AC 437 at 441 (HL).

272 *Ansari*, above note 213 at para 48.

273 The issues arose because the arrest was not made under the *Criminal Code*. Had it been, even a private citizen authorized to arrest would be entitled to use necessary force by virtue of s 25: see the discussion in Chapter 2.

might act as requested. Similarly, arrests often occur while an accused is already in custody—for example, in a police interview room, being questioned. It would be useless formalism to insist that in such cases there was some requirement for the police to touch the person in addition to pronouncing the words of arrest. Indeed, to insist on some form of touching would be inconsistent with the principle of restraint in compelling appearance discussed above. The policy argument in *Whitfield*—that police are entitled to use force to effect an arrest but that the law should not encourage its use—has some validity.[274] Similarly, as the Court has noted, the legal authority to use force if necessary often makes it in fact unnecessary to do so because it leads an accused to choose to submit.[275]

It is also preferable from the perspective of the accused, in many cases, since the fact of being arrested triggers the various rights in section 10 of the *Charter*: an accused who submits in the face of clear words of arrest is more clearly immediately entitled to those rights.

It is also reasonable to hold, as the caselaw does, that the term "words of arrest" is not restricted to the words "you are under arrest." Rather, any words that convey to the accused the meaning that they are under arrest will be sufficient. Specifically, police need not use the word "arrest" itself. The important issue is

> the substance of what the accused can reasonably be supposed to have understood, rather than the formalism of the precise words used . . . . The question is . . . what the accused was told, viewed reasonably in all the circumstances of the case.[276]

This is an understandable approach. "Don't go anywhere; you can't leave; I am charging you with theft," or something similar, would seem to be a pretty unambiguous way of communicating to a shoplifter that they are under arrest. Courts have, for example, found the "words of arrest" requirement to be satisfied when an accused was told by a customs officer that they could not leave or was told by a police officer that they were required to accompany the officer to a vehicle.[277]

However, although the words of arrest standard and flexibility over the exact words required are both reasonable in themselves, in combination they have created an ambiguity in the law. It can now be unclear, in some cases, *what* power a police officer has actually exercised. This

---

274 *Whitfield*, above note 264 at 50.

275 *Asante-Mensah*, above note 267 at para 57.

276 *Latimer*, above note 266 at para 24, quoting *R v Evans*, [1991] 1 SCR 869 at 888 [*Evans*].

277 See *R v Grossman*, [1998] BCJ No 62 (SC), and *R v Tipewan*, [1998] SJ No 238 (QB), respectively.

difficulty arises because of the concept of "de facto arrest," which the Supreme Court created in *R v Latimer*. This concept allows courts to rely on the second definition in *Whitfield* as a basis for characterizing something, after the fact, as an arrest, even though it was not meant to be one at the time. As will be pursued in a moment, at a policy level, this is a bad choice. Making matters even more complicated, however, is that there is also ambiguity in the way in which the term is used. At present, the concept is sometimes used as a way of rendering non-arbitrary what otherwise would be an arbitrary detention but on other occasions has exactly the opposite impact and is a way of showing that police have acted outside their powers. We will begin by looking at the concept's use in the first of those two ways.

In *Latimer*, the police had formed the view that the accused was responsible for his daughter's death. They decided that they wanted to take him into custody in order to question him about that; significantly, they consciously decided not to arrest him. Instead, they simply wanted to detain him for questioning, and that was what they told him: "You are being detained for investigation into the death of your daughter Tracy."[278] The important and awkward point here is that the police did not have the power to detain Latimer—or anyone—for investigation. No such power existed;[279] nonetheless, the police had not asked the accused to come for questioning but had insisted upon it and had told him that he was now in custody. That is, the police had set out to do—and, one might think, had done—something they had no legal authority to do. Not surprisingly, therefore, the accused brought a *Charter* application, claiming that there had been a violation of his right not to be arbitrarily detained. In his view, he had been detained, and there was no lawful authority for the detention, so his section 9 right was violated.

The Court rejected this section 9 claim. It held that there had been legal authority for the accused's detention and that that authority was the law of arrest. The Court acknowledged that the officers had decided not to arrest the accused and that in taking him into custody, they had used the word "detention" rather than "arrest." Nevertheless, the Court concluded: "[N]otwithstanding what the *intention* of the officers may have been, their conduct had the *effect* of putting Mr. Latimer under

278 *Latimer*, above note 266 at para 8.

279 Although no such power existed at the time, later decisions of the Court in *R v Mann*, 2004 SCC 52 [*Mann*]; *R v Clayton*, 2007 SCC 32 [*Clayton*]; and *R v Aucoin*, 2012 SCC 66 [*Aucoin*], have created powers of investigative detention in some circumstances. Even those powers, however, would not allow the police to confront a person and immediately take him to the police station for questioning.

arrest."[280] The Court supported this claim based on the second branch of the *Whitfield* test. The accused had certainly submitted to the police because he had gone with them at their request. So, if there were words of arrest, then "words of arrest plus submission" was made out. And, as noted above, the precise words do not matter; rather, the issue is "what the accused can reasonably be supposed to have understood." On the facts of the case,

> Mr. Latimer was told that he was being detained, and that he would be taken back to North Battleford to be interviewed. The police officers informed him of his right to silence and his right to counsel. They accompanied him back into his house while he changed his clothes, telling him that they were doing so because he was now in their custody.[281]

This amounted to "words of arrest," the Court ruled. Since it was coupled with the accused's submission, there was a "de facto arrest"; there was, in fact, an arrest, however it might have been presented or appeared. On the particular facts of *Latimer*, "accidental arrest" would be a better description: the officers did not mean to arrest the accused, tried not to, but did so despite their best intentions. The Court then carried on to find that the prerequisites to a legal arrest were also made out; in that event, there was no arbitrary detention.

Applying the *Whitfield* definition of arrest in the way *Latimer* does—that is, to apply the concept of arrest despite the intentions of the police—is not clearly a sensible policy. Normally, the purpose the police have in mind is seen to be quite important to settling whether or not their behaviour is authorized by law (see Chapter 2, Section B(2)). Having an improper purpose in mind, or even just the wrong purpose, has often been taken to render illegal the use of some power; for example, in *R v Caslake*, a search that could have been made properly as a search incident to arrest was found to be illegal because the officer's purpose in conducting the search had been to produce an inventory of the contents of the vehicle.[282] If the concept of de facto arrest is accepted, however, then the police purpose becomes simply irrelevant in this context. This would be inconsistent with the general approach to that subject. Later cases,

---

280 *Latimer*, above note 266 at para 24 [emphasis added].

281 *Ibid* at para 25.

282 *R v Caslake*, [1998] 1 SCR 51. See also *R v Lai*, 2019 ONCA 420 at paras 29–30, or *R v Dudhi*, 2019 ONCA 665 at para 64, holding that "the subjective component of the relevant legal standards plays an important role in ensuring that the police act for legitimate purposes and turn their minds to the legal authority they possess."

decided after the distinction between arrest powers and detention powers had become clearer than it was at the time of *Latimer*, have held that the important issue is "[t]he police power actually exercised and not . . . some other police power which may have been, but was not, exercised."[283]

Treating the police purpose as irrelevant is therefore questionable. It is noteworthy, after all, that the police had in Latimer's case set out to violate his rights. Their conscious intention had been to do something they had no authority to do. In that particular case, employing the concept of de facto arrest rendered lawful an attempt by the police to act unlawfully.

However, later cases have used the term "de facto arrest" in quite a different way. *Latimer* was decided in 1997, at a point when police powers in this regard were "all or nothing": either the police had the power to arrest, or they had no power to direct the accused's movements at all. The power to do what they purported to do—detain the accused for investigation—did not exist. The choices confronting the Court at that time, therefore, were either to conclude that the police had conducted a lawful arrest or conclude that the police had acted unlawfully. Subsequently, the Court created a power of investigative detention with its decision seven years later, in *R v Mann*,[284] and powers to detain for investigative purposes were developed further in *R v Clayton*[285] and *R v Aucoin*.[286] Because of those decisions, a middle ground now exists in which police might be authorized to interfere with an accused's liberty in a way that is less than an arrest, based on lower grounds than would be required for an arrest.[287]

Of note in this context was that in *Mann*, the Court was concerned not to allow an investigative detention power to become too open-ended but, rather, to make sure it remained in check. To make this point, the Court held that "[t]he power to detain cannot be exercised on the basis of a hunch, nor can it become a *de facto* arrest."[288] The concept of de facto arrest is being used in that quotation for the opposite purpose from *Latimer*. In *Latimer*, the point of saying that what the police did was a de facto arrest was to say that they *were* authorized. In *Mann*, however, the point being made is that the investigative detention power only allows a brief detention, and if the police detain someone for too

283 *R v Stevenson*, 2014 ONCA 842 at para 56. See also *R v Brown*, 2012 ONCA 225 [*Brown* 2012]; *R v Dhillon*, 2012 BCCA 254; and *R v Whitaker*, 2008 BCCA 174, and the discussion in Chapter 2, Section B(2).

284 *Mann*, above note 279.

285 *Clayton*, above note 279.

286 *Aucoin*, above note 279.

287 See the discussion of these powers in Chapter 3, Section C.

288 *Mann*, above note 279 at para 35.

long, they are no longer acting within that investigative detention power; instead, it has become the equivalent of an arrest, for which no authority existed. In such a case, to say "it became a de facto arrest" is to say "the police acted unlawfully." For example, the Ontario Court of Appeal in *R v McGuffie* held

> In *Mann*, at para. 35, Iacobucci J. stressed that an investigative detention was not the same thing as an arrest and could not be allowed to become "a *de facto* arrest." The significant interference with individual liberty occasioned by an arrest is justified because the police have reasonable and probable grounds to believe that the arrested person has committed an offence. Investigative detention does not require the same strong connection between the detained individual and the offence being investigated. The detention contemplated by an investigative detention cannot interfere with individual liberty to the extent contemplated by a full arrest.[289]

When used in this way, the phrase does not have the same meaning as in *Latimer*. The intention here is not to say that "the accused understood they had been placed under arrest and complied"; it is to say that the detention was of such duration that the infringement on the accused's liberty was equivalent to an arrest and therefore was unlawful. In that context, the absence of words of arrest should be irrelevant and should not lead to the conclusion that there was not a de facto arrest. To reason otherwise would be to reach the perverse conclusion that, because the police not only acted unlawfully but also failed to comply with the necessary legal requirements to exercise that unavailable power, the two wrongs cancel each other out and mean that there was no illegality.

The term "de facto arrest" has often been used in the latter way: to say that police have gone beyond the limits of a power of detention and performed a de facto arrest. For example, in *R v Strilec*, the accused was stopped while riding a dirt bike, was questioned about motor vehicle infractions, and was taken to the police officer's car in order for this to occur; all of that would have legitimately been part of a brief roadside detention. However, the accused was handcuffed and placed in the back of the police car while all of this occurred, which took the case beyond a detention to a de facto arrest.[290] Other cases have similarly considered

289 *R v McGuffie*, 2016 ONCA 365 at para 37 [*McGuffie*]. See also *R v Suberu*, 2007 ONCA 60 at para 54. The result in that case was affirmed by the Supreme Court of Canada, although for quite different reasons: *R v Suberu*, 2009 SCC 33 [*Suberu*].

290 *R v Strilec*, 2010 BCCA 198 at para 32 [*Strilec*], or *R v Orr*, 2010 BCCA 513 [*Orr*].

the amount of force used by police in determining whether a detention has passed into the realm of de facto arrest.[291]

However, it is also clear that the *Latimer* concept of a de facto arrest has not disappeared. For example, in *R v Bielli*, the police had wanted to seize money that was being transported by the accused without giving away that they were already investigating him as part of an illegal betting investigation.[292] On a ruse, they stopped his vehicle and manipulated events to present him with the choice between his vehicle being searched as part of an investigative detention or being arrested for obstruction of justice; he opted for the former. The Crown argued that the subsequent search was a search incident to arrest, taking the position that what had occurred (the accused had been handcuffed and detained for several hours) was a de facto arrest, making the search lawful. Although the Ontario Court of Appeal rejected the argument, they did so on the facts: specifically, that having opted for being detained over being arrested when given the choice, it could not be said that the accused understood he was under arrest. The Court of Appeal did not suggest, however, that there was any problem with the argument in principle. Quite the opposite: they relied on *Latimer* to conclude that "the test for a *de facto* arrest asks what the accused can reasonably be supposed to have understood in light of what he was told, viewed reasonably in all the circumstances of the case."[293]

Indeed, the Supreme Court seems to have endorsed the notion of de facto arrest as a means of making actions lawful much more recently than *Latimer*, in *R v Tim*.[294] The accused had been arrested, but that was later determined to be an unlawful arrest. His vehicle had been searched incidental to that, but that search was unlawful since the arrest was unlawful. There was then a lawful pat-down search incident to a parallel investigative detention, leading the police to discover a handgun. That discovery led to him being placed in the back of a police car, told of his *Charter* rights, and later strip-searched at the police station. Of interest in this context was that the Court found the strip search to have been a lawful search incident to arrest on the basis that being placed in the

291 See, for example, *R v Madore*, 2012 BCCA 160 [*Madore*], or *R v Squires*, 2016 NLCA 54.

292 *R v Bielli*, 2021 ONCA 222.

293 *Ibid* at para 74. See also *R v Mohamed*, 2023 ABPC 49, where a police officer testified that she had placed the accused under investigative detention. The trial judge found that this amounted to a de facto arrest but only found that to be unlawful because reasonable grounds for arrest did not exist. See also the discussion of caselaw around this issue in *R v Bassi*, 2019 BCSC 1224.

294 2022 SCC 12 [*Tim*].

police car amounted to an arrest. The Court did not use the term "de facto arrest," but it is quite clear that that is the concept they are applying. They hold:

> The officer's language and conduct conveyed clearly that the appellant was under arrest (see *R. v. Latimer*, [1997] 1 S.C.R. 217, at para. 25). His conduct had the effect of placing the appellant under arrest for possession of a prohibited firearm (*Latimer*, at para. 24).[295]

Where it has been unclear what power the police purported to exercise, it will generally be necessary to determine whether a de facto arrest in the *Latimer* sense occurred. In some contexts, the distinction is not important; the right to counsel arises whether the accused was arrested or merely detained, for example, so there will be a section 10(b) violation if it was not provided, no matter which power was in issue.[296] In most contexts, it will matter, however. *Mann* and *R v Suberu*[297] used the phrase as a kind of shorthand to indicate that the police had acted beyond their powers, essentially on the basis that it was obvious on the facts that an arrest could not be justified. However, in principle, courts can follow the example of *Latimer* and carry on to conclude that as a matter of fact what occurred was an arrest and that grounds for arrest did exist.[298]

Finally, note that this analysis does not have to be limited to the question of whether the police acted lawfully in the first place. It could also be relevant in the context of a section 24(2) analysis, going to the issue of how serious the breach was. If police have briefly detained someone unlawfully, that will be a breach of section 9, but if their unlawful behaviour rose to the seriousness of being a de facto arrest, that would weigh even more heavily in deciding whether to exclude evidence.[299]

---

295 *Ibid* at para 67.

296 *Madore*, above note 291, distinguished *Strilec*, above note 290, on this basis.

297 *Suberu*, above note 289.

298 See, for example, *R v Sanghera*, 2012 BCSC 246, aff'd 2015 BCCA 316 [*Sanghera*].

299 See, for example, *Madore*, above note 291 at para 49:

> An arrest is a more serious infringement of personal liberty than a detention, and it requires a more compelling justification on the part of police. In cases such as this one, where police lacked sufficient grounds to detain, they would necessarily have had even less basis to carry out an arrest. In this sense, an arbitrary *de facto* arrest should weigh more heavily than an arbitrary detention within the s. 24(2) analysis.

See also *Orr*, above note 290. In *Madore*, the circumstances were found not to amount to a de facto arrest, while in *Orr*, they did.

2) Powers of Arrest

a) Private Citizens and Peace Officers

Understanding the current state of powers of arrest requires a certain knowledge of its history. Today, the vast majority of arrests are conducted by professional police officers. However, this is a situation of the exception having swallowed the rule. As the Supreme Court has noted: "The concept of 'arrest' by private citizens is as old as the common law. It predates the rise of the modern police force."[300]

It will be necessary to discuss powers of arrest by both private citizens and peace officers. It is worth pausing, however, to discuss exactly what it means to say that someone is a peace officer as opposed to a private citizen since it makes a difference at many points. It has already been observed that although anyone may lay an information, informations laid by private citizens are treated differently from those laid by peace officers. Similarly, although the *Code* offers a number of protections to anyone exercising powers, some protections are provided only to peace officers.[301] And as we will discuss below, different arrest powers are available depending on whether the person arresting is a peace officer or a private citizen.

It would be more accurate to say, however, that different powers are available to a person depending on whether or not they are, at the relevant time, acting as a peace officer.[302] That is, the world does not simply divide into peace officers and non-peace officers; rather, the same person can fall into either category depending on the exact circumstances. In part, this is reflected in the fact that arrest powers are not, strictly speaking, divided into those available to peace officers and those available to private citizens. Although some arrest powers are limited to peace officers, the others are available to "any one"—that is, to peace officers and non-peace officers alike. While it is convenient to think of and refer to the latter as powers of "citizen's arrest," that is not really accurate. A

300 *Asante-Mensah*, above note 267 at para 36. As an aside, in this discussion, as in the caselaw, the term "private citizen" is used, but that term is not meant to impose a citizenship requirement. The statutory provisions talk of "any one" or of a "person."

301 For example, although s 25(1) permits anyone authorized to act under the *Criminal Code* to use reasonable force, the use of force likely to cause grievous bodily harm or death is limited in s 25(4) to peace officers and those assisting them. See Chapter 2, Section B(1).

302 See *R v Lord*, 2011 BCCA 295 at para 10 [*Lord*] (quoting the trial judge): "I would therefore conclude that the definition of "peace officer" in s. 2 of the *Criminal Code* serves only to grant additional powers to enforce the criminal law to persons who must otherwise operate within the limits of their statutory or common law sources of authority."

person who is a peace officer could, if necessary, rely on the citizen's arrest powers.

In addition, a person might be a peace officer in some circumstances but not in others. Although the term is defined in the *Criminal Code*, the Supreme Court has observed that it is not really meant as a status:

> On the level of principle, it is important to remember that the definition of "peace officer" in s. 2 of the *Criminal Code* is not designed to create a police force. It simply provides that certain persons who derive their authority from other sources will be treated as "peace officers" as well, enabling them to enforce the *Criminal Code* within the scope of their preexisting authority, and to benefit from certain protections granted only to "peace officers."[303]

"Peace officer" is defined in section 2 of the *Code*. The definition includes a police officer, of course, but is much broader. It also includes officers appointed under various other listed Acts, such as the *Customs Act*, the *Immigration and Refugee Protection Act*, the *Corrections and Conditional Release Act*, and the *Fisheries Act*. In addition, it includes a "person employed for the preservation and maintenance of the public peace," whether or not that appointment comes under a statute listed in the *Code*.[304] It includes the pilot in command of an aircraft, members of the Canadian forces who are appointed as military police and "a mayor, warden, reeve, sheriff, deputy sheriff, sheriff's officer and justice of the peace."[305]

However, the definition of peace officer does not constitute a blanket inclusion of all those listed individuals as people having a peace officer's powers under the *Code* at all times. Some limits are explicitly built in: customs officers have that status only while enforcing the relevant statutes, a pilot is a peace officer only while the aircraft is in flight, and so on. Furthermore, the Court concluded in *R v Nolan* that the definition ought not to be given the broadest interpretation possible.

In *Nolan*, a military police officer appointed under the *National Defence Act* observed the accused driving on the base (and in fact leaving the base) at a speed of 50 km/h in a 15 km/h zone. The military officer stopped the accused and made a Breathalyzer demand; the issue in the case was whether the accused had been arbitrarily detained. The accused was a civilian and so was not himself subject to the *Code of*

---

303 *R v Nolan*, [1987] 1 SCR 1212 at para 19.

304 See *Lord*, above note 302, finding that constables appointed under the *Canada Transportation Act*, SC 1996, c 10, fell within the s 2 definition of "peace officer."

305 *Criminal Code*, above note 1, s 2.

Service Discipline; he therefore argued that the military police had no power to stop him.

The Nova Scotia Court of Appeal had relied on the definition of "peace officer" in section 2 of the *Code* to find that the military officers did have the power to stop the accused and qualified as peace officers "against the world." At the time, the definition referred to "officers and men" of the Canadian Armed Forces who were "(i) appointed for the purposes of section 134 of the *National Defence Act*."[306] The Court of Appeal held that the military police had been appointed under that section, and since they therefore met the definition of "peace officer," they had the powers of peace officers in every context.

The Supreme Court held that this would amount to Parliament having created a national police force and was too expansive an approach to interpreting the definition. Rather, it held, to have been appointed for "the purposes" of the *National Defence Act* did not merely mean that the military police had been appointed under that section. It meant that they were peace officers when they were acting to fulfill the purposes of the *National Defence Act*—that is, when they were dealing with people who were themselves subject to the *Code of Service Discipline*.

On the other hand, the Court did not adopt the most restrictive interpretation of "peace officer" either. Although not willing to allow military police to qualify as peace officers against everyone at all times, the Court held that on the facts of this case, the military police stopping the accused were peace officers. An alternative part of the definition was that military police were peace officers when "employed on duties that the Governor in Council . . . has prescribed to be of such a kind as to necessitate that the officers and men performing them have the powers of peace officers." Those duties included the powers needed for the maintenance or restoration of law and order, the protection of property, and the protection of persons; stopping drunk drivers fell within those purposes. In addition, the regulations required that the military police officer must be following a specific order or practice, but this was met by the obligations imposed under the *Trespass Regulations*. Accordingly, the officers in this case did qualify as peace officers for the purpose of stopping the accused on these facts even though he was a civilian.[307]

---

306 The section now reads "officers and non-commissioned members of the Canadian Forces who are (i) appointed for the purposes of s 156 of the *National Defence Act*."

307 See also *Lord*, above note 302 at para 12, concluding that a constable appointed under the *Canada Transportation Act* by a superior court judge from Alberta remained a peace officer in British Columbia as long as his "enforcement relates to the protection of property owned, possessed, or administered by CN or the protection of persons or property on or within 500 metres of CN property."

The Court reached a similar conclusion in *R v Decorte*, where it found that two First Nations constables were acting as peace officers in stopping a driver as part of the Reduced Impaired Driving Everywhere (RIDE) program, even though they did not stop him on the reserve. The officers were not police, although they had the powers of police officers in carrying out their duties. They were appointed as First Nations constables for the Fort Williams Reserve, but that did not mean, the Court held, that they could exercise their powers only within the territorial limits of the reserve; rather, they had been empowered by statute to act "in relation to" the community they served. In this case, the checkstop had been set up just outside the reserve, so they were acting within their authority.[308]

A similar conclusion was reached in *Roberge v The Queen*. Peace officers are appointed within a particular jurisdiction; depending on the force, that might be for a particular city or for an entire province. Normally, a peace officer out of their jurisdiction loses the status of peace officer and would have to rely on the citizen's arrest power, if an arrest power existed at all. This was the argument in *Roberge*, where a Quebec police officer pursued a taxi driver into New Brunswick. However, an exception is made in the case of fresh pursuit. The Supreme Court held that a peace officer who had lawful authority to arrest a person in one province retains the status of peace officer in another province so long as "the pursuit had commenced lawfully in his jurisdiction and as long as such pursuit is fresh."[309] On the other hand, it also held:

> The police officer should endeavour to contact the local peace officers as soon as is possible, even during the pursuit, circumstances permitting. Once the local authorities have taken over the pursuit, he ceases to be a peace officer and becomes then a person assisting peace officers.[310]

b) Statutory Powers to Arrest

Beyond the issue of whether, as a matter of fact, an accused was arrested is the question of whether that arrest was lawful. An arrest can be made either with a warrant or without one.

Where a peace officer wishes to arrest a person with a warrant, they must lay an information before a justice under section 504 of the *Code* and then under section 507 seek a warrant. Section 507(4) requires the

308 *R v Decorte*, 2005 SCC 9.

309 *Roberge v The Queen*, [1983] 1 SCR 312 at 332 [*Roberge*]. The particular finding in that case was that the peace officer is still protected under s 25(4) for the use of force likely to cause death or grievous bodily harm.

310 *Ibid*.

justice to issue a summons unless it is shown that there are reasonable grounds to believe that a warrant is necessary in the public interest. The warrant can authorize the release of the person following arrest rather than keep them in custody until a bail hearing. Failing that, the warrant requires the person to be brought before a justice to answer to the charge. These issues have all been dealt with at length in sections A(2), B(1), and B(3), above.

It is worth observing that arrest powers with and without a warrant are not entirely independent of one another. For example, section 495(1)(c) (discussed below) provides for a warrantless power of arrest on the basis of reasonable grounds to believe that an arrest warrant exists. See also *R v Charles*, where Saskatchewan police were assisting Ontario police to arrest the accused, based on a warrant that had not in fact been properly endorsed to be enforceable in Saskatchewan. Nonetheless, it was found that the two Saskatchewan officers, because of the one-hour briefing they had received, had reasonable grounds to believe the accused had committed the offence and therefore had a warrantless arrest power.[311]

The issue that needs to be discussed at length here is the other arrest option, arrest without a warrant. Warrantless powers of arrest are also set out in the *Criminal Code*, specifically in sections 494 and 495.[312] The latter section sets out powers of arrest available only to peace officers. The powers in the former section are more broadly available: some to "any one" and others to property owners or their delegates. They are often referred to colloquially as the powers of "citizen's arrest," and that is not inaccurate, in the sense that they are available to private citizens. As noted above, however, in occasional fact situations, peace officers might not be able to rely on section 495 but could rely on section 494. Since they too fall within "any one," they are also entitled to use these powers.[313]

As a preliminary observation, note that the Court has, broadly speaking, adopted the view that these arrest powers must be kept within their defined limits. That is, unless an arrest power has been specifically

311 *R v Charles*, 2012 SKCA 34.

312 There is authority suggesting that one remaining common law power of arrest still exists, which is an arrest for an apprehended breach of the peace, though doubt has been cast on this view: see Chapter 2, Section B(1)(c) and *Fleming*, above note 261.

313 See, for example, *Roberge*, above note 309, where the Court observes that a peace officer might pursue someone across a provincial border and, once there, call on local police for help. At that point, the original officer becomes only a citizen but could rely on the citizen's arrest power in s 494(1)(b). See also *R v Huff* (1979), 50 CCC (3d) 324 (Alta CA) [*Huff*]. In addition, see *R v Reddy*, 2007 BCPC 384 [*Reddy*], where an off-duty peace officer was entitled to rely on the citizen's arrest power.

prescribed by the *Criminal Code* or some other statute, then no arrest power exists. This point is made clear in *R v Sharma*. The accused there was issued a ticket for selling flowers without a licence, contrary to a city bylaw. When he refused to leave the street, the officer arrested him and charged him with obstructing an officer in the execution of duty. The Court held that the officer was not permitted to act in that fashion. The only mechanism provided for enforcement of the bylaw was to issue a ticket, and the officer had not been obstructed in doing that. Furthermore, the officer was not permitted to "manufacture" an arrest power for himself by ordering the accused to stop violating the bylaw and then arresting him under the *Criminal Code* for failing to comply.[314] Indeed, even where the underlying bylaw does contain an arrest power, that means a peace officer would have the right to arrest the accused only for violating the bylaw; it does *not* permit an arrest for obstruction.[315]

We will begin with a brief overview of the individual warrantless powers of arrest and then return to consider each of them in greater depth.

i) Overview of Arrest Powers

There are two initial distinctions to be noted in the arrest provisions. The first is that between an "indictable offence" and a "criminal offence." An indictable offence is one that may be prosecuted by indictment: "may" be as opposed to "must" be; therefore, this category includes hybrid offences.[316] The category of "criminal offence," on the other hand, includes all offences in the *Criminal Code*. Put another way, "indictable offence" means indictable or hybrid offences, and "criminal offence" means indictable, hybrid, or summary conviction offences. An arrest

314 *R v Sharma*, [1993] 1 SCR 650 [*Sharma*]. Applying *Sharma*, see *R v Hayes* (2003), 65 OR (3d) 787 (CA), where a motorcyclist was asked to remove his helmet for inspection but refused to do so. The officer then arrested the accused for obstruction, but the Ontario Court of Appeal found that charge not to be made out. The provincial legislation in question created an enforcement mechanism covering this situation, and the accused had not obstructed any effort on the part of the officer to use that mechanism (because no such effort had been made). See also the discussion in *R v Hadi*, 2018 ABQB 35.

315 *Fraser*, above note 129.

316 See *Huff*, above note 313. See also the *Interpretation Act*, RSC 1985, c-I-21, s 34(1):

> Where an enactment creates an offence, (a) the offence is deemed to be an indictable offence if the enactment provides that the offender may be prosecuted for the offence by indictment.

Note that Bill C-75 expanded the number of hybrid offences quite significantly. However, this was done by making some offences that had formerly only been prosecutable by indictment into hybrid offences, so there was no expansion of arrest powers as a result.

power for criminal offences is therefore the broader one. However, very few offences in the *Code* can only be prosecuted summarily, so as a practical matter, the narrower power is usually available in criminal matters.

Second, it is necessary to distinguish between the arrestor finding a person committing an offence and the arrestor having reasonable grounds to believe that a person has committed an offence. The former requires that the arrestor has actually witnessed the offence being committed.[317] The latter category is a broader one since it requires only reasonable belief, not personal knowledge (see the discussion in Chapter 2, Section C(2)).

Earlier in this chapter, we discussed the principle of restraint in compelling appearance: the notion that the ability of the state to interfere with individual liberty should be constrained to the extent consistent with achieving the goal of public safety. Clearly, that consideration is also relevant here. Generally speaking, to allow an arrest power for criminal offences is more intrusive than to allow one only for indictable offences. Similarly, to allow an arrest on reasonable grounds is more intrusive than an arrest power based on a "finds committing" standard. The most intrusive possible arrest power, then, would be one that allowed arrest based on reasonable grounds to believe that the accused has committed any criminal offence. Appropriately, then, that is the one arrest power that is not created in any part of section 494 or 495.

Section 494(1) sets out the powers of arrest available to anyone. There are two.

First, anyone may arrest someone whom they find committing an indictable offence. Note that, as is appropriate to counterbalance the fact that this arrest power is the one most broadly available (that is, to anyone), it combines the more limited options in order to maintain restraint. That is, it is available only for some offences, not all, and it requires the stricter "finds committing" standard.[318]

The second arrest power available to anyone depends on another arrest power already existing in someone else's hands; it is, in effect, a helping provision. That is, anyone may help arrest a person who is fleeing a valid arrest by someone else. Specifically, anyone may arrest if they have reasonable grounds to believe two things: that the person to be arrested has committed a criminal offence and that that person is escaping from and being freshly pursued by someone with lawful authority to arrest them.[319]

---

317 The situation is somewhat more complicated than that, of course: see Section C(2)(b)(ii), below in this chapter.

318 *Criminal Code*, above note 1, s 494(1)(b).

319 *Ibid.*

Section 494(2) sets out specific arrest powers for those with an interest in property and for their delegates—that is, "a person authorized by the owner or by a person in lawful possession of property." This power allows the arrest of anyone the arrestor finds committing a criminal offence on or in relation to the property. Although nominally available to any property owner, realistically, this arrest power is most frequently used by private security guards, bouncers, and so on.

Anyone other than a peace officer who arrests a person is required to "forthwith deliver the person to a peace officer."[320]

The warrantless powers of arrest exclusively available to peace officers are set out in section 495. There are limits on these powers, some of which were discussed in Section B(3), above. In general terms, however, peace officers are given quite broad powers of arrest. Really, there is only one circumstance in which peace officers cannot arrest, which is the situation that on the "finds committing/reasonable grounds" and "indictable/criminal" matrix would be the most intrusive. That is, if a peace officer has only reasonable grounds to believe an offence was committed, and the offence was only a summary conviction one, then no power of arrest exists. In those circumstances, the officer must lay an information before a justice and seek a summons or warrant.

More specifically, section 495 creates three warrantless arrest powers for peace officers. The first relates to the more restricted category of indictable offences: a peace officer may arrest a person who "has committed an indictable offence" or whom they on reasonable grounds believe has committed or is about to commit an indictable offence. These requirements are not immediately very obviously distinguishable, and we will discuss in more detail below the differences between them. The second arrest power relates to the broader category of criminal offences: in this case, a peace officer can arrest only if they find the person committing the offence. The final warrantless arrest power allows a peace officer to arrest a person if they have reasonable grounds to believe there is a warrant for that person's arrest.

The arrest powers given to peace officers are subject to the terms of section 495(2) and (3), imposing some limits on them: see the discussion in Section B(3), above.

Finally, note that it is of some importance for police, in the course of making an arrest, to be specific about the particular power upon which they are relying and the basis for the arrest. This issue will be pursued further in Chapter 5, dealing with the right under section 10(a) of the *Charter* to be informed of the reason for an arrest. Beyond that, however,

---

320 *Ibid*, s 494(3).

later consideration of whether or not an arrest was lawful will depend on the actual basis upon which the police purport to rely. That is, "[a]n arrest stated to be for one described offence cannot be validated by a later reliance upon another offence for which it might have been, but was not, made."[321]

ii) Citizen's Arrest[322]

Today, the vast majority of arrests are made by peace officers, but the Supreme Court has noted that "it is the peace officer's powers which are in a sense derivative from that of the citizen, not the other way around."[323] That citizen's arrest power itself "is in direct descent over nearly a thousand years of the powers and duties of citizens in the age of Henry II in relation to the 'King's Peace.'"[324] Nonetheless, the power is more limited than that given to peace officers. First, all citizen's arrest powers are subject to the overarching requirement that it was reasonable to use the power at all.[325] Second, the circumstances in which private citizens are given the power to arrest are more limited. As the power exists today, private citizens have the power to arrest in four separate situations.

The primary citizen's arrest power is in section 494(1)(a): to arrest a person one "finds committing" an indictable offence. The meaning of "finds committing" in the citizen's arrest context was reviewed at length by the Alberta Court of Appeal in *R v Abel & Corbett*.[326] The accused in that case, Abel, believed that a person who had lived in his house, Holl, had stolen his rifle. After attempting in other ways to have the rifle returned, Abel went with several friends to Holl's residence. They entered, an altercation in which Holl was struck with a tire iron ensued, and after Holl was tied up, he told Abel where to find the rifle, which was hidden in another location. Abel and his friends then recovered the rifle and took Holl to an RCMP station. Charges were laid against most participants, but Abel and his friends argued that they had acted with legal authority—specifically, that they were performing a citizen's

---

321 *Huff*, above note 313. See also *Dumbell v Roberts*, [1944] 1 All ER 326 (CA).

322 See also the discussion in Chapter 2, Section B(4) (Agents of the Police), and in particular the discussion there of whether private citizens are required to inform an arrested person of their *Charter* rights.

323 *Asante-Mensah*, above note 267 at para 40.

324 *Ibid* at para 36, quoting from *R v Lerke* (1986), 24 CCC (3d) 129 (Alta CA).

325 *Gentles*, above note 267 at para 39: "If it is found that the security guards did have reasonable and probable grounds to arrest the appellants, a further question would arise by virtue of *Asante-Mensah*: Was it reasonable for them to exercise their power to arrest in all of the circumstances of the case?"

326 2008 BCCA 54 [*Abel*].

arrest. They argued that they had found Holl committing the offence of possession of stolen property.

The central question was whether on these facts the "finds committing" standard was met; the Court of Appeal held that it was not. First, the court noted that the citizen's arrest power in the *Code* was a codification of the power that had existed at common law: that power had insisted on a strict immediacy requirement. To have a power to arrest, the private citizen must have been "present when any felony is committed."[327] So, for example, a person finding a thief with stolen vegetables one field away from where they had been stolen had not found the person committing the theft.[328] Similarly, a person learning at 3:00 p.m. that someone in his house had committed an offence at 1:00 p.m. had no power to arrest.[329]

The common law standard, the Court of Appeal held, was still reflected in the *Criminal Code* provision. It too requires that the person arresting witness the offence. Witnessing the offence, however, does not require that the arrestor witness every element of the offence. First, the arrestor is required only to "see at least the essential features of the offence."[330] Furthermore:

> 13 It is not necessary for a citizen making an arrest under s. 494(1)(a) to have personal knowledge of all the factors that lead him to conclude *that the person is "in the process" of committing an offence*; it can be deduced from a series of circumstances that a person is apparently in the process of committing an offence, and that offence must be apparent to a reasonable person in the same circumstances.[331]

The court noted as well that the French version of the section in the *Code* referred to a person "qu'elle trouve en train de commetre un acte criminal,"

327 William Blackstone, *Commentaries on the Laws of England*, vol 5 (Oxford: Clarendon Press, 1769), quoted in *Asante-Mensah*, above note 267 at para 37, and in *Abel*, above note 326 at para 32.

328 *R v Curran* (1828), 172 ER 472.

329 *Downing v Capel* (1867), LR 2 CP 461.

330 *Abel*, above note 326 at para 50, quoting Laskin J (as he then was) concurring in *R v Dean*, [1966] 3 CCC 228 at 236 (Ont CA) [*Dean*].

331 *Abel*, above note 326 at para 54, quoting *R v Sirois*, [1999] JQ no 1079 (CA) [emphasis in *Abel*]. So, for example, in *R v Gonzalez*, [1996] OJ No 761 (Prov Div) [*Gonzalez*], one security guard saw the accused hide an item on his person, so he radioed to another security guard closer to the exit. Although the second security guard saw the accused commit the offence in the sense that he saw him leave the store while he in fact had the item, this did not count since the second security guard did not personally know that the accused had the item or that he had not paid.

which also conveyed a sense of immediacy. In addition, it referred to various other statutes setting out a "finds committing" arrest standard. These were relevant, the court held, because "Parliament clearly intended the words 'finds committing' to have the same meaning whenever used in authorizing an arrest without warrant."[332] Some of these statutes described the standard, in French, as "en flagrant délit d'infraction," which is captured in the English as "caught red-handed."[333] It is clear, therefore, that "finds committing" sets a standard requiring a close temporal connection between the commission of the offence and the arrest and requires that the arrestor be present at and witness the offence.

An important point to note here is that the person arresting must not only have witnessed the offence; they must also have made the arrest at the time of witnessing it. Nonetheless, even at common law, some gap in time between commission and arrest was permissible so long as the person who committed the offence was being pursued throughout:

> The learned Judges present were clearly of opinion that the conviction was lawful: for, as he had been seen in the out-house, *and was taken on fresh pursuit* before he had left the neighbourhood, it was the same as if he had been taken in the out-house, or in running away from it, *that it was all one transaction.*[334]

On the other hand, an unjustified delay can cause the right to arrest to lapse. In *Twan v Hudson's Bay Company*, for example, a store security guard stopped a customer who had left the store without paying for a newspaper and asked her to return to sign a trespass notice. She went with the guard and produced identification showing her name and address, and she was then permitted to leave temporarily to pick up food she had already ordered. When she returned, the detainee was asked to sign the trespass notice but refused to do so; she was told that she would therefore have to wait for the police to arrive. Upon being told that this

---

332 *Abel*, above note 326 at para 61.

333 *Ibid* at para 62. In *Abel* itself, the Court of Appeal held that the "finds committing" standard was not met. The accused reasonably believed Holl had stolen his rifle but did not find him in possession of it and had no knowledge as to where he might have hidden it in order to justify finding him in constructive possession under s 4(3)(1)(ii) of the *Code*.

334 *R v Howarth* (1828), 168 ER 1243, quoted in *Abel*, above note 326 at para 36 [emphasis in *Abel*]. See also *Reddy*, above note 313, where the accused was an off-duty police officer who was threatened with a sword. The officer fled to safety initially and then pursued the person who had brandished the sword, coming upon him minutes later, after on-duty police officers had arrested him. The court held that he was acting under the "finds committing" arrest power, although he then used excessive force.

could take as much as five hours, the detainee began to leave but was physically restrained. The Court found that the arrest occurred at this point but that there was no justification for it.[335] (See the discussion below of the citizen's arrest power in section 494(2)(b), created in 2012, which in one particular context makes provision for some delay between the time grounds for the arrest and the arrest itself.)

There is an area in the jurisprudence around section 494(1)(a) that remains ambiguous. Although the section clearly states that the power therein allows a person to arrest someone "he finds committing" an offence, some courts have held that in fact a reasonableness standard applies. That is, a literal interpretation suggests that the arrestor must be correct: the person arrested must actually have been committing an offence, or no arrest power arises. A reasonableness standard would mean that the arrest would be legal if the arrestor reasonably believed they had found the person committing an offence.

The argument for this position is based on combining section 494(1)(a) and section 25 of the *Code*. Section 494(1)(a) creates the "finds committing" citizen's arrest power. Section 25 states:

> **25** (1) Every one who is required or authorized by law to do anything in the administration or enforcement of the law
> (a) as a private person . . .
> is, if he acts on reasonable grounds, justified in doing what he is required or authorized to do.

Combining these, some courts have concluded that a person who has reasonable grounds to think that a person has committed an offence is therefore authorized to arrest.[336]

---

335 *Twan v Hudson's Bay Company* (2008), 93 OR (3d) 582 (SCJ).

336 See, for example, *Karogiannis v Poulus*, [1976] 6 WWR 197 (BCSC) [*Karogiannis*], or *Dendekker v FW Woolworth Co*, [1975] 3 WWR 429 (Alta SC). This result is similar to that in *The Queen v Biron*, [1976] 2 SCR 56 [*Biron*], which interprets the "finds committing" standard in the context of peace officer arrest powers to mean "apparently finds committing"; this issue will be discussed in Section C(2)(b)(iii), below in this chapter. *Biron* is sometimes offered as a further justification (as in *Karogiannis*), but it is not the primary argument for this interpretation. See also *R v Piao*, 2010 ONCJ 496 at para 67, where the accused argued unsuccessfully that he had performed a citizen's arrest when he seized a person who had not yet returned some video and musical equipment:

> [A] rental holdover of only a few days when the offending parties remain in contact (as here conceded by the defendant and affirmed by other evidence) does not *by itself* provide a reasonable foundation for a belief that a person's property has been stolen directly or through conversion. [Emphasis in original.]

However, other courts have questioned this conclusion, for several reasons. It has been observed that, at common law, there was a distinction between the arrest powers of a private citizen and those of a peace officer:

> At common law a police constable may arrest a person if he has reasonable cause to suspect that a felony has been committed although it afterwards appears that no felony has been committed, but that it is not so when a private person makes or causes the arrest, for to justify his action he must prove, among other things, that a felony has actually been committed.[337]

That is not to say that reasonable grounds are not relevant at all, but they are not sufficient on their own. It is still necessary that a crime was actually committed by someone even if not, as it transpires, by the person arrested.[338]

Many courts have concluded that this distinction between private citizen's arrests and peace officer arrests survives into the *Criminal Code* provisions. On this view, the law is that two distinct things must be proven:

> [A] private person who arrests an individual must satisfy the court on a balance of probabilities:
> (a) that someone committed an indictable offence, and
> (b) that the private person effecting the arrest had reasonable grounds for believing and did believe the person arrested had committed that indictable offence.[339]

This same result has been taken to follow from the combined reading of section 494(1)(a) and section 25. Section 25 invokes the "reasonable ground" standard when the person is already authorized to act by some other section, but it does not itself authorize anything. Accordingly, the

---

337 *Walters v WH Smith & Son Ltd*, [1914] 1 KB 595 at 602, quoted in *Kovacs v Ontario Jockey Club* (1995), 126 DLR (4th) 576 (Ont Ct Gen Div) [*Kovacs*]. Note that (as was discussed in Chapter 2, Section B(1)) most of the relevant cases on this section arise from private law actions for false imprisonment or false arrest where the defendant relies on legal authority as the defence.

338 See *Williams v Laing* (1923), 55 OLR 26 at 28 (SCAD), quoted in *Kovacs*, above note 337 at para 57: "The law is quite clear that in order to succeed in establishing this defence the appellants must prove first that the crime they suspected had actually been committed, not necessarily by the person detained, but by some one, and that they had reasonable ground for suspecting the person detained."

339 *Parlee (Guardian ad litem of) v Port of Call Holdings Ltd*, 2000 BCSC 548 at para 11. Adopting the same view, see *Kovacs*, above note 337; *Banyasz v K-Mart Canada Ltd* (1986), 57 OR (2d) 445 (Div Ct); and *Hayward v Woolworth* (1979), 8 CCLT 157 (Nfld SCTD).

preconditions in section 494(1)(a) must be satisfied before any question of reasonableness arises:

> The legally authorized action with which we are concerned in Section 449 [now 494] is the arresting without warrant of a person found committing a crime. Proof of the commission of a criminal act by someone is thus essential. There can be no doubt if there is no crime, there can be no justification.[340]

Only after that condition is satisfied do reasonable grounds enter, in the form of reasonable grounds to believe that it was the accused who committed the offence.

Furthermore, it is worth observing that a great deal of the caselaw on citizen's arrest, since it arises from tort actions for false imprisonment, has to do with shoplifting cases. In such cases, the two questions of whether an offence was committed and whether there are reasonable grounds to believe that the person arrested committed it tend to merge into a single question, for practical purposes: "In those cases there is usually no proof of a crime committed unless it is proof of the crime committed by the person arrested."[341] Accordingly, many of those decisions seem to overlook that the first question is a separate one to be answered. In that event, they are of less precedential value than those cases that are careful to consider the two issues distinctly.

Two things should be noted in closing about the "apparently finds committing" standard in citizen's arrest. First, note that nothing in the discussion of reasonable grounds in any of the cases suggests that this standard *replaces* the strict immediacy requirement discussed above.[342] That is, to say that the arrestor need only have reasonable grounds to believe the person committed the offence is to say that if, given the facts immediately observed by the arrestor, it was reasonable for them *to believe they had found the person committing the offence*, then section 494(1)(a) authorizes the arrest. Reasonable grounds alone will not do.[343] Second, although the "finds committing" standard is used to define

---

340 *Smart v Sears Canada* (1987), 36 DLR (4th) 756 (Nfld CA).

341 *Briggs v Laviolette* (1994), 21 CCLT (2d) 105 at para 14 (BCSC).

342 If it did, then the result in *Abel*, above note 326, for example, would not only be different, there also would have been no dispute in the first place: Abel was acknowledged to have reasonable grounds to believe that Holl was in possession of the stolen rifle, but that was not sufficient because the standard was "finds committing."

343 See, for example, *Gonzalez*, above note 331 at para 18: "Reasonable grounds in that s. [s. 494(1)(b)] includes what an arrestor is told. The 'reasonable grounds/apparently' test for 'finds committing' requires that the arrestor have all the knowledge from his own senses, excluding everything he has been told."

arrest powers by private citizens and by peace officers, the term does not necessarily have exactly the same meaning in the two contexts. The citizen's arrest power is deliberately meant to be a narrower power.[344]

The second citizen's arrest power is in section 494(1)(b). It is based only on reasonable grounds, although it also depends on a prior arrest power in someone else's hands already existing. Specifically, that section gives an arrest power to anyone who on reasonable grounds believes two things: that the person to be arrested has committed a criminal offence and that that person is escaping from and freshly pursued by someone who has lawful authority to arrest that person.

One issue that arises here is that this arrest power is based on reasonable grounds rather than the "finds committing" standard. We have discussed in Chapter 2 the meaning of "reasonable grounds," and that discussion would apply here. There are some specific observations worth making about the operation of the standard in this particular context.

First, note the significance of the fact that a person is running away—or, perhaps more accurately, note the significance it does *not* have. Flight by a suspect can contribute toward creating reasonable grounds to believe that that person has committed an offence. However, it is not by itself sufficient to establish reasonable grounds. Section 494(1)(b) separates as two distinct inquiries that (i) the suspect has committed an offence and (ii) the suspect is escaping. If the latter were sufficient to create reasonable grounds for guilt, these two requirements would be collapsed into one.[345] In *R v Volker*, for example, a security guard saw a suspect standing by a car in a parkade, and a moment later, the suspect ran off. The court held that this gave that security guard reasonable grounds to believe that the suspect was trying to escape. However, relatively few other facts were known to the accused, and he was found not to have reasonable grounds to believe the suspect had committed a criminal offence.[346]

More specifically, the fact that a person is fleeing a police officer is not sufficient, on its own, to create reasonable grounds. In *R v Gladue* (2002), for example, two police constables were responding to a call that there had been a stabbing at an outdoor festival. As they approached the scene, they saw their corporal, with his gun drawn, chasing the accused,

344 See, for example, *R v Boyd*, 2013 BCCA 19 at para 21 [*Boyd*], considering the "finds committing" power in s 495: "I am not of the view that *Abel* is a particularly apposite authority to consider on the issue arising in the case at bar. The law has always sought to circumscribe within very narrow limits the powers of a citizen to effect an arrest."

345 *R v Gladue*, 2002 ABQB 519 at para 29 [*Gladue* 2002].

346 *R v Volker*, [1994] BCJ No. 3134 (Prov Ct) [*Volker*].

who was coming toward them. They drew their own guns and ordered the accused to lie down. He did not, with the result that they used force to take control of him, and he was charged with resisting an officer in the execution of duty. The accused was acquitted, on the basis that the police officers had had no power to arrest and so were not acting in the execution of duty.

The court noted the limited information known to the arresting officers. The call they had received had said only that there had been a stabbing. The stabber had not been identified or described in any way, such as by height, weight, race, gender, or clothing. There had been no indication that the stabber was fleeing or had fled the festival. The only information they acted on was that the accused was being chased by another officer. The court rejected the suggestion that "whenever a police officer sees a superior officer chasing someone, that police officer is entitled to step in and arrest the person being chased" and acquitted the accused.[347]

That does not mean that reliance on other persons is not allowed; it will necessarily be the case if the person is arresting based on reasonable grounds. In *Kendall v Gambles Canada Ltd*, for example, the head of security for a department store thought she observed two customers hiding items in their clothes. She made a coded message over the store's public-address system that informed other employees that she was observing potential shoplifters; she then specifically pointed out the suspects to two employees and instructed them to keep an eye on her and the suspects. When she later arrested the two accused after they left the store, the two employees assisted her. In fact, the two suspects had not been shoplifting, so their false arrest claim against the head of security succeeded: no offence had been committed, which was essential to her authority to arrest under section 494(1)(a). The two employees who assisted, however, were protected by section 494(1)(b): what they had been told gave them reasonable grounds to believe that the suspects had committed an offence.[348]

The two issues of "escaping from" and "freshly pursued" are also worth considering. The Ontario Court of Appeal held in *R v Dean* that these terms ought not to be given a narrow interpretation.[349] However, that decision long predates the *Charter*, and it should be noted that giving the terms a broad interpretation amounts to authorizing more

---

347 *Gladue* 2002, above note 345 at para 40.

348 *Kendall v Gambles Canada Ltd*, [1981] 4 WWR 718 (Sask QB) [*Kendall*]. The court held that those facts also gave the employees reasonable grounds to believe the suspects were escaping from someone with authority to arrest.

349 *Dean*, above note 330.

widespread interferences with individual liberty; accordingly, it is not clear that that interpretive approach is in general the right one.

On the other hand, *Dean*'s specific interpretation of "escaping from" still seems sensible. In that case, the accused had rushed out of a coffee shop without paying his bill. Two staff members pursued him to the door and then flagged down a passing police car; that officer caught the accused and brought him back to the coffee shop. After the accused had refused several times to pay the bill, the officer arrested him. The court held that on these facts the officer was authorized under what is now section 494(1)(b). On one view, the accused was no longer "escaping" by the time he was arrested since the officer had caught him and brought him back. However, the court held that the officer certainly had been in compliance with the "escaping from and freshly pursued by" requirements at the point he had first caught the accused and so could have arrested him then. Holding that he had lost that arrest power by taking the accused back to the coffee shop to try to sort things out would require an officer "to arrest first and inquire afterwards, hardly a desirable procedure."[350]

Frequently, the proof that someone is escaping will be that they are actually running away, coupled with the inference that this is being done to avoid arrest.[351] What appears to be more important than the physical activity is the intention behind it, however. For example, in *R v Matthews*,[352] the detainee had been in an altercation with picketers while on his way into a movie theatre. The police had been called, and an officer was at the front of the movie theatre when the movie ended a few hours later. The accused went to the back door of the theatre and found the detainee there, waiting for his wife and son to return with the car. Although the detainee testified that he had left that way in order to avoid further confrontation, the court held that it was reasonable of the accused to infer that the detainee had left by the back door in order to escape detection and not talk to the police. In that event, there were reasonable grounds to think he was escaping from someone with authority to arrest him.

The meaning of "fresh pursuit" has been discussed by the Supreme Court of Canada, although not strictly in the context of section 494(1)(b). However, there is a common law exception to the rules around police

350 *Ibid* at para 8.

351 In *Volker*, above note 346 at para 47, for example, the security guard testified that he thought "why else would he run" when the accused fled, which the court took to be a reasonable inference that the accused was "escaping."

352 2001 BCPC 253.

entry into a dwelling house to effect arrest, which allows the police to enter in cases of "hot pursuit."[353] In defining "hot pursuit," the Court held:

> Generally, the essence of fresh pursuit is that it must be continuous pursuit conducted with reasonable diligence, so that pursuit and capture along with the commission of the offence may be considered as forming part of a single transaction.[354]

Seemingly, this meaning of "fresh pursuit" ought to be equally applicable in the context of section 494(1)(b).

However, "fresh pursuit" in the context of section 494(1)(b) does not require that the capture be by the same person who begins the pursuit at the commission of the offence; indeed, by definition, it will not be. Therefore, the real requirement is that someone who had authority to arrest has begun a fresh pursuit but has not finished it.

The initial pursuit need not be of any particular duration. In *Dean*, for example, the staff of the coffee shop pursued the accused only as far as the door of the coffee shop when he fled without paying because they were then able to flag down a police car. Nonetheless, this satisfied the "freshly pursued" requirement and clothed the officer with power to arrest.

On the other hand, in *R v Gonzalez*, one store security guard radioed to another that the accused had hidden an item on his person. The second security guard saw the accused leave the store without paying. The second guard chased the accused down the street and caught up with him. As discussed above, the second security guard had no "finds committing" power because he was dependent on what the first guard had told him to believe the accused had committed an offence. Those facts did give him reasonable grounds to believe the accused had committed an offence, satisfying part of section 494(1)(b). However, no evidence was led that the first guard had attempted to catch the accused personally, so it was not established that he was being freshly pursued.

Similarly, the pursuit, if commenced at one point, must still be ongoing to constitute fresh pursuit. In *R v Lawson*,[355] a taxi driver dropped off a passenger who did not pay; after some attempts to get into

353 *R v Macooh*, [1993] 2 SCR 802 [*Macooh*]. *Macooh* was an exception to rules that have since been found to violate the *Charter*: see *R v Feeney*, [1997] 2 SCR 13 [*Feeney*]. However, *Feeney* referred to and upheld the "hot pursuit" exception to the new rules formulated in that case. Subsequently, Parliament has created a warrant scheme that explicitly creates an "exigent circumstances" exception, but the common law hot-pursuit exception has also survived. See the discussion in Chapter 2, Section B(1)(d).

354 *Macooh*, above note 353 at para 24, quoting from Roger E. Salhany, *Canadian Criminal Procedure*, 5th ed (Aurora, ON: Canada Law Book, 1989) at 44.

355 [1973] OJ No 1333, 22 CRNS 215 (Prov Ct).

the rooming house to which the passenger had fled, the taxi driver left to get the police. The court held that the taxi driver had had the authority to arrest the passenger, but the police did not have authority under section 494(1)(b): the taxi driver had abandoned his pursuit in order to get the help of the police.

One might be tempted to argue that there is a certain formalism or technicality in the distinctions between some of these cases. In *Dean*, the coffee-shop staff were lucky enough to find a police officer on the street; in *Lawson*, the taxi driver had to seek one; in *Kendall*, the other store employees were authorized to arrest on reasonable grounds because the first security guard also stepped out of the store; in *Gonzalez*, quite similar reasonable grounds were not enough because the first security guard was not shown to have stepped outside the store. However, there is in fact an important principle at play. Of the three citizen's arrest powers, two (section 494(1)(a) and section 494(2)) require that the arrestor find the accused committing the offence. The section 494(1)(b) power relaxes that standard to reasonable grounds but does so because of the urgency in the situation: because it is a fast-developing situation, quick decisions need to be made. For that reason, it makes sense to be careful about interpreting the requirements in a way that reflects the urgent nature of the situation. If there is time to leave and seek the police, or if no one is actually pursuing the accused, then it is sensible to conclude that there is time for more measured reactions and therefore that the ordinary arrest rules should apply.

The final two citizen's arrest powers should be discussed together since they are variations on the same situation. Section 494(2) provides arrest powers not to all private citizens but specifically to "the owner or a person in lawful possession of property, or a person authorized by the owner or by a person in lawful possession of property." It permits such a person to arrest someone found "committing a criminal offence on or in relation to that property." "Property" is defined in section 2 of the *Code* to include both real and personal property.[356] This power is available in two separate circumstances, varying by time: the arrest can be made (1) at the time of the offence or (2) "within a reasonable time after the offence is committed" if the person "believe[s] on reasonable grounds that it is not feasible in the circumstances for a peace officer to make the arrest."[357]

This particular arrest power was changed in 2013 in reaction to a highly publicized prosecution. Up until that point, it could only be exercised on a "finds committing" basis, the standard still preserved in section 494(1)(a). In 2009, a Toronto grocery store owner witnessed a

356 *Criminal Code*, above note 1, s 2.
357 *Ibid*, s 494(2)(a) & (b).

person steal something from his store but did not arrest the person at the time. Several hours later, he saw the shoplifter return and, with the help of several others, seized the shoplifter, tied him up, and threw him in a van. This led onlookers to believe they had seen an abduction and to call the police, which resulted in the store owner being charged with an offence. It seemed to many as though he would not fall within the existing citizen's arrest power since the gap of several hours would not meet the "finds committing" standard. In reaction, a private member's bill was introduced to change the section, and that eventually became law.[358] As a result, in addition to the finds committing standard, the property owner arrest power now extends to a reasonable time after if it is not feasible to have the police make the arrest.

The property owner arrest power is often used by security personnel in stores as the authority for arresting shoplifters, but it is not limited to that situation. For example, in *Dean*, discussed above, the accused left a coffee shop without paying his bill. A waitress and a cashier were there, and the court held that they were both persons "in lawful possession of property": they "were found in complete control of the premises serving the customers and collecting payment therefore."[359] In *R v Cunningham*, the two accused were officers in charge of a ship that made trips up and down the Red and Assiniboine rivers; they were authorized under the section to arrest a youth who threw a rock at the boat from shore, breaking a window.[360]

The final point to note about citizen's arrests is the obligation in section 494(3) to "forthwith deliver the person to a peace officer." Arrest involves an imposition on liberty, and citizen's arrest is arguably the most difficult to control. In order to see to it that the detention lasts no longer than necessary, the accused is to be handed over to a state actor, the police.

"Forthwith" in this context does not mean immediately. Rather, it means as soon as "reasonably possible or practicable under all the circumstances." In *Cunningham*, for example, the accused arrested a youth who had thrown a rock and broken a window in the cruise ship they were taking up the Assiniboine River. They radioed the police, who indicated that they could not come to the scene and instructed the accused to bring the youth to the dock from which they had departed. The return

358 In fact, the store owner was found at trial to have fallen within the existing citizen's arrest power, but by that point, the *Criminal Code* had already been amended. See the discussion of the case in Steve Coughlan, "Citizen's Arrest, Property Owners, and Private Fiefdoms" (2014) 18 *Canadian Criminal Law Review* 1.

359 *Dean*, above note 330 at para 11.

360 *R v Cunningham* (1979), 49 CCC (2d) 390 (Man Co Ct) [*Cunningham*].

voyage took ninety minutes, and the boy was confined in the wheelhouse the entire time, with his ankles tied together. Nonetheless, the court held that this met the "forthwith" requirement: the accused had acted as instructed and had returned without stopping and with all reasonable speed.

Even if "forthwith" does not mean "instantly," however, it does require a timely delivery. In *R v Corbett*, the accused was assaulted by the complainant while she was in his apartment. He and a friend were able to subdue her and restrained her with tape and by tying her up. However, they did not then call the police, and she was not freed for several hours, until the police arrived after she was able to dial 911. The accused might, on these facts, have had the right to arrest the complainant. However, the court held that there was not even an air of reality to the claim that the accused was acting with lawful authority because of the extended detention.[361]

iii) Peace Officer Arrests

Section 495(1) contains a number of different arrest powers given only to peace officers. For a full understanding of the powers, it is important to recall that they are all subject to sections 495(2) and (3), which attach some limits to their proper use; that issue is discussed in Section B(3), above. Here, we will discuss at greater length the nature of the arrest powers themselves.

a. Section 495(1)(a)

Section 495(1) is limited to arrests for indictable offences. It appears to create three separate arrest powers, although they are closely related. The section allows a peace officer to arrest

> a person who has committed an indictable offence or who, on reasonable grounds, he believes has committed or is about to commit an indictable offence.

As a practical matter, the middle of these three powers—a person "who, on reasonable grounds, he believes has committed" an indictable offence—is the most used. We will discuss each of them in turn.

On a literal reading, a power to arrest anyone who *has committed* an indictable offence would be extraordinarily broad. As the British Columbia Court of Appeal has noted, if these words were to be read in isolation from the rest of the section, then

361 *R v Corbett*, 2004 BCCA 378.

> the arresting officer would not have to believe or even possess reasonable grounds for believing that the arrestee had in fact committed an offence. So long as that fact could subsequently be established, the arrest would be lawful.[362]

That literal approach to the section would in many cases render the "reasonable grounds" standard redundant since arrests made without them might still be valid. Indeed, an arrest on reasonable grounds would become relevant only in cases where it transpired that the arrestee had not in fact committed the offence. It would also allow *post facto* justification for the use of police powers, which is generally an undesirable approach.[363]

Properly, the British Columbia Court of Appeal held that such a broad reading could not be justified. Rather, it concluded, the words must be understood by looking at the arrest powers available to peace officers as a whole. Section 495(1)(b) deals with arrests made while an offence is taking place; that is, the officer finds the person committing the offence. Section 495(1)(a), the court ruled, brackets that by providing an arrest power where an indictable offence has already been committed or is about to be committed. However, the words "has committed" should be understood, in essence, to mean "has just committed"; that is, the officer witnessed the offence, but it was completed before she had a chance to intervene. The court held:

> Looking in particular at the first part of s. 495(1)(a), a peace officer is entitled to arrest a person who has committed an indictable offence. Before such an arrest can be made, the peace officer must know that the arrestee has committed an indictable offence. In order for him to know that, he must have witnessed the indictable offence occurring. Correctly construed, then, this first part of the provision covers those few situations where the arresting officer, having personally witnessed the commission of an indictable offence, could not prevent it or perfect an

---

362 *R v Klimchuk* (1991), 67 CCC (3d) 385 at 404 (BCCA) [*Klimchuk*].

363 See *Canada (Combines Investigation Branch, Director of Investigation and Research) v Southam Inc*, [1984] 2 SCR 145 at 160, speaking in the context of searches:

> Such a *post facto* analysis would, however, be seriously at odds with the purpose of s. 8. That purpose is, as I have said, to protect individuals from unjustified state intrusions upon their privacy. That purpose requires a means of *preventing* unjustified searches before they happen, not simply of determining, after the fact, whether they ought to have occurred in the first place. This, in my view, can only be accomplished by a system of *prior authorization*, not one of subsequent validation. [Emphasis added.]

> arrest before its completion. In such circumstances, s. 495(1)(b) would no longer apply because the offence was no longer being committed.[364]

Read in this way, the "has committed" standard is not a dilution of the "reasonable grounds" standard, permitting arrests on lesser grounds and allowing them to be justified after the fact. Rather, as is appropriate, "has committed" will be a stricter standard than reasonable grounds.[365] This approach is consistent with the relationship between section 495(1)(a) (generally speaking, arrests on reasonable grounds) and section 495(1)(b) (arrests based on the "finds committing" standard); it has been observed that the latter standard is stricter than the former.[366]

R v Klimchuk also notes the relationship of the rest of section 495(1)(a) to the "has committed" standard:

> The remainder of s. 495(1)(a), that is, everything after the first "or," covers those situations in which the officer did not personally witness the indictable offence or in which the indictable offence has not yet occurred. In those cases the officer is entitled to arrest if he believes on reasonable grounds that such offence has been or is about to be committed.[367]

The primary arrest power in section 495(1)(a) is the second one, the authorization given to a peace officer to arrest a person "who, on reasonable grounds, he believes has committed" an indictable offence. The most important issue to understand in looking at the power is the meaning of "reasonable grounds to believe." However, that issue was discussed at length in Chapter 2. Accordingly, only a brief summary of the power need be given here.

The leading decision on the application of this portion of section 495(1)(a) is *Storrey*.[368] In that case, the Court noted that the purpose of the standard in the arrest provision was to strike the appropriate balance between the individual's right to liberty and the need for society to be protected from crime. It stated that reasonable and probable grounds must be established in front of a justice to obtain a search warrant and that "it is even more important for the police to demonstrate that they have those same reasonable and probable grounds" in the case of warrantless arrests.[369]

---

364 *Klimchuk*, above note 362 at 405–6.

365 The approach in *Klimchuk*, *ibid*, has been referred to with approval in *Abel*, above note 326, and in *R v MD* (1994), 40 BCAC 101 (CA).

366 See *R v Janvier*, 2007 SKCA 147 at para 28 [*Janvier*].

367 *Klimchuk*, above note 362 at 406.

368 *Storrey*, above note 31.

369 *Ibid* at para 14.

A peace officer requires more than suspicion to arrest a person. On the other hand, the standard is short of a prima facie case. In addition, the fact that a person is later found to be not guilty does not mean that no reasonable grounds existed for the arrest:

> The question of reasonable and probable grounds depends upon a *bona fide* reasonable belief in a state of facts that, if true, would justify the course taken. That the supposed fact proves not to exist does not render the belief unreasonable.[370]

The Court also noted in *Storrey* that reasonable grounds consist of two components: the subjective and the objective. A peace officer must personally believe, on reasonable grounds, that the accused has committed the offence in question, and this independent belief matters. In *R v Frieburg*, for example, police had a search warrant for a house and arrested the accused before she could return to it; the only evidence from the officers was that they did so in order to make the search safer. In the absence of any evidence from those officers that they subjectively believed the accused had committed the offence, the arrest was found to be unlawful.[371] In addition, however,

> it must be objectively established that those reasonable and probable grounds did in fact exist. That is to say a reasonable person, standing in the shoes of the police officer, would have believed that reasonable and probable grounds existed to make the arrest.[372]

Finally, recall several other points about reasonable grounds that were discussed in greater length in Chapter 2: they must be specific to the offence for which the accused is arrested, they can be based on hearsay, and one officer is entitled to arrest on the basis that another officer meets the requirements for an arrest under section 495(1)(a).

The final arrest power in section 495(1)(a), an arrest on the basis that there are reasonable grounds to believe a person is "about to commit" an indictable offence, has received very little judicial attention. The reason for this is very likely that the words "about to commit" do not admit of any real ambiguity; they require a very close temporal connection. "About to commit" is obviously a much stricter test than "will commit at some point," and no real attempt to stretch its meaning seems to have been made.

Nonetheless, there are one or two observations that might be made about this arrest power. First, like the "reasonable grounds" standard

370 *R v Grotheim*, 2001 SKCA 116 at para 42.

371 *R v Frieburg*, 2013 MBCA 40.

372 *Storrey*, above note 31 at para 16.

in section 495(1)(b), the "about to commit" standard has both a subjective and an objective component. In *R v Sanghera*, for example, the accused was lawfully arrested on the basis that he was about to commit a shooting. The trial judge considered the evidence about the officer's own personal belief to satisfy the subjective standard and then considered the evidence as a whole—escalating tensions between two groups who had already fired shots at one another, a tip that the accused was in "hunt mode," and observations of the accused driving slowly and looking in other vehicles—to find that that belief was objectively reasonable.[373] Second, recall that reasonable grounds must be specific to the charge to be laid or the issue in question. That is, of course, equally true in the "about to commit" context. In *R v Warford*, for example, the police received a reliable tip that the accused would be trafficking in narcotics at a particular nightclub on a particular date at an approximate time and would be travelling there in a particular vehicle. The police stopped the accused on the date in question in the vehicle in question, at the time suggested, while the accused was driving a route that was consistent with travelling to the nightclub. The Court of Appeal held that this did constitute reasonable grounds to believe that the accused was about to commit the offence of trafficking in narcotics; the fact that the police did not believe they had enough evidence to obtain a search warrant for the accused's home did not interfere with this conclusion.[374]

A final issue is worth noting in connection with the "about to commit" standard. Recall that an arrest made on one basis cannot later be justified on the grounds that arrest on a different basis would have been permissible.[375] In many factual situations, particularly those that are fast-evolving, this limitation can be of some significance. In *Jensen v Stemmer*, for example, the police had attended at the home of a couple because the husband had reported to them that his common law partner had threatened to kill him. The police interviewed both parties and told them that one of the two would have to leave the residence; they testified that they did this because they were afraid the situation would spiral out of control. Eventually, the police arrested the wife for uttering a threat. In upholding a finding of wrongful imprisonment, the Manitoba Court of Appeal noted that the power to arrest on the "about to commit" basis could be quite relevant in the domestic-dispute context; however, it was not the basis upon which the police had in fact purported to arrest. In that event, the claimant had been wrongly imprisoned.[376]

---

373 *Sanghera*, above note 298.

374 *R v Warford*, 2001 NFCA 64.

375 *Huff*, above note 313.

376 *Jensen v Stemmer*, 2007 MBCA 42.

b. Section 495(1)(b)

Section 495(1)(b) allows a peace officer to arrest "a person whom he finds committing a criminal offence." The essential difference between the arrest powers in section (a) and (b) was laid out by the Court in *Biron*.[377] Where section 495(1)(a) primarily rests on arrests based on reasonable grounds,

> [p]aragraph (b) applies in relation to any criminal offence and it deals with the situation in which the peace officer himself finds an offence being committed. His power to arrest is based upon his own observation. Because it is based on his own discovery of an offence actually being committed there is no reason to refer to a belief based upon reasonable and probable grounds.[378]

Despite this difference, however, the Court held that section 495(1)(b) is equally to be decided based on the circumstances known to the peace officer at the time of the arrest. More specifically, the Court concluded that the "finds committing" standard does not require that the person arrested was *in fact* committing the offence; rather, it is sufficient if they were "apparently" committing it.

This question arose in *Biron* because the accused was charged with two offences: causing a disturbance by shouting and resisting a peace officer in the execution of duty. Biron was arrested at a bar during a raid to check for firearms and illegal liquor; he was uncooperative and refused to give the police his name. He was passed through several police officers before eventually getting into a scuffle with the officer, who attempted to put him in the police wagon. He was acquitted of the causing a disturbance charge because there was no evidence that he had been shouting. He appealed his conviction on the other charge based on that finding. Specifically, he argued that since he had not been committing an offence, the officer therefore could not have found him committing one. In that event, the officer did not have the power to arrest under section 495(1)(b) and so was not acting in the execution of duty.

The majority of the Court rejected this argument. They held that Biron's argument would create an unworkable situation. Therefore, they concluded that it was not actually necessary that the accused was committing an offence — merely that it appeared to the peace officer that he was doing so:

> The power of arrest which that paragraph gives has to be exercised promptly, yet, strictly speaking, it is impossible to say that an offence is

377 *Biron*, above note 336.

378 *Ibid* at 72.

> committed until the party arrested has been found guilty by the courts. If this is the way in which this provision is to be construed, no peace officer can ever decide, when making an arrest without a warrant, that the person arrested is "committing a criminal offence." In my opinion the wording used in para. (b), which is oversimplified, means that the power to arrest without a warrant is given where the peace officer himself finds a situation in which a person is apparently committing an offence.[379]

On that approach, Biron was guilty; the arresting officer was justified in thinking that the accused had committed an offence even if, as it turned out, that was not proven.

Subsequently, in *Roberge*, the Court clarified its decision in *Biron*. In that latter decision, the Court held that it was not sufficient merely for a peace officer to claim that it had been apparent the accused had been committing an offence. Rather, what was required was that "it must be 'apparent' to a reasonable person placed in the circumstances of the arresting officer at the time."[380]

Somewhat infelicitously, the Court then described the "finds committing" standard as "an officer acting 'on reasonable and probable grounds.'" It would be easy to mistake the intent behind this description and take it to be a general statement that section 495(1)(b) requires a peace officer only to have reasonable grounds to believe that the accused has committed a criminal offence. If that were the intention, then the one exception to peace officer powers of arrest—where the offence was only a summary conviction one and the peace officer only had reasonable grounds to believe the accused had committed it—would no longer be an exception.

In fact, that is not the Court's intention. A peace officer still cannot, despite *Biron*, simply arrest on reasonable belief for summary conviction offences. A peace officer who arrives at the scene of a summary conviction offence and is reliably told that the accused committed it is still not empowered to arrest. Rather, *Biron* retains the notion that the peace officer's "power to arrest is based upon his own observation."[381] It merely means that those personal observations need only give the peace officer reasonable grounds to believe the accused has committed an offence rather than requiring that the officer is ultimately proven to be correct in that assessment.

Courts of appeal certainly have held to the view that the relaxation of the "finds committing" standard in *Biron* has not reduced it to nothing

379 *Ibid* at 75.

380 *Roberge*, above note 309 at 324–25.

381 *Biron*, above note 336.

but a reasonable grounds standard. The Saskatchewan Court of Appeal has affirmed that, even given *Biron* and *Roberge*, the "finds committing" standard remains stricter than the standard for arrest for an indictable offence under section 495(1)(a).[382] As the British Columbia Court of Appeal has put it, "the arresting officer must have reasonable grounds to believe that the person to be arrested is apparently in the process of committing a crime in his or her presence."[383]

The Nova Scotia Court of Appeal has suggested that, given the decisions in *Biron* and *Roberge*, three things must be established to meet the "finds committing" standard. First, it must be shown that the police officer's knowledge is contemporaneous to the event: "[U]nlike the *reasonable and probable grounds* standard, it is not enough to believe that an offence has taken place in the past or is about to take place."[384] Second, the officer must actually observe the commission of the offence, although there is room for some ambiguity as to whether this requires the officer to *see* the offence. The accepted view seems to be that an officer can meet the "finds committing" standard if they are able to personally detect the offence in some way, by seeing, hearing, or, in some cases, smelling it.[385] To observe the smell of burnt marijuana, for example, is not a sufficient basis on its own for a peace officer to claim to find the person committing the offence of possession of marijuana since it only demonstrates that the accused had possessed marijuana in the past.[386] On the other

---

382 *Janvier*, above note 366 at para 28. See also *R v Yeh*, 2009 SKCA 112.

383 *Abel*, above note 326 at para 52, relying on *Roberge*, above note 309. See also *Janvier*, above note 366 at para 22: "*Roberge* does not eliminate the distinction between 'has committed' in s. 495(1)(a) and 'finds committing' in s. 495(1)(b) but instead is directed to the belief the officer has as to the presence of the grounds for either type of offence in order to arrest."

384 *STP v Canada (Director of Public Prosecutions Service)*, 2009 NSCA 86 at para 20 [*STP*].

385 For example, see *Boyd*, above note 344 at para 6:

> As the Crown notes in its factum, there may be some debate in the cases as to whether the power to arrest exists only when an officer sees an offence being committed or observes facts from which an inference may be drawn that an offence is being committed. It would be well to avoid undue casuistry in this area and it seems to me that a peace officer could legitimately arrest a person if it is *apparent* that an offence is being committed by such person. [Emphasis in original.]

386 See *Boyd*, *ibid*, or *Janvier*, above note 366 at paras 28 & 29:

> Thus, I conclude that the standard for arrest without a warrant for the commission of a summary conviction offence pursuant to s. 495(1)(b) is more strict than the standard for arrest for an indictable offence under s. 495(1)(a).
>
> Applying this principle to the case at hand, the police officer did not see, hear or smell Mr. Janvier committing the offence of possession of marihuana, and therefore, did not *find* him committing that offence. [Emphasis in original.]

hand, the smell of vegetative marijuana could authorize such an arrest.[387] The central point is that "there must be an objective basis for the officer's conclusion that an offence is being committed."[388]

There is some reason to be doubtful that the Court adopted the right policy with its decision in *Biron*. Note first of all the difference between the decision in *Biron* and the "finds committing" power in the case of citizen's arrests. As pointed out in the discussion of that topic, the common law requirements around this power depended on proving two things: that an offence was actually committed and that there was a reasonable basis for believing the accused had committed it. The approach in *Biron* departs from this by giving up the requirement that an offence has actually been committed.

Furthermore, as the dissent in the case observes, it is useful to distinguish two separate considerations. On the one hand, there is the question of whether a peace officer should forfeit the protection of section 25 to use reasonable force where they are "authorized by law to do anything in the administration or enforcement of the law." There are good policy reasons to think that an officer who reasonably believes they have the power to arrest should not forfeit that protection in civil proceedings even if the arrest later turns out not to have been authorized.[389]

That is quite a different question, however, from the issue of whether the accused should be guilty of resisting an officer in the execution of duty even though the officer was *not* acting in the execution of duty. In that context, the dissenting judges suggest:

> Our law has not, as I understand it, deprived the citizen of his right to resist unlawful arrest. His resistance may be at his own risk if the arrest proves to be lawful, but so too must the police officer accept the risk of having effected a lawful arrest.[390]

The decision of the majority in *Biron*, however, says that a person will be guilty of the offence of resisting arrest even if the arrest turns out to be unlawful.

These first two points are related in some sense. Note that *Biron* (abandoning the "an offence was actually committed" requirement) was decided in the context of whether the accused was guilty, whereas the great majority of citizen's arrest cases (retaining the requirement) were decided in the context of whether the person who made the arrest was protected from tort liability. It must surely seem surprising that a person's

---

387 See, for example, *R v Harding*, 2010 ABCA 180, or *R v MacCannell*, 2014 BCCA 254.

388 *STP*, above note 384 at para 22.

389 Indeed, s 25(1) specifically says a person "is, if he acts on reasonable grounds, justified in doing what he is required or authorized to do."

390 *Biron*, above note 336 at 65.

financial interest in compensation has received greater protection than their liberty interest.

A final reason to think that *Biron* was decided incorrectly—and, indeed, that it should be reversed—is that it is a pre-*Charter* case. Specifically, the *Charter*, in section 10(a), guarantees anyone arrested the right to be informed of the reason for the arrest. The Court has noted that there are two rationales for this right, the second of which is to permit the arrestee to exercise the right to consult with counsel effectively. However, that is not the primary justification:

> The right to be promptly advised of the reason for one's detention embodied in s. 10(*a*) of the *Charter* is founded most fundamentally on the notion that one is not obliged to submit to an arrest if one does not know the reasons for it.[391]

That is, the Court has specifically acknowledged that a person is entitled not to submit to—is entitled to resist—an arrest in some circumstances. Even more particularly, one must consider for what purpose an accused is entitled to be told the reason for the arrest. It would make little sense to say that as long as an accused was told of the reason for the arrest, the accused must then submit to it, even though it was patently unlawful. Rather, it would make more sense to assume that one is entitled to know of the reason precisely because one is not obliged to submit to an unlawful arrest. That conclusion is the opposite of that reached in *Biron*.

To a small extent, the Court has already limited the impact of *Biron*. In *Sharma*, as recounted earlier, the accused was a flower vendor operating without a licence. A passing police officer gave him a provincial offence ticket and ordered him to pack up and move on. When the officer returned later, the accused was still selling flowers, and the officer arrested him for obstructing an officer in the execution of duty. In fact, the bylaw under which the provincial offence ticket was issued was found to be *ultra vires*, so the accused was acquitted on that charge. The Crown argued that he was nonetheless guilty of the obstruction charge, on the *Biron* argument: although the accused had not been committing the offence, it appeared to the officer that he was doing so, so the arrest was valid. The Court rejected this argument and the analogy to *Biron*:

> *Biron* deals with apparent perpetration of an offence, not apparent offences, and as such it cannot be relied upon to confer on police the power to charge someone with obstruction where there is an apparent violation of a law which itself is invalid.[392]

---

391 *Evans*, above note 276 at para 31.

392 *Sharma*, above note 314 at para 32.

It is not entirely clear that the distinction between "apparent perpetration of an offence" and "apparent offences" is a sensible one. From the perspective of the officer, the situation is the same: a law is in place, and the accused appears to be violating it. Indeed, since the validity of a law will only ever be determined after the fact, this approach violates the rationale offered in *Biron* for adopting the "apparently finds committing" standard—that otherwise it would be impossible to say at the time of the arrest whether or not the power existed.[393] The most sensible conclusion to draw, however, is not that *Sharma* was wrongly decided. Rather, it is that *Biron* overestimates the extent to which this should really be a concern.[394]

c. Section 495(1)(c)

Section 495(1)(c) seems, at first glance, a bit of an oddity. It allows a peace officer to arrest, without a warrant, "a person in respect of whom he has reasonable grounds to believe that a warrant . . . is in force." Although this warrantless arrest based on a warrant power might seem unusual, it reflects a sensible policy. In effect, it can be seen as simply an elaboration of the arrest power on reasonable grounds in section 495(1)(a) (although it is not necessarily limited to indictable offences). If a warrant for the person's arrest has been issued, then an information has been laid before a justice alleging that that person has committed an offence, and the justice has decided that it is in the public interest to issue a warrant rather than a summons. In those circumstances, one can argue that there are "judicially certified" reasonable grounds to believe that the person has committed an offence.[395]

---

393 *Biron*, above note 336 at 75: "If this is the way in which this provision is to be construed, no peace officer can ever decide, when making an arrest without a warrant, that the person arrested is 'committing a criminal offence.'"

394 The Court in *Biron*, *ibid*, seems to have been influenced by the feeling that although Biron was acquitted of the causing a disturbance charge, he was "really" guilty of it. It states: "That he was justified in so thinking is shown by the fact that, at trial, Biron was convicted of the offence of causing a disturbance, and that his appeal from conviction resulted from the fact that the information charged only causing a disturbance 'by shouting,' which 'shouting' the judge on appeal found was not established by the evidence." The argument is not made explicitly, of course, and would be quite problematic if it were.

395 LRC, *Arrest*, above note 66 at 23–24. The Law Reform Commission recommended retention of this warrantless arrest power. Note, however, that it also adopted the view that the standard a justice must apply in deciding whether to issue process based on an information was the same reasonable grounds standard as for warrantless arrests. Not all authorities agree that the standard to be applied by a justice is as high as that: see the discussion in Section B(1), above in this chapter.

In essence, the only real thing to recognize about section 495(1)(c) is that it is exactly what it says: a power to arrest without warrant. In *Gamracy*, for example, the officer was at the accused's home to arrest him, but the officer knew only that there was a warrant for the accused's arrest, not the offence for which the warrant had been issued.[396] He also did not have a copy of the warrant with him. The Court held that the officer had complied with his obligations under the *Code*. He had the power to arrest without a warrant under section 495(1)(c) since he had reasonable grounds to believe that a warrant was in existence. He also complied with his obligation under section 29 to tell the accused the reason for the arrest when he told him merely that he was arresting him on the basis that a warrant existed. See the discussion of this issue in Chapter 2, Section B(1)(b).

At least two things are required to comply with section 495(1)(c): a reasonable belief that there is an arrest warrant, but also a reasonable belief that the person arrested is the person for whom the warrant was issued. In *R v Burke*, for example, the officer was carrying out an arrest under section 495(1)(c), and the accused insisted that the warrant was in fact for his brother, not for him. The Court upheld the trial judge's decision that the arrest was not legal on the basis that on the particular facts of the case, the necessary reasonable grounds were not established.[397] As with section 495(1), the relevant beliefs must have been subjectively held by the officer but must also have been objectively reasonable.[398]

Note as well that section 495(1)(c) is specific in stating that the warrant must be "in any form set out in Part XXVIII" and also must be in force within the territorial jurisdiction in which the person is found. The former requirement was significant in *R v Luc*, where a peace officer purported to rely on section 495(1)(c) to make a warrantless arrest on the basis that an immigration warrant existed for the accused.[399] The Court of Appeal noted that the warrants in Part XXVIII depend upon the commission or apprehended commission of an offence under the *Code*. An immigration warrant does not depend on an offence having been committed and is not listed in Part XXVIII; therefore, it could not be the basis for an arrest under section 495(1)(c).

---

396 *Gamracy*, above note 140.

397 *R v Burke*, 2009 SCC 57.

398 *R v Hiltz*, [1991] NSJ No 389 (SCAD).

399 *R v Luc*, 2004 SKCA 1117. The case is further complicated by the fact that the immigration warrant was not in fact for the accused at all but rather for someone with a superficially similar name, and the officer had made a mistake.

CHAPTER 5

THE IMPACT OF THE *CHARTER*

A. INTRODUCTION

It is trite to observe that the *Canadian Charter of Rights and Freedoms*[1] has had a dramatic impact on criminal law and procedure. Of course, that has been true in the areas of detention and arrest as much as in other areas. In particular, the most relevant rights have been those specified in section 9 and section 10. Section 9 provides that "[e]veryone has the right not to be arbitrarily detained or imprisoned." Section 10 provides that several rights arise when a person is either arrested or detained, the most important of which are "to be informed promptly of the reasons therefor" and "to retain and instruct counsel without delay and to be informed of that right."

It is interesting to note that the impact of the *Charter* has been different in kind depending on whether one is speaking of detention or arrest. In the case of section 9, *Charter* caselaw has tended to focus on whether or not a power to detain exists. Indeed, rather paradoxically, Supreme Court decisions dealing with section 9 have more often than not resulted in an expansion of police powers rather than imposing limits on them. Section 10 of the *Charter*, on the other hand, has had no significant impact on the circumstances in which police (or anyone else) can or cannot arrest. Rather, the effect of section 10 has been to impose

1 Part 1 of the *Constitution Act, 1982*, being Schedule B to the *Canada Act 1982* (UK), 1982, c 11 [*Charter*].

additional obligations on the police when they make an arrest. Those obligations include rights the police must extend to the accused at the time of the arrest as well as information the accused is entitled to be told.

We will discuss sections 9 and 10 in that order.

B. SECTION 9—ARBITRARY DETENTION

Section 9 jurisprudence was, on the whole, very late developing. There were several cases in the early days of the *Charter* that began to develop an understanding of what "arbitrary detention" might mean. However, those cases did not create an overall framework for analyzing a section 9 claim, in the way that frameworks were laid down for other rights, such as those in section 7 or 8. Some relevant questions seem not to have been explicitly asked, and a number of questions were left deliberately unanswered. Individual cases decided that a particular accused had or had not been arbitrarily detained, but without offering much guidance for future cases.[2] It was only with the Supreme Court's 2009 decision in *R v Grant* that a real structure, as opposed to a series of unrelated decisions, began to emerge, and only with the 2019 decision in *R v Le* that it was fully articulated.[3]

The approach that has been adopted parallels that of section 8 of the *Charter*, which deals with unreasonable searches. In section 8, the initial question is whether there was a search at all and, if so, whether that search was unreasonable. The issue of whether a search is "unreasonable" is determined by three questions: was the search authorized by law, was the law itself reasonable, and was the manner of search reasonable?[4] This three-part test was created at a very early stage and is referred to as the *Collins* test.[5] After several decades of individual arbitrary detention cases, in *Le*, the Court fully established a parallel approach for section 9:

> Where a detention is established, a court must consider whether the detention is arbitrary. This Court's decision in *Grant* provides guidance (at paras. 54-56), drawing from the three-part test stated in *R. v. Collins*, [1987] 1 S.C.R. 265, for assessing unreasonable searches and seizures under s. 8. Specifically, the detention must be authorized by law; the

---

2 See, for example, *R v Hawkins*, [1993] 2 SCR 157 [*Hawkins*], and *R v Chaisson*, 2006 SCC 11.

3 *R v Grant*, 2009 SCC 32 [*Grant*], and *R v Le*, 2019 SCC 34 [*Le*].

4 See, for example, *R v MacDonald*, 2014 SCC 3 at para 29, quoting *R v Mann*, 2004 SCC 52 [*Mann*].

5 *R v Collins*, [1987] 1 SCR 265 [*Collins*].

authorizing law itself must not be arbitrary; and, the manner in which the detention is carried out must be reasonable.[6]

Although both rights are now governed by similar approaches, it is noteworthy that the search-related right was consciously developed by the Court, while the detention-related right developed more by happenstance than by design. Several factors might explain this relative neglect of section 9. In part, the relatively limited utility of the section to an accused meant that it was not often argued. The first cases dealing with detention were a trio of vehicle-stop cases: *R v Dedman*,[7] *R v Hufsky*,[8] and *R v Ladouceur*.[9] Aspects of these cases will be dealt with in greater depth below, but the important point to note here is not so much the section 9 analysis as the section 1 analysis. The last of the three, *Ladouceur*, created a power for any police officer to, in the words of the dissent, "stop any vehicle at any time, in any place, without having any reason to do so."[10] The Supreme Court found that any such stop would be an arbitrary detention and would violate section 9; the majority also held, however, that this violation was saved under section 1. Given this start to section 9 jurisprudence, it is not surprising that defence counsel would infrequently find it worthwhile to devote a great deal of time to developing an arbitrary detention argument. In essence, if *that* power could be saved under section 1, it seemed unlikely that a successful section 9 argument would ever lead to a remedy.

Furthermore, defence counsel could resort to other *Charter*-based arguments that were more likely to be fruitful. If a detention was made in accordance with a statutory scheme (for example, dangerous-offender legislation),[11] then a challenge could likely be made based on life, liberty, and security of the person under section 7 or based on cruel and unusual punishment under section 12. If the detention was a more discretionary one, of a vehicle or a pedestrian, then section 8 or 10 is likely to be relevant. Specifically, if the person was detained and searched, then an argument concerning unreasonable search would likely be made. If the person was detained and made an incriminating statement, then an argument based on the right to be informed of the reason for arrest or the right to counsel would likely be made. A "pure" section 9 claim would only be necessary if the person was detained but was not searched and made no statement; in such a case, it would be unlikely that the police

6 *Le*, above note 3 at para 124.
7 [1985] 2 SCR 2 [*Dedman*].
8 [1988] 1 SCR 621 [*Hufsky*].
9 [1990] 1 SCR 1257 [*Ladouceur*].
10 *Ibid* at 1264.
11 *R v Lyons*, [1987] 2 SCR 309 [*Lyons*].

obtained any evidence as a result of the section 9 breach; therefore, it would be equally unlikely that any useful remedy would flow to the accused if a violation was made out. As a result, section 9 has tended to be secondary to most analyses—sometimes supporting a claim of a pattern of violations, but not very often significant all on its own.

Nonetheless, with *Grant*, a framework for evaluating section 9 claims has now been created. As noted above, the two central issues are (1) what is a detention and (2) when is a detention arbitrary?

1) What Is a "Detention"?

A definition of "detention" was first offered among the very earliest *Charter* cases. In *R v Therens*, the Supreme Court was called upon to decide whether an accused stopped for a Breathalyzer demand was entitled to the right to counsel; since section 10(b) says that an accused is entitled to be informed of the right to counsel "on arrest or detention," that amounted to the question of whether a Breathalyzer stop fell within the meaning of the word "detention." Although it might seem obvious that being required to stay in the company of police for an extended period of time is a detention, the pre-*Charter* decision *R v Chromiak* had concluded that a person who, while stopped, performed roadside sobriety tests and complied with a demand for a breath sample was *not* detained.[12] In *Therens*, the Court reversed that conclusion, and its reasoning is instructive in a number of regards.

One of the most significant aspects of *Therens* is its general approach to *Charter* rights rather than the particular finding it made about the meaning of detention. It had been argued that in using the word "detention," the drafters of the *Charter* should be taken to have known of and to have relied on pre-*Charter* cases—in essence, that in using the word "detention," the legislators meant "detention as it was interpreted in *Chromiak*." The Court rejected this as an approach to interpreting the *Charter*. The *Charter*, it held, was "a new affirmation of rights and freedoms and of judicial power and responsibility in relation to their protection" and, accordingly, had to be interpreted afresh.[13] In particular, the Court was quite willing to allow the word "detention" to have a broad meaning, in part because any rights based on it were subject to a section 1 analysis.[14]

---

12 *R v Chromiak*, [1980] 1 SCR 471 [*Chromiak*].

13 *R v Therens*, [1985] 1 SCR 613 at 638 [*Therens*]. This passage, and indeed all the reasoning about the meaning of the word "detention," occurs in the dissenting judgment of Le Dain J. This aspect of his reasons was adopted by the majority.

14 *Ibid* at 639.

A second important point to note is an argument that was rejected as not relevant to interpreting the meaning of detention. Section 10(c) of the *Charter* guarantees the right "to have the validity of the detention determined by way of *habeas corpus* and to be released if the detention is not lawful." It had been argued that this demonstrated that the word "detention" was meant to be limited to infringements of liberty of a long enough duration that a challenge by way of *habeas corpus* was practical. In *Therens*, however, the Court held that the term "detention" covered a wide variety of situations of varying duration, and the fact that *habeas corpus* "may not be possible in some cases, because of the limited duration of the detention, is not . . . a reason for limiting the meaning of the word 'detention' to detentions of a certain duration."[15]

Finally, *Therens* offered an approach to understanding what detention means—not so much a definition as a purposive reading of the purpose of the right. The term appears in both section 9 and section 10. *Therens* was talking about the meaning of the word in the latter context, but the Court did soon thereafter hold that the same definition applied to both sections.[16] First, the Court noted:

> In its use of the word "detention," s. 10 of the *Charter* is directed to a restraint of liberty other than arrest in which a person may reasonably require the assistance of counsel but might be prevented or impeded from retaining and instructing counsel without delay but for the constitutional guarantee.[17]

Based on this, the Court distinguished three different situations, all of which would fall within the meaning of "detention." The first was where a person was subject to physical constraint. In those circumstances, similar to an arrest, the person should be seen as detained. Second, a person would also be detained when given an order if there are legal consequences for non-compliance. It is, for example, an offence to refuse when a police officer makes a Breathalyzer demand, as in *Therens*. The Court held that it would be inaccurate to describe the person to whom the demand was made as free to refuse to comply. In that event, the person is detained.

In fact, that second category—detention by legal compulsion—was sufficient to settle the issue in *Therens*. The Court went on, however, to create a third category of detention: psychological detention. It held:

---

15 *Ibid* at 641.

16 *Hufsky*, above note 8 at 632.

17 *Therens*, above note 13 at 641–42.

> [I]t is not realistic, as a general rule, to regard compliance with a demand or direction by a police officer as truly voluntary, in the sense that the citizen feels that he or she has the choice to obey or not, even where there is in fact a lack of statutory or common law authority for the demand or direction and therefore an absence of criminal liability for failure to comply with it. Most citizens are not aware of the precise legal limits of police authority. Rather than risk the application of physical force or prosecution for wilful obstruction, the reasonable person is likely to err on the side of caution, assume lawful authority and comply with the demand. The element of psychological compulsion, in the form of a reasonable perception of suspension of freedom of choice, is enough to make the restraint of liberty involuntary. Detention may be effected without the application or threat of application of physical restraint if the person concerned submits or acquiesces in the deprivation of liberty and reasonably believes that the choice to do otherwise does not exist.[18]

The Court conveniently summarized its various conclusions from *Therens* in the subsequent case, *R v Thomsen*:

> 1. In its use of the word "detention," s. 10 of the *Charter* is directed to a restraint of liberty other than arrest in which a person may reasonably require the assistance of counsel but might be prevented or impeded from retaining and instructing counsel without delay but for the constitutional guarantee.
> 2. In addition to the case of deprivation of liberty by physical constraint, there is a detention within s. 10 of the *Charter*, when a police officer or other agent of the state assumes control over the movement of a person by a demand or direction which may have significant legal consequence and which prevents or impedes access to counsel.
> 3. The necessary element of compulsion or coercion to constitute a detention may arise from criminal liability for refusal to comply with a demand or direction, or from a reasonable belief that one does not have a choice as to whether or not to comply.
> 4. Section 10 of the *Charter* applies to a great variety of detentions of varying duration and is not confined to those of such duration as to make the effective use of *habeas corpus* possible.[19]

Although the Court was clear in *Therens* that there were three categories of detention—physical restraint, restraint by legal compulsion,

---

18 *Ibid* at 644.

19 *R v Thomsen*, [1988] 1 SCR 640 at 649.

and psychological detention —in *Grant*, the Court distinguishes only between physical detention and psychological detention. However, in speaking of the latter, they said:

> [P]sychological constraint amounting to detention has been recognized in two situations. The first is where the subject is legally required to comply with a direction or demand, as in the case of a roadside breath sample. The second is where there is no legal obligation to comply with a restrictive or coercive demand, but a reasonable person in the subject's position would feel so obligated.[20]

That is, the Court here uses the term "psychological detention" to describe *both* of the latter two categories in *Therens*.[21] There is no change in the underlying law, just in the terms used to describe it. This was not obviously a beneficial change since the *Therens* terminology was more precise, allowing the three situations to be more easily distinguished. In the following discussion, the term "psychological detention" will be used to refer only to those situations where no legal authority actually exists.

It has also been made clear that these definitions of detention apply only to relations between individuals and the state in circumstances that are closely similar to the investigation of a criminal offence. Deprivations of liberty can occur in other contexts, such as schools, where students often feel, or indeed are, compelled to go to or remain in various locations. These do not qualify as "detention" for *Charter* purposes.[22] Similarly, persons who face routine questioning by customs officials at the border are not free to leave, but this too does not qualify as a detention within the meaning of sections 9 and 10. On the other hand, those people who are taken out of the normal course of activity and subjected to a strip search *are* detained.[23]

Practically speaking, detention by physical restraint and detention by legal compulsion have provided no real challenges in application, at least at the initial stage of determining whether a detention has occurred. Psychological detention, on the other hand, has been a very difficult issue for courts to come to grips with. This is not surprising since almost by definition a psychological detention involves the police acting in circumstances where they have no specific power to act; if they did have such a power, then "detention by legal compulsion" would be in issue.

20 *Grant*, above note 3 at para 30.

21 This is also how other courts have understood *Grant*: see, for example, *R v Guenter*, 2016 ONCA 572 at para 37 [*Guenter*].

22 *R v M(MR)*, [1998] 3 SCR 393 [*M(MR)*].

23 *R v Simmons*, [1988] 2 SCR 495. See the more detailed discussion of customs detentions in Chapter 3, Section B(2)(b).

At least, it would be in issue if the police exercised that power; in some cases, it appears that police deliberately avoid using a detention power, even if it exists, in order to try to avoid triggering *Charter* rights.[24]

Claims of psychological detentions have tended to fall into one of two scenarios. First, during a formal investigation, a person might be taken (or invited) to the police station to answer questions. In some cases, in the course of questioning, a person who initially was merely a witness comes to be a suspect. Although the person might at some point be placed under arrest, there is no immediate need to do so since the person is already sitting in a room with the police. Thus, although the situation might in some abstract way have changed from a voluntary attendance to a detention, there will probably be no obvious outward manifestation of that change. In such cases, there is not likely to be a section 9 issue since any detention is probably lawful and therefore not arbitrary. However, when the person passes that metaphysical boundary between "not detained" and "detained," they are entitled under section 10(b) to have been informed of the right to counsel. Since on this scenario the person is already answering questions, the failure to comply with section 10 is potentially quite significant.

The second situation in which the question of whether a person has been psychologically detained has typically arisen in sidewalk encounters with police officers. Police not infrequently approach individuals on the street and ask them questions. Often this is done not in the course of investigating any particular offence or based on any particular suspicion about the person stopped. Also not infrequently, such sidewalk stops have led individuals to make incriminating statements or have led to searches that turned up narcotics or firearms. In these cases, the question of whether the person was or was not detained when being questioned by the police leads directly to, at least, the question of whether there was an arbitrary detention. Generally, the answer will be "yes" since no particular power to detain will be in play.

Guidelines for the former situation, the police station detention, were offered at a very early stage by the Ontario Court of Appeal in its decision in *R v Moran*. In that case the accused had been having an affair with a woman who had been murdered. He spoke with the police twice, both times at the police station rather than at his house. The police had not ruled out suicide as an explanation for the death at the time of the interviews, and although the accused was asked some questions about his whereabouts and his willingness to take a polygraph test, similar questions were asked of others. The questioning officer testified that he did

24 See, for example, *R v Seagull*, 2015 BCCA 164, where this argument was made, although unsuccessfully.

not consider the accused a suspect at the time, although the accused testified that he felt pressured by some of the questions. In fact, he was not arrested until two months later, when other evidence had turned up. The Court of Appeal held that the trial judge was correct to find that the accused had not been detained during these interviews. In doing so, it articulated factors to be applied in determining whether a person interviewed at a police station was detained, including questions such as whether the person was given a choice about where the interview would take place, whether they were escorted to the station or came on their own, whether the questions were general ones or were aimed at obtaining incriminating statements, and so on.[25] Leave to appeal to the Supreme Court was refused,[26] and as a result, the guidelines set down by the Ontario Court of Appeal tended to be employed by other courts faced with similar questions, making *Moran* for a long time the leading case in this area.

A difficulty, however, is that the *Moran* criteria were not very relevant to the other situation in which the question of psychological detention most commonly arises: the sidewalk stop. The *Moran* criteria all presume that some particular crime is already under investigation. In sidewalk stops, on the other hand, police are often talking to individuals in the absence of knowledge that any particular crime has occurred. If they did have such a reasonable suspicion, they likely would be using some common law power to formally detain the person, and psychological detention would not be in issue at all.

This situation was left largely without guidance for many years, until the Supreme Court's decision in *Grant* set out a definition that paid particular attention to the difficult issue of psychological detention in sidewalk-stop situations. In *Grant*, the accused was walking along a street. Two plainclothes officers decided that he looked suspicious because he stared at them and fidgeted with his clothes. They suggested to a uniformed officer that he have a chat with the accused, and that officer stepped out his car and blocked the accused's path, asking him what was going on and requesting identification. The two plainclothes officers then joined the uniformed one, identified themselves as police, and positioned themselves so as to obstruct the way forward. On further questioning, the accused admitted to having marijuana and a firearm, at which point, he was arrested and searched. The trial judge found on these facts that this interaction with the police did not constitute a detention; the Court of Appeal disagreed. The Supreme Court upheld the notion that the accused was detained but went further than that

25 *R v Moran* (1987), 36 CCC (3d) 225 at 258 & 259 (Ont CA) [*Moran*].

26 *R v Moran*, [1988] SCCA No 213.

particular conclusion and laid down a general set of criteria to be used in determining the detention question.

The Court had earlier observed in *R v Mann* that not every delay caused by police would constitute a detention and that not every person asked for identification by police or interviewed would necessarily be detained. This is, of course, a sensible position: police might well direct all witnesses to a traffic accident to stay to identify themselves so they can be asked at some later time what they saw, but no one would suggest that, for example, the right to counsel should arise in all such cases. In *Grant*, however, the Court was careful to try not to let this reasonable limitation on the rights that are related to detention become a large enough exception that the section failed to provide protection when it actually should. The Court noted that one of the purposes of section 9 was to guard "against incursions on mental liberty by prohibiting the coercive pressures of detention and imprisonment from being applied to people without adequate justification."[27] The central concerns, the Court held, were to preserve the accused's ability to make an informed choice about whether to walk away and about whether to speak to state authorities.

The Court concluded that the question of detention had to be decided based on an objective test rather than a subjective one. It also decided that the subjective views of the police officers should not be determinative on the detention question, although they would be relevant at other stages, such as deciding whether evidence should be excluded. Consistent with this, the Court held that "focussed suspicion, in and of itself, does not turn the encounter [into] a detention. What matters is how the police, based on that suspicion, interacted with the subject."[28] Having downplayed the police perspective on the interaction, the Court settled on a detainee-centred objective test: whether a reasonable person in the detainee's position would conclude that they had no choice but to comply.

The Court discussed a number of factors that would be relevant to this objective analysis and eventually summarized the test for psychological detention:

> 1. Detention under ss. 9 and 10 of the *Charter* refers to a suspension of the individual's liberty interest by a significant physical or psychological restraint. Psychological detention is established either where the individual has a legal obligation to comply with the restrictive request or demand, or a reasonable person would

---

27 *Grant*, above note 3 at para 20.

28 *Ibid* at para 41. Note that minimizing the significance of focused suspicion is quite consistent with the Court's refusal to uphold *Hawkins*, above note 2.

conclude by reason of the state conduct that he or she had no choice but to comply.

2. In cases where there is no physical restraint or legal obligation, it may not be clear whether a person has been detained. To determine whether the reasonable person in the individual's circumstances would conclude that he or she had been deprived by the state of the liberty of choice, the court may consider, *inter alia*, the following factors:
    a) The circumstances giving rise to the encounter as would reasonably be perceived by the individual: whether the police were providing general assistance; maintaining general order; making general inquiries regarding a particular occurrence; or, singling out the individual for focussed investigation.
    b) The nature of the police conduct, including the language used; the use of physical contact; the place where the interaction occurred; the presence of others; and the duration of the encounter.
    c) The particular characteristics or circumstances of the individual where relevant, including age; physical stature; minority status; level of sophistication.[29]

This test was formulated in the context of an "on-the-street" detention, but it is clear that it is the governing authority for psychological detentions in *any* context. Lower courts did for some time continue to rely on the *Moran* factors in police station questioning cases, but the Court has now held that

> Respectfully, the better view is that, as a result of *Grant*, *Moran* is no longer good law (S. Coughlan and G. Luther, *Detention and Arrest* (2nd ed. 2017), at p. 287), and it should no longer be applied or relied upon. In *Grant*, the test for detention was restated to direct the inquiry to the perspective of the reasonable person in the accused's shoes. In contrast, the *Moran* factors focus principally on police conduct and information that will not be readily available to the accused at the time of detention (such as the stage of the police investigation). And, while the test in *Grant* is objective, *Moran* encourages courts to consider the subjective perceptions and beliefs of the accused, thereby emphasizing considerations that play a limited (if any) role in an objective assessment (*Le*, at paras. 111–17).
>
> Further, and as noted, the scope of *Moran* is, by its own terms, confined to deciding whether a person who is questioned at a police

29 *Ibid* at para 44.

station is detained. By design, then, *Moran* applied in limited circumstances. *Grant* is comprehensive in scope, applying to every instance of alleged detention by police by addressing the full breadth of circumstances that engage the right against self-incrimination protected by s. 10 of the *Charter*, including investigative detentions (*R. v. Folker*, 2016 NLCA 1, 373 Nfld. & P.E.I.R. 49, at paras. 74-79, per White J.A. (dissenting in part)).[30]

In *Grant* itself, based on the criteria set out, the Court concluded that the accused was detained. The initial questioning by the first officer would not be a detention, although the direction to the accused to keep his hands in front of him was ambiguous. When the other two officers took up positions behind the first, however, and the nature of the questioning changed from ascertaining the appellant's identity to determining whether he had anything that he shouldn't, it became clear that the accused was detained, and indeed detained from the time of the direction about his hands. Although the tone of the questioning officer was respectful, the power imbalance of a young inexperienced person faced with three physically larger officers made the encounter inherently intimidating.

The detainee-centric approach in *Grant* is a sensible one because it eliminates consideration of the perspective of the police. Reasoning that had relied on the police perspective often incorporated an odd irony. If the police do not see themselves as performing an investigative detention, for example, and are asking questions when they do not have reasonable grounds to suspect that there is a nexus between the detainee and a recent or ongoing offence, then relying on the police perspective means that there was no detention. However, in such situations, the lack of that subjective state of mind on the part of the police also means that they are trying to act when they do not have lawful authority to do so. This would be an arbitrary detention, but only if it were a detention in the first place. If the lack of belief in grounds for a detention made it less likely that there *was* a detention, the result would be that a section 9 violation was *less* likely to be found if the police were acting without legal authority. That would be a counterintuitive and unfortunate result, and the approach in *Grant* wisely avoided it.

However, the positive impact of *Grant* is somewhat tempered by another decision handed down the same day, *R v Suberu*.[31] In *Suberu*, the police had responded to a call of two people using stolen gift cards at a liquor store; an officer who arrived encountered the accused, who was

30 *R v Lafrance*, 2022 SCC 32 at paras 27 & 28 [*Lafrance*].

31 [2009] 2 SCR 460 [*Suberu*].

on his way out of the store. The accused said words to the effect of "he did this, not me, so I guess I can go," to which the officer replied, "Wait a minute, I need to talk to you before you go anywhere," and followed the accused outside. The accused sat in the driver's seat of a minivan, and the officer engaged him in conversation, asking him questions about his connection to the events in the store, until eventually he arrested the accused. At trial and up to the Court of Appeal, the issue argued was whether the accused should have been informed of his right to counsel. The Supreme Court concluded that the words "without delay" in section 10(b) meant "immediately" and therefore that anyone who was subject to an investigative detention was immediately entitled to be informed of the right to counsel (see the discussion below). However, the majority of the Court concluded that Suberu had not, by the test in *Grant*, actually been detained; therefore, there was no section 10(b) violation.

This is perhaps a surprising result. Justice Binnie, writing in dissent, noted that the accused's question to the officer amounted to asking "can I leave," and the officer's answer amounted to "no." In those circumstances, he found it hard to see how one could conclude that a reasonable person in the accused's situation would not have felt that he had been denied choice. Justice Binnie points to the fact that interpreting "without delay" to mean "immediately" removes any flexibility for the police around the issue of the timing of a *Charter* warning and suggests that such flexibility must exist somewhere. He points to the danger that courts will avoid the consequence of being forced to find a section 10(b) violation by the stratagem of being overly strict in applying the test for whether a person has been detained; this seems to be exactly what occurred in *Suberu* itself. This is an unfortunate consequence and parallels the pattern that has arisen in search-and-seizure law: a warrantless search is unreasonable, but adopting a narrow interpretation of reasonable expectation of privacy can allow a court to conclude that a police investigative technique was not a search at all.[32]

One could see some aspects of the post-*Suberu* caselaw as fulfilling Binnie J's prediction, although one could equally perceive it as creating a new police power. The majority held in *Suberu* that "the definition of detention, as understood in these reasons, gives the police leeway to engage members of the public in non-coercive, exploratory questioning without necessarily triggering their Charter rights relating to detention."[33] Similarly, they held that "[t]his Court's conclusion in *Mann* that there was an 'investigative detention' does not mean that a detention is

32 See Steve Coughlan, "Arbitrary Detention: Whither—or Wither?—Section 9" (2008) 40 *Supreme Court Law Review* (2d) 147, pointing to the danger of this possibility.

33 *Suberu*, above note 31 at para 45.

necessarily grounded the moment the police engage an individual for investigative purposes."[34]

This distinction has become central to the reasoning in lower courts as to which side of the "sometimes murky line between general questioning (which does not trigger a detention—see *Suberu*) and a particular, focussed line of questioning (which does)"[35] a particular encounter falls. Interactions between police and a person on the street "move along a spectrum before reaching the point of detention,"[36] and if what the police were doing can be characterized as merely "exploratory questioning," then the accused was not detained. This can be true even when the police are not simply making general inquiries of people at the scene of a crime, but—as in *Suberu* itself—are limiting their investigation to a single person in order to determine their role or whether there was a crime at all. This is true even if there is no legally sufficient basis for thinking that an offence has occurred; indeed, it is the absence of any such basis that sometimes seems to mean that no detention has occurred.[37] In effect, it is as though the police have been given a *power* to engage in exploratory questioning. Strictly speaking, no such power to stop people exists, but if it is not a "detention," then it cannot be an arbitrary detention; in that event, there is no effective mechanism by which a person subject to it can object.[38]

In any event, it is now well settled that whether a psychological detention has or has not occurred depends on consideration of the three sets of factors outlined in *Grant*: the circumstances of the encounter, the nature of the police conduct, and the characteristics of the individual. The Supreme Court has expanded on the meaning and application of these factors in two subsequent significant decisions about psychological detention: *Le* in 2019[39] and *Lafrance* in 2022.[40] Both decisions, it is worth noting, concluded that the accused in the case was detained but were deeply divided, *Le* being a 3:2 split and *Lafrance* a 5:4 split.[41]

In *Le*, three police officers had gone to a housing co-operative looking for a person unrelated to the case and were told by security guards

---

34 *Ibid* at para 23.

35 *Le*, above note 3 at para 31.

36 *Guenter*, above note 21 at para 42.

37 See, for example, *Guenter*, *ibid*; *R v Bagnato*, 2011 ONSC 2440; or *R v Guce*, 2011 ONSC 2331.

38 See the discussion of "default" powers in Chapter 2, Section A(5).

39 *Le*, above note 3.

40 *Lafrance*, above note 30.

41 The Court also considered the issue of psychological detention in *R v Tessier*, 2022 SCC 35 [*Tessier*], concluding on an application of the *Grant* factors that the accused there, who had gone on request to the police station for an interview, was not psychologically detained.

that that person was not present. The officers then went to the backyard of one of the units, which was fenced in, and where the accused and four other young men were standing. Two of the officers entered the backyard through an opening while the third first walked the length of the fence and then stepped over it. It was agreed that the police had no lawful authority to enter or to investigate at that stage. The officers then asked the five young men what they were doing and asked them for identification; one of the young men was told to keep his hands visible. One of the officers testified that, about a minute into the encounter, he noticed that the accused had a satchel slung across his body, was nervous, and "bladed" away from him (that is, angled his body, seemingly to conceal the satchel). The officer demanded identification, which the accused did not have, and then asked what was in the satchel, at which point the accused fled. He was pursued and arrested, leading to charges relating to weapons and narcotics. The issue at trial was whether there was an arbitrary detention that should lead to the exclusion of the evidence; more specifically, since everyone agreed that the accused was detained at *some* point, the issue was exactly *when* the psychological detention began. The Supreme Court (in a 3:2 decision) concluded that it began the moment the officers entered the backyard.

With regard to the circumstances giving rise to the encounter, the Court noted that the police were not providing general assistance, maintaining order, or responding to unfolding events when they entered the backyard and questioned the young men. The trial judge had found that the police had legitimate investigatory purposes for entering, but the Court concluded that that would only be relevant in determining whether or not the detention was arbitrary. The test for psychological detention is detainee-centric, and "a reasonable person in the shoes of the putative detainee would not have known why these police officers were entering the property."[42] From the perspective of a reasonable person, there was no obvious cause for the police to enter the backyard, the police did not explain why they had entered, and their questions could have been asked from outside the fence, but instead they entered and began demanding identification and issuing instructions. This "would have made it clear to a reasonable observer that the police were taking control over the individuals in the backyard."[43]

The second set of factors, relating to the nature of the police conduct, also supported the view that there was a psychological detention. The police themselves were trespassers in the backyard, and even if their tone was initially cordial, "[t]he nicest of hellos could not mask the fact that

42 *Le*, above note 3 at para 37.

43 *Ibid* at para 40.

the three persons entering onto this private property were uniformed police officers acting without permission, consent or legal authorization."[44] Their manner of entry, in particular one officer stepping over the fence, would be perceived as an exercise of power. The Court also observed that it was unlikely the police would have "brazenly entered a private backyard and demanded to know what its occupants were up to in a more affluent and less racialized community."[45] The accused was not "delayed" from going anywhere, which previous caselaw had identified as a potentially relevant consideration, but this was of little relevance: he was socializing in a friend's backyard and was not intending to go anywhere.[46] There was no physical contact, but the officers positioned themselves to separate the young men and to block the exits. The *Grant* test had identified the presence of others as a relevant consideration, and in this case, the Court held that that presence contributed to the reasonable perception that there was a detention: each person in the backyard saw how the others were being treated. Finally, on this set of factors, the duration was short, which generally weighs against a detention being found, but the Court reiterated that "a single forceful act or word may be enough to cause a reasonable person to conclude that his or her right to choose how to respond has been removed."[47]

The Court in *Le* also spent some time considering the last set of factors, the particular characteristics of the individual, including age, physical stature, minority status, and level of sophistication. In that list, "minority status" had been a consideration that courts had had some difficulty coming to grips with, so the guidance in *Le* on this point is particularly helpful. Most notably, they held that the trial judge's finding that no racial profiling had occurred in this particular case was not relevant. "Racial profiling" asks about the subjective mental state of the state actor, while "psychological detention" asks about how the encounter would appear to a reasonable person. A finding that there was no racial profiling therefore went to whether any detention was arbitrary but not to whether a reasonable person would feel detained. On the other hand, the existence of racial profiling in a broader sense was relevant to that latter question, in the sense that a reasonable person would be deemed to know about how relevant race relations would affect an interaction between police officers and racialized accused. The Court then looked at various studies over many decades showing the overpolicing of minority communities and concluded that

44 *Ibid* at para 47.

45 *Ibid* at para 59, quoting Lauwers JA in dissent in the Ontario Court of Appeal.

46 *Ibid* at para 52.

47 *Ibid* at para 66, quoting *Grant*, above note 3, at para 42.

> We do not hesitate to find that, even without these most recent reports, we have arrived at a place where the research now shows disproportionate policing of racialized and low-income communities (see D. M. Tanovich, "Applying the Racial Profiling Correspondence Test" (2017), 64 *C.L.Q.* 359). Indeed, it is in this larger social context that the police entry into the backyard and questioning of Mr. Le and his friends must be approached. It was another example of a common and shared experience of racialized young men: being frequently targeted, stopped, and subjected to pointed and familiar questions. The documented history of the relations between police and racialized communities would have had an impact on the perceptions of a reasonable person in the shoes of the accused. When three officers entered a small, private backyard, without warrant, consent, or warning, late at night, to ask questions of five racialized young men in a Toronto housing co-operative, these young men would have felt compelled to remain, answer and comply.[48]

In this case, the young men testified that they personally had been frequently stopped by police, but the trial judge rejected that evidence. Nonetheless, the Court held:

> The trial judge's conclusion that these young men did not have the past experiences they described means only that he has rejected their evidence about how their personal history with the police may have affected their subjective perceptions of what they thought was happening to them when the police entered the backyard. However, the s. 9 inquiry requires an objective assessment of what *a reasonable person in the shoes of the accused* perceived about whether they were free to leave. In the absence of testimonial evidence, which is what happens when such is either rejected or was never tendered, there is still a need to inquire into how the race of the accused may have impacted the s. 9 analysis.[49]

The Court also addressed the accused's level of sophistication, in particular an argument that had frequently succeeded in previous cases: that as a person who was "no stranger to street-level encounters with the police," the accused would be familiar with the situation and that "a reasonable person with a similar experiential history would view what happened as merely another police interaction or, to put it simply, 'business as usual.'"[50] The Court soundly rejected the premise upon which this argument was based:

48 *Ibid* at para 97.

49 *Ibid* at para 106 [emphasis in original].

50 *Ibid* at para 107. The Court noted that the Ontario Court of Appeal's adoption of this argument required them to accept that the accused *had* had frequent interactions with the police, a claim that the trial judge had rejected.

> We see no good reason for the conclusion that *more* frequent encounters with the police make it *less* likely that a person feels "detained" when police approach. Such reasoning is flawed and is premised on a non-sequitur: that familiarity with police encounters breeds familiarity with the scope of police entitlement to detain and with one's *Charter* right to be free from arbitrary detention. . . .
>
> Merely because an individual has had repeated interactions with the police does not mean that the individual has acquired a level of sophistication in dealing with the police. Indeed, in our view, it is more reasonable to anticipate that frequency of police encounters will typically foster *more*, not *less*, "psychological compulsion, in the form of a reasonable perception of suspension of freedom of choice" (*Therens*, at p. 644). Individuals who are frequently exposed to forced interactions with the police more readily submit to police demands in order to move on with their daily lives because of a sense of "learned helplessness" (M. E. P. Seligman, "Learned Helplessness" (1972), 23 *Annu. Rev. Med.* 407, at p. 408, as discussed in *R. v. Lavallee*, [1990] 1 S.C.R. 852). That is, when individuals have repeated exposure to unwanted experiences from a more powerful source, they learn to simply acquiesce and try to get through the unwanted experience by getting it over with as quickly and peaceably as possible.
>
> In this case, Mr. Le's experience with the police tends to *support* a finding that he *was* detained when the police entered the backyard. While most Canadians have infrequent or no experience with police encounters, we ought not to be naïve to the reality that others' encounters with police will not only be frequent, but also unpleasant. Any previous experiences would not attenuate the power imbalance or reduce the coercive force of multiple police officers entering a private backyard without explanation or authority. A reasonable person who has been stopped by the police on multiple prior occasions would more likely perceive that it is necessary to simply submit to police demands.[51]

Finally, and consistent with relying on the views of the reasonable person rather than the accused's subjective state of mind, the Court found Le to have been psychologically detained despite his own testimony that up to a certain point he felt free to leave.[52]

In *Lafrance*, a team of eleven police officers, many of whom were wearing bulletproof vests and carrying firearms, arrived at the accused's residence at 6:50 a.m. to execute a search warrant. They entered the house, went to the accused's bedroom, woke him, and directed him to

---

51 *Ibid* at paras 108–10 [emphasis in original].

52 *Ibid* at paras 111–21.

dress and leave his house immediately. He was met outside by an officer who had been assigned to interview him. The accused obtained permission to retrieve his cat, which had gone outside, and was then asked to come to the police station to give a statement, which he was told was "completely voluntary." The accused agreed to do so and chose to go with the officers in their car rather than get to the station in some other way. At the station, he was escorted through two controlled-access key-carded doors to an interview room, where he was left alone for at least seventeen minutes. The door was unlocked, but the accused had not been told that, and when he asked to use the washroom, he was escorted there and back. Applying the *Grant* factors, the Court concluded that the accused had been psychologically detained.

With regard to the circumstances, the Court noted that "it is inconceivable that a reasonable person in Mr. Lafrance's shoes—woken and confronted by armed police officers in his home telling him to leave—would believe that they had arrived to 'provid[e] general assistance,' 'maintai[n] general order' or make 'general inquiries.' The reasonable person would immediately understand that he or she is being singled out for investigation."[53] The search warrant meant that the police were authorized to act as they had, but that did not affect how a reasonable person would perceive the situation, except perhaps that the existence of the warrant would demonstrate that there was a targeted investigation. The trial judge had begun the analysis from the point at which the officer had spoken to the accused outside his home, but the Court held that this was incorrect: that was an extension of the events that had begun with the police entry.

The nature of the police conduct—specifically, telling the accused that choosing to come to the station would be voluntary—militated against a finding of psychological detention and indeed was given significant emphasis by the dissenting judges.[54] The majority, however, declined to regard that as determinative, noting that "[i]t is entirely possible that such an assurance, given at a very specific point and time of the interaction with the police, might lose any significance to a reasonable

53 *Lafrance*, above note 30 at para 32.

54 The dissent holds at *ibid*, para 123:

> But police statements to such effect are not merely "a single consideration among others," as the majority suggests (para. 39). In our view, as the New Brunswick Court of Appeal stated in *R. v. Way*, 2011 NBCA 92, 377 N.B.R. (2d) 25, "detention will certainly be much more difficult to establish when such information has been genuinely provided" (para. 40). This is consistent with the role of unambiguous police statements that an individual is free to leave as contemplated by this Court in *R. v. Grant*, 2009 SCC 32, [2009] 2 S.C.R. 353, at paras. 32 and 39.

person in the detainee's circumstances once the entirety of the encounter is accounted for."[55] In this case, where the statement occurred in the context of being awakened by armed peace officers, being supervised at all times (including while finding his cat), and having no practical alternative for getting to the police station other than in the police car, it did not turn the tide. There was no reliance by the police on physical contact, but "the presence of others" was a significant factor—specifically, the presence of other police officers at virtually all times. The majority pointed out that "others" was not limited to civilian bystanders and could include police officers. Finally, under this factor, the place and duration of the encounter favoured a finding of detention. It began in the early morning with an intrusion into the accused's home, which is reasonably seen as more coercive and intimidating. It continued as he was driven to the station, although the majority noted that this did not mean that being driven by police automatically amounted to a detention.[56] It then continued through a three-and-a-half-hour interview, all of which taken together would contribute to a reasonable person's belief that they were not free to leave.

In looking at the particular circumstances of the accused, the Court noted that he was young (nineteen years old) and unsophisticated in circumstances where he needed to be aware of his rights. Perhaps surprisingly, the Court finds that the accused's "lack of experience with the police and unfamiliarity with his *Charter* rights bolsters" the case for detention.[57] This might be difficult to reconcile with the rejection in *Le* of the argument that experience with the police would make a reasonable person less likely to feel detained; both arguments seem to rest on the same assumption. Most interesting in this set of factors, however, is the Court's discussion of the accused's status as an Indigenous person. On the one hand, they note that "[t]he assessment of whether an Indigenous person was detained must be mindful of '[g]enerations of systematic racism, discriminatory policies and practices directed at Indigenous people' and of the role of police in implementing these policies and practices."[58] On the other hand "[a] court cannot simply assume that all Indigenous people's experiences with the police are *Charter* non-compliant or otherwise oppressive. And not all Indigenous people will be vulnerable, at all or in the same way, when interacting with police."[59] They concluded:

---

55 *Ibid* at para 36.

56 *Ibid* at para 49.

57 *Ibid* at para 62.

58 *Ibid* at para 57 [citation omitted].

59 *Ibid* at para 58 [citations omitted].

> Taking the foregoing and the record of this case into account, it would appear that Mr. Lafrance's Indigenous background played no significant role in shaping his perception of his obligation to cooperate with the police on March 19. But, to be clear, that is not the question. Again, the inquiry is *objective*, not grounded in his subjective impressions. The question, then, is whether the reasonable person in Mr. Lafrance's position would understand his or her options as limited to cooperating by reason of an Indigenous background. On this slender record, and absent any evidence to the contrary regarding Mr. Lafrance's circumstances, his Indigenous background is a factor that weighs somewhat in favour of detention, albeit not heavily. This accounts for what I have already described as the overrepresentation of Indigenous peoples in the criminal justice system, and the "relational aspect" of the interaction between Indigenous people and police that must always be borne in mind.[60]

In conclusion, note that there is one other relevant issue regarding psychological detention that does not relate to the *Grant* test: the fleeing suspect. In *Therens*, when the Court first spoke of psychological detention, they described it as being when "the person concerned *submits or acquiesces* in the deprivation of liberty and reasonably believes that the choice to do otherwise does not exist."[61] A number of courts have therefore taken submission or acquiescence as an absolute requirement for a psychological detention, independent of the *Grant* test. It has sometimes been treated as a kind of threshold step, its absence meaning that no further analysis was necessary. In *R v Nesbeth*, for example, police saw an accused in an apartment complex and called to him to stop, but he instead ran away. He was eventually tackled, and the Ontario Court of Appeal found that he was not detained until that point; he had not been psychologically detained prior to that because "while there was a demand: 'Stop, police,' the element of compliance with the demand was missing."[62] In *R v Ratt*, the police yelled at the accused that he was under arrest and to stop; instead, he ran away. Relying on *Nesbeth* and other cases, the Saskatchewan Court of Appeal concluded that there had been no psychological detention:

> [A] reasonable person in Mr. Ratt's circumstances would have concluded that he or she had no choice but to comply with that command. What is missing, however, is the second component of the *Grant* test.

---

60 *Ibid* at para 59.

61 *Therens*, above note 13 at para 57 [emphasis added].

62 *R v Nesbeth*, 2008 ONCA 579 at para 16. To similar effect, see *R v Atkins*, 2013 ONCA 586 [*Atkins*].

> Mr. Ratt did not submit or acquiesce—even briefly—to the peace officer's commands.[63]

Similarly, in *R v Julom*, the Alberta Court of Appeal refused to find that an accused who hid from police when they approached him had been detained, on the grounds that "[t]he appellant's conduct in this case was the *opposite* of submission or compliance."[64]

That argument has some intuitive appeal, but it should not be adopted, for two main reasons. First, although the particular passage from *Therens* gives a foundation for the argument, it is not supported by the Court's subsequent decisions. Second, for a variety of reasons, it would be a bad policy decision.

Consider first the Court's statements about psychological detention in the key cases. *Therens* did refer to submission, but the accused there had in fact submitted, so that particular aspect of the test was arguably *obiter*. More importantly, the Supreme Court has stopped mentioning a need for acquiescence and implicitly has decided cases as though no such requirement exists. For example, in *Lafrance*, quoting *Le*, the Court described psychological detention by saying that "a detention exists in situations where a reasonable person in the accused's shoes would feel obligated to comply . . . and that they are not free to leave."[65] Both decisions make repeated reference to the definition of psychological detention, neither of them (either the majority or the dissenters) mentioning acquiescence.[66] Earlier in *Grant*, although the Court did quote *Therens*, it set out its three-part test for deciding whether a person was psychologically detained without making any reference to acquiescence. In *Lafrance*, the Court said that "*Grant* is comprehensive in scope."[67]

Furthermore, *Le* discusses *Therens* in a way that implies that the accused's submission is not required. In the context of rejecting the

---

63 *R v Ratt*, 2020 SKCA 19 at para 37. "Even briefly" is a reference to an argument that has been used to counter the "no acquiescence" argument in some cases, that an accused has *momentarily* acquiesced before fleeing: see, for example, *R v Reddy*, 2010 BCCA 11, or *R v Dunkley*, 2016 ONCA 597.

64 *R v Julom*, 2022 ABCA 198 at para 33 [emphasis in the original]. See also *R v Saretzky*, 2020 ABCA 421.

65 *Lafrance*, above note 30 at para 21, quoting *Le*, above note 3 at para 26 [ellipses in *Lafrance*].

66 See, for example, *Le*, above note 3 at paras 25, 26, or 233, or *Lafrance*, above note 30 at paras 21 & 22.

67 *Ibid* at para 28. The Court said this in the context of precluding reliance on *Moran*, above note 25, on the basis that "*Moran* encourages courts to consider the subjective perceptions and beliefs of the accused, thereby emphasizing considerations that play a limited (if any) role in an objective assessment" (at para 27).

claim that the detainee's subjective perceptions are highly relevant, the Court says that *Therens* is misleading:

> Prior to *Grant*, the objective nature of the test may have been unclear. For example, in *Therens*, this Court held that a detention will arise when an individual "submits or acquiesces in the deprivation of liberty and reasonably believes that the choice to do otherwise does not exist" (p. 644)—a statement that may have suggested that the analysis focuses on the reasonableness of an individual's subjective perceptions. But in *Grant*, this Court clarified that the analysis is objective.[68]

This suggests that there is no acquiescence requirement since it says that the accused's own state of mind is not the issue. Even more strongly suggesting that the Court does not see acquiescence as a requirement is the fact that in *Le*, the accused *did not* acquiesce but rather fled. If that were fatal to his claim to be psychologically detained, one would expect the point to have been mentioned, at least by the dissent.

Second, insisting on acquiescence would be a bad policy decision, for several reasons. That approach to psychological detention would put it out of step with physical detention or detention by legal compulsion. A person who does not submit to physical restraint but instead breaks free of an arresting officer and escapes is nonetheless in custody.[69] A driver who is signalled to stop but does not do so faces legal consequences for that failure.[70] The fact that a suspect does not comply with either physical detention or detention by legal compulsion does not lead to the conclusion that the person was not detained; it would therefore be reasonable to treat psychological detention in the same way.

Indeed, and related to that point, if the police have no authority to detain an individual, then that person is constitutionally entitled to leave. The Supreme Court has held that the most fundamental purpose of section 10(a) of the *Charter*, the right to be informed of the reason for an arrest or detention, is to support the right not to submit to a detention if one does not know the reason for it.[71] Similarly, the Court held in *R v Chehil* that

---

68 *Le*, above note 3 at para 114.

69 *R v Whitfield*, [1970] SCR 46.

70 Section 320.17 of the *Criminal Code*, RSC 1985, c C-46 [*Code*], makes it a criminal offence to flee police in a vehicle, and various motor vehicle acts impose a legal obligation to stop when signalled to do so: see, for example, the *Traffic Safety Act*, RSA 2000, c T-6, ss 157(1) and 166, or the *Motor Vehicle Act*, RSBC 1996, c 318, s 73.

71 *R v Evans*, [1991] 1 SCR 869 at para 26 [*Evans*].

> Nor should the exercise of *Charter* rights, such as the right to remain silent or to walk away from questioning made outside the context of a detention, provide grounds for reasonable suspicion. These rights become meaningless to the extent that they are capable of forming the basis of reasonable suspicion. Individuals should not have to sacrifice privacy to exercise *Charter* rights.[72]

Furthermore, focusing on actual submission gives an inappropriately subjective nature to the concept of psychological detention. It is perfectly obvious that a person could think "I am required to stop but I am not going to"; the mere fact that a person does not *submit* to a compulsion does not mean that that person does not *perceive* a compulsion.[73] More importantly, it is not the suspect's subjective perception that matters. It is even clearer that the accused could subjectively decide to flee even though the reasonable person would perceive an obligation to submit, and it is the reasonable person test that governs.[74]

Finally, and most importantly, failing to treat psychological detention in the same way as physical detention or detention by legal compulsion has an inappropriate impact on *Charter* analysis. If police physically detain a person—for example, by an arrest—and that person breaks free and flees, they would be able to argue that they were entitled to resist the arrest because it was unlawful. If police attempted to detain a person by legal compulsion when they were not lawfully entitled to do so, that person could refuse to comply and point to the unlawfulness of the police action as a justification. In each of those cases, the accused

---

72 *R v Chehil*, 2013 SCC 49 at para 44 [*Chehil*].

73 See, for example, *Atkins*, above note 62, where police officers called the accused, a young Black male, over to talk to them, but instead of complying, he fled in the opposite direction. There is room to disagree over whether the reasons the police had for stopping him—he appeared to be withdrawn and overdressed for the weather—amounted to reasonable suspicion. The focus of the decision, however, was not whether the detention was arbitrary but whether there *was* a detention. The analysis focuses (wrongly, in light of the later decision in *Le*) on the accused's subjective reaction, but leaving that aside, the Ontario Court of Appeal noted at para 10: "The fact that the appellant ran may well be some evidence that he believed that he had no choice but to comply, and instead of complying, decided to escape." Nonetheless, that court carried on to say, "However, as the trial judge recognized, if the appellant did not acquiesce or submit to any deprivation of liberty, there could be no detention."

74 Worth noting as well is that it will often be open to debate as to whether a person was chased because they ran or ran because they were chased. See, for example, *R v Ford*, 2011 ONSC 5658, where police chased the accused, a Black male. The police testified that they chased him because they suspected him to be a different Black male wanted for bank robbery, while the accused testified that he ran because he feared the police were going to shoot him.

would be claiming a section 9 violation: that the police had detained them but had done so arbitrarily. When, however, courts reason that a person who does not submit to a psychological detention is not, because of the non-submission, detained, it becomes impossible for the accused to argue section 9.

Imagine, for example, a person of colour walking along the street and being directed by a peace officer to stop, but perceiving—rightly—that it was an instance of racial profiling. Under section 9, that would unquestionably be arbitrary,[75] and the person should be able to complain of it. But if acquiescence is a prerequisite to psychological detention, the person is faced with two equally unacceptable options: comply with the unlawful demand or decline to comply and thereby forfeit any ability to complain of the unlawfulness. The option of exercising the liberty simply to walk uninterrupted down the street will have disappeared. If acquiescence is essential before there is a detention, then no matter how arbitrary the police action might have been, the question of arbitrariness would never come to court. If the accused was not detained, there could be no section 9 claim. To insist on submission or acquiescence, therefore, is to prevent a person who rightly claims that the police were trying to effect an unlawful detention from making that argument; that is a bad policy decision.

2) When Is a Detention Arbitrary?

The "arbitrariness" portion of section 9 claims is to be addressed by a structure parallel to that created in *R v Collins* for assessing section 8 claims. The *Collins* test says, "A search will be reasonable if it is authorized by law, if the law itself is reasonable and if the manner in which the search was carried out is reasonable."[76] In the search context, that overarching approach was established from the very start, and the subsequent caselaw was all developed in light of it. In contrast, the parallel approach that now exists for section 9 was left consciously undecided for many years and was developed gradually. As a result, it was only with the *Le* decision in 2019 that the Court fully articulated the test:

> Where a detention is established, a court must consider whether the detention is arbitrary. This Court's decision in *Grant* provides guidance (at paras. 54–56), drawing from the three-part test stated in *R. v. Collins*, [1987] 1 S.C.R. 265, for assessing unreasonable searches and seizures under s. 8. Specifically, the detention must be authorized by law; the

75 "[A] detention based on racial profiling is one that is, by definition, not based on reasonable suspicion": *Le*, above note 3 at para 78.

76 See *Collins*, above note 5 at para 23.

> authorizing law itself must not be arbitrary; and, the manner in which the detention is carried out must be reasonable.[77]

We will consider each of those three issues in turn. Doing so, however, involves a certain amount of "retrofitting" of the caselaw. Because the Court had not expressly set out those three questions as separate issues at an early stage, it is necessary now to classify cases as falling under headings that did not exist at the time they were decided. This problem is exacerbated by the fact that many powers of detention were created at common law, which for practical purposes has tended to collapse the distinctions between whether there was a power to act, whether it was reasonable for there to be such a power, and whether the power was exercised in a reasonable manner.[78] This will sometimes make it difficult, in the discussion below, to determine exactly how some particular issues, such as racial profiling, should be taken into account. This failure to have had an overall structure for so long also continues to cause confusion even in more recent cases.

a) Is the Detention Authorized by Law?

The first question, whether the detention is authorized by law, sounds like an obvious step. The equivalent point for section 8, that "unreasonable search" and "unlawful search" mean the same thing, was established in some of the earliest *Charter* decisions about unreasonable search and seizure.[79] However, *Grant* was the first case to make fully clear that the same approach applies to section 9. In fact, the failure to have established this point earlier means that much of the section 9 caselaw prior to 2009 is not entirely reliable.

It is important to see that the first question includes two different considerations: that if the detention *is* authorized by law, it passes the first stage, but also that if it is *not* authorized by law, it fails the first stage. The first half of that equation had never really been controversial. As noted earlier, the technique of finding a detention lawful as a means of avoiding a section 9 violation led to the creation of new common law powers of detention.[80] For that reason and others, the rule that "a lawful detention is not an arbitrary one" was used routinely.

The controversial point was the second half of equating "arbitrary" and "unlawful": that a detention would be arbitrary simply because it failed to comply with the law. In fact, many courts had denied that that

77 *Le*, above note 3 at para 124.

78 See the discussion of this issue in Chapter 3, Section C(3).

79 See *R v Kokesch*, [1990] 3 SCR 3, and *Collins*, above note 5.

80 See the discussion in Chapter 2, Section A(4).

was so. In *R v Duguay*, for example, the Ontario Court of Appeal had held that a police officer might arrest someone on grounds that fell just short of being reasonable and that such an arrest, "though subsequently found to be unlawful, could not be said to be capricious or arbitrary."[81] The Supreme Court did not comment in any way on this issue when it upheld the result in *Duguay*, but the appeal dealt only with the issue of exclusion of evidence, so this point did not arise.[82] On other occasions, the Court deliberately left the issue aside. In *R v Latimer*, for example, it commented that "[u]nlawful arrests may be inherently arbitrary . . . [but] it is not necessary to address that question."[83]

With *Grant*, however, the Court fully and consciously committed itself to both halves of the equation: unlawful detentions are arbitrary, and vice versa. It held:

> A lawful detention is not arbitrary within the meaning of s. 9 (*Mann*, at para. 20), unless the law authorizing the detention is itself arbitrary. Conversely, a detention not authorized by law is arbitrary and violates s. 9.[84]

In fact, the Court had said something similar two years earlier in *R v Clayton*.[85] There, however, the observation was made in passing, without reference to the fact that this was a point deliberately left undecided in earlier cases. In *Grant*, the Court referred explicitly to that unsettledness and to the suggestion in *Duguay* that an unlawful detention was not necessarily arbitrary and commits itself consciously to the opposite view.

---

81 *R v Duguay* (1985), 50 OR (2d) 375 and 382 (CA) [*Duguay*]. It is probably fair to say that the majority opinion among courts of appeal had been that unlawfulness did not automatically amount to arbitrariness. See, for example, *R v Campbell*, 2003 MBCA 76 at para 42:

> In summary, appellate courts in Canada have accepted the proposition that an unlawful arrest will not necessarily constitute an arbitrary detention. What must be determined is whether the arrest was "capricious, despotic or unjustified," or whether there were "near grounds" or articulable cause for the detention. See also *R v Ingle*, 2007 BCCA 445, and *R v Perello*, 2005 SKCA 8.

82 *R v Duguay*, [1989] 1 SCR 93.

83 *R v Latimer*, [1997] 1 SCR 217 at para 26 [*Latimer*].

84 *Grant*, above note 3 at para 54.

85 2007 SCC 32 at para 19 [*Clayton*]:

> If the police conduct in detaining and searching Clayton and Farmer amounted to a lawful exercise of their common law powers, there was no violation of their *Charter* rights. If, on the other hand, the conduct fell outside the scope of these powers, it represented an infringement of the right under the *Charter* not to be arbitrarily detained or subjected to an unreasonable search or seizure.

In light of that unambiguous clarification of the law, it is unfortunate that, at least among trial courts, *Duguay* continues sometimes—although decreasingly—to be cited for the now-incorrect proposition that an unlawful detention is not automatically an arbitrary one.[86]

There has also been confusion over this same issue caused by the fact that "arbitrariness" is a principle of fundamental justice under a section 7 analysis, although its meaning in that context is entirely different from that in section 9. Nonetheless, the Alberta Court of Appeal in particular has repeatedly relied on the section 7 definition of "arbitrary" (that the law bears no relation to its objective) when considering section 9 claims and therefore continues to contemplate, despite the clear rejection of the possibility in *Grant*, that there could be a detention that "is unlawful even if not arbitrary."[87] This error arises, it seems, precisely from the fact that the overall structure of a section 9 claim was not settled for several decades. Until *Grant*, it was not clear that a court had to ask first, "Did some law authorize this state action?" and then second, "Was that law itself arbitrary?" As will be discussed below, if the section 7 definition of "arbitrariness" were to be relevant anywhere, it would be in answering that second question. But on the overall structure of section 9 that has now been developed, there is often no need even to ask the second question. If the action was not authorized by law—that is, it was unlawful—then a section 9 violation has been established. It would only be if some law did purport to authorize the action that it would be necessary to consider whether that law itself was arbitrary, and only at that stage that one would ask (if, in fact, the section 7 definition were to be used at all, which is not currently the law) whether the law bore some relation to its objective. But concluding that there was no further

---

86 See, for example, *R v Fortune*, 2012 BCSC 2031; *R v Unka*, 2012 NWTTC 9; *R v Dimitrov*, 2013 SKPC 148; *R v Berry*, 2013 ONCJ 406; *R v Antosh*, 2013 SKPC 81; *R v Kachmarski*, 2014 SKQB 39; *R v Wenham*, 2014 ONSC 994; *R v Harrigan*, 2014 NWTTC 4; *R v White*, 2015 ABPC 77; or *R v Khatra*, 2017 BCPC 462. Of course, some courts do explicitly note that *Duguay* has been overtaken in this regard: see, for example, *R v Cameron*, 2016 SKPC 3.

87 *R v Zolmer*, 2019 ABCA 93 at para 52 [*Zolmer*]. See also the majority decision in *R v Vassell*, 2015 ABCA 409 [*Vassell*], which relies on s 7 caselaw to determine the arbitrariness issue in the s 9 argument, thereby concluding that the unlawful detention was not arbitrary. The dissenting judge pointed to *Grant* in arguing that the majority erred. The Supreme Court of Canada reversed the result in *R v Vassell*, 2016 SCC 26, but on the basis of a trial within a reasonable time argument that explicitly did not consider the s 9 issue. See as well *R v Upright*, 2020 ABCA 227 at para 13 [*Upright*], in which the Alberta Court of Appeal again uses the s 7 definition of "arbitrary" from *Canada (Attorney General) v Bedford*, 2013 SCC 72 [*Bedford*], rather than the s 9 definition of "arbitrary" from *Grant*, above note 3.

section 9 violation at that second step would not retroactively cure the violation at the first step.

This confusion is one example of a point noted in the introduction to this section, that it can be difficult in the section 9 context to neatly separate the issues involved in the three different steps of the analysis. Another example is the impact of racial profiling. That issue will be discussed below under "Is the Manner in Which the Detention Was Carried Out Reasonable?" because it is most naturally thought of as improperly using a power that does in fact exist (and is discussed at much greater length in Chapter 2, Section B(3)). However, the Supreme Court held in *Le* that "a detention based on racial profiling is one that is, by definition, not based on reasonable suspicion."[88] One could therefore think of the issue as the detention not being authorized by law in the first place.

b) Is the Law Itself Arbitrary?

The second question in the analysis, is the law itself arbitrary, was in fact one of the earliest points addressed in section 9 analysis; this happened more than twenty years before *Grant*, in *Hufsky*. At the time, the question was not being considered in the context of a three-step analysis, but nonetheless the Court did turn its mind to what would make a law arbitrary for section 9 purposes. It is necessary to say "for section 9 purposes" because it has subsequently been decided that there is, under section 7 of the *Charter*, a principle of fundamental justice that a law cannot be arbitrary: see the discussion below.[89]

In *Hufsky*, the Court was concerned with a provincial highway traffic act provision that permitted police to stop vehicles at random. It had no difficulty concluding that the accused, stopped under this power, was detained. The Court did not specifically ask whether his detention was authorized by law, although, of course, it was, by the relevant highway traffic act. The issue was whether his detention under this power was arbitrary. The Court held that it was. The statute did not create any criteria as to which cars could be stopped and left the matter entirely in the discretion of the individual police officer. The Court found this to be arbitrary and set out the definition that led it to this conclusion: "A discretion is arbitrary if there are no criteria, express or implied, which

88 *Le*, above note 3 at para 78.

89 The Court considered arbitrariness as a principle of fundamental justice in a number of cases without, for some time, settling on an exact definition: see the discussion of this point in *Canada (Attorney General) v PHS Community Services Society*, 2011 SCC 44 [*PHS*]. The Court finally settled on a definition of "arbitrary" for s 7 purposes in *Bedford*, above note 87.

govern its exercise."[90] It also carried on to find the section 9 violation in that case to be justified under section 1, but nonetheless it established the definition of "arbitrary."

This definition has been applied by the Court in a number of other cases. First, and unsurprisingly, it was used in other vehicle-stop cases.[91] In *R v Swain*, in dealing with a law that required the automatic detention of a person found not guilty by reason of insanity, the Court noted: "The duty of the trial judge to detain is unqualified by any standards whatsoever. I cannot imagine a detention being ordered on a more arbitrary basis."[92] In *R v Pearson* and in *R v Morales*, the Court used this definition to assess aspects of the *Criminal Code*'s bail provisions in the section 9 analysis.[93] In *Lyons*, it was used to assess the dangerous-offender provisions.[94] Justice Binnie, dissenting in *Clayton*, used it to find that his proposed new common law power of detention was arbitrary (but saved under section 1).[95]

The important point to note is that the Court has not merely said that not being governed by any criteria is one way to be arbitrary. Rather, it actually does intend that "not governed by any criteria" is the definition of "arbitrary" for section 9 purposes. In *Lyons*, for example, the accused challenged the dangerous-offender provisions of the *Code* under sections 7, 9, and 12. The Court rejected the section 9 claim, noting that the provisions did set out criteria governing when an offender could be designated as dangerous. It carried on to say: "If these criteria are themselves unconstitutional, it is because they otherwise fail adequately to safeguard the liberty of the individual, not because they are arbitrary."[96] On this approach, the section 9 question reduces to whether criteria exist at all; if they do, the detention is not arbitrary. Questions relating to the content of the criteria would fall to be decided under some other section, such as section 7 or 12.[97]

---

90 *Hufsky*, above note 8 at 633. The Court reaffirmed this criterion more recently: see *R v Nolet*, 2010 SCC 24 at para 22 [*Nolet*].

91 *R v Wilson*, [1990] 1 SCR 1291; *Ladouceur*, above note 9; *R v Macooh*, [1993] 2 SCR 802; and *R v Mellenthin*, [1992] 3 SCR 615.

92 *R v Swain*, [1991] 1 SCR 933 at 1012.

93 *R v Pearson*, [1992] 3 SCR 665 [*Pearson*]; *R v Morales*, [1992] 3 SCR 711 [*Morales*].

94 *Lyons*, above note 11.

95 *Clayton*, above note 85 at para 67.

96 *Lyons*, above note 11 at 347. *Lyons* was actually decided prior to *Hufsky*, above note 8, but is consistent with the approach articulated in the latter case.

97 See also *Pearson*, above note 93 at 699–700, and *Morales*, above note 93 at 740–41 and 747, for other instances where the fact that the provisions had some criteria led directly to the conclusion that the provisions did not violate s 9.

This is unproblematic as far as it goes; the difficulty is that this does not go far enough if this were meant to be the end of the analysis. This point can be seen most easily by thinking, again, about racial profiling. Because of the roving random-stop power upheld in *Ladouceur*, or based on various pieces of provincial legislation, police have the authority to stop any car they like, without the need to point to a reason for the stop. One cannot say, therefore, that in stopping a vehicle because of the race of the driver, the police will have acted arbitrarily if that term simply means "without criteria." Those officers will have used objectionable and improper criteria but not *no* criteria. If the complete basis for assessing section 9 is that articulated in *Grant*—for a detention to be non-arbitrary, it must be authorized by a law which is itself non-arbitrary[98]—and the definition of "arbitrary" is that in *Hufsky*, then racial profiling would not violate section 9 (or, at least, would not violate this aspect of the test). Nonetheless, it seems obvious that if anything ought to allow us to say that a law itself is arbitrary, it would be racial profiling.

In fact, the Supreme Court has noted this point in passing, although it has never developed it. In *Ladouceur*, having upheld the very broad roving random-stop power, the Court observed that if the power to make such stops was used based on race, that would be a misuse of the power that would constitute a *Charter* violation.[99] Similarly, in *R v Storrey*, the Court held:

> [T]here is no indication that the arrest was made because a police officer was biased towards a person of a different race, nationality or colour, or that there was a personal enmity between a police officer directed towards the person arrested. These factors, if established, might have the effect of rendering invalid an otherwise lawful arrest.[100]

Subsequently, in *Chehil*, although in the context of a search, the Court warned against allowing "discriminatory profiling" to enter into the reasonable suspicion standard.[101] Note that—although in *Chehil* itself there was no *Charter* violation—this was not addressing an instance of a discretionary decision by an officer but a concern that the guidelines themselves "capture a high percentage of . . . racially marginalized groups."[102]

---

98 *Grant*, above note 2 at para 56.

99 In fact, this point is made in the dissenting judgment and attributed to the majority: "[R]acial considerations may be a factor too. My colleague states that in such circumstances, a *Charter* violation may be made out." *Ladouceur*, above note 9 at 1267.

100 *R v Storrey*, [1990] 1 SCR 241 at 251–52 [*Storrey*].

101 *Chehil*, above note 72 at para 42.

102 *Ibid* at para 20.

This illustrates a number of things. First, it shows once again that the failure to have established an overarching framework at the start has made section 9 caselaw more complicated than it needs to be. Second, it shows that although "no criteria" is the only definition articulated for when a law will be arbitrary, it is not in fact the only definition being used in practice. Third, it shows the necessity for the third step, which has since been firmly established: whether the manner of detention was reasonable.

However, a few other comments are also in order. It would, for example, be possible to argue that there is actually no problem with having "no criteria" as the sole test for the arbitrariness of a law even if it is inadequate as a complete solution; just as in *Lyons*, it might be that the objectionable content of the criteria used is a matter for other *Charter* sections, such as section 7 or 15.[103] That would be a bit counterintuitive, and racial profiling is clearly a legitimate section 9 issue, but it is not an impossible approach.

A second option would be to change the definition of "arbitrary" so that it takes into account the nature of the criteria used, not simply their existence. As mentioned above, "arbitrariness" is also a principle of fundamental justice under section 7. Although references to that principle date back to at least the *Rodriguez v British Columbia (Attorney General)* decision in 1993,[104] it took some time for the Court to settle on a definition.[105] The Court has now determined in *Bedford* that, for section 7 purposes,

> [a]rbitrariness asks whether there is a direct connection between the purpose of the law and the impugned effect on the individual, in the sense that the effect on the individual bears some relation to the law's purpose. There must be a rational connection between the object of the measure that causes the s. 7 deprivation, and the limits it imposes on life, liberty, or security of the person (Stewart, at p. 136). A law that imposes limits on these interests in a way that bears *no connection* to its objective arbitrarily impinges on those interests.[106]

If this definition were used in the section 9 context, then racial profiling and other similar misuses of power would become arbitrary.

---

103 See, for example, *R v Cruickshank*, 2014 SKPC 88, which treats the racial profiling claim in that case as a matter for those sections rather than for s 9.

104 [1993] 3 SCR 519.

105 In *Chaoulli v Quebec (Attorney General)*, 2005 SCC 35, members of the Court who considered the issue split 3:3 on the proper definition of "arbitrariness" as a principle of fundamental justice. In *PHS*, above note 89, the Court noted this unsettledness without settling this dispute.

106 *Bedford*, above note 87 at para 111.

There has been no suggestion from the Court that this discussion in the section 7 context ought to also extend to section 9. However, there is some intuitive attraction to the notion that the same term should have the same meaning in two different *Charter* sections, even if the term does not explicitly appear in one of them. Also, no section 9 case in which it was necessary to consider the question, "Is the law itself arbitrary?" has reached the Supreme Court since they settled this section 7 dispute, so adopting that definition is at least possible.

However, for several reasons, this does not seem like the best approach. First, to do so carries some danger. Think again about the reasoning in *Duguay*: that police action could fall just short of the necessary standard and therefore not be arbitrary even though it was unlawful. That logic was explicitly rejected in *Grant*, but adopting the *Bedford* definition of "arbitrary" would risk reintroducing it. An officer who arrests for reasons falling slightly short of reasonable grounds, or who conducts an investigative detention on grounds slightly less than reasonable suspicion, is not acting "in a way that bears *no connection*" to the objective of those powers. It would therefore be easy to conclude that such a detention was not an arbitrary one, although this result would run directly contrary to what *Grant* dictated.

In principle, this danger could be avoided by remembering that this definition of arbitrary would only be relevant at the second stage of asking, "Is the law itself arbitrary?": the first stage (asking, "Was the detention authorized by law?") could still guard against unlawful detentions. However, there would still be the risk that courts would not see this distinction.[107] This risk is heightened by the current approach to creating common law powers of detention, which tends to collapse into a single step the questions of whether a detention was authorized by law and whether the law was arbitrary. Where the Court simply creates a law in a case, it is unlikely to then find that the law it has just created is arbitrary and cannot be saved.[108]

A second reason not to take this approach is that there are really two separate questions involved. The *Collins* test for searches, "Was the law itself reasonable?" and "Was the manner of search reasonable?" distinguishes between the questions of whether the law is acceptable in the abstract and whether a law that is acceptable in the abstract is used in an unacceptable manner. The same two questions arise in the detention context. Whether the law itself should not exist or should exist but is

107 See the discussion above in Section B(2)(a) of the Alberta Court of Appeal decisions in *Vassell*, above note 87; *Upright*, above note 87; and *Zolmer*, above note 87, making exactly this error.

108 See the discussion in Chapter 3, Section C(3).

being misused are different questions. Incorporating the way in which the law is used into the question of whether the law is arbitrary unnecessarily eliminates that distinction.

c) Is the Manner in Which the Detention Was Carried Out Reasonable?

As noted above, for many years the governing approach to section 9 was not settled, and even in 2009, when *Grant* articulated a portion of that approach, this particular step was not mentioned. Its role in the analysis was only authoritatively confirmed with *Le* in 2019: "the detention must be authorized by law; the authorizing law itself must not be arbitrary; and, the manner in which the detention is carried out must be reasonable."[109] However, even before *Le*, many lower courts had relied on essentially this criterion in deciding that an accused had been arbitrarily detained.

In *Brown v Durham (Regional Municipality) Police Force*, for example, the Ontario Court of Appeal found that a stop made using the *Highway Traffic Act* would not violate section 9 even if the police had other purposes beyond highway traffic ones for making it. It carried on to say:

> If, however, one of the purposes motivating a stop and detention is improper, then in my view the stop is unlawful even if highway safety concerns also factor into the decision to make the stop and detention.[110]

The court continued:

> While I can find no sound reason for invalidating an otherwise proper stop because the police used the opportunity afforded by that stop to further some other legitimate interest, I do see strong policy reasons for invalidating a stop where the police have an additional improper purpose. Highway safety concerns are important, but they should not provide the police with a means to pursue objects which are themselves an abuse of the police power or are otherwise improper. For example, it would be unacceptable to allow a police officer who has valid highway safety concerns to give effect to those concerns by stopping only vehicles driven by persons of colour. Section 216(1) of the HTA does not, in my view, authorize discriminatory stops even where there is a highway safety purpose behind those stops.[111]

---

109 *Le*, above note 3 at para 124.

110 *Brown v Durham (Regional Municipality) Police Force* (1998), 131 CCC (3d) 1 at para 34 (Ont CA) [*Brown*]. Note that this approach seems to have been endorsed by the Supreme Court: see the discussion of *Nolet*, above note 90, in Chapter 2, Section B(2).

111 *Brown*, above note 110 at para 38.

Based on this, courts have relied on "improper purpose" as a basis for finding a section 9 violation. In *R v Herter*, for example, the trial judge found that a peace officer arbitrarily detained the accused by keeping him in the "drunk tank" for more than seven hours. It was not that there was no justification for doing so, in the sense that the accused was not intoxicated; he was. However, the trial judge concluded that the officer had acted in this way solely out of frustration at the accused's uncooperativeness.[112] In these cases, there is nothing wrong with the underlying law; rather, there is found to be a section 9 violation based on the way in which that law was used.

Furthermore, even before the third step was articulated in *Le*, the Court had, with its decisions in *R v Aucoin* and *R v MacKenzie*, provided support for its existence, although in a way that creates some ambiguity.[113] In *Aucoin*, the Court confirmed that the earlier decision in *Clayton* had created a general power to detain.[114] It also found that the particular detention in that case was an arbitrary one that violated section 9. In characterizing the issue to be addressed, the Court had held:

> I do not see this case as turning on whether Constable Burke had the *authority* to detain the appellant in the rear of his police cruiser, having lawfully stopped him for a regulatory infraction. Rather, the question is whether he was justified in *exercising it* as he did in the circumstances of this case.[115]

This passage certainly sounds as though it is saying that *Aucoin* is about the third-step equivalent to the *Collins* test of whether the manner of the detention violated section 9. Similarly, in *MacKenzie*, the majority held:

> To return to the facts here, it is unnecessary to consider whether the manner of the appellant's detention was reasonably necessary in the circumstances. Unlike *R. v. Aucoin*, 2012 SCC 66, [2012] 3 S.C.R. 408, there is no suggestion here that the manner in which he was detained (being asked to sit by the side of the road while the sniff was conducted) was not reasonably necessary in the circumstances.[116]

---

112 *R v Herter*, 2006 ABPC 221, rev'd 2007 ABQB 756. The reversal is difficult to understand given that it seems to amount to simply reversing the trial judge's findings of fact with no reference to standard of review: see Steve Coughlan, "*R v Herter*: Annotation" (2007) 53 *Criminal Reports* (6th) 287 at 288–89. In addition, see *R v Hardy*, 2015 MBCA 51, also arguing unsuccessfully that the accused was detained merely as a punitive measure: see the review of caselaw in that decision.

113 *R v Aucoin*, 2012 SCC 66 [*Aucoin*]; *R v MacKenzie*, 2013 SCC 50 [*MacKenzie*]. See the further discussion of this point in Chapter 3, Section C(5)(b).

114 *Aucoin*, above note 113.

115 *Ibid* at para 35 [emphasis in original].

116 *MacKenzie*, above note 113 at para 39.

This passage too confirms that a third step of asking about the manner of the detention is part of the section 9 analysis. However, the ambiguity arises from the way in which this is phrased in *MacKenzie*: not, "Was the manner in which the detention was carried out arbitrary?" but "Was it reasonably necessary?" That the detention was "reasonably necessary" is one of the criteria for the general power to detain at issue in those cases; the passage could equally be read, therefore, as asking whether the detention was authorized by law in the first place.

The point is not entirely clear, but it seems most plausible to say that instances of racial profiling should be found to violate section 9 based on this step of the test. The Court observed in *Le* that "racial profiling is primarily concerned with the motivation of the police. It occurs when race or racial stereotypes about offending or dangerousness are used, consciously or unconsciously, to any degree in suspect selection or subject treatment."[117] That approach makes it sound as though the issue is why the police officer is using an available power, not whether the power is in fact available in the first place. Similarly, the Court's definition of "racial profiling" seems to support that same conclusion:

> Racial profiling is any action taken by one or more people in authority with respect to a person or group of persons, for reasons of safety, security or public order, that is based on actual or presumed membership in a group defined by race, colour, ethnic or national origin or religion, without factual grounds or reasonable suspicion, that results in the person or group being exposed to differential treatment or scrutiny.
>
> Racial profiling [also] includes any action by a person in a situation of authority who applies a measure in a disproportionate way to certain segments of the population on the basis, in particular, of their racial, ethnic, national or religious background, whether actual or presumed.[118]

Again, this focus on "appl[ying] a measure in a disproportionate way" seems to focus on the state of mind leading to the *use* of a power, not to whether the power exists.

However, the point is not entirely free from doubt. As noted above, the Court also said in *Le* that "a detention based on racial profiling is one that is, by definition, not based on reasonable suspicion."[119] On that approach, one would say that racial profiling is an instance of the

117 *Le*, above note 3 at para 76.

118 *Ibid* at para 77, quoting *Quebec (Commission des droits de la personne et des droits de la jeunesse) v Bombardier Inc (Bombardier Aerospace Training Center)*, 2015 SCC 39.

119 *Le*, above note 3 at para 78.

detention being unlawful as opposed to being conducted in an unreasonable way.

Either approach, of course, would lead to the conclusion that a successful racial profiling claim leads to a successful section 9 claim, which is the more important point. See the more complete discussion of racial profiling in Chapter 2, Section B(3).

C. SECTION 10—THE RIGHT TO BE INFORMED OF THE REASONS FOR DETENTION AND THE RIGHT TO COUNSEL

1) Introduction

Section 10 of the *Charter* reads as follows:

> Everyone has the right on arrest or detention
> (a) to be informed promptly of the reasons therefor;
> (b) to retain and instruct counsel without delay and to be informed of that right; and
> (c) to have the validity of the detention determined by way of habeas corpus and to be released if the detention is not lawful.

While the section 10(c) right to *habeas corpus* is beyond the scope of this book—our primary focus is "on the street encounters"—the rights under section 10(a) and (b) are intricately entwined with the section 9 right relating to arrest and detention.[120] Indeed, breaches of these two rights may well in themselves result in the arrest and detention being held unlawful. In Chapter 3, we discussed the concept of "detention," which triggers the applicability of the section 10 rights. We will not repeat that discussion here. It is worth saying, however, that section 10(a) and (b) rights have been treated as "gateway" rights in the sense that the Court has indicated that their purpose is to ensure that suspected persons are able to enjoy their other rights. By informing suspects why they are detained or arrested and allowing them to speak to counsel, suspects are able to enjoy their rights, in particular their right to silence in regard to the matter under investigation.

Therefore, based on the detention of the suspect, the suspect needs to be placed in a position to decide whether to exercise the right to silence

120 See, generally, Tim Quigley, *Procedure in Canadian Criminal Law*, 2d ed (Toronto: Thomson Carswell, 2005) ch 15.2, and Robert J. Sharpe, *The Law of Habeas Corpus*, 3d ed (Oxford: Clarendon Press, 2011). See also *May v Ferndale Institution*, 2005 SCC 82.

in the face of police suspicion and desire to secure evidence. Having said that, there are significant situations in which the Court has determined that section 1 of the *Charter* legitimately limits the right to counsel, a subject covered in Chapter 3.[121] The Supreme Court has generally limited the right to counsel in "screening" situations in impaired-driving cases. Furthermore, as discussed in Chapter 2, the issue as to whether these rights apply to non-police detentions has not been settled. Below, we will offer additional comments on this issue.

It is worth recognizing the interaction between sections 9 and 10. Earlier in this chapter, we discussed section 9, which deals with whether there was any legal authority to detain or arrest the individual. If there was not, then there will already have been a violation of the accused's *Charter* rights, so they will potentially be entitled to a remedy. Whether or not there was legal authority, however, the mere fact of arrest or detention triggers the rights in section 10(a) and (b). The police must then (in accordance with the requirements to be discussed below) inform the person of the reason for the detention and the right to counsel.

As a practical matter, this often means that there will be violations of both section 9 and section 10 on a single fact pattern. In particular, when a psychological detention is at issue, very frequently that is because the police had no lawful authority to detain; if they did, they likely would have used that power. In practice, then, psychological detentions often turn out to be arbitrary ones for that reason. Furthermore, in those cases, the police generally will not have said to the accused "you are detained" or given a reason for it and will not have told the accused of the right to counsel; accordingly, there will be violations of section 10(a) and (b) as well.

On the other hand, it is also quite possible for the rights to be violated independently. An accused might be explicitly but unlawfully arrested or detained and given their section 10 rights, in which case there is a violation only of section 9. Alternatively, an accused might have been lawfully arrested or detained, but there could be some failure to comply with the requirements of section 10, a scenario discussed below.

The most obvious "triggers" for section 10 are a formal arrest, made under one of the powers set out in the *Criminal Code*, or a detention of the sort discussed in Chapter 3, but the right arises no matter what the source of the state interference.[122] For some time, it had remained

121 See the discussion of limits on the right to counsel in impaired-driving cases in Chapter 3, Section B(2)(a).

122 See, for example, *R v Sabados*, 2015 SKCA 74 [*Sabados*], where a breath sample demand was made of an accused who was subject to a condition in a recognizance requiring him to provide one on request. Rejecting the Crown's argument

unclear whether an investigative detention under *Mann* triggered the right to counsel; however, in *Suberu*, the Supreme Court of Canada decided authoritatively that such detentions do trigger section 10.[123]

There is an issue of timing to be noted with regard to the rights in section 10. The right to be informed of the reason under section 10(a) arises "promptly," and the right to contact counsel under section 10(b) arises "without delay." Of those two phrases, probably "promptly" conveys a greater sense of urgency, but even the phrase "without delay" means "immediately." Any other interpretation, the Court held in *Suberu*, would not serve the purposes of mitigating the legal disadvantage and legal jeopardy faced by detainees. To allow some period of permissible delay before complying with section 10(b) would create an "ill-defined and unworkable" standard: "What constitutes a permissible delay is abstract and difficult to quantify, whereas the concept of immediacy leaves little room for misunderstanding."[124]

Nonetheless, there is some scope for delay, exceptionally, in section 10. The Court noted in *R v Mian* that exceptional circumstances could justify a delay in providing a detainee with the informational rights in section 10(b).[125] Exactly what will constitute "exceptional circumstances," however, is not fully decided; in *Mian*, the Court declined to consider whether the need to protect the integrity of an ongoing investigation would fall into that category.[126] *Mian* also declined to decide whether exceptional circumstances could ever justify not complying with the right in section 10(a) to inform a person of the reason for a detention or an arrest.[127] There is no established list of justifications, but lower courts have tended to be understanding of delay in informing a person of their section 10 rights

---

that in these circumstances s 10(b) did not arise, the Saskatchewan Court of Appeal held at para 20:

> The right to counsel under s. 10(*b*) of the *Charter* is engaged whenever an individual is arrested or detained, regardless of the reason for that arrest or detention or the possible evidence that could be produced as a result of that arrest or detention.

123 *Suberu*, above note 31.

124 *Ibid* at para 42.

125 *R v Mian*, 2014 SCC 54 at para 74 [*Mian*].

126 *Ibid* at para 74. In *Mian*, the police had not immediately provided the accused, who had been arrested for possession of a narcotic, with his right to counsel because they did not want to jeopardize the more central investigation of a different person. The Court did not decide whether this would constitute an exceptional circumstance because on the facts it was not shown that the concern arose.

127 *Ibid*.

when the officer has legitimate safety concerns.[128] In addition, it has sometimes been found that there can be delay in informing a person of the reason for the detention where it is impracticable to do so promptly.[129]

Furthermore, although an accused must generally be *informed* immediately of the right to contact counsel, that is not the same thing as actually *contacting* counsel immediately; often there is some delay (for example, to arrive at the police station) before this occurs. As the Court noted in *R v Taylor*:

> The duty to inform a detained person of his or her right to counsel arises "immediately" upon arrest or detention (*Suberu*, at paras. 41-42), and the duty to facilitate access to a lawyer, in turn, arises immediately upon the detainee's request to speak to counsel. The arresting officer is therefore under a constitutional obligation to facilitate the requested access to a lawyer at the first reasonably available opportunity.[130]

See the further discussion in Section C(3)(c), below in this chapter.

As a final introductory point, note that although initial arrests and detentions are the most obvious triggers for section 10, they are not the only ones. As noted earlier, in some cases, the interaction between police and an individual will be more properly seen as a series of linked detentions, and in such cases, police have an obligation to keep the individual informed of the evolving reason they are detained. In addition, in some cases, changed circumstances might mean that a person is entitled to a second opportunity to consult with counsel. That is a complicated and evolving situation in the law, however, which is discussed at length below in Section C(3)(d).

---

128 See, for example, *R v Boliver*, 2014 NSCA 99 at paras 11–21; *R v Nguyen*, 2016 BCCA 32 at paras 59–61 [*Nguyen* 2016]; or *R v Gonzales*, 2017 ONCA 543 at para 128. See also *R v Mohamed*, 2023 ABPC 49, where an officer approached two men, suspecting them to have been involved in a shooting that had just occurred. It was found to be reasonable of her to have delayed complying with s 10 before backup arrived but no longer reasonable after that point.

129 See, for example, *R v Hamdan*, 2017 BCSC 467, where a five-to-six-minute delay in telling the accused the reason for his detention was found not to violate s 10. The accused had been arrested on six terrorism-related charges, and the officer had waited until he got the agitated accused to the police van to read him the "arrest script," a document describing the six charges, which took him seven minutes to read out.

130 *R v Taylor*, 2014 SCC 50 at para 24 [*Taylor*]. See *R v DMR*, 2014 BCSC 63 [*DMR*], for a useful review of circumstances that have been held to justify delay in some cases.

2) Section 10(a)—Right to Be Informed of the Reasons for Detention

Section 10(a) gives a person the right to be "informed promptly of the reasons" for an arrest or detention. It has been noted that there are two distinct ways in which this right might be violated:

> Breaches of s. 10(a) can be "temporal" or "informational." A temporal breach occurs if an arrested or detained person is not promptly informed of the reasons for their detention. An "informational" breach arises if the reasons for their detention are not adequately communicated.[131]

The possibility of a temporal breach (an issue that is shared with section 10(b)) was discussed in the previous section. Here, we will look at the issue of informational breaches and exactly what it is that needs to be conveyed to a detainee.

The right to be informed of the reason for an arrest did not get very much attention in the early *Charter* cases. It was a right that was recognized at common law. In *Christie v Leachinsky*, the House of Lords set out the following on the point:

> 1. If a policeman arrests without warrant on reasonable suspicion of felony, or of other crime of a sort which does not require a warrant, he must in ordinary circumstances inform the person arrested of the true ground of arrest. He is not entitled to keep the reason to himself or to give a reason which is not the true reason. In other words, a citizen is entitled to know on what charge or on suspicion of what crime he is seized.
> 2. If the citizen is not so informed, but is nevertheless seized, the policeman, apart from certain exceptions, is liable for false imprisonment.
> 3. The requirement that the person arrested should be informed of the reason why he is seized naturally does not exist if the circumstances are such that he must know the general nature of the alleged offence for which he is detained.
> 4. The requirement that he should be so informed does not mean that technical or precise language need be used. The matter is a matter of substance, and turns on the elementary proposition that in this country a person is, *prima facie*, entitled to his freedom and is only required to submit to restraint on his freedom if he knows

131 *R v Roberts*, 2018 ONCA 411 at para 63. See also *R v Sanclemente*, 2021 ONCA 906 at para 129.

in substance the reason why it is claimed that this restraint should be imposed.

5. The person arrested cannot complain that he has not been supplied with the above information as and when he should be, if he himself produces the situation which makes it practically impossible to inform him, *eg*, by immediate counter-attack or by running away.[132]

The House of Lords was decidedly of the view that such a rule was necessary to protect the person arrested and particularly to allow the person arrested to determine whether the arrest was lawful:

> If another person has a lawful reason for seeking to deprive him of that liability, that person must as a general rule tell him what the reason is, for, unless he is told, he cannot be expected to submit to arrest or be blamed for resistance. The right to arrest and the duty to submit are correlative.[133]

Of course, the information thus provided allows the arrested person to know on what ground they are arrested and assists in their decision as to whether they should remain silent in the face of the allegation in question. Note that being told the *grounds* for the arrest is not the same thing as knowing the exact *charge* that will be laid.[134]

Before the enactment of section 10(a), the Supreme Court had thrown some doubt on whether Canadian law required full compliance with the law set out in *Christie v Leachinsky*. In *R v Gamracy*,[135] the accused was arrested and told that he was being arrested on a warrant that the officer did not have with him, nor did the officer know for what offence the warrant had been issued. Nonetheless, the Court found compliance with section 29(2) of the *Criminal Code*, which says:

> **29**(2) It is the duty of every one who arrests a person, whether with or without a warrant, to give notice to that person, where it is feasible to do so, of
> (*a*) the process or warrant under which he makes the arrest; or
> (*b*) the reason for the arrest.

---

132 *Christie v Leachinsky*, [1947] 1 All ER 567 at 572–73 (HL), Simon LJ [*Christie*].

133 *Ibid* at 578, Lord DuParcq.

134 See *R v S (WEQ)*, 2018 MBCA 106 at para 28:

> [P]olice officers are not required to articulate a specific offence at the time they arrest a suspect. Rather, the authorities suggest that as long as the police officers articulate the substance of the offence that they have in mind to the suspect and those offences are hybrid or indictable offences, then the officers' arrest of the accused, without a warrant but on reasonable grounds, will be valid.

135 [1974] SCR 640 [*Gamracy*].

The majority in *Gamracy* held that advising the suspect that there was a warrant for his arrest was sufficient compliance with the section and that although *Christie* was

> no doubt an interesting one in the English context and naturally entitled to the greatest respect, I think it should be said that such cases afford no assistance in determining the true meaning and effect to be given to ss. 450(1) and 29 of the Canadian *Criminal Code* and I do not think that any further comment is necessary.[136]

The arrest in *Gamracy* was, according to the Court, warrantless since the officer did not have the warrant with him; thus, only section 29(2)(b) was applicable. The section was to be read disjunctively, so the officer met its requirements by telling the accused that "the reason for the arrest" was that there was a warrant for his arrest. Accordingly, the officer was in the execution of duty when he arrested the accused, who was therefore convicted of assaulting the officer when he resisted the arrest. The dissenting justices disagreed with the majority that informing the accused that there was a warrant without also telling him what the warrant was for was sufficient compliance.

Caselaw surrounding section 10(a) casts severe doubt on whether *Gamracy* should still be seen as good law. After the *Charter* came into force, the majority of the Supreme Court of Canada in *Evans* said in relation to section 10(a):

> The right to be promptly advised of the reason for one's detention embodied in s. 10(a) of the *Charter* is founded most fundamentally on the notion that one is not obliged to submit to an arrest if one does not know the reasons for it: *R. v. Kelly* . . . . A second aspect of the right lies in its role as an adjunct to the right to counsel conferred by s. 10(b) of the *Charter*. As Wilson J. stated for the Court in *R. v. Black* . . . "[a]n individual can only exercise his s. 10(b) right in a meaningful way if he knows the extent of his jeopardy." In interpreting s. 10(a) in a purposive manner, regard must be had to the double rationale underlying the right.[137]

Therefore, in the majority's view, the double rationale included encouraging submission to lawful arrests and allowing meaningful exercise of the right to counsel. An accused who is merely told that the reason for their arrest is that there is a warrant might have had the first of these rationales satisfied, but certainly not the second. Indeed, it has

---

136 *Ibid* at 645.

137 *Evans*, above note 71 at 886–87, McLachlin J citing *R v Kelly* (1985), 17 CCC (3d) 419 at 424 (Ont CA); and *R v Black*, [1989] 2 SCR 138 at 152–53 [*Black*].

specifically been held that section 10(a) reflects the right set out in *Christie*, which *Gamracy* had distinguished.[138]

The Court's decision in *Evans*[139] also casts more light on the content of and approach to section 10(a). Evans was described by the Court as a youth (but who would appear to have been twenty years old on the date of his arrest) and as of "borderline" intelligence, being mentally the age of a fourteen-year-old. On the facts in *Evans*, although they found several breaches of the right to counsel, the majority ruled that the police had complied with section 10(a) since, in its view, Evans had understood why he was arrested and why he was being investigated. The accused had originally been told that he was arrested for drug offences when in fact he was being investigated in relation to a homicide. His section 10(b) right was violated because he should have been rewarned of the right to counsel when the nature of his detention changed. However, the majority found no violation of section 10(a), the right to be informed of the reason for the detention. They held that by the time the relevant statements had been made, the accused was aware that it was in fact the homicide in which the police were interested. To them, the crucial issue was

> what the accused can reasonably be supposed to have understood, rather than the formalism of the precise words used . . . . The question is whether what the accused was told, viewed reasonably in all the circumstances of the case, was sufficient to permit him to make a reasonable decision to decline to submit to arrest, or alternatively, to undermine his right to counsel under s. 10(b).[140]

Justice Sopinka, in dissent in relation to section 10(a), was not so accepting of the accused's understanding. He held that because the police had not been as explicit in explaining that it was not the drug charge in which they were interested as they had been in originally concocting the drug charge as the reason for his detention, the accused's section 10(a) right had been breached. To the dissenting justice, the purpose of section 10(a) was "to enable the person under arrest or detention to immediately undertake his or her defence, including a decision as to what response, if any, to make to the accusation."[141]

Subsequent to *Evans*, the Supreme Court seemingly continued to downplay the effect of section 10(a). In *Latimer*,[142] discussed in Chapter 4, the Court stressed that section 10(a) required only "that a person

138 *R v Nguyen*, 2008 ONCA 49 at para 16 [*Nguyen* 2008].
139 *Evans*, above note 71.
140 *Ibid* at 888.
141 *Ibid* at 875.
142 *Latimer*, above note 83.

'understand generally the jeopardy' in which he or she finds himself or herself,"[143] and therefore it was acceptable on the facts that Latimer knew he was being investigated in relation to his daughter's death and that he "was in an extremely grave situation as regards his daughter's death."[144] On the other hand, the Court did suggest that "it would be a gross interference with individual liberty for persons to have to submit to arrest without knowing the reasons for that arrest."[145]

Perhaps the low watermark for section 10(a) rights is the argument, accepted by at least some lower courts, that non-compliance with section 10(a) is permissible if it would be obvious to the accused why they were being detained: "[w]here the reason for the arrest is obvious in the circumstances surrounding the arrest, no such obligation exists."[146] It has been held, for example, that if a person had been drinking and driving erratically late at night, there was no violation of section 10(a) where the police officer did not inform the accused of the reason he was stopped because he must have known it was due to a concern over impaired driving.[147] Similarly, it has been held that a person arrested after a fight at a bar must know that the reason was because of an assault and therefore need not be informed.[148]

However, this view is far from universally accepted. It has been argued that this approach inappropriately relies on the common law rule in *Christie* rather than the text of section 10(a) or the language of Supreme Court decisions dealing with it, which talk about what the accused was "advised" or "told" or "informed."[149] Courts have held that the question for section 10(a) is not what the accused knows but whether the police have complied with their obligation to inform the accused. It has been pointed out, for example, that most lawyers or police officers would "know" of their right to counsel, but that does not relieve police of the obligation to inform an accused nonetheless, and that the same result

143 *Ibid* at para 28, quoting *R v Smith*, [1991] 1 SCR 714 at 728 [*Smith* 1991]. In *Smith* 1991, the Supreme Court held that an accused was not denied his s 10(a) rights when the police failed to inform him that his victim had died. The Court was of the view (at para 33) that "Smith was aware that his situation was one of the most grave seriousness."

144 *Latimer*, above note 83 at para 31. In a similar vein, see *R v Goodkey*, 2015 BCCA 64, where informing the accused that he was being arrested for "smuggling" without specifying anything more was found to be compliance with s 10(a).

145 *Latimer*, above note 83 at para 28.

146 *R v Boden*, 2014 BCSC 66 at para 54.

147 *R v Kumarasamy*, 2011 ONSC 1385.

148 *R v Nguyen*, 2014 BCSC 1499. *Nguyen* was upheld (*Nguyen* 2016, above note 128), but this issue was not before the British Columbia Court of Appeal.

149 See the very thorough analysis of this issue in *R v Evans*, 2015 ONCJ 305.

should follow for section 10(a).[150] In Ontario in particular, it is well recognized that there are competing lines of authority on this issue.[151]

In part, it might be that this ambiguity flows from the finding in *Evans* that the precise words used to satisfy section 10(a) do not matter and that the police need not say any particular thing to the accused as long as it is reasonable to find that the accused did understand.[152] For example, in *Smith* 1991, the Court held:

> The fact that the accused knew that he was in jeopardy for a most serious offence distinguishes this case from one in which the description given minimizes the legal consequences of the acts committed by the person under detention. In such cases the description by the police may allay the concerns that the detainee might otherwise have. It would then be wrong for the court to conclude that the detainee ought to have inferred from the circumstances the extent of his or her jeopardy.[153]

However, there is a significant difference between "the words giving the reason for detention were not precise" and "no reason for the detention was given." Similarly, that the detainee can be supposed to have understood despite misleading statements by the police (and therefore it can be concluded that the accused was not in fact misled) raises very different considerations from whether the detainee understood despite a failure by the police to comply with their section 10(a) obligations.

The better view is that no "obviousness" exception should exist. Quite apart from the problematic "you know what you did" attitude behind such an exception, requiring the police to inform a detainee is more consistent with the caselaw. For example, the Court, when creating the power of investigative detention in *Mann*, said that "[a]t a minimum, individuals who are detained for investigative purposes must therefore be advised, in clear and simple language, of the reasons for the detention."[154] Similarly, in *R v Orbanski; R v Elias*, the Court held that "every motorist

---

150 *R v Mueller*, 2018 ONSC 2734 at para 21 [*Mueller*]. See also *R v Hayatibahar*, 2022 ONSC 1281, adopting the approach in *Mueller*. Similarly, see *R v Koma*, 2015 SKCA 92 at para 95: "[W]hile Mr. Koma might be reasonably *presumed* to have had a general understanding of why he was being detained given the circumstances, it is clear from the record that the constable never actually *told* Mr. Koma why he was being detained." [Emphasis in original.]

151 See, for example, *R v Gardner*, 2021 ONSC 3468 at para 38: "There is no question that the *Mueller* and *Kumarasamy* decisions, both penned by eminent jurists, offer different perspectives about the scope of a detainee's s. 10(a) *Charter* rights." Similarly, see *R v O'Reilly*, 2022 ONCJ 176 at para 62.

152 See the discussion of *Evans*, above note 71, earlier in this section.

153 *Smith* 1991, above note 143 at 730.

154 *Mann*, above note 4.

would fully expect 'to be informed promptly of the reasons' why he or she is being stopped."[155]

It makes sense that, obvious or not, the police have some obligation to indicate to the detainee the reason for the detention. As the Ontario Court of Appeal noted in *Nguyen* (2008):

> It is clear, therefore, that while the main purpose of s. 10(a) is to inform an individual of why he or she is being detained, it also has an important secondary aspect as an adjunct to the right to counsel conferred by s. 10(b). Specifically, the purpose of s. 10(a) is also to inform an individual of the extent of his or her jeopardy such that he or she can exercise the right to counsel conferred by s. 10(b) in a meaningful way.[156]

The Court stressed that, "[o]nce detained, an individual is at the mercy of state actors" and that "the breach of the obligation to provide that information cannot be considered a trivial matter."[157]

Finally, for this section, note that the right under section 10(a) is intimately connected with the right to counsel since unless the accused understands their jeopardy, they are in no position to decide whether to seek counsel. Furthermore, a waiver of the right to counsel might be invalid where there is a breach of section 10(a).[158] Lastly, as noted in Chapter 3, in many situations, an accused's detention will in fact be a series of discrete detentions based on the successive use of different police powers. As an officer proceeds to a different and discrete investigation, section 10(a) might well reapply and require additional information to be given to the accused.[159]

3) Section 10(b)—The Right to Counsel

a) Introduction

Section 10(b) creates the right upon arrest or detention to "retain and instruct counsel without delay and to be informed of that right." The content of the right to counsel has been the subject of considerable discussion by the Supreme Court, but the Court summarized its overall approach in *R v Sinclair*:

---

155 *R v Orbanski; R v Elias*, 2005 SCC 37 at para 31.

156 *Nguyen* 2008, above note 138 at para 20.

157 *Ibid* at para 21.

158 *Ibid*.

159 See, for example, *R v Pearson*, 2012 ABCA 239, where what was initially a traffic stop changed in character when the officer formed suspicions that the accused was in possession of narcotics. The change in the nature of the detention entitled the accused to be told under s 10(a) of this new reason.

> The purpose of the right to counsel is "to allow the detainee not only to be informed of his rights and obligations under the law but, equally if not more important, to obtain advice as to how to exercise those rights": *R. v. Manninen*, [1987] 1 S.C.R. 1233, at pp. 1242-43. The emphasis, therefore, is on assuring that the detainee's decision to cooperate with the investigation or decline to do so is free and informed. Section 10(*b*) does not guarantee that the detainee's decision is wise; nor does it guard against subjective factors that may influence the decision. Its purpose is simply to give detainees the opportunity to access legal advice relevant to that choice.
>
> Section 10(*b*) fulfills its purpose in two ways. First, it requires that the detainee be advised of his right to counsel. This is called the informational component. Second, it requires that the detainee be given an opportunity to exercise his right to consult counsel. This is called the implementational component. Failure to comply with either of these components frustrates the purpose of s. 10(*b*) and results in a breach of the detainee's rights: *Manninen*. Implied in the second component is a duty on the police to hold off questioning until the detainee has had a reasonable opportunity to consult counsel. The police obligations flowing from s. 10(*b*) are not absolute. Unless a detainee invokes the right and is reasonably diligent in exercising it, the correlative duties on the police to provide a reasonable opportunity and to refrain from eliciting evidence will either not arise in the first place or will be suspended: *R. v. Tremblay*, [1987] 2 S.C.R. 435, at p. 439, and *R. v. Black*, [1989] 2 S.C.R. 138, at pp. 15455.
>
> Once informed of his right to consult counsel, the detainee may waive the right, deciding not to avail himself of the opportunity to consult that has been provided. The right to choose whether to cooperate with the police, the basic purpose of s. 10(*b*), has been respected in the event of a valid waiver, and there is consequently no breach.[160]

More succinctly, in *R v Willier*,[161] the Court said:

> The purposes of s. 10(*b*) serve to underpin and define the rights and obligations triggered by the guarantee. In *Bartle*, Lamer C.J. summarized these rights and obligations in terms of the duties imposed upon state authorities who make an arrest or effect a detention (p. 192). Section 10(*b*) requires the police
>
> (1) to inform the detainee of his or her right to retain and instruct counsel without delay and of the existence and availability of legal aid and duty counsel;

160 *R v Sinclair*, 2010 SCC 35 at paras 26–28 [*Sinclair*].

161 2010 SCC 37 at paras 29 & 30 [*Willier*].

> (2) if a detainee has indicated a desire to exercise this right, to provide the detainee with a reasonable opportunity to exercise the right (except in urgent and dangerous circumstances); and
> (3) to refrain from eliciting evidence from the detainee until he or she has had that reasonable opportunity (again, except in cases of urgency or danger).
>
> The first duty is an informational duty, while the second and third duties are implementational in nature and are not triggered until detainees indicate a desire to exercise their right to counsel. As explained in *R. v. Suberu*, 2009 SCC 33, [2009] 2 S.C.R. 460, these duties are triggered immediately upon an individual's arrest or detention, as "the concerns about self-incrimination and the interference with liberty that s. 10(*b*) seeks to address are present as soon as a detention is effected" (para. 41).

The following discussion will pursue these questions of informational and implementational duties, in addition to other related questions. Specifically, we will look at the rules around having an additional consultation with counsel, at the extent to which a detainee can consult their counsel of choice, the duty on a detainee to be reasonably diligent in exercising their right and the related issue of waiver, and finally the issue of privacy in consulting with counsel.

Before turning to those issues, however, it is worth noting a thing that section 10(b) does not provide: the right to have counsel present during an interrogation: "[d]etainees do not have a right to obtain, and police do not have a duty to facilitate, the continuous assistance of counsel."[162] This point was settled in cases that have come to be referred to as the "right to counsel trilogy": *Sinclair*,[163] *R v McCrimmon*,[164] and *Willier*.[165] For the most part, these cases simply left the law unchanged from what it was prior to them; they reflect an unsuccessful attempt by defence counsel to expand the protection given by section 10(b). However, as the majority in *Sinclair* observed, "we take the settled view to the effect that the right to counsel is essentially a one-time matter with few recognized exceptions."[166]

The lesson to take away from the right to counsel trilogy is that section 10(b) generally only has an impact at the time the accused is detained or arrested but not afterward (but see the discussion below in

162 *R v Dussault*, 2022 SCC 16 at para 33 [*Dussault*].
163 *Sinclair*, above note 160.
164 2010 SCC 36 [*McCrimmon*].
165 *Willier*, above note 161.
166 *Sinclair*, above note 160 at para 64.

Section C(3)(d) about additional consultations with counsel). Defence counsel in particular must be careful to take this into account by recognizing that a detainee's initial consultation with counsel is also likely to be the only one and therefore to be careful about providing the most complete advice possible.

b) Informational Duties

The most obvious informational duty in section 10(b) is that explicitly stated in it: the right "to retain and instruct counsel without delay *and to be informed of that right*" (emphasis added). Jurisprudence from the Supreme Court, however, has made clear that the police do not satisfy their informational duties by informing an accused of the simple fact that they have the right to counsel. In *R v Brydges*,[167] the Court found that section 10(b) also contained the right to be informed of the existence of whatever legal aid and duty counsel systems are in place in the province of arrest. Later, in *R v Bartle*,[168] the Court held that the information a suspect is entitled to receive from the police includes any 1-800 number that is provided by the legal aid plan in place in that jurisdiction.

In practice, as a result of the Supreme Court decisions, police forces have created cards that are to be read to suspects upon arrest and detention. A typical police card in use in Canada reads as follows:

> You have the right to retain and instruct a lawyer without delay. This means that before we proceed with our investigation you may call any lawyer you wish or a lawyer from a free legal advice service immediately. If you want to call a lawyer from a free legal advice service, we will provide you with a telephone and you can call a toll-free number for immediate legal advice. If you wish to contact any other lawyer, a telephone and telephone books will be provided for you. If you are charged with an offence, you may apply to Legal Aid for assistance. Do you understand: (*Record answer*).[169]

One can see that this police service has removed any reference to duty counsel, which is replaced here with "free legal advice service," presumably to make the information more accessible to the average detained person. Note as well that this caution makes no mention of remaining silent. The section 10(b) caution includes no such requirement, although there is a right to silence protected by section 7 of the *Charter*. Under the

167 [1990] 1 SCR 190 [*Brydges*].

168 [1994] 3 SCR 173 [*Bartle*].

169 The text of this card comes from the Calgary Police Service. See, for example, *R v Clarke*, 2019 ABPC 38 at para 8, and *R v Roberts*, 2022 ABKB 748 at para 13 [*Roberts* 2022].

voluntariness analysis of the common law confessions rule, if a person has not been told of their right to silence, that is "*prima facie* evidence that they were unfairly denied their choice to speak to the police," and the Crown would have the burden of rebutting that presumption.[170] However, such a failure has no consequence for section 10 purposes.

We will see below that implementational duties arise only if the detainee has first expressed a desire to exercise the right to counsel. That is not true of the informational duties, however, which arise in all cases. Rather than try to determine whether the detainee might be interested in contacting duty counsel or whether they would qualify for legal aid, the Court has directed that police should simply inform all detainees of all of this information:

> [B]ecause the purpose of the right to counsel under s. 10(*b*) is about providing detainees with meaningful choices, it follows that a detainee should be fully advised of available services *before* being expected to assert that right, particularly given that subsequent duties on the state are not triggered unless and until a detainee expresses a desire to contact counsel. In my opinion, the purpose of the right to counsel would be defeated if police were only required to advise detainees of the existence and availability of Legal Aid and duty counsel *after* some triggering assertion of the right by the detainee.[171]

In *Latimer*, the Court explained:

> The informational component of s. 10(b) is of critical importance because its purpose is to enable a detainee to make an informed decision about whether to exercise the right to counsel, and to exercise other rights protected by the *Charter*, such as the right to silence. In *R. v. Brydges*, [1990] 1 S.C.R. 190, this Court engrafted two requirements upon the informational component: first, information about access to counsel free of charge provided by provincial Legal Aid where an accused meets financial criteria with respect to need, and second, information about access to duty counsel, who provide immediate and temporary legal advice to all accused, irrespective of financial need.[172]

However, although the police must *inform* all detainees of the right to counsel, that is not the same thing as imposing an obligation on the police to make sure that an accused *understands* the right to counsel. The Court held in *Bartle* that

170 *Tessier*, above note 41 at para 9.

171 *Bartle*, above note 168 at para 21 [emphasis in original].

172 *Latimer*, above note 83 at paras 33–34.

> absent special circumstances indicating that a detainee may not understand the s. 10(b) caution, such as language difficulties or a known or obvious mental disability, police are not required to assure themselves that a detainee fully understands the s. 10(b) caution.[173]

The majority did also say that

> [i]f the circumstances reveal, however, that a particular detainee does not understand the standard caution, the authorities must take additional steps to ensure that the detainee comprehends the rights guaranteed by s. 10(b), and the means by which they can be exercised.[174]

In *Evans*, for example, the accused had a mental deficiency bordering on mental retardation, and since the police were aware of his mental incapacity, they were required to take "special care" in the circumstances.[175] The Court held:

> I am satisfied that the police did not comply with s. 10(b). It is true that they informed the appellant of his right to counsel. But they did not explain that right when he indicated that he did not understand it. A person who does not understand his or her right cannot be expected to assert it. The purpose of s. 10(b) is to require the police to communicate the right to counsel to the detainee. In most cases one can infer from the circumstances that the accused understands what he has been told. In such cases, the police are required to go no further (unless the detainee indicates a desire to retain counsel, in which case they must comply with the second and third duties set out above). But where, as here, there is a positive indication that the accused does not understand his right to counsel, the police cannot rely on their mechanical recitation of the right to the accused; they must take steps to facilitate that understanding.[176]

---

173 *Bartle*, above note 168 at para 19.

174 *Ibid* at para 39.

175 *Evans*, above note 71 at 890. In *Latimer*, above note 83 at para 38, the Court also said:

> I hasten to add that there will be cases in which it will be necessary to provide more information to an accused or detained person than was provided to Mr. Latimer about the means to access duty counsel. For example, a young person, or even more obviously an individual who is visually impaired, may require more assistance from the police than Mr. Latimer. As well, someone whose facility in the language of the jurisdiction is not sufficient to understand the information provided about duty counsel may require more explicit information than was provided to Mr. Latimer. This list of examples should not be taken to be exhaustive.

176 *Evans*, above note 71 at 891.

On the other hand, in *R v Whittle*, a case in which the accused was mentally ill, the Court found section 10(b) to have been satisfied since the accused was fit to stand trial:

> In exercising the right to counsel or waiving the right, the accused must possess the limited cognitive capacity that is required for fitness to stand trial. The accused must be capable of communicating with counsel to instruct counsel, and understand the function of counsel and that he or she can dispense with counsel even if this is not in the accused's best interests. It is not necessary that the accused possess analytical ability. The level of cognitive ability is the same as that required with respect to the confession rule and the right to silence. The accused must have the mental capacity of an operating mind as outlined above.[177]

Related to this, police must not actively cause confusion about the meaning of an accused's right to counsel. In *R v Burlingham*, the Court found that the police had undermined the accused's understanding by belittling his counsel. This resulted in him, when offered a plea bargain, accepting the advice of a "random lawyer"[178] instead of that of his own lawyer, who knew the facts of the case but was unavailable on the weekend. The Court held that this did not amount to compliance with section 10(b):

> 10(b) specifically prohibits the police, as they did in this case, from belittling an accused's lawyer with the express goal or effect of undermining the accused's confidence in and relationship with defence counsel. It makes no sense for s. 10(b) of the *Charter* to provide for the right to retain and instruct counsel if law enforcement authorities are able to undermine either an accused's confidence in his or her lawyer or the solicitor-client relationship.[179]

The Court elaborated on this issue of undermining legal advice in *R v Dussault*. In that case, the accused's lawyer had told the interrogating officer that he was coming to the police station in order to provide advice to the accused in person since he did not seem to understand what he was being told over the phone. The police did not allow the lawyer to see the accused when he arrived, on the basis that the phone call constituted compliance with section 10(b). They also misled the accused by saying, in response to one of his several inquiries about his lawyer's arrival, that the lawyer "isn't at the front of the station."[180] While strictly true, this ignored the fact that the lawyer had come to the station and waited for

---

177 *R v Whittle*, [1994] 2 SCR 914 at para 51.

178 *R v Burlingham*, [1995] 2 SCR 206 at para 16 [*Burlingham*].

179 *Ibid* at para 14.

180 *Dussault*, above note 162 at para 49.

more than two hours, and upon leaving had left a note indicating his willingness to return. The Court found this to satisfy the *Sinclair/Burlingham* exception of "undermining legal advice."

In reaching that conclusion, they noted that *Sinclair* had talked about undermining legal advice, while *Burlingham* had spoken of undermining confidence in counsel, but they concluded that these two things can "produce the same effect."[181] They also held that undermining counsel was not limited to intentional belittling of the sort in *Burlingham* since an accused's confidence in the advice could be undermined even without that. Furthermore, it does not matter whether the police intended to undermine the legal advice; it is only a question of whether the *effect* of their behaviour was to do so. The Court concluded:

> Simply put, the purpose of s. 10(b) is to provide the detainee with an opportunity to obtain legal advice relevant to their legal situation. As noted earlier, the legal advice is intended to ensure that "the detainee's decision to cooperate with the investigation or decline to do so is free and informed." The legal advice received by a detainee can fulfill this function only if the detainee regards it as legally correct and trustworthy.[182]

See the further discussion of *Dussault* and the issue of undermining legal advice below in Section C(3)(d), below, discussing additional consultations with counsel.

Note that the standard warning quoted above refers to the accused being allowed to contact "any lawyer you wish." On the implementational side, the accused has a right to counsel of choice, subject to some limitations: see the discussion in Section C(3)(d), below. On the informational side, it has been held that the caution does not need to *specify* that the accused has the right to choose counsel.[183] It has also been suggested that the informational component should contain information about the right to consult counsel in private, although that point is not settled.[184] The issue of privacy in the actual implementation of the right to counsel is discussed further in Section C(3)(c), below.

---

181 *Ibid* at para 38.

182 *Ibid* at para 45.

183 See *R v Grouse*, 2004 NSCA 108 at paras 22–23.

184 The current state of the law is well captured in *R v Notay*, 2021 ABQB 706 at para 137:

> The applicable cases have recommended, but stopped short of requiring, police officers to expressly advise a detainee that his right to consult with counsel includes a right to do so in private. The prevailing view is that a failure to advise the accused of their right to instruct counsel in private does not, in and of itself, amount to a breach of s. 10(b) (*R v Rudolph* (1986), 32 CCC (3d) 179 (Alta QB) at pp. 182-84 (Alta. Q.B.); *R v Haudegand* (1989), 77

The *Youth Criminal Justice Act* contains a special provision on the right to counsel that specifies obligations relating to informing an accused young person of the right to counsel and provides the right to have a parent or guardian present. In addition, the section requires a written waiver of the rights it details.[185]

Finally, a valid waiver of the informational components of section 10(b) will be a rarity. Waiver of implementational duties will be discussed below and is a difficult area. However, the Court has concluded that waiver will arise with regard to informational duties only in exceptional circumstances. The reason for this is quite straightforward. A valid waiver depends on the accused having been fully informed of the nature of the right they are waiving.[186] Only in unusual circumstances would an accused be fully informed of the content of the right without having been told of the informational components. This could happen, however—for example, when it becomes necessary to rewarn an accused in the middle of an interrogation because the nature of the jeopardy has changed. In such cases, it might be safe not to mention again the telephone number for duty counsel, for instance.

Because a waiver is meant to be rare, police might have an additional informational obligation if the detainee attempts to waive the right to counsel. As has been noted, where a detainee has asserted the right to counsel, implementational duties (discussed in the next section) arise. Where a detainee has asserted the right to counsel but then later decides not to exercise it, police have an obligation to inform the detainee of these implementational duties; this is referred to as a "*Prosper* warning," which is discussed at greater length below.[187] The Court has explained:

> Thus, when a detainee, diligent but unsuccessful in contacting counsel, changes his or her mind and decides not to pursue contact with a lawyer, s. 10(*b*) mandates that the police explicitly inform the detainee of his or her right to a reasonable opportunity to contact counsel and of the police obligation to hold off in their questioning until then. This additional informational obligation, referred to in this appeal as the

---

Sask R 280 (QB) at pp. 280-82). However, in *R v Jackson* (1993), 15 OR (3d) 709 (CA), Goodman J.A. held that the police may be required to provide such advice in certain circumstances.

See also *R v Parrill* (1998), 169 Nfld & PEIR 28 (Nfld CA) [*Parrill*], and *DMR*, above note 130, holding at para 53 that the failure to mention privacy is not a violation of s 10(b).

185 *Youth Criminal Justice Act*, SC 2002, c 1, s 146. See, generally, *R v LTH*, 2008 SCC 49.

186 *Bartle*, above note 168.

187 *R v Prosper* (1994), 92 CCC (3d) 353 (SCC) [*Prosper*]. See Section C(3)(g), below in this chapter.

> duty to give a "*Prosper* warning," is warranted in such circumstances so as to ensure that a detainee is informed that their unsuccessful attempts to reach counsel did not exhaust the s. 10(*b*) right, to ensure that any choice to speak with the police does not derive from such a misconception, and to ensure that a decision to waive the right to counsel is fully informed.[188]

However, no similar duty arises when an accused has initially indicated a desire to speak to counsel of their choice and then later decides to speak to duty counsel instead.[189]

c) Implementational Duties

As already noted, when an accused asserts the right to counsel, two correlative duties arise for the police: to facilitate that contact and to hold off from attempting to elicit evidence from the accused until a reasonable opportunity has been provided. These obligations were established at a very early stage, when the Court ruled in *R v Manninen* in 1987 that

> 10(b) imposes at least two duties on the police in addition to the duty to inform the detainee of his rights. First, the police must provide the detainee with a reasonable opportunity to exercise the right to retain and instruct counsel without delay. The detainee is in the control of the police and he cannot exercise his right to counsel unless the police provide him with a reasonable opportunity to do so. This aspect of the right to counsel was recognized in Canadian law well before the advent of the *Charter*.[190]

The Court then noted the second implementational duty:

> Further, s. 10(b) imposes on the police the duty to cease questioning or otherwise attempting to elicit evidence from the detainee until he has had a reasonable opportunity to retain and instruct counsel. The purpose of the right to counsel is to allow the detainee not only to be informed of his rights and obligations under the law but, equally if not more important, to obtain advice as to how to exercise those rights. In this case, the police officers correctly informed the respondent of his right to remain silent and the main function of counsel would be to confirm the existence of that right and then to advise him as to how to exercise it. For the right to counsel to be effective, the detainee must

---

188 *Willier*, above note 161 at para 32.

189 *Ibid* at paras 38–39.

190 *R v Manninen*, [1987] 1 SCR 1233 at 1241 [*Manninen*].

> have access to this advice before he is questioned or otherwise required to provide evidence.[191]

The Court emphasized that the police had an obligation to "facilitate" contact with counsel where the desire to contact counsel is asserted by the detainee.[192]

An important point to note here is that these correlative implementational duties arise only where the accused expresses an interest in having counsel. All the informational duties arise automatically and for all accused, whether or not that person expresses an interest in counsel. In contrast, the duties to facilitate contact with counsel and to hold off from eliciting evidence do not arise unless they are triggered by the accused requesting counsel.

The "request" might be perfectly explicit. Manninen, for example, very specifically said, "I ain't saying anything until I see my lawyer. I want to see my lawyer."[193] However, a less straightforward expression of interest in counsel might also be sufficient. Brydges, for example, upon being told of the right to counsel, said, "Well. Do they have any free Legal Aid or anything like that up here. . . . Won't be able to afford anyone, hey? That's the main thing."[194] The Supreme Court upheld the trial judge's finding that this response amounted to a request for counsel and therefore triggered the correlative duties.

However, even if the request can be implicit, there must be some sort of assertion of the right by the accused, or the implementational duties do not arise. As the Supreme Court concluded in *R v Baig*:

> [O]nce the police have complied with s. 10(*b*), by advising the accused without delay of his right to counsel without delay, there are no correlative duties triggered and cast upon them until the accused, if he so chooses, has indicated his desire to exercise his right to counsel.[195]

The Court there also noted that "absent proof of circumstances indicating that the accused did not understand his right to retain counsel when he was informed of it, the onus has to be on him to prove that he

191 *Ibid* at 1242–43. The obligation to not "elicit" evidence was discussed in the context of the s 7 right of silence in *R v Broyles*, [1991] 3 SCR 595 at paras 31–34 [*Broyles*].

192 This requirement was stressed in the pre-*Charter* judgment in *R v Brownridge*, [1972] SCR 926, where Laskin J, as he then was, in a minority concurring judgment, spoke of a "correlative obligation" upon the police to facilitate contact with counsel.

193 *Manninen*, above note 190 at 1241.

194 *Brydges*, above note 167 at 195.

195 *R v Baig*, [1987] 2 SCR 537 at 540.

asked for the right but it was denied or he was denied any opportunity to even ask for it."[196]

The current state of the law leaves both factual and legal ambiguity.

As a matter of fact, sometimes it is difficult to state authoritatively whether or not a detainee has requested counsel. For example, in *R v Culotta*, the accused was asked whether she wished to call a lawyer and replied, "No, my parents should be here soon. We have a family lawyer."[197] In the Ontario Court of Appeal, the majority of two judges took that to be declining counsel, while the dissenting judge (who said the question the accused was asked was whether she wanted to speak to a lawyer "now") held that her reply could reasonably be understood to be a request to speak to her family lawyer. On appeal, the Supreme Court split, three judges siding with the Court of Appeal majority and two with the dissent.[198]

Although the Supreme Court has given no direct guidance about such situations, there are relevant lower court decisions. In *R v Small*, for example, the accused had an ambiguous conversation with the officer who cautioned him, and the Alberta Court of Appeal concluded that because of the ambiguity, "the police officer was obliged to pursue the issue further and to either obtain a clear and unequivocal waiver or afford the Appellant a reasonable opportunity to exercise his right to counsel."[199] Other courts have followed this reasoning, but it has not been universally adopted.[200] This is an area where guidance from the Supreme Court would be useful.

Legally, a single factual situation could potentially be covered by two different rules that could lead to different results. One rule is that an accused must assert the right to counsel: if a detainee gives an unclear response after being cautioned, a court might therefore say the right was

---

196 *Ibid*, adopting the statement from *R v Anderson* (1984), 10 CCC (3d) 417 (Ont CA).

197 *R v Culotta*, 2018 ONCA 665 at para 8.

198 *R v Culotta*, 2018 SCC 57.

199 *R v Small*, 1998 ABCA 85 at para 34.

200 Lower courts in Alberta have followed this approach: see, for example, *R v Nixon*, 2006 ABPC 194; *R v Kehoe*, 2010 ABPC 255; or *R v Gendron*, 2017 ABPC 63. It has also been followed in other provinces: see, for example, *R v Seehra*, 2009 BCPC 194 at para 10: "Where a detainee's response to the question is ambiguous, the peace officer must either provide the person with the opportunity to call counsel . . . or the officer must ask further questions of the person to determine whether he wishes to contact counsel." The Ontario Court of Appeal in *R v JWC*, 2011 ONCA 550, was presented with the argument that an ambiguous reply from a detainee imposes a duty on police to clear up the ambiguity (at para 21), but their analysis instead focuses on whether the detainee understood his right to counsel, which is a different question.

not asserted. However, the standard for finding a waiver of the right to counsel is very high: in the face of an unclear response, a court might say that there was no clear waiver.[201] Ambiguous statements such as "we have a family lawyer" have been taken *not* to be an assertion of the right, while an arrestee explicitly refusing to call counsel because there would be "no point" has been found not to be a valid waiver.[202] Depending on whether a court applies the "assertion" rule or the "waiver" rule, therefore, a different result might flow from the same set of facts..

The Supreme Court has not addressed this issue, although lower courts have. For example, in *R v Owens*, the accused replied "no, not right now" when asked if he wanted to contact counsel and in the end never did. The trial judge found no section 10(b) violation, but the summary conviction appeal court judge found that there was no unequivocal waiver of the right. The Ontario Court of Appeal, however, held that the first question was whether the accused had ever *asserted* the right to counsel, and it was open to the trial judge to find that the accused's ambiguous reply was not an assertion of the right.[203] One could well argue that the police should be obliged to ask *all* detainees whether they want to exercise the right as a part of the standard caution. However, the Supreme Court has not looked at the issue in this way but rather has suggested that only where the accused asserts their right to counsel (with or without being asked) do the implementational duties arise.[204]

The first correlative duty is to facilitate access with counsel, and this must be done at "the first reasonably available opportunity" or "as soon as practicable."[205] The Court explained in *Taylor*:

> The duty to inform a detained person of his or her right to counsel arises "immediately" upon arrest or detention (*Suberu*, at paras. 41–42), and the duty to facilitate access to a lawyer, in turn, arises immediately upon the detainee's request to speak to counsel. The arresting officer is therefore under a constitutional obligation to facilitate the requested access to a lawyer at the first reasonably available opportunity. The

201 See, for example, *R v Liddel*, [2008] BCPC 143, or *R v King*, [2009] BCPC 26.

202 See, respectively, *Brydges*, above note 167, and *Clarkson v The Queen*, [1986] 1 SCR 383 [*Clarkson*], discussed below in Section C(3)(g).

203 *R v Owens*, 2015 ONCA 652. See Tim Quigley, "*R v Owens*: Annotation" (2015) 23 *Criminal Reports* (7th) 266, arguing that not everyone is likely to know that additional rights flow from an initial assertion of a desire to speak to counsel and suggesting that removing the requirement for asserting the right would be more in keeping with the purpose of s 10(b).

204 See, generally, Steve Coughlan, "When Silence Isn't Golden: Waiver and the Right to Counsel" (1991) 33 *Criminal Law Quarterly* 43.

205 *Nguyen* 2016, above note 128 at para 61.

> burden is on the Crown to show that a given delay was reasonable in the circumstances (*R. v. Luong* (2000), 271 A.R. 368 (Alta. C.A.), at para. 12). Whether a delay in facilitating access to counsel is reasonable is a factual inquiry.[206]

The rationale for such an immediate right was also set out in *Taylor*: "[T]o reduce the possibility of accidental self-incrimination and to refrain from eliciting evidence from the individual before access to counsel has been facilitated."[207]

Although the rule is that the accused must be allowed to contact counsel immediately, the caselaw has recognized that in exceptional circumstances, contact might not occur immediately. Where there are concerns over the destruction of evidence, public or police safety, or some other urgent or dangerous circumstance, access to counsel might be delayed. However, "[g]eneral or theoretical concern for officer safety and destruction of evidence will not justify a suspension of the right to counsel . . . . Rather, the assessment of whether a delay or suspension of the right to counsel is justified involves a fact specific contextual determination."[208] This means that the police cannot rely on a general policy but "must actually turn their mind to the specific circumstances of the case."[209] If such justifications exist, however, then the delay in allowing access does not violate the *Charter*.

For example, in *R v Montgomery*, the accused was arrested in a parking lot on drug-trafficking charges but was not permitted to call counsel until several hours later at the police station, although he had a cellphone with him and could have called immediately. The British Columbia Court of Appeal upheld the decision that there had been no violation of section 10(b):

> The police considered the arrest to be one of high risk. The appellant was believed to be associated with an organization that used violence. It would have been difficult for the police to ensure that the call was not used for an improper purpose and to provide the appellant with privacy at the scene of his arrest while ensuring that he was secure.[210]

---

206 *Taylor*, above note 130 at para 24.

207 *Ibid* at para 28.

208 *R v La*, 2018 ONCA 830 at para 39 [citations omitted]. See also *R c Tremblay*, 2021 QCCA 24 [*Tremblay* QCCA], and *R v Shang En Wu*, 2017 ONSC 1003, a very thorough lower court decision frequently cited in these discussions. See as well *Freddi c R*, 2021 QCCA 249 [*Freddi*], handed down on the same day as *Tremblay* QCCA.

209 *R v Rover*, 2018 ONCA 745, at para 33 [*Rover*].

210 *R v Montgomery*, 2009 BCCA 41 at para 35.

Similarly, in *R v Ashby*, the accused was not allowed to make a call from the roadside. She had been arrested on drug trafficking charges, and the police were aware that backup vehicles sometimes accompanied couriers, so there were safety concerns.[211] On the other hand, in *R v Tremblay*, the suggestions that an accused might ingest something that could affect a breath test or that officers would have to wait on the side of the road to monitor her were found only to be general or theoretical concerns that did not justify delay.[212]

Independent of whether a delay itself is justified, it has also been suggested that the failure to inform an accused of the reasons for the delay or to advise the accused when they might be allowed to speak to counsel might also violate section 10(b), but this point has not yet been determined.[213]

One context in which delay in providing access to counsel has often arisen has been where a person has been arrested and a search is associated with the arrest. The same case-specific circumstances analysis must be undertaken in this situation: "concerns of a general or non-specific nature applicable to virtually any search cannot justify delaying access to counsel."[214] As a generalization, courts have tended to be more sympathetic to allowing access to counsel to be delayed while an existing search is completed but less sympathetic to allowing delay while a search warrant is obtained. Even when such delay is allowed, however, police "must take reasonable steps to minimize the delay in granting access to counsel."[215] Indeed, courts have pointed out that the better practice might be for police to obtain a search warrant before carrying out an arrest:

> [I]f the police determine that some delay in allowing an arrested person to speak to counsel is justified to permit execution of the warrant, then they must consider whether it is necessary to arrest the individual before they execute the warrant. The police cannot create a justification for delaying access to counsel by choosing, for reasons of convenience or efficiency, to arrest an individual before seeking, obtaining and executing a search warrant. Police efficiency and convenience cannot justify delaying an arrested person's right to speak with counsel for several hours.[216]

---

211 *R v Ashby*, 2013 BCCA 334.

212 *Tremblay* QCCA, above note 208.

213 *R v Griffith*, 2021 ONCA 302 at footnote 1 in the decision [*Griffith*].

214 *R v Russell*, 2020 ABCA 90 at para 19. See also *R v Badu*, 2022 ABCA 267.

215 *Griffith*, above note 213 at para 38 [citations omitted]. See also *R v Pino*, 2016 ONCA 389, and *R v Patterson*, 2006 BCCA 24, suggesting that in such cases the search should be expedited.

216 *Rover*, above note 209 at para 33. To similar effect, see *R c Archambault*, 2012 QCCA 20 at para 40, quoting the trial judge to the effect that the police were

Where the detainee deliberately obstructs the police or makes the investigation difficult, a court might find the accused to have not been reasonably diligent in attempting to contact counsel and, in any event, is unlikely to grant a section 24(2) remedy.[217] A detainee could potentially attempt to contact someone else in order to get help in obtaining counsel, but in that event the detainee would have to make clear to the police that that was the purpose of the contact.[218]

This "immediately" question asks, in effect, about the first reasonably available opportunity for an accused to have a private conversation by telephone with counsel. When the Court began to articulate these rules, telephone access was limited to landlines, so often consultation with counsel could not occur until the detainee had been taken to a police station. This was not necessarily true even then,[219] and of course with the ubiquity of cellphones, the limiting factor now is more likely to be privacy than it is the technical capacity to make the call: see the discussion of privacy below at Section C(3)(h).

In *Taylor* itself, the accused had been arrested at the roadside for impaired driving causing bodily harm and had indicated that he wanted to contact counsel. He was initially taken to the hospital rather than back to the police station; he seemed unharmed, but a paramedic prevailed upon him to be checked out. As it transpired, evidence against him was gathered at the hospital, but the police made no efforts while there to allow him to reach counsel. In finding that this violated the accused's section 10(b) rights, the Court noted that

> Mr. Taylor could have been given the opportunity to speak to counsel at the hospital if Cst. MacGillivray had remembered to do so. He made no mention of any practical obstacles to access, such as a medical

---

"caught in a tactical disadvantage created solely by their own decision to arrest the accused. That does not create or imply exceptional circumstances that could justify an exception to the duties imposed upon police officers by the Constitution."

217 See *R v Tremblay*, [1987] 2 SCR 435 [*Tremblay*]. See the discussion of reasonable diligence in Section C(3)(f), below in this chapter.

218 *R v KWJ*, 2012 NWTCA 3. See, for example, *Lafrance*, above note 30, where the accused asked to speak to his father since that was his only chance of getting a lawyer. It was agreed that this amounted to a request for counsel.

219 See, for example, *Manninen*, above note 190 at para 22, where the accused was arrested at a simonizing establishment and questioned for some period; the Court noted that the accused could have used the telephone there. See also *R v Dombrowski* (1985), 44 CR (3d) 1 at 9 (Sask CA): "In this case, the arresting officers had no right to limit the appellant's opportunity to contact counsel until they returned to the detachment office. With the availability of a telephone at the business premises of Co-op Implements, there was no justification for limiting or delaying the opportunity."

> emergency, the absence of a phone, or even problems in providing sufficient privacy to Mr. Taylor.
>
> There is, in fact, virtually no evidence about what logistical or medical barriers stood between Mr. Taylor and a phone call to his lawyer.[220]

The officer had no obligation to offer his own phone, but nonetheless some effort had to be made to facilitate contact with counsel.

Two final points should be made regarding the first correlative duty. First, the discussion here has focused on when the detainee can *begin* trying to contact counsel. However, a further aspect of a "reasonable opportunity" looks at how long a detainee can *continue* to try to reach counsel, which relates to whether or not the accused is entitled to counsel of choice. See the further discussion of this issue in Section C(2)(e), below in this chapter.

Second, a particular issue arises in the context of the right to counsel and investigative detentions. Where actual contact with counsel is to occur, practicalities might mean that this will take a bit of time. However, the power of investigative detention only authorizes a brief detention. The result is that the theoretical time limit for investigatively detaining the accused might have expired before contact with counsel could occur. In *Suberu*, the Court rejected the notion that this meant that there could be some delay in providing the right to counsel in investigative detention cases, instead reaffirming that the right arises "immediately."[221] However, also in *Suberu*, the Court avoided the question of whether there was a *Charter* violation from the failure to inform in that case by finding that the accused had not been detained. This particular problem point therefore lingers. The Ontario Court of Appeal, however, has observed in *obiter*:

> It may be that, if a police officer can afford a detained person an opportunity to exercise his s. 10(b) rights only by significantly prolonging an investigative detention, the police officer must release the detained person rather than breach s. 9 of the Charter. I leave that question for another case.[222]

We turn now to the second correlative duty, the obligation to hold off from eliciting evidence.

In *Manninen* itself, the police questioned the accused despite him having asserted the right to counsel. In finding the section 10(b) violation, the Court noted that "where a detainee has positively asserted his

---

220 *Taylor*, above note 130 at paras 29–30.

221 *Suberu*, above note 31 at para 41.

222 *R v McGuffie*, 2016 ONCA 365 at para 47.

desire to exercise his right to counsel and the police have ignored his request and have proceeded to question him, he is likely to feel that his right has no effect and that he must answer."[223] The obligation to hold off extends beyond asking questions, however. For example, in *R v Ross*, the accused should not have been asked to take part in a lineup.[224] In *R v Prosper*, the accused should not have been required to take a Breathalyzer test.[225] In *R v Bagherli*, an accused, having asserted the right to counsel, was directly asked, "Will you provide samples of your breath?" and he declined, leading him to be charged with refusal; this too was found to be a violation of section 10(b).[226] In *R v GTD*, the standard caution used by the police to inform an accused of their right to silence concluded with "do you wish to say anything," and this too was a violation of the duty to hold off.[227]

Where the obligation to "hold off" from eliciting evidence does arise, it generally takes priority over the investigative needs of the police. In *Prosper*, the accused was arrested on a weekend for impaired driving and asserted the right to counsel, but due to unusual circumstances at the time, no legal aid lawyer would be available until regular office hours. Although waiting until that time would mean that the police would be unable to administer a Breathalyzer test within the required time, this was "simply one of the prices which has to be paid by governments which refuse to ensure that a system of '*Brydges* duty counsel' is available to give detainees free, preliminary legal advice on an on-call, 24-hour basis."[228]

d) Additional Opportunity to Contact Counsel

In *Sinclair*, the Court held that "we take the settled view to the effect that the right to counsel is essentially a one-time matter with few recognized exceptions."[229] As a general proposition, that means that a detainee must be given a reasonable opportunity to consult with counsel; however, once that initial consultation has occurred, even if it is very brief, section 10(b) has been satisfied. This had tended to be the practice since the inception of the right, but the approach was authoritatively confirmed with the "right to counsel trilogy" in 2010.[230] Until recently, one would have said that this parsimonious approach to the right was firmly

223 *Manninen*, above note 190 at para 25.
224 *R v Ross*, [1989] 1 SCR 3 [*Ross*].
225 *Prosper*, above note 187.
226 *R v Bagherli*, 2014 MBCA 105.
227 *R v GTD*, 2018 SCC 7.
228 *Prosper*, above note 187 at para 45.
229 *Sinclair*, above note 160 at para 64.
230 *Ibid*; see also *McCrimmon*, above note 164 at para 22, and *Willier*, above note 161.

entrenched, but the 5:4 majority decision in *Lafrance* in 2022 might herald a more welcoming approach to additional consultations. We will first consider the right to counsel trilogy and the rules it laid out and then at the end consider whether *Lafrance* has changed any of that.

In essence, the right to counsel trilogy resulted from an unsuccessful attempt by defence counsel to expand the protection given by section 10(b). That attempt was sparked in response to two other decisions by the Court, *R v Oickle*[231] and *R v Singh*.[232] It is not necessary to go into either of those cases at length to understand the general role they played: *Oickle* limited the protection offered by the confessions rule to a person being interrogated, while *Singh* limited the protection offered to that same person by the right to silence. Justice Binnie, dissenting in *Sinclair*, described these two cases as "trump cards" given to the police in their "endurance contest with the detainee."[233] Because the accused had been left with very few resources to draw on when being interrogated, defence counsel argued for what amounted to a change in the law: that section 10(b) should be seen as guaranteeing the assistance of counsel during an interrogation.

The majority, in a very divided Court, rejected this position. No lower courts had held that section 10(b) included such a right. The language of the section ("to retain and instruct counsel") did not imply counsel's presence during an interrogation. The purpose of the section—to inform the detainee of their rights and provide the detainee with an opportunity to get legal advice on how to exercise them—did not require the presence of counsel during an interrogation. Finally, although other countries had adopted such a rule, that was not a persuasive reason for Canada to do so. Thus, the majority of the Court concluded that, as a general proposition, an accused was entitled to an initial opportunity to consult with counsel on arrest or detention but was guaranteed nothing more.

This will be true even if that initial consultation with counsel was brief. In *Sinclair*, the accused (charged with murder) had only two

---

231 2000 SCC 38 [*Oickle*].

232 2007 SCC 48 [*Singh*].

233 *Sinclair*, above note 160 at para 92:

> [I]n their endurance contest with the detainee, the police are now given three trump cards. The first is *Oickle* itself, which sets a substantial hurdle to making inadmissible a confession on the basis of involuntariness. The second is *R. v Singh*, 2007 SCC 48, [2007] 3 SCR 405, which allows the police to prolong the endurance contest despite repeated assertions of the right to silence by the detainee and the frequently expressed desire to return to his cell.

Justice Binnie concluded that the decision in *Sinclair* itself was the third trump card.

three-minute telephone conversations with counsel; *McCrimmon* had one five-minute conversation; *Willier* (also charged with murder) had a three-minute conversation and a one-minute telephone conversation. Nonetheless, in each case, the accused was found to have had what section 10(b) guaranteed them: a reasonable opportunity to contact counsel. The Court has found that the length of time the accused spends consulting is not, itself, a relevant consideration. The real issue is the adequacy of the advice but no duty to monitor that could be imposed on the police.[234] As a result, "unless a detainee indicates, diligently and reasonably, that the advice he or she received is inadequate, the police may assume that the detainee is satisfied with the exercised right to counsel and are entitled to commence an investigative interview."[235]

The majority rejected proposals that would have allowed a detainee an additional consultation with counsel on any relatively unrestricted basis. However, they did not exclude completely the possibility of additional consultations. They held that that right would only arise if there were a change in circumstances: "What is required is a change in circumstances that suggests that the choice faced by the accused has been

---

234 The Court held in *Willier*, above note 161 at para 41, that

> [w]hile s. 10(*b*) requires the police to afford a detainee a reasonable opportunity to contact counsel and to facilitate that contact, it does not require them to monitor the quality of the advice once contact is made. The solicitor-client relationship is one of confidence, premised upon privileged communication. Respect for the integrity of this relationship makes it untenable for the police to be responsible, as arbiters, for monitoring the quality of legal advice received by a detainee. To impose such a duty on the police would be incompatible with the privileged nature of the relationship. The police cannot be required to mandate a particular qualitative standard of advice, nor are they entitled to inquire into the content of the advice provided. Further, even if such a duty were warranted, the applicable standard of adequacy is unclear. As this Court recognized in *R. v G.D.B.*, 2000 SCC 22, [2000] 1 S.C.R. 520, at para. 27, there is a "wide range of reasonable professional assistance," and as such what is considered reasonable, sufficient, or adequate advice is ill-defined and highly variable.

235 *Ibid* at para 42. To similar effect, see *R v Edmonton*, 2014 ABCA 186. See also *R v Beauregard*, 2016 ABCA 37, where an officer asked the accused whether he was "done" as opposed to whether he had contacted a lawyer. The police were entitled to accept at face value his claim that he was even though in fact he had only spoken to his mother. However, see also *R v Badgerow*, 2008 ONCA 605 at para 46, where the Ontario Court of Appeal held that although the police "cannot be expected to be mind readers," nonetheless, "they are not entitled to ignore statements by an accused that raise a reasonable prospect that the accused has not exercised his or her s. 10(b) rights. Rather, where an accused makes such a statement, the police must be diligent in ensuring that an accused has a reasonable opportunity to exercise his or her rights, and may not rely on answers to ambiguous questions as a basis for assuming that an accused has exercised his or her rights."

significantly altered, requiring further advice on the new situation, in order to fulfill the purpose of s. 10(*b*) of providing the accused with legal advice relevant to the choice of whether to cooperate with the police investigation or not."[236] In *Sinclair*, the Court suggested three examples of such situations: where the detainee was invited to take part in a non-routine procedure that was not likely to have been anticipated during the initial consultation; where the nature of the detainee's jeopardy changed during the detention; or where there was reason to think the detainee did not understand the right to counsel. In theory, that was not a closed list of potential changed circumstances, although in practice, it has tended to operate as one.[237] Failing one of those circumstances, or in principle some other similar changed circumstance, the accused is only entitled to one opportunity to consult with counsel.[238] We will discuss each of those in turn.

First, an accused will be entitled to a new consultation with counsel when a non-routine procedure, such as a lineup or a polygraph, is proposed. Because that procedure will not have been in the contemplation of counsel when the initial advice was given, a further opportunity for advice is necessary to serve the purpose of providing counsel.[239] It is not necessary that the procedure actually be performed; the fact that the accused is asked to consent to it is sufficient.[240] Whether a procedure qualifies as "non-routine," of course, is a matter of judgment. A DNA test has been found to be non-routine.[241] So has asking an arrestee for the password to their cellphone.[242] However, both asking an accused to take part in a re-enactment of the crime and recording the accused's voice in order to compare it to a wiretap have been found to be functionally no different from simply taking a statement and therefore not to be non-routine.[243] A

236 *Sinclair*, above note 160 at para 65.

237 *Ibid* at para 49. See *R v Tahmasebi*, 2020 ONCA 47, as an example of one of the relatively few cases considering whether a fourth category should be created.

238 Although there is no general s 10 right to consult with counsel again on request, in *McCrimmon*, above note 164 at para 22, the Court noted (at para 36) that if police continue an interview despite repeated requests from an accused for it to end so that he can speak to counsel, it could, in some cases, raise an issue about the voluntariness of any statement given.

239 *Ibid* at para 50.

240 *R v Briscoe*, 2015 ABCA 2 at para 89.

241 *Ibid*.

242 *R v Boutros*, 2018 ONCA 375 at para 27.

243 See, respectively, *R v Ashmore*, 2011 BCCA 18, and *R v Wu*, 2010 ABCA 337. See also *R v Fogarty*, 2015 NSCA 6 [*Fogarty*], where the accused could contact counsel before submitting to a drug recognition evaluation (DRE). He was later asked to provide a blood sample and argued that this was a new procedure. However, the Court of Appeal concluded that the very purpose of the DRE was to

request for blood samples after a drug recognition evaluation demand has been made is not something unexpected.[244] The Court has also noted that "the common police tactic of gradually revealing (actual or fake) evidence to the detainee in order to demonstrate or exaggerate the strength of the case against him" is not a basis for a renewed caution.[245]

Second, an accused is also entitled to be recautioned if there is a change in jeopardy. For example, in *Evans*,[246] the accused had been arrested on a marijuana charge and taken to the police station for questioning. In fact, the real interest of the police was a murder they believed Evans's brother had committed, and they hoped to elicit information from Evans. When the accused was arrested, he was properly told of the reason—that is, the arrest for marijuana—in accordance with section 10(a). As the interview continued, however, the police began to form the view that Evans himself was likely responsible for the murder. In those circumstances, the Court held that the accused's section 10 rights were retriggered. It stated that when there is a "fundamental and discrete change in the purpose of the investigation, one involving a different and unrelated offence or a significantly more serious offence than that contemplated at the time of the warning," then the police must restate the accused's right to counsel.[247] The rationale for this rewarning was that the nature of the accused's jeopardy had changed, so the accused's initial decision as to whether it was necessary to consult counsel might equally change. So, for example, in *R v Moore*, the Ontario Court of Appeal found the accused entitled to a second consultation with counsel when a charge of assault with a weapon was added to a dangerous driving causing bodily harm charge, even though it was based on the same facts and the offences had the same maximum penalty: "[T]he assault with a weapon charge

---

determine whether to seek a blood sample, so counsel would have had that issue in mind in initially advising the accused.

In contrast, see *R v TGH*, 2014 ONCA 460 at para 40, where police obtained a general warrant, nine months after an arrest, to take photographs of the accused's anus to look for a skin flap. The Ontario Court of Appeal concluded that even if this could be considered a single detention, the accused was entitled to a new consultation with counsel:

> The examination authorized by the general warrant was about as far from a "routine procedure" as one could get. No one would suggest that the appellant's lawyer, when he was advising the appellant at the time of his arrest, could have anticipated an order in the terms of the general warrant and given the appellant the appropriate advice.

244 *Fogarty*, above note 243.

245 *Sinclair*, above note 160 at para 60.

246 *Evans*, above note 71.

247 *Ibid* at 893.

significantly increased the appellant's alleged moral blameworthiness in relation to the charge in that it required proof that he acted intentionally to harm the van driver, rather than simply that his driving constituted a marked departure from the norm. This, in turn, markedly increased the potential penalty that the appellant faced."[248]

Furthermore, an accused is entitled to a new warning if there is reason to question whether the detainee understood their right to counsel. This would arise if something the accused says or does suggests that they do not understand the right or, alternatively, if the police actively undermine the accused's understanding. In *Burlingham*, for example, the police belittled the accused's counsel over the course of a weekend while the accused was in custody, suggesting that he was interested only in money, with the goal of undermining the accused's confidence in and relationship with defence counsel.[249] Since this could nullify the advice the accused received, a new opportunity to consult with counsel arose.[250]

A different instance of retriggering the right to counsel (and one not included in the right to counsel trilogy list of exceptions) is also found in *Burlingham*. The accused had been arrested for murder, had been properly cautioned, and indeed had spoken with counsel. He was held over a weekend and, at a certain point in the interrogation, was offered a plea bargain. The Court held that this constituted the kind of change in jeopardy envisioned in *Evans* and therefore that the accused's section 10(b) right to consult with counsel arose again at that point. Indeed, they held that such an offer of a plea bargain could not be made directly to an accused and must be made to counsel or to the accused with counsel present.[251]

The lesson to take away from the right to counsel trilogy is that section 10(b) only amounts to a right with an impact at the time the accused is detained or arrested, but generally not afterward. Defence counsel in particular must be careful to take this into account by recognizing that a detainee's initial consultation with counsel is also likely to be the only one and therefore to be careful about providing the most complete advice possible.

However, there are signs that courts, particularly the Supreme Court, might be moving toward an attitude that shows more openness toward the notion that an accused should have freer access to an additional consultation with counsel. This can be seen in two recent decisions, *Dussault*[252] and *Lafrance*.[253]

248 *R v Moore*, 2016 ONCA 964 at para 10.

249 *Burlingham*, above note 178.

250 *Sinclair*, above note 160 at para 52.

251 *Burlingham*, above note 178 at para 21.

252 *Dussault*, above note 162.

253 *Lafrance*, above note 30.

In *Dussault*, the accused was arrested for murder and arson and was connected by telephone to a lawyer. That lawyer concluded that Dussault was not understanding the advice he was being given and told the arresting officer, over the phone, that he was coming to the station to complete the consultation in person. In fact, the lawyer was not allowed to speak to Dussault again, despite his arrival and Dussault's queries about where his lawyer was. An interesting argument was that presented by the Quebec Court of Appeal in finding a section 10 violation: they did not see this as an issue of a *second* consultation at all. To assume that *any* initial telephone contact between an arrestee and a lawyer satisfied the requirements of section 10

> would allow police to assert that the right was exhausted if a suspect successfully reached counsel by telephone and the lawyer said little more than that she would come immediately to the station to advise the suspect more fully. The present case is not far removed from that possibility.[254]

For the Quebec Court of Appeal, the *initial* consultation had not taken place, so there was a section 10 violation. The Supreme Court upheld that result but did not address that reasoning; they found it "unnecessary to decide whether the police were entitled to presume that the phone conversation constituted a 'complete' consultation."[255] Instead, the Court unanimously held that this was an instance that fell within the already-established exception from *Sinclair* of undermining the right to counsel. The lawyer had said he would come to the police station and had done so, and the accused had repeatedly asked after the lawyer, but the police gave the accused the impression that his lawyer had never arrived. On that basis, they found a section 10 violation.

Dussault, in the reasoning unanimously adopted, does not show any change in attitude toward how freely counsel should be made available. But the decision in *Lafrance* only a few months later might well do so, and, indeed, a key dispute between the five-judge majority and the four-judge dissent is whether the reasoning adopted departs from that in the right to counsel trilogy.

Lafrance was arrested for murder, had a short conversation by telephone with a legal aid lawyer, and then was interrogated.[256] Several hours into the interview, he asked to speak to his father, indicating that "Legal

254 *Dussault c R*, 2020 QCCA 746 at para 34. The Alberta Court of Appeal in *R v Lafrance*, 2021 ABCA 51, referred approvingly to this approach from *Lafrance*, at para 55.

255 *Dussault*, above note 162 at para 28.

256 The following discussion is drawn from Steve Coughlan, "Is the Right to Counsel a Nuisance?" (2023) 27:1 *Canadian Criminal Law Review* 37.

Aid told him 'to get a lawyer before [he] continue[s] talking' to sit down and talk about his situation."[257]

The dissent would have found that the police had not violated Lafrance's right to counsel. He had been asked whether he understood the advice he had been given and replied that he did, which in their view settled things:

> The fact that a detainee demonstrates hesitancy or concern during an interview or interrogation is not, on its own, sufficient to establish that he or she did not have a full opportunity to consult with counsel. It is assumed that the legal advice received was sufficient in relation to how the detainee should exercise his or her rights in the context of the police investigative interview.[258]

The majority breaks new ground with its decision. It does not do so by purporting to change any rules; the reasoning is presented as simply an application of *Sinclair*. The majority reaches a different conclusion, however, because it adopts a different view of the purpose of the right to counsel. Specifically, the majority makes clear that the mere fact that the arrestee has received advice cannot be taken as determinative:

> The caselaw reveals two general approaches to assessing detainees' understanding of s. 10(b) advice. The first—narrower, relative to the second—tends to focus on the fact of the earlier consultation or, where applicable, on a detainee's assertion of his or her right to silence . . . . The second approach inquires into "the overall context," or "the situation 'on the ground'" . . . that properly inform the reasonable perceptions of police of whether detainees understand their right to silence and how to exercise it . . . *R. v. Hunt*, 2020 ONCJ 627, at para. 51 (CanLII): "In most cases, it can be inferred from the circumstances that the detainee understands what he or she has been told, but where there are circumstances where the detainee may not understand his or her [right to counsel], the police must take steps to facilitate that understanding [*including*] *giving consideration to the detainee's understanding and capacity to understand*."[259]

The majority favours the second approach: the one that looks beyond "the fact of the earlier consultation" to "the situation on the ground."

The disagreement in *Lafrance* is over the purpose of section 10(b). The majority says that the purpose is "to mitigate the imbalance between

---

257 *Lafrance*, above note 30 at para 17. All members of the Court agreed that the request to speak to his father amounted to a renewed request for counsel.

258 *Ibid* at para 176 [citations omitted].

259 *Ibid* at para 74 [emphasis in *Lafrance*; citations omitted].

the individual and the state."[260] The dissent say that that is too ambitious a purpose, and the purpose is merely "to provide [the detainee] *an opportunity* to mitigate [the] legal disadvantage relative to the state," not to actually mitigate it.[261] Both cohorts claim to be following the dictates of the right to counsel trilogy.

On the second (and secondary) issue of whether *Lafrance* is consistent with the right to counsel trilogy, the dissent's argument is probably the stronger:

> The majority suggests that s. 10(b)'s purpose is to mitigate the imbalance between the individual and the state, similar to the purposes of s. 9 (see the majority's reasons, at paras. 76–77). This is not accurate. To the contrary, this Court in *Sinclair* expressly rejected this view, stating at paras. 30–31:
>
> > Mr. Sinclair argues that the purpose of s. 10(*b*) is broader than this. In his view, accepted by our colleagues LeBel and Fish JJ., the purpose of s. 10(*b*) is to advise the detainee on how to deal with police questions. The detainee, it is argued, is in the power of the police. *The purpose of s. 10*(b) *is to restore a power-balance between the detainee and the police in the coercive atmosphere of the police investigation. On this view, the purpose of the right is not so much informational as protective.*
> >
> > *We cannot accept this view of the purpose of s. 10*(b). As will be discussed more fully below, this view of s. 10(*b*) goes against 25 years of jurisprudence defining s. 10(*b*) in terms of the right to consult counsel to obtain information and advice immediately upon detention, but not as providing ongoing legal assistance during the course of the interview that follows, regardless of the circumstances. [Emphasis added.][262]

It is therefore probably more accurate to see *Lafrance* as changing the underlying rules, despite its claims not to do so. The majority ruling, since it looks to whether a second consultation is needed to offset actual imbalance rather than merely asking whether as a matter of fact there was a conversation between the accused and a lawyer, will make it less likely that a single short phone call will always be sufficient. As the majority says:

> The degree of imbalance between police and detainee will of course vary from case to case, depending on the particular circumstances of

260 *Ibid* at paras 78ff and 168ff.

261 *Ibid* at para 169, paraphrasing *Willier* and emphasizing "an opportunity."

262 *Lafrance*, above note 30 at para 168.

> the detainees themselves. Specific characteristics of individual detainees (described as "vulnerabilities" in the context of police interrogation) can influence the course of custodial interviews. Investigating officers and reviewing courts must be alive to the possibility that these vulnerabilities, which may relate to gender, youth, age, race, mental health, language comprehension, cognitive capacity or other considerations, coupled with developments that may occur in the course of police interrogation, will have rendered a detainee's initial legal advice inadequate, impairing his or her ability to make an informed choice about whether to cooperate with the police. In such situations, *Sinclair* requires that an accused is entitled to an additional consultation to even the playing field.[263]

More simply, the long-standing view, which would have been continued by the dissent in *Lafrance*, was that the fact that the detainee had spoken to a lawyer was, by itself, sufficient to exhaust the right to counsel and to mean that some special justification needed to be found for a further consultation. The majority approach makes it possible to find that the right was not exhausted in the first place, despite the conversation with counsel, and therefore makes it more likely that the detainee could obtain further advice.[264]

e) Reasonable Opportunity to Contact Counsel of Choice

It is trite to note that the accused is allowed more than one phone call. Even before the *Charter*, the accused could make as many phone calls as necessary to obtain advice. In *R v Louttit* in 1974, the Manitoba Court of Appeal said: "The 'one phone call' rule is a fiction propagated by Hollywood. Reasonable conduct by the police is always required, and that may in appropriate circumstances require that a plurality of phone calls be permitted."[265] This position was expressly adopted by the Ontario Court of Appeal after the *Charter* in *R v Pavel*.[266]

---

263 *Ibid* at para 79.

264 See, for example, *Roberts* 2022, above note 169, one of the earliest cases to discuss at any length the impact of *Lafrance* and holding at para 76 that "[a] narrow inquiry into whether a detainee was advised of their rights is insufficient to discharge the implementational component of section 10(b); rather, police must be satisfied that the detainee *understood* their legal advice" [emphasis in original]. In that case, it was clear to the police that the accused had cognitive difficulties, and he made statements suggesting that he had misunderstood the legal advice he had been given. The approach taken by police in the face of this, the judge held, amounted to "essentially usurping the role of his lawyer" (at para 145) and meant that his right to counsel had been undermined.

265 *R v Louttit*, [1974] MJ No 76 (CA).

266 (1989), 36 OAC 328 (CA).

The system prefers allowing a detainee to contact counsel of choice, but that is not a constitutional requirement; rather, section 10(b) guarantees a detainee a reasonable *opportunity* to contact counsel of choice. As long as that reasonable opportunity is provided, the *Charter* right has been satisfied, and an accused will eventually be expected to contact some other lawyer. As the Court held in *McCrimmon*:

> If the chosen lawyer is not immediately available, the detainee has the right to refuse to contact another counsel and wait a reasonable amount of time for counsel of choice to become available. Provided the detainee exercises reasonable diligence in the exercise of these rights, the police have a duty to hold off questioning or otherwise attempting to elicit evidence from the detainee until he or she has had the opportunity to consult with counsel of choice. If the chosen lawyer cannot be available within a reasonable period of time, the detainee is expected to exercise his or her right to counsel by calling another lawyer, or the police duty to hold off will be suspended.[267]

The duty to hold off means that police must not attempt to elicit evidence until the accused has had a reasonable opportunity to contact counsel of choice, which requires them to, for example, wait a reasonable period of time for that lawyer to call back if the accused has attempted contact. That raises the question of what constitutes a reasonable period of time. The Court has observed that

> [w]hat amounts to a reasonable period of time depends on the circumstances as a whole, including factors such as the seriousness of the charge and the urgency of the investigation. It is also informed by the purpose of the guarantee. The right to counsel upon arrest or detention is intended to provide detainees with immediate legal advice on his or her rights and obligations under the law, mainly regarding the right to remain silent. As Lamer J. (as he then was) aptly noted in *R. v. Brydges*, [1990] 1 S.C.R. 190 at p. 206:
>
>> It is not always the case that immediately upon detention an accused will be concerned about retaining the lawyer that will eventually represent him at a trial, if there is one. Rather, one of the important reasons for retaining legal advice without delay upon being detained is linked to the protection of the right against self-incrimination. This is precisely the reason that there is a duty on the police to cease questioning the

267 *McCrimmon*, above note 164 at para 17.

> detainee until he has had a reasonable opportunity to retain and instruct counsel.[268]

Because duty counsel systems are in place, after a certain length of time and in most circumstances, a detainee would be expected to make use of that service. If the detention is in relation to a routine Breathalyzer test, for example, there is unlikely to be any reason that the accused would obtain better advice about their immediate obligations from their own lawyer than from duty counsel, although even then there is no urgency until the limitation period for conducting the test approaches.[269] On the other hand, if the charge is a more serious one and there is no urgency, a much longer wait would be appropriate.[270]

The fact that there is no absolute right to counsel of choice is significant beyond the initial consultation. It means that if the detainee does consult with duty counsel rather than wait for their own lawyer, then the section 10(b) right has been satisfied; as noted above, unless there is some change in circumstance, the person does not have any further right to consult with counsel.[271] That is, even if the detainee later wishes to speak with their own lawyer, having consulted duty counsel earlier will ordinarily have exhausted the protection offered by section 10(b).[272]

It was argued that police should have a duty to inform a detainee of this fact: that if a detainee initially requests counsel of choice but subsequently opts for duty counsel, the police should be required to inform that person of their obligation to hold off. This additional informational obligation would be similar to a "*Prosper* warning," discussed below.[273] However, in *Willier*, the Court rejected that argument, noting that the obligation in *Prosper* arises when a detainee who has asserted the right to counsel later expresses a willingness to proceed without advice from any lawyer. They held:

---

268 *Ibid* at para 18.

269 See *R v Richfield* (2003), 175 OAC 54 at para 12 (CA), and *R v Van Binnendyk*, 2007 ONCA 537 at paras 9–10. See also *R v Traicheff*, 2007 ONCJ 564 at para 27, where waiting only twenty-three minutes before requiring the accused to contact other counsel was insufficient.

270 See *Black*, above note 137 at 155, where the Court was of the view that a delay of eight hours was not unreasonable where the charge was first-degree murder. In *Burlingham*, above note 178, the Court held that where the interrogation occurred on the weekend, the police should have waited until the Monday since they were aware that the accused's lawyer was unavailable until then. Similarly, in *Clarkson*, above note 202, the Court held that the police interrogation should have been delayed until the accused sobered up.

271 See the discussion in Section C(3)(a), above in this chapter.

272 *McCrimmon*, above note 164.

273 See Section C(3)(g), below in this chapter.

> The circumstances of this case are not analogous. The concerns animating the provision of a *Prosper* warning do not arise when a detainee is unsuccessful in contacting a specific lawyer and simply opts to speak with another. In no way did Mr. Willier attempt to relinquish his right to counsel and thus any opportunity to mitigate his legal disadvantage. He made no attempt to waive his s. 10(*b*) right. Instead, unsuccessful in contacting Mr. Royal, he exercised his right to counsel by opting to speak with Legal Aid. As such, the police were under no obligation to provide him with a *Prosper* warning, and its absence fails to establish a *Charter* breach.[274]

On the other hand, lower courts have attempted to limit this impact of *Willier* by stressing that it only applies when the later choice to call duty counsel can genuinely be said to be that of the accused.[275] Furthermore, where police are found to have steered a detainee toward duty counsel rather than counsel of choice, that will be a violation of section 10.[276] In addition, where police take control of the process of contacting counsel or undertake to the accused to contact their counsel of choice, special obligations are then imposed on the police to do so properly.[277] The Ontario Court of Appeal has held that

---

274 *Willier*, above note 161 at para 39.

275 See, for example, *R v Jhite*, 2021 ONSC 3036 at para 43 [*Jhite*]:

> [T]he police cannot mislead the detainee by suggesting that they do not have the option of waiting for their preferred lawyer or that their only option is speaking with duty counsel: *Willier*, at para. 43. Further, the police must refrain from pressuring the detainee to forego consulting their lawyer of choice in favour of speaking instead with duty counsel: at para. 43. In other words, the decision to forego the detainee's preferred counsel for duty counsel must result from *the detainee's choice*. The decisions of Ontario courts both before and after *Willier* are consistent with the approach it endorsed. [Emphasis in original.]

276 See, for example, *R v Kumarasamy* (2002), 22 MVR (4th) 234 (Ont SC); *R v Vernon*, 2015 ONSC 3943; *R v Michael*, 2017 ONSC 4579; *R v Lewis*, 2019 ONSC 5919; *R v Singh*, 2020 ONSC 1342; *R v Dickson*, 2021 ONSC 6374; or *R v Barwis*, 2022 ABQB 581.

277 *Jhite*, above note 275 at paras 29 & 30, holds that:

> In some jurisdictions, including Peel Region, the police *do not* provide detainees with the means to contact counsel of choice. For example, police do not provide detainees with access to a phone and the Internet or a lawyers' directory. Instead, the police have assumed responsibility for locating the lawyer's phone number and calling them. Detainees only have access to the telephone once the lawyer is on the line. In jurisdictions where police take that approach, a detainee's ability to exercise their right to counsel of choice and do so with reasonable diligence mostly depends on the police.
>
> Where police assume control over the means for contacting counsel of choice, their efforts must reflect the same reasonable diligence expected of

> [w]here the police assume the responsibility of making first contact, rather than providing the detainee with direct access to a phone or internet connection, they must be taken to have "assumed the obligation to pursue [the detainee's] constitutional right to [access counsel] as diligently as she would have."[278]

That point leads directly to the next issue to be discussed, reasonable diligence.

f) Duty upon Accused to Be Reasonably Diligent

If the detained individual asserts the wish to speak to counsel, a duty for the detained individual to be reasonably diligent then arises. When there is a failure to be reasonably diligent in attempting to contact counsel, the implementational duties will be suspended, and police can continue their investigation.[279] The policy behind this is not unreasonable: a detainee should not be able to simply pretend to exercise the right to counsel as a means of frustrating a police investigation, particularly where timeliness is at issue (such as with use of a Breathalyzer). However, what the failure to be reasonably diligent means has engendered considerable confusion in the jurisprudence.

A failure to be reasonably diligent operates in a similar way to a waiver of the right to counsel. It allows the police to continue their investigation by asking questions of the accused or taking bodily samples or breath tests from the accused. Where the accused is found not to have been reasonably diligent, no breach of section 10(b) will be found even though the accused never expressly waived their right to counsel and never spoke to counsel. Unfortunately, there do not appear to be the same protections in place in this area as there are in the waiver cases (discussed below) in terms of the accused's need to understand the consequences of giving up the right. In *Tremblay*, the Court said:

> Generally speaking, if a detainee is not being reasonably diligent in the exercise of his rights, the correlative duties set out in this Court's decision in *R. v. Manninen*, [1987] 1 S.C.R. 1233, imposed on the police in a situation where a detainee has requested the assistance of counsel

---

> detainees . . . . Requiring anything less would risk encouraging only token efforts by the police and imperilling the right to counsel of choice. [Emphasis in original; citations omitted.]

See also *R v Pileggi*, 2021 ONCA 4 [*Pileggi*], and *R v Ector*, 2018 SKCA 46.

278 *R v Jarrett*, 2021 ONCA 758 at para 43 [citations omitted]. See also *R c Blackburn-Laroche*, 2021 QCCA 59 at para 143.

279 *R v Luong*, 2000 ABCA 301 at para 12.

are suspended and are not a bar to their continuing their investigation and calling upon him to give a sample of his breath.[280]

A majority of the Supreme Court applied this requirement on the facts of *R v Smith* (1989), where the majority was of the view that Smith's "most casual" attitude to the exercise of his right to counsel resulted in the suspension of the right.[281] At 9:00 p.m., the accused decided not to call his lawyer when he found only his lawyer's office telephone number in the telephone book, and he thus advised the police that he would contact his lawyer in the morning. Despite the police requests that he try the number, the accused refused and simply told them he would call the next day. On the facts, while the accused clearly asserted his desire to speak to counsel, he took no steps beyond looking in the phone book to attempt to do so, despite police encouragement. Here the "suspension" of the right operated so as to no longer require the police to hold off questioning the accused. Accordingly, in *Smith* 1989, the four-person majority held Smith's later statement to be admissible in evidence as not being obtained in breach of the right to counsel.[282]

To fully analyze the duty to be reasonably diligent, it is necessary to first discuss the principles applicable to the waiver of the right to counsel.

g) Waiver of the Right to Counsel

The section 10(b) law on the issue of waiver of the right to counsel was built upon the Supreme Court's earlier decisions relating to waiver of statutory protections.[283] Indeed, it is useful to note that waiver is not unique to section 10(b) since the issue arises throughout *Charter* jurisprudence and in particular in the context of so-called consent searches.[284] On the whole, it is true to say that upon detention, in the absence of a suspect actually receiving advice from counsel, there will be a breach of the right to counsel in the absence of a valid waiver unless the accused is not reasonably diligent in exercising the right. The caselaw at times

280 *Tremblay*, above note 217 at 439. See also *Ross*, above note 224 at 11, and *Black*, above note 137 at 154.

281 *R v Smith*, [1989] 2 SCR 368 at 391 [*Smith* 1989].

282 For a similar result, see *R v Payeur*, 2005 BCPC 155.

283 See *Korponay v Canada (AG)*, [1982] 1 SCR 41 [*Korponay*].

284 See, generally, in the context of waiver of the s 8 right to be free from unreasonable search and seizure: *R v Borden*, [1994] 3 SCR 145 at 164–65; *R v Wills* (1992), 7 OR (3d) 337 (CA); *R v Luc*, 2004 SKCA 117; *R v Perello*, 2005 SKCA 8; *R v Sewell*, 2003 SKCA 52; *R v Rutten*, 2006 SKCA 17; *R v Williams* (1995), 58 BCAC 53 (CA); and *R v Deprez* (1994), 97 Man R (2d) 272 (CA). See, generally, Glen Luther, "Consent Search and Reasonable Expectation of Privacy: Twin Barriers to the Reasonable Expectation of Privacy in Canada" (2008) 41 *University of British Columbia Law Review* 1.

has suggested that the actions of the accused might "implicitly" waive counsel, but whenever the argument arises, the Court has made clear that waiver will not readily be implied. In *Clarkson v The Queen*, the majority said:

> Given the concern for fair treatment of an accused person which underlies such constitutional civil liberties as the right to counsel in s. 10(b) of the *Charter*, it is evident that any alleged waiver of this right by an accused must be carefully considered and that the accused's awareness of the consequences of what he or she was saying is crucial. Indeed, this Court stated with respect to the waiver of statutory procedural guarantees in *Korponay v. Attorney General of Canada* . . . that any waiver ". . . is dependent upon it being clear and unequivocal that the person is waiving the procedural safeguard and is doing so with full knowledge of the rights the procedure was enacted to protect and of the effect the waiver will have on those rights in the process."[285]

In *Evans*, the accused made an unsuccessful attempt to call his lawyer and then provided a written statement. The majority held that he had not implicitly waived his right to counsel. The Crown had stated that the appellant was given the choice of contacting his lawyer later or proceeding with the written statement and that he agreed to continue with the written statement. It argued that this "cured" the earlier section 10(b) violations, with the result that the written confession was obtained in conformity with section 10(b) of the *Charter* as his actions amounted to an implicit waiver of his right to consult with counsel. The majority disagreed:

> Such an argument could only succeed if it were concluded that by making the written confession the appellant had waived his s. 10(b) right. In *Manninen*, *supra*, this Court held that a person may implicitly, by words or conduct, waive his or her rights under s. 10(b). The Court cautioned, however, that "the standard will be very high" (at p. 1244) and referred to its judgment in *Clarkson v. The Queen*, [1986] 1 S.C.R. 383, where it was held that for a voluntary waiver to be valid and effective it must be premised on a true appreciation of the consequences of giving up the right . . . . I am not satisfied that he appreciated the consequences of making the written statement and thereby waiving his right to counsel or, to put it another way, that he waived his right "with full knowledge of the rights the procedure was enacted to protect and of the effect the waiver will have on those rights in the process": *Korponay v. Attorney*

285 *Clarkson*, above note 202 at 394, citing *Korponay*, above note 283 at 49 [emphasis omitted].

> *General of Canada*, [1982] 1 S.C.R. 41, at p. 49, as cited in *Clarkson v. The Queen*, supra, at p. 395 (emphasis deleted). Accordingly, I am of the view that the written statement was also taken in violation of the appellant's s. 10(b) right.[286]

In *Evans*, of course, the accused suffered from "subnormal mental capacity," and in *Clarkson*, the accused was significantly intoxicated. These factors therefore cause some confusion for the situation of an accused who is not impaired by alcohol or drugs and who is of "normal" capacity. The Court, in stressing the incapacity issues present in the two cases, seemingly left open the possibility that an accused who knows they are allowed to wait to speak to counsel but who goes along with the police's desire to proceed to questioning waives the right to counsel.

However, in *Ross*, a case where there were no particular special circumstances about the accused, the Supreme Court was clear that an implicit waiver should not be found when the purpose of the right to counsel is "contradicted":

> [T]hat the accused did not refuse to participate in the line-up cannot by itself amount to a waiver of the right to counsel. The very purpose of the right to counsel is to ensure that those who are accused or detained be advised of their legal rights and how to exercise them when dealing with the authorities. It would contradict this purpose to conclude that a detained or accused person has waived the right to counsel simply by submitting, before being instructed by counsel, to precisely those attempts to secure the detainee's participation from which the police should refrain. Here, the appellants were unable to make an informed decision about participating in the line-up because they were ignorant of their legal position, not having been advised by their lawyers. Nor did the police even give them the choice as to whether they should participate. In the circumstances, therefore, to conclude that the appellants had waived their rights by participating in the line-up would render the right to counsel nugatory.[287]

One special case in which the issue of waiver can raise concerns, and where the problems in the interplay between "reasonable diligence" and "waiver" can be particularly acute, is in what has come to be called a "*Prosper* warning." We will first consider *Prosper* warnings themselves and then look at how they interact with the other potentially inconsistent rules.

As already noted, if a detainee asserts the right to counsel, then the police have a duty to hold off from investigating until a reasonable

---

286 *Evans*, above note 71 at 893.

287 *Ross*, above note 224 at 14–15.

opportunity to do so has been provided. In *Prosper*, the accused had requested counsel but, after some unsuccessful attempts, then indicated that he had changed his mind and would proceed without counsel. The Court held that in such circumstances, an additional informational duty was imposed on the police before the alleged waiver of counsel would be valid; the detainee had to be specifically informed of the police duty to hold off. The Court held:

> Given the importance of the right to counsel, I would also say with respect to waiver that once a detainee asserts the right there must be a clear indication that he or she has changed his or her mind, and the burden of establishing an unequivocal waiver will be on the Crown: *Ross*, at pp. 11-12. Further, the waiver must be free and voluntary and it must not be the product of either direct or indirect compulsion. This Court has indicated on numerous occasions that the standard required for an effective waiver of the right to counsel is very high: *Clarkson v. The Queen*, [1986] 1 S.C.R. 383, *Manninen*, and *Evans*. As I said in *Bartle*, at pp. 192-94 and 206, a person who waives a right must know what he or she is giving up if the waiver is to be valid.[288]

The Court also stated:

> In circumstances where a detainee has asserted his or her right to counsel and has been reasonably diligent in exercising it, yet has been unable to reach a lawyer because duty counsel is unavailable at the time of detention, courts must ensure that the *Charter*-protected right to counsel is not too easily waived. Indeed, I find that an additional informational obligation on police will be triggered once a detainee, who has previously asserted the right to counsel, indicates that he or she has changed his or her mind and no longer wants legal advice. At this point, police will be required to tell the detainee of his or her right to a reasonable opportunity to contact a lawyer and of the obligation on the part of the police during this time not to take any statements or require the detainee to participate in any potentially incriminating process until he or she has had that reasonable opportunity. This additional informational requirement on police ensures that a detainee who persists in wanting to waive the right to counsel will know what it is that he or she is actually giving up.[289]

The Court articulated the conditions in which a *Prosper* warning is required based on the facts of that case, but later decisions from lower courts have clarified some aspects of it, indicating that it is not as limited

288 *Prosper*, above note 187 at para 44.
289 *Ibid* at para 43.

as the precise situation dealt with there. For example, *Prosper* arose in circumstances where no duty counsel system was available at the time, but *Prosper* warnings are required even in provinces where such systems do exist.[290] In *Prosper*, the accused was explicit about his change of mind, but this is not an absolute requirement: "[I]f it is *apparent* that a detainee has changed his mind about wanting to speak to counsel without delay, and no other legal impediments to the right to a *Prosper* warning are operating, that warning must be given."[291] Furthermore, the accused need not have changed their mind about contacting counsel entirely: an accused who initially expresses a desire to speak to counsel of choice and then agrees to speak to duty counsel (while still intending to speak with their own lawyer eventually) is entitled to a warning.[292] Put another way, the issue is whether the accused can be said to have abandoned their efforts to speak to counsel *without delay*.[293]

To return to the issue of inconsistency in application, then, the rules are that waiver of the right to counsel will only be found where it is clear and unequivocal.[294] But on the other hand, an accused must be reasonably diligent in exercising the right to counsel or they lose the protection of section 10(b), and a lack of reasonable diligence can be found relatively easily. While either waiver or a lack of reasonable diligence leads to the loss of *Charter* protection, a lack of reasonable diligence is much more likely to be found than waiver, but there are many sets of facts to which either analysis could be applied. That situation creates great potential for confusion.

For example, reasonable diligence was at issue in *R v Jones*. The facts are succinctly set out in the Alberta Court of Appeal's judgment:

> On arriving at the police station, the police officer took the appellant to a private phone room which contained a working telephone, phone books and a list of lawyers who had indicated their availability for consultation. The police officer explained the use of the phone, and told the appellant to knock on the door when he was finished.
>
> Seven minutes later, the appellant knocked on the door. The police officer noted that the appellant was not speaking on the phone, and

290 *R v Basko*, 2007 SKCA 111 [*Basko*].

291 *R v Fountain*, 2017 ONCA 596 at para 44 [*Fountain*] [emphasis in original].

292 *Ibid* at para 41.

293 *Ibid* at para 37.

294 As a further example, see *Sabados*, above note 122, where the accused had a condition in a recognizance that required him to provide a breath sample upon demand from an officer. While not deciding the point, the Saskatchewan Court of Appeal expressed great skepticism over whether agreeing to such a condition could be seen as a waiver of the right to counsel before providing any such sample.

> entered the room. He asked the appellant whether the appellant had reached his lawyer. When the appellant responded that he had not been able to reach him, the police officer again advised the appellant about the available list of legal aid lawyers and the phone book and advised that he could contact another lawyer. The appellant responded that he did not wish to speak to anyone else; that he wished to speak only to the named lawyer. The appellant did not indicate that he required more time, and did not suggest that he required any assistance. The police officer assumed from the appellant's act of knocking on the door and the appellant's response that the appellant had terminated his efforts to reach a lawyer. The officer requested that the appellant accompany him to the breathalyser where the appellant provided samples of his breath for analysis.[295]

On these facts, the Court of Appeal agreed with the trial judge that there was no violation of the accused's section 10 rights. Specifically, they held that "[t]he burden is on the detainee to establish reasonable diligence," and on these facts he had not done so.[296] That finding had two consequences: first, it meant that the police duty to hold off no longer applied, and second, it meant that the accused was not entitled to a *Prosper* warning since establishing "reasonable diligence" is a prerequisite for that warning to arise. In the abstract, the finding that a detainee who made minimal efforts to contact counsel was not reasonably diligent is a plausible one, so the reasoning in *Jones* is defensible. However, if the analysis had been undertaken through a waiver lens—as the dissenting judge held it should have been[297]—it is difficult to imagine the same conclusion being reached. The onus then would have been on the Crown to establish that the detainee was fully informed of his rights in order to meet the very high standard for waiver. The accused's arguments that the officer should have asked why he had been unable to reach his lawyer and whether he needed more time, or that the officer should have told him of the duty to hold off rather than simply mention the existence of duty counsel, would be much more persuasive in that context. The result in this case, then, and in similar cases, can be settled not by the facts, or even by the law, but by which set of legal rules a court decides to apply.

In contrast to *Jones*, but also demonstrating the scope for confusion caused by the current rules, is the Ontario Court of Appeal decision in

295 *R v Jones*, 2005 ABCA 289 at paras 3–4 [*Jones*], leave to appeal to SCC refused [2005] SCCA No 538.

296 *Jones*, above note 295 at para 8.

297 *Ibid* at para 14: "The issue in this appeal is whether the Crown established that the Appellant had clearly and unequivocally waived his right to counsel before the police compelled him to submit to a breathalyser test."

R v Fountain.[298] The accused there had been arrested and indicated that he wished to speak to his own lawyer. It transpired that that lawyer would not be available until the next morning, and about six hours after the arrest, an officer asked the accused whether he wanted to wait to speak to his own lawyer in the morning or to call Legal Aid then; the accused said he would wait until the next day. The officer then questioned him, and about ninety minutes into that questioning—and after the accused had asked "this is an illegal interrogation without me speaking to a lawyer, is it not?"—the accused called Legal Aid. The trial judge found no section 10(b) violation, concluding that the accused had not been reasonably diligent in exercising his right, that he had waived his right, and that no *Prosper* warning had been required. The Ontario Court of Appeal found all of those conclusions to be in error.

It could not be said that the accused was failing to be reasonably diligent because he was not being obstinate, trying to impede the investigation, or signalling that he was not serious about wanting counsel without delay. He had been offered a choice of waiting or of speaking to Legal Aid immediately and had taken one of the options offered. Nothing showed that the accused knew what rights he was giving up when he did agree to call Legal Aid, especially as he had not been given a *Prosper* warning. And (for reasons discussed above) the trial judge's bases for saying that no *Prosper* warning was required (the accused had not explicitly said he no longer wanted to speak to his own counsel and indeed *did* still want to speak to his own counsel) were incorrect. The Court of Appeal noted in particular that "the submission that Mr. Fountain did not change his mind about wanting to speak to counsel is difficult to square with the trial judge's alternative finding that Mr. Fountain waived his right to counsel."[299]

One cannot realistically see *Jones* and *Fountain* as irreconcilable, but they do show how very different analyses can be applied to similar facts. The facts are, of course, not identical: although both accused indicated that they only wanted to speak to their counsel of choice, Fountain was more assertive about the issue, which makes any finding that he had given up on counsel of choice less likely. On the other hand, Fountain did also speak with duty counsel, unlike Jones, which could easily have swayed things in the opposite direction. And for the Alberta Court of Appeal, the fact that Jones did not, for example, expressly ask for more time showed a lack of reasonable diligence, while the Ontario Court of Appeal had required a basis for concluding that the accused's desire to wait for his own lawyer was some sort of ruse.

298 *Fountain*, above note 291.

299 *Ibid* at para 43.

Also showing the scope for confusion and variability is the Saskatchewan Court of Appeal decision in *R v Basko*.[300] The accused had been detained at a routine traffic stop and taken back to the police station for a Breathalyzer test, where he had been properly informed of the right to counsel. He indicated that he wished to speak to a lawyer and through the officers made three attempts in an eight-minute period to call Legal Aid. However, the phone was busy on each occasion, and the accused then indicated that he knew what they would say, that he would call the next day, and that he wished to get it over with. The trial judge concluded that in the circumstances, the accused had been entitled to a *Prosper* warning, so there was a section 10(b) violation. The Court of Appeal disagreed, holding that the facts of this case were the same as those in *Jones* and therefore that, as in *Jones*, the accused should be found to have waived his section 10(b) right. But, of course, that was not the basis of the reasoning in *Jones*, which instead had found a lack of reasonable diligence.

These cases illustrate the confusion that exists in Canadian law because of the basic inconsistency between stating, at one and the same time, that the standard for waiver is high (and that the onus to prove it is on the Crown)[301] and that an accused must be reasonably diligent in exercising the right to counsel (and has the burden of proving a *Charter* violation).[302] The two tests can both apply to the same types of fact situations and can in many cases (although not here) equally be adopted as the "correct" method of analysis, but, frustratingly, they will lead to opposite conclusions.[303]

Standard police right-to-counsel cards may in fact be clearer and fairer about this issue than the courts have been. For example, the Calgary Police Service card says about the *Prosper* warning:

> FORMAL WAIVER: Where a detainee indicates a desire to contact a lawyer and then changes their mind OR there are concerns that the waiver of the right to counsel was not clear and unequivocal. READ THIS: You have the right to a reasonable opportunity to contact a lawyer. I am obliged not to take a statement from you or ask you to participate in any process that might provide evidence against you until you are certain about whether you want to exercise this right. Do you

---

300 *Basko*, above note 290 at paras 13–16.

301 *Ibid* at para 44.

302 This burden comes from *Collins*, above note 5 at 277, and the general principles underlying s 24(2), which requires an accused to prove a breach of rights.

303 See Steve Coughlan, "*R v Basko*: Annotation" (2007) 52 *Criminal Reports* (6th) 360.

> understand? (*Record answer*) Do you want to waive your right to contact a lawyer? (*Record answer*).[304]

Of course, it is a good practice for the police to be clear about the waiver if they wish evidence subsequently obtained to be admissible. Such a practice also has the salutary effect of ensuring that an accused truly wishes to waive their right. The restatement of the obligation to hold off investigating pending the exercise of the right is a significant part of this process. Otherwise, the questioning of the accused can be seen as coercive in the sense that many accused will feel obligated to answer since they have not received legal advice concerning the right to silence.

h) Privacy When Consulting Counsel

Pre-*Charter*, the Supreme Court held in *R v Jumaga*[305] that there was no obligation on the police to afford privacy for a detainee to consult with counsel in the absence of a request by the accused. Although the Court has never explicitly reversed that finding (or, indeed, considered *Jumaga* at all), it is clear that the same is not true under the *Charter*: a reasonable opportunity to consult counsel means a reasonable opportunity to do so in private. Indeed, the need to provide privacy can be one of the justifications leading to some delay.[306]

In *Taylor*, for example, the accused was arrested following a traffic accident, requested counsel, but was taken to the hospital for observation before being taken to the police station; he was only allowed to contact counsel once he had arrived at the station. The trial judge had concluded that this did not violate section 10(b) since the accused could not have had privacy at the hospital; the Supreme Court found that there was no evidence for this factual conclusion and therefore that there had been a section 10(b) violation. It held:

> An individual who enters a hospital to receive medical treatment is not in a *Charter*-free zone. Where the individual has requested access to counsel and is in custody at the hospital, the police have an obligation under s. 10(*b*) to take steps to ascertain whether private access to a phone is in fact available, given the circumstances. Since most hospitals

---

304 This is from the Calgary Police Service right-to-counsel card in use as of January 2010. See above note 169.

305 [1977] 1 SCR 486 [*Jumaga*].

306 See, for example, *Nguyen* 2016, above note 128. See also *Pileggi*, above note 277 at para 77: "[I]t is difficult to fathom how the police could have accommodated a private conversation at the appellant's home. Consultation in private is a vital component of the s. 10(*b*) right. . . . The appellant's right to consult counsel in private would have been compromised by attempting to facilitate contact at the house while a search was underway."

have phones, it is not a question simply of whether the individual is in the emergency room, it is whether the Crown has demonstrated that the circumstances are such that a private phone conversation is not reasonably feasible.

The result of the officers' failure to even turn their minds that night to the obligation to provide this access, meant that there was virtually no evidence about whether a private phone call would have been possible, and therefore no basis for assessing the reasonableness of the failure to facilitate access.[307]

While not explicitly overruling *Jumaga*, the Court's reasoning in *Taylor* hinges on the fact that the right to consult with counsel includes the right to do so privately. This is true both in the conclusion that there was no need to provide an opportunity to contact counsel before reaching the hospital (because privacy was not possible until then) and that he should have been allowed to contact counsel before reaching the police station (because privacy was possible before then).

Many courts of appeal have explicitly considered this issue and reached the conclusion that there is a right to consult in private. In *R v Playford*, the Ontario Court of Appeal dealt with the issue in this way:

> In my opinion, the right to retain and instruct counsel without delay carries with it the right to do so in privacy. It would defy common sense to expect an accused person to instruct counsel properly when his instructions can be overheard by other persons and in particular by police officers. Such lack of privacy might even seriously prejudice his ability to retain counsel. Retention of counsel usually requires some explanation by the accused of the circumstances which have led to his arrest.[308]

The Ontario court expressly agreed with the decision in *R v Lepage*,[309] where the Nova Scotia Appellate Division had distinguished the pre-*Charter* decision in *Jumaga*. In fact, the Appellate Division expressly adopted the dissenting judgment of Laskin CJC, who had said:

> [T]he fact that it may have to be limited in some cases does not call for an unqualified denial of any privacy in all cases. I do not think that it can reasonably be made a condition that an accused be shown to have asked for it before consideration is given to providing it. Once an accused has requested that he be permitted to consult counsel, that should carry with it, to the knowledge of the police, a right to have the consultation in private, so far as circumstances permit. The right

307 *Taylor*, above note 130 at paras 34–35.

308 *R v Playford* (1987), 40 CCC (3d) 142 (Ont CA).

309 (1986), 32 CCC (3d) 171 (NSCA) [*Lepage*].

> to counsel is diluted if it can only be secured by adding request to request. I would not put the police in an adversary position on this question; they are better placed than the ordinary person (who has been detained or arrested and is in police custody) to recognize what the right to counsel imports, and they should be alert to protect that right as an important element in the administration of justice through law, for which they are as much accountable as any others involved in the judicial process.[310]

The Nova Scotia Court also said:

> Even to obtain the minimal advice by means of a telephone a person detained or arrested must be free to discuss the circumstances of his detention with counsel. If he cannot do so for fear of making admissions in the presence of the police then, obviously, his right to instruct counsel has been limited. In such circumstances the right under the *Charter* has been violated. In my view, the right to privacy is inherent in the right to retain and instruct counsel under s. 10(b) of the *Charter*.[311]

In that case, the officer stood five to six feet away while the accused called counsel from his own telephone. A breach of the right was found by the court.

The New Brunswick Court of Appeal summarized the position thus in *R v O'Donnell*:

> It is settled law that the right to retain and instruct counsel, under s. 10(b) of the *Charter*, includes a corollary right to consult in private. Without the requisite degree of privacy, the constitutional right to counsel becomes illusory. Although waiver of the right is a possibility, the issue does not arise in the present case. While the amount of privacy need not be great, at a minimum, an accused must be able to converse with his or her lawyer without the conversation being overheard. Moreover, those who exercise their right to counsel are not required to request privacy or greater privacy than what the police are willing to provide. Furthermore, the right to consult in private extends to legal advice that is sought over the telephone and it matters not whether the advice sought is of minimal scope (whether to provide breath samples).[312]

That court, however, stressed that the breach of privacy must be proven, which it held required a factual finding that the police did in fact overhear

---

310 *Jumaga*, above note 305 at 494–95, Laskin CJC dissenting.

311 *Lepage*, above note 309 at 176–77.

312 *R v O'Donnell*, 2004 NBCA 26 at para 4.

the conversation with the lawyer.[313] Furthermore, in *R v Standish*, the British Columbia Court of Appeal found no breach of privacy where the accused required and obtained the assistance of the police in placing calls to counsel, holding that privacy "starts after the accused reaches his lawyer to seek his advice."[314]

Other courts have concluded that the accused need not actually be overheard for there to be a violation of privacy. The accused in *R v Coaster* was an inmate in a correctional facility charged with second-degree murder in the death of a fellow inmate and was allowed to telephone counsel. However, he was placed in a room with the door left partly open so that an officer could see him. The accused had been told that the officer would stand far enough away not to hear him but testified that he did not believe he could not be overheard. The Manitoba Court of Appeal found that the proper test was not whether it was probable that the accused could be overheard but whether the detainee had a reasonable belief that he could not speak to counsel in private—unless it could be shown that the detainee was, in fact, able to speak to counsel in private. As Coaster had used the opportunity to try to make an unauthorized call to his girlfriend, the Court of Appeal concluded that he did not have a reasonable belief that his conversation would be overheard.[315]

Finally, note that the *right* to privacy when consulting counsel is not the same as a *requirement* that the accused can only consult counsel privately and is not a foundation for categorically denying the right to counsel until privacy is possible. There is authority suggesting that a detained person should be given the option of foregoing privacy in order to consult with counsel at an earlier point: "Detained persons can legally waive their right to counsel. Why could they not do so partially?"[316]

4) Section 10 and Non-state Actors

There is a question about section 10 of the *Charter*, which, quite surprisingly after more than four decades of *Charter* jurisprudence, has no entirely clear answer: do security guards, loss prevention officers, and

313 See also *Parrill*, above note 184. Cases tend to concern whether the arrestee can be overheard by police, but a lack of privacy could equally be caused by, for example, the risk of being overheard by fellow inmates: *R v Hassan*, 2023 ONSC 1300.

314 *R v Standish* (1988), 41 CCC (3d) 340 at 343 (BCCA).

315 *R v Coaster*, 2014 MBCA 108.

316 *Freddi*, above note 208 at para 49. See also *DMR*, above note 130 at para 54, or *R v Fedan*, 2014 BCSC 2119 at para 47.

other private policing services need to inform detainees of their rights under section 10?[317]

In part, this question is unsettled because it is several intermingled questions; in part, however, it simply has not been authoritatively decided by the Supreme Court. The answer, depending on how one approaches the issue, can depend on whether the actor is or is not a state agent, on what power the actor is exercising (different conclusions might be reached with regard to searches and arrests, for example), on how the terms "detention" and "arrest" are to be interpreted, and on the consequences of a failure to provide a *Charter* caution.

In Chapter 2, we discussed the issue of the *Charter*'s application to non-state actors[318] and the main authorities from the Supreme Court—*R v Broyles*[319] and *R v Buhay*[320] in particular—which consider when a private citizen is acting as an agent of the police. In *Broyles*, the issue was whether statements made by the accused to a friend who was talking to him at the instigation of police was in fact a state agent and whether the *Charter* therefore applied to his actions. In *Buhay*, the issue was whether bus station security guards who searched a locker and then contacted police about drugs they had found were state agents. The central point pursued in Chapter 2 was that the *Charter*, by way of section 32, applies to "state" actors, and therefore *if* the private citizens in those cases were state agents, then the *Charter* would apply. That point is authoritatively determined. What is unsettled is the converse: if a person is *not* a state agent, does that necessarily mean that the *Charter* does not apply?

Part of the unsettledness seems to stem from an occasional failure in courts to recognize that those are two distinct questions. Some decisions consider the issue of whether the actor was a state agent and then, having decided that the person was not, stop the analysis.[321] That approach unconsciously assumes that the rule "the *Charter* never applies to non-state actors" has been established when, at least in theory, that is not the case. In *Buhay*, for example, although the Court looked at whether the security guards were state agents, they also considered whether the *Charter* might apply to the activities of the security guards because they could "be ascribed to those of the government."[322]

317 On this issue and similar related ones, see Steven Penney, "State Action in Action: The *Charter*'s Application in Criminal Investigations" (2023) 27:2 *Canadian Criminal Law Review* 61.

318 See Chapter 2, Section B(4).

319 *Broyles*, above note 181.

320 2003 SCC 30 [*Buhay*].

321 See, for example, *R v Jacobs*, 2014 ABCA 172, although it is a decision about search powers.

322 *Buhay*, above note 320 at paras 28 & 29.

It is therefore possible that a non-state actor might nonetheless be exercising a power given by the state and that on that basis the *Charter* would apply. The *Criminal Code* gives private persons the power of "citizen's arrest," and indeed, in section 494(2), employees of property owners have been given specific powers to arrest in certain circumstances. The power of citizen's arrest is discussed at length in Chapter 4.[323] Does this grant of power mean that the *Charter* should apply where it might not otherwise apply?

The decision that is most often cited in answering that question positively is that of the Alberta Court of Appeal in *R v Lerke*,[324] a 1986 decision involving an arrest and search by a tavern supervisor at a licensed drinking establishment. The Court of Appeal said as follows:

> In my view the arrest of a citizen is a governmental function whether the person making the arrest is a peace officer or a private citizen. I reach this conclusion from a consideration of the long legal history of citizen's arrest from its common law origins to the statutory expression of the present powers of arrest contained in the *Criminal Code of Canada* or in the *Petty Trespass Act*.[325]

After a review of the history of citizen and police arrest powers, the court was of the view that "when one citizen arrests another, the arrest is the exercise of a governmental function to which the *Canadian Charter of Rights and Freedoms* applies."[326] However, other courts of appeal have reached the opposite conclusion, deciding that the *Charter* does not apply to citizen's arrests. For example, in *R v Skeir*, the Nova Scotia Court of Appeal, relying on the Supreme Court's analysis of the place of security guards in *Buhay*, held that the *Charter* did not require a store security guard to comply with section 10(b) of the *Charter*.[327] Similarly, the Ontario Court of Appeal, in a very brief decision in *R v NS*, held that

> we are satisfied on the authority of *R. v. Buhay* (2003), 174 C.C.C. (3d) 97, paragraphs 25–31 (S.C.C.) that the security guards could not be considered police agents or otherwise be subject to the limitation of the *Charter*.[328]

---

323 See Chapter 4, Section C(2)(b)(ii).

324 (1986), 24 CCC (3d) 129 (Alta CA) [*Lerke*].

325 *Ibid* at 134.

326 *Ibid* at 136.

327 *R v Skeir*, 2005 NSCA 86 [*Skeir*].

328 *R v NS*, 2004 OJ No 290 (CA) at para 1. See also *R v AMJ*, 1999 BCCA 366, which is unsympathetic to the notion of s 10 arising in a citizen's arrest but is deciding a different issue.

In essence, some courts see *Lerke* as having been implicitly overruled by *Buhay*. However, the Alberta Court of Appeal does not regard matters that way. In *R v Dell*, a bouncer detained a man after seeing him with cocaine.[329] The Alberta Court of Appeal found that *Lerke* had not been overruled by the Supreme Court of Canada:

> As I read *Buhay*, it does not determine that the *Charter* has no application to a citizen's arrest by a private person. *Buhay* involved a search and seizure, not a citizen's arrest, and *Lerke* was neither considered nor mentioned. There is but a passing reference to arrest in paragraph 31. The Supreme Court confirmed the existence of the government function exception in *Buhay*, noting that it may derive from an express delegation or an abandonment of state powers to a citizen.[330]

They also noted of the reasoning in *Skeir* that "the specific government function exception relied on in *Lerke*, and recognized in *Buhay*, was not canvassed."[331] In addition, the Court noted that only a few months after *Buhay*, the Supreme Court had handed down its decision in *R v Asante-Mensah*. In that decision, the Court observed that "we are not called on in this case to address the question whether a citizen's arrest could be construed as state action for purposes of the *Charter* . . . and, if so, what consequences might flow from that ruling."[332] If the Supreme Court saw its own decision in *Buhay* as having settled the issue of the applicability of the *Charter* to citizen's arrests, it would not, a few months later, describe that as an open question.

The Alberta Court of Appeal in *Dell*, however, proceeded to distinguish *Lerke* on the basis that the common law power to conduct an investigative detention did not arise from statute. In the majority's view, the fact that the investigative detention by a bouncer was not an arrest meant that he was not relying on the statutory power to arrest; thus, *Lerke* did not apply. On that approach, a private citizen performing an arrest is required to give the detainee their section 10 rights, but a private citizen performing some other sort of detention is not required to do so. That approach has been adopted in some courts.[333] In the particular context of *Dell*, that is problematic because the very fact that the bouncer

---

329 *R v Dell*, 2005 ABCA 246 [*Dell*].

330 *Ibid* at para 17.

331 *Ibid* at para 12.

332 *R v Asante-Mensah*, 2003 SCC 38 at para 77.

333 See, for example, *Nguyen* 2016, above note 128, where the British Columbia Court of Appeal upheld a decision that the actions of bouncers at a nightclub did not give rise to s 10 rights because the bouncers had only detained, not arrested, the accused. They relied on *R v Asp*, 2011 BCCA 433, in reaching this conclusion.

had not arrested but only detained the accused should have led to the conclusion that his action was unlawful; we pointed out in Chapter 2 that the power to investigatively detain can be given only to the police at common law.[334] However, that does not mean that there are never situations in which private citizens can lawfully detain someone.

This leads to a further intermingled issue: the definition of "detention." In *R v Shafie*,[335] the accused was charged with theft. The Crown sought to introduce a statement made by the accused to a private investigator in a private office. The investigator did not provide the accused with his section 10(b) rights. The Ontario Court of Appeal ruled that there was no need for the investigator to do so because the accused was not "detained" by the investigator: "[T]he weight of judicial opinion ... is that actions that, at the hands of the police or other state or governmental agents, would be a detention, do not amount to a detention within the meaning of s. 10(b) of the *Charter* when done by private or non-governmental persons."[336]

Indeed, the Supreme Court of Canada reached the same conclusion in *R v M(MR)*. In that case, a student was suspected of selling drugs at a school event and was called into the office by the vice-principal, with a police officer present. The Court concluded that the vice-principal was not acting as an agent of the police, although the *Charter* did apply nonetheless since the vice-principal was independently a state actor. The accused was not given his section 10 rights when he was brought into the office at the instance of the vice-principal, although he was given them when the police officer arrested him. The Court concluded that there was no section 10 violation on those facts because the vice-principal's actions did not constitute a "detention" for section 10 purposes:

> Detention has been defined to include a "deprivation of liberty by physical constraint" or "when a police officer or other agent of the state assumes control over the movement of a person by a demand or direction which may have significant legal consequence and which prevents or impedes access to counsel" (*R. v. Therens*, [1985] 1 S.C.R. 613, at p. 642). Even if the compelled attendance of a student at a principal's office or some other form of restraint by a school authority could be understood as falling within the strict terms of the definition of "detention" set out in *Therens*, it should not be considered as

334 The test for the creation of common law police powers is based on the statutory duty of the police to investigate crime. See Chapter 2, Section B(4), and the text accompanying note 373.

335 (1989), 47 CCC (3d) 27 (Ont CA) [*Shafie*].

336 *Ibid* at 34.

> "detention" for the purposes of s. 10(*b*). In my view that section was not meant to apply to relations between students and teachers, but rather to relations between individuals and the state, usually focused upon the investigation of a criminal offence. The right to counsel provided in s. 10(*b*) was designed to address the vulnerable position of an individual who has been detained by the coercive power of the state in the course of a criminal investigation, and is thus deprived of his or her liberty and placed at risk of making self-incriminating statements (*R. v. Bartle*, [1994] 3 S.C.R. 173, at p. 191). Its application in the school context is inappropriate and would lead to absurd results. As a result, there was no detention for Charter purposes in this case, and thus no violation of s. 10(*b*) can be found.
>
> Once again, it must be stated that if the vice-principal had been acting as an agent of the police, or if the police officer himself had taken any active role in detaining the appellant, it might well be that the appellant was detained within the meaning of s. 10(*b*). However, on the facts presented in this case, the appellant was not detained prior to his arrest by Constable Siepierski. He was properly cautioned and instructed as to his right to counsel at the time of the arrest. Therefore, I find that there was no violation of the appellant's s. 10(*b*) rights.[337]

This approach is subtly different from saying that private citizens do not have to inform a detainee of their *Charter* rights on detention: it is saying that if the interference with liberty is carried out by a private citizen, it is not actually a "detention," so there are no *Charter* rights in the first place. Note, of course, that this same argument could not be made if the private citizen carried out an arrest, which certainly would have to meet the definition of "arrest" in section 10. Therefore, this alternate route would arrive at the same conclusion as *Dell's* interpretation of *Lerke*: private citizens must inform those they deal with of section 10 rights in the case of an arrest but not a detention.

Finally, note that on one view of the matter, it might not be very important whether section 10 actually applies in the case of private citizen arrests or detentions. The central consequence of a failure to inform a detainee of their rights is the possibility that this will be a breach of the *Charter* that might lead to a remedy under section 24, such as exclusion of a statement given at the time. It is possible that that same result might follow whether or not there was explicitly a section 10 violation.

In *R v Harrer*,[338] the Supreme Court of Canada said that when a statement given to a foreign police officer is obtained in breach of the

337 *M(MR)*, above note 22 at paras 67–68.

338 [1995] 3 SCR 562.

right to counsel, it might be excluded if its admission in evidence would result in an unfair trial. This is so even though that foreign officer is not bound by the *Charter*. The right to a fair trial is protected by section 11(d) of the *Charter* and is a principle of fundamental justice under section 7. The majority was clear that such exclusion would not be the result of section 24 of the *Charter*, but

> I would reject the evidence on the basis of the trial judge's duty, now constitutionalized by the enshrinement of a fair trial in the *Charter*, to exercise properly his or her judicial discretion to exclude evidence that would result in an unfair trial.[339]

It seems, therefore, that while the issue of the right to counsel as it might be applied to private security officers is unlikely to apply in the same detailed way as with police officers, there could be times when the failure to provide rights similar to those enshrined in section 10(a) and (b) might result in an unfair trial. Indeed, in *Buhay*, the leading authority on "state agents," the Supreme Court expressly referred to *Harrer* and other cases when it said:

> Before turning to s. 24(2), I wish to address briefly the approach taken by the Court of Appeal in this case. I will make two observations. First, we do not have to decide whether there would have been a "search" by the police had the security guards not replaced the contents inside the locker but had held it in a corner cupboard. This is not what they did here. Had they done so, we might have had to adapt the test in *Broyles*, *supra*, to determine if and when the security guards would have become state agents or, alternatively, if the "mere transfer of control" in that case could have been characterized as a "seizure" by the police within the meaning of s. 8.
>
> Second, and more importantly, I wish to stress that even if the reasoning of the Court of Appeal were sound and that there had been no search and seizure triggering s. 8 of the *Charter*, remedies other than under the *Charter* might be available in such a case to an accused seeking exclusion of the impugned evidence. Indeed, even in the absence of a *Charter* breach, judges have a discretion at common law to exclude evidence obtained in circumstances such that it would result in unfairness if the evidence was admitted at trial, or if the prejudicial effect of admitting the evidence outweighs its probative value (see, in the context of confessions: *Rothman v. The Queen*, [1981] 1 S.C.R. 640, at p. 696, *per* Lamer J., as he then was; *R. v. Oickle*, [2000] 2 S.C.R. 3, 2000 SCC 38, at para. 69, *per* Iacobucci J.; see also J. Sopinka, S. N. Lederman and A. W. Bryant, *The*

339 *Ibid* at para 21.

> *Law of Evidence in Canada* (2nd ed. 1999), at pp. 339–40); see also, in other contexts, *R. v. Harrer*, [1995] 3 S.C.R. 562, *per* La Forest J.; *Caucci*, *supra*, at paras. 13 and 17; Sopinka, Lederman and Bryant, *supra*, at pp. 30-33). Such an argument was not advanced in this case as the appellant maintained throughout that he was entitled to a *Charter* remedy for a s. 8 violation. In light of my conclusion on the s. 8 issue, it is not necessary to explore further whether this common law discretion could have extended to the exclusion of real evidence in circumstances such as here. Rather, we must turn to whether the marijuana illegally seized by the police should be excluded under s. 24(2) because its admission "would bring the administration of justice into disrepute."[340]

Therefore, even if section 10 did not strictly apply on a particular set of facts, it might nonetheless be the case that the admission of evidence discovered as a result of the failure to inform the accused of the right to counsel would render the trial unfair.[341] In that event, the evidence should be excluded anyway, which would have been the only value in finding that section 10 applied. The result is that, at a bottom-line level, any non-applicability of section 10 might be a distinction without a difference.

---

340 *Buhay*, above note 320 at paras 39–40.

341 It has been suggested that cases such as *Shafie*, above note 335, which allow evidence to be admitted even though no right to counsel was given, might be seen to be wrongly decided on this basis: see Glen Luther, "Of Excision, Amplification and Standing: Making Sense of the Law of Evidence in the Context of Challenges to Warranted Searches" (2006) 11 *Canadian Criminal Law Review* 1.

APPENDIX I

REASONABLE BELIEF

Reasonable Grounds for Arrest Made Out

R v Debot, [1989] 2 SCR 1140: The police received confidential information from an informant concerning a future drug deal. The informant had previously provided useful information to the police (Cst. G) and was considered by the police to be reliable. The informant provided details said to have been received directly from one of the parties to the drug transaction indicating the date, time, location, type of drug, and names of the parties to the offence. The police established visual surveillance of the anticipated site of the drug deal; a vehicle known to the police was observed along with persons entering/exiting the premises; and Cst. G, by radio to an off-site officer (Sgt. B), confirmed that the accused was the registered owner of the vehicle. Sgt. B then instructed other officers to intercept and search the vehicle. On these facts, Cst. B had reasonable and probable grounds to believe that the accused had drugs in his possession, despite reliance on hearsay from other officers. An officer instructed to carry out a search by another officer is entitled to assume that the officer ordering the search has reasonable grounds.

The tip provided by the informant was compelling and detailed: it went beyond mere rumour; the informant was reliable and not paid or facing charges; and the police surveillance corroborated the information received.

R v Wong, [1990] 3 SCR 36 (*obiter* conclusion on reasonable grounds for arrest for unlawful gaming): The police entered a recently vacated room in which the furniture had been rearranged to be "suitable for gambling"; they located many slips of paper in a garbage bin written in Chinese characters; the slips were similar to other notices known to be distributed elsewhere in the city; and hotel records showed that the accused had rented the same room on two other occasions that month.

R v Storrey, [1990] 1 SCR 241: Reasonable grounds to arrest for aggravated assault were made out by the accused's possession and ownership of a relatively unusual and uncommon car of the type used during the crime; (1) the accused had been stopped by the police on several occasions driving that car; (2) the accused had a past record of violence; and (3) the accused closely resembled the picture of another person picked out by the victims as their assailant.

R v Stillman, [1997] 1 SCR 607: Reasonable grounds to arrest for murder were made out where

> (a) he was the last person seen with the deceased on the evening of her disappearance; (b) he could not, or at least did not, account for his whereabouts between 9:00 p.m. and 11:30 p.m. on that evening when he returned to his residence; (c) when the appellant returned home he was wet and cold, his clothes were muddy and he had a scratch over his eye and blood on his face consistent with having been in a scuffle. When the deceased's body was found she appeared to have been physically beaten; (d) the appellant claimed to have been in a fight with some "Indians," but this story changed over time; (e) the appellant's worried and disturbed reaction to the police helicopter which was searching the river close to where the deceased was found; (f) immediately following the appellant's observation of the helicopter he left a suicide note and fled; (g) the appellant made a statement to Constable Cole saying, "I tried to stop her from killing herself. I left her there"; and (h) the RCMP received a report from two motorists that they had seen the deceased on the bridge crossing the Oromocto River and that she was with a male who met the description of the appellant (at para 31).

R v Latimer, [1997] 1 SCR 217: Reasonable grounds to arrest for murder were made out:

> Objectively, the reasonable person in the position of the arresting officer would have concluded there were reasonable grounds for arrest. Those grounds included:
>
> > the carbon monoxide in Tracy's blood, strongly suggesting that she had been poisoned; the fact that it was extremely unlikely that Tracy's death had been accidental; the fact that,

> because of Tracy's physical condition, her death could not have been suicide; and finally, the fact that the accused had both opportunity and motive (at para 27).

Hill v Hamilton-Wentworth Regional Police Services Board, 2007 SCC 41: Reasonable grounds for arrest on robbery charges were made out where the police had a Crime Stoppers tip; identification of the accused by a police officer based on a surveillance photo; several eyewitness identifications (some tentative, others more solid); a potential sighting of the accused near the site of a robbery by a police officer; eyewitness evidence that the robber appeared to be Aboriginal (which the accused was); and the belief of the police that a single person committed all ten robberies. The reasonable grounds were made out, although the police also had received an anonymous Crime Stoppers tip implicating two other people for the robbery. The accused, in fact, had not committed the robberies and unsuccessfully sued for negligent investigation.

R v Nolet, 2010 SCC 24: The police had reasonable grounds to arrest for possession of the proceeds of crime. They found a tractor-trailer driving with an empty load, without appropriate registration, operating outside of its jurisdiction, and with expired decals and a deficient logbook. There was a passenger along for the ride, and the cargo hold appeared to have been altered. When the officer then found a duffle bag with $115,000 in cash, he had reasonable grounds to believe that it was the proceeds of crime. (See *R v Perello*, 2005 SKCA 8, below, where the discovery of $55,000 in cash was not sufficient to create reasonable grounds.)

R v Loewen, 2011 SCC 21: Reasonable grounds to arrest for indictable offence of possessing more than thirty grams of marijuana were made out when he was stopped while driving:

> [4] . . . The trial judge held that Sergeant Topham had reasonable grounds to believe that Mr. Loewen was in possession of sufficient marijuana to constitute an indictable offence, having regard to the totality of the evidence, including the smell of burnt marijuana in the car and the sum of $5,410 found in Mr. Loewen's pocket, mostly in $20 bills, which suggested that he was involved in the drug trade.

R v Whyte, 2011 SCC 49: Reasonable grounds to believe that the accused was in possession of a firearm were made out. The police had received a tip that a Black male, possibly named "Jay," would be coming from Toronto to Windsor for a transaction related to firearms and drugs, might be accompanied, and would go to a particular address. A car, which had been rented in Toronto, driven by a Black male wearing a track suit and accompanied by a Black woman, arrived at that Windsor address; the car's occupants went inside for thirty minutes and then left and drove away. The vehicle was followed back to Toronto, at which point the investigation was handed over to Toronto police, who located the vehicle by an apartment building. Two Black men (one wearing a track suit) and a Black woman were seen going to the car. One of the men was carrying a shoebox and was seen to go to the trunk of the vehicle, remove the spare tire, and place the shoebox where the spare tire had been. The officer testified that shoeboxes are often used to transport guns, drugs, or money. The car was stopped, the occupants were arrested, and three handguns were found in the shoebox.

The tipster was conceded by the defence to be credible, which was one of the major factors in considering a tip. In addition, this was a tip about firearms and drugs, and the informer had given tips about firearms and drugs in the past. Travelling in a car from Toronto to Windsor and staying only thirty minutes were suspicious behaviour, and the fact that it was a rental car could contribute to reasonable grounds. Although the occupants had not been under surveillance for the entire period, a Black male wearing a track suit and a Black female were associated with the vehicle in both Windsor and Toronto. Finally, the shoebox was handled in a suspicious manner, which, coupled with the tip and the other confirmatory information, meant that the reasonable grounds to believe standard was met.

R v MacDonald, 2014 SCC 3: Reasonable grounds to believe that there was an imminent threat to the safety of the public or the police were made out. The police attended at the accused's condominium door in response to a noise complaint. The first time the police came to the door, the accused slammed it shut and swore at them. On the second occasion, the accused opened the door about sixteen inches, allowing the police to see only the right side of his body and face. The officer could see that MacDonald had his hand behind his leg and was clearly holding an object and that what he was holding was "black and shiny" and therefore could have been a weapon. When twice asked what he had behind his back, he refused to answer or to provide any explanation. The majority concluded that this gave the officer reasonable grounds to believe that there was an imminent safety threat and therefore authorized him to conduct a safety search. The dissent objected that this amounted to a watering down of the reasonable grounds standard and that these facts amounted, at best, to reasonable suspicion; the dissent would also have held that safety searches could be conducted based on reasonable suspicion.

R v Beaver, 2022 SCC 54: Reasonable grounds to arrest an accused for murder were made out, on a 5:4 split in the Court. The police were investigating a death that had been reported by the two accused to 911.

The circumstances of the death were seen as suspicious by the experienced police officer and by the medical examiner. The two accused had a motive due to a recent history of conflict and violence in the townhouse that the three of them shared, which had led to altercations all that week. They also had the opportunity to kill the accused because they lived with him, were the last known persons to see him alive, and were the persons who claimed to have discovered his body.

R v Warford, 2001 NFCA 64: The police received a "tip" that the accused would be driving to a local nightclub, at a particular time, to sell cocaine. The informant had provided reliable information to the police on approximately six occasions over a period of about eighteen months. The tip identified the date on which the accused had received cocaine and identified the vehicle in which he would be driving to the nightclub. The police observed the accused leave his residence in that vehicle at the indicated time and date, and he began to drive on a route consistent with going to the named nightclub. The police had reasonable grounds to arrest when they stopped the vehicle a short distance from the nightclub. (See, in contrast, *R v Zammit* (1993), 13 OR (3d) 76 (CA), below.)

R v MAL (2003), 173 CCC (3d) 439 (Ont CA): The police had reasonable grounds to arrest the accused for seven carjackings from Asian victims in plazas in Scarborough where they had the following evidence: the accused had previously been convicted of a very similar carjacking involving an Asian victim, which had occurred at a plaza where one of these seven carjackings had occurred; three of the four cars recovered by the police were found a short distance from the residence of the respondent's girlfriend, which was in the same general area where the various plazas were located; the accused and two companions were seen in the plaza where one of the robberies occurred about an hour and a half before the robbery, and his behaviour had been described by a witness as "suspicious"; in May, a police surveillance unit observed the accused in the plaza where one of the robberies had taken place the previous February; in late May and early June, the accused was seen in another of the plazas where one of the robberies had occurred. That robbery took place in April. The accused approached a vehicle in a manner that caused the driver (who was Asian) to call 911. That witness had seen the accused approach his car in a similar manner on an earlier occasion, and he also saw him a third time. The accused's race, age, and height were consistent with the very general descriptions given by most of the victims of the carjackings.

Potential weaknesses in eyewitness identification evidence that would be relevant at trial were not relevant to determining whether the police had reasonable grounds to arrest.

R* v *Bracchi, 2005 BCCA 461: There were reasonable grounds to arrest an accused where the police had received information from several sources that the accused was involved in cocaine trafficking. They observed him leave his house at night and drive some distance without his lights on, taking a circuitous route, and sometimes speeding, from which they concluded that he was trying to avoid being noticed. The accused was heading toward an address known as "the compound": the police had in the past stopped about twenty vehicles leaving that address, and all but one had been found to have cocaine. In addition, the police had in the past stopped a vehicle leaving the accused's address and had found cocaine, which the driver indicated he had bought from the accused. When the accused turned onto the street where the compound was located, the police had reasonable grounds to believe that he was delivering cocaine.

R* v *Rajaratnam, 2006 ABCA 333: The police had reasonable grounds to arrest for possession of a narcotic on the basis that the accused, encountered at a bus station, (1) purchased his ticket in a false name, at the last minute, with cash; (2) could not provide a credible explanation regarding the timing and duration of his trip; (3) became nervous when the police noticed that the name on his identification and ticket did not match; (4) had checked a bag that smelled of Bounce fabric softener, which was known by the police to be an agent used to camouflage the smell of drugs; and (5) tagged that bag with a false name. (Note the comment of Binnie J in *R v Kang-Brown*, 2008 SCC 18 at para 88, with regard to last-minute ticket purchases in cash: "This is a factor developed in the original Jetway program at airports where ordinary travellers usually book air transportation in advance and do not pay for an expensive ticket in cash (see, e.g., *Monney*). I think we can take judicial notice of the fact that people travelling by bus frequently buy their tickets not long before boarding. There is no evidence that cash payments are unusual.")

R* v *Johnson (2006), 213 OAC 395 (CA): Reasonable grounds to arrest for possession of a narcotic for purposes of trafficking were made out when the police, in a location frequently used for drug trafficking, saw a person they knew to be a crack-cocaine user approach the accused, saw the two acknowledge one another in a guarded fashion, saw the accused show a small item in his cupped hands, and then saw both men walking off together.

R* v *MacEachern, 2007 NSCA 69: There were reasonable grounds to arrest an accused for possession of narcotics when he walked in a large arc around a drug-sniffer dog and that dog twice gave a positive indication for the presence of drugs on the accused.

R v Webster, 2008 BCCA 458: The smell of burned marijuana combined with seeing what appears to be a marijuana cigarette behind the accused's ear gives reasonable grounds to arrest for possession of marijuana. (See *R v Janvier*, 2007 SKCA 147, below, holding that the smell of burned marijuana alone does not give reasonable grounds with regard to current possession.)

R v Baddock, 2008 BCCA 48: Police received information from an informant about a dial-a-dope operation; the officer believed the informant to be reliable on the basis of past information received that had resulted in arrests when the officer had been able to purchase drugs by calling the phone numbers provided by the informant. The police called the number and arranged a meeting to buy drugs and were told that a small white car would arrive at a McDonald's parking lot fifteen minutes after the call. Within the stated timeline, a white Honda Civic arrived and parked in front of the McDonald's, and the driver and his passenger waited for two minutes without ever exiting the vehicle before driving away. The police officer followed the accused's car and stopped him. As he approached the vehicle, the officer redialled the dial-a-dope number and, upon reaching the vehicle, observed that the accused's phone was ringing in his hand. On these facts, the officer had reasonable suspicion justifying stopping the car before he redialled the dial-a-dope number and had reasonable grounds to arrest after that.

R v Canlas, 2014 ABCA 160: Reasonable grounds to believe that the accused possessed narcotics were made out when the accused was stopped while driving and the following facts were established (at para 4):

> (a) when the Suburban door first opened Cst. Shule noted a faint odour of raw marijuana, (although no marijuana was located during the subsequent search);
> (b) he observed a large can of air freshener in the passenger side door compartment, which he knew was often used to conceal drug odours;
> (c) he observed fast food wrappers littering the vehicle, consistent with drug couriers being unwilling to leave their vehicle to eat while travelling;
> (d) when he asked Mr. Canlas why he was speeding, the reply was to get to a basketball tournament in Saskatoon which was to start two hours later, at 5 pm that day; however, neither Mr. Canlas nor his passenger was able to provide the location of where they were to play nor the schedule or plans for the tournament nor the full name of their coach;
> (e) a parka lay across the backseat concealing what was beneath it. When Constable Shule returned to the Suburban after running a

document search in his own police vehicle, he noted a basketball had been produced and placed on top of the parka which he interpreted as an effort to support the occupants' earlier claims that they were headed to a basketball tournament. He testified that he found this action extremely odd;

(f) the two occupants appeared very nervous to Cst. Shule when he first spoke to them, continually rubbing their hands over their limbs. This state increased rather than decreased as the interaction continued, which in the constable's experience was inconsistent with what usually happened, where a stopped driver is initially nervous but then calms as he talks to the police; and,

(g) the two occupants initially became vague when asked for further details about the basketball tournament; when later questioned separately they provided inconsistent information as to the details of the tournament and as to their own occupations.

There was evidence that the arresting officer was very familiar with the odour of marijuana.

Reasonable Grounds for Arrest Not Made Out

R* v *Greffe, [1990] 1 SCR 755: Reasonable grounds for a search were not made out. The RCMP received a tip that the accused was importing an unknown quantity of heroin to Calgary from Amsterdam and instructed customs officers to question/detain the accused. The accused was arrested and subjected to a body-cavity search. The informer provided details of the accused's name, the nature of the offence, flight information, and a physical description of the accused and the accused's clothing.

> With respect, a conclusion that the police had reliable information about the Appellant's attempt to import heroin must be based on more than the fact of a subsequent recovery of the drugs. There must be an independent inquiry into the source and reliability of the confidential information in order to determine whether, in the totality of the circumstances, there existed reasonable and probable grounds to believe the appellant was carrying the heroin or whether there was mere suspicion. Relevant to this inquiry is whether the information received contains sufficient detail to ensure that it is based on more than mere rumour or gossip, whether the source or means of knowledge is revealed and whether there is any indicia of the reliability of the source of the information, such as the supplying of reliable information in the past (at para 24).
>
> [T]he record reveals no evidence to support the existence of the grounds beyond a conclusory statement by the police (at para 47).

R v Feeney, [1997] 2 SCR 13: Reasonable grounds to arrest for murder were not made out.

> The salient facts known to the police prior to their entry of the trailer are as follows: (a) it appeared that Boyle's truck had been stolen before being in an accident, and Cindy Potter claimed to have seen "Michael" walking near the site of the accident; (b) Kelly Spurn told police that he assumed the appellant had crashed Boyle's truck since the appellant had crashed earlier that morning in about the same place with a different truck; and (c) Dale Russell told police that the appellant came home around 7:00 a.m. after drinking all night and that the appellant had earlier crashed a vehicle at the spot where Boyle's truck was found. In my view, these facts did not constitute reasonable and probable grounds to arrest the appellant for the murder of Boyle. Whether or not the appellant had been involved in two similar truck accidents, or might have stolen Boyle's truck, does not raise reasonable and probable grounds to believe that he had murdered Boyle. This evidence may have pointed to the appellant as a suspect, but these facts without more do not justify an arrest. When the police entered the trailer, objectively reasonable and probable grounds for an arrest, as opposed to grounds for prima facie suspicion, did not exist (at para 36).

R v Tim, 2022 SCC 12: There were no reasonable grounds to arrest an accused for possession of a controlled substance. The arresting officer saw the accused swipe a pill to the ground and seem to be trying to hide it from the officer's view. He recognized the pill as gabapentin, which he had seen traded among people on the street and believed was a controlled substance. The officer was incorrect in thinking gabapentin was a controlled substance, and reasonable grounds cannot be based on a mistake of law.

R v Zammit (1993), 13 OR (3d) 76 (CA): There were no reasonable grounds to arrest an accused for possession of narcotics based on a tip from a confidential informer that the accused would come into possession on a particular date. The informer's "tip" contained no details (such as the source of the drugs or the location and time of delivery) to ensure that it was based on more than mere rumour, and there was no evidence that the informer disclosed their source or means of knowledge. The accused had no reputation for involvement in drugs and no previous convictions for drug-related offences. The officer had never dealt with the informer before, and the only corroboration went to innocuous matters, such as the address of the accused, a description of him and of his motor vehicle, and the name and address of his workplace. These were matters that probably would have been known by anyone familiar with the accused. (See, in contrast, *R v Warford*, 2001 NFCA 64, above.)

R* v *Perello, 2005 SKCA 8: The discovery of $55,000 in cash in a vehicle registered in another province than the one it was being driven in does not give reasonable grounds to believe that the accused is committing the offence of possession of the proceeds of crime.

R* v *Janvier, 2007 SKCA 147: The smell of burned marijuana in a vehicle does not give reasonable grounds to believe that the driver is currently in possession of further unburned marijuana. The smell of raw marijuana would be a direct sensory impression, which would give reasonable grounds to believe that a person possesses raw marijuana. The smell of burned marijuana might indicate that the person had possessed marijuana in the past, but to prove current possession, two further inferences would be necessary: that the driver was the person who burned the earlier marijuana and that a person who has recently smoked marijuana probably has more. Neither inference can automatically be drawn. (See, in contrast, *R v Webster*, 2008 BCCA 458, discussed above, holding that the smell of burned marijuana emanating from a vehicle *does* meet the reasonable suspicion standard in relation to either the offence of possession of marijuana or impaired driving and so authorizes an investigative detention.)

R* v *Brown, 2012 ONCA 225: Reasonable grounds to arrest for trafficking in narcotics were not made out. An officer noticed a 6'7" "male black" fully extend his right arm with a closed fist toward a second person on the street. The second person did not extend their hand toward the appellant or reciprocate in any way to the gesture made by the appellant but then turned abruptly and walked away. The accused crossed the street and had his right hand by his side, still closed. The officer testified that based on his experience, he believed that the accused was concealing drugs in his hand. The Ontario Court of Appeal acknowledged that officer experience could be relevant but held that reasonable grounds were nonetheless not made out:

> 14 In our view, however, there must be something in the conduct observed by the officer, placed in the context of the rest of the circumstances, that lends some objective justification or verification to the officer's belief. Section 495 of the *Criminal Code* and, more importantly, s. 9 of the *Charter* demand that the belief be "reasonable," meaning that a reasonable person standing in the shoes of the police officer be able to see the grounds for the arrest. Without this objective component, the scope of the police power to arrest would be defined entirely by the police officer's perception of the relevant circumstances. The individual's constitutional right to be left alone by the state cannot depend exclusively on the officer's subjective perception of events regardless of how accurate that perception might be. The issue is not the correctness

> of the officer's belief, but the need to impose discernable objectively measurable limits on police powers.
>
> 15 The appellant's interaction with the person facing him on the city sidewalk does not, in our view, provide any objective basis upon which to believe that the two persons were engaged in a drug transaction. Nor does the fact that the two persons then walked away from each other make that interaction any more suspicious. Officer Manafo's evidence that the second person may have walked away from the appellant because he or she caught sight of the police cruiser is speculation.
>
> 17 Officer Manafo put some emphasis on the way in which the appellant held his right hand both during and after the interaction with the other person. Without some explanation from Officer Manafo as to why these actions were of some particular significance in the drug world, they do not elevate the circumstances to reasonable and probable grounds to arrest the appellant.

The officer also testified that the actions took place in a high-crime area, but the Court of Appeal described the evidence supporting that contention (at para 18) as "thin to say the least."

R v Santos, 2022 SKCA 50: The arrest for trafficking in narcotics made during a traffic stop was not based on reasonable grounds. The officer had pointed to a number of factors that he said his training and experience led him to believe that the accused was transporting narcotics. These included that he was driving a rented vehicle, he was travelling from Calgary to Winnipeg along the Trans-Canada Highway, and he had an energy drink in the cup holder, fast-food wrappers on the floor, and a factory-installed luggage cover in place. The Saskatchewan Court of Appeal found that those things were "so commonplace with travelers who are doing nothing illegal that they contribute little to the base of a reasonable belief in criminal activity" (at para 33). Other factors, such as that the accused volunteered the reason he was driving a rented vehicle without being asked, was making a trip from Calgary to Winnipeg and back in four days, and had trouble finding the rental agreement in the vehicle, did not raise suspicion. The officer also detected a small amount of cannabis, but nothing in the evidence suggested that this was in a quantity beyond which it was legal for the accused to possess it. Finally, a computer check showed that the accused had been dealt with by police on fifteen occasions, which was the most potentially incriminating information, but one of those occasions was a complaint initiated by the accused that his car had been stolen, and none of the entries showed that he had ever been convicted, charged, or even arrested for any drug-related offences.

APPENDIX II

REASONABLE SUSPICION*

Reasonable Suspicion Standard Met

R* v *Mann, [2004] 3 SCR 59: Shortly before midnight, the police received a dispatch call describing a break and enter in progress in downtown Winnipeg. The suspect was described as a twenty-one-year-old Aboriginal male, approximately 5'6", weighing 165 pounds, wearing a black jacket with white sleeves, and was believed to be "Zachary Parisienne." A short while later, the police observed the accused walking away from the site of the offence. The Court found that the reasonable suspicion standard was met because the accused closely matched the description and was only two or three blocks from the crime scene a short time after the offence. It also stated that the high-crime nature of a neighbourhood is not itself a basis to detain someone and is relevant only if it shows the connection of an accused to a particular crime.

R* v *Chehil, 2013 SCC 49: Reasonable suspicion that the accused was in possession of narcotics was established. The police checked the passenger manifest for a WestJet flight arriving in Halifax looking for particular characteristics, based upon which they selected the accused's bags to be subject to a sniffer-dog search. The Court noted that many of the characteristics that were relied upon were individually capable of innocent explanation but that nonetheless, taken together, were capable

* This appendix deals only with reasonable suspicion in the context of investigative detentions. There is also caselaw using the reasonable suspicion standard in other contexts, such as customs stops or approved-screening-device demands.

of amounting to reasonable suspicion. This was particularly the case because the officers testified that most people meeting this constellation of factors had been proven to be drug couriers, and that assertion was not challenged on cross-examination. The constellation of factors relied upon was as follows: (1) the travel was on a one-way ticket; (2) the flight originated in Vancouver; (3) the appellant was travelling alone; (4) the ticket was purchased with cash; (5) the ticket was the last one purchased before the flight departed; (6) the appellant checked one piece of luggage; (7) the flight was overnight; (8) the flight took place mid- to late-week; and (9) drug couriers prefer less expensive airlines, such as WestJet.

R v MacKenzie, 2013 SCC 50: Reasonable suspicion that the accused was transporting narcotics was established, but in a close-to-the-line decision where the Court split 5:4 over the issue. The accused was driving on the Trans-Canada Highway; he slowed down quickly when he saw a police car and pulled over to the side of the road without having been directed to do so. The officer described the accused as showing some of the highest nervousness he had ever seen even though the offence being investigated was only a minor traffic infraction. The accused's eyes were pinkish and his hands were trembling, which the officer knew from his experience were consistent with marijuana use. Finally, the accused was doing a trip with a fast turnaround between Calgary and Regina, which the officer knew to be a drug route. These facts gave rise to the reasonable *possibility*, rather than *probability*, of criminal behaviour, which was all that was necessary for the reasonable suspicion standard.

R v Stairs, 2022 SCC 11: Reasonable suspicion justifying a search incident to arrest of the area proximate to the accused in his home was established, but only on a 5:4 split by the Court. Police were responding to a report of a person striking a female passenger in his car and had found that car at an unknown home, which they entered when no one answered. A woman with fresh injuries emerged from the basement living room, and the accused ran from that room across the hallway to the laundry room, barricading himself in there rather than complying with the commands of the police. He was known to have a history of violence, and the offence being investigated was a violent one. Reasonable suspicion justifying a visual scan of the room that the accused had left before being arrested, to confirm that no one else was present and that there were no weapons or hazards, was made out. The dissenting judges argued that the officer's own testimony that he did not search until he felt it was safe and that "*you never really know*" what you will find showed that the officer acted only on a generalized concern.

R v Greaves, 2004 BCCA 484: An officer on duty received a report of an assault at a liquor store, perpetrated by a Black male and several White males who had fled eastbound. The dispatch record indicated one Black male and five White males, the Black male being described as eighteen years of age and six feet tall, with a skinny build and short black hair, wearing a light T-shirt and black pants. The officer arrived at the store within five minutes and found no one. He went east, where two blocks away he encountered a Black male (the accused) with two White males. The accused did not closely fit the description of the Black male described on the dispatch record, but the officer testified that he considered the grouping of a Black male with two White males unique for that part of the city. The three men were drinking beer and discarded the bottles upon seeing the officer; when he made eye contact with him, they proceeded to jaywalk, apparently to avoid the officer. These facts were found to objectively justify a detention.

R v Scott, 2004 NSCA 141: Early in the morning, a woman robbed a convenience store wearing a ski mask and then fled the scene. The RCMP arrived and traced footprints in the fresh snow from the store to an apartment building. As the officers approached the parking lot of the apartment building, they saw what they described as a red- or wine-coloured Grand Prix or Grand Am car, moving at an unusually high speed, leaving the parking lot. The officers radioed for assistance to locate and stop the car. Shortly afterward, other officers spotted a wine-coloured Grand Prix enter a gas station. The police had reasonable suspicion and were entitled to detain the vehicle and its occupants.

R v Bui, 2005 BCCA 482: Two accused were detained at Vancouver International Airport. The officer who detained Bui had twice previously investigated arrests of him (both of the prior two arrests occurring on the same day as one another), both at the Vancouver International Airport. In one, the accused had been smuggling cigarettes, and in the other, he had been in possession of six pounds of marijuana. On that previous occasion, Bui had not exited the terminal through the arrivals level but had gone up to the departures level, where he was stopped, which was the route he was taking on this occasion. He had flown from Toronto on the previous occasion and on this date. On the previous occasion, Bui had given a Toronto address of and claimed to be related to a woman (the co-accused, Vu) whom the constable had arrested once in the Vancouver airport for possession of illegal cigarettes. He had seen Vu in the airport, acting suspiciously and failing to board her flight to Toronto, the day before he had previously arrested Bui, and he had later been informed that she had attempted to claim baggage that was subsequently found to contain fifty pounds of marijuana. On this occasion, Vu was on the same flight from Toronto as Bui and exited the plane directly behind him, but it appeared to the constable that they were pretending not to know one another, although Bui's travel itinerary showed the two of them to be travelling on the same itinerary. In addition, they appeared to be nervous and maintained prolonged eye contact with the constable. Finally, the officer knew that the Vancouver–Toronto route was commonly used to smuggle cigarettes and money in one direction and marijuana in the other.

With regard to Vu, in addition to having arrested her previously for possession of illegal cigarettes, the officer had on an earlier occasion observed her behave suspiciously at the Vancouver airport, culminating with her and another woman failing to board their flight to Toronto; their abandoned baggage was found to contain about fifty pounds of marijuana. He had also been informed by another police officer that someone named Muoi Thi Vu had tried to claim that baggage in Toronto. Bui had given Vu's name as his next of kin. The itinerary and tickets that both were travelling on had been issued by a travel agency in Toronto that was implicated in nearly half of the smuggling investigations on which the constable had worked. Finally, neither Bui nor Vu had any checked baggage. On these facts, the constable had reasonable suspicion with regard to each accused.

R v Duong, 2006 BCCA 325: A police officer saw the accused seated in a parked car in an area with a high incidence of property crime; twenty minutes later, the same officer saw that the accused and the vehicle remained in the same location. The accused was said to be looking out the window and possibly waiting for someone. The officer approached the accused to inquire what he was doing and then asked him to produce his driver's licence, which he did. The officer observed in plain view a car stereo that appeared to have its wires cut situated behind the passenger's seat. The officer asked about the ownership of the stereo and the car, to which the accused indicated that both belonged to his friend; the officer testified that it took longer to provide answers to these questions than it did to answer the least-pointed questions. The officer also testified that the accused appeared slow and nervous and that there was a change in his demeanour, facial expression, and pattern of speech. The Court of Appeal found that the officer did objectively have reasonable suspicion about the car stereo.

R v Schell, 2006 SKCA 128: In the early morning hours, an RCMP officer positioned his vehicle one half block from the entrance to a bar in a small Saskatchewan town with his parking lights on to deter drunk driving.

The officer observed two men leave the bar and walk around a corner; shortly thereafter, a white truck (which had been parked near the bar when the officer arrived) drove past. The officer followed the truck for three or four blocks, observing nothing abnormal about how the truck was being driven before stopping it. Given that it was around the time the bar was to close and the patrons were leaving, and that the officer saw the accused leave the bar and shortly thereafter saw a vehicle he had previously identified leave the immediate vicinity of the bar and proceed down the street, there were reasonable grounds to detain.

R v Baddock, 2008 BCCA 48: A police officer received information about a dial-a-dope operation, which he believed to be reliable on the basis of past tips from the same informant. The officer called the number and arranged to buy drugs from a small white car, which would arrive at a McDonald's parking lot fifteen minutes later. Within the stated timeline, a white Honda Civic arrived and parked in front of the McDonald's, waited for two minutes, and then drove away. The police followed the car and stopped it. As he approached the vehicle, the officer redialled the dial-a-dope number, and upon reaching the vehicle, he observed that the accused (the driver) had a phone in his hand, which was ringing. On these facts, the officer had reasonable suspicion justifying stopping the car before he redialled the dial-a-dope number and had reasonable grounds to arrest after that.

R v Nesbeth, 2008 ONCA 579: At 11:00 p.m., six police officers entered an apartment complex described by the officers as "plagued by drug use, drug sales, robberies, guns and gang violence." Two officers in a stairwell detected a strong odour of freshly smoked marijuana, and when the officers reached the ninth floor landing, the landing door opened and the respondent entered. The respondent seemed surprised when he saw the officers and immediately and very tightly clenched the knapsack he was carrying. One of the officers asked the respondent, "Hey buddy, what are you doing?" The respondent replied, "Oh shit," turned around, opened the door, and began to run. The officers ran after him across the ninth floor. On the way, the respondent grabbed a shopping cart and attempted to knock it over in front of one of the pursuing officers. The pursuing officers were repeatedly yelling, "Stop, police." During the chase, the accused threw away the knapsack. He was not detained until he was apprehended by the police. By that time, the facts known to the police included that the accused had immediately bolted when he saw the uniformed officers, had used some force in an attempt to impede the officers' progress by throwing a shopping cart in their way, had thrown away a knapsack he had been tightly holding up until then, that it was late at night, and that the respondent was in the stairwell of a building known to be located in a high-crime area. (Note the observation in *Mann*, above, at para 47, that "the presence of an individual in a so-called high crime area is relevant only so far as it reflects his or her proximity to a particular crime. The high crime nature of a neighbourhood is not by itself a basis for detaining individuals.")

R* v *Bramley, 2009 SKCA 49: The police stopped the accused's vehicle for speeding. The officers then spoke to the driver and made a number of observations from the circumstances and the answers. These facts were as follows:

(a) The respondents lived in Surrey, British Columbia, and were coming from that city. Constable Donison knew Surrey to be a known point of origin for illegal drugs.
(b) The respondents were travelling to Regina, a known destination point in the movement of illegal drugs.
(c) The respondents were driving a car that had been rented by a third party. Constable Donison understood this to be a practice used by drug traffickers.
(d) Mr. Bramley said that he did not have enough money to rent a car, a $260 charge, but was nonetheless on a trip to Regina to visit friends.
(e) Mr. Bramley lived in Surrey, but the renter of the vehicle, whom he identified as his wife, was noted on the rental agreement as being from Markinch, Saskatchewan. This is not the usual husband-and-wife arrangement.
(f) The rental agreement appeared to be improperly completed in that, on the endorsement concerning additional drivers, Mr. Bramley's name was in the place where the renter was to sign.
(g) Both Mr. Bramley and Mr. Schiller were described as being nervous when they were stopped. While acknowledging that people pulled over in traffic stops are often nervous at first, Constable Donison said that such nervousness typically subsides as the stop progresses. In contrast, Mr. Bramley became more nervous over time.
(h) Between the time the respondents sped past Constable Donison's parked cruiser and the time they were pulled over, Mr. Schiller had put his long hair up under his baseball cap. This was unusual and appeared to be an attempt by Mr. Schiller to make himself look more conservative.
(i) Both respondents had criminal records involving drug offence convictions. This included convictions, dated in Mr. Bramley's case, for possession for the purposes of trafficking in both Saskatchewan and British Columbia. (As noted earlier, counsel did not question or put in issue the propriety of Constable Donison asking Mr. Schiller, a

passenger in the rental vehicle, for his driver's licence. The legality of that request is not an issue in this appeal.)

The Saskatchewan Court of Appeal held that these facts did give rise to reasonable suspicion. However, since it was reasonable suspicion with regard to a suspected offence rather than a known offence, the *Mann* test for investigative detention was not made out. (Note: the Saskatchewan Court of Appeal subsequently reversed its view on this issue, in *R v Yeh*, 2009 SKCA 112, holding that investigative detentions could be made out in the case of suspected offences.)

R v Wunderlich, 2014 ABCA 94: Reasonable suspicion regarding narcotics was made out. The accused was stopped because his vehicle had crossed over the fog line onto the shoulder of the highway and the vehicle did not have mud flaps. The officer noted that (1) the vehicle had a "very lived-in look"; (2) there was a mattress and a jerry can in the bed of the truck, which indicated to him that the accused did not want to leave the vehicle unattended; (3) there were numerous air fresheners hanging from the rear-view mirror, several of which were emitting odour; (4) a large dog was present; (5) the accused said that he was travelling from Vancouver, British Columbia, to Regina, Saskatchewan, but he was not on the most direct route; (6) the accused claimed that he planned to go hunting, but the officer knew that the hunting season was not open for non-residents; and (7) the appellant appeared to be overly nervous for a traffic stop as his carotid artery was pulsating, and he became increasingly nervous as the stop continued. In addition, the officer determined that a similar roadside inquiry had been made by the Vancouver police on 30 September 2010, but the accused had told the officer that he left Vancouver on 28 September 2010. The accused remained nervous and then changed his story about his travel plans to one more consistent with the highway he was on. Although some of the individual indicators were neutral, collectively, in context, and with the officer's training and experience, the factors raised a reasonable suspicion that the accused was involved in drug-related activity.

R v Mooiman and Zahar, 2016 SKCA 43: Reasonable suspicion that the accused was in possession of narcotics was made out. An officer stopped a vehicle travelling from Saskatoon, Saskatchewan, to Richmond, British Columbia. The accused was the passenger in the vehicle and had a freshly lit cigarette in his mouth; the officer testified that in his experience people generally discard their cigarettes when they are stopped by the police rather than light fresh ones, and he had been taught that cigarette smoke can be used to mask the odour of alcohol or narcotics in a vehicle. Both the driver and the passenger appeared to be very nervous, which was unusual since a passenger does not face any jeopardy in a traffic stop. In addition, there were fast-food wrappers on the floor boards of the truck, and the officer said that fast-food wrappers were a common marker in the transport of narcotics via motor vehicle. Based on these facts, the officer did a computer check and discovered entries associating the driver and the passenger with drug activity. At that point, reasonable suspicion was established.

Reasonable Suspicion Standard Not Met

R v Chaisson, 2006 SCC 11: A police officer noticed the accused and a passenger sitting in a darkened automobile behind a closed service station. The service station was adjacent to a restaurant that had just closed and to another that was open. The officer approached the parked automobile in his unlit cruiser. Based on the fact that the occupants were so absorbed in what they were doing that they did not notice him arrive, and on their shocked reaction when they noticed his presence, the officer decided to search the vehicle. On these facts, the officer did not have reasonable suspicion justifying a detention.

R v Calderon (2004), 188 CCC (3d) 481, 23 CR (6th) 1 (Ont CA): The police stopped a vehicle at 3:00 a.m. on the Trans-Canada Highway. A Canadian Police Information Centre check showed the vehicle to be a rental car, and it had a large trunk. The officers observed two cellular telephones, a pager on the belt of the passenger, road maps, fast-food wrappers on the floor of the car, and a large amount of luggage on the back seat instead of in the trunk. The officers testified that they had taken a drug interdiction course, which caused them to rely on these factors as indicators that the occupants of the car might be drug traffickers. The evidence was that they had stopped between sixty and 120 cars based on these indicators in the past and had never before found drug traffickers. The Court of Appeal held that there was no reasonable suspicion. Most of the purported indicators were neutral and might be found in anyone's car. The Court of Appeal held that, given the neutrality and apparent unreliability of the indicators, their presence could not amount to reasonable grounds for detention.

R v Houben, 2006 SKCA 129: The police were patrolling a residential neighbourhood in Saskatoon at 2:30 a.m. and observed a vehicle on four occasions travelling in different directions; they stopped the accused on the fourth occasion. The officers testified that the accused was doing nothing untoward at the time of the stop. The trial judge found that the officer stopped the driver to satisfy his curiosity; that there was nothing amiss with the accused's driving; that, in the officer's view and from experience, "undesirables" were active between 2:00 a.m. and 5:00 a.m.; that the area where the accused was stopped was not a high-crime area, nor was it known to be frequented by prostitutes; and that the police were not engaged in a specific investigation of any crime at the time of the stop.

R v Nguyen, 2008 SKCA 160: The three accused were stopped for travelling too fast for road conditions. The officer detected nervousness, noted that the vehicle was rented, and there was a smell of cologne in it, and decided to detain the accused for a drug investigation. The Court of Appeal held that these facts were not sufficient to give reasonable suspicion:

> 14. Before a police officer can detain a person for investigative purposes, there must be some aspect of the circumstances, relied upon by the officer, to permit a future judicial assessment as to whether a crime has been or is being committed or is about to be committed, as a first step in the *Mann* analysis. (See the judgment of Binnie J. in *Kang-Brown*.) An ongoing police investigation, a reported crime, or an odour of contraband of sufficient strength, as examples, might lead a judge to conclude in assessing police conduct after the fact that, at the point of detention, a crime has been or is being committed or is about to be committed. None of these indicia of a recent or ongoing criminal offence are present in this case.
>
> 20. When the Nguyen vehicle was stopped in this case, the only activity under investigation was that of travelling too fast for road conditions. When Duy Nguyen was subsequently placed under investigative detention for some other crime in relation to drugs, the only indicia of criminal activity beyond the speeding infraction was excessive nervousness, a strong odour of cologne and a rented car. Such nebulous and ambiguous factors—even when taken together—cannot meet the criteria of *Mann* and *Simpson* so as to establish the existence of a recent or ongoing criminal offence.

R v NO, 2009 ABCA 75: Shortly after midnight, an officer saw the accused exit his car and enter an apartment building that had two glass doors. Another male, who had been sitting on the stairs inside the second door, reached his hand through that door to the respondent's hand. A brief hand-to-hand exchange occurred. The male disappeared into the building, and the respondent returned to his car. The officer then detained the accused for a drug investigation. The Alberta Court of Appeal held that these facts did not make out reasonable suspicion. The time was not so late that it could form part of the necessary constellation of circumstances objectively justifying detention. The officer could not see what had been handed off, and neither the fact that it was small or that no words were exchanged gave rise to reasonable suspicion. The officer did not know the individual he detained or the building he entered. He had testified that apartment blocks in the area were plagued with drug transactions in their lobbies, but his evidence about the location and type of building where such events occurred was too vague to contribute to reasonable grounds to detain. The court noted that the officer had not specified the size of the area or the types or numbers of apartment blocks in it and held:

> With such specificity, there may be other facts when a detention could be justified. But on these facts, such a general approach gives rise to a grave risk of police interference with lawful activities. As Iacobucci J. stated in *Mann*, the high crime nature of a neighbourhood, alone, is not enough. Even though some apartment buildings in a neighbourhood may be known to the police as havens of drug activity, that does not mean that anyone who enters any apartment building in an ill-defined area or neighbourhood can objectively be suspected of criminal activity (at para 40).

R v Reddy, 2010 BCCA 11: The accused was a passenger in a vehicle that was parked outside the home of a known drug dealer, and his statement as to how long he had been there conflicted with information provided by an unknown 911 caller. In addition, the accused was known to have been, eight months earlier, a passenger in a vehicle in which machetes were found. These facts were not sufficient to give rise to reasonable suspicion that the accused was in breach of a probation order requiring him not to have a cellphone or a pager.

R v McCammon, 2013 MBCA 68: Police observed the accused's car at approximately 2:00 a.m. on a road on the outskirts of Winnipeg. Nothing about the manner in which the accused was driving was of concern to the officers, and prior to approaching the vehicle, they ascertained through a computer check that the vehicle had not been reported stolen. The officers decided to stop the vehicle because they thought it was suspicious that there was a vehicle in that area at that time of night. The officers asked the driver what she was doing in that area at that time of night, and she replied that she had driven to the park to show her wife where she walked the dog as she was to be deployed by the military out of the country shortly thereafter. No reasonable suspicion arose on these facts.

R v Ahmed-Kadir, 2015 BCCA 346: An officer who conducted a clearing search for safety purposes of an apartment she had been called to in connection with a domestic disturbance did not have reasonable suspicion.

The officer had been dispatched to the apartment in response to a domestic dispute complaint involving two parties. When she arrived, two officers were in the hallway dealing with a woman whose identity she did not know, while another officer was in the living room dealing with a man whose identity she did not know. In both cases, matters appeared to be under control. On these facts, there was no basis for reasonable suspicion that there might be other persons in the apartment who could pose a threat.

TABLE OF CASES

INDEX

For individual cases, please see the Table of Cases, included in this volume. Entries in italics indicate a table.

ABOUT THE AUTHORS

Steve Coughlan is a professor at the Schulich School of Law, Dalhousie University. He is the author of *Criminal Procedure* (Irwin Law, 2008, 2012, 2016, and 2020) and many other books, as well as a co-author of the *Annual Review of Criminal Law*. He is one of the editors of *Criminal Reports* and is a co-author of the National Judicial Institute Criminal Law Essentials e-letter. He is the recipient of a number of teaching awards, including the Association of Atlantic Universities Distinguished Teacher Award. In 2019, he was named by *Canadian Lawyer* magazine as one of the Twenty-Five Most Influential People in the Justice System.

Glen Luther, QC, is a professor at the College of Law, University of Saskatchewan. He has previously taught at several law schools, including Osgoode Hall Law School, the University of Calgary, and Victoria University in New Zealand. He has extensive criminal litigation experience in Alberta and Saskatchewan and has argued cases at all levels of courts. Professor Luther has received several awards for teaching excellence and in 2009 was appointed Queen's Counsel by the Government of Saskatchewan.

Printed and bound by CPI Group (UK) Ltd, Croydon, CR0 4YY

15/09/2026

14962401-0006